*Third Edition*

# ADOLESCENCE

## Laurence Steinberg

Temple University

McGraw-Hill, Inc.

New York   St. Louis   San Francisco   Auckland   Bogotá
Caracas   Lisbon   London   Madrid   Mexico   Milan
Montreal   New Delhi   Paris   San Juan
Singapore   Sydney   Tokyo
Toronto

## ADOLESCENCE

2 3 4 5 6 7 8 9 0 **AGM AGM** 9 0 9 8 7 6 5 4 3 2

ISBN 0–07–061218-8

This book was set in New Baskerville by Ruttle, Shaw & Wetherill, Inc.
The editors were Jane Vaicunas and James R. Belser;
the designer was Jo Jones;
the cover was designed by John Hite;
the production supervisor was Kathryn Porzio.
The photo editor was Barbara Salz.
Arcata Graphics/Halliday was printer and binder.

*Cover photograph:* © Bill Bachman, 1990/Photo Research, Inc.

*To*
*the Memory of*
*John P. Hill (1936–1988)*

**PHOTO CREDITS**

Introduction: Susan Lapides/Design Conceptions; Part One: Laima Druskis/Photo Researchers; Chapter 1: Bill Bachman/Photo Researchers; Chapter 2: Susie Fitzhugh/Stock, Boston; Chapter 3: John Moore/The Image Works; Part Two: Jerry Howard/Stock, Boston; Chapter 4: Arthur Tress/Photo Researchers; Chapter 5: Hazel Hankin/Stock, Boston; Chapter 6: Ursula Markus/Photo Researchers; Chapter 7: Joel Gordon; Part Three: Joel Gordon; Chapter 8: Dion Ogust/The Image Works; Chapter 9: Bob Daemmrich/The Image Works; Chapter 10: Jeffry Myers/Stock, Boston; Chapter 11: Carol Palmer/The Picture Cube; Chapter 12: David M. Grossman/Photo Researchers; and Chapter 13: Michael Siluk/The Image Works.

Library of Congress Cataloging-in-Publication Data

Steinberg, Laurence D., (date).
    Adolescence / Laurence Steinberg.—3rd ed.
       p.        cm.
    Includes bibliographical references and indexes.
    ISBN 0-07-061218-8
    1. Adolescence.    2. Adolescent psychology.    3. Teenagers—United
    States—Social conditions.    4. Personality in adolescence.
    5. Developmental psychology.    I. Title.
    HQ796.S826        1993
    305.23'5—dc20                                     92-15734

# About the Author

**Laurence Steinberg** is Professor of Psychology at Temple University. He graduated from Vassar College in 1974 and received his Ph.D. in Human Development and Family Studies from Cornell University in 1977. A Fellow of the American Psychological Association's Division of Developmental Psychology, Professor Steinberg has taught previously at the University of California, Irvine and the University of Wisconsin–Madison. He is the author of numerous scholarly articles on adolescent development as well as the books *When Teenagers Work: The Psychological and Social Costs of Adolescent Employment* (with Ellen Greenberger), *Infancy, Childhood, and Adolescence: Development in Context* (with Jay Belsky), and *You and Your Adolescent: A Parent's Guide for Ages 10 to 20* (with Ann Levine).

# Contents
# in Brief

# Contents

# *Preface*

*T*he first time I was asked to teach a semester-long course in adolescent development in 1976 my graduate advisor—who at that time had been teaching adolescent development for ten years—took me aside. "Getting them to learn the stuff is easy," John said, smiling. "Unfortunately, you'll only have about three weeks to do it. It'll take you ten weeks just to get them to *unlearn* all the junk they're sure is true."

He was right. I would present study after study documenting that turmoil isn't the norm for most adolescents, that most teenagers have relatively good relationships with their parents, that adolescence isn't an inherently stressful period, and so on, and my students would nod diligently. But five minutes later someone would tell the class about his or her cousin Billy, who had either run away from home, attempted to set his parents' bedroom on fire, or refused to say a word to either his mother or his father for eight years.

As most instructors discover, teaching adolescent development is both exhilarating and exasperating. Every student comes into class an expert; for many of them, adolescence wasn't very long ago. No good instructor wants to squelch the interest and curiosity most students bring with them when they first come into a class. But no conscientious teacher wants to see students leave with little more than the preconceptions they came in with and an even firmer conviction that social scientists who study human development are out of touch with the "real" world.

Urie Bronfenbrenner once wrote that the science of child development had found itself caught between "a rock and a soft place"—between rigor and relevance. Teachers of adolescent development find themselves in the same boat. How do you present scientific research on adolescent development in ways students find interesting, believable, relevant, and worth remembering when the term is over? I hope this book will help.

## *About the Third Edition*

About the time of the publication of the first edition of *Adolescence,* the study of development during the second decade of the life cycle suddenly became a hot topic. New journals, devoted exclusively to the study of adolescence, began publication; established journals in the field of child and adolescent development became deluged with submissions; more and more well-trained scholars specializing in the study of adolescent development appeared on the scene. During the four years between the publication of the first and second editions of this text, our understanding of adolescent development expanded dramatically. This expansion continued—even accelerated—between the publication of the second and third editions.

The third edition of this textbook reflects this new and more substantial knowledge base. Although the book's original organization has been retained, the material in each chapter has been significantly updated and revised. More than 400 new studies have been cited.

In some areas of inquiry, issues that were unresolved at the time of the earlier editions have been settled by newer and more definitive studies. In many cases, conclusions that had been tentatively accepted by the field were abandoned in favor of more contemporary views. For instance, when the first edition went to press, most scholars conceived of various aspects of problem behavior—drug use, unprotected sex, delinquency, for example—as being more or less independent phenomena, and theorists went out of their way to treat these issues under separate headings. By the time of the second edition, however, our theories of adolescent problem behavior had changed substantially, because the weight of the evidence began to indicate that the various problem behaviors associated with adolescence are indeed highly interrelated. New theories linking these problem areas to one another necessitated discussing them in a unified, coherent fashion. Accordingly, *Adolescence* was revised to reflect this change in perspective, and Chapter 13, "Psychosocial Problems in Adolescence," devoted entirely to psychosocial problems was added. This chapter has been retained and substantially updated in the third edition.

In yet other areas, our knowledge has expanded so dramatically that several altogether new sections were added to the text. Readers will find expanded sections on hormonal influences on behavior, physical health, information processing, adolescent risk-taking, noncollege-bound adolescents (sometimes referred to as the "Forgotten Half"), the impact of divorce and remarriage, peer crowds, social competence training, student engagement, adolescent leisure activities, ethnic identity, individuation and ego development, attachment, AIDS, achievement attributions, eating disorders, and adolescent depression. In addition, the expansion of knowledge during the past decade about adolescents from minority groups has permitted increased coverage of the ways in which the course of development during adolescence is affected by ethnicity and culture. These additions, corrections, and expansions are natural responses to the development of new knowledge in a dynamic and growing scientific field.

This edition of *Adolescence* retains a feature that ran throughout the last edition. A box in each chapter considers in detail whether a particular pattern of adolescent development is different for boys and girls. I emphasize the word "whether" here, for in many instances the scientific evidence suggests that the similarities between the sexes are far more striking than the differences. Some of the topics I examine are whether there are sex differences in the impact of early pubertal maturation, in cognitive abilities, in rates of depression, in relations with mothers and fathers, and in the nature of the transition into adulthood.

## Adolescent Development in Context

If there is a guiding theme to *Adolescence,* it is this: adolescent development cannot be understood apart from the context in which young people grow up. Identity crises, generation gaps, and peer pressure may be features of adolescent life in contemporary society, but their prevalence has more to do with the nature of our society than with the nature of adolescence as a period in the life cycle. In order to understand how adolescents develop in contemporary society, students need first to understand the world in which adolescents live and how that world affects their behavior and social relationships. I have therefore devoted a good deal of attention in this book to the contexts in which adolescents live— families, peer groups, schools, and work settings—to how these contexts are changing, and to how these changes are changing the nature of adolescence.

## Organization

The overall organization of this book has not changed since the last edition. Specifically, the chapters on psychosocial development during adolescence are separate from those on the context of adolescence. In this way, the psychosocial concerns of adolescence—identity, autonomy, intimacy, sexuality, and achievement—are presented as central developmental concerns that surface across, and are affected by, different settings.

This book contains an introduction and thirteen chapters, which are grouped into three parts: the *fundamental biological, cognitive, and social changes of the period* (Part One); the *contexts of adolescence* (Part Two); and *psychosocial development during the adolescent years* (Part Three). The introduction presents a model for studying adolescence developed by the late John Hill that serves as the organizational framework for the text. I have found the framework to be extremely helpful in teaching adolescent development, and I highly recommend using it. However, if the model does not fit with your course outline or your own perspective on adolescence, it is possible to use the text without using the framework. Each chapter is self-contained, so it is not necessary to assign chapters in the sequence in which they are ordered in the text. However, if you choose to use the model presented in the introduction, it may be helpful to follow the text organization.

## Theory and Methods

One of the things you will notice about *Adolescence* when you thumb through the contents is that the ubiquitous chapters on "theories of adolescence," and "research methods" are missing. The chapter titles are indeed missing, but the material isn't. After teaching adolescence for many years, I am convinced that students seldom remember a word of the chapters on theory and methods because the information in them is presented out of context. Therefore, although there is plenty of theory in this text, it is presented when it is most relevant, in a way that shows students how research and theory are related. At the beginning of the chapter on intimacy, for example, Sullivan's perspective on intimacy (and on psychosocial development in general) is presented, and then the relevant research is examined. Similarly, the research methods and tools employed in the study of adolescence are discussed in the context of specific studies that illustrate the powers—or pitfalls—of certain strategies. My approach has been to blend theory, research, and practical applications in a way that shows students how the three depend on each other. However, for students unfamiliar with theories in developmental psychology, I have included an Appendix that gives an overview of this material.

## Acknowledgments

Revising a textbook at a time when so much new information is available is a challenge that requires much assistance. Over the years my students have suggested many ways in which the text might be improved, and I have learned a great deal from listening to them. I am especially grateful to Jill Wittmer, who ably tracked down much of the new research published in the four years between editions; and to several colleagues, including Ganie DeHart, State University of New York at Geneseo; Karen G. Howe, Trenton State College; Patricia A. Jarvis, Illinois State University; Narina Nunez Nightingale, University of Wyoming; Robert E. Schell, State University of New York at Oswego; O. Suthern Sims, Jr., Mercer University, Georgia; Peg Hull Smith, University of Toledo; and Dennis Thompson, Georgia State University, who carefully reviewed the third edition and suggested a variety of ways in which the text might be revised. I also wish to thank my colleagues at McGraw-Hill, Barry Fetterolf, Renee Leonard, and Jane Vaicunas, who helped develop the book. I am also grateful to the many colleagues across the country who took the time to write during the past seven years with comments and suggestions based on their first-hand experiences using *Adolescence* in the classroom.

Finally, thanks, as always, to Wendy and Benjamin.

*Laurence Steinberg*

# ADOLESCENCE

# ADOLESCENT DEVELOPMENT IN CONTEXT

*I* magine you are a member of the state legislature, considering a bill that has been submitted by the Subcommittee on Educational Policy. The bill would lower the age at which adolescents could voluntarily leave school from age 16 to age 14. In essence, it would eliminate compulsory high school in your state, making formal education after the age of 14 entirely optional and leaving the decision to attend high school to each young person.

The floor is open for questions. You ask the subcommittee's chair why the majority of her group favors the change. You explain that you represent a district in one of the state's largest cities and you are worried that your constituents will feel that letting teenagers out of school early will only add to the growing problems of delinquency and unemployment.

The chair motions to one of the panel's legal experts to respond to your question. The lawyer replies that adolescents are old enough to make their own decisions about whether to continue their education and indicates that it may be unconstitutional to hold people in school if they don't want to be there. "Besides," he says, "what evidence is there that staying in high school helps find jobs?" He passes the microphone to an anthropologist who specializes in the study of young people in other cultures. She cites examples of many societies in which young people marry, have children, and work by the time they are 14 years old. Another panel member, a historian, points out that as recently as seventy years ago in this country, most individuals left school before the age of 14.

Another historian, however, who has dissented from the panel's recommendation, interrupts the speaker. "Things are not the same in this country today as they were seventy years ago," she points out. "And things are certainly different here from what they are in societies in which people become adults at the age of 14. We have to make decisions about adoles-cents on the basis of the world they live in *today*, not the one they lived in seventy years ago."

You want to hear from some of the psychologists on the panel. "Are 14-year-olds emotionally ready to make important decisions about their futures?" you ask. "Are 16-year-olds more mature than 14-year-olds, or is there little difference between adolescents who are only two years apart?" The psyhologists on the panel disagree with each other. One replies that she wonders whether even *16-year-olds* are capable of making important decisions about their futures: she vehemently opposes changing the age at which adolescents may leave school. In fact, she thinks the age should be *raised* to 18. The other psychologist, however, is less certain; he argues that it is hard to make generalizations about adolescents because individuals develop at such different rates. "Some 14-year-olds," he says, "are more mature than many 18-year-olds. Shouldn't they be given the chance to choose what they want to do? Furthermore," he adds, "adolescents' parents undoubtedly will help their children make decisions about whether to stay in school. The 14-year-olds won't be facing the dilemma on their own."

After listening to the panel members speak about the bill, you realize that you have never thought much about adolescence before. It has always seemed natural that there is a period of time between childhood and adulthood when people are not quite children any more but not yet ready to live as adults. Isn't adolescence supposed to be a time when people have "identity crises," when they agonize over dates and popularity in school and argue with their parents about staying out late or doing this school-work? How could people with these concerns be capable of deciding something as important as whether or not to continue in school?

At the same time, though, you think for a moment about adolescence in other places and at other times. Adolescents in this country may agonize over the junior prom while they flip hamburgers at the local fast food restaurant, but in some parts of the world, teenagers are fighting in wars, tending to housefuls of younger siblings, or working in factories to support their aging relatives. In responsibility, if not status, those adolescents carry the same burdens as their adult counterparts.

Perhaps you have heard stories about someone in your family's past whose adolescence was markedly different from your own. At the age of 13, for example, my grandfather left his family and smuggled himself in the back of a haywagon out of Russia and ultimately came to Ellis Island in New York City—without knowing a soul, or a word of English. At the same age, I, on the other hand, growing up some 50 years later and less than 20 miles from Ellis Island, was worrying about such weighty matters as whether my classmates would laugh at the new braces on my teeth.

Although 13-year-olds all over the world surely share certain things in common, it is obvious that generalizing about the nature of adolescence is no easy task, which makes decisions about lowering the school-leaving age quite difficult. As you read on, think about the things that adolescents all share in common and those that make their adolescent experiences remarkably different from each other.

## A Multidisciplinary Approach to Adolescence

What is the nature of adolescents' identity development in a changing world? How should society deal with problems of youth unemployment, adolescent AIDS, teenage pregnancy, or juvenile delinquency? What is the best way to prepare young people for the roles of adulthood? Should adolescents be required to obtain their parents' consent in order to receive contraceptives? When *should* adolescents be permitted to leave school legally?

At the turn of the century, the majority of teenagers left school before the age of 14. Like many of their contemporaries, these adolescents were employed full-time in factories. *(Culver)*

Answering these questions requires a thorough understanding of adolescents' psychological development, and in this book we will examine how—and why—people's hopes and plans, their fears and anxieties, and their questions and concerns change as they grow into adulthood. But answering these difficult questions also requires knowledge of how individuals develop physically, how their relationships with parents and friends change, how young people as a group are viewed and treated by society, how adolescence in our society differs from adolescence in other cultures, and how the nature of adolescence itself has changed over the years. In other words, a complete understanding of adolescence in contemporary society depends on being familiar with biological, social, sociological, cultural, and historical perspectives on adolescence.

In this book, we look at adolescence from a *multidisciplinary* perspective—a perspective that draws on a variety of disciplines. Each provides a view of adolescence that helps, in its own way, to further our understanding of this period of the life cycle. We will look at contributions to the study of adolescence made by biologists, psychologists, educators, sociologists, historians, and anthropologists. The challenge ahead of us in this book is not to try to determine which perspective on adolescence is best, but to find ways in which to integrate contributions from different disciplines into a coherent and comprehensive viewpoint on the nature of adolescent development in contemporary society.

## The Boundaries of Adolescence

Let's begin with a fairly basic question. When does adolescence begin and end? Perhaps we can gain some insight into this question by examining the word itself.

The word *adolescence* is Latin in origin, derived from the verb *adolescere*, which means "to grow into adulthood." In all societies, adolescence is a time of growing up, of moving from the immaturity of childhood into the maturity of adulthood. Adolescence is a period of transitions: biological, psychological, social, economic. It is an exciting time of life. Individuals become interested in sex and become biologically capable of having children. They become wiser, more sophisticated, and better able to make their own decisions. Adolescents are permitted to work, to get married, and to vote. And eventually, adolescents are expected to be able to support themselves financially.

As you can see in the accompanying box, there are a variety of different boundaries that one might draw between childhood and adolescence, and between adolescence and adulthood. Although it may seem frustrating, it is nevertheless the case that determining the beginning and ending of adolescence is more a matter of opinion than absolute fact. Whereas a biologist would place a great deal of emphasis on the attainment and completion of puberty, an attorney would look instead at important age breaks designated by law, while an educator might draw attention to differences between students enrolled in different grades in school. Is a biologically mature fifth-grader an adolescent or a child? Is a 20-year-old college student who lives at home an adolescent or an adult? It all depends on the boundaries one uses.

It probably makes more sense to think of development during adolescence as involving a series of passages from immaturity into maturity. Some of these passages are long and some are short; some are smooth and others are rough. And not all of them occur at the same time. Consequently, it is quite possible—and perhaps even likely—that an individual will mature in some respects before he or she matures in others. The various aspects of adolescence have different beginnings and different endings for every individual. Every young person is a child in some ways, an ad-

Social scientists who study adolescence usually differentiate among three periods: *early adolescence* (approximately 11 through 14 years of age), *middle adolescence* (15 through 18 years), and *late adolescence* (18 through 21 years). *(David S. Strickler/Picture Cube; Rick Smolan/Stock, Boston)*

olescent in other ways, and an adult in still others.

## EARLY, MIDDLE, AND LATE ADOLESCENCE

Although adolescence may span a ten-year period, most social scientists and practitioners recognize that so much psychological and social growth takes place during this decade, it makes more sense to view the adolescent years as composed of a series of phases than as one homogeneous stage. The 13-year-old whose interests center around Batman and baseball, for example, has little in common with the 18-year-old who is contemplating marriage, worried about pressures at work, and beginning a college career.

Social scientists who study adolescence usually differentiate among **early adolescence,** which covers the period from about age 11 through age 14, **middle adolescence,** from about age 15 through age 18, and **late adolescence** (or *youth,* as it is sometimes known), from

about age 18 through age 21 (Kagan and Coles, 1972; Keniston, 1970; Lipsitz, 1977). These divisions, as you may have guessed, correspond to the way in which our society groups young people in educational institutions; they are the approximate ages that customarily mark attendance at middle or junior high school, high school, and college. In discussing development during adolescence, we will need to be sensitive not only to differences between adolescence and childhood, or between adolescence and adulthood, but to differences among the various phases of adolescence itself.

## A Framework for Studying Adolescent Development

In order to organize information from a variety of different perspectives, this book uses a framework that is based largely on a model suggested by the late psychologist John Hill

## THE BOUNDARIES OF ADOLESCENCE

One problem that students of adolescence encounter early is a fundamental one: deciding when adolescence begins and ends, what the boundaries of the period are. Different theorists have proposed various markers, but there is little agreement on this issue. Here are some examples of the ways in which adolescence has been distinguished from childhood and adulthood that we shall examine in this book. Which boundaries make the most sense to you?

|  | When adolescence begins | When adolescence ends |
| --- | --- | --- |
| Biological | Onset of puberty | Becoming capable of sexual reproduction |
| Emotional | Beginning of detachment from parents | Attainment of separate sense of identity |
| Cognitive | Emergence of more advanced reasoning abilities | Consolidation of advanced reasoning abilities |
| Interpersonal | Beginning of a shift in interest from parental or peer relations | Development of capacity for intimacy with peers |
| Social | Beginning of training for adult work roles, family roles, and citizen roles | Full attainment of adult status and privileges |
| Educational | Entrance into junior high school | Completion of formal schooling |
| Legal | Attainment of juvenile status | Attainment of majority status |
| Chronological | Attainment of designated age of adolescence (e.g., 13 years) | Attainment of designated age of adulthood (e.g., 20 years) |
| Cultural | Entrance into period of training for a ceremonial rite of passage | Completion of ceremonial rite of passage |

(1983). The framework is organized around three basic components: the *fundamental changes* of adolescence, the *contexts* of adolescence, and the *psychosocial developments* of adolescence.

## THE FUNDAMENTAL CHANGES OF ADOLESCENCE

What, if anything, is distinctive about adolescence as a period in the life cycle? According to Hill, there are three features of adolescent development that give the period its special flavor and significance: (1) the onset of puberty, (2) the emergence of more advanced thinking abilities, and (3) the transition into new roles in society. We refer to these three sets of changes—biological, cognitive, and social—as the *fundamental changes of adolescence*. And they are changes that occur universally; virtually without exception, all adolescents in every society go through them.

**Biological transitions**    The chief elements of the biological changes of adolescence—which together are referred to as **puberty**—involve

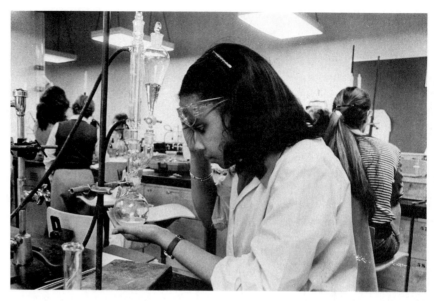

The development of more sophisticated thinking abilities is one of the most striking changes to take place during adolescence. *(Elizabeth Hamlin/Stock, Boston)*

changes in the young person's physical appearance (including breast development in girls, the growth of facial hair in boys, and a dramatic increase in height for both sexes) and the attainment of reproductive capability—the ability to conceive children (Brooks-Gunn and Reiter, 1990).

Chapter 1 describes the impact of puberty on the adolescent's psychological development and social relations. Puberty requires adaptation on the part of the young people and those around them. The adolescent's self-image, for example, may be temporarily threatened by marked changes in physical appearance. The body changes, the face changes, and not surprisingly, the way the adolescent feels about himself or herself changes. Relationships inside the family are transformed by the adolescent's greater need for privacy and by his or her interest in forming intimate relationships with peers. Girls may suddenly feel uncomfortable about being physically affectionate

with their fathers, and boys with their mothers. And of course, adolescents' friendships are altered by newly emerging sexual impulses and concerns.

**Cognitive transitions**   The word *cognitive* is used to refer to the processes that underlie how people think about things. Memory and problem solving are both examples of cognitive processes. Changes in thinking abilities, which are dealt with in Chapter 2, constitute the second of the three fundamental changes of the adolescent period. The emergence of more sophisticated thinking abilities is one of the most striking changes to take place during adolescence. Compared with children, for example, adolescents are much better able to think about hypothetical situations (that is, things that have not yet happened but will, or things that may not happen but could) and are much better able to think about abstract concepts, such as friendship, democracy, or morality (Keating, 1990).

The implications of these cognitive changes are also far-reaching. The ability to think more capably in hypothetical and abstract terms affects the way adolescents think about themselves, their relationships, and the world around them. We will see, for example, that teenagers' abilities to plan ahead, to argue with their parents, to solve chemistry problems, and to resolve moral dilemmas are all linked to changes in the way they think. Even the way that day-to-day decisions are made is affected. For the first time, individuals become able to think in logical ways about what their lives will be like in the future, about their relationships with friends and family, and about politics, religion, and philosophy.

**Social transitions** All societies distinguish between individuals who are thought of as children and those who are seen as ready to become adults. Our society, for example, distinguishes between people who are "underage," or minors, and people who have reached the age of majority. It is not until adolescence that individuals are permitted to drive, marry, and vote. Such changes in rights, privileges, and responsibilities—which are examined in Chapter 3—constitute the third set of fundamental changes that occur at adolescence: social changes. In some cultures, the social changes of adolescence are marked by a formal ceremony—a **rite of passage.** In others, the transition is less clearly demarcated. Still, a change in social status is a universal feature of adolescence. (Ford and Beach, 1951).

Society's redefinition of the individual provokes reconsideration of the young person's capabilities and competencies. As the young person's treatment by society changes, so do relationships around the home, at school, and in the peer group. Changes in social status also permit the young person to enter new roles and engage in new activities, such as marriage

and work, which dramatically alter his or her self-image and relationships with others. The adolescent, on the verge of becoming an adult, has choices to consider that previously did not exist for him or her.

## The Three Fundamental Changes of Adolescence

**BIOLOGICAL TRANSITIONS**

**COGNITIVE TRANSITIONS**

**SOCIAL TRANSITIONS**

## THE CONTEXTS OF ADOLESCENCE

Although all adolescents experience the biological, cognitive, and social transitions of the period, the *effects* of these changes are not uniform for all young people. Puberty makes some adolescents feel attractive and self-assured, but it makes others feel ugly and self-conscious. Being able to think in hypothetical terms makes some youngsters thankful that they grew up with the parents they have, but it prompts others to run away in search of a better life. Reaching 18 years of age prompts some teenagers to enlist unhesitatingly in the army or apply for a marriage license, but for others, becoming an adult is frightening and unsettling.

If the fundamental changes of adolescence are universal, why are their effects so varied? Why aren't all individuals affected in the same ways by puberty, by changes in thinking, and by changes in social and legal status? The answer lies in the fact that the psychological impact of the biological, cognitive, and social changes of adolescence is shaped by the environment in which the changes take place (Bronfenbrenner, 1979). In other words, psychological development during adolescence is a product of the interplay between a set of three very basic and universal changes and the context in which these changes are experienced.

Consider, for example, two 14-year-old girls growing up in neighboring communities. When Alice went through puberty, around age 13, her parents responded by restricting her social life because they were afraid that Alice would become too involved with boys and neglect her schoolwork. Alice felt that her parents were being unfair and also foolish. She rarely had a chance to meet any boys she wanted to date, anyway. All the older boys went to the high school across town. Even though she was in the eighth grade, she was still going to school with fifth-graders. And she couldn't meet anyone through work, either. Her school would not issue work permits to any student under the age of 16.

Maria's adolescence was very different. For one thing, when she had her first period, her parents took her aside and discussed sex and pregnancy with her. They explained how different contraceptives worked and made an appointment for Maria to see a gynecologist in town in case she ever needed to discuss something with a doctor. Although she was still only 14 years old, Maria knew that she would begin dating soon, because in her community the junior and senior high schools had been combined into one large school, and the older boys frequently asked the younger girls out. In addition, since there was no prohibition at her school against young teenagers working, Maria decided to get a job; she knew she would need money to buy clothes if she was going to start dating.

Two teenage girls. Each goes through puberty, each grows intellectually, and each moves closer in age to becoming an adult. Yet each grows up under very different circumstances: in different families, in different schools, with different groups of peers, and under different work conditions. Both are adolescents, but their adolescent experiences are markedly different. And as a result, each girl's psychological development will follow a different course.

Alice's and Maria's worlds may seem quite different from one another. Yet the two girls share many things in common, at least in comparison to two girls growing up in different parts of the world or in different historical eras. Imagine how different your adolescence would have been if you had grown up without going to high school and had had to work full-time from the age of 12. Imagine how different it would have been to grow up 100 years ago—or how different it will be to grow up 100 years from today. And imagine how different adolescence is for a youngster whose family is very poor and for one whose family is very rich. Even siblings growing up within the same family have different growing-up experiences, depending on their birth order within the family and various other factors (Daniels et al., 1985). You can see that it is impossible to generalize about the nature of adolescence without taking into account the surroundings and circumstances in which young people grow up.

## The Four Contexts of Adolescence

**FAMILIES**

**PEER GROUPS**

**SCHOOLS**

**WORK AND LEISURE**

For this reason, the second component of our framework is the *context of adolescence*. In modern societies, there are four main contexts that affect the development and behavior of young people: families, peer groups, schools, and work and leisure settings. The nature and structure of these contexts dramatically affect the way in which the fundamental changes of adolescence are experienced. To the extent that one adolescent's world differs from another's, the two young people will have very different experiences during the adolescent years.

Although young people growing up in modern America share some experiences with young people all over the world, their development is distinctively different from that of young people in other societies, because their families, peer groups, schools, and work settings are different. In other words, the contexts of adolescence are themselves shaped and defined by the larger society in which young people live. In this book, we shall be especially interested in how the contexts of adolescence have changed in Western society, and in the implications of these changes for adolescent development.

As in discussions of young people's psychological development, it is important when discussing families, peer groups, schools, and work and leisure settings to differentiate among the phases of adolescence. Take adolescent peer groups, for example. During early adolescence, peer groups are usually composed of teenagers of the same sex. During middle adolescence, peer groups become a context in which males and females interact. And during late adolescence, the large peer groups of earlier phases begin to disintegrate.

Let us now briefly survey how the contexts of adolescence have changed as society has changed.

**Families** Frequent moves, high rates of divorce, increasing numbers of single-parent households, and more and more working mothers have become characteristic of family life in contemporary America (Furstenberg, 1990). In Chapter 4, we look at these changes and try to assess how they are affecting young people's psychological development.

**Peer groups** Over the last 100 years, age-segregated peer groups—groups of people of the same age who spend most of their time together—have come to play an increasingly important role in the socialization and development of teenagers (Brown, 1990). But has the rise of peer groups been a positive or negative influence on young people's development? In Chapter 5, we discuss how peer groups are changing adolescence in contemporary America.

**Schools** Chapter 6 surveys schools as a context for adolescent development. Since the 1930s, Americans have turned more and more to schools as a setting to occupy, socialize, and educate adolescents (Entwistle, 1990). But how good a job are schools doing? And how should schools for adolescents be structured? These are two of the many difficult questions we will be examining.

**The Workplace** If you've been to a fast-food restaurant lately, you know that many of today's teenagers are working. But did you know that more adolescents are working now than at any other time in the last forty years (Greenberger and Steinberg, 1986)? In Chapter 7, we look at the world of adolescent work and at how part-time jobs are affecting young people's psychological development and well-being. We also take a look at adolescents' leisure activities, as well.

## PSYCHOSOCIAL DEVELOPMENT DURING ADOLESCENCE

Five sets of development concerns are paramount during adolescence: **identity; autonomy; intimacy; sexuality;** and **achievement.** These five sets of *psychosocial issues*, as well as

The nature of adolescence is shaped profoundly by the context in which young people grow up. This young migrant worker in Texas will experience adolescence very differently from an affluent teenager living in the suburbs. *(Bob Daemmrich/Image Works)*

certain psychosocial problems that may arise at adolescence, constitute the third, and final, component of our framework. Theorists use the word **psychosocial** to describe aspects of development that are both psychological and social in nature. Sexuality, for instance, is a psychosocial issue because it involves psychological change (that is, changes in the individual's emotions, motivations, and behavior) as well as changes in the individual's social relations with others.

Of course, identity, autonomy, intimacy, sexuality, and achievement are not concerns that arise for the first time during the adolescent years; and psychological or social problems can and do occur during all periods of the life cycle. Nor do psychosocial concerns disappear when the adolescent becomes an adult. These five sets of issues are present throughout the entire life span, from infancy through late adulthood. They represent basic developmental challenges that all people face as they grow and change: discovering and understanding who they are as individuals (identity); establishing a healthy sense of independence (autonomy); forming close and caring relationships with other people (intimacy); expressing sexual feelings and enjoying physical contact with others (sexuality); and being successful and competent members of society (achievement).

## The Psychosocial Issues And Problems of Adolescence

IDENTITY

AUTONOMY

INTIMACY

SEXUALITY

ACHIEVEMENT

PSYCHOSOCIAL PROBLEMS

Although these are not new concerns to the adolescent, development in each of these areas takes a special turn during the adolescent years. Understanding how and why such psychosocial developments take place during adolescence is a special concern of social scientists interested in this age period. We know that individuals form close relationships before adolescence, for example, but why is it during adolescence that intimate relationships with opposite-sex agemates first develop? We know that infants struggle with learning how to be independent, but why during adolescence do individuals need to be more on their own and make some decisions apart from their parents? We know that children fantasize about what they will be when they grow up, but why is it not until adolescence that these fantasies give way to serious concerns?

Part Three of this book (Chapters 8–13) discusses changes in each of the five psychosocial areas and examines several common psychosocial problems.

**Identity**  Chapter 8 deals with changes in identity, self-esteem, and self-conceptions. At adolescence, a variety of important changes in the realm of identity occur (Harter, 1990). The adolescent may wonder who he or she really is and where he or she is headed (Erikson, 1968). Coming to terms with these questions may involve a period of role experimentation—a time of trying on different personalities in an attempt to discover one's true self. The adolescent's quest for identity is a quest not only for a personal sense of self, but for recognition from others and from society that he or she is a special and unique individual.

**Autonomy**  Adolescents' struggle to establish themselves as independent, self-governing individuals—in their own eyes and in the eyes of others—is a long and occasionally difficult process, not only for young people but for those around them, too. Chapter 9 focuses on three sorts of concerns that are of special importance to developing adolescents: becoming less emo-

Individuals usually establish intimate relationships with opposite-sex peers for the first time during adolescence. Changes in the expression of intimacy along with changes in the areas of identity, autonomy, achievement, and sexuality constitute the main psychosocial developments of the adolescent years. *(Susan Lapides/Design Conceptions)*

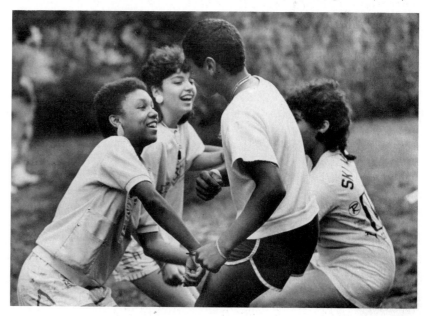

tionally dependent on parents, becoming able to make independent decisions, and establishing a personal code of value and morals (Douvan and Adelson, 1966; Steinberg, 1990).

## A Framework for Studying Adolescent Development

**FUNDAMENTAL CHANGES**

**CONTEXTS**

**PSYCHOSOCIAL ISSUES AND PROBLEMS**

**Intimacy**    During adolescence, important changes take place in the individual's capacity to be intimate with others, especially with peers. As we shall see in Chapter 10, friendships emerge for the first time during adolescence that involve openness, honesty, loyalty, and exchanging confidences, rather than the mere sharing of activities and interests (Savin-Williams and Berndt, 1990). Dating takes on

increased importance, and as a consequence, so does the capacity to form a relationship that is trusting and loving.

**Sexuality**    Sexual activity generally begins during the adolescent years. Becoming sexual is an important aspect of development during adolescence—not only because it transforms the nature of relationships between adolescents and their peers but also because it raises for the young person a range of trying and difficult questions. Chapter 11 discusses these concerns, including efforts to incorporate sexuality into a still developing sense of self, the need to resolve questions about sexual values and morals, and coming to terms with the sorts of relationships into which one is prepared—or not prepared—to enter (Katchadorian, 1990). We also look at sex education, contraceptive use, and the dangers of sexually-transmitted diseases.

**Achievement**    In Chapter 12, we examine changes in individuals' educational and vocational behavior and plans. Important decisions—many with long-term consequences—about schooling and careers are made during adolescence. Many of these decisions depend on adolescents' achievement in school, on their evaluations of their own competencies and capabilities, on their aspirations and expectations for the future, and on the direction and advice they receive from parents, teachers, and friends (Henderson and Dweck, 1990).

**Psychosocial problems**    In Chapter 13, we look at four sets of problems typically associated with adolescence: drug and alcohol use, delinquency, depression, and eating disorders. In each case, we examine the prevalence of the problem, the factors believed to contribute to its development, and approaches to prevention and intervention.

The illustration at left puts together the three pieces of the framework that we have been discussing: changes, contexts, and adolescent psychosocial development.

## *Stereotypes versus Scientific Study*

One of the oldest debates in the study of adolescence is whether adolescence is an inherently stressful time for individuals. G. Stanley Hall, who is generally acknowledged as the father of the modern study of adolescence, likened adolescence to the turbulent, transitional period in the evolution of the human species from savagery into civilization. "Adolescence is a new birth," Hall wrote. "Development is less gradual, suggestive of some ancient period of storm and stress" (1904, p. 6). Long before Hall, in the eighteenth century, French philosopher Jean-Jacques Rousseau had described adolescence by drawing an analogy to a violent storm: "As the roaring of the waves precedes the tempest, so the murmur of rising passions announces the tumultuous change. . . . Keep your hand upon the helm," he warned parents, "or all is lost" (Rousseau, 1762/1911, pp. 172–173).

Although neither Hall or Rousseau had any scientific evidence that adolescence was any more stormy than childhood or adulthood, their portrayal of teenagers as passionate, fickle, and unpredictable individuals persists. For example, people still tend to think of adolescence as a difficult and stressful time. A 12-year-old girl once told the author that her mother had been telling her that she was going to go through a difficult time when she turned 14—as if some magical, internal alarm clock was set to trigger "storm and stress" on schedule.

The girl's mother wasn't alone in her view of adolescence, of course. Sometime this week, turn on the television and note how teenagers are depicted. If they are not portrayed as ju-

venile delinquents—the usual role in which they are cast—adolescents are depicted as sex-crazed idiots (if they are male), mindless schoolgirls (if they are female), or tormented lost souls, searching for their place in a strange, cruel world (if they aren't delinquent, sex-crazed, or mindless). Adolescents are one of the most stereotyped groups in American society, and as a consequence, they are one of the most misunderstood (Adelson, 1979). One recent study demonstrated that most of the undergraduates enrolled in an adolescent development course believed that adolescence was an inherently stressful period (Holmbeck and Hill, 1988). After completing the course, however—which, incidentally, used this textbook—the students were less likely to endorse this view.

Movies such as *Rebel Without a Cause* have contributed to the stereotype that adolescence is an inherently difficult time. Scientific studies have shown this stereotype to be untrue. *(Culver)*

Your experiences as a teenager were the product of a unique set of cultural and historical forces at work in the context in which you came of age. Long after he enters adulthood, this Moscow adolescent will forever remember having to hoard vegetables underneath the living room sofa during the Soviet food shortages of the 1990s. *(Ursula Markus/Photo Researchers)*

You have no doubt come into this course with many convictions about adolescence. These beliefs are based in part on your own experiences as a teenager and in part on the images of adolescents to which you have been exposed over the years—in books, on film, and in television. As one team of writers pointed out, even scientists' portrayal of teenagers is influenced by the broader social and historical context in which they work. During periods of economic downturns, for instance, scholars depict adolescents as immature, unstable, and in

need of more schooling, whereas during periods of war, the same age group is portrayed as mature, responsible, and competent (Enright et al., 1987). Presumably, these characterizations serve a broader, if hidden, agenda—during depressions, there are fewer jobs to go around, and adults may "need" to see adolescents as incapable of working, whereas the reverse is true during wartime, when even youngsters are needed to help in factories and on farms.

One of the goals of this book is to provide you with a more realistic understanding of adolescent development in contemporary society—an understanding that reflects the best scientific knowledge available. Some of the results of this scientific research will not mesh with your own experiences and beliefs; others will.

As you read the material, you *should* think about your personal experiences as an adolescent, but you should also try to look beyond them and be willing to question the "truths" about teenagers that you have grown accustomed to believing over the years. This does not mean that your experiences were not valid ones, or your recollections inaccurate. Rather, your experiences as a teenager were the product of a unique set of forces that have made you the individual you are today. The person who sits next to you in class—or the person who right now, in some distant region of the world, is thinking back to his or her adolescence—was probably exposed to different forces than you, and probably had a different set of adolescent experiences as a consequence.

## Summary

1. A thorough understanding of adolescent development in contemporary society depends on being familiar with numerous perspectives on adolescence. Among the most important are those drawn from psychology, biology, history, sociology, education, and anthropology.

2. Adolescence is a transitional period. Rather than viewing adolescence as having a specific beginning and a specific ending, it makes more sense to think of the period as being composed of a series of passages—biological, psychological, social, and economic—from immaturity into maturity.

3. Three features of adolescence give the period its special flavor and distinctiveness: the biological changes of puberty, the emergence of more advanced thinking abilities, and the transition of the individual into new roles in society. These three sets of universal changes are referred to as the "fundamental" changes of adolescence.

4. Although the fundamental changes are universal, they occur in a given social context that varies from individual to individual and across space and time. The most important elements of the context of adolescent development are the family, the peer group, schools, and work and leisure settings.

5. Five sets of psychosocial concerns are paramount during adolescence. These issues involve self-discovery and understanding (identity), establishing a healthy sense of independence (autonomy), forming close and caring relationships with others (intimacy), expressing sexual feelings and enjoying physical contact with others (sexuality), and being successful and competent members of society (achievement). Although these are not new concerns in adolescence, development in each of these areas takes a special turn during the adolescent years.

6. There are a number of specific psychosocial problems that we associate with adolescence, although they affect only a minority of young people. Among the most important are drug and alcohol use, delinquency, depression, and eating disorders.

7. Although it is commonly believed that adolescence is an inherently difficult time, there is little scientific support for this idea. Adolescence is a period of change, but not necessarily stress. One important goal of the study of adolescence is understanding the factors that make the period difficult for some individuals, but not for others.

## Key Terms

achievement
autonomy
early adolescence
identity
intimacy
late adolescence

middle adolescence
psychosocial
puberty
rite of passage
sexuality

## For Further Reading

FELDMAN, S., AND ELLIOTT, G. (EDS.) (1990). *At the threshold: The developing adolescent.* Cambridge: Harvard University Press. An up-to-date collection of summaries of what is known about various aspects of adolescent development.

HILL, J. (1983). Early adolescence: A research agenda. *Journal of Early Adolescence, 3,* 1–21. Psychologist John Hill discusses his framework for understanding adolescent development.

KENISTON, K. (1970). Youth: A "new" stage of life. *American Scholar, 39,* 631–641. In this article, Kenneth Keniston explains why late adolescents, or youths, must be distinguished from younger adolescents.

KETT, J. (1977). *Rites of passage: Adolescence in America, 1790 to the present.* New York: Basic Books. The history of adolescence in America, with an emphasis on how people's conception of this stage in the life cycle has changed.

SPACKS, P. *The adolescent idea.* (1981). New York: Basic Books. A thorough examination of how writers, philosophers, and scientists have looked at adolescence over the years.

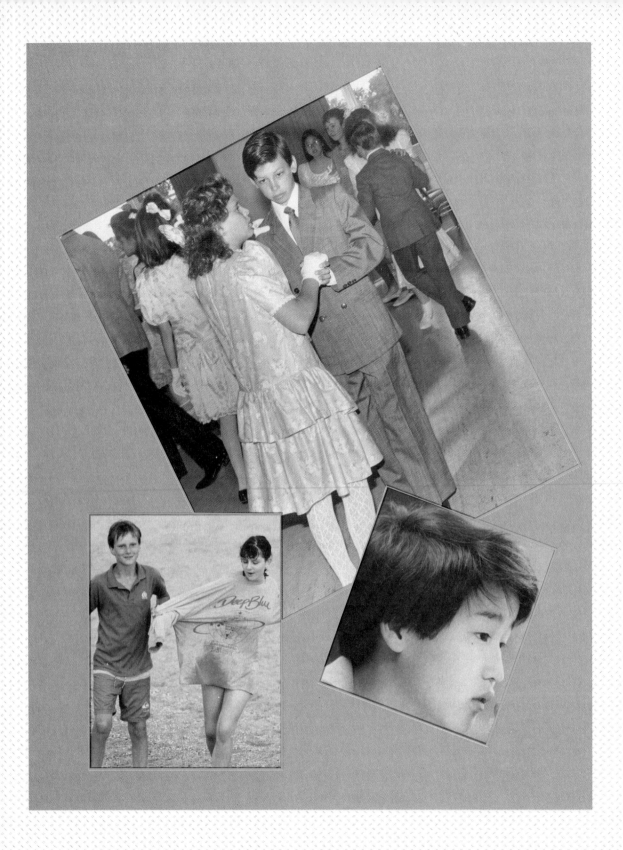

# One

# THE FUNDAMENTAL CHANGES OF ADOLESCENCE

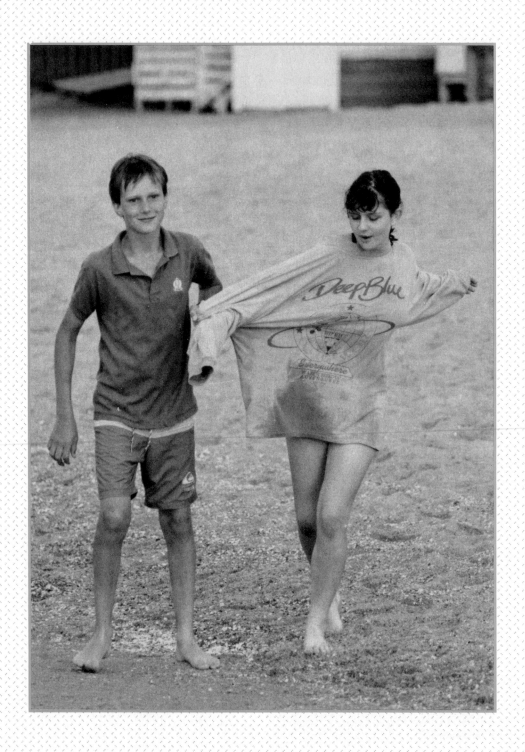

# BIOLOGICAL TRANSITIONS

According to an old joke, there are only two things in life that one can be sure of—death and taxes. To this brief list one might add puberty—the physical changes of adolescence—for, of all the developments that take place during the second decade of life, the only truly inevitable one is physical maturation. Not all adolescents experience identity crises, rebel against their parents, or fall head over heels in love, but virtually all undergo the biological transitions associated with maturation into adult reproductive capability.

Puberty, however, is considerably affected by the context in which it occurs. Physical development is influenced by a host of environmental factors, and the timing and rate of pubertal growth varies across regions of the world, socioeconomic classes, ethnic groups, and historical eras. Today, in contemporary America, the average girl reaches **menarche**—the time of first menstruation—between her twelfth and thirteenth birthdays. But among the Lumi people of New Guinea, the typical girl does not reach menarche until after 18 years of age (Eveleth and Tanner, 1976). Imagine how great a difference those five years make in transforming the nature of adolescence. Picture how different American high schools would be if sexual maturation did not occur until after graduation!

Physical and sexual maturation profoundly affect the way in which adolescents view themselves and the way in which they are viewed and treated by others. Yet the social environment exerts a tremendous impact on the meaning of puberty and on its psychological and social consequences. In some societies, pubertal maturation brings with it a series of complex initiation rites, which mark the passage of the young person into adulthood socially as well as physically. In other societies, recognition of the physical transformation from child into adult takes more subtle forms. Parents may merely remark that "our little boy has become a man" when they discover that he needs to shave. Early or late maturation may be cause for celebration or cause for concern, depending on what is admired or derogated in a given peer group at a given point in time. In the fifth grade, developing breasts may be a source of embarrassment; but in the ninth grade, it may be just as embarrassing *not* to have developed breasts.

In sum, even the most universal aspect of adolescence—puberty—is hardly universal in its impact on the young person. In this chapter, we examine just how and why the environment in which adolescents develop exerts its influence even on something as fundamental as puberty.

## Puberty: An Overview

*Puberty* derives from the Latin word *pubertas*, which means "adult." Technically, the term refers to the period during which an individual becomes capable of sexual reproduction, that is, it denotes the series of biological changes leading up to reproductive capability. More broadly speaking, however, *puberty* is used as a collective term to refer to all the physical changes that occur in the growing girl or boy as the individual passes from childhood into adulthood.

The following are the five chief physical manifestations of puberty (Marshall, 1978):

1. A *rapid acceleration in growth*, resulting in dramatic increases in both height and weight.
2. The further *development of the gonads*, or sex glands, which are the testes in males and the ovaries in females.
3. The *development of secondary sex characteristics*, which involve changes in the genitals and breasts, and the growth of pubic, facial, and axillary (body) hair, and the further development of the sex organs.

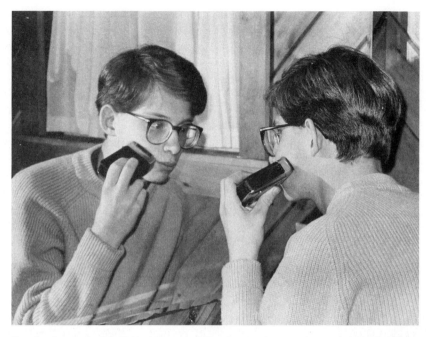

The development of facial hair is one of the changes in secondary sex characteristics that occur at puberty. Changes in appearance at puberty are the result of hormonal changes in the endocrine system, many of which take place long before the external signs of puberty are evident. *(Mark Antman/Image Works)*

4. *Changes in body composition*, specifically, in the quantity and distribution of fat and muscle.
5. *Changes in the circulatory and respiratory systems*, which lead to increased strength and tolerance for exercise.

Each of these sets of changes is the result of developments in the endocrine and central nervous systems, many of which begin years before the external signs of puberty are evident—some, even before birth.

## Onset and Termination

Puberty may appear to be rather sudden, judging from its external signs, but in fact it is part of a gradual process that begins at conception.

(Petersen and Taylor, 1980). You may be surprised to learn that no new hormones are produced and no new bodily systems develop at puberty. Rather, some hormones that have been present since before birth increase, and others decrease.

Hormones play two very different roles at adolescence: **organizational** and **activational** (Coe, Hayashi, and Levine, 1988). Long before adolescence—in some cases, prenatally—hormones *organize* the brain in ways that may not be manifested in observable behavior until puberty. For example, sex differences in levels of certain hormones during the development of the fetus may predetermine different patterns of behavior for males and females that may not actually appear until adolescence. Studies of sex differences in adolescent aggression, for example, show that these differences are likely due to the impact of prenatal hormones, rather than to hormonal changes at puberty. In other words, the presence or absence of certain hormones early in life may "program" the brain and the nervous system to develop in certain ways later on. Because we may not see the resulting changes in behavior until adolescence, it is easy to conclude mistakenly that the behaviors are due to the hormonal changes specific to puberty. In reality, however, exposure to certain hormones before birth may set a sort of "alarm clock" that does not go off until adolescence. Just because the alarm clock "rings" at the same time that puberty begins does not mean that puberty caused the alarm to go off.

Other changes in behavior at adolescence occur, however, because of changes in hormone levels at puberty—these hormonal changes are said to *activate* the changes in behavior. For instance, the increase in certain hormones at puberty is thought to stimulate the development of secondary sex characteristics, such as the growth of pubic hair. Still other changes are likely to be the result of an interaction between organizational and activational effects. Hormones present during the development of the fetus may organize a certain set of behaviors (our brains may be set up to have us later engage in sexual behavior, for example), while changes in hormones at puberty may be needed to actually activate the pattern (that is, it may not be until puberty that individuals become motivated to engage in sex).

## THE ENDOCRINE SYSTEM

The **endocrine system** produces, circulates, and regulates levels of hormones in the body. Hormones are highly specialized substances secreted by one or more endocrine glands. Glands are organs that stimulate particular parts of the body to respond in specific ways. Just as hormones are specialized to carry "messages" to particular cells in the body, so are the body's cells designed to receive hormonal messages selectively. For example, one of the many effects of the hormone adrenaline, secreted by the adrenal gland, is to stimulate the heart to increase its activity. The heart responds to adrenaline but not to all other hormones.

The endocrine system receives its instructions to increase or decrease circulating levels of particular hormones from the central nervous system, chiefly, the brain. The system works somewhat like a thermostat. Hormonal levels are "set" at a certain point, just as you might set a thermostat at a certain temperature. By setting your room's thermostat at 60°F, you are instructing your heating system to go into action when the temperature falls below this level. Similarly, when a particular hormonal level in your body dips below the endocrine system's **set point** for that hormone, secretion of the hormone increases; when the level reaches the set point, secretion temporarily stops. And, as is the case with a room thermostat, the setting level for a particular hormone can be adjusted up or down, depending on environmental or internal bodily conditions.

A **feedback loop** of this sort figures very importantly at the time of the onset of puberty. Long before early adolescence—in fact, during infancy—a feedback loop develops involving the **pituitary gland** (which controls hormone levels in general), the **hypothalamus** (the part of the brain that controls the pituitary gland), and the gonads, (in males, the **testes;** in females, the **ovaries**). The gonads release the "sex" hormones—**androgens** and **estrogens** (see Figure 1.1). Although one typically thinks of androgens as "male" hormones and estrogens as "female" hormones, both types of hormones are produced by each sex, and both are present in males and females at birth. During adolescence, however, the average male produces more androgens than estrogens, and the average female, more estrogens than androgens (Petersen and Taylor, 1980).

The hypothalamus responds to the levels of

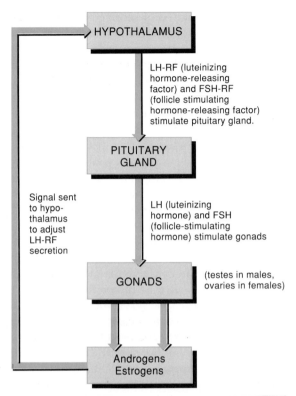

**FIGURE 1.1** Levels of sex hormones are regulated by a feedback system composed of the hypothalamus, pituitary gland, and gonads. (Grunbach et al., 1974)

sex hormones circulating in the body. Your endocrine system is set to maintain certain levels of androgens and estrogens. When these levels fall below the set points, the hypothalamus stimulates the pituitary, which, in turn, stimulates the release of sex hormones by the gonads. When sex-hormone levels reach the set point, the hypothalamus responds by inhibiting its stimulation of the pituitary gland.

## ENDOCRINAL CHANGES AT PUBERTY

Is is probably more accurate to say that our brain inhibits puberty before adolescence than to say that it stimulates puberty at adolescence (Brooks-Gunn and Reiter, 1990). During in-

fancy, the set point for sex hormones is fixed so that very low levels of sex hormones will be maintained. But at puberty, there is a change in this feedback system. The hypothalamus appears to lose a certain degree of sensitivity to the sex hormones, and consequently, it takes higher and higher levels of these substances to trigger the hypothalamus to inhibit the pituitary gland. It is as if a thermostat that had previously been set at 60°F were now set at 80°F and required a lot more fuel to reach the set point. Right before puberty, the hypothalamus begins to lose sensitivity to the sex hormones and, consequently, permits levels of these hormones to rise. As far as is known, this gradually decreasing sensitivity of the hypothalamus to sex hormones is the chief mechanism in initiating the onset of puberty. But the cause of this change in hypothalamic sensitivity is not well understood (Grumbach, Roth, Kaplan, and Kelch, 1974). Studies do show, however, that the onset of puberty is affected by the adolescent's psychological and physical health. Stress, excessive exercise, and excessive thinness can all delay the onset of puberty (Frisch, 1983; McClintock, 1980).

Interestingly, a number of recent studies suggest that social, as well as physical, factors may influence the onset of maturation, especially in girls. One study, for example, found that girls who were emotionally closer to their parents before puberty matured at a slower rate than girls who were more distant (Steinberg, 1988). Another researcher found that girls who grew up in homes from which the father was absent—because of divorce or death, for example—matured at an earlier age than girls whose father was present (Surbey, 1989). In general, among humans and other mammals, living in proximity to one's close biological relatives appears to slow the process of pubertal maturation (Surbey, 1989). Although it may seem surprising that something as biological as puberty can be influenced by factors in our social environment, scientists have long known that our social relationships can indeed affect our biological functioning. One of the best-known examples of this is that women who live together—such as dormitory roommates—find that their menstrual periods begin to synchronize over time (McClintock, 1971).

At puberty, the pituitary also secretes hormones that act on the thyroid and the adrenal cortex and hormones that stimulate overall bodily growth. The release of these substances is also under the control of the hypothalamus. The thyroid and adrenal cortex, in turn, secrete hormones that cause various physical (somatic) changes to take place at puberty.

## Somatic Development

The effects of the endocrinological changes of puberty on the adolescent's body are remarkable. Consider the dramatic changes in physical appearance that occur during the short span of early adolescence. One enters puberty looking like a child and within four years or so has the physical appearance of a young adult. During this relatively brief period of time, the average individual grows nearly 12 inches taller, matures sexually, and develops an adult-proportioned body.

### CHANGES IN STATURE AND THE DIMENSIONS OF THE BODY

The simultaneous release of growth hormone, thyroid hormones, and androgens stimulates rapid acceleration in height and weight. This dramatic increase in stature is referred to as the **adolescent growth spurt.** What is most incredible about the adolescent growth spurt is not so much the absolute gain of height and weight that typically occurs, but the speed with which the increases take place. Think for a moment of how quickly very young children grow. At the time of **peak height velocity**—the

time at which the adolescent is growing most rapidly—he or she is growing at the same rate as a toddler. For boys, peak height velocity averages about 4.1 inches (10.5 centimeters) per year; for girls, about 3.5 inches (9.0 centimeters) (J. Tanner, 1972).

Figure 1.2 shows just how remarkable the growth spurt is in terms of height. The graph on the left presents information on absolute height and indicates that, as you would expect, the average individual increases in height throughout infancy, childhood, and adolescence. As you can see, there is little gain in height after the age of 18. But look now at the right-hand graph, which shows the average increase in height *per year* over the same age span. Here you can see the acceleration in height at the time of peak height velocity.

Figure 1.2 also indicates quite clearly that the growth spurt occurs, on the average, about two years earlier among girls than among boys. In general, as you can see by comparing the two graphs, boys tend to be somewhat taller than girls before age 11, girls taller than boys between ages 11 and 13, and boys taller than girls from about age 14 on. You may remember what this state of affairs was like during fifth or sixth grades. Sex differences in height at this age can be a concern to many young adolescents when they begin socializing with members of the opposite sex, especially to tall, early-maturing girls and short, late-maturing boys.

Much of the height gain is due to an increase in torso length, rather than leg length. The sequence in which various parts of the body grow is fairly regular. Extremities—the head, hands, and feet—are the first to accelerate in growth. Then follows accelerated growth in the arms and legs, followed by torso and shoulder growth. Consequently, "a boy stops growing out of his trousers (at least in length) a year before he stops growing out of his jackets" (J. Tanner, 1972, p. 5). During

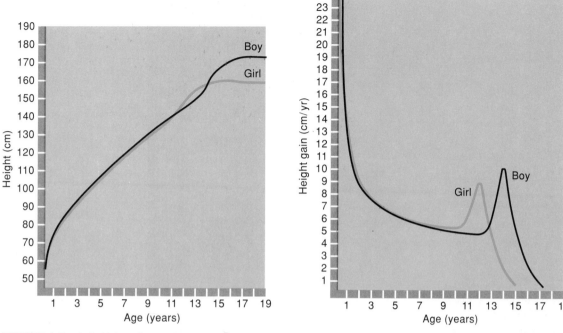

**FIGURE 1.2** *Left:* Height (in centimeters) at different ages for the average male and female youngster. *Right:* Gain in height per year (in centimeters) for the average male and female youngster. Note the adolescent growth spurt. (Adapted from Marshall, 1978)

puberty, the composition of the skeletal structure also changes, with bones becoming harder and more brittle. One of the markers of the end of puberty is the closing of the ends of the long bones in the body, which terminates growth in height.

Young adolescents often appear out of proportion physically—as if their noses or legs were growing faster than the rest of them. No, it's not an optical illusion. The parts of the body do not all grow at the same rate or at the same time during puberty. This **asynchronicity in growth**—can lead to an appearance of awkwardness or gawkiness in the young adolescent, who may be embarrassed by the unmatched accelerated growth of different parts of the body. It is probably little consolation for the young adolescent to be told that an aes-

thetic balance probably will be restored within a few years; nevertheless, this is what usually happens.

The spurt in height at adolescence is accompanied by an increase in weight that results from an increase in both muscle and fat. However, there are important sex differences along these latter two dimensions. In both sexes, muscular development is rapid and closely parallels skeletal growth; but muscle tissue grows faster in boys than in girls (see Figure 1.3). Body fat increases for both sexes during puberty, but more so for females than for males, and at a somewhat faster rate for girls, especially during the years just before puberty. For boys, there is actually a slight decline in body fat just before puberty. The end result of these sex differences in growth is that boys finish

During puberty there is a rapid acceleration in height and weight, known as the "adolescent growth spurt." Adolescents do not all experience this spurt at the same age, however, resulting in a difference in appearance among young teenagers who are classmates. *(Janice Fullman/Picture Cube)*

adolescence with a muscle-to-fat ratio of about 3:1, but the comparable ratio for girls is approximately 5:4. This has important implications for understanding why sex differences in strength and athletic ability often appear for the first time during adolescence. Before puberty, there are relatively few sex differences in muscle development and only slight sex differences in body fat.

Accompanying these gains in strength are increases in the size and capacity of the heart and lungs and, consequently, in exercise tolerance. In all these areas, the rate and magnitude of the gains favor males over females.

By the end of puberty, boys are stronger, have "larger hearts and lungs relative to their size, a higher systolic blood pressure, a lower resting heart rate, a greater capacity for carrying oxygen to the blood, . . . a greater power for neutralizing the chemical products of muscular exercise, such as lactic acid," higher blood hemoglobin, and more red blood cells (Petersen and Taylor, 1980, p. 129).

It is tempting to attribute these sex differences purely to hormonal factors, because androgens, which increase during puberty in males at a much faster rate than in females, are closely linked to growth along these phys-

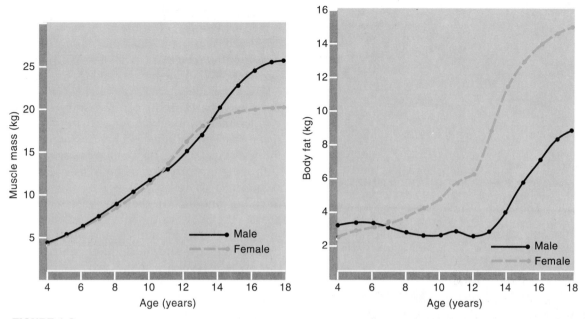

**FIGURE 1.3**  During preadolescence, important sex differences emerge in body composition that continue through adolescence. Figures reflect muscle and body fat for individuals of average height at each age. Note the changes in muscle mass (left) and body fat (right). (Adapted from Grumbach et al., 1974)

ical dimensions. But no studies have examined the role that sex differences in exercise patterns and diet may play. As Petersen and Taylor (1980) point out, there are strong social pressures on girls to curtail "masculine" activity—including some forms of exercise—at adolescence. Moreover, adolescent girls' diets are generally less nutritionally adequate than those of boys. Both factors could result in sex differences in muscular development and exercise tolerance. Sex differences in physical maturation are influenced by a variety of factors, of which hormonal differences are but one part of an extremely complicated picture.

Along with many other of the body's organs, the brain changes in size and structure at puberty. Studies show that brain growth and maturation continue well into adolescence, with different regions of the brain undergoing growth "spurts" at different times during ad-

olescence (Brooks-Gunn and Reiter, 1990). At one time it was believed that these spurts were linked to specific changes in thinking abilities—some writers even proposed that early adolescents should not be taught demanding subject matter because their brains had not matured sufficiently! Careful studies have not substantiated this idea, however. Although important intellectual changes take place in adolescence, as you will read in Chapter 2, these developments do not seem linked in any one-to-one correspondence to specific changes in the brain's size or structure (Keating, 1990).

## SEXUAL MATURATION

Puberty brings with it a series of developments associated with sexual maturation. In both boys and girls, the development of the so-called **sec-**

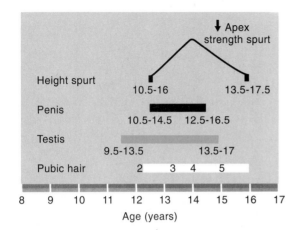

**FIGURE 1.4**  The sequence and approximate ages of the major changes at puberty among males. (Adapted from Tanner, 1972)

**ondary sex characteristics** is typically divided into five stages, often called **Tanner stages.**

**Sexual maturation in boys**  The sequence of developments in secondary sex characteristics among boys is fairly orderly (see Figure 1.4). Generally, the first stages of puberty involve growth of the testes and scrotum, accompanied by the first appearance of pubic hair. Approximately one year later, the growth spurt in height begins, accompanied by growth of the penis and further development of pubic hair—now of a coarser texture and darker color. The five pubertal stages of penis and pubic hair growth in boys are shown in Figure 1.5.

The emergence of facial hair—first at the corners of the upper lip, next across the upper lip, then at the upper parts of the cheeks and in the midline below the lower lip, and finally along the sides of the face and the lower border of the chin—and body hair are relatively late developments in the pubertal process. The same is true for the deepening of the voice, which is gradual and generally does not occur until very late adolescence. During puberty, there are changes in the skin as well; the skin

becomes rougher, especially around the upper arms and thighs, and there is increased development of the sweat glands. This latter development often gives rise to acne, skin eruptions, and increased oiliness of the skin.

During puberty there are slight changes in the male breast—to the consternation and embarrassment of many boys. Breast development is largely influenced by the estrogen hormones. As noted earlier, both estrogens and androgens are present in both sexes and increase in both sexes at puberty—although in differing amounts. In the male adolescent, the areola (the area around the nipple) increases in size, and the nipple becomes more prominent. Some boys show a slight enlargement of the breast, although in the majority of cases this development is temporary.

Other, internal changes occur that are important elements of sexual maturation. At the time that the penis develops, the seminal vesicles, the prostate, and the bilbo-urethral glands also enlarge and develop. The first ejaculation of seminal fluid generally occurs about one year after the beginning of acclerated penis growth, although this is often culturally, rather than biologically, determined (J. Tanner, 1972).

**Sexual maturation in girls**  The sequence of development of secondary sex characteristics among girls (shown in Figure 1.6) is somewhat less regular than it is among boys. Generally, the first sign of sexual maturation is the elevation of the breast—the emergence of the so-called breast bud. In about one-third of all adolescent girls, however, the appearance of pubic hair precedes breast development. The development of pubic hair follows a sequence similar to that in males—generally, from sparse, downy, light-colored hair to more dense, curled, coarse, darker hair. Breast development often occurs concurrently and generally proceeds through several stages. In the

**Penis and Scrotum**

Penis
Scrotum
Glans
(Head)
Testes

1    2    3    4    5

*Stage 1:*    The infantile state that persists from birth until puberty begins. During this time the genitalia increase slightly in overall size but there is little change in general appearance.
*Stage 2:*    The scrotum has begun to enlarge, and there is some reddening and change in texture of the scrotal skin.
*Stage 3:*    The penis has increased in length and there is a smaller increase in breadth. There has been further growth of the scrotum.
*Stage 4:*    The length and breadth of the penis have increased further and the glans has developed. The scrotum is further enlarged and the scrotal skin has become darker.
*Stage 5:*    The genitalia are adult in size and shape. The appearance of the genitalia may satisfy the criteria for one of these stages for a considerable time before the penis and scrotum are sufficiently developed to be classified as belonging to the next stage.

**Pubic Hair**

1    2    3    4    5

*Stage 1:*    There is no true pubic hair, although there may be a fine velus over the pubes similar to that over other parts of the abdomen.
*Stage 2:*    Sparse growth of lightly pigmented hair, which is usually straight or only slightly curled. This usually begins at either side of the base of the penis.
*Stage 3:*    The hair spreads over the pubic symphysis and is considerably darker and coarser and usually more curled.
*Stage 4:*    The hair is now adult in character but covers an area considerably smaller than in most adults. There is no spread to the medial surface of the thighs.
*Stage 5:*    The hair is distributed in an inverse triangle as in the female. It has spread to the medial surface of the thighs but not up the linea alba or elsewhere above the base of the triangle.

**FIGURE 1.5**    The five pubertal stages for penile and pubic hair growth. (From Morris and Udry, 1980)

bud stage, the areola widens and the breast and nipple are elevated as a small mound. In the middle stages, the areola and nipple become distinct from the breast and project beyond the breast contour. In the final stages, the areola is recessed to the contour of the breast, and only the nipple is elevated. The female breast undergoes these changes at pu-

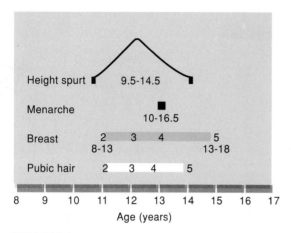

Height spurt    9.5-14.5

Menarche         10-16.5

Breast     2     3    4       5
         8-13           13-18

Pubic hair    2    3   4    5

8   9   10   11   12   13   14   15   16   17

Age (years)

**FIGURE 1.6** The sequence and approximate ages of the major changes at puberty among females. (Adapted from Tanner, 1972)

berty regardless of changes in breast size. Changes in the shape and definition of the areola and nipple are far better indicators of sexual maturation among adolescent girls than is breast growth alone. The five stages of breast and pubic hair growth in girls are shown in Figure 1.7.

As in the case among boys, puberty brings important internal changes for the adolescent girl that are associated with the development of reproductive capacity. In girls, these changes involve development and growth of the uterus, vagina, and other aspects of the reproductive system. In addition, there is enlargement of the labia and clitoris.

As is apparent in Figure 1.6, the growth spurt is likely to occur during the early and middle stages of breast and pubic hair development. Menarche, the beginning of menstruation, is a relatively late development. Hence it is incorrect to use menarche as a marker for the onset of puberty among girls. A great deal of pubertal development has taken place long before the adolescent girl begins to menstruate. Generally, full reproductive function does not occur until several years

after menarche, and regular ovulation follows menarche by about two years (Hafetz, 1976).

## Timing and Tempo

You may have noted that, thus far, no mention has been made about the "normal" ages at which various pubertal changes are likely to take place. The truth is that the variations in the timing of puberty—the age at which puberty begins—and in the tempo of puberty—the rate at which maturation occurs—are so great that it is misleading to talk even about "average" ages.

### VARIATIONS IN THE TIMING AND TEMPO OF PUBERTY

The onset of puberty can occur as early as 8 years in girls and 9½ in boys, or as late as 13 in girls and 13½ in boys. In girls, the interval between the first sign of puberty and complete physical maturation can be as short as one and one-half years or as long as six years. In boys, the comparable interval ranges from about two years to five years (J. Tanner, 1972). Within a totally normal population of young adolescents, some individuals will have completed the entire sequence of pubertal changes before others have even begun. In more concrete terms, it is possible for an early-maturing, fast-maturing youngster to complete pubertal maturation by the age of 10 or 11—two years before a late-maturing youngster has even begun puberty, and *seven years* before a late-maturing, slow-maturing youngster has matured completely!

There is no relation between the age at which puberty begins and the rate at which pubertal development proceeds. Furthermore, the timing of puberty has little to do with the ultimate adult stature or bodily dimensions of the individual. Late maturers, for example, at-

### Breasts

1. No breast development.

2. The first sign of breast development has appeared. This stage is sometimes referred to as the breast budding stage. Some palpable breast tissue under the nipple, the flat area of the nipple (areola) may be somewhat enlarged.

3. The breast is more distinct although there is no separation between contours of the two breasts.

4. The breast is further enlarged and there is greater contour distinction. The nipple including the areola forms a secondary mound on the breast.

5. Size may vary in the mature stage. The breast is fully developed. The contours are distinct and the areola has receded into the general contour of the breast.

### Pubic Hair

1. No pubic hair.

2. There is a small amount of long pubic hair chiefly along vaginal lips.

3. Hair is darker, coarser, and curlier and spreads sparsely over skin around vaginal lips.

4. Hair is now adult in type, but area covered is smaller than in most adults. There is no pubic hair on the inside of the thighs.

5. Hair is adult in type, distributed as an inverse triangle. There may be hair on the inside of the thighs.

**FIGURE 1.7** The five pubertal stages for breast and pubic hair growth. (From Marshall and Tanner, 1969)

# NORA EPHRON'S "A FEW WORDS ABOUT BREASTS"

For many adolescent girls, developing breasts later than their friends is a real cause for concern. Looking back, that concern may seem funny, but for many girls it was anything but funny at the time, as author Nora Ephron recalls:

I was about six months younger than everyone else in my class, and so for about six months after it began, for six months after my friends had begun to develop (that was the word we used, develop), I was not particularly worried. I would sit in the bathtub and look at my breasts and know that any day now, any second now, they would start growing like everyone else's. They didn't. "I want to buy a bra," I said to my mother one night. "What for?" she said. My mother was really hateful about bras, and by the time my third sister had gotten to the point where she was ready to want one, my mother had worked the whole business into a comedy routine. "Why not use a Band-Aid instead?" she would say. It was a source of great pride to my mother that she had never even had to wear a brassiere until she had her fourth child, and then only because her gynecologist made her. It was incomprehensible to me that anyone could ever be proud of something like that. It was the 1950s, for God's sake. Jane Russell. Cashmere sweaters. Couldn't my mother see that? "I am too old to wear an undershirt." Screaming. Weeping. Shouting. "Then don't wear an undershirt," said my mother. "But I want to buy a bra." "What for?"

I suppose that for most girls, breasts, brassieres, that entire thing, has more trauma, more to do with the coming of adolescence, with becoming a woman, than anything else. Certainly more than getting your period, although that, too, was traumatic, symbolic. But you could see breasts; they were there; they were visible. Whereas a girl could claim to have her period for months before she actually got it and nobody would ever know the difference.

I started with a 28 AA bra. I don't think they made them any smaller in those days, although I gather that now you can buy bras for five-year-olds that don't have any cups whatsoever in them; trainer bras they are called. My first brassiere came from Robinson's Department Store in Beverly Hills. I went there alone, shaking, positive they would look me over and smile and tell me to come back next year. An actual fitter took me into the dressing room and stood over me while I took off my blouse and tried the first one on. The little puffs stood out on my chest. "Lean over," said the fitter. (To this day, I am not sure what fitters in bra departments do except to tell you to lean over.) I leaned over, with the fleeting hope that my breasts would miraculously fall out of my body and into the puffs. Nothing.

"Don't worry about it," said my friend Libby some months later, when things had not improved. "You'll get them after you're married."

"What are you talking about?" I said.

"When you get married," Libby explained, "your husband will touch your breasts and rub them and kiss them and they'll grow."

That was the killer. Necking I could deal with. But it had never crossed my mind that a man was going to touch my breasts, that breasts had something to do with all that, petting, my God, they never mentioned petting in my little sex manual about the fertilization of the ovum. I became dizzy. For I knew instantly—as naive as I had been only a moment before—that only part of what she was saying was true: the touching, rubbing, kissing part, not the growing part. And I knew that no one would ever want to marry me. I had no breasts. I would never have breasts.

*Source:* Nora Ephron, *Crazy Salad* (New York: Knopf, 1975), pp. 4–6.

tain the same average height as early maturers (Marshall, 1978).

## GENETIC AND ENVIRONMENTAL INFLUENCES

What factors underlie the tremendous variations in the timing and tempo of puberty? Why do some individuals mature relatively early and others relatively late? One can point to both genetic and environmental factors.

Researchers who study variability in the onset and timing of puberty approach the issue in two ways. One strategy involves the study of differences among individuals (that is, studying why one individual matures earlier or faster than another). The other involves the study of differences among groups of adolescents (that is, studying why puberty occurs earlier or more rapidly in certain populations than in others). Let us first consider research on differences among individuals.

**Individual differences in pubertal maturation**
Differences in the timing and rate of puberty among individuals growing up in the same general environment are chiefly due to genetic factors. Comparisons between individuals who are genetically identical (identical twins) and individuals who are not reveal patterns of similarity in pubertal maturation indicating that the timing and tempo of an individual's pubertal maturation are largely inherited (Marshall, 1978).

Despite this powerful influence of genetic factors, the environment plays an important role. In all likelihood, every individual inherits a predisposition to develop at a certain rate and begin pubertal maturation at a certain time. But this predisposition is best thought of as an upper and lower age limit, rather than as a fixed absolute. Whether the genetic predisposition each person has to mature around a given age is actually realized, and when within the predisposed age boundaries he or

she actually goes through puberty, are subject to the influence of the environment. In this respect, the timing and rate of pubertal maturation are the product of an interaction between nature—the genetic makeup—and nurture—the environmental conditions under which one has developed.

Although we saw earlier that contextual factors such as social relationships can affect the timing of puberty, by far the two most important environmental influences on pubertal maturation are nutrition and health. Puberty occurs earlier among individuals who are better nourished throughout their prenatal, infant, and childhood years. Similarly, delayed puberty is more likely to occur among individuals with a history of protein and/or caloric deficiency. Chronic illness during childhood and adolescence is also associated with delayed pu-

Girls, on average, reach puberty about two years earlier than boys. As a consequence, young adolescent girls are often taller than same-aged boys. *(Elizabeth Crews)*

berty, as is excessive exercise. For example, girls in ballet companies or in other rigorous training programs often mature later than their peers (Frisch, 1983). Generally speaking, then, after genetic factors, of the onset of puberty is the overall physical well-being of the individual from conception through preadolescence (Marshall, 1978).

**Group differences in pubertal maturation**
Researchers typically study group differences in puberty by comparing average ages of menarche in different regions. Most of these studies have indicated that genetic factors play an extremely small role in determining group dif-

ferences in pubertal maturation (Eveleth and Tanner, 1976). Differences among countries in the average rate and timing of puberty are likely to be due more to differences in their environments than to differences in their populations' gene pools.

The influence of the broader environment on the timing and tempo of puberty can be seen in more concrete terms by looking at three sorts of group comparisons: (1) comparisons of the average age of menarche across countries, (2) comparisons among socioeconomic groups within the same country, and (3) comparisons within the same population during different eras. (Although menarche does

**FIGURE 1.8** The average menarcheal age of adolescent girls varies in different regions of the world. (Adapted from Eveleth and Tanner, 1976)

| 1 | Mainly African descent |
| 1 | Mainly Asiatic descent |
| (1) | Mainly European descent |
| 1 | Native inhabitants of Australia (Aborigines), Near East, India, N. Africa, and S. America |

not signal the onset of puberty, researchers often use the average age of menarche when comparing the timing of puberty across different groups or regions.)

First, consider variations in the age of menarche across different regions of the world. Figure 1.8 presents median menarcheal ages throughout the world, across regions that vary considerably in typical dietary intake and health conditions. As you can see, the average age at menarche generally is lower in those countries where individuals are less likely to be malnourished or suffer from chronic disease. For example, in Western Europe and in the United States, the median menarcheal age

ranges from about 12.5 years to 13.5 years. In Africa, however, the median menarcheal age ranges from about 14 years to about 17 years. The range is much wider across the African continent because of the much greater variation in environmental conditions there.

Figure 1.9 presents evidence bearing on differences *within* groups. When we look within a specific region, we find that, almost without exception, girls from affluent homes reach menarche before economically disadvantaged girls. In comparisons of affluent and poor youngsters from the United States, Hong Kong, Tunis, Baghdad, and South Africa, differences in the average menarcheal ages of economically advantaged and disadvantaged youngsters within each of these regions range from about 6 months to about 18 months.

Finally, we can examine environmental influences on the timing of puberty by looking at changes in the average age of menarche over the past two centuries. Because nutritional conditions have improved during the past 150 years, we would expect to find a decline in the average age at menarche over time. This is indeed the case, as can be seen in Figure 1.10. Generally, "children have been getting larger and growing to maturity more rapidly" (Eveleth and Tanner, 1976, p. 260). This pattern, referred to as the **secular trend,** is attributable not only to improved nutrition but also to better sanitation and the control of infectious disease. In most European countries maturation has become earlier by about 3 to 4 months per decade. For example, in Norway 150 years ago, the average age of menarche may have been about 17 years. Today, it is about 13 years. Similar declines have been observed over the same time period in other industrialized nations and, more recently, in developing countries as well, although at least one writer has suggested that 100 years ago menarche may have occurred earlier than age 17 (Bullough, 1981).

The secular trend in pubertal maturation appears to be leveling off in most industrialized

The age at which adolescents mature physically varies around the world. On average, teenagers in highly industrialized countries, like Japan, mature earlier than their counterparts in developing nations, where health and nutritional problems slow physical growth. *(R. M. Collins, III/Image Works)*

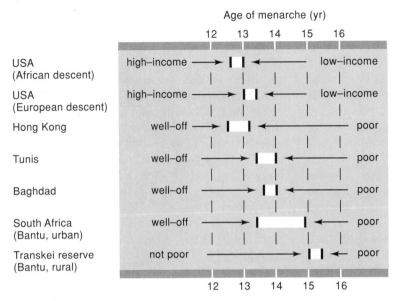

**FIGURE 1.9**  The average menarcheal age of adolescent girls varies across different social classes. (Eveleth and Tanner, 1976)

nations, however. This suggests that environmental conditions in these parts of the world have improved to the point where the average age of menarche is approaching its genetically bound lower limit. For example, no substantial changes in average menarcheal age have been reported during the past twenty-five years in Oslo, Norway, or London, England. You can lay to rest any fears you might have that children in future generations will go through puberty before they leave kindergarten. In all likelihood, the average age at menarche will not decline much below 12 years.

## The Psychological and Social Impact of Puberty

Puberty's psychological and social impact occurs through a cyclical, or reciprocal, process. Physical maturation affects the adolescent's self-image and behavior, and this in turn prompts changes in the behavior of others. For example, a boy who has recently gone through puberty may feel shy about his changed body and seek more privacy at home when he is dressing or bathing. He closes his door more often and is more modest around his parents than he used to be. If they are responsive to his discomfort, his parents will change their routines around the house. Before entering his room, they will knock and wait to see if he is dressed—something they did not have to do before.

The process works in the other direction as well. The adolescent's changed physical appearance may elicit new sorts of behavior from peers, parents, and others, and these new reactions may prompt the adolescent to adjust his or her behavior and self-image. An adolescent girl who has recently matured physically may find herself suddenly receiving the attention of older boys who had not previously paid

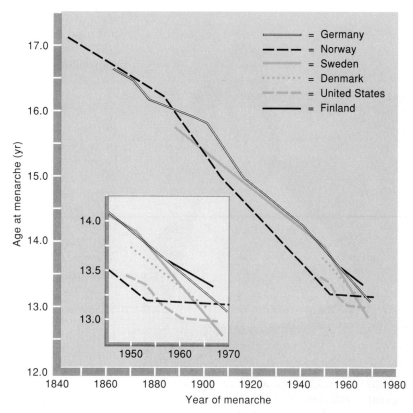

**FIGURE 1.10** The age at menarche has declined considerably over the past 150 years. This decline is known as the secular trend. (Adapted from Eveleth and Tanner, 1976)

her much heed. In consequence, she will start to feel more attractive and confident. Moreover, she must now make decisions about how much time she wishes to devote to dating and how she should handle herself when out on a date.

Young people's reactions to the changes brought on by puberty, and others' reactions to them, are influenced by the broader social environment. Contemporary society's views of puberty and physical maturation are expressed through television commercials, newspaper and magazine advertisements, and depictions of young adolescents in films and other media.

People cannot help but be influenced by these images, and the expectations they associate with puberty as well as the meaning they give it determine the reactions it brings out in them. Consider, for example, the treatment of menstruation in each of the advertisements reprinted on page 46. What sorts of reactions might each of the ads foster?

Researchers have generally taken two approaches to studying the psychological and social consequences of puberty. One approach is to look at individuals who are at various stages of puberty, either **cross-sectionally** (in which groups of individuals at different stages of pu-

Youngsters went through puberty at a later age 100 years ago than they do today. The increasingly earlier maturation of young people is referred to as the *secular trend.* (Bettmann Archive)

berty are compared) or **longitudinally** (in which the same individuals are tracked over time as they move through the different stages of puberty). Studies of this sort examine the *immediate impact* of puberty on the young person's psychological development and social relations. Researchers might ask, for example, whether youngsters' self-esteem is higher or lower during puberty than before or after.

A second approach compares the psychological development of early and late maturers. The focus of these studies is not so much on the absolute impact of puberty but on the effects of *differential timing* of the changes. Here, a typical question might be whether early maturers are more popular in the peer group than late maturers.

## THE IMMEDIATE IMPACT OF PUBERTY

Studies of the psychological and social impact of puberty indicate that physical maturation, regardless of whether it occurs early or late, affects the adolescent's self-image, mood, and relationships with parents. The short-term consequences of puberty may be most taxing on the adolescent's family, however, and less significant for the adolescent's self-perceptions or mood (Simmons and Blyth, 1987; Steinberg, 1987a).

In a longitudinal study of changes in self-esteem during the early adolescent years, sociologist Roberta Simmons and her colleagues found that going through puberty may lead to modest declines in self-esteem among adolescent girls but only when accompanied by other changes that require adaptation on the part of the young person (Simmons, Blyth, Van Cleave, and Bush, 1979). Among the nearly 800 youngsters who were studied, those who showed the greatest declines in self-esteem between sixth and seventh grade were girls who began menstruating, began dating, and had to change schools all during the same year. (Boys did not show the same adverse effects of going through puberty, but we should remember that few boys are likely to begin puberty during the transition into junior high school.) This research suggests that puberty may be a potential *stressor* that has temporary adverse psychological consequences for girls, but only when it is coupled with other changes that necessitate adjustment. By itself, however, puberty appears to have only modest effects on girls' and boys' self-image (Simmons and Blyth, 1987). Indeed, recent studies suggest that the impact of puberty on adolescents' psychological functioning is to a great extent shaped by the social context in which puberty takes place (Brooks-Gunn and Reiter, 1990).

Although an adolescent's self-image could be expected to be changed during a time of dramatic physical development, it could also be the case that self-esteem or self-image is a reasonably stable characteristic, with long and sturdy roots reaching back to childhood. For this reason, some researchers have turned their attention to the impact of puberty on more transient states, such as mood. One reason for this choice is that adolescents are thought to be moodier, on average, than adults. One study (Csikszentmihalyi and Larson, 1984), in which adolescents' moods were monitored repeatedly by electronic pagers, for example, showed that adolescents' moods fluctuate during the course of the day more than the moods of adults (see Figure 1.11). Many adults assume that adolescent moodiness is directly related to the hormonal changes of puberty. (Petersen, 1985). Is there any scientific evidence that the hormonal changes of puberty cause adolescents to be moody, or, for that matter, that these hormonal changes affect the adolescent's psychological functioning or behavior at all?

A number of studies have examined this question. One team of investigators has found that high levels of **adrenal androgens** may be related to sadness, aggression, and rebelliousness in adolescent boys (Susman et al., 1987) but that increases in levels of sex hormones, such as testosterone, may be related to better adjustment for male adolescents (Nottelmann, Susman, Inhoff-Germain, and Chrousos, 1987). Another team of scientists has found that rapid increases in estrogen may be related to depression among early adolescent girls (Brooks-Gunn and Warren, 1987). These effects seem strongest early in puberty, when the system is being "turned on" (Brooks-Gunn and Reiter, 1990) and when hormonal levels are highly variable (Eccles et al., 1988). However, the researchers cautiously point out that the connection between hormones and mood is not

strong and that we need to understand better how environmental and biological factors interact in influencing adolescents' mood and behavior.

An excellent illustration of the way in which hormones and environment interact at puberty comes from the work of psychologist Jeanne Brooks-Gunn and her colleagues (Brooks-Gunn, 1987, 1989; Brooks-Gunn, Warren, and Rosso, 1991), who have been studying the development of psychological problems, such as depression and aggression, in young girls around the time of puberty. Although rapid increases in hormones early in puberty are associated with depressed mood in girls, it turns out that stressful life events, such as problems in the family, in school, or with friends, play a far greater role in the development of depression than do hormonal changes. Moreover, as she and others point out, it is quite possible that changes in the environment—in levels of stress, for instance—may affect hormonal activity, which in turn may affect adolescents' mood. The evidence for a direct and strong link between the hormonal changes of adolescence and changes in young people's mood is very weak.

Interestingly, not only is there little evidence that adolescents' moodiness is due to the "storm and stress" of "raging" hormones, there is also research that questions the very idea that adolescents are inherently moodier than children. Psychologists Mihaly Csikszentmihalyi and Reed Larson (1986; Larson and Lampman-Petraitis, 1989) had teenagers carry electronic pagers similar to the ones physicians carry, and they paged them periodically throughout the day. When the adolescents were paged, they filled out forms noting how they were feeling, what they were doing, where they were, and whom they were with. By looking at changes in mood across activities and settings, the researchers were able to determine the correlates of adolescent moodiness.

Their findings suggest that adolescent mood

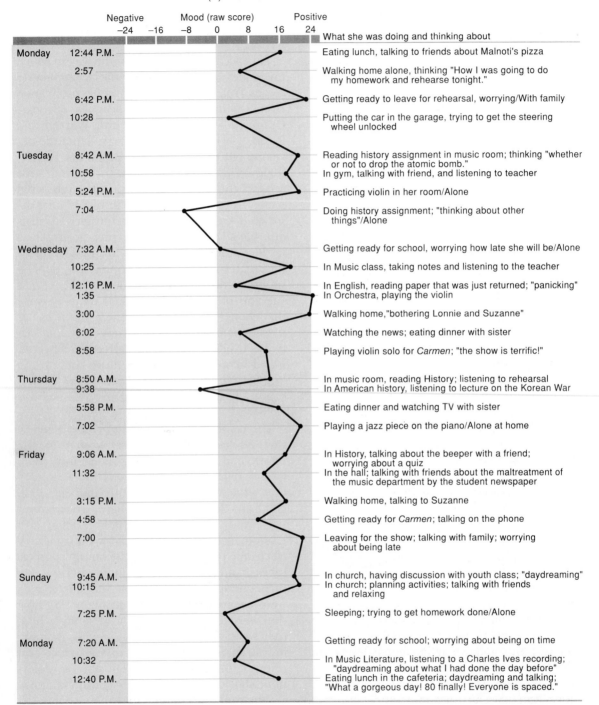

**(A) The Week of Katherine Tennison**

| | | What she was doing and thinking about |
|---|---|---|
| Monday | 12:44 P.M. | Eating lunch, talking to friends about Malnoti's pizza |
| | 2:57 | Walking home alone, thinking "How I was going to do my homework and rehearse tonight." |
| | 6:42 P.M. | Getting ready to leave for rehearsal, worrying/With family |
| | 10:28 | Putting the car in the garage, trying to get the steering wheel unlocked |
| Tuesday | 8:42 A.M. | Reading history assignment in music room; thinking "whether or not to drop the atomic bomb." |
| | 10:58 | In gym, talking with friend, and listening to teacher |
| | 5:24 P.M. | Practicing violin in her room/Alone |
| | 7:04 | Doing history assignment; "thinking about other things"/Alone |
| Wednesday | 7:32 A.M. | Getting ready for school, worrying how late she will be/Alone |
| | 10:25 | In Music class, taking notes and listening to the teacher |
| | 12:16 P.M. | In English, reading paper that was just returned; "panicking" |
| | 1:35 | In Orchestra, playing the violin |
| | 3:00 | Walking home,"bothering Lonnie and Suzanne" |
| | 6:02 | Watching the news; eating dinner with sister |
| | 8:58 | Playing violin solo for *Carmen*; "the show is terrific!" |
| Thursday | 8:50 A.M. | In music room, reading History; listening to rehearsal |
| | 9:38 | In American history, listening to lecture on the Korean War |
| | 5:58 P.M. | Eating dinner and watching TV with sister |
| | 7:02 | Playing a jazz piece on the piano/Alone at home |
| Friday | 9:06 A.M. | In History, talking about the beeper with a friend; worrying about a quiz |
| | 11:32 | In the hall; talking with friends about the maltreatment of the music department by the student newspaper |
| | 3:15 P.M. | Walking home, talking to Suzanne |
| | 4:58 | Getting ready for *Carmen*; talking on the phone |
| | 7:00 | Leaving for the show; talking with family; worrying about being late |
| Sunday | 9:45 A.M. | In church, having discussion with youth class; "daydreaming" |
| | 10:15 | In church; planning activities; talking with friends and relaxing |
| | 7:25 P.M. | Sleeping; trying to get homework done/Alone |
| Monday | 7:20 A.M. | Getting ready for school; worrying about being on time |
| | 10:32 | In Music Literature, listening to a Charles Ives recording; "daydreaming about what I had done the day before" |
| | 12:40 P.M. | Eating lunch in the cafeteria; daydreaming and talking; "What a gorgeous day! 80 finally! Everyone is spaced." |

Mood (raw score): Negative −24 −16 −8 0 8 16 24 Positive

**FIGURE 1.11**   (A and B)   Fluctuations in two adolescents' moods over the course of a week. (Csikszentmihalyi and Larson, 1984)

## (B) The Week of Gregory Stone

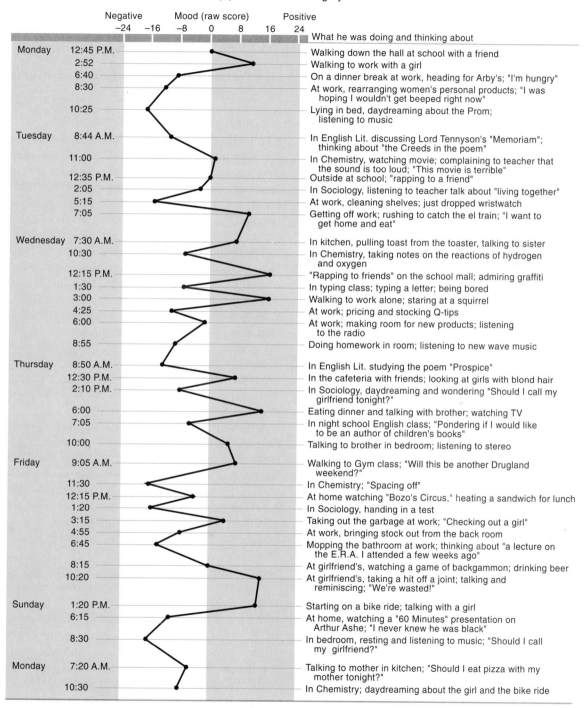

| | | Mood (raw score) | |
|---|---|---|---|
| | Negative | | Positive |
| | −24  −16  −8  0  8  16  24 | | What he was doing and thinking about |

| | | |
|---|---|---|
| Monday | 12:45 P.M. | Walking down the hall at school with a friend |
| | 2:52 | Walking to work with a girl |
| | 6:40 | On a dinner break at work, heading for Arby's; "I'm hungry" |
| | 8:30 | At work, rearranging women's personal products; "I was hoping I wouldn't get beeped right now" |
| | 10:25 | Lying in bed, daydreaming about the Prom; listening to music |
| Tuesday | 8:44 A.M. | In English Lit. discussing Lord Tennyson's "Memoriam"; thinking about "the Creeds in the poem" |
| | 11:00 | In Chemistry, watching movie; complaining to teacher that the sound is too loud; "This movie is terrible" |
| | 12:35 P.M. | Outside at school; "rapping to a friend" |
| | 2:05 | In Sociology, listening to teacher talk about "living together" |
| | 5:15 | At work, cleaning shelves; just dropped wristwatch |
| | 7:05 | Getting off work; rushing to catch the el train; "I want to get home and eat" |
| Wednesday | 7:30 A.M. | In kitchen, pulling toast from the toaster, talking to sister |
| | 10:30 | In Chemistry, taking notes on the reactions of hydrogen and oxygen |
| | 12:15 P.M. | "Rapping to friends" on the school mall; admiring graffiti |
| | 1:30 | In typing class; typing a letter; being bored |
| | 3:00 | Walking to work alone; staring at a squirrel |
| | 4:25 | At work; pricing and stocking Q-tips |
| | 6:00 | At work; making room for new products; listening to the radio |
| | 8:55 | Doing homework in room; listening to new wave music |
| Thursday | 8:50 A.M. | In English Lit. studying the poem "Prospice" |
| | 12:30 P.M. | In the cafeteria with friends; looking at girls with blond hair |
| | 2:10 P.M. | In Sociology, daydreaming and wondering "Should I call my girlfriend tonight?" |
| | 6:00 | Eating dinner and talking with brother; watching TV |
| | 7:05 | In night school English class; "Pondering if I would like to be an author of children's books" |
| | 10:00 | Talking to brother in bedroom; listening to stereo |
| Friday | 9:05 A.M. | Walking to Gym class; "Will this be another Drugland weekend?" |
| | 11:30 | In Chemistry; "Spacing off" |
| | 12:15 P.M. | At home watching "Bozo's Circus," heating a sandwich for lunch |
| | 1:20 | In Sociology, handing in a test |
| | 3:15 | Taking out the garbage at work; "Checking out a girl" |
| | 4:55 | At work, bringing stock out from the back room |
| | 6:45 | Mopping the bathroom at work; thinking about "a lecture on the E.R.A. I attended a few weeks ago" |
| | 8:15 | At girlfriend's, watching a game of backgammon; drinking beer |
| | 10:20 | At girlfriend's, taking a hit off a joint; talking and reminiscing; "We're wasted!" |
| Sunday | 1:20 P.M. | Starting on a bike ride; talking with a girl |
| | 6:15 | At home, watching a "60 Minutes" presentation on Arthur Ashe; "I never knew he was black" |
| | 8:30 | In bedroom, resting and listening to music; "Should I call my girlfriend?" |
| Monday | 7:20 A.M. | Talking to mother in kitchen; "Should I eat pizza with my mother tonight?" |
| | 10:30 | In Chemistry; daydreaming about the girl and the bike ride |

swings parallel their changes in activities. Over the course of a day, a teenager may shift from elation to boredom, back again to happiness, and then to anger. But this shifting appears to have more to do with shifts in activities—elated when seeing a girlfriend, bored in social studies class, happy when having lunch with his friends, and angry when assigned extra work at the fast-food restaurant—than with internal, biological changes. More important, comparisons of youngsters between the ages of 9 and 15 did not show increases in moodiness during the transition into adolescence. Although adolescents may be moodier than adults, it is probably because they change activities and contexts more often than adults do.

All in all, research on the immediate impact of puberty on individual psychological functioning has not indicated very strong effects. In contrast, research on the impact of puberty on *family relationships* has pointed to a more consistent pattern, namely, that puberty appears to increase distance between parents and children (Steinberg, 1990). Several studies show that as youngsters mature from childhood toward the middle of puberty, distance between them and their parents increases and conflict intensifies, especially between the adolescent and his or her mother (Hill et al., 1985a, 1985b; Steinberg, 1987a, 1988). Although conflict may diminish after the adolescent growth spurt, adolescents and their parents do not immediately become as close as they were before the adolescents entered puberty.

Because this connection between pubertal maturation and parent-child distance is not affected by the age at which the adolescent goes through puberty—in other words, the pattern is seen among early as well as late maturers—it seems that something about puberty in particular may transform the parent-child bond. To date, we do not know whether this effect is due to the hormonal changes of puberty, to

changes in the adolescent's physical appearance, or to changes in psychological functioning that in turn affect family relationships. One writer has pointed out that puberty increases distance between children and their parents in most species of monkeys and apes and that the pattern seen in human adolescents may have some evolutionary basis (Steinberg, 1987b).

Whatever the underlying mechanism, one way to interpret these studies is that puberty can upset psychological and social balances that are established during childhood, causing temporary periods of disruption. During childhood, for example, individuals develop a certain self-image that is suddenly shaken in early adolescence. It may take some time for them to integrate the changes brought about by puberty into their self-concept, and during this period of integration, their self-esteem and self-image may suffer.

Similarly, families develop patterns of relationships during a son's or daughter's childhood that are comfortable and workable, but they may find that puberty disrupts the patterns to which they have grown accustomed. They have developed a certain way of discussing things and a certain way of including the children in family discussions. But as the children go through puberty, they may want to be treated more like adults. They may want to have more of a say in family decisions. Consequently, families may experience a temporary period of conflict or tension when sons and daughters enter early adolescence. It may take some time for the individual and the family to achieve a new equilibrium that takes into account the changes brought on by puberty.

Puberty may have an effect on relationships in the peer group, too. One study of adolescents' *social networks*—the people they are most likely to see and spend time with—found that adolescents who were physically mature were less likely than their less developed peers to name adults as people who were important to them and more likely to name other adolescents (Garbarino, Burston, Raber, Russell, and Crouter, 1978). This finding suggests that pubertal maturation may be an important influence in shifting adolescents' interests and energies toward the peer group. Boys and girls who are physically mature are more likely than less mature agemates to be involved in cross-sex activities such as having a boyfriend or girlfriend or going out on dates (Crockett and Dorn, 1987), although this depends on the social norms of the adolescent's peer group and the prevailing expectations about the age at which teenagers should begin dating (Dornbusch et al., 1981; Gargiulo et al., 1987).

## THE IMPACT OF MENARCHE AND FIRST EJACULATION

Several studies have focused specifically on girls' attitudes toward and reactions to menarche and boys' reactions to their first ejaculation. The onset of menstruaton is "not just one of a series of physiological events during puberty, but is also a sociocultural event . . . imbued with special meaning" (Brooks-Gunn and Ruble, 1979). Cultural beliefs concerning menarche and the specific information a young woman receives from parents, teachers, friends, and health practitioners all influence how she greets and experiences menarche (Brooks-Gunn and Ruble, 1982).

In Western culture, many young women have developed a negative image of menstruation before reaching adolescence and enter puberty with ambivalent attitudes about menarche—a mixture of excitement and fear (Ruble and Brooks-Gunn, 1982). Adolescent girls' attitudes toward menarche are less negative today than they appear to have been in the past (Ruble and Brooks-Gunn, 1982; Greif and Ulman, 1982), a change that may be attributable to the more open and less mysterious presentation of information about menstruation in schools and in the media in recent years. In general, among today's adolescent girls, menarche is typically accompanied not only by gains in social maturity, peer prestige, and self-esteem, but also by heightened self-consciousness (Brooks-Gunn and Reiter, 1990). As you will read later in this chapter, however, the impact of menarche on the young adolescent's psychological development depends in part on whether she matures early or late, relative to her peers.

Interestingly, one set of studies, by psychologists Diane Ruble and Jeanne Brooks-Gunn, indicates that a strong negative bias toward menstruation before menarche may actually be associated with greater menstrual discomfort. Menstrual symptoms are reported to be more severe among women who expect menstruation to be uncomfortable, among girls whose mothers lead them to believe that menstruation will be an unpleasant or uncomfortable experience, and in cultures that label menstruation as an important event. In addition, girls who experience menarche early, relative to their peers, or who are otherwise unprepared for puberty report more negative reactions to the event (Rierdan, Kobb, and Stubbs, 1989; Ruble and Brooks-Gunn, 1982).

Far less is known about boys' reactions to their first ejaculation, an experience that we might consider analagous to menarche in girls. Although most boys are not very well prepared for this event by their parents or other adults, first ejaculation does not appear to cause undue anxiety, embarrassment, or fear. It is interesting to note, however, that in contrast to girls, who generally tell their mothers shortly after they have begun menstruating and tell their girlfriends soon thereafter, boys do not discuss their first ejaculation with either parents or friends (Gaddis and Brooks-Gunn, 1985). The apparent secrecy surrounding this event may be due to the fact that the first ejaculation is actually more upsetting than boys

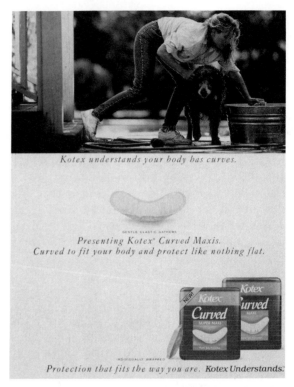

One sign that attitudes toward menstruation have changed in the last twenty-five years is that advertisements for tampons and sanitary napkins have become far more explicit and far less mysterious. As a consequence, adolescent girls receive very different messages about the meaning of maturation today from twenty or thirty years ago. Here are two excerpts from magazine advertisements for sanitary napkins—one from 1951, the other from 1991. *(KOTEX is a registered trademark of Kimberly-Clark Corporation. These advertisements reprinted by permission. All rights reserved)*

are willing to admit or to the fact that it is perceived as relatively unimportant.

## THE IMPACT OF EARLY OR LATE MATURATION

Adolescents who mature relatively early or relatively late stand apart from their peers physically and may, as a consequence, elicit different sorts of reactions and expectations from those around them. Moreover, individual adolescents may be all too aware of whether they

are early or late relative to their agemates, and their feelings about themselves are likely to be influenced by their comparisons. In short, early and late maturers may be treated differently by others, may view themselves differently, and may as a result behave differently. As we shall see, early and late maturation have different consequences in the immediate present and in the long run, different consequences in different contexts, and, most important, different consequences for boys and girls.

**Early versus late maturation among boys**
The first studies to compare early- and late-maturing boys suggested that it was an advantage to mature earlier than one's peers. Drawing on data collected as part of the Oakland Growth Study (a longitudinal study begun earlier this century and continuing today), psychologist Mary Jones and her colleagues compared early- and late-maturing boys on a variety of psychological tests and measures of interpersonal relationships (Jones, 1957, 1965; Jones and Bayley, 1950; Mussen and Jones, 1957, 1958). They found that late maturers were seen by their peers as more childish and were less popular and less likely to have held leadership positions. On personality measures, late-maturing boys exhibited stronger feelings of inadequacy, higher needs for autonomy, more negative self-concepts, more childishness, less self-control, less responsibility, and less self-assurance.

Research conducted since these early studies has confirmed their feelings, though with several modifications. With regard to self-image and popularity, early-maturing boys clearly have an advantage over their more slowly developing peers (Petersen, 1985). With regard to *behavior*, however, early maturers may be more likely than their peers to get involved in problem or deviant activities, including truancy, minor delinquency, and problems at school (Duncan, Ritter, Dornbusch, Gross, and Carlsmith, 1985), and are somewhat more likely to be involved with substance use (Anderson and Magnusson, 1990; Silbereisen, Kracke, and Crockett, 1990). One reasonable guess is that boys who are more physically mature develop friendships with older peers and that these friendships lead them into activities that are problematic for the younger boys.

With regard to *mood*, one interesting reanalysis of old data indicated that early-maturing boys may have more problems than research had indicated. Psychologist Harvey Peskin

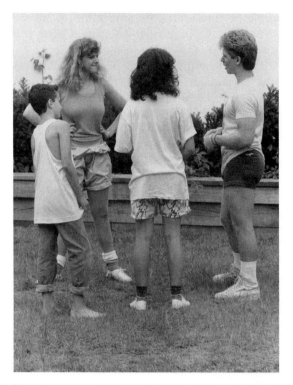

These adolescents are all the same chronological age, despite their markedly different physical appearances. Among boys, early maturation is associated with greater popularity and higher self-esteem. Although early maturing girls are also more popular with their peers, they report more emotional difficulties than young women who mature later. *(Alan Carey/Image Works)*

(1967) argued that researchers might have been confusing two different comparisons: early versus late maturers (the comparisons they were interested in) and postpubertal versus pubertal youngsters (a comparison they were making inadvertently). Perhaps, he reasoned, the apparently greater childishness and lower self-esteem of late-maturing boys found in the earlier studies were due not to their relatively late maturation but to the fact that they were still going through puberty at the time the personality measures were taken. It would be interesting, Peskin suggested, to see what the early-maturing youngsters were like *at the time they were going through puberty.*

Peskin found that early and late maturers were very similar when each was examined one year before pubertal onset. But at the time of pubertal onset and one year later as well, the late maturers showed significantly higher ratings on measures of intellectual curiosity, exploratory behavior, and social initiative. Interestingly, early maturers experienced more frequent and intense temper tantrums during puberty (Livson and Peskin, 1980).

Late maturers, Peskin argued, have the advantage of a longer preadolescent period, giving them more time to "prepare" psychologically for the onset of puberty. This preparation may be important if, as noted earlier, rapid increases in hormones at puberty provoke changes in mood. Many theorists believe that the middle childhood and preadolescent years are extremely important periods for the development of coping skills—skills that prove valuable during adolescence and adulthood. Although puberty by no means marks the end of the growth of coping abilities, it does come as an abrupt interruption to the more relaxed preadolescent era. A later puberty, and hence a longer preadolescence, might allow for coping skills to develop more fully before adolescence. This may account in part for the apparently better coping skills demonstrated by late maturers—not only during puberty but, as you will read, later, as adults.

**Early versus late maturation in girls**  The initial research on this issue, again conducted by researchers working on the Oakland Growth Study, suggested that in contrast to boys, early-maturing girls were at a disadvantage—although the findings were far less consistent than they were in the studies of boys (Jones, 1949; Jones and Mussen, 1958). Briefly, early-maturing girls were found to be "less popular, less poised, less expressive, and

more submissive, withdrawn, and unassured then [their] agemates" (Livson and Peskin, 1980, p. 71). Like the late-maturing boys, the early-maturing girl is out of step with her peers. And since girls mature about two years earlier than boys, the early-maturing girl is not only more physically advanced than her female peers but far more advanced than nearly all of her male classmates as well. In these studies, the late-maturing girls were more likely to be seen as attractive, sociable, and expressive.

As is the case for research on early- and late-maturing boys, recent research on girls has tended to corroborate the findings of the earlier studies, but we have learned a good deal more about the development of early-maturing girls in the ensuing years. A number of studies find that early-maturing girls have more emotional difficulties than do girls who mature on time or late (Aro and Taipale, 1987; Simmons and Blyth, 1987), a finding that has been confirmed in several Western countries. These difficulties seem to have a great deal to do with girls' feelings about their height and weight, because early maturers are, almost by definition, taller and heavier than their late-maturing peers (Petersen, 1988). In societies that define as physically attractive the thin, "leggy" woman, a late-maturing girl will look more like this image than an early-maturing girl will.

However, whether earlier maturation has a negative effect on the young girl's feelings about herself appears to depend on the broader context in which maturation takes place. For example, studies of American girls generally find that early-maturing girls have lower self-esteem and a poorer self-image, because of our cultural preference for thinness and our national ambivalence about adolescent sexuality (Brooks-Gunn and Reiter, 1990). In Germany, however, where sex education is more open and attitudes toward adolescent sexuality less conflicted, early maturing girls are found to have *higher* self-esteem (Silbereisen, Petersen, Albrecht, and Kracke, 1989). Interestingly, even *within* the United States, the impact of physical maturation appears to depend on the social context in which teenagers live. One study of suburban Chicago youngsters, for example, found that girls' body image was significantly higher in one community than in another—despite comparable levels of physical maturation between the two groups. One factor that differentiated the two communities was "cliquishness": In the more cliquish high school, girls were less satisfied with the way they looked (Richards, Boxer, Petersen, and Albrecht, 1990).

Although some early-maturing girls may have self-image difficulties, their popularity with peers is not jeopardized. Indeed, some studies indicate that early maturers are more popular than other girls, especially, as you would expect, when the index of popularity includes popularity with boys (Simmons, Blyth, and McKinney, 1983). Ironically, it may be in part because early maturers are more popular with boys that they report more emotional upset: At a very early age, pressure to date and, perhaps, to be involved in a sexual relationship, may take its toll on the adolescent girl's mental health. Consistent with this, one team of researchers (Blyth, Simmons, and Zakin, 1985) found that early-maturing girls in schools with older peers (for example, sixth-graders who were in a school that had seventh- and eighth-graders, too) were psychologically worse off than early-maturing girls who were in the highest grade in their school (for example, sixth-graders who were in an elementary school.) Again, we see the importance of context.

Like their male counterparts, early-maturing girls are also more likely to become involved in deviant activities, including delinquency, drug and alcohol use, more likely to have school problems, and more likely to experience early sexual intercourse (Aro and Taipale, 1987; Caspi and Moffitt, in press; Mag-

nusson, Statin and Allen, 1986). This is true in Europe as well as the United States (Silversen et al., 1989). These problems appear to arise because early-maturing girls are more likely to spend time with older adolescents, especially older adolescent boys, who initiate them into activities that might otherwise be delayed (Magnusson et al., 1986). Interestingly, one set of studies indicates that girls' *perceptions* of their maturational timing (whether they *think* they are early, late, or on-time) may be more important in influencing their behavior and their feelings about themselves than their actual maturational timing (Petersen et al., in press; Petersen, Graber, and Sullivan, 1990). Adolescents who perceive themselves to be earlier maturers may see themselves as ready to engage in "adult" behaviors, such as smoking, drinking, and drug use. As you will read in a moment, although most of these behavioral differences disappear by the time the late-maturing girls have completed puberty, the earlier involvement of early-maturing girls in certain behaviors may have important long-term repercussions.

**Long-term consequences**  Do the psychological and interpersonal differences between early and late maturers observed during adolescence persist into adulthood? Do early-maturing boys remain more popular and self-confident as adults, for example?

In order to answer these questions, a series of follow-up studies conducted some twenty-five years later looked at the adult personalities of males who had been studied during adolescence (Livson and Peskin, 1980). At age 38, the early maturers were more responsible, cooperative, self-controlled, and sociable. At first glance, it appeared as if the benefits of early maturation had carried over well into adulthood.

Yet the picture was not so clear-cut. By adulthood, some of the advantages had turned into disadvantages. True, the early maturers

# THE SEXES: THE EFFECTS OF EARLY MATURATION

Researchers are still trying to make sense of the complicated pattern of findings that emerges from comparisons of early and late maturers, but one fact is clear: Early maturation brings many more advantages for boys than it does for girls, and in many respects, it may be a disadvantage for girls to go through puberty sustantially earlier than their peers. Psychologists have offered several explanations for this sex difference. The explanations all are compatible, but they derive from very different premises.

One explanation might be termed the "deviance" hypothesis (Simmons and Blyth, 1987). Simply put, youngsters who stand far apart from their peers—in physical appearance, for instance—may experience more psychological distress than adolescents who blend in more easily. Studies of adolescents who stand out physically in other ways—obese students or students who attend schools in which they are clearly in a racial minority—support the view that standing out too much can be an unfortunate disadvantage (Blyth et al., 1980; Simmons, Blyth, and McKinney,

1983). Because girls mature earlier than boys, on average, early-maturing girls mature much earlier than their male and female agemates. This presumably makes them stand out at a time when they would rather fit in and may make them more vulnerable. This explanation would also account for the lower self-esteem of late-maturing boys, who are "deviant" toward the other extreme.

A second explanation focuses on "developmental readiness." Here the notion is that psychological distress results when youngsters have experiences before they are psychologically "ready" for them (Simmons and Blyth, 1987). If puberty is a challenge that requires psychological adaptation by the adolescent, perhaps younger adolescents are less able to cope with the challenge than older ones. Because puberty occurs quite early among early-maturing girls (some may begin maturing at age 8 or 9 and experience menarche at age 10), it may tax their psychological resources. Early maturation among boys, because it occurs at a much later age, would pose

*continued on next page*

did appear more confident and responsible. But they had also grown up to be more conforming, conventional, and humorless. Their peers who had been late maturers remained somewhat more impulsive and assertive but turned out to be more insightful, more inventive, and more creatively playful. What had happened?

One interpretation is that because of their more adultlike appearance, the early-maturing boys had been pushed into adult roles earlier than their peers. They were more likely to be asked to assume responsibility, take on leadership positions, and behave in a more "grown-up" manner. But this early press toward adulthood may have come too soon and stifled a certain amount of creativity and risk taking.

Have you gone to any gatherings of old high school classmates? Did you discover that some of the people whom you had remembered as extremely mature and socially successful during high school have turned out to be not all that interesting a few years after graduation? Perhaps too much leadership, responsibility, social success, and "maturity" during the high school years interferes with the sort of psycholess of a problem. The **developmental readiness** hypothesis has been used to account for the finding that older (eighth-graders) youngsters fare better during the transition from elementary to secondary school than younger (sixth grade) ones do. This perspective also helps to account for the fact that in puberty, late-maturing boys seem more able to control their temper and their impulses (Peskin, 1967).

A final explanation concerns the cultural desirability of different body types (Petersen, 1988). Early maturation for girls means leaving behind the culturally admired state of thinness. As you read earlier, for girls, the ratio of fat to muscle increases dramatically at puberty. Many girls feel distressed when they mature because they gain weight, and early maturers experience this weight gain when most of their peers are still girlishly thin. One interesting study showed that in ballet companies—where thinness is even more important than in the culture at large—late maturers, who can retain the "ideal" shape much longer than earlier maturers, have fewer psychological problems than even on-time girls (Brooks-Gunn and Warren, 1985). Boys at puberty, in con-

trast, move from a culturally undesirable state for males—being short and scrawny—to a culturally admired one—being tall and muscular. Early maturers enjoy the special advantage of being tall and muscular before their peers and therefore are more likely to react well to puberty. The fact that the effects of early maturation on girls' self-esteem vary across cultures suggests that contextual factors need to be taken into account in explaining this pattern of sex differences.

Whatever the explanation, the fact that early-maturing girls are at heightened risk for temporary psychological problems, at least in the United States, is an important fact for parents and school counselors to bear in mind. Unfortunately, as long as our culture overvalues thinness and encourages the view that women should be judged on the basis of their physical appearance rather than their abilities, values, or personality, the risks of early puberty will probably persist. Adults can help by being supportive, by helping the early-maturing girl to recognize her strengths and positive features—physical and nonphysical alike—and by preparing her for puberty before it takes place.

logical development that makes for interesting and creative adults. As we shall see in a later chapter, many psychologists believe that adolescents may benefit in the long run from having an extended period of time during which they are *not* being pushed into adulthood.

Success and social status may come too easily and too early for early-maturing boys, leaving them with less need to develop creative or flexible solutions to life's problems and less time to experiment with new roles and identities. In contrast, late-maturing youngsters, experiencing more difficulty in achieving social standing

and recognition because of their immature physical appearance, may be forced to develop more inventive means of problem solving and greater cognitive and social flexibility. In other words, the greater difficulty that late maturers face as early adolescents may lead to their developing coping skills that prove useful when they reach adulthood. Unfortunately, however, at least one study of late-maturing boys indicates that heavy drinking may be "coping" behavior that persists into young adulthood (Andersson and Magnusson, 1990).

One study of the adult personalities of

women who had been either early or late maturers suggests interesting parallels between the personality development of early-maturing girls and late-maturing boys (Peskin, 1973). Both sets of youngsters may have self-esteem problems during adolescence, but both appear to be somewhat more psychologically advanced than their peers during adulthood. Like the late-maturing boys, early-maturing girls may be forced to develop coping skills during adolescence that have some long-term positive effects.

At the same time, however, more recent research indicates that the earlier involvement of of early-maturing girls in problem behavior may adversely affect their long-term educational achievement. In one study of Swedish girls, for example, the researchers found that the school problems of early-maturing adolescent girls persisted, leading to the development of negative attitudes toward school and lower educational aspirations. In young adulthood, there were marked differences between the early- and late-maturing girls' levels of education; for example, the late-maturing girls were twice as likely as early-maturing girls to continue beyond the compulsory minimum number of years of high school (Magnusson et al., 1986).

## Physical Health in Adolescence

Although puberty is undoubtedly the most important biological development of the adolescent decade, concerns about the physical health and well-being of young people are far broader than those involving reproductive maturation. In the last decade, the field of **adolescent health** has grown rapidly, as health educators and health care practitioners have come to better understand that the health care needs of young people differ from those of children and adults in important respects.

Adolescence is a paradox as far as physical health is concerned. On the one hand, adolescence is one of the healthiest periods in the life span, characterized by a relatively low incidence of disabling or chronic illnesses (e.g., asthma, cancer) compared with other periods of life, fewer short-term hospital stays, and fewer days in which individuals stay home sick in bed. Moreover, in the past fifty years, rates of death and disability due to illness and disease during adolescence have decreased substantially, and new medical technologies and better health care delivery have improved the physical well-being of children, especially those with chronic illness and disabling medical conditions (Gans, 1990). Although one in fifteen adolescents in the United States is chronically ill (the main causes of disability in adolescence are mental disorders, such as depression; respiratory illnesses, such as asthma; and muscular and skeletal disorders, such as arthritis), disabled and handicapped teenagers are better cared for today and live much longer than their counterparts did previously (Gans, 1990).

On the other hand, however, adolescence is a period of relatively great physical risk due to unhealthy behaviors (such as drug use), violence (both self-inflicted and inflicted by others), and risky activity (such as unprotected sexual intercourse). Moreover, adolescents are far less likely than adults to seek and receive medical and dental care (Millstein, 1988). In some senses, then, many of the improvements we have made in preventing and treating the traditional "medical" problems of the period—those having to do with chronic illnesses—have been offset by what some scientists call the "new morbidity and mortality" of adolescence (Hein, 1988). Contributors to this new morbidity and mortality include accidents (especially automobile accidents), suicide, homicide, substance abuse (including tobacco and alcohol use), and sexually transmitted diseases (including AIDS).

The contrast between the "old" and "new"

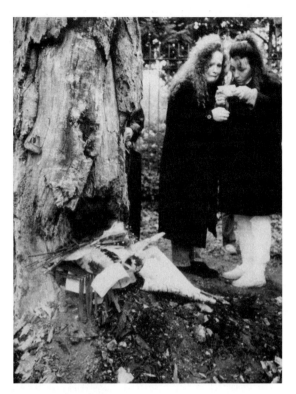

Much of the progress we have made in the prevention and treatment of medical problems during adolescence has been offset by the "new morbidity and mortality" of adolescence. Automobile accidents are a leading cause of death in adolescence. These friends of victims of a car crash are examining a photograph of the accident while standing at the scene of the crash. *(Lee Romero/ The New York Times)*

cent are due to homicide, suicide, or some other violent act or injury (Gans, 1990).

The consensus among health care experts is that the most significant threats to the health of today's youth are due to psychosocial rather than natural causes (Gans, 1990, p. 15). Unlike many other periods of the life span (such as infancy or old age), when we are more vulnerable to disease and illness, most of the health problems of teenagers are preventable. As a result of this recognition, the focus in the field of adolescent health has shifted away from traditional medical models (in which the emphasis was on the assessment, diagnosis, and treatment of disease) toward more community-oriented, educational approaches (in which the emphasis is on the prevention of illness and injury and the promotion of good health). In other words, instead of asking how we can best treat sick youngsters, experts in adolescent health care are now asking how we can encourage adolescents and children to take the steps necessary to prevent illness and disability and live more healthy lives. Such efforts include education about alcohol and other drug use, accident prevention, safe sex, and proper nutrition.

Among the most encouraging of the latest wave of prevention and promotion efforts are those that involve school-linked, or **school-based health centers.** These centers, located in or adjacent to schools, provide such services as physical examinations, the treatment of minor injuries, health education programs, dental care, and counseling related to substance abuse, sexuality, and mental health. They often are set up to serve economically disadvantaged youth, who generally are less likely to receive medical and dental care than their more affluent counterparts.

School-based centers have become increasingly popular because they are positioned to address the most pressing problems in adolescent health care: the fact that most adolescent health problems are preventable, the fact that

mortalities is readily apparent. Although the death rate due to natural causes (such as disease or illness) fell 90 percent between 1933 and 1985 among adolescents, the death rate due to violence and injury remained stable, and even increased somewhat between 1950 and 1985. Fifty years ago, illness and disease accounted for more than twice as many deaths among teenagers as violence or injury, but the reverse is true today. According to recent estimates, nearly 40 percent of all teenage deaths are due to car accidents, and another 30 per-adolescents underutilize conventional medical services, and the fact that adolescents often want their health care needs to remain confidential. Although the development of these centers has generated controversy in a number of communities because some school-based centers distribute contraceptives (a practice, that, as we shall see in a later chapter, upsets many adults), studies show that the vast majority of visits to these centers are for physical examinations, acute illnesses (e.g., influenza, strep throat), and minor emergencies (Millstein, 1988). Currently, there are about 150 school-based health centers for adolescents in the United States, and their systematic evaluation is now under way.

## Summary

1. The term "puberty" refers to the physical changes that occur in the growing girl or boy as the individual passes from childhood into adulthood. The chief physical manifestations are the growth spurt, the further development of the gonads, the development of secondary sex characteristics, changes in body composition, and changes in circulation and respiration.

2. The onset of puberty is regulated by a feedback loop in the endocrine system, involving the hypothalamus, the pituitary, and the gonads—ovaries in females; testes in males.

3. One of the most important physical changes of puberty is the development of secondary sex characteristics—changes in outward appearance that signal the onset of reproductive maturity. These changes include the growth of pubic hair, changes in the appearance of the sex organs, and breast development.

4. There is considerable variation in the timing and tempo of puberty. As a result, a group of adolescents of the same chronological age will contain youngsters whose physical maturity varies considerably. The most important influence on the timing of maturation is genetic. But in addition, adolescents who have been well-nourished and healthy during childhood go through puberty earlier than their peers. Because of improvements in nutrition and health care, young people mature earlier today than they did centuries ago, a phenomenon known as the "secular trend."

5. Although puberty may cause temporary disruption in the adolescent's social relationships, research has not shown that puberty is inherently stressful or associated with dramatic changes in mood or behavior. More important than puberty itself is how puberty is viewed within the context in which the adolescent matures, and the extent to which the adolescent has been prepared psychologically for the biological changes of the era.

6. Psychologists have long been interested in the consequences of early versus late physical maturation. In general, early maturation brings with it more social advantages for boys and girls, and very early maturation may be somewhat of a liability for girls, at least in the United States. For both sexes, however, early physical maturation is associated with more problem behavior, including drug and alcohol use, delinquency, and precocious sexual activity. This may be because early maturers see themselves as being more adult and, consequently, as being more entitled to engage in these activities.

7. Today, in contrast to fifty years ago, the most important physical health problems in adolescence have psychosocial rather than natural causes. This "new morbidity and mortality" of adolescence is caused by such preventable phenomena as automobile accidents, violence, substance abuse, and unprotected sex. New approaches to adolescent health care, emphasizing prevention and health promotion instead of treatment, are being studied. Among the most important innovations are school-based health centers.

## Key Terms

activational role of
hormones
adolescent growth
spurt
adolescent health
adrenal androgens
adrenal cortex
androgens
asynchronicity in
growth
basal metabolism rate
cross-sectional design
developmental readi-
ness
endocrine system
estrogens
feedback loop

gonadotropins
hypothalamus
longitudinal design
menarche
organizational role of
hormones
peak height velocity
pituitary gland
school-based health
centers
secondary sex charac-
teristics
secular trend
set point
Tanner stages
testes
thyroid

## For Further Reading

ADAMS, G., GULOTTA, T., AND MONTEMAYOR,
R. (EDS.). (1988). *Advances in adolescent devel-*
*opment* (Vol. 1). Beverly Hills: Sage. The first
volume of this series, an annual collection
of articles on research and theory, focuses
on biological development during adolescence and its implications for psychological
functioning.

BROOKS-GUNN, J., AND REITER, E. (1990). The
role of pubertal processes. In S. Feldman
and G. Elliott (Eds.), *At the threshold: The*
*developing adolescent.* Cambridge: Harvard
University Press. An excellent summary of
the literature on the psychological consequences of puberty.

GANS, J. (1990). *America's adolescents: How*
*healthy are they?* Chicago: American Medical
Association. One of the best summaries of
the state of health among today's adolescents.

MARSHALL, W. (1978). Puberty. In F. Faulkner
and J. Tanner (Eds.), *Human growth* (Vol. 2).
New York: Plenum Press. A good overview
of the hormonal and somatic changes of puberty.

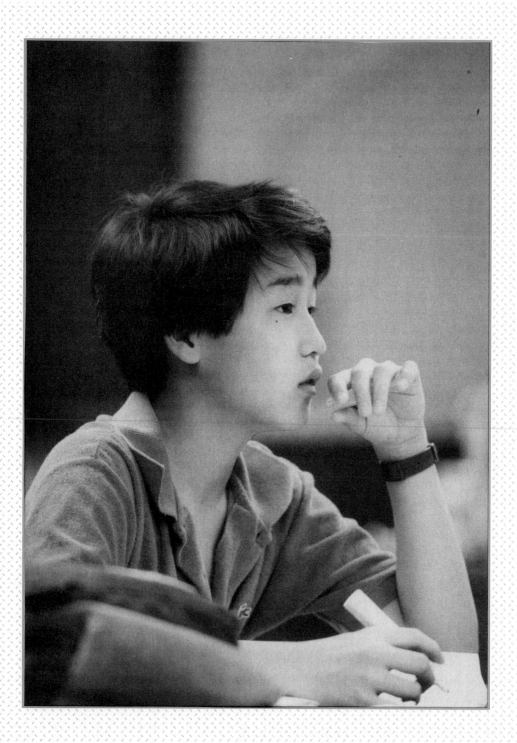

# COGNITIVE TRANSITIONS

Changes in cognition, or thinking, represent the second in a set of three fundamental changes that occur at adolescence—the other being the biological changes of puberty and the transition of the adolescent into new social roles. Like developments in the other two domains, the cognitive transitions of adolescence have far-reaching implications for the young person's psychological development and social relations. Indeed, the expansion of thought during adolescence represents as significant an event and as important an influence on adolescents' development and behavior as puberty.

## Changes in Cognition

Most people would agree that adolescents are "smarter" than children. Not only do teenagers *know* more than children—after all, the longer we live, the more opportunities we have to acquire new information—but adolescents actually *think* in ways that are more advanced, more efficient, and generally more effective. This can be seen in five chief ways. First, during adolescence individuals become better able than children to think about what is possible, instead of limiting their thought to what is real. Second, they become better able to think about abstract things. Third, during adolescence individuals begin thinking more often about the process of thinking itself. Fourth, adolescents' thinking tends to become multidimensional, rather than limited to a single issue. Finally, adolescents are more likely than children to see things as relative, rather than absolute (Keating, 1980, 1990). Let's look at each of these advantages—and some of their implications—in greater detail.

### THINKING ABOUT POSSIBILITIES

The adolescent's thinking is less bound to concrete events than is that of the child. Children's thinking is oriented to the here and now—that is, to things and events that they can observe directly. But adolescents are able to consider what they observe against a backdrop of what is possible. Put another way, for the child, what is possible is what is real; for the adolescent, what is real is but one subset of what is possible. Children, for example, do not wonder, the way adolescents often do, about the ways in which their personalities might change in the future or the ways in which their lives might be affected by different career choices. For the young child, you are who you are. But for the adolescent, who you are is just one possibility of who you could be.

This does not mean that the child is incapable of imagination or fantasy. Even young children have vivid and creative imaginations. Nor does it mean that children are unable to conceive of things being different from the way they observe them to be. Rather, the advantage that adolescents enjoy over children when it comes to thinking about possibilities is that adolescents are able to move easily between the specific and the abstract, to generate alternative possibilities and explanations *systematically*, and to compare what they actually observe with what they believe is possible.

We can illustrate this development by looking at the following problem. How would you approach it?

> Imagine four poker chips, one red, one blue, one yellow, and one green. Make as many different combinations of chips, of any number, as you can. Use the notations R, B, Y, and G to record your answers. (Adapted from Elkind, Barocas, and Rosenthal, 1968)

How did you tackle this problem? Did you need to use real poker chips to solve the problem? Probably not. In all likelihood, you used some sort of system, beginning perhaps with the case of zero chips (don't worry, a lot of people forget this one) then proceeding on to one-chip combinations (R, B, Y, G), two-chip combinations (RB, RY, RG, BY, BG, YG), three-chip combinations (RBY, RBG, RYG, BYG), and finally the single four-chip combination (RBYG). More important, you probably did not approach the problem haphazardly. You probably employed an abstract system for generating possibilities that you had in mind before being faced with the poker chip problem—a system that you can apply across a variety of similar tasks. Athough preadolescent children might be able to solve the problem correctly—in the sense that they might, with luck, generate all the possible combinations— children are far less likely than teenagers to employ a systematic approach (Neimark, 1975).

The adolescent's ability to reason systematically in terms of what is possible comes in handy in a variety of scientific and logical problem-solving situations. The study of mathematics in junior and senior high school (algebra, geometry, and trigonometry), for instance, often requires that you begin with an abstract or theoretical formulation—for example, "the square of a right triangle's hypotenuse is equal to the sum of the squares of the other two sides" (the Pythagorean theorem). This theorem, after all, is a proposition about the possible rather than the real. It is a statement about *all possible* right triangles, not just triangles that we might actually observe. In mathematics, we learn how to apply these theorems to concrete examples (that is, real triangles). Scientific experimentation—in biology, chemistry, and physics—also involves the ability to generate possibilities systematically. In a chemistry experiment in which you are trying to

## DELIA EPHRON'S "HOW TO WORRY"

One of the more unfortunate outcomes of the adolescent's increased facility in thinking about possibilities is the potential to get lost in them— not just in thinking about them, but in worrying about them. Author Delia Ephron has devised an adolescent's guide, "How to Worry":

Worry that if you neck too much, you'll get mononucleosis.

Worry that if you masturbate, you'll get pimples.

Worry that if you masturbate, you'll get brain damage.

Worry that if you masturbate, you'll go blind.

Worry that in a long kiss, you'll have to breathe through your nose and your nose will be stopped up.

Worry that there's a right way to dress and you don't know it.

Worry that you won't like the food at other people's houses.

Worry that when you go to the bathroom, people will hear. Worry that the lock on the door doesn't work. Worry that someone will walk in.

If you are a girl, worry that your breasts are too round. Worry that your breasts are too pointed.

If you are a boy, worry that you will get breasts.

*Source:* Delia Ephron, *Teenage Romance, Or How to Die of Embarrassment* (New York: Viking, 1981), pp. 87–88.

identify an unknown substance by performing various tests, you must first be able to imagine alternative possibilities for the substance's identity in order to know what tests to conduct.

The adolescent's use of this sort of thinking is not limited to scientific situations. We see it in the types of arguments adolescents employ, in which they are more able than younger children to envision and therefore anticipate the possible responses of an opponent and to have handy a counterargument or a series of counterarguments (Clark and Delia, 1976). Many parents believe that their children become more argumentative during adolescence. What probably happens is that their children become *better arguers*. During adolescence, other people's points of view are not accepted unquestioningly but are evaluated against other theoretically possible beliefs.

Related to the adolescent's increased facility with thinking about possibilities is the development of hypothetical thinking. Hypothetical thinking is what is sometimes called "if-then" thinking. In order to think hypothetically, you need to see beyond what is directly observable and reason in terms of what might be possible.

The ability to think through hypotheses is an enormously powerful tool. Being able to plan ahead, being able to see the future consequences of an action, and being able to provide alternative explanations of events are all dependent on being able to hypothesize effectively.

Thinking in hypothetical terms also permits us to suspend our beliefs about something in order to argue in the abstract. Being capable of assuming a hypothetical stance is important when it comes to debating an issue, since doing so permits us to understand the logic behind the other person's argument, without necessarily agreeing with its conclusion. Playing devil's advocate, for example—that is, formulating

Success in games such as chess requires the sort of advanced reasoning abilities that typically do not develop until adolescence. *(Evan Johnson/Jeroboam)*

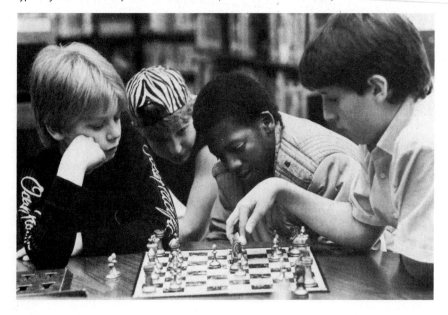

a position contrary to what you really believe in order to challenge someone else's reasoning—requires the ability to think in hypothetical terms.

Of course, hypothetical thinking also has implications for the adolescent's social behavior. It helps the young person to take the perspective of others by enabling him or her to think through what someone else might be thinking or feeling, given that person's point of view. ("If I were in his shoes, then I would feel pretty angry.") Hypothetical thinking helps in formulating and arguing one's viewpoint, because it allows adolescents to think a step ahead of the opposition—a cognitive tool that comes in quite handy when dealing with parents. ("If they come back with 'You have to stay home and clean up the garbage,' then I'll remind them about the time they let Susan go out when she had chores to do.") And hypothetical thinking plays an important role in decision-making abilities, because it permits the young person to plan ahead and to forsee the consequences of choosing one alternative over another. ("If I choose to go out for the soccer team, then I am going to have to give up my part-time job.")

## THINKING ABOUT ABSTRACT CONCEPTS

The appearance of more systematic, *abstract* thinking is the second notable aspect of cognitive development during adolescence. We noted earlier that children's thinking is more concrete and more bound to observable events and objects than is that of adolescents. This difference is clearly evident when we consider the ability to deal with abstract concepts— things that cannot be experienced directly through the senses.

For example, adolescents find it easier than

The gains in logical reasoning that take place in adolescence make young people much bettter at explaining and defending their arguments. *(Andrew Brilliant/Picture Cube)*

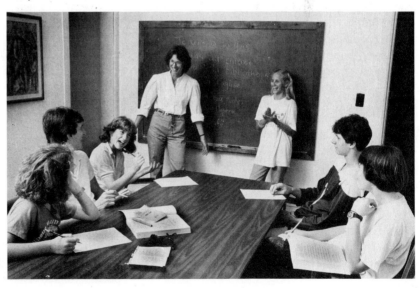

children to comprehend the sorts of higher-order, abstract logic inherent in puns, proverbs, metaphors, and analogies. When presented with verbal analogies, children are more likely than adolescents to focus on concrete and familiar associations among the words than on the abstract, or conceptual, relations among them.

Consider the following analogy, for example:

Sun : Moon : : Asleep : ?
a. Star
b. Bed
c. Awake
d. Night

Instead of answering "awake"—which is the best answer of the four given above—children would be more likely to respond with "bed" or "night," since both of these words have stronger associations with the word *asleep*. It is generally not until early adolescence that individuals are able to discern the abstract principles underlying analogies—in the one above, the principle involves antonyms—and therefore solve them correctly (Sternberg and Nigro, 1980).

The adolescent's greater facility with abstract thinking also permits the application of advanced reasoning and logical processes to social and ideological matters. This is clearly seen in the adolescent's increased facility and interest in thinking about interpersonal relationships, politics, philosophy, religion, and morality—topics that involve such abstract concepts as friendship, faith, democracy, fairness, and honesty. The growth of social thinking—generally referred to as **social cognition**—during adolescence is directly related to the young person's improving ability to think abstractly. Later in this chapter, we will examine the ways in which social thinking improves in adolescence.

## THINKING ABOUT THINKING

A third noteworthy gain in cognitive ability during adolescence involves thinking about thinking itself, a process sometimes referred to as **metacognition.** Metacognition often involves monitoring one's own cognitive activity during the process of thinking—when you consciously use a strategy for remembering something (such as Every Good Boy Deserves Fun, for the notes of the treble clef in reading music), or when you appraise your own comprehension of something you are reading before going on to the next paragraph. Not only do adolescents "manage" their thinking more than children, they are also better able to explain to others the processes they are using. For instance, in the poker-chip problem mentioned earlier, an adolescent would be able to describe his strategy to you ("First I took the single-chip possibilities, then I took the different pairs . . ."), whereas a child would probably just say "I thought of everything I could."

Another interesting way in which thinking about thinking becomes more apparent during adolescence is in increased introspection, self-consciousness, and intellectualization. When we are introspective, after all, we are thinking about our own emotions. When we are self-conscious, we are thinking about how others think about us. And when we intellectualize, we are thinking about our own thoughts. All three processes play an important role in the adolescent's psychological growth. As we shall see in Chapter 8, for example, these processes permit the sorts of self-examination and exploration that are important components of the young person's attempt to establish a coherent sense of identity.

These intellectual advances may occasionally result in problems for the young adolescent, particularly before he or she adjusts to having such powerful cognitive tools. Being able to introspect, for instance, may lead to periods of extreme self-absorption—a form of "adolescent egocentrism" (Elkind, 1967). Adolescent egocentrism results in two particular problems in thinking that help to explain some of the seemingly odd beliefs and behaviors of teenagers. The first, the **imaginary audience,** involves having such a heightened sense of self-consciousness that the teenager imagines that his or her behavior is the focus of everyone else's concern and attention. For example, a teenager who is going to a concert with 4,000 other people may worry about dressing the right way because "everybody will notice." Given the cognitive limitations of adolescent egocentrism, it is difficult indeed to persuade a young person that the "audience" is not all that concerned with his or her behavior or appearance.

A second related problem is called the **personal fable.** The personal fable revolves around the adolescent's egocentric (and erroneous) belief that his or her experiences are unique. For instance, a young man whose relationship with a girlfriend had just broken up might tell his sympathetic mother that she could not possibly understand what it feels like to break up with someone—even though breaking up is something that most people have experienced plenty of times during their adolescent and adult years. Sometimes holding on to a personal fable can actually be quite dangerous, as in the case of a sexually active adolescent who believes that pregnancy simply won't happen to her or a careless driver who believes that he will defy the laws of nature by taking hairpin turns on a road at breakneck speed. Much of the risk-taking behavior engaged in by adolescents can be explained partly in terms of the personal fable.

Although the concept of adolescent egocentrism rings true, several researchers have found it difficult to confirm that the various manifestations of adolescent egocentrism, such as the imaginary audience or the personal fable, actually increase during early adolescence (Gray and Hudson, 1984; Riley, Adams, and Neilsen, 1984). If anything, it appears that individuals become *less* egocentric as they develop more sophisticated abstract-thinking abilities. One problem with these studies, as Elkind points out (1985), is that they rely on fairly simple questionnaires to assess rather complicated belief systems invoked in real-life situations. For example, it is easy to imagine that the same adolescent who worried about being seen by "everyone" at a rock concert might not appear so egocentric in his responses to a hypothetical dilemma posed in a questionnaire. This difference, of course, would raise doubts about whether adolescent egocentrism *is* an entirely cognitive phenomenon, since we would expect that cognitive deficiencies would show up in questionnaire assessments. It may be that Elkind is right about the increased prevalence of egocentrism during early adolescence but wrong about the processes that underlie it (Lapsley and Murphy, 1985). One guess is that adolescents are egocentric for emotional, not cognitive reasons.

## THINKING IN MULTIPLE DIMENSIONS

A fourth way in which thinking changes during adolescence involves the ability to think about things in a multidimensional fashion. Whereas children tend to think about things one aspect at a time, adolescents can see things through more complicated lenses. For instance, when a certain hitter comes up to the plate in a baseball game, a preadolescent who knows that the hitter has a good home-run record might exclaim that the batter will hit the ball out of the park. An adolescent, however, would consider the hitter's record in relation to the specific pitcher on the mound, and weigh both factors, or dimensions, before making a prediction (perhaps this player hits homers against left-handed pitchers but strikes out against righties).

The ability to think in multidimensional terms is evident in a variety of different situations. Obviously, adolescents can give much more complicated answers than children to questions such as "Why did the Civil War begin?" or "How did Jane Austen's novels reflect the changing position of women in European society?" Thorough answers to these sorts of questions require thinking about several dimensions simultaneously.

But, as is the case with other gains in cognitive ability, the increasing capability of individuals to think in multiple dimensions has consequences for their behavior and thinking outside of academic settings, too. As you will read in a later section, adolescents describe themselves and others in more differentiated and complicated terms ("I'm both shy and extroverted") and find it easier to look at problems from multile perspectives ("I know that's the way you see it, but try to look at it from his point of view"). Being able to understand that people's personalities are not one-sided, or that social situations can have different interpretations, depending on one's point of view, permits the adolescent to have far more sophisticated—and complicated—relationships with other people.

One interesting manifestation of adolescents' ability to look at things in multiple dimensions concerns the development of children's understanding of sarcasm. As an adult, you understand that the meaning of a speaker's statement is communicated by a combination of what is said, how it is said, and the context in which it is said. If I turned to you during a boring lecture, rolled my eyes, and said, in an exaggeratedly earnest tone, "This is the most interesting lecture I've ever heard," you would know that I actually meant just the opposite. But you only would know this if you paid attention to my inflection and to the context, as well as the content, of my statement. Only by attending simultaneously to multiple dimensions of speech can we distinguish between the sincere and the sarcastic. Because our ability to think in multidimensional terms

improves during adolescence, we would predict that so also would our ability to understand when someone was being sarcastic.

In one study designed to look at this question, children, adolescents, and adults were presented with different stories, in which an interaction between two people was followed by a remark that was sincere, deliberately deceptive, or sarcastic (Demorest, Meyer, Phelps, Gardner, and Winner, 1984). The participants in the study were then asked what the true meaning and intent of the remark were. Before age 9, children had difficulty picking out sarcastic remarks. Individuals' understanding of sarcasm increased somewhat between 9 and 13, and continued to increase during the adolescent years.

## ADOLESCENT RELATIVISM

A final aspect of thinking during adolescence concerns the way in which adolescents look at things. Children tend to see things in absolute terms—in black and white. Adolescents, in contrast, tend to see things as relative. They are more likely to question others' assertions and less likely to accept "facts" as absolute truths.

This increase in relativism can be particularly exasperating to parents, who may feel as if their adolescent children question everything just for the sake of argument. Difficulties often arise, for example, when adolescents begin seeing their parents' values that they had previously considered absolutely correct ("Moral people do not have sex before they are married") as completely relative ("Times change, Dad").

Adolescents' belief that everything is relative can become so overwhelming that they may begin to become extremely skeptical about many things (Chandler, 1987). In fact, once adolescents begin doubting the certainty of things that they had previously believed, they may come to feel as if everything is uncertain, or that no knowledge is completely reliable.

Whereas children tend to see things in absolute terms—as black or white— adolescents tend to see things as relative. The development of relativisitic thinking in adolescence can be exasperating for parents, who may feel that their adolescent children question everything they say, just for the sake of argument. *(Billy E. Barnes/ Stock, Boston)*

Some theorists have suggested that adolescents pass through such a period of extreme skepticism on the way toward reaching a more sophisticated understanding of the complexity of knowledge.

## Theoretical Perspectives on Adolescent Thinking

Although there is general agreement that adolescents' thinking is different and more advanced than children's in the ways we have just described, there is far less consensus about the processes underlying the cognitive differences between children and adolescents. Part of the lack of agreement stems from the different points of view theorists have taken toward the issue of cognitive development in general. Because researchers working from different theoretical perspectives have posed different research questions, used different tasks to measure cognitive growth, and emphasized some aspects of cognitive activity more than others, their studies provide different but theoretically compatible pictures of mental development during adolescence. The three theoretical viewpoints that have been especially important are the **Piagetian,** the **psychometric,** and the **information-processing** perspectives. Although these three perspectives on adolescent thinking begin from different assumptions about the nature of cognitive development in general, each point of view provides valuable insight into why thinking changes during adolescence. And, in recent years, a number of theorists have attempted to integrate elements of all three approaches into a unified theory (e.g., Case, 1985). Let's look first at the contribution of each perspective.

## THE PIAGETIAN VIEW OF ADOLESCENT THINKING

Generally, theorists who take a **Piagetian,** or **cognitive-developmental,** view of intellectual development argue that cognitive development proceeds in a stagelike fashion, that adolescent thinking is qualitatively different from the type of thinking employed by children, and that during adolescence, individuals develop a special type of thinking that they use in a variety of situations.

According to Piaget, cognitive development proceeds through four stages: the **sensorimotor** period (from birth until about age 2), the **preoperational period** (from about age 2 until about age 5), the period of **concrete operations** (from about age 6 until early adolescence) and, finally, the period of **formal operations** (from adolescence through adulthood). These stages are presented in Table 2.1. Each stage is characterized by a particular type of thinking, earlier stages of thinking being incorporated into new, more advanced, and more adaptive forms

of reasoning. According to Piaget, transitions into higher stages of reasoning are most likely to occur at times when the child's biological readiness and the increasing complexity of environmental demands interact to bring about cognitive disequilibrium.

Given the emphasis that Piaget placed on the interaction between biological change and environmental stimulation in provoking intellectual growth, it comes as no surprise that early adolescence—a time of dramatic biological maturation and equally noteworthy changes in environmental demands—is viewed in Piagetian theory as an extremely important period in cognitive development.

Piaget believed that at the heart of formal-operational thinking was the use of an abstract system of **propositional logic**—a system based on theoretical, or formal, principles of logic (hence the term *formal operations*). Formal reasoning can be just as easily applied to hypothetical events as it can to real ones; is just as effective in dealing with abstract concepts as with concrete things; and is just as useful for thinking about alternatives to what really exists as it is for thinking about reality itself. Consider the significance of being able to understand the following example of propositional logic:

If A is true or B is true, then C is true.

---

### TABLE 2.1

#### THE FOUR STAGES OF COGNITIVE DEVELOPMENT ACCORDING TO PIAGET

| Stage | Approximate ages | Chief characteristics |
|---|---|---|
| Sensorimotor | Birth–2 years | Discovery of relationships between sensation and motor behavior |
| Preoperational | 2–7 years | Use of symbols to represent objects internally, especially through language |
| Concrete operations | 7–11 years | Mastery of logic and development of "rational" thinking |
| Formal operations | 11 years + | Development of abstract and hypothetical reasoning |

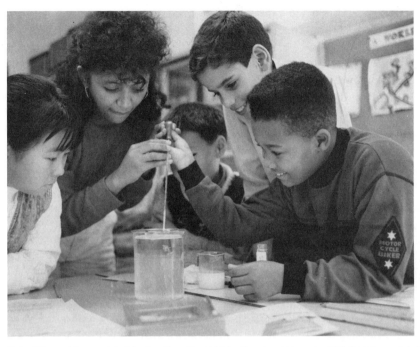

Scientific problem solving is greatly enhanced by the development of "if-then," or hypothetical, thinking at adolescence. *(Joel Gordon)*

This is a logical relationship that is encountered in all sorts of situations, ranging from scientific problem solving (for example, "If the solution turns blue or yellow, then it must contain the mineral copper") to understanding social relationships ("If Bob asks Susan out or if Judy calls me to do something this Friday night, then Bob and Judy must have broken up"). Once the *form* of the logic is understood—that *either* A or B is sufficient to demonstrate that C is true—it can be applied to all sorts of events—real as well as possible, concrete as well as abstract—merely by changing what A, B, and C stand for. While concrete operational thinkers are able to imagine alternative and hypothetical situations, they are unable to think about them in as systematic a way as formal operational thinkers can.

Just because adolescents can employ prop-ositional logic, however, does not mean that they are always consciously aware of doing so. In the example given above, for instance, we would hardly expect that an adolescent who is trying to figure out whether two friends are still "going steady" consciously runs through the As, Bs, and Cs of propositional logic. But you do not have to be aware of using propositional logic to use it effectively.

**The growth of formal-operational thinking** Piagetian theorists believe that the use of propositional logic—the formation of formal-operational thinking—is the chief feature of adolescent thinking that differentiates it from the type of thinking employed by children. We noted before that adolescents' thinking can be distinguished from the thinking of children in several respects—among them, thinking about possibilities, in thinking multidimensionally, and in thinking about abstract concepts. The connection between these types of thinking and the development of formal operations is clear: In order to think about alternatives to what really exists, in order to think in multi-dimensional terms, and in order to systematically think about concepts that are not directly observable, you must have a system of reasoning that works just as well in abstract, imagined, and complicated situations as it does in concrete ones. The system of propositional logic provides the basis for precisely this sort of reasoning.

The development of formal thinking appears to take place in two steps. During the first step, characteristic of early adolescence, formal thinking is apparent, but it has a sort of "now you see it, now you don't" quality to it. Young adolescents may demonstrate formal thinking at some times but at others be able to think only in concrete terms; they may use formal operations on some tasks but not on others; they may reason formally under some but not all testing situations. Virtually all adolescents go through this period of "emergent formal operations" (Kuhn et al., 1977).

It is not until middle or even late adolescence that formal-operational thinking becomes consolidated and integrated into the individual's general approach to reasoning. Moreover, the attainment of "consolidated formal operations" is not universal. That is, although the initial appearance of formal thinking appears to be widespread among young adolescents, the final and complete development of formal reasoning is less common—according to some estimates, only about 60 percent of college students consistently demonstrate formal thinking on tests used to measure formal-operational thought (Neimark, 1975). It would seem, then, that the child is in a state of cognitive equilibrium during the late portion of the concrete-operational period and enters a period of disequilibrium and biological

readiness during early adolescence—when formal-operational thinking appears in its rudimentary, emergent form. Subsequently, if levels of environmental stimulation are sufficient, formal-operational abilities are consolidated and permanently developed sometime during middle or late adolescence.

Under what conditions will formal-operational thinking become fully consolidated? Piaget suggested that formal operations are more likely to develop among adolescents encountering an environment that demands the use of formal-operational skills. Taking science courses, for example, that demand hypothetical reasoning might stimulate the growth of formal-operational abilities. He also felt that formal thinking is more likely to be employed in problem-solving situations with which the individual has some degree of familiarity. Some adolescents might be more likely to employ formal-operational reasoning in scientific problem solving, for example, while others might be more apt to use it in social situations. Some adolescents might be expected to use formal-operational thinking spontaneously, while others might require prompting.

Thus, while all adolescents have the *potential* to develop formal-operational thinking, and most can and do demonstrate it from time to time, not all adolescents (or, for that matter, all adults) employ formal-operational thinking regularly and in a variety of situations. The extent to which consolidated formal-operational thinking appears depends on the environmental demands placed on adolescents as they develop and on the conditions under which their reasoning is assessed.

The Piagetian perspective on cognitive development during adolescence has stimulated a great deal of research on how young people think. Generally, the concept of formal operations as defined by Piaget and his followers appears to account for many of the changes in thinking observed during the adolescent years. Specifically, the theory of formal operations helps to explain why adolescents are better able than children to think about possibilities, to think multidimensionally, and to think about thoughts.

Where the Piagetian perspective on adolescent cognitive development appears to fall short is in its claim that cognitive development proceeds in a stagelike fashion and that the "stage" of formal operations is the stage of cognitive development characteristic of adolescence. Rather, research suggests that advanced reasoning capabilities (which may or may not be synonymous with what Piaget termed "formal operations") develop gradually and continuously from childhood through adolescence and beyond, probably in more of a quantitative fashion than was proposed by Piaget. Rather than talking about a "stage" of cognitive activity characteristic of adolescence, then, it appears to be more accurate to depict these advanced reasoning capabilities as skills that are employed by older children more often than younger ones, by some adolescents more often than other adolescents, and by individuals when they are in certain situations more often than when they are in other situations.

## THE PSYCHOMETRIC VIEW OF ADOLESCENT THINKING

Compared to Piagetian theorists, *psychometricians* have taken a far more quantitative view of cognitive development during the adolescent years. The term *psychometric* refers to these researchers' concern with the *measurement* of mental functioning. Unlike Piagetian theorists, who have been most interested in discovering the cognitive competencies that all adolescents share in common, psychometric theorists have been most interested in assessing individual differences in intellectual abilities.

**The measurement of IQ** The most widely used measures of what individuals know are intelligence, or IQ (for "intelligence quotient"),

tests. A variety of such tests exists, including the Stanford-Binet, the Wechsler Intelligence Scale for Children (WISC-III), and the Wechsler Adult Intelligence Scale (WAIS-R).

The IQ test is one of the most widely used—and most widely misused—psychological instruments ever developed. Initially developed by the French psychologist Alfred Binet in 1905, the first intelligence test was devised in response to the French government's interest in better predicting which children would profit from formal schooling. Thus although Binet's test—and the many others that would be developed over the years—was designed to yield a measure of "intelligence," the test was devised with a very specific type of "intelligence" in mind: the type of intelligence it takes to succeed in formal educational institutions. Even the best IQ tests used today measure only a very specific type of intelligence.

An individual's performance on an IQ test is usually presented not as a raw score but as a relative score in comparison to the scores of other individuals of the same age and from approximately the same cohort (a *cohort* is a group of people born during the same historical era). Comparison scores are collected every so often, so that the comparison group for individuals taking the test at any given time is valid, representative, and up-to-date. The score of 100 is used to designate the midway point: An IQ score below 100 indicates a poorer test performance than half of the comparison group; a score above 100 indicates a better performance than half the comparison group. In other words, the higher an individual's IQ, the smaller the number of agemates who perform equally or better on the same test.

Although an individual's score on an intelligence test is often reported in terms of his or her overall IQ, intelligence tests are actually comprised of a series of tests, and it is usually possible to look at performance in different areas independently. The WISC and the

Standardized intelligence tests, or IQ tests, are often used to study individual differences in cognitive abilities during adolescence. Critics of such tests argue that they measure just one type of intelligence—"school smarts"—and neglect other equally important skills, such as social intelligence, creativity, and "street smarts." *(Arthur Grace/ Stock, Boston)*

WAIS, for example, each contain two groups of tests: *verbal* tests, which include measures of vocabulary, general information, comprehension, and arithmetic abilities; and *performance* tests, which include block design, mazes, picture completion, and picture arrangement.

The IQ test represents only one of many ways of assessing intelligence in adolescence. Indeed, many theorists have argued that its exclusive focus on "school-smarts"—the sorts of abilities that are related to scholastic success—yields a one-sided picture of what it means to be an intelligent person. Two of the more recent attempts to expand on this narrow definition come from the work of Robert Sternberg (1988) and Howard Gardner (1983).

Sternberg has proposed a **triarchic theory of intelligence.** He has argued that a thorough assessment of an individual's intellectual capabilities requires that we look at three distinct, but interrelated types of "intelligence": *componential intelligence,* which involves our abilities to acquire, store, and process information; *experiential intelligence,* which involves our abilities to use insight and creativity; and *contextual intelligence,* which involves our ability to think practically. Componential intelligence is closest to the type of intelligence measured on traditional intelligence tests. Experiential intelligence is closest to what we call creativity. Contextual intelligence is closest to what we might call "street smarts." All individuals have all three types of intelligence, but some individuals are stronger in one respect than in others.

You probably can think of individuals who are good test-takers, but not particularly creative or sensible. According to Sternberg's model, these individuals would be high in componential intelligence, but low in experiential and contextual intelligence.

More important, Sternberg's view forces us to look at individuals who are not good test-takers, but who are creative or street-smart, as being equally intelligent as individuals who score high on IQ tests—but intelligent in a different way. He argues that society needs individuals with all types of intelligence and that it is time we started assessing—and encouraging—experiential and contextual intelligence as much as we do componential intelligence.

Gardner's view of intelligence also stresses that there is more to being smart than being "book-smart." He has proposed that there are seven types of intelligence: verbal, mathematical, spatial, kinesthetic (movement), self-reflective, interpersonal, and musical. According to his view, for example, outstanding athletes such as the basketball star "Magic" Johnson, have a well-developed kinesthetic intelligence, which allows them to control their bodies and process the movements of others in extraordinarily capable ways. Although conventional tests of intelligence emphasize verbal and mathematical abilities, these are not the only types of intelligence that we possess—nor are they the only types that we should value.

**Intelligence test performance in adolescence**
Although ideas about the existence of different forms of intelligence have become popular in the last decade, most research in the psychometric tradition has employed traditional IQ tests to investigate the nature of intelligence during adolescence. Assessments based on IQ tests have been used to examine two seemingly similar but actually very different questions. First, how *stable* are IQ scores during adolescence? Second, do the sorts of mental abilities

assessed via intelligence tests *improve* during adolescence?

It is easy to confuse these questions. At first glance, they seem to be asking the same thing. But consider this: Individuals' IQ scores remain remarkably stable during the adolescent years, yet during the same time period, their mental abilities improve dramatically. Although this might seem contradictory, it is not. Studies of stability examine changes in individuals' *relative* standing over time, whereas studies of change examine changes in individuals' *absolute* scores.

Take height, for example. Children who are taller than their peers during middle childhood are likely to be taller than their peers during adulthood as well; children who are about average in height remain so throughout childhood and adulthood; and children who are shorter than their peers at one point in time are likely to be shorter than their peers later on. Height, therefore, is a very stable trait. But this does not mean that individuals don't grow between childhood and adolescence.

Like height, scores on intelligence tests are characterized by high stability and a good deal of change during childhood and adolescence. To the first question posed above—How stable are individuals' IQ scores during the adolescent years?—the answer, then, is very stable. Consider the pattern of correlations between an individual's intelligence test scores at various points during childhood and his or her score at age 18 (see Figure 2.1).

As you can see, from about age 1 to about age 5, intelligence test scores are not highly correlated with scores at age 18. Between ages 5 and 11, scores are moderately correlated with scores at age 18. From early adolescence on, however, scores are very highly correlated with scores at age 18. The pattern of correlations, then, indicates that intelligence test scores become increasingly stable during childhood and are remarkably stable during adolescence. To put it more concretely, youngsters who score

**FIGURE 2.1**  Average correlations between individuals' intelligence test scores at various ages from 1 to 17 and their scores at age 18. By age 11, the correlation is over .90. (Adapted from Bayley, 1949)

higher than their peers on intelligence tests during early adolescence are likely to score higher throughout the adolescent years.

A 10-year-old whose score is average for his age would have an IQ of about 100. If his score was stable—that is, if he remained about average in comparison with his peers—his score would remain at about 100. Even if he became more intelligent over time, as any normal child would, his IQ score probably would not change very much, because the score would always reflect his performance *relative* to his peers. If his abilities increased at the same rate as his agemates', his relative standing would not change. In other words, when an individual's IQ scores are fairly stable, a graph of those scores over a period of time produces a relatively straight horizontal line.

For most individuals, this is indeed what happens. But a study by Robert McCall and his colleagues suggests that not everyone follows this pattern of high stability (McCall, Applebaum, and Hogarty, 1973). After graphing many individuals' IQ scores during child-

hood and adolescence, these researchers were able to identify five different patterns—some very stable but others very unstable. Their findings are shown in Figure 2.2. As expected, most individuals fell into cluster number 1— that is, their scores were extremely stable over the 17-year period. But many youngsters' scores fluctuated considerably. In fact, the scores of individuals in cluster number 4 changed by as much as 30 points over the course of adolescence! In other words, although *most* adolescents' IQ scores remain stable throughout adolescence, not all do.

In absolute terms, however, do mental abilities increase during adolescence? Figure 2.3 shows the growth of mental abilities as assessed by standardized tests. As you can see, abilities assessed by conventional IQ tests increase dramatically through childhood and adolescence, reaching a plateau sometime during early adulthood. Thus despite the fact that IQ scores remain stable during adolescence, individuals

**FIGURE 2.2**  For some individuals, IQ scores fluctuate very little during childhood and adolescence. But for others, variations of 20 or 30 points occur. Here are five common patterns of change in IQ scores during childhood and adolescence. (Adapted from McCall et al., 1973)

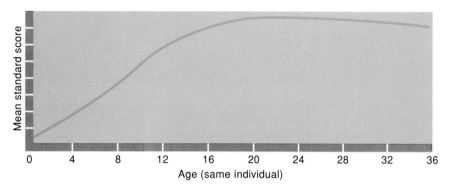

**FIGURE 2.3** The growth of mental abilities from birth to age 36. (Adapted from Bayley, 1949)

do become smarter as they get older—a fact that argues strongly in favor of educational interventions designed to stimulate intellectual development during adolescence. In fact, at least one study shows that extended schooling enhances individuals' performance on standardized tests of intelligence (Shavit and Featherman, 1988). Whereas individuals who had dropped out of school early showed unchanging—and relatively lower—scores on intelligence tests during adolescence, students who remained in school, especially those in the more advanced tracks, showed impressive gains in verbal ability over time.

Another widely-used—and equally controversial—measure of aptitude in adolescence is the Scholastic Aptitude Test, or SAT. (An *aptitude test* is designed to predict a student's future performance, not the student's current level of achievement.) Thus, the SAT was designed not to measure an adolescent's present level of accomplishment, but to predict his or her likelihood of success in college. Like the IQ test, therefore, the SAT is a measure of "school-smarts" (or, in Sternberg's framework, componential intelligence), and scores on this test should be so viewed. It does not measure such important characteristics as insight, creativity, or practical intelligence.

Given that the SAT was created in order to predict high school students' college success, it is only fair that it be evaluated in this light. How well does the SAT predict success in college courses? The answer is, "well, but not perfectly." Knowing an individual's SAT scores helps to foretell how well he or she will do in college, but it is only one of many useful predictive factors. Because of this, most college admissions committees rely on many pieces of information about an applicant's academic record, including the difficulty of the student's high school curriculum and the student's class rank, in addition to SAT scores (Moll, 1986).

Psychometric approaches to cognitive development provide as adequate an account of observed changes in thinking during adolescence as do Piagetian ones. Indeed, performance on measures of formal operations and on standardized intelligence tests are correlated with one another. In fact, some theorists believe that formal operations tests and standard IQ tests measure the same sorts of abilities (Keating, 1980). But the psychometric approach to cognitive development in adolescence does not assume a stagelike growth of intelligence; differences in thinking between adolescents and children are seen as differences in quantity, not quality.

## THE SEXES: ARE THERE DIFFERENCES IN MENTAL ABILITIES AT ADOLESCENCE (ANYMORE)?

For many years, it had been asserted that there were sex differences in mental abilities, and that these differences emerge for the first time during adolescence (Maccoby and Jacklin, 1974). Although adolescent males and females did not show *overall* differences in IQ scores, studies showed that females enjoyed a small advantage in tests of verbal ability, whereas males had a small advantage in tests of spatial ability and, to a lesser extent, mathematics. What was especially interesting about the pattern, however, was that it appeared that boys' and girls' scores on math and verbal tests were comparable before puberty.

A number of explanations had been offered for this pattern of sex differences, and, in particular, for their emergence in early adolescence. One explanation was based on the hormonal changes of puberty. As noted in the previous chapter, levels of androgens and estrogens change at puberty in different degrees for males and females. Because individuals with higher androgen levels score better on tests of spatial ability—this is true whether they are male or female—it has been argued that the male advantage in tests of spatial ability at adolescence may be due to their higher level of androgens (Petersen, 1979).

A second explanation focused on the fact that girls are more likely, on average, to mature earlier than boys. It had been speculated that the development of certain brain functions was altered by the onset of puberty and, specifically, that the onset of puberty curtailed some developments in the structure of the brain that are related to spatial ability. Since girls mature earlier than boys, it was reasoned that their development of spatial abilities may be curtailed earlier (Waber, 1977). If this theory were true, however, one would expect that early-maturers in general—whether male or female—would show worse spatial abilities than later-maturers. But this turns out not to be the case, casting doubt on the idea that females' earlier maturation is the reason for their poorer performance on tests of spatial intelligence (Newcombe and Dubas, 1987).

A third account—that sex differences in mental abilities are social, not biological, in origin—actually has received the most support. The argument here is that boys and girls are rewarded for different interests and for showing different abilities. During elementary school, boys and girls take the same courses and would therefore be expected to show similar intellectual strengths and weaknesses. But once young people begin

*continued on next page*

## THE INFORMATION-PROCESSING VIEW OF ADOLESCENT THINKING

During the past two decades, a new view of cognitive development during adolescence has emerged, partly in response to criticisms of the Piagetian and psychometric perspectives. Some scientists point out that neither the Piagetian nor the psychometric approach has been es-

pecially helpful in pinpointing exactly *what* it is that changes as individuals mature into and through adolescence. If we are left only with the conclusion that cognitive growth between childhood and adolescence is due to changes in "logical reasoning abilities" or "general mental abilities," we have not moved a great deal closer to understanding which *specific* aspects of intellectual development during adolestaking elective courses, males and females may be led down different educational paths by their guidance counselors, parents, and friends. Males, for example, are more likely to be encouraged to pursue advanced course work in math and science, whereas females are more likely to be steered away from these classes (Fennema and Sherman, 1977). Consistent with this explanation, one study found that differences in individuals' mathematical abilities are more closely related to their attitudes toward math than to their gender (Paulsen and Johnson, 1983). If, beginning in adolescence, girls are told, implicitly or explicitly, that math is not interesting, their performance in this area may decline.

Perhaps the clearest support for the idea that sex differences in mental abilities are socialized rather than biologically determined comes from several very recent examinations of males' and females' test scores. According to Carol Jacklin, who in 1974 had coauthored the initial study documenting reliable sex differences in mental abilities, by the end of the 1980s, many of the gains in males' and females' performance either had vanished or diminished substantially (Jacklin, 1989). This was particularly true with regard to verbal abilities, but appeared also to be the case with regard to math abilities (Hyde and Linn, 1988; Marsh, 1989). The fact that these more recent contrasts of males' and females' scores have shown much smaller sex differences than was found in earlier studies suggests to many experts that changes in sex-roles and educational opportunities that have taken place in recent decades are now beginning to be reflected on measures such as the SAT (Feingold, 1988).

It appears now that the only reliable sex difference in mental abilities during adolescence is in the area of spatial ability, but new research indicates that this is not a uniquely adolescent phenomenon. The male advantage on tests of spatial performance emerges before age 10 and is more or less constant during the adolescent years (Johnson and Meade, 1987). For reasons that predate adolescence, then—reasons that may be biological, social, or, most likely, both— boys score slightly higher than girls on tests measuring spatial intelligence. Even this difference is quite modest, however. And, who knows? Five years from now, sex differences in spatial abilities may have gone the way of sex differences in math and verbal abilities.

cence are the most important ones. Just what is it about the ways that adolescents think about things that makes them better problem solvers than children? This question has been the focus of researchers working from a third theoretical vantage point: the information-processing perspective.

Information-processing researchers apply the same techniques to understanding human reasoning that computer scientists employ in writing programs. Suppose that you were asked to develop a computer program to solve the poker chip problem presented earlier in this chapter. A first step in the program might involve determining how many different colored chips are contained in the set. But as you know if you have ever written a computer program, this first step is actually quite compli-

Recent studies of sex differences in mental abilities have shown that the old gender gap in math abilities, favoring boys, has disappeared. Male and female adolescents also score equally well on tests of verbal ability. *(Jean-Claude Lejeune)*

It is possible to look at human information processing in much the same way. When broken down into its component processes, human thinking involves such "subprograms" as paying attention to a stimulus, encoding information, retrieving information, comparing different pieces of information, and making decisions based on such comparisons. Obviously, deficiencies in any of these component functions will interfere with accurate problem solving. In the poker chip problem, for example, not perceiving the colors correctly will cause mistakes to be made. The ways in which component processes are combined also will affect the results. For example, if we try to compare the two chips' colors before storing the color of the first chip in memory, we will not be able to solve the problem.

Some arrangements of component processes are not only more accurate than others, they are more efficient. Suppose you have successfully determined that the first two poker chips you have examined are indeed different in color. What is your next step? Do you compare the third chip with both the first and second chips before moving on to the fourth chip, or do you compare the third with the first and then compare the fourth with the first? If you work this problem out, you will find that one approach is more efficient than the other.

cated when broken down into discrete tasks. It involves (1) taking the first chip and perceiving what color it is, (2) storing this information in memory, (3) considering the second chip and deciding what color it is, (4) storing this information in memory, (5) retrieving the color of the first chip from memory, (6) retrieving the color of the second chip from memory, (7) comparing these two bits of information, (8) determining whether the colors are the same or different, and (9) storing the results of the comparison in memory. And these nine steps take us only as far as comparing the first two chips. Imagine how involved a program would have to be in order to perform more complicated tasks!

**Changes in information-processing abilities during adolescence**   Studies of changes in specific components of information-processing have focused on four sets of gains that appear to occur during adolescence. Taken together, these gains help to explain why adolescents are better than children at abstract, multidimensional, and hypothetical thinking. First, there are advances in individuals' ability to pay *attention.* Improvements are seen both in **selective attention,** in which adolescents must focus in on one stimulus (such as a reading assignment) and tune out another (such as the electronic beeping of a younger brother's video game), and in **divided attention,** in which adolescents must pay attention to two sets of stimuli at the same time (such as studying while listening to music) (Higgins and Turnure, 1984; Schiff and Knopf, 1985). Improvements in attention mean that adolescents are better able than children to concentrate and stay focused on complicated tasks.

Second, during adolescence our *memory* abilities improve. This is reflected in both **short-term memory** (being able to remember something for a brief period of time, such as 30 seconds) and in **long-term memory** (being able to recall something from a long time ago) (Keating, 1990). When we think of the importance of memory in problem solving, we typically think of having to retrieve facts that we deliberately have memorized—one aspect of long-term memory. For example, can you recall the name of the stage of thinking that precedes the stage of "formal operations" in Piaget's theory? (If not, refer back to page 66.)

But short-term memory is extremely important in problem solving as well. For example, in order to solve multiple-choice questions successfully, you need to be able to remember each alternative answer long enough to compare it to the other choices as you read through them. Think for a moment of how frustrating it would be to solve a multiple-choice problem if, by the time you had read the final alternative answer, you had forgotten the first one!

One illustration of how improvements in short-term memory might account for adolescents' advantages over children in problem-solving comes from studies of individuals' solutions to problems involving analogies (Sternberg, 1977; Sternberg and Nigro, 1980; Sternberg and Rifkin, 1979). Through a series of experiments in which different types of analogies were presented to third-graders, sixth-graders, ninth-graders, and college students, Sternberg and his colleagues examined age differences in the use and organization of

cognitive processes. The major difference between younger and older subjects concerned the incomplete nature of the younger ones' information processing. Although older and younger subjects appeared to use similar processes, the older ones employed them in a far more exhaustive fashion. For example, in determining the relation between pairs of terms, the third- and sixth-graders tended to curtail their information processing prematurely, before all possible relations had been considered.

The researchers attribute this premature termination to information overload in short-term memory. Because adolescents are able to hold more information in immediate memory than children can, they are more successful in the sorts of tasks (such as analogies) that require repeated comparisons between newly encoded information and information that has been stored previously. Running out of storage space before all of the necessary information has been encoded will result in information-processing errors.

A third component of information processing that improves during adolescence involves improvements in individuals' *organizational strategies* (Siegler, 1988). Adolescents are more "plan-ful" than children—they are more likely to approach a problem with an appropriate information-processing strategy in mind. Psychologist Ann Brown (1975), for example, has suggested that the use of mnemonic devices and other organizational strategies helps to account for differences in the performance of older and younger children on tasks requiring memory, and moreover, why older children are better able to judge *when* the use of such strategies is likely to be helpful and when it is not. For instance, think for a moment about how you approach learning the information in a new textbook chapter. After years of school, you are probably well aware of particular strategies that work well for you (underlining, highlighting, taking notes, writing in the margin of the textbook) and you go into a reading as-

The information-processing perspective on cognitive development draws an analogy between human reasoning abilities and information processing performed by computers. Recent studies have found that the development of more advanced thinking abilities during adolescence may be due to growth in memory capacity. *(Michael F. Kullen/ Picture Cube)*

signment with these strategies in mind. Because children are not as "plan-ful" as adolescents, their learning is not as efficient.

Finally, individuals' *knowledge about their own thinking processes* improves during adolescence. We noted earlier that one of the most important gains to occur in adolescence is in the realm of **metacognition**—thinking about thinking. Adolescents are more likely than children to think about their own thoughts—a tencency, as we saw, that helps to explain their greater self-consciousness. But from an information-processing perspective, adolescents' heightened self-consciousness results from advances in basic metacognitive abilities. Self-consciousness may be more a cognitive than emotional phenomenon: for the first time, the adolescent is *capable* of "thinking about thinking about thinking."

Of course, advances in metacognition are more a blessing than a curse. Because adoles-

cents are better able to think about their own thoughts, they are much better at monitoring their own learning processes. For example, during the course of studying, adolescents are more able than children to step back from time to time and assess how well they are learning the material. Doing this enables them to pace their studying accordingly—to speed up and skim the material if they feel that they are learning it easily, or to slow down and repeat a section if they feel that they are having a hard time (e.g., Baker & Brown, 1984).

## NEW DIRECTIONS FOR THEORIES ABOUT ADOLESCENT THINKING

There is no doubt that many specific aspects of information processing improve during the adolescent years. What remains to be seen is whether and how understanding these specific cognitive gains can help account for the broader changes in thinking described at the beginning of this chapter—in abstraction, in hypothetical thinking, or in relativism, for example. To many theorists, the *quantitative* approach to thinking advocated by information-processing theorists leaves something out: the intuitive feeling that adolescents think in a way that is *qualitatively* different from children. Even if there is no evidence for a separate "stage" of thinking characteristic of adolescence, there may still be room for viewing adolescent thinking as different, not simply more advanced, than that of children.

Several researchers have attempted to integrate findings on improvements in adolescents' information-processing abilities within a cognitive-developmental framework similar to Piaget's. Case (1985), for example, has argued that the gains in attention, memory, metacognition, and organization enjoyed during the adolescent years permit the individual to think in a more "automatic" way. For instance, think about how automatically you drive a car now in contrast to when you were first learning how. This **automatization** of thinking frees up cognitive resources for the adolescent that enable her or him to approach problems in a structurally more sophisticated way. In other words, as basic elements of information processing become more automatic—second nature, we might say—the adolescent is better able to devote conscious cognitive processes to more complicated tasks.

Whether we should think of this as a shift in quality or quantity is impossible to answer definitively. In general, the distinction between changes in quantity and changes in quality is fraught with definitional problems. Take the perception of color, for instance (Keating, 1980). Suppose you were presented with a series of cards, each of a different color, and asked to sort colors that were "different" into separate piles. Like most people, you would probably agree that blue and green are qualitatively different colors—that is, that the difference in color between a green card and a blue card cannot be described merely in quantitative terms (that is, one color cannot be described as more "something" than the other). Yet if you were to take a blue card and a green card and separate them by a series of cards of various shades of blue-green arranged in a sequence from the most "bluish" blue-green to the most "greenish," the difference between green and blue would seem quantitative, not qualitative. The distinction between differences in quality and differences in quantity depends largely on how we go about measuring the phenomenon in question.

## Adolescent Thinking In Context

As our understanding of adolescent thinking has expanded, researchers have begun to look beyond laboratory experiments and standardized tests in an effort to examine how the cognitive changes of adolescence actually affect teenagers' day-to-day thoughts and actions. Do advances in propositional logic or information-processing abilities make a difference in the real world? In order to look at this issue, psychologists and educators have studied the practical side of adolescent thinking in three domains: in social situations, in risk-taking, and in the classroom.

### CHANGES IN SOCIAL COGNITION

Many of the examples of adolescent thinking we have looked at in this chapter have involved reasoning about scientific problems or physical objects. But the same sorts of gains in intellectual abilities observed in young people's thinking in these realms are apparent in their reasoning about social phenomena as well. **Social cognition** is the term used to refer to this sort of cognitive activity—thinking about people, thinking about social relationships, and thinking about social institutions (Lapsley, 1989).

It is not difficult to imagine that adolescents' advanced abilities in thinking about possibilities, thinking in multiple dimensions, and thinking about abstract concepts make them more sophisticated when it comes to reasoning about social matters. Compared with those of children, adolescents' conceptions of interpersonal relationships are more mature, their understanding of human behavior is more advanced, their ideas about social institutions and organizations are more complex, and their ability to figure out what other people think is far more accurate. As we shall see in subsequent chapters, gains in the area of social cognition help to account for many of the psychosocial advances typically associated with adolescence—advances in the realms of identity, autonomy, intimacy, sexuality, and achievement.

Studies of social cognition during adolescence typically fall into three categories: studies of **impression formation,** which examine how individuals form and organize judgments about other people; studies of **role taking,** which examine how, and how accurately, individuals make assessments about the thoughts and feelings of others; and studies of morality and **social conventions,** which examine individuals' conceptions of justice, social norms, and guidelines for social interaction.

**Impression formation**   During preadolescence and adolescence, individuals' impressions of other people develop in five main directions (Hill and Palmquist, 1978). First, impressions become progressively *more differentiated*. Adolescents are more likely than children to describe people—themselves as well as others—in more narrowly defined categories and with more differentiated attributes. Whereas children tend to use fairly global descriptors, such as gender and age, adolescents are more likely to describe people in terms of such things as

interests and personality characteristics. A second trend in the development of impression formation is toward *less egocentric* impressions. Adolescents are more likely to be aware that their impressions of others are personal viewpoints and therefore subject to disagreement. Third, impressions of other people become *more abstract*—that is, they become less rooted in such concrete attributes as physical characteristics or personal possessions and more tied to such abstract things as attitudes and motives. Fourth, individuals come to make *greater use of inference* in their impressions of others. Compared with children, adolescents are more likely to interpret the feelings of others and infer the motives, beliefs, and feelings of others, even when specific information of this sort is not directly observable. Finally, adolescents' impressions of others are *more highly organized*. Adolescents are more likely than children, for example, to make judgments of others that link personality traits to the situations in which they are likely to be expressed ("She's impatient when she works with other people") and to reconcile apparently discrepant information about people into a more complex impression ("He's friendly toward girls but not at all toward boys.") As we shall see in Chapter 10, the development of more advanced impression-formation skills has important implications for the development of intimate relationships.

**Role-taking abilities**   Related to these gains in impression-formation abilities are considerable improvements in the adolescent's ability to view events from the perspective of others. According to Robert Selman (1980), who has studied the development of role-taking extensively, children become better able as they grow older to step back from their own point of view and see that others may view an event from a different, but equally valid, perspective. Not only are adolescents more capable of discerning another person's perspective on some issue or event, they are also better able to understand that person's perspective on their own perspective.

According to Selman, role-taking ability progresses through a series of stages. During the preadolescent stage in the development of role taking, youngsters can put themselves in others' shoes but do not yet see how the thoughts and feelings of one person may be related to the thoughts and feelings of another. During early adolescence, with the progression into what Selman calls *mutual* role taking, the young adolescent can be an objective third party and see how the thoughts or actions of one person can influence those of another. In thinking about two of her friends, for instance, an adolescent at this level would be able to look at their relationship and see how each person's behavior affects the other's.

Later in adolescence, we see the development of role taking that is *in-depth and societal* in orientation. The adolescent at this level understands that the perspectives people have on each other are complicated, often unconscious, and influenced by larger forces than individuals can control, including each person's position in society or within a social institution. For example, you are able to understand that your perspective on the instructor teaching your class is influenced not only by your own personality and the instructor's, but by forces inherent in the way the relationship of professor and student is defined.

Ultimately, these gains in role-taking abilities lead to improvements in communication, as the adolescent becomes more capable of formulating his or her arguments in terms that are more likely to be understood by someone whose opinion may be different. One study (Clark and Delia, 1976), for example, looked at how well youngsters of different ages were able to persuade other people to do something for them—convincing their parents to buy them a new stereo, for instance. The researchers found that adolescents were more likely to

use reasoning that pointed out advantages to their parents ("If I have my own stereo in my room, you won't be bothered by my music.") than reasoning that simply stated the case from their own point of view ("I really need to have my own stereo. All the other kids do."). A major shift in reasoning took place during early adolescence, coinciding with the transition into the stage of "mutual" role taking. Although one might think that parents might find dealing with a more persuasive teenager more difficult, studies suggest that when adolescents are able to take their parents' perspective in an argument, family communication becomes more effective and satisfying (Silverberg, 1986).

**Conceptions of morality and social convention**  The realization that individuals' perspectives vary, and that their opinions may differ as a result, leads to changes in the ways that issues regarding morality and social convention are approached. Changes in moral reasoning during adolescence have been investigated extensively, and we examine this body of research in detail in Chapter 9. Briefly, during childhood, moral guidelines are seen as absolutes emanating from such authorities as parents or teachers; judgments of right and wrong are made according to concrete *rules*. During adolescence, however, such absolutes and rules come to be questioned, as the young person begins to see that moral standards are subjective and based on points of view that are subject to disagreement. Later in adolescence comes the emergence of reasoning that is based on such *moral principles* as equality, justice, or fairness—abstract guidelines that transcend concrete situations and can be applied across a variety of moral dilemmas (Kohlberg, 1976).

The development of individuals' understanding of social conventions—the social norms that guide day-to-day behavior—follows a similar course (Turiel, 1978). During middle

Gains in role-taking abilities allow the adolescent to evaluate a speaker's words in terms of the speaker's perspective and vested interests. *(Susan Lapides/Design Conceptions)*

childhood, social conventions—such as waiting in line to buy movie tickets—are seen as arbitrary and changeable, but adherence to them is not; compliance with such conventions is based on rules and on the dictates of authority. When you were 7 years old, you might not have seen why people had to wait in line to buy movie tickets, but when your mother told you to wait in line, you waited. By early adolescence, however, conventions are seen as arbitrary and changeable in both their origins and their enforcement; conventions are merely social expectations. As an adolescent, you begin to realize that people wait in line because they are expected to, not because they are forced to. Indeed, young adolescents often see social conventions as *nothing but* social expectations and, consequently, as insufficient reasons for compliance. You can probably imagine youngsters in their midteens saying something like this: "Why wait in a ticket line simply because other people are lined up? There isn't a *law* that forces you to wait in line, is there?"

Gradually, however, adolescents begin to see social conventions as means used by society to regulate people's behavior; conventions may be arbitrary, but we follow them because we all share an understanding of how people are expected to behave in various situations. In fact, high schoolers see conventions as so ingrained in the social system that individuals follow them partly out of habit. We wait in line for theater tickets not to comply with any "rule" but because it is something we are accustomed to doing.

Ultimately, individuals come to see that social conventions serve a function in coordinating interactions among people. Social norms and expectations are derived from and maintained by individuals' having a common perspective and agreeing that, in given situations, certain behaviors are more desirable than others, because such behaviors help society and its institutions to function more smoothly. Without the convention of waiting in line to buy movie tickets, the pushiest people would always get tickets first. The older adolescent can see that waiting in line doesn't only benefit the theater, it preserves everyone's right to a fair chance to buy tickets. In other words, we wait in line patiently because we all agree that it is better if tickets are distributed fairly.

Table 2.2 summarizes some of the important differences in social cognitive abilities between preadolescents and adolescents. As you can see, across all four domains, thinking becomes more abstract, more hypothetical, and more relativistic between childhood and adolescence.

Taken together, these gains in social cognitive abilities help to account for gains in individuals' social competence during adolescence. Some research has shown, for example, that adolescents who have more sophisticated social cognitive abilities (i.e., more advanced role-taking abilities, more sophisticated impression formation skills) actually behave in more socially competent ways (Ford, 1982). Although there is more to social competence than social cognition, being able to understand social relationships in a more advanced way is an important component of being able to behave in a more advanced way.

## TABLE 2.2

DIFFERENCES BETWEEN PREADOLESCENT AND ADOLESCENT THINKING IN FOUR SOCIAL COGNITIVE DOMAINS

| Domain | Preadolescent thought | Adolescent thought |
| --- | --- | --- |
| Impressions of Others (e.g., *Barenboim*) | Global, egocentric, concrete, disorganized, and haphazard | Differentiated, objective, abstract, and organized into coherent whole |
| Role Taking (e.g., *Selman*) | Able to put self in other's shoes but difficulty seeing how one person's perspective affects another's | Able to take "third party" perspective (mutual) and to see the bigger, societal picture |
| Moral Reasoning (e.g., *Kohlberg*) | Morals are based on concrete rules handed down by authorities | Morals come out of agreements between people or out of abstract principles |
| Social Conventions (e.g., *Turiel*) | Conventions are based on the rules and dictates of authorities | Conventions are based on expectations or grow out of social norms |

## ADOLESCENT RISK-TAKING

A second practical application of research on adolescent thinking involves the study of adolescent risk-taking. In the previous chapter, we noted that many of the health problems of the adolescent period are the result of behaviors that can be prevented—behaviors such as substance abuse, reckless driving, or unprotected sex. Some writers have suggested that we look at these behaviors as resulting from decisions that adolescents make—for instance, decisions to drink alcohol, to drive fast, or to have intercourse without using contraception—and that we need to better understand the cognitive processes behind such decision making. One line of research has attempted to examine whether adolescents make risky decisions because of deficiencies in their developing cognitive abilities (Furbey and Beyth-Marom, 1990).

A number of writers have looked at adolescent risk-taking from a perspective called **behavioral decision theory** (Fischoff, 1988; Kahneman, Slovic, and Tversky, 1982). According to this theory, all behaviors can be analyzed as the outcome of a process that involves (1) identifying alternative choices; (2) identifying the consequences that follow each choice; (3) evaluating the desirability of each possible consequence; (4) assessing the likelihood of each possible consequence; and (5) combining all of this information according to some decision rule.

So, for example, an adolescent girl who is trying to decide whether to sleep with her boyfriend for the first time would (1) identify the choices (sleep with him or not sleep with him); (2) identify the consequences (sleeping with him may solidify our relationship but it exposes me to the possibility of getting pregnant or contracting AIDS, whereas not sleeping with him may risk the relationship but I won't feel guilty for doing something I don't really want to do); (3) evaluate the desirability of each consequence (getting pregnant would be a ter-

rible thing, not respecting myself would be a terrible thing, losing my boyfriend would be a bad thing, but not a terrible one); (4) assess the likelihood of each consequence (I probably won't get pregnant because we'll be careful, I probably will feel guilty, he probably won't break up with me anyway); and (5) combine all of the information according to some decision rule (all things considered, I think I'll wait).

From the perspective of behavioral decision theory, then, it is important to ask whether adolescents use different processes than adults in identifying, estimating, and evaluating various behavioral options and consequences. If risky decisions are the result of faulty information processing—in attention, memory, metacognition, or organization, for example—perhaps it would make sense to train these basic cognitive abilities as a means of lessening adolescent risk-taking.

According to most studies, however, adolescents make decisions using the same basic cognitive processes as do adults (Furbey and Beyth-Marom, 1990). This is true even around issues as complicated as deciding whether to abort a pregnancy (Lewis, 1987). The major gains in information processing appear to occur between childhood and adolescence, rather than between adolescence and adulthood (Keating, 1990). If this is the case, then, why do adolescents behave in ways that are excessively risky?

The answer may involve the different ways in which adolescents and adults evaluate the desirability of different consequences. For example, an individual's decision to try cocaine at a party may involve evaluating a number of different consequences, including the legal and health risks, the pleasure the drug will induce, and the way in which one will be judged by the other people present (positively and negatively). Whereas an adult and an adolescent may both consider all of these consequences, the adult may place relatively more weight on the health risks of trying the drug, while the adolescent may place relatively more weight on the social consequences of not trying. Although an adult may see an adolescent's decision to value peer acceptance more than health as "irrational," an adolescent may see the adult's decision as equally incomprehensible. Behavioral decision theory reminds us that all decisions—even risky ones—can be seen as "rational," once we understand the ways in which individuals estimate and evaluate the consequences of various courses of action.

In all likelihood, of course, neither adolescents' nor adults' decisions are always made in as straightforward or rational a way as suggested by behavioral decision theory. Nevertheless, this approach has opened up a new way of thinking about adolescent risk-taking. Instead of looking at "risky" decisions as the result of irrational or faulty judgment, experts are now trying to understand where and how adolescents obtain the information they use in reaching their conclusions, and how accurate the information is. If, for example, adolescents underestimate the likelihood of getting pregnant following unprotected sex, sex education efforts might focus on teaching teenagers the actual probability.

## ADOLESCENT THINKING IN THE CLASSROOM

Given the sorts of changes in thinking that occur during the adolescent years, one would hope that schools and teachers adapt their methods and curricula to better mesh with the developing cognitive abilities of their students. In theory, adolescents' ability to think in more advanced ways—whether in terms of abstraction, multidimensionality, relativism, or some other dimension—should permit them to think more critically about a wide range of issues. Yet, the prevalence of **critical thinking** among American high school students—thinking that is in-depth, analytical, and discriminating—has been less than staggering, as we shall see in later chapters on school and on achievement. Most assessments of adolescent achievement in

recent years indicate that American youth have difficulty thinking in the sophisticated ways that our theories and research suggest they ought to be capable of.

To what can we attribute this gap between theory and practice? According to some writers, our educational system does not encourage or stimulate the type of thinking that adolescents have the potential for. Although research indicates that it is possible to stimulate the development of formal operational thinking, for example (e.g., Danner and Day, 1977; Siegler, Liebert, and Liebert, 1973), few junior or senior high school classes are set up to do so. Rather than encouraging adolescents to think in abstract or relativistic ways, for instance, most secondary school classes reward the rote memorization of concrete facts and the parroting back of the teacher's "correct" answer. According to one expert, opportunities for real give-and-take in adolescents' schools account for less than 10 percent of the total time spent on instruction. At a time when individuals are becoming capable of seeing that most issues are too complicated to have one "right" answer, an educational program that stifles this developing ability works against the adolescent's developmental inclinations. Although attempts have been made to make the instruction of adolescents more compatible with our understanding of their cognitive development, these efforts have not been widespread (Linn, 1987).

Similar criticisms have been levelled against schools' lack of attempt to deliberately enhance adolescents' information-processing skills. As our society becomes more information-dependent—some social commentators have talked about information "overload"—it is important that adolescents learn how to better manage and utilize this wealth of data. A number of writers have argued that schools can and should teach adolescents ways of focusing attention, improving short- and long-term memory, organizing information, and monitoring thought processes (Baron and Sternberg,

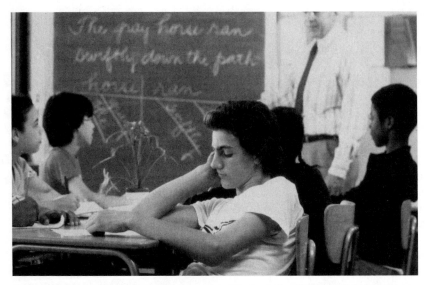

Although schools, in theory, could play an important role in stimulating intellectual development, few secondary school classes encourage critical thinking or advanced reasoning. It is little surprise that many high school students find classes dull and boring. *(Richard Hutchings/Photo Researchers)*

1987; Gagne, 1985; Glazer and Bassok, 1989). In other words, these experts believe that information-processing skills can be taught and that educators should make more of a conscious effort to do so. Moreover, they point to recent advances in research on adolescent information-processing as providing the foundation for an overhaul of our secondary school curricula.

## *Summary*

1. Changes in cognition, or thinking, are the second of three sets of fundamental changes that occur at adolescence. Adolescents show five main advantages in thinking over children: in thinking in terms of what is possible, not only what is real; in thinking about abstract things; in thinking about the process of thinking itself (referred to as metacognition); in thinking in multidimensional terms; and in seeing knowledge as relative, rather than as absolute.

2. Several theories have been proposed about the processes that underlie the development of more advanced thinking in adolescence. The three main viewpoints are Piagetian, or cognitive-developmental; psychometric; and information-processing. According to the Piagetian view, the development of more sophisticated thinking at adolescence is due to the development of advanced logical abilities. Piaget believed that adolescence marked the transition into a qualitatively different way of reasoning—a stage of thinking based on "formal operations." In contrast to the "concrete operational" child, the formal operational adolescent is able to employ an abstract system of logic in a variety of social and scientific situations.

3. Researchers working from the psychometric perspective have focused on the measurement and assessment of individual differences in mental abilities, and in particular, in intelligence. In recent years, several theorists have proposed alternatives to the view that intelligence can be adequately captured on standard-

ized tests, arguing that true intelligence is defined by skills in addition to those assessed in tests of "school smarts," such as the IQ test or the SAT.

4. Adolescent thinking also has been described from the information-processing perspective. According to this view, advances in thinking at adolescence are due to quantitative increases in such skills as memory, attention, metacognition, and organization. Information-processing theorists attempt to break down problem solving into its specific components in order to better understand exactly what it is that develops as individuals mature intellectually.

5. The cognitive developments of adolescence are reflected in young people's behavior in real-world situations as well as in laboratory experiments. One area of inquiry that has received a good deal of attention is the development of social cognition. Studies show that thinking about social relationships and social institutions—like thinking in general—becomes more abstract, more multidimensional, and more relativistic over the adolescent period.

6. Researchers also have examined adolescent risk-taking from a cognitive point of view. Contrary to popular wisdom, which holds that adolescents are "bad" decision makers, recent studies suggest that adolescents make decisions in much the same way that adults do. Young people sometimes behave in risky ways not because of faulty decision making, but because they evaluate the possible consequences of their actions differently than adults do.

7. Research on cognitive development in adolescence suggests a number of ways that schools might change in order to make classroom instruction better matched to the developing capabilities of adolescent students. Unfortunately, however, little has been done to change the way that adolescents are taught, and few high school programs are designed to stimulate the development of formal operations or more sophisticated information-processing skills.

## Key Terms

aptitude test
automatization
behavioral decision theory
cognitive-developmental (Piagetian)
concrete operations
divided attention
formal operations
imaginary audience
impression formation
information processing
long-term memory

metacognition
personal fable
preoperational period
propositional logic
psychometric
role taking
selective attention
sensorimotor
short-term memory
social cognition
social conventions
triarchic theory of intelligence

## For Further Reading

BARON, J., AND STERNBERG, R. (1987). *Teaching thinking skills: Theory and practice.* New York: Freeman. Applications of our understanding of information processing to classroom instruction.

ELKIND, D. (1978). Understanding the young adolescent. *Adolescence, 13,* 127–134. In this article, David Elkind explains how adolescents' social behavior can be understood in terms of their cognitive development.

KEATING, D. (1990). Adolescent thinking. In S. Feldman and G. Elliott (Eds.), *At the threshold: The developing adolescent.* Cambridge: Harvard University Press. A comprehensive overview of what is known about the development of thinking during the adolescent years.

LAPSLEY, D. (1989). Continuity and discontinuity in adolescent social cognitive development. In R. Montemayor, G. Adams, and T. Gullota (Eds.), *Advances in adolescence research* (Vol. 2). Beverly Hills, Calif.: Sage. A recent review of research on the development of social cognition in adolescence.

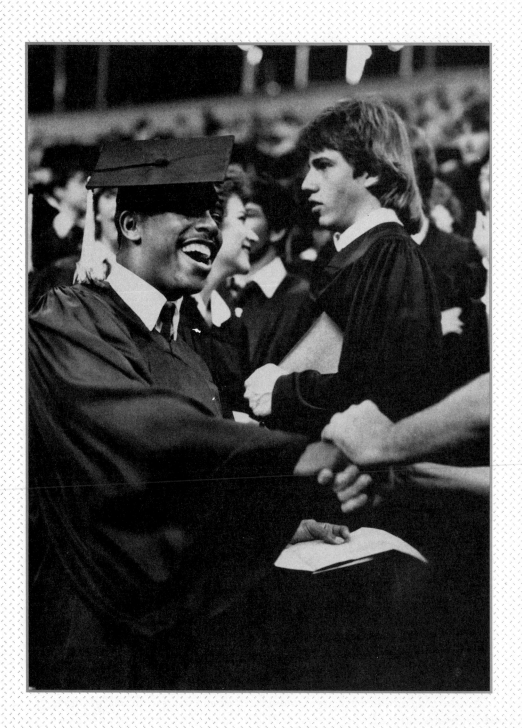

# SOCIAL TRANSITIONS

A mong the Thonga (an agrarian society in the southeastern region of Africa), at the time of her first menstruation, the adolescent girl goes to an older woman of her choosing and announces that she has come of age (Ford and Beach, 1951). At this point, a seclusion period of one month commences, and

> three or four girls, undergoing the initiation ceremony together, are shut up in a hut, and when they come out, must always wear over their face a veil consisting of a very dirty and greasy cloth. Every morning they are led to the pool, and their whole body is immersed in the water as far as the neck. Other initiated girls or women accompany them, singing obscene songs, and drive away with sticks any man who happens to be on the road, as no man is allowed to see a girl during this period. . . . When the cortege of women accompanying the initiated has returned home, the nubile girls are imprisoned in the hut. They are teased, pinched, scratched by the adoptive mothers or by other women; they must also listen to the licentious songs which are sung to them. . . . They are also instructed in sexual matters, and told that they must never reveal anything about the blood of the menses to a man. . . . At the end of the month the adoptive mother brings the girl home to her true mother. She also presents her with a pot of beer. A feast takes place on this occasion. (Junod, 1927, cited in Ford and Beach, 1951, p. 175)

Along with the biological changes of puberty and changes in thinking abilities, changes in social roles and status constitute yet another universal feature of development during adolescence. All societies differentiate among individuals on the basis of how old they are (although not all use chronological age as the defining criterion).

In all societies, adolescence is a period of social transition for the individual. Over the course of the adolescent years, the individual ceases to be viewed by society as a child and comes to be recognized as an adult. Although the specific elements of this social passage from childhood into adulthood vary considerably from one society to another, the presence during adolescence of some sort of recognition that the individual's status has changed—a **social redefinition** of the individual—is universal.

This social redefinition at adolescence is certainly less vivid and less ceremonial in contemporary America than it is among the Thonga. We do not seclude young people from the rest of society at the onset of puberty, nor, with the exception of certain religious ceremonies, do we generally mark the passage into adulthood with elaborate rituals. But just because the social transition into adulthood is less explicit in contemporary society than it is in many traditional cultures does not mean that the passage is any less significant. Indeed, some theorists have argued that the nature of adolescence is far more influenced by the way in which society defines the economic and social roles of young people than by the biological changes of puberty.

The study of social transitions at adolescence provides an interesting vehicle through which we can compare adolescence across different cultures and historical epochs. While certain features of the social passage from childhood into adulthood are universal, considerable differences exist between the processes of social redefinition in contemporary society and in more traditional cultures. In examining some of these differences, you will come to understand better how the way in which society structures the transition of adolescents into adult roles influences the nature of psychosocial development during the period.

Because young people go through puberty earlier today than 100 years ago, and because they tend to stay in school longer, the adolescent period has been lengthened and the transition into adulthood prolonged. Today, young people are caught between the world of childhood and the world of adulthood for an extremely long time, with only a vague sense of when—and how—they become adults. Indeed, in the minds of many social scientists who study adolescence in modern society, the social passage of young people into adult roles is too long, too vague, and too rocky (National Commission on Youth, 1980; Nightingale and Wolverton, 1988).

## Social Redefinition and Psychosocial Development

Like the biological and cognitive transitions of adolescence, the social transitions have important consequences for the young person's psychosocial development. Indeed, from a sociological or cultural perspective, it is social redefinition at adolescence—rather than, for example, puberty as such—that has the most profound impact on the individual's development and behavior. In the realm of *identity*, for example, attainment of adult status may transform the young person's self-concept, causing him or her to feel more adultlike and to think more seriously about future work and family roles. Doing for the first time such things as reporting to work, going into a bar, or registering to vote all make us feel older and more mature. In turn, these new activities and opportunities may prompt self-evaluation and introspection.

Becoming an adult member of society, accompanied as it is by shifts in responsibility, independence, and freedom, also has an impact on the development of *autonomy*. In contrast to the child, the adolescent-turned-adult is permitted to make a wider range of decisions that may have serious long-term consequences. A young woman who has reached the drinking age, for example, must decide how she should handle this new privilege. Should she go along with the crowd and drink every weekend night, or should she follow her parents' example and abstain from drinking? And in return for the privileges that come with adult status, adolescents are expected to behave in a more responsible fashion. Receiving a driver's license carries with it the obligation of driving safely. Thus the attainment of adult status provides chances for the young person to exercise autonomy as well as chances to develop a greater sense of independence.

Changes in social definition often bring with them changes in the sorts of relationships and interpersonal behaviors that are permitted and expected. Social redefinition at adolescence is therefore likely to raise new questions and concerns for the young person about *intimacy*—including, in particular, such matters as dating and marriage. Many parents prohibit their children from dating until they have reached an "appropriate" age. And not until the **age of majority** (the legal age for adult status) are individuals allowed to marry without first gaining their parents' permission. In certain societies, young people may even be *required* to marry on becoming adults. A marriage may have been arranged while they were children, and they will be expected to marry as soon as they have been initiated into adulthood.

Status changes at adolescence may also affect development in the domain of *sexuality*. In contemporary society, for example, laws governing sexual behavior (such as the definition of statutory rape) typically differentiate between individuals who have and have not attained adult status. By becoming an adult in a legal sense, the young person may be confronted with the need for new and different decisions about sexual activity. One problem currently facing society is whether sexually active individuals who have not yet attained adult *legal* status should be able to make independent decisions about such "adult" matters as abortion and contraception.

Finally, reaching adulthood often has important implications in the realm of *achievement*. For instance, in contemporary society, it is not until adult status is attained that one can enter the labor force as a full-time employee. Not until young people have reached a designated age are they permitted to leave school of their own volition. In less industrialized societies, becoming an adult typically entails entrance into the productive activities of the community. Taken together, these shifts are likely to prompt changes in the young person's skills, aspirations, and expectations.

## Adolescence as a Social Invention

Because so many of the psychological changes of adolescence are linked to the changes that accompany society's redefinition of the individual, many writers have argued that adolescence, as a period in the life cycle, is mainly a social invention (e.g., Lapsley et al., 1985). These **inventionists** point out that although the biological and cognitive changes characteristic of the period are important in their own right, adolescence is defined primarily by the ways in which society recognizes (or does not recognize) the period as distinct from childhood or adulthood.

Many of our images of adolescence are influenced by the fact that we draw lines between adolescence and childhood (for instance, the boundary between elementary and secondary school) and between adolescence and adulthood (for instance, the age at which one can hold a job). Inventionists stress that it is because we *see* adolescence as distinct that it in fact exists as such. They point to other cultures and other historical periods in which adolescence is either not recognized at all or is viewed very differently. As we shall see later in this chapter, many of these theorists view the behaviors and problems characteristic of adolescence in contemporary society as having to do with the particular way that adolescence is defined by society, rather than the result of the biological or cognitive givens of the period.

This is an entirely different view than that espoused by writers such as G. Stanley Hall, for example, who saw the psychological changes of adolescence as driven by puberty, and, as a result, by biological destiny.

According to the inventionist view, the origins of adolescence as we know it in contemporary society are closely linked to the industrial revolution of the middle of the nineteenth century. Prior to that time, in the agricultural world of the sixteenth or seventeenth century, children were treated primarily as miniature adults, and people did not make precise distinctions among children of different ages (the term *child* referred to anyone under the age of 18 or even 21). Children provided important labor to their families, and they learned early in their development the roles they were expected to fulfill later in life. The main distinction between children and adults was not based on their age or their abilities, but on whether they owned property (Modell and Goodman, 1990). As a consequence, there was little reason to label some youngsters as "children" and others as "adolescents"—in fact, the term adolescent was not widely used before the nineteenth century.

With industrialization, however, came new patterns of work and family life. Adolescents were among the most dramatically affected by these changes. First, because the economy was changing so rapidly, away from the simple and predictable life known in agrarian society, the connection between what individuals learned in childhood and what they would need to know in adulthood became increasingly uncertain. Although a father may have been a farmer, for instance, his son would not necessarily follow in his footsteps. One response to this uncertainty was that parents, especially in middle-class families, encouraged adolescents to spend time preparing for adulthood within socially organized institutions, such as schools. Instead of working side by side with their parents and other adults at home, as was the case before industrialization, nineteenth-century adolescents were increasingly more likely to spend their days with peers of the same age, preparing for the future.

Inventionists have been quick to point out that the redefinition of adolescence as a time of preparation, rather than participation, suited society's changing economic needs as well. One initial outcome of industrialization was a shortage of job opportunities, because machines were used to replace workers. Although adolescents provided inexpensive labor, they were competing with adults for a limited supply of jobs. One way of protecting adults' jobs was to remove adolescents from the labor force, by turning them into full-time students. In order to accomplish this, society needed to begin discriminating between individuals who were ready for work and those who were not. And although there was very little factual basis for the distinction, society began to view adolescents as less capable and as more in need of guidance and training—as a way of rationalizing what was little more than age discrimination. Individuals who earlier in the century would have been working side by side with adults were now seen as too immature or unskilled to carry out similar tasks. As noted in the introductory chapter, our view of adolescents' capability and maturity has changed dramatically when their labor has been sorely needed, such as during wartime (Enright et al., 1987).

A less cynical view of the events of the late nineteenth century emphasizes the genuine desire of some adults to protect adolescents from the dangers of the new workplace, rather than the selfish desire to protect adults' jobs from teenagers. Industrialization brought with it worrisome changes in community life, especially in the cities. Many factories were dangerous working environments, filled with new and unfamiliar machinery. The disruption of small farming communities and the growth of large urban areas because of the shift from agriculture to industry was accompanied by increases in crime and in "moral degeneracy."

**Child protectionists** argued that young people needed to be kept away from the labor force for their own good. In addition to the rise of schools during this time, the early twentieth century saw the growth of many organizations aimed at protecting young people, such as the Boy Scouts and similar adult-supervised youth clubs (Modell and Goodman, 1990).

For whatever the reason, it was not until the late nineteenth century—about 100 years ago—that adolescence came to be viewed as we view it today: a lengthy period of preparation for adulthood, in which young people, in need of guidance and supervision, remain economically dependent on their elders. This view started within the middle class—where parents had more to gain by keeping their children out of the labor force and educating them for a better adulthood—but it spread quickly throughout much of society. Because the workplace has continued to change in ways that make the future uncertain, the idea of adolescence as a distinctive period of preparation for adulthood has remained intact.

Two relatively recent modifications of our definition of adolescence also have given rise to new terminology and ideas. The first of these concerns the use of the term **teenager,** which was not employed until about fifty years ago. In contrast to the term "adolescent," teenager connotes a more frivolous and light-hearted age, during which individuals concern themselves with cars and cosmetics. An important social change that gave rise to the invention of the "teenager" was the increased affluence and economic freedom enjoyed by American adolescents during the late 1940s and early 1950s. Advertisers recognized that these young people represented an important consumer group and, with the help of the new publications such as *Seventeen* magazine, began cultivating the image of the happy-go-lucky teenager as a means of targeting ad campaigns toward the lucrative adolescent market (Greenberger and Steinberg, 1986).

A second term whose acceptance grew as a

Although adolescence was "invented" during the late 19th century, it was not until the middle of this century that our present-day image of the "teenager" was created. An important contributor to this image was the mass media—magazines such as *Seventeen* cultivated the picture of the happy-go-lucky teenager as a way of targeting advertisements toward the lucrative adolescent market. *(Reprint from Seventeen Magazine. Copyright by K-III Magazines Corporation. All rights reserved.)*

result of recent social change is **youth.** The term "youth" was used long before "adolescent." But, prior to industrialization, "youth" had a very vague and imprecise meaning, and could refer to someone as young as 12 or as old as 24 (Modell and Goodman, 1990). During the 1960s, however, the growth of the college population and the rise in student activism across the country focused attention on individuals who were somewhere between adolescence and young adulthood—those in the 18-

to 22-year-old range. Many adults referred to the changes they saw in attitudes and values among college students as the "youth movement." One theorist went so far as to argue that "youth" is a separate stage in the life cycle, psychologically as well as chronologically distinct from adolescence and adulthood (Keniston, 1970). Indeed, many college students are unsure about whether they are adolescents or adults, since they may feel mature in some respects (e.g., keeping up an apartment, being involved in a serious dating relationship) but immature in others (e.g., having to depend on parents for economic support, having to have an advisor approve class schedules). The lengthening of formal schooling in contemporary society has altered the social definition of adolescence, because the majority of young people continue their education past high school and are forced to delay their transition into many adult work and family roles.

It is important to note that when we say that adolescence (or the teenager, or youth) is in part a social invention, we do not mean that its significance is in any way diminished, or that it is somehow less real than if it were an entirely biological phenomenon. "Democracy," after all, is a social invention, too, but its creation and development have had profound effects on the way that we live. As with other social inventions, the notion that there should be a distinct period of adolescence has endured over time and has had important and very concrete repercussions. But as with other social constructs, the nature of adolescence changes over time, and it will continue to change as we revise our notions of what it means to grow from childhood into adulthood.

## Changes in Status

"The most casual survey of the ways in which different societies have handled adolescence makes one fact inescapable," wrote anthropologist Ruth Benedict in her classic work, *Patterns of Culture*. "[E]ven in those cultures which have made the most of the trait, the age upon which they focus their attention varies over a great range of years. . . . The puberty they recognize is social, and the ceremonies are a recognition in some fashion or other of the child's new status of adulthood. . . . In order to understand [adolescence] . . . we need . . . to know what is identified in different cultures with the beginning of adulthood and their methods of admitting to the new status" (Benedict, 1934, p. 25). Changes in social definition at adolescence typically involve a two-sided alteration in status. On the one hand, the adolescent is given certain privileges and rights that are typically reserved for the society's adult members. On the other hand, this increased power and freedom generally are accompanied by increased expectations for self-management, personal responsibility, and social participation.

We can find examples of this double shift in social status in all societies, across a variety of interpersonal, political, economic, and legal arenas.

## CHANGES IN INTERPERSONAL STATUS

In many societies, individuals who have been recognized as adults are usually addressed with adult titles. They also are expected to maintain different sorts of social relationships with their parents, with the community's elders, and with young people whose status has not yet changed. On holidays such as Thanksgiving, for example, some large families set two tables: a big table for the adults and a smaller, "children's" table. When a young person is permitted to sit at the big table, it is a sign that he or she has reached a new position in the family. These interpersonal changes are typically accompanied by new interpersonal obligations—for example, being expected to take care of and set a proper example for the younger members of the family.

## CHANGES IN POLITICAL STATUS

With the attainment of adult status, the young person is often permitted more extensive participation in the community's decision making. Among the Navaho (Southwestern United States), for example, it is only following a formal initiation ceremony that adolescents are considered members of the Navaho People and permitted full participation in ceremonial life (Cohen, 1964). In contemporary America, attaining the age of majority brings the right to vote. But in return for this increased power usually come new obligations. Young adults are expected to serve their communities in cases of emergency or need. And training for warfare is often demanded of young men once they attain adult status (Benedict, 1934).

## CHANGES IN ECONOMIC STATUS

Attaining adult status also has important economic implications that again entail obligation as well as privilege. In some societies, only adults may own property and maintain control over their income (Miller, 1928). In many American states, for example, any income that a youngster earns before the age of 16 is technically the property of the young person's parents.

Entrance into certain work roles is also restricted to adults. In most industrialized societies, employment is regulated by child labor laws, and the attainment of a prescribed age is a prerequisite to employment in certain occupations. Among the Tikopia (Melanesia), one of the first privileges accorded boys when they reach adolescence is accompanying older males on fishing expeditions, as members of the crew (Fried and Fried, 1980). In most communities, however, once they have attained the economic status and rights of adults, young people are expected to contribute to the economic well-being of their community. They are depended on to participate in the community's produc-

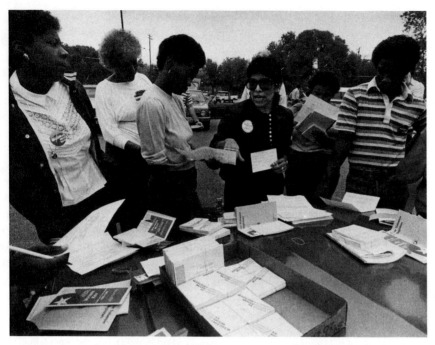

One privilege that accompanies the young person's transition into adult status in contemporary society is the right to vote. *(Bob Daemmrich/Image Works)*

tive activities and to carry out the labor expected of adults. In contemporary society, the young adult's economic responsibilities to the broader community may entail having to pay taxes for the first time. In some families, adolescents who are permitted to work must contribute to their family's support.

## CHANGES IN LEGAL STATUS

In most societies, not until adult status is attained is the young person permitted to participate in a variety of activities that are typically reserved for adults. Gambling, purchasing alcoholic beverages, and driving are but three of the many privileges we reserve in America for individuals who have reached the legal age of adulthood. In many cultures, the eating of certain foods is restricted to individuals who have been admitted to adult society (Mead, 1928).

Once an adolescent is designated as an adult, however, he or she is also subject to a new set of laws and must expect to be treated differently by the legal institutions of the society from how he or she was treated as a child. In the United States, for example, crimes by young adolescents are generally adjudicated in a separate juvenile justice system, which operates under different rules and principles from the system that applies to adults. Unfortunately, development during the adolescent years is so rapid and so variable that it is difficult to know at what chronological age a line should be drawn between legally viewing someone as an adult and viewing someone as a child (Gold and Petronio, 1980).

Many other issues surrounding the legal status of adolescents remain vague and confusing. For example, courts have ruled that teenagers have the right to obtain contraceptives without their parents' approval. But they also have up-

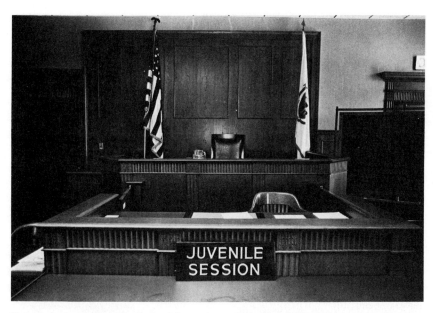

The criminal activities of young adolescents are typically adjudicated in a separate juvenile justice system. Difficulties inherent in grouping individuals together on the basis of chronological age, however, have raised questions about how well this system works. Still today, the legal status of adolescents remains vague, confusing, and inconsistent. *(J. Berndt/Stock, Boston)*

held laws forbidding adolescents access to cigarettes or to magazines that, while vulgar, were not considered so obscene that they were outlawed among adults (Zimring, 1982). In general, legal decisions have tended to restrict the behavior of adolescents when the behavior in question is viewed as potentially damaging to the young person (buying cigarettes, for example) but have supported adolescent autonomy when the behavior is viewed as having potential benefit (using contraceptives).

## The Process of Social Redefinition

Social redefinition at adolescence is not a single event, but a series of events that may occur over a relatively long time. In contemporary America, the process of redefinition typically begins at the age of 15 or 16, when the young person is first permitted to drive, to work, and to leave school. But the social redefinition of the adolescent continues well into the young adult years in many parts of the country. Some privileges, such as voting, are not conferred until the age of 18, and others, such as purchasing alcoholic beverages, are not conferred until the age of 21, five or six years after the redefinition process begins. Even in societies that mark the social redefinition of the young person with a dramatic and elaborate **initiation ceremony,** the social transformation of the individual from a child into an adult may span many years, and the initiation ceremony may represent just one element of the transition. In fact, the initiation ceremoney usually marks the beginning of a long period of training and preparation for adulthood rather than the adolescent's final passage into adult status (Cohen, 1964).

In many cultures, the social redefinition of

### TABLE 3-1

SOME CONSEQUENCES OF ATTAINING ADULT STATUS

|  | In traditional societies | In contemporary societies |
| --- | --- | --- |
| Interpersonal | Addressed with "adult" title by other members of community | Permitted to sit with grownups for special occasions |
| Political | Permitted to participate in community decision making | Eligible to vote |
| Economic | Permitted to own property | Permitted to work |
| Legal | Permitted to consume certain foods | No longer dealt with in a separate juvenile justice system |

young people occurs in groups. That is, the young people of a community are grouped with peers of approximately the same age—a cohort—and move through the series of status transitions together. One of the results of such age-grouped social transitions is that very strong bonds are formed among youngsters who have shared certain rituals. In many American high schools, for example, attempts are made to create "class spirit" or "class unity" by fostering bonds among students who will be graduated together. In many Mexican-American communities adolescent girls together participate in an elaborate sort of "coming out" celebration, called the *quinceañera*. On college campuses, fraternities and sororities may conduct group initiations that involve difficult or unpleasant tasks, and special ties may be forged between "brothers" or "sisters" who have pledged together.

## COMMON PRACTICES IN THE PROCESS OF SOCIAL REDEFINITION

Although the specific ceremonies and signs of social redefnition at adolescence vary from one culture to another, several general themes characterize the process in all societies. First, social redefinition usually entails the *real or symbolic separation of the young person from his or her*

*parents.* In traditional societies, this may take the form of **extrusion:** During late childhood, children are expected to begin sleeping in households other than their own. Youngsters may spend the day with their parents, but they spend the night with friends of the family, with relatives, or in a separate residence reserved for preadolescent youngsters (Cohen, 1964). In America, during earlier times, it was customary for adolescents to leave home temporarily and live with other families in the community, either to learn specific occupational skills (i.e., as apprentices) or to work as domestic servants (Kett, 1977). Interestingly, the "placing out" of adolescents from their parents' home often coincided with puberty (Katz, 1975). In contemporary societies, the separation of adolescents from their parents takes somewhat different forms. They are sent to summer camps, to boarding schools, or, as is more common, to live at college.

A second aspect of social redefinition at adolescence entails the *accentuation of physical and social differences between males and females.* (Ford and Beach, 1951). This accentuation of differences occurs partly because of the physical changes of puberty and partly because adult work and family roles are generally highly sex-differentiated. Many societies separate males and females during religious ceremonies, have

The boys of the Mandingo tribe are initiated in an elaborate group ritual. First, their courage is tested by a "ghost." Then they are circumcised in a group ceremony. Following the circumcision, they live together in a special hut, separated from the tribe, until they have completed their religious instruction. Group rituals often create lifelong bonds among the members of the group. *(Arthur Tress/Photo Researchers)*

individuals begin wearing sex-specific articles of clothing (rather than clothing permissible for either gender), and keep males and females apart during initiation ceremonies. Some traditional societies employ a practice called **brother-sister avoidance:** After puberty, a brother and sister may not have any direct contact or interaction until one or both are married (Cohen, 1964).

The separation of males and females is not limited to social redefinition in traditional societies. In earlier times in America (and to a certain extent in many other industralized societies today), males and females were separated during adolescence in educational institutions, either by excluding adolescent girls from secondary and higher education, grouping males and females in different schools or different classrooms, or having males and females follow different curricula. In present-day America, many of these practices have been discontinued, but some elements of accentuated sex differentiation and sex segregation during adolescence still exist: in residential arrangements, in styles of dress, in athletic activities, and in household chores (Hill and Lynch, 1983; Medrich, Roizen, Rubin, and Buckley, 1982; White and Brinkerhoff, 1981). And many contemporary ceremonies designed to recognize the young person's passage into adulthood are either limited to one sex or the other (e.g., debutante balls or the quinceañera, each of which is for young women) or somehow differentiate between males and females (e.g., the Bar Mitzvah and the Bat Mitzvah ceremonies for Jewish males and females, respectively).

Third, social redefinition at adolescence typically entails the *passing on of cultural, historical, and practical information* from the adult generation to the newly inducted cohort of young people. This information may concern (1) matters thought to be important to adults but of limited utility to children (for example, information on the performance of certain tasks); (2) matters thought to be necessary for adults but unfit for children (for example, information regarding sex); or (3) matters concerning the history or rituals of the family or community. In traditional societies, initiates are often sent to some sort of "school" in which they are instructed in the productive activities of the community (hunting, fishing, farming). Following puberty, boys and girls receive instruction about sexual relations, moral behavior, and societal lore (Fried and Fried, 1980; Miller, 1928). In contemporary society, too, adolescence is a time of instruction in preparation for adulthood. Elementary school students, for example, are generally not taught a great deal about sexuality, work, or financial matters; such coursework is typically reserved for high

school students. We also restrict entrance into certain "adult" activities (such as sexually explicit movies) until the adolescent is believed to be old enough to be exposed to them.

Because formal initiation ceremonies are neither very common nor very meaningful in modern society, students sometimes overlook important similarities between the processes of social redefinition in traditional and contemporary societies. Practices like extrusion, brother-sister avoidance, and scarification are alien and seem odd to us. But if we look beneath the surface, at the meaning and significance of each culture's practices, we find many common threads. In contemporary society, for example, our own form of "brother-sister avoidance" begins at puberty: Once adolescents have reached puberty, brothers and sisters are more likely to seek privacy from each other when dressing or bathing. And while we do not practice anything as "alien" as scarification, we do have our share of body rituals which often are not seen until adolescence and which might seem equally alien to someone unfamiliar with our society: the punching of holes in earlobes (ear piercing), the scraping of hair from faces or legs (shaving), and the application of brightly colored paints to lips, eyes, and cheeks (putting on make-up)!

## VARIATIONS IN SOCIAL TRANSITIONS

Different societies recognize and orchestrate the passage into adult status at different times and in different ways. In this respect, although the presence of social redefinition in a general sense is a universal feature of adolescent development, there is considerable diversity in the nature of the transition. Examining social redefinition from cross-cultural and historical perspectives provides a valuable means of contrasting the nature of adolescence in different social contexts. Two very important dimensions along which societies differ in the process of social redefinition are in the explicitness, or *clarity*, of the transition and in the smoothness, or *continuity*, of the passage.

**Variations in clarity**  Initiation ceremonies are in many ways religious ceremonies. As such, they are most often employed in societies in which a shared religious belief unites the community and structures individuals' daily experiences. Universal, formal initiation ceremonies therefore have never been prevalent in American society, largely because of the heterogeneity of the population and the general separation of religious experience from everyday affairs.

There are, however, factors other than the presence of formal rites of passage that determine how clear the transition into adult status is to the young person and society. One such factor concerns the extent to which various aspects of the status change occur at about the same time for an individual and during the same general time period for adolescents growing up together (Elder, 1980). When transitions into adult work, family, and citizenship roles occur close in time, and when most members of a cohort experience these transitions at about the same age, the passage into adulthood takes on greater clarity. If all young people were to graduate from high school, enter the labor force, and marry at the age of 18, this age would be an implicit boundary between adolescence and adulthood, even without a formal ceremony. But when different aspects of the passage occur at different times, and when adolescents growing up in a similar environment experience these transitions in different order and along different schedules, the boundary between adolescence and adulthood is made more cloudy.

*The clarity of social redefinition in contemporary society*  When did you become an adolescent? When did you (or when will you) become an

adult? If you are like most individuals in contemporary society, your answers to these questions will not be clearcut. We have no formal ceremonies marking the transition from childhood into adolescence, nor do we have any to mark the passage from adolescence into adulthood. Although in many religious, cultural, and social groups the young American adolescent may undergo an initiation ceremony of sorts—the confirmation, the bar mitzvah, the quinceañera, and the "coming out" parties of debutantes are some examples—rarely does this rite have much significance outside the youngster's family, circle of friends, or religious community. School graduation ceremonies perhaps come the closest to universal rites of passage in contemporary society, but school graduation does not bring with it many meaningful or universal changes in social status, responsibilities, or privileges. As a result, social redefinition in contemporary society does not give the adolescent any clear indication of when his or her responsibilities and privileges as an adult begin.

Attaining adult status is essentially an individual matter in contemporary society, and the absence of clearcut and universal markers of the passage make the process confusing. It is often difficult for young people to tell when they have reached adulthood. In many states, for example, the age for starting employment is 15; for leaving high school, 16; for attending restricted (R-rated) movies, 17; for voting, 18; and for drinking 21. We have few universal markers of adulthood—adolescents are treated as adults at different times by different people in different contexts. A young person may be legally old enough to drive, but his parents may feel that 16 is too early and refuse to let him use the family car. Another may be treated like an adult at work, where she works side by side with people three times her age, but she may be treated like a child at home. A third may be viewed as an adult by her mother but

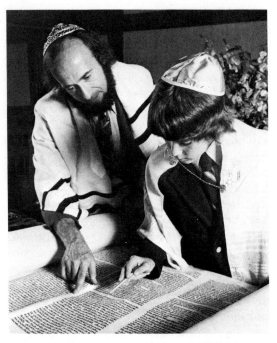

Formal rites of passage from childhood into adolescence or from adolescence into adulthood are rare in contemporary society. Certain religious ceremonies, such as the Confirmation or the Bar Mitzvah (pictured here), are as close as we come to initiation rites in contemporary America. *(Peter Southwick/Stock, Boston)*

entrance into a new position in the community (Ford and Beach, 1951). For boys, such ceremonies may take place at the time of puberty, at the attainment of a designated chronological age, or at a time when the community decides that the individual is ready for the status change. For girls, initiation is more often linked to puberty and, in particular, to the onset of menstruation. In both cases, the initiation ceremony serves to ritualize the passing of the young person out of childhood and, if not directly into adulthood, into a period of training for it.

In many initiation ceremonies, the adolescent's physical appearance is changed, so that other members of the community can distinguish between initiated and uninitiated young people. For example, new types of clothing may be worn following initiation; or some sort of surgical operation or scarification (the intentional creation of scars on some part or parts of the body) may be performed to create a permanent means of marking the individual's adult status. In most traditional societies, there is no mistaking which individuals are adults and which still children.

*The clarity of social redefinition in previous eras* Historical documents concerning life in early nineteenth-century America indicate that the transition into adulthood may actually have been then even more disorderly and cloudy than it is today. According to historian Joseph Kett (1977), many young people at that time moved back and forth between school, where they were viewed as children, and work, where they were viewed as adults. Moreover, timetables for the assumption of adult roles varied considerably from one individual to the next, because they were highly dependent on family and household needs rather than on generally accepted age patterns of school, family, and work transitions. An adolescent might have been working and living away from home, but if his family needed him—because, let's say,

as a child by her father. It is little wonder, in light of the mixed and sometimes contradictory expectations facing young people, that for many adolescents the transition into adult roles is a difficult passage to navigate. According to social psychologist Kurt Lewin (1948), the adolescent in modern society is a **marginal man,** caught in a transitional space betwen childhood and adulthood.

*The clarity of social redefinition in traditional cultures* Unlike the case in contemporary society, social redefinition at adolescence is clearly recognized in most traditional cultures. Typically, the passage from childhood into adolescence is marked by a formal initiation ceremony, which publicly proclaims the young person's someone became ill—he would leave his job and move back in with his parents. During the middle of the nineteenth century, in fact, many young people were neither enrolled in school nor working, occupying a halfway stage that was not quite childhood but not quite adulthood (Katz, 1975). As we noted earlier, industrialization left many young people excluded from the labor force, and only those adolescents from affluent families were able to afford private school. Descriptions of adolescent idleness during the era are strikingly reminiscent of descriptions of unemployed, out-of-school youth today. Indeed, concern about juvenile misbehavior was one factor that encouraged the development of public high schools.

One study comparing adolescents' transitions today with those of their counterparts 100 years ago indicates that the passage into adulthood may have been more prolonged as well as less clearly defined during the latter part of the nineteenth century than it is today.

Using census data and historical documents, social historian John Modell and his colleagues compared the timing and patterning of adolescents' transitions in 1970 with those in 1880 (Modell, Furstenberg, and Hershberg, 1976). The researchers examined five transitions, all of which can be thought of as indicators of the passage into adulthood: exit from school, entry into the labor force, departure from home, first marriage, and the establishment of an independent household. They were interested in the extent to which these transitions were negotiated along a common timetable and clustered around a narrow age period.

Compared with contemporary youth, adolescents living in the late nineteenth century underwent family-related transitions (leaving home, getting married, and setting up an independent household) much later, and school- and work-related transitions (leaving school and entering the labor force) much earlier. In other words, the passages into adulthood were

Generally speaking, young people 100 years ago left their parents' household, married, and set up their own households at a later age than they do today. In these respects, the transition of adolescents into adulthood was more prolonged than it is now. *(Culver)*

much more spread out over time. Although in recent years, there has been an increase in the average age at marriage, the timing of family-related and nonfamily-related transitions have converged, and the age range during which young people make these transitions is narrower and more universal now than it was 100 years ago (Modell and Goodman, 1990). Interestingly, though, there are some sex differences in the way in which different elements of the transition are ordered, as the box on pp. 106–107 describes.

In this respect, it appears as if the transition into adult status today has greater uniformity, if not greater clarity, than it did during much of the nineteenth century. As Modell and his colleagues suggest, those "who see today's period of youth as extended, normless, [and] lacking bounds" would do well to compare the structure of the adolescent passage as it exists today with that of 100 years ago (Modell, Furstenberg, and Hershberg, 1976, p. 31).

**Variations in continuity**   A second way in which the process of social redefinition varies across cultural and historical contexts is along the dimension of *continuity*—the extent to which the adolescent's transition into adulthood is gradual or abrupt (Benedict, 1934). Gradual transitions, in which the adolescent assumes the roles and status of adulthood bit by bit, are referred to as **continuous transitions.** Transitions that are not so smooth and in which the young person's entrance into adulthood is more sudden are referred to as **discontinuous transitions.** Children who grow up working on the family farm and continue this work as adults have a continuous transition into adult work roles. In contrast, children who do not have any work experience while they are growing up and who enter the labor force for the first time when they graduate from college have a discontinuous transition into adult work roles.

*The continuity of the adolescent passage in contemporary society*   Transitions into adulthood in contemporary society are more discontinuous than in other cultural or historical contexts. Young people in general are given little preparation before their entrance into adult status in the roles they will be expected to fulfill. Rather, in contemporary society, we tend to exclude young people from the world of adults; we give them little direct training for adult life and then thrust them rather abruptly into total adult independence.

Consider three of the most important roles of adulthood that individuals are expected to carry out successfully—the roles of worker, parent, and citizen. In all three cases we find that adolescents in contemporary society receive little preparation for these positions. Young people are segregated from the workplace throughout most of their childhood and early adolescent years and receive little direct training in school relevant to the work roles they will likely find themselves in as adults. The transition into adult work roles, therefore, is fairly discontinuous for most young people in contemporary society.

The transition of young people into adult family roles is even more abrupt than is their transition into work roles. Prior to actually becoming a parent, most young people have little training in child rearing or other related matters. Families are relatively small today, and youngsters are likely to be close in age to their siblings; as a result, few opportunities exist for participating in child-care activities at home. Schools generally offer little if any instruction in family relationships and domestic activities. And with childbirth generally taking place in hospitals rather than at home, few young people today have the opportunity of observing a younger sibling's birth.

Passage into adult citizenship and decision-making roles is also highly discontinuous in contemporary Western society. Adolescents are permitted few opportunities for independence and autonomy in school and are segregated from most of society's political institutions until they complete their formal education. Young people are permitted to vote once they turn 18 years old, but they have received little preparation for participation in government and community roles before this time.

Some fifty years ago, anthropoligist Ruth Benedict (1934) pointed out that the degree of stress individuals experience at adolescence is related to the degree of continuity they experience in making the transition into adulthood; the more discontinuous the passage, the more stressful it is likely to be. Benedict's view suggests that adolescent turmoil, if it exists, is more likely due to environmental than biological factors. It is little surprise, then, that some young people today have difficulty in assuming adult roles and responsibilities. Instead of being gradually socialized into work, family, and citizenship positions, adolescents in modern society typically are segregated from activities in these arenas during most of their childhood and youth. Yet young people are supposed to be able to perform these roles capably on reaching the age of majority. With little preparation in meaningful work, adolescents are expected to find, get, and keep a job immediately after completing their schooling. With essentially no training for marriage or parenting, they are expected to form their own families, manage their own households, and raise their own children soon after they reach adulthood. And without any previous involvement in community activities, they are expected on reaching the age of majority to vote, pay taxes, and behave as responsible citizens.

Discontinuity may be exacerbated by rapid community growth and social change. According to one study, rapid industrialization and expansion may more negatively affect adolescents than adults, however. (Freudenberg, 1984). This researcher compared teenagers and adults living in a rapidly growing boomtown in the Rocky Mountains with their counterparts in three nearby communities. Although there were few differences among adults, the boomtown teenagers were more likely than other teenagers to feel alienated and dissatisfied. One explanation is that the rapid expansion of the community was especially stressful for the teenagers, who, because of the influx of newcomers, were forced to cope with ever-changing cliques and crowds in school. Adults may have been buffered against some of the ill effects of expansion by well-established social networks and longstanding friendships and sources of social support.

*The continuity of the adolescent passage in traditional cultures*  The high level of discontinuity found in contemporary America is not characteristic of adolescence in traditional societies. Consider the socialization of young people in Samoa, for example. From early childhood on, youngsters are involved in work tasks that have a meaningful connection to the work they will perform as adults. They are involved in the care of younger children, in the planting and harvesting of crops, and in the gathering and preparation of food. Their entrance into adult work roles is gradual and continuous, with work tasks graded to children's skills and intelligence. Young people are charged with the socialization of their infant brothers and sisters, particularly during middle childhood, when they are not yet strong enough to make a substantial contribution to the community's fishing and farming activities. Gradually, young people are taught the fundamentals of weaving, boating, fishing, building, and farming. By the time they have reached late adolescence, Samoan youngsters are well trained in the tasks they will need to perform as adults (Mead, 1928).

Such continuity is generally the case in societies in which hunting, fishing, and farming are the chief work activities. As Margaret Mead (1928) has observed, the emphasis in these so-

# THE SEXES: SIMILARITIES AND DIFFERENCES IN THE TRANSITION INTO ADULTHOOD

The transition from adolescence to adulthood is marked by several related changes in social roles. Among the most important events in this transition are the completion of formal schooling, entrance into the full-time labor force, marriage, and parenthood. One way to think about the transition into adulthood, therefore, is to think about the transition out of one role—that of student—and into three others—those of worker, spouse, and parent (Marini, 1984).

Because these four transitions do not occur simultaneously, it is interesting to ask how they might be related to one another over time. Do most individuals finish school before taking on a full-time job, or does entry into the world of work precede leaving school? How do transitions into family roles, such as spouse and parent, link up with nonfamily transitions? For instance, do individuals become "adults" in nonfamily roles (that is, by leaving school and entering the workforce) before or after they become adults with respect to family roles? Is one sequence more common than another?

Sociologist Margaret Marini has examined these questions by looking at the way in which role transitions during young adulthood are ordered in contemporary America. Using data collected as a part of a longitudinal follow-up of individuals who had been high school students during the late 1950s (and who had participated in one of the most famous studies of adolescents ever conducted, *The Adolescent Society* [Cole-

man, 1961], which you will read about in Chapter 5), Marini was able to look at the relations among the role transitions out of school and into work, marriage, and parenthood. Although Marini found that about half of all males and females followed one particular sequence of role transitions, she also found several important differences between males' and females' patterns that have implications for understanding sex differences in educational and occupational attainment.

The most common sequence followed for both sexes was exit from school, followed by entrance into work, entrance into marriage, and then into parenthood, in that order. But half of all the individuals did not follow this "normative" path toward adulthood. One-fifth of the women and nearly one-third of the men had taken a full-time job before finishing school; some worked while in school, and others left school for a time and returned later. One-fifth of the women and nearly one-quarter of the men married before finishing school, and about one in ten men and women had married and become parents before their education was finished.

In general, the longer an individual stayed in school, the less likely he or she was to follow the expected sequence—primarily because longer schooling made it more likely that one of the other transitions would occur before education was completed. At the turn of the century, for example, the average age by which the majority of individuals had completed school was still a

*continued on next page*

cieties is on informal education in context rather than on formal education in schools. Children are typically not isolated in separate educational institutions, and they accompany the adult members of their community in daily

activities. Adolescents' preparation for adulthood, therefore, comes largely from observation and "hands-on" experience in the same tasks that they will continue to carry out as adults. Typically, boys learn the tasks per-few years younger than the average age by which even the youngest members of the generation had married. By 1930, however, individuals were staying in school longer and marrying earlier, so that there were large numbers of individuals who were leaving school and marrying at about the same age. By 1960, these trends had continued to the point where substantial numbers of individuals were marrying *before* finishing their education. Although between 1960 and 1980, the tendency toward younger and younger marriages that had characterized the first half of the century began to reverse itself, the average age at which individuals completed their education continued to increase. As a result, the timeframe within which individuals finished school and got married remained fairly narrow (Modell and Goodman, 1990).

A similar pattern is found when we look at individuals' entrance into the labor force. Although individuals are staying in school longer than they did 100 years ago, they have barely delayed their entry into the labor force. These findings counter the widely held belief that entering into work or family commitments before finishing school necessarily impedes educational attainment. As Marini notes, we need more research on the long-term occupational experiences of students who marry or work before completing school.

Why were men somewhat more likely than women to interrupt or combine their schooling with work or family commitments? Women who went on to higher levels of education were especially likely to delay taking on family roles.

Apparently, men found it easier than women to become both spouse and parent while still in school. Marini suggests that women's traditional family roles—and, in particular, their greater involvement in domestic responsibilities —make it more diffcut for them to move between student and nonstudent roles and make marriage and parenthood "less compatible with the continuation of education for women than for men" (Marini, 1984, p. 78). As she writes, "Although for men the continuation of education does not permit direct fulfillment of the traditional male role of provider, because of its future payoff for the well-being of the family, it is viewed as an investment in the family's future. Women's educational and occupational pursuits tend to be viewed as secondary to those of their husbands" (p. 78).

Because becoming a spouse and parent interrupts the process of educational attainment more for women than for men, it may be more important for women to delay taking on family roles until after they have finished school, or they risk compromising their careers. Indeed, in other articles, Marini has pointed out that the earlier transition into parenthood among women than men and its greater educational cost for women are main factors in the generally lower occupational attainment of women (Marini, 1978). Although it is *possible* for men and women to marry and become parents before they stop being students, the costs of deviating from the "normative" sequence are not equal for the two sexes.

formed by adult men, and girls those performed by adult women. Where work activities take adults out of the community, it is not uncommon for children to travel with their parents on work expeditions (Miller, 1928).

*The continuity of the adolescent passage in previous eras* During earlier periods in American history, the transition into adult roles and responsibilities began at an earlier age and proceeded along a more continuous path than generally is

In societies in which hunting, farming, and fishing are the primary work activities, young people often are taught the skills they will need as adult workers by accompanying—and observing—their elders in daily activities rather than by attending school. *(Owen Franken/Stock, Boston)*

the case today. This is especially true with regard to work. During the eighteenth century, of course, and well into the early part of the nineteenth century, when many families were engaged in farming, a good number of adolescents were expected to work on the family farm and learn the skills necessary to carry on the enterprise. Some youngsters, generally boys, accompanied their fathers on business trips, learning the trades of salesmanship and commerce (Kett, 1977)—a pattern reminiscent of that found in many traditional societies.

Many other young people left home relatively early—some as early as age 12—to work for nonfamilial adults in the community or in nearby villages (Katz, 1975; Kett, 1977). Even

as recently as the mid-nineteenth century, it was common for young adolescents to work as apprentices, learning skills and trades in preparation for the work roles of adulthood; others left home temporarily to work as servants or to learn domestic skills. The average nineteenth-century youngster left school well before the age of 15 (Modell, Furstenberg, and Hershberg, 1976).

However, census data and historical documents—such as letters, diaries, and community histories—indicate that while adolescents of 100 years ago took on full-time employment earlier in life than they typically do today, they were likely to live under adult supervision for a longer period than is usual in contemporary society. That is, although the transition into work roles may have occurred earlier in the nineteenth century than in the twentieth century, this transition was made in the context of semi-independence rather than complete emancipation (Katz, 1975; Kett, 1977; Modell and Goodman, 1990). This semi-independent period—which for many young people spanned the decade from about ages 12 to 22, and even beyond—may have increased the degree of continuity of the passage into adulthood by providing a time during which young people could assume certain adult responsibilities gradually (Katz, 1975). The semi-independence characteristic of adolescence in the nineteenth century had largely disappeared by 1900 (Modell and Goodman, 1990).

Socialization for family and citizenship roles may also have been more continuous in previous historical eras. Living at home during the late adolescent and early adult years, particularly in the larger families characteristic of households 100 years ago, contributed to the preparation of young people for future family life. It was common for the children in a family to span a wide age range, and remaining at home undoubtedly placed the older adolescent from time to time in child-rearing roles (President's Science Advisory Committee, 1974). As opposed to today's adolescents, who typically have little experience with infants, adolescents 100 years ago were more likely to have fed, dressed, and cared for their younger siblings. They were also expected to assist their parents in maintaining the household (Modell, Furstenberg, and Hershberg, 1976), and this experience probably made it easier for young people to manage when they eventually established a home separate from their parents. One recent study indicates that leaving one's parents' home earlier and living independently before marriage encourages young women to develop less traditional attitudes, values, and plans than their counterparts who live with their parents as young adults (Waite et al.,

1986). Interestingly, individuals from single-parent homes and stepfamilies tend to leave home at an earlier age than do their peers whose biological parents remained married (Mitchell, Wister, and Burch, 1989).

Recent reports of changes in home-leaving are noteworthy, however, and suggest that this aspect of the transition into adulthood may be changing: On average, individuals are living with their parents longer today than was the case 30 years ago; more than half of all 20- to 24-year-olds either live with or are supported by their parents, up from 40 percent in 1960 (Kutner, 1988). Most experts attribute this trend to the increased cost of housing, which makes it difficult for individuals to move out from their parents' home (or their financial support) and establish a separate residence.

The current impact of the economy on adolescents' home-leaving reaffirms the importance of looking at the broader context in defining what "normal" adolescence is. Because in 1960 it was the exception to live at home past high school, we tended to view individuals who did so as being less independent than their peers. But now that living at home has become the norm, we no longer view it as an index of maturity. Above all, we need to keep in mind that because adolescence *is* in part societally defined, its nature changes along with society.

Indeed, some massive historical events such as the war in the Persian Gulf or the economic recession of the early 1980s may temporarily alter the nature of the adolescent passage and produce exceptions to general historical trends. One such event was the Great Depression of the early 1930s. Sociologist Glen Elder, Jr., has examined the impact of growing up during this era on adolescents' behavior and development (Elder, 1974), and many of his findings are relevant to the issue of continuity in the adolescent passage. Elder looked at the data collected during the Depression as part of a longitudinal study of individuals living in

Social and economic changes can transform the nature of the adolescent's transition into adulthood. The increased cost of housing in recent decades, for example, has made it more difficult for young people to move out from their parents' home and establish a separate residence. As a result, individuals are living with their parents longer today than was the case 30 years ago. Scientists do not yet know how this change is affecting individuals' psychosocial development. *(Blair Seitz/Photo Researchers)*

Oakland, California. The group Elder focused on was born between 1920 and 1921 and thus were preadolescents during the worst years of the Depression.

Elder found that youngsters whose families experienced economic hardship during these years were more likely to be involved in adult-like tasks at an earlier age than their more privileged peers. Boys, for example, were more likely to work and help support their families; girls were more likely to play a major role with household chores. And both boys and girls were more likely to marry and enter into full-time employment relatively early.

Thus some aspects of the semi-independent stage of adolescence that had become uncommon by 1930 may have reappeared during the Great Depression. For many youngsters growing up during this time period, the adolescent passage may have resembled that of an earlier era.

## The Transition into Adulthood

We do not know for certain whether the discontinuity characteristic of the passage into adulthood today impedes the adolescent's psychosocial development and responsible assumption of adult roles. But many social scientists have speculated that these consequences may result. Identity development, to take one example, is probably made more difficult by the higher levels of confusion and inconsistency that surround the social passage into adulthood in modern society. Erik Erikson (1968) and other theorists view identity devel-

Major historical events, such as the Great Depression, may temporarily alter the transition to adulthood. During the Depression, many adolescent boys had to leave school and enter the work force full-time at an unusually early age. Many adolescent girls also were forced to leave school early, in order to assume adult responsibilities at home. *(Bettmann Newsphotos)*

opment during adolescence as the result of the interplay between the young person's growing self-awareness and society's changing view of him or her. It is not difficult to see, then, how an "identity crisis" might be intensified by not knowing whether one is an adult or a child or when the change in social definition takes place.

In recent years, observers of adolescence in America have suggested that the discontinuity in the passage into adulthood has become so great that many youngsters, especially those not bound for college, are having problems negotiating the passage into adult roles (Hamburg, 1986; National Commission on Youth, 1980; William T. Grant Foundation, 1988). One national commission wrote that we had so neglected the needs of noncollege-bound adolescents that their report called them "The Forgotten Half" (William T. Grant Foundation, 1988). These observers point to problems many young people experience in developing a coherent sense of identity, establishing a healthy sense of autonomy, and making informed decisions about commitments to family and work. They note that the lack of clarity and continuity in the transition into adulthood may contribute to some of the problems faced by adolescents in contemporary society and as well to some of the problems faced by contemporary society in dealing with young people (Conger, 1977a). Many social scientists believe that our relatively high rates of divorce, family violence, youth unemployment, juvenile delinquency, and teenage alcoholism stem in part from the confusing and contradictory nature of the passage into adulthood in modern society (National Commission on Youth, 1980).

## SPECIAL TRANSITIONAL PROBLEMS OF MINORITY YOUTH

No discussion of the transitional problems of young people in America today is complete without noting that youngsters from some minority groups—African-American, Hispanic-American, and American Indian youth, in particular—have more trouble negotiating the

transition into adulthood than do their white and Asian-American counterparts. Youngsters from minority backgrounds make up a substantial and growing portion of the adolescent population in America. By the end of this century, about 15 percent of the youth population will be African-American and another 13 percent Hispanic-American. Approximately 4 percent of the youth population will be composed of Asian-American, Pacific Islander, and American Indian youth. In other words, about one-third of the youth population in the year 2000 will be from minority groups (Wetzel, 1987; and see Figure 3.1). By the year 2020, minority children will account for nearly half of all U.S. children (Pallas et al., 1984).

Growing up in poverty may profoundly impair youngsters' ability to move easily between adolescence and adulthood. Poverty is associated with failure in school, unemployment, and out-of-wedlock pregnancy, all of which contribute to transition difficulties. Because

**FIGURE 3.1**   By the end of this century, youngsters from minority backgrounds will comprise about one-third of the U.S. adolescent population. (Wetzel, 1987)

Projected U.S. youth population in the year 2000

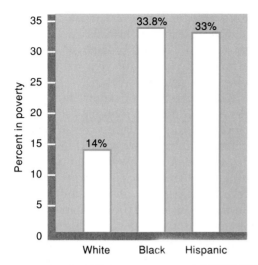

**FIGURE 3.2**  Poverty rates of 16–21-year-olds, 1985. (Wetzel, 1987)

minority youngsters are more likely than other teenagers to grow up in poverty, they are more likely than other youths to encounter transitional problems during middle and late adolescence (see Figure 3.2). As you will read in later chapters, school dropout rates are much higher among Hispanic-American and American Indian teenagers than other groups, and college enrollment is lower among African-American, Hispanic-American, and American Indian youth than other young people. Youth unemployment is much higher among African-American, Hispanic-American, and American Indian groups than other groups. African-American and Hispanic-American youth are more likely to be victimized by crime than other young people. And rates of out-of-wedlock births are higher among African-American and Hispanic-American teenagers than among white teenagers (Wetzel, 1987). All of these factors disrupt the transition into adulthood by limiting individuals' economic and occupational success. Poverty impedes the transition to adulthood among *all* teenagers, regardless of race, of course, but because mi-

nority youth are more likely to grow up poor, they are more likely to have transition problems.

The situation is particularly grave for disadvantaged, minority youngsters growing up in the inner city (Wilson, 1987). Many of these young people grow up without knowing *a single adult* "whose stable employment supports an even modest standard of family life" (Wilson, cited in Nightingale and Wolverton, 1988, p. 10). As two writers for the Carnegie Council on Adolescent Development noted with depressing clarity:

> Those who have succeeded in attaining a solid standard of living often have moved away from the city to the suburbs, further depriving young people of role models. Such young people have no experience working or living among people with . . . different kinds of jobs and their choices are limited to poorly paying and unrewarding jobs or quick money from drug running. Often the only role models available in areas of concentrated poverty are gang members or drug dealers, who appear to have what adolescents desperately want, respect and money.
>
> In these neighborhoods, often adult women were adolescent mothers themselves. Their daughters, in turn, may see a child of their own as the only hope for affection and respect, and perhaps even stability. However, the babies quickly become demanding toddlers. Usually the fathers of these children do not marry or provide family support. Too early child-bearing can have disastrous consequences for both mother and child, including dropping out of school and long-term unemployment for the mother, and low birth-weight and other health problems for the child (Nightingale and Wolverton, 1988, p. 10).

A variety of suggestions have been offered for making the transition into adulthood smoother for all young people, including restructuring secondary education, expanding work and volunteer opportunities, and increasing contact between adolescents and adults so that more observational learning can take place. Some groups have called for expanded opportunities in the workplace as a way of making the high school years more of a "bridge" between adolescence and adulthood (Carnegie Council on Policy Studies in Higher Education, 1980). Other groups have suggested that adolescents be encouraged to spend time in voluntary, nonmilitary service activities—such as staffing day-care centers, working with the elderly, or cleaning up the environment—for a few years after high school graduation so that they can learn responsibility and adult roles (Children's Defense Fund, 1989). Still others have called for more extensive pregnancy- and dropout-prevention programs so that fewer young people enter adulthood at an economic disadvantage (Hayes, 1987).

As you read this book, give some thought to how adolescence ought to be structured. Should we have some sort of initiation ceremony that signifies when young people have become adults? Should we rethink the purpose of high school? What do you think is the best way to prepare adolescents for the responsibilities they will face as adults?

## Summary

1. Changes in social definition comprise the third set of fundamental transformations that define adolescence as a period of development. Although the specific elements of the social passage from childhood into adulthood vary from one society to another, all societies recognize that the social status of the individual changes during the adolescent period.

2. Some writers, called "inventionists," have argued that adolescence is more a social invention than a biological or cognitive phenomenon. They suggest that our conception of adolescence—whether it exists as a separate period and what its nature is—is determined largely by forces in the broader social environment. Changes in the broader environment, therefore, can change the very nature of adolescence.

3. Adolescence as we know it in contemporary society has its roots in the industrial revolution of the nineteenth century. Prior to that time, children were viewed as miniature adults, and adolescents provided important labor for their families. With industrialization, however, new patterns of work and family life led to the exclusion of young people from the labor force and the lengthening of formal schooling and adolescents' economic dependence on their elders.

4. Changes in the individual's social definition at adolescence typically revolve around changes in status in four domains: interpersonal, political, economic, and legal. In each of these domains, individuals are given greater privileges but are expected to take increased responsibility for self-management and social participation.

5. Certain themes are commmon to the process of social redefinition across many societies. These include the real or symbolic separation of young people from their parents; the accentuation of differences between males and females; and the passing on of cultural, historical, or practical information deemed important for adulthood.

6. The process of social definition varies from society to society in its clarity. In some societies, as well as within certain religious and cultural groups, adolescence is marked by a formal initiation ceremony and specific rites of passage, which clearly mark the redefinition of the individual. In others, however, the transition from childhood into adulthood is vague and poorly defined. This absence of clarity is especially the case in contemporary industrialized societies.

7. In addition to clarity, societies also vary in the extent to which the passage into adoles-

cence is continuous or discontinuous. In a continuous passage, the adolescent assumes the roles and status of adulthood bit by bit, with a good deal of preparation and training along the way. In a discontinuous passage, the adolescent is thrust into adulthood abruptly, with little prior preparation. Contemporary industrialized societies generally are characterized by a discontinuous passage into adulthood.

8. Many social commentators have argued that the vague and discontinuous nature of the adolescent passage in contemporary society has contributed to numerous psychological and behavioral problems among today's youth. These difficulties are more severe among adolescents who are not bound for college, and especially so among minority youth living in the inner city. A number of commissions have recommended that we re-examine the structure of schools and expand work and service opportunities for young people as a means of addressing these problems.

## Key Terms

age of majority
brother-sister avoidance
child protectionists
continuous transition
discontinuous transition
extrusion
initiation
inventionists
marginal man
social redefinition
teenage
youth

## For Further Reading

ENRIGHT, R., AND LAPSLEY, D. (EDS.). (1985). *Early adolescence throughout American history.* Complete issue of the *Journal of Early Adolescence,* 5. A collection of articles examining adolescence from colonial America until the present.

KETT, J. (1977). *Rites of passage: Adolescence in America, 1790 to the present.* New York: Basic Books. An extensive discussion of how adolescence in America has changed over the last two centuries.

MEAD, M. (1928). *Coming of age in Somoa.* New York: Morrow. Margaret Mead's classic discussion of adolescence in the South Pacific and what we can learn about our own society by studying a more traditional one.

MODELL, J., AND GOODMAN, M. (1990). Historical perspectives. In S. Feldman and G. Elliott (Eds.), *At the threshold: The developing adolescent.* Cambridge: Harvard University Press. An excellent overview of the recent history of adolescence, with an emphasis on its definition in the United States and the United Kingdom.

WILLIAM T. GRANT FOUNDATION, Commission on Work, Family, and Citizenship. (1988). *The forgotten half: Non-college youth in America.* Washington: William T. Grant Foundation. A blue-ribbon commission's report on the status of the neglected half of the youth population.

WILSON, W. (1987). *The truly disadvantaged: The inner city, the underclass, and public policy.* Chicago: University of Chicago Press. A detailed examination of the problems faced by youth and adults growing up under grave disadvantage.

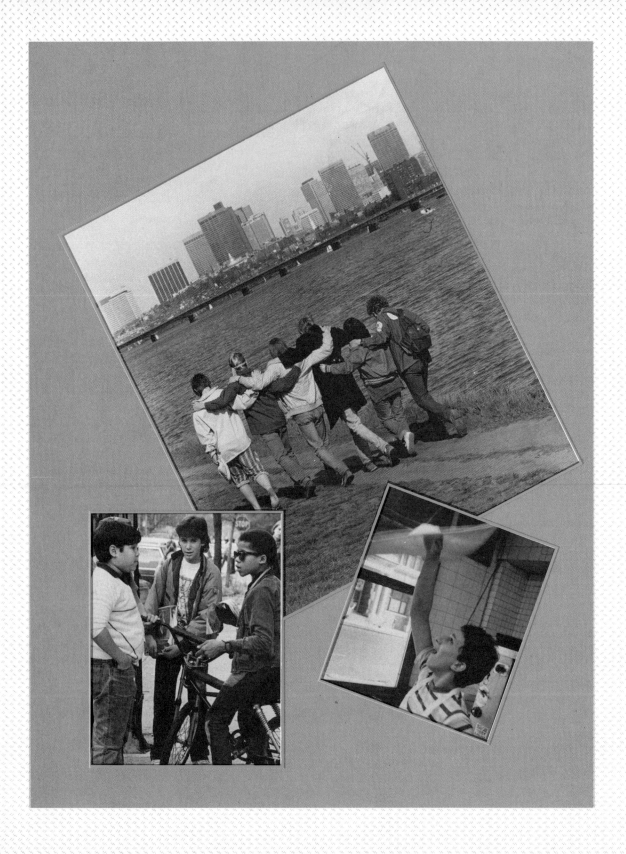

# THE CONTEXTS
# OF
# ADOLESCENCE

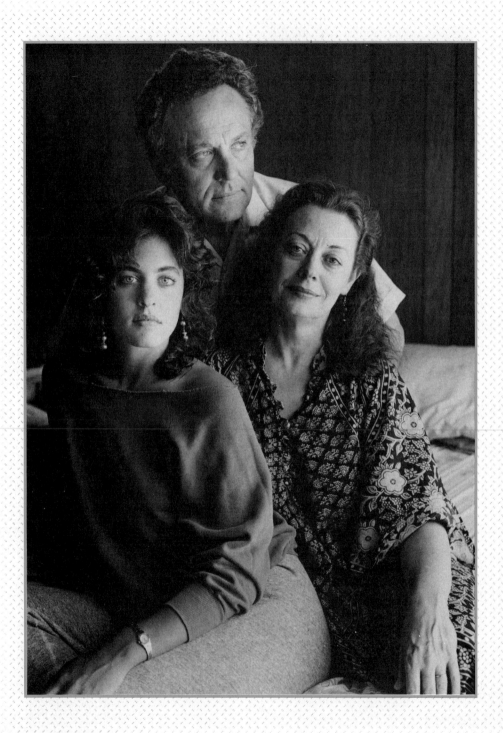

# FAMILIES

*I*n the eyes of many, the American family by 1990 had become an endangered species, and children and adolescents were bearing the costs of the family's demise. According to some observers, the all-too-familiar problems of young people—low achievement test scores, high rates of alcohol and drug use, sexual precocity, violence in the schools—were due to the progressive fragmentation of the family (e.g., Uhlenberg and Eggebeen, 1986).

Others, less pessimistic, argued that the family had not died but *changed*. They noted that although the family of the 1950s—two parents (with mother at home), three children, and a station wagon—had become less common, new forms of family life, commendable in their own right, were emerging. The family of the 1950s, these observers pointed out, was not very well suited for life in the 1990s, and there was little reason to lament its disappearance.

There is no question that in America and in many comparably industrialized countries, the family has undergone a series of profound changes during the past quarter-century. Rising rates of divorce, increases in maternal employment, and accelerating geographic mobility all have dramatically altered the world in which children and adolescents grow up. And, although some of the most striking trends in family life slowed during the 1980s, they did not reverse, by any means. Between 1980 and 1990, for example, the number of American single parents grew by 41 percent and the number of divorced mothers grew at a rate of nearly 2 percent per year (*The New York Times*, 1991). Nevertheless, questions as to whether these changes have weakened the family's influence over young people or, in one way or another, have harmed young people are difficult to answer. Yes, the family has changed—but so has society. This chapter and the three that follow focus on the changing nature of

adolescence in contemporary society. As you will see, it is not only the family that has changed.

Amidst all this talk of change, it is important to bear in mind two very fundamental points about young people and their families that have *not* changed very much at all. First, the family remains an extremely important influence on adolescent development. As an influence on the development of identity, autonomy, or achievement, for example, few forces are as significant as the young person's family. And second, regardless of the family's structure or composition—one parent or two, natural or reconstituted, employed mother or not—having positive and warm family relationships stands out as one of the most powerful predictors and correlates of healthy psychosocial growth during the adolescent years. In this chapter, we take a close look at families during adolescence and at why they exert such an important influence on development.

## The Changing American Family

The family does not exist in a social vacuum. As a consequence, it is impossible to discuss the changing nature of the family in America without putting these changes into broader perspective. Changing rates of divorce, single parenthood, and maternal employment during the past thirty years are not isolated trends but the results of a constellation of historical, economic, and ideological shifts that took place following World War II. Like the other contexts in which adolescents develop, the structure and nature of the family has changed as society has changed. Chief among the social transformations that have affected the contemporary family most profoundly have been changes in the world of work, changes in attitudes toward sex roles, changes in patterns of housing, and changes in individuals' values and priorities.

## THE CHANGING NATURE OF WORK

Following World War II, the chief growth in the American labor force was concentrated in retail and service jobs. Many of these jobs were part-time, and most of the people who took them were women (Ginzberg, 1977). The trend toward increasing participation of women in the world of work was evident by 1950. Increasingly, women—many of whom had children—were drawn into the labor force. As a consequence, the familiar pattern of family life—the man as sole wage earner, the woman as housewife—became less prevalent as America moved into the 1960s (Bronfenbrenner, 1975).

## THE WOMEN'S MOVEMENT

It is crucial to distinguish between part-time and full-time work in discussions of the impact of women's employment on family life. As social scientists George Masnick and Mary Jo Bane (1980) point out, it is only when women's participation in the labor force becomes a full-time, permanent attachment to work that patterns of family life change in any dramatic way. Many women who were in the labor force part-time during the 1950s and 1960s structured their work hours in a way that altered patterns of family life very little. It was not until the early 1970s that year-round, full-time employment—perhaps the best indicator of involvement in the labor force—became prevalent among women and, in particular, among women with schoolaged children. A good deal of this increase in full-time work among American women was no doubt due to economic factors, but a major contributing force was the widespread and far-reaching impact of the women's movement. In the minds of many, in

fact, the women's movement was the single most significant change of the 1970s (Conger, 1981).

## CHANGING PATTERNS OF HOUSING

A third trend that had an important impact on the family relates to changing patterns of housing. As increasing numbers of families moved from rural to urban areas during the first half of this century, and from urban to suburban areas during the 1950s and 1960s, nuclear families became increasingly isolated—from each other and from the extended family. Many families moved into single-family dwellings, cut off from neighbors and relatives. While the extended family household was never particularly popular in America, earlier in this century family members were more likely to live near one another, and extended family networks (if not households) played an important role in child rearing. Residential mobility was not very common. In today's highly mobile society, "half of all families in the United States move every five years" (Conger, 1981, p. 1475). In day-to-day terms, these changed patterns of housing have left the family more detached from other people and other institutions that can provide support during times of emotional stress or material need.

## CHANGING VALUES AND PRIORITIES

During the past thirty years, Americans' values and priorities have changed, and these changes have affected family life in profound ways. Two components of this value shift stand out. First, people became more preoccupied with themselves and their needs as individuals and less concerned about the needs of others. Second, and related to this first shift, Americans became more tolerant of behavior that veered from socially determined norms and standards (Conger, 1981).

The phenomenal rise of the suburbs during the 1950s and 1960s resulted, in part, in the isolation of families from neighbors and relatives. Some experts believe that this isolation has left many families without adequate sources of support when they are under stress. *(Bill Owens/Archive)*

The impact of this value shift on family life was dramatic. One of the most important trends identified by demographers in their predictions of changes in household composition and family structure during the remainder of this century is the remarkable diversity that is coming to characterize American family life. At the simplest level, diminished concern with adherence to society's ideal pattern of behavior permitted individuals to pursue a wider variety of family forms than had been socially acceptable in the past. Self-fulfillment, rather than social obligation, became the driving force behind individuals' familial and marital decisions. Cohabitation, divorce, remarriage, single par-

enthood, reconstituted families, having children out of wedlock—all of these lifestyles became more acceptable and more accepted (some, of course, more than others). The traditional nuclear family form not only became less prevalent, it also became less idealized as the morally correct way to live. In 1960, demographers observe, there was a "typical" family form in this country: a married couple with children and with the man as the sole full-time worker. Today, this structure is but one of many accepted family forms (Masnick and Bane, 1980). In 1955, for example, nearly two-thirds of all households "consisted of a working father, a housewife mother, and two or more school age children" (Hodgkinson, 1985, p. 3). By 1985, the proportion had dropped to 7 percent. This trend continued as the 1980s drew to a close (*The New York Times*, 1991).

*OR 67%*

## The Adolescent's Family Today

Just how dramatic have the changes in American family life been over the past forty years? Consider three of the most important shifts: increases in the rate of divorce, increases in the number of single parents, and increases in the rate of mothers' employment. These shifts have transformed the nature of family life for many young people.

As you can see from Figure 4.1, the rate of divorce had increased markedly since 1950 and rose steadily, and at times rapidly, until 1980. (The divorce rate increased most dramatically after 1965 and peaked around 1980.) By 1979, the divorce rate in the United States was the highest in the world (Hetherington, 1981). Between 1980 and 1990, the rate of divorce remained more or less constant, rising somewhat in some years but falling in others. Demographers (social scientists who study changes in the composition of the population) estimate

**FIGURE 4.1** The divorce rate rose dramatically between 1960 and 1980 and has more or less leveled off since then.

that nearly half of all American children born during the late 1970s and early 1980s—the teenagers of the 1990s—will experience their parents' divorce and will spend approximately five years in a single-parent household. In addition, a sizeable percentage of youngsters will spend time in a single-parent household from birth, since they are born outside of marriage (Furstenberg, 1990). All told, about 60 percent of children born in the early 1980s will spend some time in a single-parent household before the end of adolescence.

There are important racial differences in these patterns, however. African-American youngsters are far more likely than other youngsters to experience parental divorce and to be born outside of marriage, but they are far less likely to experience their parents' remarriage (Furstenberg et al., 1983). As a consequence, whereas well over half of all African-American children at any given time are residing with one parent, the percentage is about one in three among Hispanic-American adolescents and about one in five among white youngsters (Furstenberg, 1990).

Because more than 75 percent of divorced parents remarry, the majority of youngsters whose parents separate also experience living in a stepfamily at some time. And, because the rate of divorce is higher for second marriages than first marriages, the majority of youth whose parents remarry will experience yet a second divorce. Moreover, because divorces generally occur faster in remarriages, many children must confront a second divorce before they have finished adapting to having a stepparent.

Our recognition of the fact that today's adolescents often experience a series of household reorganizations during their development has changed the way social scientists study adolescence and the changing family. As Mavis Hetherington, an expert on adolescence and divorce, has written, "Divorce and remarriage should not be viewed as single static events but as part of a series of transitions modifying the lives and development of children" (Hetherington et al., 1989, p. 303). As we shall see, much of the recent work on this topic has examined how young people adapt to these family transitions and has sought to identify the factors most important in distinguishing between adolescents who do, and do not, show ill effects. When youngsters live with only one of their natural parents, either in single-parent or in two-parent households, it is nearly always with the mother; only about 10 percent of children whose parents have been divorced live with the father (Furstenberg, 1990).

An additional trend worth noting concerns maternal employment. Figure 4.2 indicates that, among women with school-aged children, fulltime employment has increased steadily since 1950 (Masnick and Bane, 1980). Today, nearly three-quarters of all married women 75% with school-aged children are employed outside the home. And the rate, not surprisingly, is even higher among single mothers, over 80 percent of whom work.

**FIGURE 4.2** The employment of mothers with school-aged children has increased steadily since 1950.

Many individuals are certain that the answer to these questions is, "For the worse." But before we jump to this conclusion, it is important to raise two considerations. First, although increases in adolescents' problems over the period between 1950 and 1980—as tapped by such indicators as drug use, suicide, and poor school achievement, for example—occurred alongside many of these shifts in family life, it is difficult to say that the family changes *caused* the changes in adolescent behavior. Social scientists who have argued that the decline in family life has led to these problems (e.g., Uhlenberg and Eggebeen, 1986) have had a hard time explaining why adolescents' psychological and behavioral well-being took a turn for the *better* in the early 1980s, despite the continued "demise" of the family (see Furstenberg, 1990). Moreover, the one group of young people whose psychological and behavioral profile improved most markedly in the past 10 years—poor, minority youngsters—experienced the most dramatic "decline" in family life during this time.

Second, because the conditions under which divorce, father absence, and maternal employment take place vary tremendously from family to family, it is hard to generalize about their effects on adolescents. To some young people, divorce may bring a welcome end to family conflict and tension; to others, it may be extremely psychologically disruptive. Some young people living with their mothers see their fathers more often than do their peers who live in homes where the father ostensibly is present. And while for some adolescents, having an employed mother may mean curtailed family time and less contact with her, for others, a mother who is employed may provide an important role model and added opportunities to take on responsibility around the household. In other words, the variations *within* different family structures are likely to be more important than the differences *among* them. This is apparent when we look at how adoles-

In summary, few adolescents live in the idealized—perhaps even romanticized—family structure that was common before 1960: the two-parent family with the father as the only wage earner. In fact, less than 15 percent of all adolescents live in this sort of arrangement. Today, more adolescents live in single-parent households, almost invariably with their mothers; and in most cases those mothers work. Of the young people living in two-parent families, a substantial number—close to 15 percent—live with only one of their natural parents (Furstenberg, 1990).

## Adolescent Development and the Changing Family

To what extent has the changed nature of the American family changed the nature of adolescent development? How do divorce, absent fathers, and working mothers affect adolescents' development?

cents are affected by parental divorce and re-marriage, and by parental employment.

## DIVORCE AND REMARRIAGE

The recognition that divorce and remarriage can be better understood as family transitions than as static events has focused researchers' attention on adolescents' adaptation to these changes over time and on the identification of factors that seem to make a difference. In general, most studies show that the period of greatest difficulty for most children and adolescents is, as you would think, right around the time of the disruption itself. Although many young people show signs of difficulty immediately after the divorce or remarriage—among them, problems in school, more behavior problems, and more anxiety—by the time two years have passed, the majority of children whose parents have divorced or remarried have adjusted to the change and behave comparably to their peers whose parents have remained married (Hetherington et al., 1989).

Most researchers believe that this temporary period of disturbance is due to a combination of factors, including the exposure of the children to marital conflict (Peterson and Zill, 1986), disorganization or dramatic changes in parenting practices (Fauber et al., 1990; Forehand et al., 1990), or marked increases in the degree of economic stress experienced by the household (Furstenberg, 1990). One reason we suspect these factors is that children living in intact families (i.e., families in which no divorce has occurred) are also harmed by marital conflict, disrupted parenting (especially parenting that is too lenient, too harsh, or inconsistent), and family stress, such as loss of income. In other words, the adverse temporary effect of divorce or remarriage on youngsters' well-being appears due to the heightened conflict, disorganization, and stress surrounding the event, and not to the divorce or remarriage per se. Once the family has had a chance to estab-

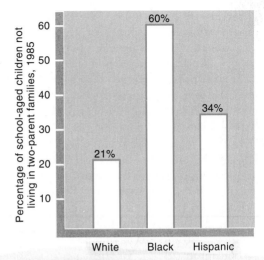

**FIGURE 4.3** The proportion of youngsters living in single-parent households varies a great deal across racial and ethnic groups. (Furstenberg, 1990)

lish a calmer, more organized, and more secure routine, many of the problems diminish.

There are interesting differences among children in how vulnerable they are to these short-term effects, however. Some children show more difficulty than others. In general, in families that divorce during childhood or preadolescence, boys, younger children, children with a difficult temperament, children who do not have supportive relationships with adults outside the immediate family, and children who end up in the custody of a parent of the opposite sex all show more immediate problems than do girls, older children, easygoing youngsters, or children who live with the same-sex parent. Taken together, studies indicate that young boys who live with their mother following a divorce have the roughest time, particularly if they have a difficult temperament to begin with (Hetherington, 1991). Especially interesting, if somewhat disheartening, is the finding that contact after the divorce between the child and his or her noncustodial father does *not* seem to reduce the adverse effects of marital dissolution. Financial support from fathers, however, does seem to be associated with less problem behavior (Furstenberg, Morgan, and Allison, 1987).

The short-term effects of remarriage also appear to vary among children, although not necessarily in the same ways as the short-term effects of divorce. In general, girls show more difficulty in adjusting to remarriage than boys, and older children more difficulty than younger children. One explanation for this is that both boys and younger children have more to gain from their mother's remarriage than do girls or older children, who may have become accustomed to having a single mother (Hetherington, 1991). In the case of remarriage, as in the case of divorce, temperamentally more difficult youngsters have a harder time than more easy-going ones (Hetherington, 1991).

Social scientists have also looked at the longer-term consequences of divorce (in this case, longer-term means more than two or three years). These studies, for example, might look at elementary school children whose parents had divorced when their child was in preschool, or at adolescents whose parents had split up during the child's elementary school years. Presumably, if the adverse effects of divorce are solely attributable to the immediate problems of adjusting to a new household structure, these effects would dissipate by the time a few years had elapsed.

Research on the longer-term consequences of parental divorce has yielded very interesting findings, and in recent years, psychologists have changed their view. Initially, studies of children whose parents divorced early in life suggested that most of the adverse effects disappeared within three years. Research on elementary school children whose parents had divorced earlier indicated that after a few years, the children were functioning essentially as well as children whose parents had remained married (Hetherington, 1981).

More recent research on adolescents, however, indicates that this conclusion may be somewhat optimistic. Specifically, some studies show that individuals whose parents divorce during preadolescence continue to demonstrate adjustment difficulties during early adolescence, even after two or three years (e.g., Hetherington, 1990). And others find that adolescents whose parents divorced early in the child's life may show adjustment problems as teenagers that were not present earlier.

The problems typically seen in greater frequency among adolescents from divorced homes include higher rates of drug and alcohol use, more behavior problems, and poorer school performance in adolescence (Allison and Furstenberg, 1989; Weinmann, Steinberg, and Dornbusch, 1991), as well as negative effects on interpersonal relationships with members of the opposite sex in late adolescence and young adulthood, including higher rates of divorce (e.g., Hetherington, 1972; McLanahan and Bumpass, 1988; Wallerstein and Blakeslee, 1989). These do not appear to be ameliorated by parental remarriage; adolescents from stepfamilies score similarly on measures of adjustment as do adolescents from single-parent, divorced homes (Allison and Furstenberg, 1989; Dornbusch et al., 1985; Steinberg, 1987d). Interestingly, these longer-term studies do *not* find sex differences in adjustment problems, nor do they suggest that male adolescents benefit from residing with their father (Buchanan and Maccoby, 1990). Rather, it appears that both male and female adolescents fare better in dual custody or in the custody of their mother.

To what can we attribute these "sleeper" effects—effects of divorce that may not be apparent until much later in the child's development? Two possible explanations come to mind. The first is that the ways in which adjustment difficulties might be expressed may not surface until adolescence. For example, social scientists believe that increased drug use and higher rates of early pregnancy are consequences of the lower level of parental mon-

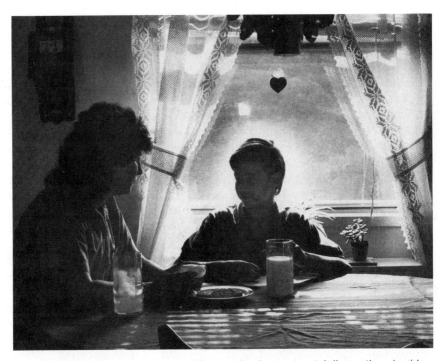

In the short term, boys have greater difficulty adjusting to parental divorce than do girls, particularly if the divorce takes place in childhood or preadolescence. Studies of the long-term effects of divorce, however, indicate that adolescents—females as well as males—whose parents divorced earlier tend to have higher rates of behavior problems and somewhat poorer school performance. *(Rae Russel)*

itoring found in divorced homes (e.g., Dornbusch et al., 1985; McLanahan and Bumpass, 1988). But because younger children—even poorly monitored ones—are unlikely to use drugs or be sexually active, no matter what their family background, the effect of the poor monitoring is not seen until adolescence, when individuals might begin using drugs and having sex.

A second explanation concerns the particular developmental challenges of adolescence (Sessa and Steinberg, 1991). Adolescence is a time during when individuals first begin experimenting with intimate, heterosexual relationships. If having one's parents divorce or being exposed to marital conflict early in life affects one's conceptions of relationships or views of commitment (Belsky, Steinberg, and Draper, 1991; Franklin et al., 1990), it makes sense that some of the effects of early parental divorce will not be manifested until the adolescent begins dating and getting seriously involved with others of the opposite sex. These initial forays into intimate relationships may recall old and difficult psychological conflicts that had remained latent for some time (see Wallerstein and Blakeslee, 1989).

**Special problems of adolescents in stepfamilies** Although it is difficult to make sweeping generalizations about the impact of divorce, single parenthood, or maternal employment on the development of the adolescent, several recent studies indicate that adolescents growing up in step-families—especially if the remarriage has occurred during early adolescence rather than childhood—may have more problems than their peers (Zill, 1984). For example, youngsters growing up in single-parent homes are more likely than those in intact homes to be involved in delinquent activity, but adolescents in step-families are even more at risk for this sort of problem behavior than are adolescents in single-parent families (Dornbusch et al., 1985). Early adolescents in step-families also are more susceptible to pressure from their peers to commit delinquent acts than are other youngsters (Steinberg, 1987d).

According to one study (Garbarino et al., 1984), adolescents in stepfamilies may be especially vulnerable to child abuse. You may know that child abuse is a significant national problem, but did you know that nearly half of all reported cases involve adolescents? According to a survey conducted by the National Center on Child Abuse, adolescent maltreatment accounts for 47 percent of the known cases of abuse and neglect—even though adolescents account for only 38 percent of the American population under the age of 18 (Garbarino, Sebes, and Schellenbach, 1984).

Remarriage during the adolescent years may be extremely stressful when families are unable to accommodate the new stepparent relationship. Given what we know about family reorganization and change during adolescence, having to integrate a new type of relationship into a family system that is already undergoing a great deal of change may be more than some families can cope with. Many adolescents find it difficult to adjust to a new authority figure moving into the household, especially if that person has different ideas about rules and discipline. This appears to be especially true when the adolescent in question is already somewhat vulnerable, either because of previous psychological problems or because of a very recent divorce or other stressful event.

By the same token, many stepparents find it difficult to join a family and not be accepted immediately by the children as the new parent. Stepparents may wonder why love is not forthcoming from their stepchildren. In extreme cases, relationships between adolescents and stepparents can become so strained that family violence results. Although many stepfathers and their adolescent stepchildren do establish positive relations, the lack of a biological connection between stepparent and stepchild, coupled with the stresses associated with divorce and remarriage, may make this relationship especially vulnerable to problems.

According to E. Mavis Hetherington, a psychologist who has done extensive research on family disruption in adolescence, it may be helpful if stepfathers build a close relationship with their stepchildren slowly, and defer in matters of discipline to the children's biological mother early on: "In the beginning of a remarriage, stepdads should be like polite strangers in their new wife's home and talk to the teen-age kids, but not intervene or exercise too much control over their lives. There's too much hostility in the kids who at that age want independence, not control" (quoted in Nordheimer, 1990, p. C6).

The findings of this research underscore the need—particularly as remarriage becomes a more common part of American family life—to understand the special problems that may arise in the course of family reorganization. As our understanding of stepfamily relationships grows, it should become easier to anticipate stepfamily problems before they occur, prepare families in the process of reorganization for the transition they are about to make, and provide special services for families who need help.

## PARENTAL EMPLOYMENT AND ADOLESCENT ADJUSTMENT

The increase in women's participation in the labor force has prompted a good deal of research on the effects of maternal employment on adolescent development. This label "maternal employment" is a misnomer, of course, because most children whose mothers work have fathers who are employed as well. It is important to remember that most studies of "maternal employment" are really studies of the impact of having *both* parents employed, and not simply studies of the impact of having an employed mother. We do not know what the impact of "paternal" employment by itself is, because there are too few families in this country with employed mothers and nonemployed fathers to make a comparison.

Adolescents whose mothers are employed differ from those whose mothers are not, in several respects. In general, maternal employment during adolescence has quite positive effects on daughters but more mixed or negligible effects on sons, especially in middle-class and professional families (Bronfenbrenner and Crouter, 1982). Not surprisingly, in these social classes, girls whose mothers work outside the home have higher career aspirations than do girls whose mothers do not work, but this is not necessarily the case for boys (Hoffman, 1974). Because daughters are more likely than sons to identify with their mother, girls' occupational plans are more influenced by having a mother work than are boys'.

One especially interesting finding conerns the impact of maternal employment on adolescents' academic achievement. Here a number of studies have found that in middle-class and upper-middle-class homes, full-time maternal employment during the high school years is associated with lowered school performance among boys, but not among girls (Bronfenbrenner and Crouter, 1982). This effect is not found in homes where mothers work part-time, nor is it found in working-class or lower-class households. Presumably, the added income from mother's work in poorer families makes up for any negative effects it has on boys' schooling.

Researchers have been puzzled by this sex

Maternal employment has quite positive effects on the development of adolescent females, who have higher career aspirations than girls whose mothers are not employed. The impact of maternal employment on sons is mixed, however, especially in middle-class or professional families. *(Spencer Grant/Stock, Boston)*

difference. Why are boys, but not girls, adversely affected in school by full-time maternal employment? One explanation concerns the impact of maternal employment on parental monitoring, in general, and in relation to school, in particular (Bogenschneider and Steinberg, 1989; Crouter et al., 1990). We know that boys are more adversely affected by less vigilant parental monitoring than girls, because boys tend to be more active and more prone to get into trouble. We also know that children who are monitored more carefully by their parents tend to do better in school than their peers (Steinberg, Elmen, and Mounts, 1989). If one effect of having two parents work full-time is to interfere with parental monitoring, it may have a more negative effect on boys than girls.

A second explanation concerns the effect of having two parents work on adolescents' family relationships. At least one study finds that boys whose mothers work have more arguments with their mothers and with their siblings than do boys whose mothers are not employed (Montemayor, 1984). Interestingly, this does not appear to be due to mothers' work stress (Galambos and Maggs, 1990) but, instead, to the increased demands for household work placed on the children of working mothers (Montemayor, 1984). Boys may react more negatively than girls to having to help out around the house, and this may contribute to family arguments. If conflict at home depresses school performance, this may help explain why boys whose mothers work full-time do less well in school.

Above all, however, studies indicate that the way in which the family *perceives* the mother's employment may be the most important factor. Children whose mothers are happily employed are much more likely to benefit from the experience than children whose mothers would prefer not to work or who have jobs with which they are unhappy. When a mother is happy to be working, and her spouse and family are appreciative of it, her youngster is more likely to develop self-reliance and independence (Hoffman, 1974).

Although psychologists have focused their attention on the effects of maternal employment on adolescent development, in recent years there has been an upsurge in interest in the relation between *parents'* employment and adolescent well-being, and, in particular, in the ways in which adolescents' mental health is affected by changes in their family's financial situation. Much of this research was stimulated by the economic recession of the early 1980s, during which many adults became unemployed, and many families lost substantial income.

To date, the studies of family income loss and adolescent adjustment suggest a number of parallels with the research on divorce and remarriage. Like divorce, income loss tends to be associated with disruptions in parenting, which in turn lead to increases in adolescent problem behaviors, including irritability, academic difficulties, and delinquency (Elder et al., 1984, 1986; Lempers et al., 1989). But, as is the case with divorce, the sex of the adolescent seems to play an important moderating role. For girls, financial difficulty is likely to lead to more demands for maturity and increased responsibility around the house (perhaps to take over some of mother's duties while she works or looks for employment) (Elder, 1974; Flanagan, 1990). This may contribute to their developing more pessimistic expectations about their own occupational futures, since they may develop more traditional views and find it difficult to envision a satisfying career outside the home (Galambos and Silbereisen, 1987). For boys, in contrast, disruptions in family finances seem to lead to more frequent conflict, especially with fathers (Elder et al., 1985; Flanagan, 1990). Boys whose fathers have been laid off may lose respect for them and challenge their authority. The resulting disruption in family functioning may lead to more involvement in problem behavior and more *irresponsibility*.

## The "Generation Gap"

One of the most frequently asked questions in the study of families during adolescence concerns **intergenerational conflict,** or as it is more commonly known, the "generation gap." In what sense is there a gap between adolescents and their parents, and how wide is it? In order to answer these questions, it is important to distinguish among family relationships, values and attitudes, and personal tastes. In some of these respects, there is indeed a schism between the generations. But in others, there is not.

Contrary to myth, the overwhelming majority of young people feel close to their parents, respect their parents' judgment, and feel that their parents love and care about them. The notion that severe intergenerational conflict is common during adolescence is largely a misconception. *(Erika Stone)*

If we consider the quality of adolescents' *relationships* with their parents, we find that there is very little gap between young people and their elders. Study after study on this issue has shown that although some adolescents and their parents have serious interpersonal problems, the overwhelming majority of adolescents feel close to their parents, respect their parents' judgment, feel that their parents love and care about them, and have a lot of respect for their parents as individuals (Steinberg, 1990). In one study, for example, three-quarters of the adolescent respondents agreed with the statements, "I can count on my parents most of the time" and "When I grow up and have a family, it will be in at least a few

ways similar to my own" (Offer, Ostrov, and Howard, 1981). If intergenerational conflict exists, it is not of the sort that seriously affects the quality or closeness of most adolescents' family relationships.

To be sure, there are times when adolescents and parents have their problems. But so are there times when younger children and their parents have problems and when adults and their parents do also. To date, no studies demonstrate that family problems are any more likely to occur during adolescence than at other times in the life span. Most systematic studies indicate that among the 25 percent of teenagers and parents who report having problems, about 80 percent had problematic relations during childhood (Rutter et al., 1976). Thus only about 5 percent of families who enjoy positive relations during childhood can expect to develop serious problems during adolescence.

When we look at intergenerational differences in *values and attitudes*, we also find little evidence in support of a generation gap—or at least, of a schism as large as many people have been led to believe exists. Adolescents and their parents have similar beliefs about the importance of hard work, about educational and occupational ambitions, and about the personal characteristics and attributes they feel are important and desirable (Conger, 1977a). Indeed, when it comes to more basic values—concerning religion, work, education, and the like—diversity *within* the adolescent population is much more striking than are differences between the generations. Socioeconomic background, for instance, has a much stronger influence on individuals' values and attitudes than does age, and adolescents are more likely to share their parents' values than those of other teenagers who are from a different background. Wealthy adolescents growing up in affluent suburbs, for example, have educational and career plans that resemble their parents' plans for them, and their plans are very different from those of poor adolescents growing up in less prosperous areas (Conger, 1977a).

In matters of *personal taste* there is often a gap between the generations, however. It is most clearly seen in styles of dress, preferences in music, and patterns of leisure activity. Adolescents are more likely to be influenced by their friends than by their parents in these matters, and as a consequence, disagreements and differences in opinion between old and young often result. Indeed, it is over these matters that much of the bickering that occurs in families takes place (Montemayor, 1983). A mother and her daughter may argue about such things as the daughter's curfew, how the daughter spends her spare time, whether the daughter keeps her room clean enough, or what sorts of clothes the daughter wears. Unlike values, which develop gradually over time and are shaped from an early age, preferences and tastes are far more transitory and subject to the immediate influences of the social environment. Because adolescents spend a great deal of time with their friends (and because a good deal of that time is spent in social activities in which taste in clothes, music, etc., is especially important) teenagers' tastes are likely to be shaped to a large measure by forces outside the family.

A recent series of studies helps illuminate the causes of these conflicts between parents and teenagers over mundane issues, such as household chores, clothing, and the adolescent's choice of friends. We saw in earlier chapters that this sort of bickering and squabbling between parents and teenagers was more likely to occur during early adolescence than during any other period (Steinberg, 1990). What is it about *early* adolescence that may explain this pattern?

According to research by Judith Smetana (1988, 1989; Smetana et al., in press), a major contributor to adolescent-parent arguments is the fact that teenagers and their parents define the issues of contention very differently. Parents are likely to see these issues as issues of "right and wrong"—not in a moral sense, but as matters of custom or convention. For instance, a mother who disapproved of her daughter's outfit may say, "People just don't dress that way to go to school." Adolescents, in contrast, are likely to define these same issues as matters of personal choice. The daughter may respond by saying, "*You* might not dress this way for school, but *I* do."

Smetana believes that teenagers and their parents often clash more over the definition of the issue (that is, as a matter of custom versus a matter of personal choice) than over the specific details. The struggle, then, is over who has the authority—and whose "jurisdiction" the issue falls into. Because early adolescence is a time during which adolescents' reasoning abilities are changing—recall the dramatic cognitive developments discussed in Chapter 2—there are changes in the ways that individuals understand family rules and regulations. A child who is willing to accept his parents' views of right and wrong—who doesn't question his mother when she says that "we do not leave clothes on the floor"—grows into an adolescent who understands that some issues are matters of personal choice, rather than social convention ("It's my room, so why should it bother you?").

Obviously, if parents and teenagers define day-to-day issues differently to begin with, resolving conflicts is going to be quite difficult. According to some experts, it is important for parents and teenagers to begin by trying to understand each other's point of view and attempting to jointly define the disagreement as a problem that both sides are eager to resolve, bypassing the question of whose "authority" it is. This is far more effective than struggling through a battle of wills, particularly because the adolescent and parent are beginning from entirely different premises. By working together to find solutions that both parties can live with ("I'll pick up my clothes twice a week and whenever company is coming over, and

One source of conflict between teenagers and parents involves the different ways that they define the same issues. Making sure that the adolescent's bedroom is tidy often is seen by parents as an area over which parents have "jurisdiction"—an issue of "right and wrong." Teenagers, however, tend to see their rooms as their own private space, and decisions about neatness as matters of personal choice. *(Joan Albert/ Image Works)*

I'll keep my bedroom door closed when the room is messy; in return, you won't nag me about my room"), parents and teenagers can work through many of these disputes (Steinberg and Levine, 1990).

## Family Relationships at Adolescence

Although it is incorrect to characterize adolescence as a time of conflict in most families, it is important to keep in mind that adolescence is a period of change and reorganization in family relationships. It is to these processes of change and reorganization in the adolescent's family that we now turn.

## THE FAMILY AS A SYSTEM

You may remember from high school science classes that living organisms and their environments function as systems. The family is a system, too—a system in which relationships change in response to the changing needs and concerns of family members and in response to changes in the family's relationship with the larger society (Minuchin, 1974). And like other systems, families attempt to maintain a sense of *equilibrium,* or balance, in their relationships.

Certain implicit understandings develop within families—concerning which family members have decision-making power, how much privacy different individuals can expect to have, how much freedom and control each family member has, and the like—and these understandings form the unwritten rules according to which the system operates. Family members may not be aware of the rules under which their family works, but outsiders are usually able to see what sorts of principles and norms a family system follows.

The tendency for family systems to try to maintain their established patterns of behavior is challenged from time to time by changes to which they must adapt. When someone new moves into the household, the members of the system must find a way to reorganize and re-establish workable types of relationships and patterns of activity. (This is one of the difficulties families have following a divorce or remarriage, for example.) And when a family member changes in one way or another—psychologically or emotionally, for example—the change usually has reverberations throughout the family system.

Often, following a change in a family system, the family goes through a period of imbalance, or *disequilibrium,* before it adjusts to the change. These periods of disequilibrium can be difficult for families. They may sense that old ways of relating to one another are no longer working, but they may not realize why. Establishing new ways of dealing with one another may take some time (Steinberg, 1990). Only after a new and different equilibrium is established may the family feel comfortable again.

Relationships in families always change most dramatically during those times when individual family members are changing or when the family's circumstances are changing, since it is during these times that the family's previously established equilibrium will be upset. During these times, it is *healthy* for family relationships to change, for through such changes families restore balance to the system. Not surprisingly, one period in which family relationships usually change a great deal is adolescence.

## THE LIFE CYCLE OF FAMILIES

A family in its "infancy" is different from a family in its "adolescence." Like individuals, families move through a life cycle, a **family life cycle**—that is, various developmental phases in which new issues arise and different concerns predominate (Rodgers, 1973). Each stage of the family life cycle is different from those that came before and those that will follow. The life cycle of families is presented in Figure 4.4.

The concerns and issues characteristic of families at adolescence arise not just because of the changing needs and concerns of the young person, but also because of changes in the adolescent's parents and because of changes in the needs and functions of the family as a unit. Consequently, in order to understand the changing nature of family relation-

**FIGURE 4.4**   Stages of the family life cycle.

Although adolescence need not be a time of difficulty for the family, it is almost always a period of change in family relationships. *(Rae Russel)*

ships during the adolescent years, we must take into account not only characteristics of the developing young person, but characteristics of the adolescent's parents and of families at this stage as well.

## THE ADOLESCENT'S PARENTS

Today, the typical parent is between 35 and 45 years old when his or her first child enters early adolescence. It is important therefore to consider psychological development during this period of adulthood and ask how the concerns characteristic of this age may contribute to the changing nature of family relationships at adolescence. A growing body of evidence suggests that the decade between 35 and 45 is a potentially difficult time for many adults. Indeed, some theorists have gone so far as to describe it as a time of "midlife" crises (Farrell and Rosenberg, 1981; Levinson, 1978).

If we look at the nature of these midlife

crises in some detail, we find that the developmental concerns of parents and adolescents are complementary (Steinberg, 1988b). First, consider the issue of biological change. At the same time that adolescents are entering into a period of rapid physical growth, sexual maturation, and ultimately, the period of the life span that society has labeled one of the most physically attractive, their parents are beginning to feel increased concern about their own bodies, about their physical attractiveness, and about their sexual appeal. (Gould, 1972).

A second overlap of crises concerns perceptions of time and the future. At the same time that adolescents are beginning to develop the capability to think systematically about the future and do, in fact, begin to look ahead, their parents are beginning to feel that the possibilities for change are limited. While adolescents' ideas about the future are becoming more expansive, their parents' ideas are probably becoming more limited. Bernice Neugarten, who has studied adult personality development extensively, suggests that an important shift in time perspective takes place during midlife: before this phase in the life cycle, we tend to measure time in terms of how long we have been alive; after midlife, we are more likely to see things in terms of how much longer we have to live (Neugarten, 1975). One reason for this shift may be that midlife adults are reminded of their mortality because they see their own parents aging.

Finally, consider the issue of power, status, and entrance into the roles of adulthood. Adolescence is the time when individuals are on the threshold of gaining a great deal of status. Their careers and marriages lie ahead of them, and choices seem limitless. For their parents, in contrast, many choices have already been made—some successfully, others perhaps less so. Most adults reach their occupational plateau—the point at which they can tell how successful they are likely to be—during midlife, and many must deal with whatever gap exists between their early aspirations and their actual achievements (Gould, 1972). In sum, for adolescents, this phase in the family life cycle is a time of boundless horizons; for their parents, it is a time of coming to terms with choices made when they were younger.

This overlap of crises is likely to have an impact on family relationships. A father who is worried about his own physical health suddenly feels uncomfortable about playing tennis each weekend with his growing son, as they did for years when the son was younger. They may have to find new activities that they can share together. An adolescent girl with big plans for the future finds it difficult to understand why her father seems so cautious and narrow-minded when she asks him for advice. She may react by turning to her friends more often. An adolescent boy finds his mother's constant attention annoying; he doesn't see that to her, his interest in independence signifies the end of an important stage in her career as a parent. In fact, the adolescent's

desire for autonomy in particular may be especially stressful for parents (Small et al., 1988). While none of these situations may cause family conflict, each requires a period of adjustment on the part of parents and their children.

This generalization must be tempered by the fact that recent decades have seen important changes in both the age at which individuals marry and the age at which they have their first child. The average age at marriage has increased by more than two years since 1970, for both men (who now tend to marry in their late 20s) and women (who tend to marry in their mid-20s). And whereas it had been common in the past for couples to begin having children soon after marriage, proportionately more couples today are delaying childbearing until they have become established in their careers. As a consequence of both of these changes, adults tend to be older today when their children reach adolescence than was the case two decades ago. Although psychologists have studied the impact of this change on parents' relationships with their infants (e.g., Parke, 1988), we do not know how being an older parent affects relationships during adolescence.

Although many theorists have speculated that parents' mental health at midlife is affected by the development of their adolescent children, few studies have examined this issue directly. One exception is found in the work of psychologist Susan Silverberg (Silverberg and Steinberg, 1987; Silverberg and Steinberg, 1990; Steinberg and Silverberg, 1987). According to these studies, parents may be somewhat adversely affected by the transition of their child into adolescence, especially if the child is of the same sex. Mothers of daughters and fathers of sons, for example, show more psychological distress, report less satisfaction with their marriage, and experience more intense midlife identity concerns as their children begin to mature physically, get involved in dating

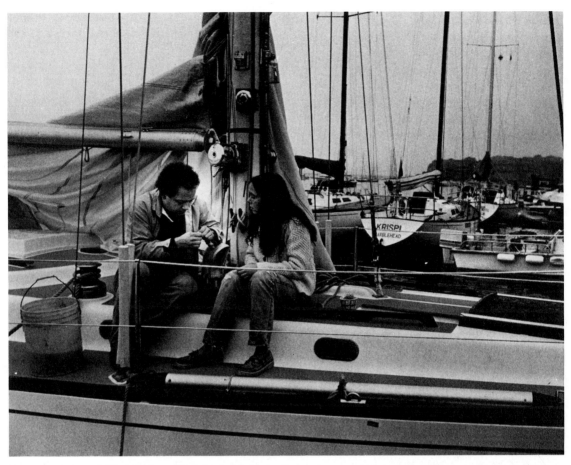

For many adults, midlife is a time of heightened introspection and personal reevaluation. Because many parents are at this stage in the life cycle when their children are teenagers, the so-called "midlife crisis" of adulthood may coincide with the "identity crisis" of adolescence. *(Ellis Herwig/Stock, Boston)*

relationships, and distance themselves from their parents emotionally. Interestingly, however, her studies indicate that parents who are deeply involved in work outside the home may be buffered against some of these negative consequences. Having a satisfying job may help parents more successfully negotiate the family's transition into their child's adolescence.

Along similar lines, studies also show that parents who have high self-esteem have better relationships with their adolescents than do parents who think more poorly of themselves (Small, 1988). Mothers with high self-esteem, in particular, grant their adolescent more autonomy and communicate more effectively, and this, in turn, contributes to greater satisfaction on the part of the teenager. When adolescents are more satisfied with the degree of autonomy their parents grant them, they are less likely to challenge their parents, and their parents report less stress at home as a result.

## CHANGES IN FAMILY NEEDS AND FUNCTIONS

It is not only individual family members who undergo change during the family's adolescent years. The family as a unit changes as well in its economic circumstances, its relationship to other social institutions, and its functions. One of the most important changes undergone by the family during adolescence is financial: Family finances are likely to be strained during adolescence. Children grow rapidly during puberty, and clothing for adolescents is expensive. Keeping up with the accoutrements of the peer culture—the records, cosmetics, and high-priced home video, computer, and stereo equipment—may push a family budget to the limit. Many families also begin saving money for large anticipated expenditures, such as the adolescent's college education. And in some families, parents may find themselves having to help support their own parents at a time when their children are still economically dependent. These financial demands require adjustment on the part of the family system.

In addition to these financial pressures, the adolescent's family must cope with the increasing importance of two new contexts in which the young person spends time and invests energy: the peer group and, later in adolescence, the workplace. During the early stages of the life cycle, the child's social world is fairly narrow, and the family is the central setting. As the child grows, the school begins to take on increased significance, and relationships and concerns revolving around school must be balanced with those revolving around the family. During late childhood and early adolescence, however, the peer group becomes a setting in which close ties are formed. Families may have a tough time adjusting to the adolescent's increasing interest in forgoing family activities for peer activities. They may have arguments about the teenager's reluctance to give up time with his or her friends for family outings.

Finally, important changes in family functions also take place during adolescence. During infancy and childhood, the functions and responsibilities of the family are fairly clear: nurturance, protection, and socialization. While all of these roles are still important during adolescence, adolescents are more in need of support than nurturance, of guidance than protection, of direction than socialization. Making the transition from the family functions of childhood to the family functions of adolescence is not necessarily easy, for the shift often upsets the equilibrium established during childhood. The transition is further complicated in contemporary society, where preparation for adulthood—one of the chief tasks of adolescence that was once carried out primarily by the family—is increasingly done by other institutions, such as the school. Many families may feel at a loss to figure out just what their role during adolescence is. A 16-year-old girl once told the author that she wasn't sure whether she needed her parents any more, now that she could drive and had a job at the local fast-food restaurant.

## TRANSFORMATIONS IN FAMILY RELATIONS

Together, the biological, cognitive, and social transitions of adolescence, the changes experienced by adults at midlife, and the changes undergone by the family during this stage in the family life cycle set in motion a series of transformations in family relationships. Think for a moment about the relationship between parents and a 12-year-old and that between parents and an 18-year-old. In most families, there is a movement during adolescence from patterns of influence and interaction that are asymmetrical and unequal to ones in which parents and their adolescent children are on a more equal footing. And there is some evidence that early adolescence—when this shift toward more egalitarian relationships first begins—may be a time of temporary disequilibrium in the family system.

Studies of family interaction suggest that early adolescence may be a time during which young people begin to try to play a more forceful role in the family but when parents may not yet acknowledge the adolescents' input. As a result, young adolescents may interrupt their parents more often but have little impact. By middle adolescence, however, teenagers act and are treated much more like adults. They have more influence over family decisions, but they do not need to assert their opinions through interruptions and similarly immature behavior.

Increases in the assertiveness and influence of adolescents as they get older are consistent with their changing needs and capabilities. It is adaptive for families to permit these changes to happen, because it is through such changes that adolescents learn to be more mature and independent. In fact, there is some evidence that families who resist making changes in their patterns of interaction during adolescence are more likely to experience such problems as juvenile delinquency (Alexander, 1973). This further corroborates the idea that family systems must be able to adapt when changes in family members or family circumstances make such adaptation necessary.

The adolescent's biological and cognitive maturation may play a role in unbalancing the family system during early adolescence. Several researchers have demonstrated that family relationships change during puberty, with conflict between adolescents and their parents increasing—especially between adolescents and their mothers—and closeness between adolescents and their parents diminishing somewhat (Hill et al., 1985a, 1985b; Holmbeck and Hill, in press; Paikoff, Brooks-Gunn, and Warren, in press; Steinberg, 1981, 1987, 1988; Susman et al., 1987). Although puberty seems to distance adolescents from their parents, it is not associated with familial "storm and stress." The conflict is more likely to take the form of bickering over day-to-day issues such as household chores than outright fighting. Similarly, the

diminished closeness is more likely to be manifested in increased privacy on the part of the adolescent and diminished physical affection between teenagers and parents, rather than any serious loss of love or respect between parents and children (Montemayor, 1983, 1986). Research suggests that the distancing effect of puberty is temporary, though, and that relationships may become less conflicted and more intimate during late adolescence. In any event, it does appear that early adolescence may be a somewhat more strained time for the family than earlier or later.

Other researchers have emphasized changes in the adolescents' cognitive abilities and how these changes may reverberate throughout the family. We noted earlier in this chapter that changes in the ways adolescents view family rules and regulations may contribute to increased conflict between them and their parents (Smetana, 1988, 1989). Research also indicates that early adolescence is a time of changes in youngsters' views of family relationships and in family members' expectations of each other. For example, one study asked adolescents of different ages to characterize their actual and "ideal" families in terms of how close and dominant different family members were (Feldman and Gehring, 1988). With age, the gap between adolescents' actual and "ideal" portraits widened, indicating that as they became older, adolescents became more aware of their families' shortcomings—at least in comparison to what they believed a perfect family was like. This realization does not necessarily lead adolescents to reject their parents, but it does lead to a more balanced, and probably more accurate, appraisal of them (Youniss and Smollar, 1985).

Psychologist W. Andrew Collins (1988, 1990) has studied the changes in children's and parents' expectations for each other that take place during adolescence and how "violations" of these expectations can cause family conflict. A child may enter adolescence expecting that it will be a time of great freedom, for example,

Tension and misunderstanding in the family during adolescence sometimes result from unfulfilled expectations of parents or children. Popular television programs, such as *The Cosby Show*, may portray family life in ways that do not mesh with individuals' actual experiences, leading them to wonder whether their own family is "normal." At the same time, however, programs such as *The Cosby Show* often model positive parent-child communication, which may help parents and adolescents learn to get along better. *(© 1988 National Broadcasting Co., Inc. For Editorial Use Relative to NBC TV Network Broadcast Only. All Other Rights Reserved.)*

whereas her parents may view the same period as one in which tighter reins are necessary. Alternatively, another child, perhaps influenced by such television shows as *The Cosby Show* or *Family Ties*, may imagine that adolescence will be a time of increased closeness and shared activities in the family, only to be disappointed to find that his or her parents have been looking forward to having time to themselves. It is easy to see how differences in expectations about what adolescence is going to be like can escalate into arguments and misunderstandings. For this reason, psychologists have been studying the sorts of beliefs children and parents have about adolescence and where they turn for sources of information (Steinberg, 1990).

## Family Relationships and Adolescent Development

Thus far we have looked at the sorts of issues and concerns faced by families during the adolescent years. We have seen that adolescence is not usually a time of dire conflict in most households, but we have also seen that families must be able to adapt to the social and psychological changes that arise at this time in the family life cycle.

In our focus on those experiences that all families share, however, we have not addressed the very important questions of how relationships differ from family to family and whether these differences have important consequences for the developing adolescent. Some parents are stricter than others. Some adolescents are given a great deal of affection, while others are treated more distantly. In some households, decisions are made through open discussion and verbal give-and-take, while in others, parents lay down the rules and children are expected to follow them. To what extent are different patterns of family relationships associated with different patterns of adolescent development? Are some styles of parenting more likely to be associated with healthy development than others? In this section, we look at variations in parenting practices and their correlates in adolescent behavior.

It is important to bear in mind that although our tendency is to see child behavior as the result of parent behavior, socialization is actually a two-way, not a one-way, street (Bell, 1968). It is a known fact, for example, that parents who employ physical punishment (spanking, hitting, etc.) are more likely to have aggressive adolescents (Bandura and Walters, 1959). But we cannot be sure whether (1) physical punishment leads to adolescent aggression; (2) adolescent aggression leads to parents using physical punishment; (3) some other factor is correlated with parents using physical punishment and with adolescent aggression (a genetic predisposition to behave aggressively that adolescents inherit from their parents); or (4) some combination of these causal and correlational factors is at work. Thus when we look at the findings concerning parenting practices and adolescent development, we must remember that just as parents affect their adolescents' behavior, so do adolescents affect their parents' behavior.

## PARENTING STYLES AND THEIR EFFECTS

There are a variety of ways to characterize parents' behavior toward their children. One of the most useful approaches derives from the work of psychologist Diana Baumrind (1978). According to her work and that of others in this vein, two aspects of the parent's behavior toward the adolescent are critical: *parental responsiveness* and *parental demandingness* (Maccoby and Martin, 1983). Responsiveness refers to the degree to which the parent responds to the child's needs in an accepting, supportive manner. Demandingness refers to the extent to which the parent expects and demands mature, responsible behavior from the child. Parents vary on each of these dimensions. Some are warm and accepting while others are unresponsive and rejecting; some are demanding and expect a great deal of their child while others are permissive and demand very little.

Because responsiveness and demandingness are more or less independent of each other—that is, it is possible for a parent to be very demanding without being responsive and vice versa—it is possible to look at various combinations of these *two* dimensions (see Figure 4.5). Many studies of parents and children indicate that the fourfold classification scheme presented in Figure 4.5 is very important in understanding the impact of parents' behavior on the child, and psychologists have given labels to the four different prototypes presented in the table. A parent who is very responsive but not at all demanding is labeled *indulgent,* whereas one who is equally responsive but also very demanding is labeled *authoritative.* Parents who are very demanding but not responsive are *authoritarian;* parents who are neither demanding nor responsive are labeled *indifferent.*

Working-class parents tend to place more emphasis on obedience in raising their children than do middle-class parents. One reason is that obedience is adaptive in working-class settings; a successful laborer is one who can take orders. *(Billy E. Barnes/ Stock, Boston)*

These four general patterns are described below:

    **Authoritative** parents are warm but firm. They set standards for the child's conduct but form expectations that are consistent with the child's developing needs and capabilities. They place a high value on the development of autonomy and self-direction but assume the ultimate responsibility for their child's behavior. Authoritative

**FIGURE 4.5** A scheme for classifying parenting types. (Maccoby and Martin, 1983)

|  |  | **Demandingness** | |
|  |  | High | Low |
| **Responsiveness** | High | Authoritative | Indulgent |
|  | Low | Authoritarian | Indifferent |

parents deal with their child in a rational, issue-oriented manner, frequently engaging in discussion and explanation with their children over matters of discipline.

    *'75% of parent*  **Authoritarian** parents place a high value on obedience and conformity. They tend to favor more punitive, absolute, and forceful disciplinary measures. Verbal give-and-take is not common in authoritarian households, because the underlying belief of authoritarian parents is that the child should accept without question the rules and standards established by the parents. They tend not to encourage independent behavior and, instead, place a good deal of importance on restricting the child's autonomy.

    **Indulgent** parents behave in an accepting, benign, and somewhat more passive way in matters of discipline. They place relatively few demands on the child's behavior, giving the child a high degree of freedom to act as he or she wishes. Indulgent parents are more likely to believe that control is an infringement on the child's freedom that may interfere with the child's healthy development. Instead of actively shaping their child's behavior, indulgent parents are more likely to view themselves as resources which the child may or may not use.

**Indifferent** parents try to do whatever is necessary to minimize the time and energy that they must devote to interacting with their child. In extreme cases, indifferent parents may be neglectful. They know little about their child's activities and whereabouts, show little interest in their child's experiences at school or with friends, rarely converse with their child, and rarely consider their child's opinion when making decisions. Rather than raising their child according to a set of beliefs about what is good for the child's development (as do the other three parent types) indifferent parents are "parent-centered"—they structure their home life primarily around their own needs and interests.

The categorization proposed by Baumrind provides a useful way of summarizing and examining some of the relations between parenting practices and adolescent psychosocial development. Generally speaking, young people raised in authoritative households are more psychosocially competent than peers who have been raised in authoritarian, indulgent, or indifferent homes: Adolescents raised in authoritative homes are more responsible, self-assured, adaptive, creative, curious, socially skilled, and successful in school. Adolescents raised in authoritarian homes, in contrast, are more dependent, more passive, less socially adept, less self-assured, and less intellectually curious. Adolescents raised in indulgent households are often less mature, more irresponsible, more conforming to their peers, and less able to assume positions of leadership. Adolescents raised in indifferent homes are often impulsive and more likely to be involved in delinquent behavior and in precocious experiments with sex, drugs, and alcohol (Lamborn et al., 1991; Pulkkinen, 1982). In general, the effects of nonresponsiveness tend to be slightly worse among girls than boys, whereas the ef-

fects of nondemandingness tend to be slightly worse among boys than girls. Although occasional exceptions to these general patterns have been noted, the evidence linking authoritative parenting and healthy adolescent development is remarkably strong, and it has been found in studies of a wide range of ethnic and socioeconomic groups (Dornbusch et al., 1987; Maccoby and Martin, 1983; Steinberg et al., 1991).

Why is authoritative parenting associated with healthy adolescent development? First, authoritative parents provide a nice balance between restrictiveness and autonomy, which on the one hand provides the young person with opportunities to develop self-reliance but on the other hand sets the sorts of standards, limits, and guidelines that developing individuals need. The authoritative family is more able than other families to adjust to new stages of the family life cycle. Because authoritative parents are flexible in their approach to parenting, they tend to shape and tailor their demands and expectations to suit the changing needs and competencies of the adolescent, a process that is likely to help the young person's continued development (Hill, 1980). Authoritative parents, for instance, are more likely to give children more independence gradually as they get older, which helps children develop self-reliance. One study, for example, found that authoritative parenting led to the development of psychological maturity, which in turn led to school success (Steinberg et al., 1989).

Second, because authoritative parents are more likely to engage their children in verbal give-and-take, they are likely to promote the sort of intellectual development that provides an important foundation for the development of psychosocial competence. Family discussions in which decisions, rules, and expectations are explained help the child to understand social systems and social relationships. This understanding plays an important part in

## THE SEXES: ARE THERE SEX DIFFERENCES IN ADOLESCENTS' FAMILY RELATIONSHIPS?

One question frequently asked by researchers is whether and in what ways there may be sex differences in patterns of family relationships. Do daughters and sons have different sorts of relationships with their mothers and fathers? Now that several studies have been completed, we have a tentative answer to this question, and it is a surprising one.

In general, differences between the family relations of sons and daughters are minimal. Although there are occasional exceptions to the rule, sons and daughters report similar degrees of closeness to their parents, similar amounts of conflict, similar types of rules (and disagreements about those rules), and similar patterns of activity (Hill and Holmbeck, 1987; Montemayor and Brownlee, 1987; Youniss and Ketterlinus, 1987). Observational studies of interaction between parents and adolescents indicate that sons and daughters interact with their parents in remarkably similar ways (Cooper and Grotevant, 1987; Hauser et al., 1987).

Does this mean that sex differences in the family are absent? Not entirely. These same studies also indicate that the sex of the adolescent's parent may be a more important influence on family relationships than the sex of the adolescent. Many studies suggest that teenagers—males and females alike—have very different types of relationships with mothers and fathers. One of the best of these studies was conducted by psychologists James Youniss and Jacqueline Smollar (1985). They found that adolescents tend to be closer to their mother than their father and feel more comfortable talking to their mother about problems and other emotional matters. Fathers are more likely to be perceived as relatively distant authority figures who may be consulted for "objective" information (such as help with homework) but who are rarely sought for support or guidance (such as help for problems with a boyfriend or girlfriend). Interestingly, adolescents also fight more often with their mothers than their fathers, but this higher level of conflict does not appear to jeopardize the closeness of the mother-adolescent relationship. It seems safe to say that relationships between adolescents and their mothers are more emotionally intense in general, and this intensity has both positive and negative manifestations (Apter, 1990).

*continued on next page*

the development of reasoning abilities, role taking, moral judgment, and empathy (Baumrind, 1978). The extensive discussion characteristic of authoritative households stimulates the adolescent's thinking.

Third, because authoritative parenting combines moderate control with a good deal of warmth, children are more likely to identify with their parents. In fact, one of the strongest predictors of identification between children and their parents is warmth in the parent-child relationship. We are more likely to identify with and imitate people who treat us with warmth and affection. A child raised warmly by parents who value self-direction will imitate his or her mother and father and display a similar preference for independence (Hill, 1980).

Finally, the child's own behavior may play a role in shaping authoritative parenting practices (Lewis, 1981a). Children who are responsible, self-directed, curious, and self-assured elicit from their parents warmth, flexible guidance, and verbal give-and-take. In contrast,

One of the most interesting findings to emerge from these studies concerns the father-daughter relationship in particular. Most researchers have found that this relationship is especially distant. Although we are not quite sure of the reasons—some theorists have speculated that unconscious taboos against incest may make it difficult for fathers and daughters to remain close after puberty, while others have suggested that the general emotional inexpressiveness of fathers may put daughters off more than sons (Youniss and Ketterlinus, 1987)—it seems clear that this relationship is the flattest, emotionally speaking, in the family. Whether and in what ways this may affect the daughter's development is not known.

Why should mothers and fathers have such different sorts of relationships with their adolescent children? One explanation concerns differences in the socialization of men and women. We know, for example, that women in Western cultures are socialized to be more emotionally expressive than men, and this may give them talents and capabilities that permit them to form closer relationships with their children. Growing up in a household in which mothers are emotionally accessible and fathers are emotionally distant only furthers this tendency, for this provides role models for adolescents to imitate. A some-what different explanation concerns differences in the maternal and paternal roles. The mother's role in this culture traditionally has included more of an "expressive," or emotional, component, whereas the father's role may be more "instrumental" (Parsons, 1949). Moreover, until relatively recently, patterns of work and family life were so different for mothers and fathers that it may have been difficult for fathers—whatever their socialization—to form close relationships with their children. Mothers may be closer than fathers simply because they spend more time with their children as their children develop, and time together may foster and strengthen emotional bonds.

Whatever the explanation, however, the consistency with which studies of parents and adolescents uncover different patterns of relations for mothers and fathers is striking—especially in light of changes that have taken place in sex roles in contemporary society. Although we cannot be sure of the origins of these differences, we are fairly confident that they exist, even in today's families. In discussing the parent-adolescent relationship, we clearly need to pay attention to sex differences—not necessarily differences between sons and daughters, but between mothers and fathers.

children who are aggressive, dependent, or less psychosocially mature in other ways may provoke parents' behavior that is excessively harsh, passive, or distant. Parents may enjoy being around children who are responsible and independent, for example, and may treat them more warmly. In contrast, children who are continually acting up make their parents short-tempered, impatient, or distant. In other words, the relationship between adolescent competence and authoritative parenting may be the result of a reciprocal cycle in which the child's psychosocial maturity leads to authoritative parenting, which in turn leads to the further development of maturity.

## INDIVIDUALITY AND ATTACHMENT IN THE ADOLESCENT'S FAMILY

Several recent studies of verbal interaction between adolescents and their parents have examined factors in the parent-child relationship that contribute to heathy adolescent development. In these studies, families are asked to discuss a problem together, and their interaction is taped and later analyzed. Psychologists Catherine Cooper and Harold Grotevant (Cooper et al., 1983; Grotevant and Cooper, 1985, 1986) have noted that families with psychologically competent teenagers interact in ways that permit family members to express their individuality yet remain attached, or connected, to other family members. In these families, verbal give-and-take is the norm, and adolescents (as well as parents) are encouraged to express their own opinions. At the same time, however, the importance of maintaining close relationships in the family is emphasized, and individuals are encouraged to consider how their actions may affect other family members.

Rather than viewing attachment and autonomy as opposites, Cooper and Grotevant's studies as well as those of other researchers (Campbell et al., 1984; Litovsky and Dusek, 1985) indicate that the path to healthy psychological development is likely to combine the two. In other words, adolescents appear to do best when they grow up in a family atmosphere that permits the development of individuality against a backdrop of close family ties. In these families, conflict between parents and adolescents can play a very important and positive role in the adolescent's social and cognitive development, because individuals are encouraged to express their opinions in an atmosphere that does not risk severing the emotional attachment (Cooper, 1988). In Chapter 10, we will look more closely at the nature of attachment between parents and adolescents.

Other researchers have also found that healthy adolescent development is associated with particular patterns of verbal interaction. Psychiatrist Stuart Hauser and his colleagues (Hauser et al., 1984) have drawn a distinction between "enabling" and "constraining" patterns of interchange in the family. **Enabling interactions** include explanation, problem

Adolescents' relationships with siblings are rated high in affection and companionship, but they are also rated high in conflict. Proximity between siblings provokes both positive and negative interactions. _(Peter Menzel/Stock, Boston)_

solving, and empathy. **Constraining interactions** are distracting, judgmental, or devaluing of a family member's opinion. Not surprisingly, adolescents who grow up in homes to which the family tends to interact in enabling ways score higher on measures of psychological development than those who grow up in relatively more constraining families.

## ADOLESCENTS' RELATIONSHIPS WITH SIBLINGS

Far more is known about adolescents' relations with their parents than about their relations with brothers and sisters. In general, studies suggest that sibling relationships may have characteristics that set them apart from both other family relationships, such as that between adolescents and their parents, and other relationships with peers, such as those between adolescents and their close friends (Furman and Buhrmester, 1985; Raffaelli and Larson, 1987). In one study, for example, young adolescents were asked to rate several different types of relationships (for example, with parents, siblings, friends, grandparents) along similar dimensions. As you can see in Figure 4.6, sibling relationships were rated like those with parents for companionship and importance, but they were rated more like friendships with respect to power, assistance, and how satisfying the relationship is. One striking difference between sibling and other types of relationship involves conflict; adolescents report far higher levels of conflict with brothers and sisters than they do with anyone else. Because siblings live in close proximity to each other, they may have added opportunities for both positive and negative interaction.

One topic of interest to researchers interested in adolescents and their siblings concerns how closely siblings resemble each other in intelligence, personality, and interests. Because siblings share some genetic influences (because they have the same parents) and at least some environmental influences (because they have grown up in the same household), you might think that they would be more alike than different. But new research suggests that adolescents growing up in the same family are actually quite different from each other—far more than would be expected given their supposedly similar genetic and environmental histories. For example, siblings' scores on standard measures of personality traits are virtually uncorrelated (Plomin and Daniels, 1987). Indeed, the findings concerning differences between siblings are so consistent that one team of investigators wrote recently that "two children in the same family are as different from one another as are pairs of children selected randomly from the population" (Plomin and Daniels, 1987, p. 1).

Why might siblings be so different from each other? One explanation is offered by behavioral geneticists Robert Plomin and Denise Daniels (Daniels et al., 1985; Plomin and Daniels, 1987). They have found that siblings growing up in the same family experience their environment very differently. One brother may describe his family as very close-knit, while another may have exerienced it as very distant. One girl describes her family life as plagued with argument and conflict; her sister describes it as peaceful and agreeable. In other words, even though we may assume that children growing up in the same family have shared the same environment, this may not really be the case.

Siblings may experience the same family environment differently for a variety of reasons. First, parents may treat their children differently because of their own conscious and unconscious preferences, differences in their children's temperaments, or changes in their child-rearing philosophies over time. Second, the family may itself be at different stages in its own development, and this may affect children differently. For instance, it may be different to be raised by older parents than by younger

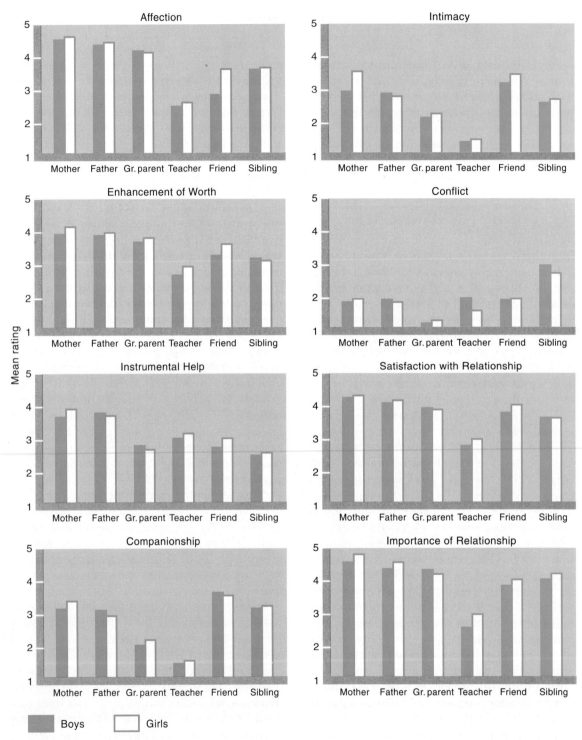

**FIGURE 4.6** These graphs show similarities and differences among adolescents' relationships with parents, friends, siblings, and significant others. (Furman and Buhrmester, 1985)

ones, and children born later in the family's history may have parents who treat them differently because of this. Finally, differences in the family's circumstances at different times may affect the way that siblings are raised. A child who is raised during a time of financial strain may have very different experiences from a sibling who grows up when the family is more comfortable.

Plomin and Daniels have found that siblings actually do describe their upbringings as very different and, moreover, that these differences in experiences are related to different patterns of development. In general, better adjusted adolescents were more likely than their siblings to report that their relationship with their mother was close, that their relations with brothers or sisters were friendly, that they were involved in family decision making, and that they were given a high level of responsibility around the house (Daniels et al., 1985).

## Summary

1. Any discussion of the role of the family in adolescent development must take into account the ways in which family life has changed in the past 50 years. Among the most important contributors to these changes have been the changing nature of work, the women's movement, changing patterns of housing, and the changing values and priorities of adults.

2. Three of the most important changes that have occurred among families with adolescents concern the increase in the rate of divorce, the increase in the prevalence of single parent households, and the increased participation of mothers in the labor force. Half of all children who will become teenagers during the 1990s will experience their parents' divorce, and more than half of these youngsters will experience living in a stepfamily. Well over half of all children born in the late 1970s or early 1980s will spend at least part of their childhood or adolescence in a single-parent household. The vast majority will have mothers who are employed outside the home.

3. Research on divorce and remarriage indicates that the period of greatest difficulty is the time immediately after the event. Hardest hit by divorce are young boys in the custody of their mother. Although most youngsters ultimately adapt to divorce or remarriage, new research indicates that certain adjustment or behavior problems may appear or reappear in adolescence. These include academic problems, increased drug and alcohol use, and difficulties in romantic relationships.

4. Research on maternal employment indicates that the effects depend on the sex of the adolescent and the attitude of the mother toward her work. Maternal employment has positive effects on daughters, but mixed effects on sons, especially where school performance is concerned. Children whose mothers are happy with their employment are more likely to benefit than are children whose mothers don't wish to work or dislike their jobs. Adolescents whose families have suffered severe economic losses may be at heightened risk for problem behavior.

5. The notion that a wide gap exists between the generations is largely a myth. When parents and adolescents do disagree, it tends to be over mundane, day to day issues, and not over major values or priorities. Many disagreements between parents and teenagers stem from the different perspectives that they bring to the discussion: Parents typically see the issues as matters of "right" or "wrong," whereas adolescents see them as matters of personal choice.

6. Adolescence is a time of renegotiation in family relationships, with adolescents gaining increasingly more power and becoming increasingly more assertive. Many of these changes in family relations affect the psychological well-being of the adolescent's middle-aged parents as well as the teenager. In gen-

eral, parents who have some strong interests outside the family and who have a positive sense of self-esteem cope better with the changes of adolescence than do other parents.

7. Psychologists have identified four basic styles of parenting during adolescence: Authoritative, authoritarian, indulgent, and indifferent. In general, adolescents from authoritative homes fare the best, whereas adolescents from indifferent homes fare worst. The healthiest families are those that permit the adolescent to develop a sense of individuality while staying emotionally attached to the family at the same time.

8. In general, adolescents' relations with siblings are different than those with parents or with friends. Interestingly, research suggests that adolescents are often quite dissimilar from their brothers and sisters, despite the strong genetic and environmental influences they share.

## Key Terms

| | |
|---|---|
| authoritarian parenting | indifferent |
| authoritative parenting | parenting |
| constraining inter- | indulgent |
|    actions | parenting |
| enabling interactions | intergenerational |
| family life cycle | conflict |
| generation gap | midlife crisis |

## For Further Reading

APTER, T. (1990). *Altered loves: Mothers and daughters during adolescence.* New York: St. Martin's Press. An intensive look at the dy-

namics of mother-daughter relationships in adolescence.

COLLINS, W. A. (1990). Parent-child relationships in the transition to adolescence: Continuity and change in interaction, affect, and cognition. In R. Montemayor, G. Adams, and T. Gullotta (Eds.), *Advances in adolescent development: Volume 2. The transition from childhood to adolescence.* Beverly Hills, CA: Sage. A thorough review of the literature on transformations in family relationships in early adolescence.

FURSTENBERG, F. (1990). Coming of age in a changing family system. In S. Feldman and G. Elliott (Eds.), *At the threshold: The developing adolescent.* Cambridge: Harvard University Press. An extensive overview of the implications of recent trends in family life in the United States for adolescent development.

HETHERINGTON, E. M., STANLEY-HAGAN, M., AND ANDERSON, E. (1989). Marital transitions: A child's perspective. *American Psychologist, 44,* 303–312. A summary of recent research on children's and adolescents' reactions to divorce and remarriage.

STEINBERG, L., AND LEVINE, A. (1990). *You and your adolescent: A parent's guide for ages 10 to 20.* New York: Harper & Row. A practical discussion of family relations and adolescent development aimed at parents of teenagers.

# PEER GROUPS

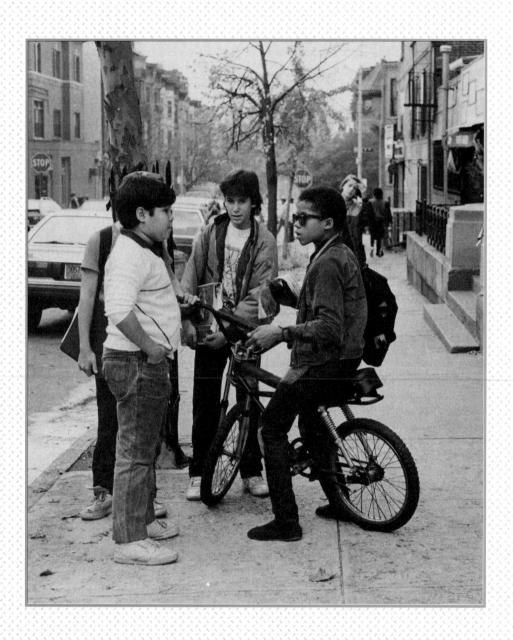

PEER
GROUPS

*I*t is about 8:30 in the morning. A group of teenagers congregate in the hallway in front of their first period classroom. They are discussing their plans for the weekend. As the first period bell sounds, they enter the classroom and take their seats. For the next 4 hours—until there is a break in their schedule for lunch—they will attend class in groups of about thirty—thirty adolescents to one adult.

At lunch, the clique meets again to talk about the weekend. They have about 45 minutes until the first afternoon period begins. After lunch, they spend another 2 hours in class—again, in groups of about thirty. The school day ends, and the clique reconvenes. They are going over to someone's house to hang out for the rest of the day. Everyone's parents are working. They are on their own. At about 6 o'clock, they disperse and head home for dinner. A few will talk on the phone that night. Some will get together to study. They will see one another first thing the next morning.

When you stop to think about it, adolescents in modern society spend a remarkable amount of time with their peers. In fact, American teenagers spend more time talking to their friends each day than in any other activity (Csikszentmihalyi, Larson, and Prescott, 1977). High school students spend twice as much of their time each week with peers as with parents or other adults—even discounting time in class (Brown, 1990). Virtually all adolescents spend most of each weekday with their peers while at school, and the vast majority also see or talk to their friends in the afternoon, in the evening, and over the weekend (Medrich et al., 1982). Even when adolescents work in part-time jobs, they are more likely to work with people their own age than with adults (Greenberger and Steinberg, 1986). And studies show that adolescents' moods are most positive when they are with their friends (Larson, 1983).

American society is very *age-segregated*. From the time youngsters enter school at the age of 5 until they graduate at age 18 or so, they are grouped with children their own age. They have little contact with people who are older or younger, outside of relatives. Because schools play such an important role in determining children's friendships, age grouping carries over into after-school, weekend, and vacation activities. Little League, scouting, church groups—all are structured in a way that groups people together by age.

In contemporary society, **peer groups** have become an increasingly important context in which adolescents spend time. Modernization has led to more and more age segregation—in schools, in the workplace, and in the community. Today's teenagers spend far more time in the exclusive company of their peers than their counterparts did in the past. Indeed, the rise of peer groups in modern society gives adolescence in contemporary America some of its most distinctive features. And the role of peers in shaping adolescent psychosocial development has become increasingly important.

For these reasons, understanding how adolescent peer groups form and what takes place within their boundaries is critical to understanding adolescent development in contemporary society. No discussion of adolescent identity development is complete without an examination of how and why teenagers derive part of their identity from the group they spend time with. No discussion of adolescent friendship is complete without an examination of teenagers' cliques and how they are formed. And no discussion of adolescent sexuality is complete without an examination of how, and when, peer groups change from same-sex groups to mixed-sex groups.

In the previous chapter, by looking at the family *in context* and *as a context*, we were better able to understand how families affect the development of young people. Our discussion of peer groups follows a similar organization.

# Adolescent Peer Groups in Modern Society

Contact between adolescents and their peers is found in all cultures. But not all societies have peer groups that are as narrowly defined and age-segregated as those in modern-day America. While adolescent peer relationships are universal, age-segregated peer groups are not. In earlier times, for example, interactions among youngsters occurred largely in the context of mixed-age groups composed of infants, children, and adolescents (Hartup, 1977). And much interaction among children occurred in the presence of their parents, because adults and children were not isolated from one another during the day. Even today, in societies that are less industrialized, young people spend a good part of the day in contact with their elders.

In contemporary America, however, age segregation is the norm. Indeed, the nature of adolescent psychosocial development in contemporary society cannot be understood without a full appreciation of just how prominent adolescents' peer groups are. Changes in the schools, changes in the workplace, and changes in the family have all led to the progressive separation of adolescents from adults and, consequently, to the rise of adolescent peer groups. Let's look at some of these changes, which have contributed to making widespread age segregation a part of life in contemporary America.

## CHANGES IN THE SCHOOLS

Educators first developed the idea of free public elementary education, with students grouped by age and achievement level, in the middle of the nineteenth century (President's Science Advisory Committee, 1974). In so doing, they established an arrangement that would eventually touch all American youngsters and encourage the development and maintenance of age-segregated peer groups. However, it was not until the second quarter of this century that most adolescents were directly affected by educational age grouping. Attending elementary school may have been common, but until 1930 or so, high school was a luxury available only to the very affluent. Adolescent peer groups based on friendships formed in school were not prevalent until fifty or sixty years ago.

We do not know for sure if not being in school hindered the development of adolescent peer groups. Perhaps peer groups were composed of young people living in the same neighborhood or working together. But we can be fairly certain that the forces encouraging adolescents to associate almost exclusively with people of exactly the same age were not as strong at the beginning of the century as they are today. Youngsters who were not in school were generally working and living at home, where they were likely to have a good deal of contact with adults and children (Modell, Furstenberg, and Hershberg, 1976). Even those youngsters from families wealthy enough to send their children to high school typically attended academies where children of different ages were mixed together, and it was not uncommon during the nineteenth century for "peer groups" to be composed of individuals ranging in age from 14 to 20 (President's Science Advisory Committee, 1974).

With the rise of free secondary education during the second quarter of this century, school attendance in age-grouped educational institutions became the norm for most American adolescents. Today, virtually all American adolescents spend the years between ages 12 and 16 in age-grouped junior and senior high schools, and fewer than 25 percent leave school before graduating at the age of 17 or 18 (William T. Grant Foundation, 1988). The impact

*— OTHER STATISTICS SAY 40-50% DROP*

The physical separation of teenagers and adults has increased during the past four decades, owing to changing patterns of housing and employment. In contemporary society, many adolescents spend a good deal of their free time without contact with adults. *(Paul Conklin/ Monkmeyer)*

of this educational age grouping on adolescents' social life is dramatic. In one survey, in which seventh- through tenth-grade students were asked to list the people who were important to them, over two-thirds of the same-sex peers they mentioned were from the same grade in their school (Blyth, Hill, and Thiel, 1982).

Participation in age-segregated organized activities—particularly among young adolescents—persists today. One study found that close to 80 percent of sixth-graders are involved in at least one nonschool club, extracurricular activity group, or youth organization in which they are likely to have contact only

with peers of the same age (Medrich et al., 1982). Furthermore, more than half of all young people currently continue their education in colleges and universities, many of which have fairly strong age groupings (although the groupings are not as narrowly defined as those in elementary or secondary schools). In short, as a result of changes in educational institutions over the last century, the vast majority of adolescents and youth in America now spend most of every weekday in the company of young people who, if not their exact age, are older or younger by very little.

## CHANGES IN THE WORKPLACE

A second set of factors related to the rise of adolescent peer groups during this past century concerns changes in the workplace, or more precisely, changes in the relationship between work and other aspects of daily life. With industrialization came more stringent and more carefully monitored child labor laws, which restricted adolescents' participation in the world of work (Bakan, 1972; Modell and Goodman, 1990). Because the implementation of tougher child labor laws coincided with the rise of secondary education, adolescents and adults (who had once shared the same daily activity—work) went their separate ways. Adolescents spent the day in school, adults at work.

In addition, the disappearance of the household as a workplace moved many adults who had been employed in family enterprises out of the home during the day and into work settings. Improvements in transportation made it possible for more and more adults to leave home each day and travel long distances to work; suburbs grew rapidly. Thus home and work became geographically separated, and as a consequence, adolescents and adults saw less and less of each other. Between dawn and dusk each weekday, America's suburbs are filled with people under the age of 18. Not surprisingly, studies of adolescents' social ties show that suburban youngsters have fewer adult friends than do their urban or rural counterparts (Garbarino et al., 1978).

The segregation of adolescents from adults was also fueled by the rise in maternal employment. For example, the proportion of employed mothers of children between the ages of 6 and 17 living in two-parent households rose from 26 percent in 1948 to 68 percent in 1984. The movement of mothers out of the home and into the workplace furthered the trend, already set in motion by suburbanization, toward the development of residential neighborhoods dominated by young people during weekday mornings and afternoons. Today, between 2 and 10 million school-aged youngsters—about 15 percent of all children in this age range—come home from school to houses with no adults present (Goleman, 1988). In all likelihood, the proportion of so-

called "latchkey" children among 14- to 18-year-olds is even higher, although precise figures are not available. Later in this chapter we examine how the changing nature of adolescents' after-school environment may affect their susceptibility to peer pressure.

## CHANGES IN THE POPULATION

Perhaps the most important factor influencing the rise of adolescent peer groups was the dramatic growth of the teenage population during the 20-year period between 1955 and 1975. Following the end of World War II, many parents wanted to have children as soon as possible, creating what has come to be called the postwar "baby boom." The products of this baby boom became adolescents during the 1960s and early 1970s, creating an "adolescent boom" for about 15 years. As you can see from Figure 5.1, the size of the population aged 15

**FIGURE 5.1** The percentage of the U.S. population comprised of 15- to 19-year-olds reached its highest level in 1975. It will begin to increase again by the turn of this decade. Figures in parentheses indicate the number of 15- to 19-year-olds, in millions. (From United Nations Population Division, 1976)

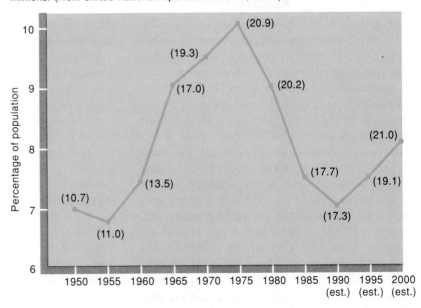

to 19 nearly doubled between 1955 and 1975 and, more important, rose from less than 7 percent of the total population to over 10 percent. During the mid-1970s, one out of every seven Americans was a teenager (United Nations, Population Division, 1976). One reason for the growth of peer groups, therefore, was the sheer increase in the number of peers that young people had. This trend, as you can see, turned downward in 1975, and the relative size of the adolescent population decreased until 1990. But during the last decade of this century—when the products of the baby boom have adolescents of their own, the size of the teenage population is expected to increase once again. In Chapter 13, we will look at one theory that links fluctuations in adolescent problems, such as crime and suicide, to changes in the size of the teenage population (Easterlin, 1980).

## The Adolescent Peer Group: A Problem or a Necessity?

There is no doubt about it: Peer groups play a more prominent role in adolescents' lives today than at any other time in history. But is the rise of peer groups in modern society a problem that needs to be remedied, or is it an inevitable—perhaps even necessary—part of life in contemporary America? This question has sparked some of the hottest arguments in the study of adolescence during the past twenty-five years (Brown, 1990). On one side are those who say that age segregation has led to the development of a separate "youth culture," in which young people maintain attitudes and values that are different from—even contrary to—those of adults. On the other side are those who argue that industrialization and modernization have made peer groups more important, that adults alone can no longer pre-pare young people for the future, and that peer groups play a vital and needed role in the socialization of adolescents for adulthood. Let's look at both sides of the debate.

### IS THERE A SEPARATE YOUTH CULTURE?

Among the most vocal proponents of the view that age segregation has fueled the development of a separate—and troublesome—"youth culture" was sociologist James Coleman, whose book *The Adolescent Society* (1961) presented the findings of an extensive study of the social worlds of ten American high schools. Even though this book is more than 30 years old, its influence on our views of adolescent peer groups remains strong. "Our adolescents are cut off, probably more than ever before, from the adult society," Coleman wrote. "They are still oriented toward fulfilling their parents' desires, but they look very much to their peers for approval as well. Consequently, our society has within its midst a set of small teenage societies, which focus teenage interests and attitudes on things far removed from adult responsibilities, and which may develop standards that lead away from those goals established by the larger society" (1961, p. 9).

What were these "teenage interests and attitudes," that Coleman was referring to, and how did they differ from the interests and attitudes of adults? Coleman felt that the most significant differences concerned the value placed on academic success. While parents felt that academic achievement should be a priority for their youngsters, adolescents lived in a social world in which academic success was frowned on, in which doing well in school did not earn the admiration of peers. Although their parents may have been pleased by straight-A report cards, the high school students studied said that being a good student carried little weight with their friends.

"What does it take to get into the leading

crowd in this school?" When Coleman asked adolescents from ten different high schools this question, he found that their answers were very consistent. For boys, overall, the most important determinants of prestige were personality and athletic success as well as having a good reputation and good looks; for girls, getting into the leading crowd depended on personality, good looks, and clothes. Good grades, particularly for girls, were near the bottom of the list.

Coleman also found that social and athletic success were more likely to make adolescents feel good about themselves than academic success. Getting into the most popular crowd in the school made adolescents feel confident and self-assured. Doing well academically, however, did not make people more popular and did not boost adolescents' self-esteem. The less the students in a school valued academic achievement, the lower the opinion that academically successful students had about themselves. In fact, in schools in which scholastic achievement was not valued very highly, bright students were likely to be "underachievers"— that is, they were likely to perform worse in classes than would be expected on the basis of their ability. In other words, in these schools, getting good grades was a real liability, and in order to remain popular, bright students worked below their level of capability.

*The Adolescent Society* was written nearly thirty years ago, but many of its findings have been corroborated in more recent studies (e.g., Eitzen, 1975). It probably is fair to say that academic achievement is not valued any more by American teenagers today than it was thirty years ago. Indeed, there are some indications that, if anything, it is valued even less. As you can see in Figure 5.2, for example, academic achievement is considered less important than appearance, personality, or athletic achievement among contemporary adolescents—just as it was during the 1950s (Crockett et al., 1984).

**FIGURE 5.2** Percentage of boys (top) and girls (bottom) during the early 1980s who cited appearance, athletic achievement, academic achievement, and personality as qualities important for popularity.

Not all studies have replicated these results, however. One study of Canadian adolescents, for example, found that the majority of students preferred to be remembered as outstanding students (rather than great athletes or popular adolescents), and other studies have found that students' preferences for how they will be remembered vary a great deal by sex, age, and where they fit into the social structure of the school (Brown, 1990). These studies indicate that the world of adolescents is not dominated by *one* youth culture, as Coleman had suggested, but by several different youth *cultures*. Some of these cultures are anti-intellectual, but others are very positively oriented toward school.

At the time of its publication, though, the findings of *The Adolescent Society* were interpreted to mean that age segregation had so strengthened the power of the peer group that American adolescents had become alienated and unfamiliar with the values of adults. No longer were young people interested in the things their parents wanted for them. Teenagers had become separated from adult society to such an extent that they established their own society—a separate youth culture that undermined parents' efforts to encourage academic excellence and placed emphasis on sports, dating, cars, and partying. Unless steps were taken to integrate adolescents into the world of adults—such as shortening the school day and expanding opportunities for adolescents to work—society was going to have a difficult time preparing young people for adulthood. How could adolescents growing up in the "adolescent society," without sufficient contact with their elders, become responsible, diligent, and competent adults?

Many social scientists agreed with Coleman's observations. Growing problems—such as youth unemployment, teenage suicide, juvenile crime and delinquency, drug and alcohol use, and premarital pregnancy—were all attributed to the rise of peer groups and the isolation of adolescents from adults. Many observers of the adolescent scene noted that all of these problems increased dramatically after 1940, as peer groups became more prominent and age segregation more prevelent (Bronfenbrenner, 1974).

Debates about the increasing orientation of American adolescents toward the peer group and away from adults are generally fueled by rhetoric rather than hard evidence. Many social commentators had suggested that peer groups had become more and more powerful during the late 1960s, but much of this was speculation. One study, however, looked at this issue directly, by contrasting the peer orientation of young people at three different points in time. Identical questionnaires assessing how much adolescents looked to their parents and friends for advice on a range of issues were given to groups of teenagers from the same community in 1963, 1976, and 1982 (Sebald, 1986). As might have been predicted, between 1963 and 1976 adolescents became more oriented toward their peers and less toward their parents. Between 1976 and 1982, however, this trend reversed itself somewhat, as adolescents' orientation toward their peers diminished. During this later period, boys' orientation toward their parents increased, but girls' continued to decline, although at a less dramatic rate.

Interestingly, this period of heightened peer orientation during the late 1960s coincided with a time during which several politically oriented youth movements were prominent and visible in the media (Braungart, 1979). Similarly, the decline in peer orientation during the 1970s occurred during a time of a notable decline in youth activism. One might speculate that adolescents' orientation toward peers may ebb and flow with the prominence of youth movements. If this is the case, peer orientation probably was stronger in the late 1980s than during the late 1970s because political activism among youth appeared to increase earlier in the 1980s. As B. Bradford Brown (1990), an

Studies show that in most high schools, athletic and social success are more reliable routes to popularity with peers than is academic success. *(Polly Brown/Picture Cube)*

expert on adolescent peer groups, has noted, the nature and strength of adolescent peer influence varies a great deal from one historical period to the next. We must be cautious about generalizing images of adolescent peer pressure derived from one point in time to all generations of young people.

These cautions notwithstanding, it seems obvious to even the most casual observer that peers play a more important role in the lives of adolescents in modern society than they did in previous eras. But has the rise of adolescent peer groups in modern society really been the cause of so many problems? Unfortunately, this question is very difficult to answer. While it is true that age segregation has increased over the last fifty years, society has changed in other ways during this same time—ways that may also have contributed to increases in such problems as crime and drug use. Adolescents are pressured to grow up faster today than they were fifty years ago (Elkind, 1982). In many regards, the world is a far more stressful place to grow up in now than it was in the past. Families move every few years. Divorce is commonplace. The economy seems to change from month to month, and competition to get a good job is fierce. Is it any wonder that problems such as suicide and alcohol abuse are on the rise?

To be sure, contemporary adolescents spend more *time* in peer groups than adolescents did in past eras. But we do not know if today's young people are any more susceptible to the influence of their friends than their counterparts were previously, nor do we know if teenagers are any worse off because peer groups have come to play a more prominent role in modern society. In fact, studies of peer pressure indicate that most teenagers feel that their friends are likely to pressure them *not* to use drugs or engage in sexual activity. Adolescents do, however, report a good deal of pressure to drink alcohol, and this pressure increases during the adolescent years (Brown, Clasen, and Eicher, 1986). Adolescents exert both positive and negative influences on each other, and it is incorrect to describe the peer group as a monolithic, negative influence. Indeed, some theorists have suggested that peer groups are inevitable and *necessary* byproducts of modernization. Let's now take a look at their point of view.

## THE NEED FOR PEER GROUPS IN MODERN SOCIETY

In less industrialized societies, political, economic, and social institutions revolve around the family. Your occupation, your choice of a spouse, your place of residence, your treatment under society's laws, and your participation in governing the community are all tied to who your relatives are. Individuals' family ties determine whom they can trade with and how much they pay for various commodities. In short, how adults are expected to behave depends on which family they come from.

Because all adults are not expected to behave in the same way in these kinship-based societies, it is not possible to educate or social-

ize all young people in one large group, because they all have to learn somewhat different sets of norms. When norms for behavior vary from person to person they are called **particularistic norms.** Suppose, for example, that the rules for driving were particularistic—that the rules of the road were different for every person. Perhaps people from families who had lived in the community for a long time would be allowed to drive at 75 miles an hour, but people from families who were new to the area would have to drive at 55. Under a particularistic system such as this, having driver education courses for high school students wouldn't make much sense, because each student would have to learn a different set of rules.

In societies in which norms are particularistic, grouping adolescents by age and sending them off to school is not effective strategy for socializing them for adulthood, since their family ties, not their age, determine what their rights and responsibilities are. The socialization of adolescents in kinship-based societies is best accomplished in family groups, where elders can pass on the values and norms particular to the family to their younger relatives.

In contemporary societies, things are quite different. Modernization has eroded much of the family's importance as a political, social, and economic unit. Generally speaking, in modern society, all individuals are expected to learn the same set of norms, because the rules governing behavior apply equally to all members of the community. These norms are called **universalistic norms.** When you walk into a department store to buy something or when you go into a voting booth to vote, it generally makes no difference who your relatives are. Whom you are permitted to marry, what kind of work you do, where you live, and how you are treated under the law are not based on family lineage. The norms that apply to you apply to everyone.

Under these circumstances, it is not wise to limit the socialization of adolescents to the family, because doing so does not ensure that all youngsters will learn the same set of norms. In societies that require individuals to learn universalistic norms, it is more efficient to group by age all of the individuals who are to be socialized together (Eisenstadt, 1956). Teaching is better done in schools than left up to individual families. One of the reasons we have driver education classes, for example, is that our rules for driving are universalistic—the same for everyone—and we need to make sure that individuals learn a common set of regulations, not simply the ones their parents teach them.

As the family has become a less important political and economic institution, universalistic norms have come to replace particularistic ones. And this has required a change in the way in which adolescents are prepared for adulthood. Modernization has not just created age groups—it has made them absolutely *necessary*. Without systematic age grouping in schools, it would be impossible to prepare young people for adulthood. And because age grouping in schools carries over into activities outside of school, the need for universal, school-based education has created age-segregated peer groups.

Some theorists do not see this as a bad thing. They feel that as society has become more technologically advanced, adolescents have come to play a valuable role in preparing one another for adulthood. According to the anthropologist Margaret Mead (1978), the way in which young people are best socialized for adulthood depends on how fast their society is changing. In some cultures, cultural change is so slow that what a child needs to know to function as an adult changes very little over time. Mead called these **postfigurative cultures.** In postfigurative cultures, the socialization of young people is accomplished almost exclusively through contact between children and their elders, because the way in which older generations have lived is almost identical

to the way in which subsequent generations will live.

Imagine, for a moment, growing up in a world in which you had to know only what your grandparents knew in order to survive. In this age of computers, video discs, robotics, and space shuttles, growing up in a world in which very little changes in fifty years seems almost impossible to imagine. Fifty years ago, television had barely been on the market. Yet strange as it may seem to us now, most societies until fairly recently have been postfigurative—and they still are in much of the developing world. In other words, until fairly recently, adolescents could learn what they needed to know to be successful adults exclusively from their elders.

During the past 100 years, contemporary societies have shifted away from being postfigurative cultures. They have become **cofigurative cultures.** In cofigurative cultures, the socialization of young people is accomplished not merely through contact between children and their elders but through contact between people of the same age. In cofigurative cultures, society changes so quickly that much of what parents are able to teach their children may be outdated by the time their children become adults. Today, we live in a cofigurative society. For adolescents in contemporary America, peers have become role models as important as parents and grandparents. As a result, adolescents increasingly need to turn to members of their own generation for advice, guidance, and information.

If you were a teenager living in a postfigurative culture, you might ask your grandfather for advice on how to hunt or farm. But if you were a teenager in today's cofigurative culture, to whom would you turn for advice on how to use a computer—your friends, who probably have grown up with computers in their homes and schools, or your grandparents, who may never even have seen a computer?

Mead believed that as society became even

In postfigurative societies, cultural change is slow. As a result, the socialization and education of adolescents is performed almost exclusively by their elders. In cofigurative societies, such as ours, where cultural change takes place at a faster rate, much of the socialization and education of adolescents is performed by peers. *(George Bellerose/Stock, Boston) (Harry Wilkes/Stock, Boston)*

more rapidly changing, cofigurative cultures would be replaced by **prefigurative cultures,** in which young people would become adults' teachers. We already may be living in a prefigurative culture. Instead of parents asking, "Why can't Johnny read?" teenagers ask, "Why can't Mom and Dad program the VCR?"

Do these analyses mean that the adolescents of the future will cease to profit from having close relationships with adults? Of course not. Young people will always need the support, affection, and advice of their elders. But understanding how peer groups have been made necessary by modernization casts the issue of age segregation in a new light. Despite what-

ever problems may have been caused by the rise of peer groups in contemporary society, there may be little we can do to make adolescent peer groups less prominent.

## AFTER-SCHOOL ACTIVITIES AND ADOLESCENT PEER GROUPS: THE "LATCHKEY" PROBLEM

Adults' concerns about the problems associated with adolescent age-segregation change from era to era. During the 1960s, adults worried that the separation of young from old had given rise to "antiestablishment" political ideas. During the 1970s, concerns were not so much about the youth culture's politics, but its morals (or lack of them), as adults were alarmed by young people's apparent tolerance for drug use and their permissive attitudes toward sex. (Forget, for the time being, that *adults* became more tolerant toward drugs and permissive toward sex during the 1970s, too.) During the past decade, the segregation of young people from their elders has once again emerged as a social issue warranting media attention (e.g., Baker and Gore, 1989; Goleman, 1988). This time the concern is couched in debates about so-called "latchkey" youngsters.

As noted earlier, changes in patterns of work and family life have resulted in a large number of young people who are not supervised by their parents after school. While some of these youngsters are involved in school- or community-based programs that provide adult supervision, others spend their after-school hours away from adults, in their homes, with friends, or simply "hanging out" in neighborhoods and shopping malls. Psychologists have debated whether these latchkey youth are profiting from these opportunities for self-management (e.g., Rodman et al., 1985, 1988) or potentially heading for trouble (Long and Long, 1983).

The answer is complicated. In general, most studies show that children who care for themselves after school are not different from their peers when it comes to psychological development, school achievement, and self-conceptions (e.g., Galambos and Garbarino, 1985; Rodman et al., 1985; Vandell and Corasaniti, 1988). These studies argue against the view that having to care for oneself contributes in positive ways to the development of self-reliance or personal responsibility. In addition, several studies suggest that latchkey children are more likely to be involved in problem behavior and use more drugs and alcohol than children who are supervised after school by adults (Galambos and Maggs, in press; Richardson et al., 1989; Steinberg, 1986). Taken together, these studies seem to suggest that

latchkey arrangements may have more costs than benefits.

One limitation of studies on latchkey youth is that they typically lump together all children who take care of themselves after school, even though there are important differences *within* the latchkey population (Steinberg, 1986). Several studies that have recognized these differences have shown, for example, that the setting in which an adolescent cares for him- or herself makes a difference: Latchkey youngsters who go straight home after school are far less likely to engage in problem behavior than their peers who go to a friend's house or who just "hang out" (Galambos and Maggs, in press; Steinberg, 1986). In addition, these same studies find that latchkey youngsters who are raised in an "authoritative" style by their parents (as we saw in Chapter 4, authoritative parents are warm but firm) and who are monitored by their parents from a distance—via telephone check-ins, for example—are no more susceptible to problem behavior than are children whose parents are home with them.

Taken together, these studies suggest that while latchkey after-school arrangements probably do not hold great benefits for youngsters, they need not cause problems, either. Experts advise parents of school-age youngsters to help make sure the experience is not harmful by providing clear instructions about the child's after-school activities and whereabouts, asking the child to check in with an adult as soon as he or she gets home, and teaching the child how to handle emergencies, should they arise (Steinberg and Levine, 1990).

## The Nature of Adolescent Peer Groups

### CHANGES IN PEER GROUPS DURING ADOLESCENCE

Visit any elementary school playground and you will readily see that peer groups are an important feature of the social world of child-hood. But even though peer groups exist well before adolescence, during the teenage years they change in significance and structure. Four specific developments stand out (Brown, 1990).

First, as we noted earlier, there is a sharp increase during adolescence in the sheer amount of time individuals spend with their peers and in the relative time they spend in the company of peers versus adults. If we count school as being a setting in which adolescents are mainly with agemates, well over half of the typical adolescent's waking hours are spent with peers, as opposed to only 15% with adults—including parents (a good deal of the remaining time is spent alone or with a combination of adults and agemates). When asked to list the people in their life who are most important to them—what psychologists call their **significant others**—nearly half of the people adolescents mention are people of the same age. By sixth grade, adults other than parents account for less than 25 percent of the typical adolescent's **social network**—the people he or she interacts with most regularly. And among early-maturing teenagers, this figure is only about 10 percent (Brown, 1990).

Second, during adolescence, peer groups function much more often without adult supervision than they do during childhood (Brown, 1990). Groups of children typically play where adults are present, or in activities that are organized or supervised by adults (e.g., Little League, Brownies), whereas adolescents are granted far more independence. A group of teenagers may go off to the mall on their own, or to the movies, or will deliberately congregate at the home of someone whose parents are out.

Third, during adolescence increasingly more contact with peers is with opposite-sex friends. During childhood, peer groups are highly sex-segregated, a phenomenon known as **sex cleavage.** This is especially true of chil-dren's peer activities in school and other settings organized by adults, although somewhat less so of their more informal activities, such as neighborhood play (Maccoby, 1988). During adolescence, however, an increasingly larger proportion of an individual's "significant others" are opposite-sex peers, even in public settings (Brown, 1990). As we shall see in a later section, this movement toward opposite sex peers seems to stimulate changes in the structure of the peer group.

Finally, whereas children's peer relationships are limited mainly to pairs of friends and relatively small groups—three or four children at a time, for example—adolescence marks the emergence of larger collectives of peers, or "crowds." (Adolescents still have close friendships, of course, which we shall look at in Chapter 10.) In junior high school cafeterias, for example, the "popular" crowd sits in one section of the room, the "brains" in another, and the "druggies" in yet a third (see Eder, 1985). These crowds typically develop their own minicultures, which include particular styles of dressing, talking, and behaving. Studies show that it is not until early adolescence that individuals can confidently list the different crowds that characterize their schools and reliably describe the stereotypes that distinguish the different crowds from each other (Brown, 1990).

These changes in peer relations have their origins in the biological, cognitive, and social transitions of adolescence. Puberty, as we have seen, stimulates adolescents' interest in opposite-sex relationships and serves to distance them from their parents, which helps to explain why adolescents' social networks increasingly include more opposite-sex peers and fewer adults. The cognitive changes of adolescence permit a more sophisticated understanding of social relationships, an understanding which may allow the sort of abstract categorization that leads to grouping individuals into crowds. And changes in social definition may stimulate changes in peer relations as a sort of adaptive response: The larger, more anonymous social setting of the secondary school, for instance, may force adolescents to seek out individuals whom they perceive as having common interests and values, perhaps as a way of recreating the smaller, more intimate groups of childhood (Brown, 1990). Instead of floundering in a large, impersonal high school cafeteria, the adolescent who belongs to the "cheerleader" crowd, or even the "nerds," may head directly for her or his place at a familiar table.

## CLIQUES AND CROWDS

In order to better understand the significance of peer relations during adolescence, it is helpful to think of adolescents' peer groups as organized around two related, but different, structures (Brown, 1990). **Cliques** are small groups of between two and twelve individuals—the average is about five or six—generally of the same sex and, of course, age (Dunphy, 1975; Hollingshead, 1949/1975). Cliques can be defined by common activities (e.g., the "drama" group, a group of students who study together regularly, etc.) or simply by friendship (e.g., a group of girls who have lunch together every day or a group of boys who have known each other for a long time). The importance of the clique, whatever its basis, is that it provides the main social context in which adolescents *interact* with each other. The clique is the social setting in which adolescents "hang out," talk to each other, and form close friendships. Some cliques are more open to outsiders than others (i.e., the members are less "cliquish"), but virtually all cliques are small enough so that the members feel that they know each other well and appreciate each other more than people outside the clique do (Brown, 1990).

Cliques are quite different in structure and purpose than **crowds.** Crowds are "large, *rep-utation-based* collectives of similarly stereotyped individuals who may or may not spend much time together" (Brown, 1990, p. 177). In contemporary American high schools, typical crowds are "jocks," "brains," "nerds," "populars," "druggies," and so on. The labels for these crowds may vary from school to school ("jocks" versus "sportos," "populars" versus "preppies"), but their generic presence is commonplace, and you can probably recognize these different types of crowds from your own school experience. In contrast to cliques, crowds are not settings for adolescents' intimate interactions or friendships, but, instead, serve to locate the adolescent (to himself and to others) within the social structure of the school. As well, the crowds themselves tend to form a sort of social hierarchy or map of the school, and different crowds are seen as having different degrees of status or importance.

Membership in a crowd is based mainly on reputation and stereotype, rather than on actual friendship or social interaction. This is very different from membership in a clique, which, by definition, hinges on shared activity and friendship. In concrete terms—and perhaps ironically—an adolescent does not have to actually have "brains" as friends, or to hang around with "brainy" students, to be a member of the "brain" crowd. If he dresses like a "brain," acts like a "brain," and takes honors courses, then he is a "brain," as far as his crowd membership goes. The fact that crowd membership is based on reputation and stereotype can be very difficult for individual adolescents, who may find themselves stuck in a crowd that they do not wish to belong to (or that they do not see themselves as a part of).

The extent to which crowds are viewed in stereotypic terms is illustrated vividly in Figure 5.3. As you can see, "socies" are seen by the vast majority of individuals as dressing stylishly (84 percent agreement), cliquish (86 percent), positive about school (61 percent), very active in school affairs (58 percent), hanging out in

S = Socies     J = Jocks     D = Druggies     T = Toughs     N = Nerds     No = Normals     B = Brains

Dress and grooming

Socializing style

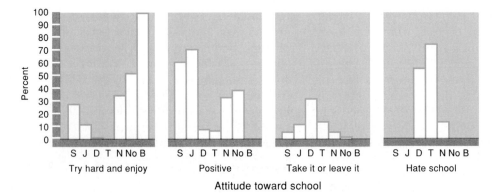

Attitude toward school

**FIGURE 5.3** Degree of agreement about characteristics of various crowds. (Brown, B., Lohr, M., & Trujillo, C. (1983). *Adolescent peer-group stereotypes, member conformity, and identity development.* Paper presented at the meeting of The Society for Research in Child Development, Detroit, MI.)

S = Socies      J = Jocks      D = Druggies      T = Toughs      N = Nerds      No = Normals      B = Brains

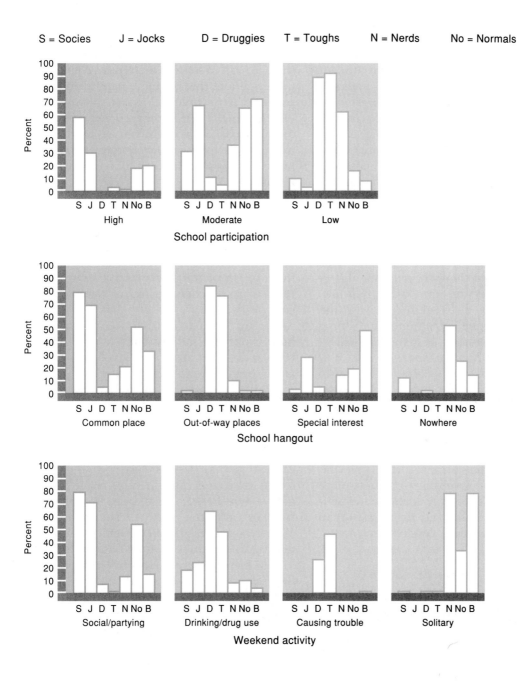

the common areas of the school (81 percent), and partying on weekends (79 percent). "Brains" are stereotyped, but in different ways: They are seen as dressing neatly (55 percent), "not with it" (69 percent), very invested in school (100 percent), moderately active in school affairs (72 percent), hanging out in special-interest settings (49 percent), and spending weekends alone (78 percent). Whether each and every "socie" or "brain" fits these characterizations doesn't really matter. What is more important, perhaps, is that their peers believe that they do.

Psychologists used to believe that crowds were little more than clusters of cliques (e.g., Dunphy, 1963), but they now see these different structures as serving entirely different purposes. Because it is based on activity and friendship, the clique is the important setting in which the adolescent learns social skills— how to be a good friend to someone else, how to communicate with others effectively, how to be a leader, how to enjoy someone else's company, or even how to break off a friendship that is no longer satisfying. These and other social skills are important in adulthood as well as in adolescence. In contrast, because crowds are based on reputation and stereotype, and not interaction, they probably contribute more to the adolescent's sense of identity and self-conceptions—for better and for worse—than to his or her actual social development.

## CHANGES IN CLIQUE AND CROWD STRUCTURE OVER TIME

Studies of the structure of adolescents' peer groups often make use of a research technique called **participant observation.** In this approach, the researcher establishes rapport with a group of individuals in order to infiltrate and eventually join the group. In *Inside High School* (Cusick, 1973), for example, the author pretended to be a newcomer to the community and attended high school for a year to learn

more about the adolescents' social world. As an observer who is also a participant, the researcher can observe the group's behavior under conditions that are more natural and more private than would otherwise be the case. Overhearing a ten-minute conversation in a high school locker room can be more informative than interviewing a student for three hours if the student feels uncomfortable or uneasy.

Observational studies (for example, Dunphy, 1963) of young people indicate that there are important changes in the structure of cliques and crowds during the adolescent years. Although the best research we have on this process of transformation is quite dated, many of the general patterns it reveals ring true today.

During early adolescence, adolescents' activities revolve around same-sex cliques. Adolescents at this stage are not yet involved in parties and typically spend their leisure time with a small group of friends, playing sports, talking, or simply hanging around.

Somewhat later, as boys and girls become more interested in one another—but before dating actually begins—boys' and girls' cliques come together. This is clearly a transitional stage. Boys and girls may go to parties together, but the time they spend there actually involves interaction with peers of the *same* sex. When youngsters are still uncomfortable about dealing with members of the opposite sex, this setting provides an opportunity in which adolescents can learn more about opposite-sex peers without having to be intimate and without having to risk losing face. It is not unusual, for example, at young adolescents' first mixed-sex parties, for groups of boys and girls to position themselves at opposite sides of a room, watching each other but seldom interacting.

The peer group then enters a stage of structural transformation, generally led by the clique leaders. As youngsters become interested in dating, part of the group begins to divide off into mixed-sex cliques, while other individuals remain in the group but in same-sex cliques. The shift into dating is usually led by the clique leaders, with other clique members following along. For instance, a clique of boys whose main activity is riding dirt bikes may discover that one of the guys they look up to has become more interested in going out with girls on Saturday nights than hanging out at the local racing track. Over time, they will begin to follow his lead, and their crowd at the track will become smaller and smaller.

During middle adolescence, mixed-sex cliques become more prevalent. In time, the peer group becomes composed entirely of heterosexual cliques. One clique might consist of the drama students—male and female students who know each other from acting together in school plays. Another might be composed of four girls and four boys who like to drink on the weekends. The staff of the school yearbook might make up a third.

What about those adolescents who are not interested in starting to date or in mixed-sex activities? What happens to them when clique activities begin to change? Many leave the group as its interests turn toward dating, either remaining together in a smaller same-sex clique or forming a few close friendships with same-sex peers. Others are left behind by their peers who are interested in moving on to dating. They may stop getting invitations or telephone calls about weekend activities. Not keeping up with the peer group's transition from same-sex activities into mixed-sex ones is one of the most common reasons for peer rejection during adolescence (Dunphy, 1963).

Finally, during late adolescence, the peer group begins to disintegrate. Pairs of dating adolescents begin to split off from the activities of the larger group. The larger peer group is replaced by loosely associated sets of couples. Couples may go out together from time to time, but the feeling of being in a crowd has disappeared. This pattern—in which the cou-

ple becomes the focus of social activity—persists into adulthood.

When viewed from a structural point of view, the peer group's role in the development of intimacy is quite clear. Over time, the structure of the peer group changes to become more in keeping with adolescents' changing needs and interests. As we shall see in Chapter 10, the adolescent's capacity for close relationships develops first through friendships with peers of the same sex. Only later does intimacy enter into opposite-sex relationships. Thus the structure of the peer group changes during adolescence in a way that parallels the adolescent's development of intimacy: As the adolescent develops increasing facility in close relationships, the peer group moves from the familiarity of same-sex activities to contact with opposite-sex peers but in the safety of the larger group. It is only after adolescent males and females have been slowly socialized into dating roles—primarily by modeling their higher-status peers—that the safety of numbers is no longer needed and adolescents begin pairing off.

There also are changes in adolescents' conceptions of crowds during this time. Many of these changes reflect the growing cognitive sophistication of the adolescent, as we described in Chapter 2. For example, as adolescents mature intellectually, they come to define crowds more in terms of abstract and global characteristics (i.e., "preppies," "nerds," "jocks") than in terms of concrete, behavioral features (i.e., "the ballet crowd," "the Nintendo crowd," "the kids who play basketball on Arcadia Street") (O'Brien and Bierman, 1988). As you know, this shift from concrete to abstract is a general feature of cognitive development in adolescence. In addition, as adolescents become more cognitively capable, they become more consciously aware of the crowd structure of their school and their place in it (Brown, 1990).

As crowds become increasingly more salient influences on adolescents' view of their social

As young people become more interested in opposite-sex relationships, the structure of the adolescent peer group changes. During early adolescence, peer activities typically revolve around same-sex cliques; boys' and girls' cliques may merge, but interaction between the sexes is limited. By late adolescence, large peer groups have begun to break down and are replaced by loosely associated sets of couples. *(George Gardner/Image Works) (Ellis Herwig/Picture Cube)*

world, such crowds come to play an increasingly important role in structuring adolescent social behavior (O'Brien and Bierman, 1988). By ninth grade, there is nearly universal agreement among students in a school about their school's crowd structure, and students' assessment of the strength of peer group influence is very high. Between ninth and twelfth grade, however, the significance of the crowd structure begins to decline, and the salience of peer pressure wanes. As we shall see in Chapter 9, this pattern of an increase and then a decline in the salience of peer crowds parallels developmental changes in adolescents' susceptibility to peer pressure. In other words, as crowds become more important in defining the teenager's social world—between early and middle adolescence—adolescents become more likely to accede to their influence. As crowds become less important, however—between middle adolescence and late adolescence—their influence over the individual adolescent's behavior weakens as well (Brown, 1990; Gavin and Furman, 1989).

Just as the changes in the structure of cliques play a role in the development of intimacy during adolescence, changes in the salience of crowds over the adolescent years play an important role in adolescent identity development. In Chapter 8, we shall see that adolescence is frequently a time for experimentation with different roles and identities. During the early adolescent years, before the adolescent has "found" himself, the crowd provides an important basis for self-definition (Newman and Newman, 1976). By locating himself within the crowd structure of his school—through his style of dress, language, or choice of hangouts—an adolescent wears a "badge" that says, "This is who I am." At a time when he may not actually know just "who" he is, associating with a crowd provides the adolescent with a rudimentary sense of identity.

As the adolescent becomes more secure about her identity as an individual, however,

the need for affiliation with a crowd diminishes. Indeed, by the time she has reached high school, the older adolescent is likely to feel that remaining a part of a crowd *stifles* her sense of identity and self-expression (Larkin, 1979; Varenne, 1982). The breakup of the larger peer group in late adolescence may both foreshadow and reflect the emergence of each adolescent's unique and coherent sense of self (Brown, 1990).

## *Adolescents and Their Crowds*

### THE SOCIAL MAP OF ADOLESCENCE

We noted earlier that the idea of a single "youth culture" has not held up very well in research conducted since the publication of *The Adolescent Society* some thirty years ago. Most ethnographic studies of high schools indicate that the social world of adolescents is far more multifaceted than this (e.g., Cusick, 1973). (An **ethnography** is an observational study in which the researcher spends time in a natural setting, such as high school, and records detailed field notes describing individuals' behavior and interactions. Ethnographic techniques are widely used by anthropologists in their studies of other cultures.) One helpful scheme for mapping the social world of adolescent crowds was suggested by Rigsby and McDill (1975) and later modified by Brown (1990).

According to this model, adolescents' crowds can be placed along two dimensions: how involved they are in the institutions controlled by adults, such as school and extracurricular activities; and how involved they are in the informal, peer culture. (See Figure 5.4). "Jocks" and "populars," for example, are quite involved in the peer culture, but they are also very involved in the institutions valued by adults (sports and school organizations, for ex-

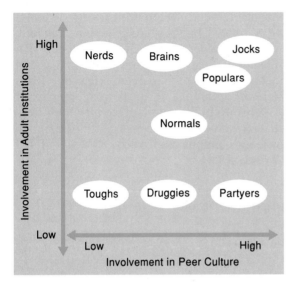

**FIGURE 5.4** A model for mapping the social world of adolescent peer groups. (From Brown, 1990)

amount about the individual's behavior and values. This is because crowds contribute to the definition of norms and standards for such things as clothing, leisure, and tastes in music. Being a jock means more than simply being involved in athletics. Jocks wear certain types of clothes, listen to certain types of music, spend Saturday nights in certain hangouts, and use a particular slang when they talk. They accept many of the values of the adults around them but also value many elements of the contemporary peer culture.

Another way of putting this is that adolescents' crowds serve as **reference groups.** They provide their members with an identity in the eyes of *other* adolescents. Adolescents judge one another on the basis of the company they keep. Individuals become branded on the basis of whom they hang around with. Such labels as "jocks," "brains," "socies," "druggies," and "leathers" serve as shorthand notations—accurate or inaccurate—to describe what someone is like as a person and what he or she holds as important.

Crowd membership is important not only because crowds are used by adolescents when talking about one another, but also because membership in a crowd is often the basis for an adolescent's own identity. A girl who runs with the "preppies" identifies herself as a "preppy" by wearing the preppy "uniform," shopping in the preppy stores, and speaking the preppy language. After a while, "preppiness" becomes a part of her own self-concept; she wouldn't think of dressing or talking in a different way. Or consider the boys whose clique is held together because none of them likes school. By having their attitude toward school continually reinforced by one another, the boys' feelings about school become strengthened, and not liking school becomes a part of each boy's identity. Even if something very positive happens at school, it becomes difficult for someone in the clique to admit that it makes him feel good about himself. Doing

ample). "Brains" and "nerds," in contrast, are also involved in adult-controlled organizations (in their case, academics) but tend to be less involved in the peer culture. "Partyers" are on the opposite side of the map from "nerds": these adolescents are very involved in the peer culture but not involved in adult institutions. "Toughs" and adolescents who are members of delinquent gangs are not involved in either the peer culture or adult institutions. Other crowds, such as "normals" or "druggies" fall somewhere between these extremes. This conceptualization points to an important limitation of Coleman's view of a monolithic adolescent society: His description of adolescents as fun-loving and antiestablishment accurately described *one segment* of the adolescent society—a segment known in some schools as "partyers"—but not all young people in general.

## CROWDS AS REFERENCE GROUPS

Knowing where an adolescent fits into the social system of the school can often tell us a fair well on a test or receiving a compliment from a teacher is likely to be dismissed as unimportant.

Because the adolescent's peer group plays such an important role as a reference group and a source of identity, the nature of the crowd with which an adolescent affiliates is likely to have an important influence on his or her behavior, activities, and self-conceptions. Psychologist B. Bradford Brown and his colleagues have studied how peer group membership—that is, *which* peer group the adolescent affiliates with—may affect the adolescent's development and behavior. Although most adolescents feel pressure from their friends to behave in ways that are consistent with their crowd's values and goals, the specific nature of the pressure varies from one crowd to another. Adolescents who are part of the druggie crowd report much more peer pressure to engage in misconduct, for example, than do adolescents from the jock crowd (Clasen and Brown, 1985).

Crowd membership can also affect the way adolescents feel about themselves. Adolescents' self-estem is higher among students who are identified with peer groups that have relatively more status in their school. In the high schools that Brown has studied, the "jocks" and "socies" are highest in status, the "druggies" and "toughs" lowest. Students who were identified with the jock or socie group had higher self-esteem than those identified with the druggie or tough group (Brown and Lohr, 1987). As the authors wrote, "Crowds are not merely fertile grounds for bolstering self-esteem through identity testing or building supportive social relationships. Crowd labels also provide one feedback on one's comparative standing among peers, which in turn may enhance or depreciate self-esteem" (1987, p. 53).

Researchers do not yet know how the social structure of adolescent crowds differs for minority and nonminority adolescents, because most of the research to date has been conducted in predominantly white high schools.

There is some evidence, however, that in racially integrated high schools, the adolescents may divide first across ethnic lines, and then, into the more familiar adolescent crowds within ethnic groups. Thus, in a large urban high school there may be separate groups of African-American jocks and White jocks, Hispanic-American populars and African-American populars, and so on. Interestingly, in multiethnic schools, adolescents from one ethnic group are less likely to see crowd distinctions within other ethnic groups than they are in their own group. Thus, to white students all Asian-American adolescents are part of the "Asian" crowd, whereas the Asian-American students see themselves as divided into "brains," "populars," and so on (Brown and Mounts, 1989).

There is also reason to believe that the meaning associated with belonging to different crowds may vary between ethnic groups. According to one team of researchers, for example, in predominantly African-American high schools, adolescents who are in the "brain" crowd are ridiculed (Fordham and Ogbu, 1986). In the inner-city schools they studied, students who were high achievers were labeled "brainiacs" and ostracized for "acting white." Similarly, in some schools it may be admirable to be a "jock," while in others it may be frowned upon. Thus, the values we associate with being in one crowd as opposed to another may not be constant across all school contexts.

## Adolescents and Their Cliques

What draws adolescents into one clique and not another? What factors influence who forms cliques with whom? Because cliques serve as a basis for adolescents' friendships and play an important role in their social development, many researchers have studied the determinants of clique composition.

## SIMILARITY AS THE BASIS FOR CLIQUE COMPOSITION

The most important influence on the composition of cliques is similarity. Adolescents' cliques typically are composed of people who are the same age, the same race, from the same socioeconomic background, and at least during early and middle adolescence, of the same sex.

**Age segregation**   Age grouping in junior and senior high schools makes having friends who are substantially older or younger unlikely. A tenth-grader who is enrolled in tenth-grade English, tenth-grade math, tenth-grade history, and tenth-grade science simply does not have many opportunities to meet adolescents who are in different grades. Age segregation in adolescents' cliques does indeed appear to be due mostly to the structure of schools (Shrum et al., 1988). When an adolescent's friends come from a different school, those friends are just as likely to be younger or older as they are to come from the same grade (Blyth, Hill, and Thiel, 1982).

**Sex segregation**   During the early and middle adolescent years, cliques also tend to be composed of adolescents of the same sex. This so-called **sex cleavage** begins in childhood and continues through most of the adolescent years, although the sex cleavage is stronger among white students than among black students (Hallinan, 1981; Sagar et al., 1983) and weakens later in adolescence (Shrum et al., 1988). The causes of sex segregation in adolescents' cliques are more interesting than the causes of age segregation, because schools do not separate boys and girls into different classes. Why, then, do adolescent males and females separate themselves into different cliques?

First, cliques are formed largely on the basis of shared activities and interests. Generally speaking, preadolescent and early adolescent boys and girls are interested in different things. It is not until adolescents begin dating that boys' cliques and girls' cliques mix, presumably because dating provides a basis for common activity.

A second reason for the sex cleavage in adolescent peer groups concerns young adolescents' sensitivity about sex roles. Over the course of childhood, boys and girls become increasingly concerned about behaving in ways that are judged to be sex-appropriate. When boys show an interest in dolls, they are often told either explicitly, by parents, friends, and teachers, or implicitly, by television, books, and other mass media, "Little boys don't play with dolls. Those are for girls." And when girls start wrestling or roughhousing, they are often reprimanded and told to "act like ladies."

As a consequence of these continual reminders that there are boys' activities and girls' activities, early adolescents—who are trying to establish a sense of identity—are very concerned about acting in sex-appropriate ways. This makes it very difficult for an adolescent girl to be part of a boys' clique, whose activities are likely to be dominated by athletics and other physical activities, and for a boy to be a part of a girls' clique, whose activities are likely to revolve around clothing, grooming, and talking about boys (Schofield, 1981). Adolescents who go against prevailing sex-role norms by forming friendships with members of the opposite sex may be teased about being "faggots" or ostracized by their peers because they are "strange." Ironically, once dating becomes the norm, adolescents who *don't* have relationships with peers of the opposite sex become the objects of equally strong suspicion and social rejection.

**Social class segregation**   One of the most important studies ever undertaken of adolescents' peer groups is *Elmtown's Youth* (1949/1975). In this study of adolescents in the midwestern community of "Elmtown," sociologist August Hollingshead examined the relation between the social position of adolescents' families and the composition of teenagers' cliques. He was interested in determining whether adolescents' cliques were segregated along class lines.

Hollingshead used such indicators as income, residence, and reputation in the community to sort families into five different **social class** groups. In the highest class were families who were very affluent, lived in the best neighborhoods, and were known in the community as powerful and respected families. These "upper-class" families had lived in the community for a long time and belonged to all the exclusive clubs and organizations. In the "lower class" were families who were poor, lived on the "wrong" side of town, and were not highly thought of in the community. In between these extremes were three groups of families: the hard-working but not very well off "working-class" families; the comfortable but not especially affluent "middle-class" families; and the "upper-middle-class" families, who had money but did not quite have the reputation and prestige of the families in the highest class.

Hollingshead found that adolescents do in fact associate chiefly with peers from the same social class. More than 60 percent of each adolescent's close friendships in Elmtown High School were between teenagers from the same background. Of the remaining clique relationships, the vast majority were between adolescents of adjacent social classes (for example, "middle-class" adolescents with "upper-middle-class" adolescents). Almost never did adolescents from one social class associate with students from a class that was two steps higher or lower (see Figure 5.5).

Hollingshead found similar patterns when he looked at adolescents' best friends and dating relationships: Rarely were social class lines

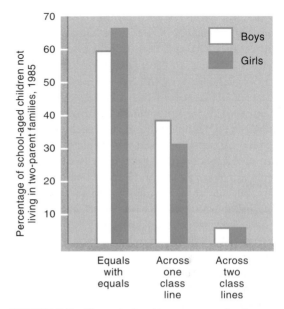

**FIGURE 5.5**  The majority of teenagers are in cliques with adolescents from the same socioeconomic background. Virtually no cliques cross two class lines. (Hollingshead, 1949/1975)

crossed, and when they were, it was virtually always between adolescents of adjacent classes. Moreover, adolescents became even more class conscious as they got older.

Social class was also important in shaping the status hierarchy of the school. Hollingshead asked the adolescents to list those students who were the leaders in extracurricular and social activities and those who were shunned by most of their classmates. Over 40 percent of the leaders came from the two highest social classes, even though only 9 percent of the student body were from these social groups. Only 14 percent of the leaders came from the two lowest classes, even though over half the students in the school were from these social groups. And adolescents from the lower classes were far more likely to be among those who were shunned—in fact, students from the two lowest classes constituted virtually all of this group.

Several other studies conducted since the time of *Elmtown's Youth* have confirmed the importance of social class in influencing an adolescent's status in the peer group of the high school. But subsequent research has shown the pattern to be somewhat different from that suggested by Hollingshead. In *The Adolescent Society* (1961), the study on the "youth culture" of ten different high schools discussed earlier, James Coleman also looked at some of the same questions examined in *Elmtown's Youth*. Overall, as in "Elmtown," adolescents from wealthier backgrounds were proportionately more likely to occupy leadership positions in their schools. The student government leaders, the team captains, the presidents of different clubs and activities, and the students who were in the leading crowd usually came from the more affluent families. But this pattern was more characteristic of some schools than others. Specifically, Coleman found that the dominance of high school activities by middle- and upper-middle-class students is most likely to occur in communities with a high proportion of middle- and upper-middle-class families. In communities dominated by working-class families, however, middle-class adolescents have less of an advantage over the other students. In this respect, then, the social structure of the high school mirrors the social structure of the broader community in which the high school is found.

This finding has important implications for understanding how the location of an adolescent's school can have an impact on his or her social life and psychosocial development. A youngster from a poor family probably has less of a chance to become a leader in a middle-class school than in a school located in a working-class or poor neighborhood. Opportunities to develop responsibility, leadership skills, and self-confidence are more restricted for poor youngsters than they are for their affluent peers, particularly in schools dominated by middle-class families.

**Race segregation**   Race is not a strong determinant of clique composition during childhood, but like social class, it becomes increasingly powerful as youngsters get older (Shrum et al., 1988). By middle and late adolescence, adolescents' peer groups typically are racially segregated. This appears to be the case, although somewhat less so, even within desegregated schools (Schofield, 1981).

There are several explanations for racial separation in adolescents' peer groups. First, because adolescents' cliques are often segregated along socioeconomic lines, peer groups that appear to be segregated because of race actually may be separated on the basis of class, since disproportionately higher numbers of minority youngsters come from economically poorer families. This explanation helps to account for the race cleavage in desegregated schools, which often bring together youngsters not only of different racial backgrounds but from varying economic backgrounds and neighborhoods as well. Even among adolescents who do have cross-racial friendships at school, few report seeing that friend outside of school (Dubois and Hirsch, 1990).

Another reason for the strong racial split in adolescents' cliques appears to be the differential levels of academic achievement of white and black adolescents (Schofield, 1981). Adolescents who are friends usually have similar attitudes toward school, similar educational aspirations, and similar school achievement levels (Berndt, 1982). Racial differences in school achievement may lead to racial separation in adolescent peer groups through tracking and other mechanisms (Hallinan and Williams, 1989).

A third reason, according to one study of adolescents in a recently desegregated school, is attitudinal. In this school, the white adolescents perceived their black peers as aggressive, threatening, and hostile. The black students felt that the white students were conceited, prejudiced, and unwilling to be friends with

Generally speaking, peer groups become more racially segregated as individuals get older. Adolescents' peer groups, for example, are more segregated than are those of children. *(Spencer Grant/Picture Cube)*

them. These perceptions, which fed on each other, made the formation of interracial peer groups unlikely. The more the white students felt that the black students were hostile, the more the white students acted distant and kept to themselves. But the more the white students acted this way, the more likely the black students were to feel rejected, and the more hostile they became. In many schools, adolescents' lack of familiarity with youngsters from other racial groups results in misperceptions of the others' attitudes and motives, and this misunderstanding limits interracial interaction (Schofield, 1981). In general, white students are less apt to initiate contact with black students than vice versa (Sagan et al., 1983).

One way out of this cycle of misunderstanding is to bring white and black youngsters together from an early age, before they have had time to build up prejudices and stereotypes.

Interracial school busing, for example, has been far more successful in communities that began such programs during elementary school than in districts that implemented them for the first time at the high school level. If white and black children grow up together from an early age, they are less likely to misunderstand each other and less likely to go off into separate peer groups purely on the basis of race.

## SHARED INTERESTS AS A BASIS FOR CLIQUE FORMATION

Thus far we have seen that adolescents' cliques are usually composed of adolescents who are the same age, in the same grade in school, from the same social class, and of the same race. But what about factors beyond these? Do adolescents who associate with one another also share

# THE SEXES: WHY ARE THERE SEX DIFFERENCES IN INTERRACIAL CONTACT?

Two findings from studies of adolescent peer groups emerge over and over again. First, a strong "sex cleavage" limits the interaction between adolescent boys and girls—at least, until dating begins. And second, adolescents have very little contact with peers from other races, even when they attend desegregated schools that have been developed to increase cross-racial interaction.

One curiosity that has been uncovered, as noted in this chapter, is that, although the "race cleavage" seems to characterize boys' as well as girls' interaction, it is much stronger among adolescent girls than boys. Specifically, although boys and girls alike are likely to interact more often with adolescents of the same race, the likelihood of white boys interacting with black boys is much greater than the likelihood of white girls interacting with black girls. Indeed, several studies suggest that cliques of young-adolescent black girls are among the most socially isolated of all adolescent groups (Damico and Sparks, 1986). This isolation seems to work both ways: White students of both sexes are less likely to talk to black girls than to any other group, and black girls are less likely than any other group to initiate contact with whites.

No one is quite sure why black females face this predicament, but at least three hypotheses may be offered. One researcher has suggested that a special tension exists between white and black girls that does not exist between white and black boys (Schofield, 1982). She suggests that as sex and romance become more important during early adolescence, students become increasingly competitive for the attention of opposite-sex students. Although both boys and girls seek this attention, it may be more important for girls, who may rely more on the prestige derived from dating popular boys as an index of their social status in school. Boys, in contrast, may look to athletics more for status and may be slightly less concerned about getting the attention of girls in their classes. The heightened concern for male attention introduces a greater level of competition into adolescent girls' social relations, and this competition may underlie white and black girls' reluctance to interact.

An alternative explanation concerns the special role that white girls may play in the communication network of the school. One team of researchers (Damico and Sparks, 1986) has suggested that from an early age white girls try to develop personalized relationships with their teachers. By junior high school, these girls may have become an important source of "inside information" for students in the school about teachers and classes. Thus white girls may find themselves more centrally located within the school's social network than black girls. Black girls may receive fewer social overtures from other students because they are perceived as less tied into the school's network.

Finally, sex differences in the degree to which peer interaction is racially segregated may be based in differences between the activity patterns of girls and boys in general. As you will read in Chapter 10, adolescent boys are more likely than girls to spend time in large group activities, such as sports, and girls are more likely to spend time talking in pairs or in small groups. The large group activities of boys may simply provide greater opportunities for cross-racial interaction to take place—as when white and black students are on the same team, for example. In contrast, the focus of adolescent girls on more intimate peer relations may make them less likely to interact with individuals whom they perceive—correctly or not—to have different values and norms for behavior. In other words, sex differences in the structure of adolescent peer activities may make cross-racial contact easier for boys than girls.

certain interests and activities? Generally speaking, they do. Two factors appear to be especially important in determining adolescent clique membership and friendship patterns: orientation toward school and orientation toward the teen culture. These factors parallel those that distinguish crowds from each other, as we discussed earlier.

**Orientation toward school**    Adolescents and their friends tend to be similar in their attitudes toward school, in their school achievement, and in their educational plans (Berndt, 1982; Epstein, 1983b). Adolescents who earn high grades, study a great deal, and plan to go on to college usually have friends who share these activities and aspirations. One reason for this is that how much time a student devotes to schoolwork affects his or her involvement in other activities. Someone who is always studying will not have many friends who are out late at night partying, because the two activities conflict. By the same token, someone who wants to spend afternoons and evenings out having fun will find it difficult to remain friends with someone who prefers to stay home and study. Students also may influence each other's academic performance. Given two students with similar records of past achievement, the student whose friends do better in school is likely to achieve more than the student whose friends do worse (Epstein, 1983).

**Orientation toward the teen culture**    Adolescents and their friends generally listen to the same type of music, dress similarly, spend their leisure time in similar types of activities, and have similar patterns of drug use (Berndt, 1982). It would be very unlikely, for example, for a "jock" and a "druggie" to be part of the same clique, because their interests and attitudes are so different. In most high schools, it is fairly easy to see the split between cliques—in how people dress, where they eat lunch, how much they participate in the school's activities,

and how they spend their time outside of school.

Because leisure activities seem to be such a strong determinant of clique composition, many adults have expressed concern over the influence of peers in the socialization of delinquent activity and drug and alcohol use. Parents often feel that if their youngster runs with the wrong crowd, he or she will acquire undesirable interests and attitudes. They express concern, for instance, when their child starts spending time with peers who seem to be less interested in school or more involved with drugs. But which comes first, joining a clique or being interested in a clique's activities? Do adolescents develop interests and attitudes because of who their friends are, or is it more the case that people with similar interests and tastes are likely to become friends?

This question has been examined by social psychologist Denise Kandel (1978) in a longitudinal statewide study of New York high school students. Students completed a battery of questionnaires once during the beginning weeks of a school year and again toward the end of the year. They answered questions concerning a range of activities and interests, including delinquency, drug use, and educational aspirations. In addition, through the use of an intricate coding system that kept information anonymous and confidential, respondents provided the identities of their close friends. By examining patterns of attitudinal and behavioral change over the course of the school year and comparing these shifts with patterns of friendship formation and change, Kandel was able to determine whether adolescents were attracted to one another because of their initial similarity or whether they became similar as a result of the friendship.

Kandel found that both *selection*—choosing a friend on the basis of similarity—and *socialization*—becoming more similar as a result of the friendship—are at work. Moreover, on almost every dimension studied—including de-

Leisure activities, tastes in music and dress, and patterns of drug and alcohol use are strong determinants of clique composition during adolescence. Teenagers tend to have friends who share their tastes, attitudes, and interests. *(Joel Gordon)*

linquency, drug use, and attitudes toward school—selection and socialization operated with about equal weight. In other words, similarity among adolescent friends is about equally due to their selecting one another as friends to begin with as it is to the influence that friends have on one another.

This finding has important implications for understanding the composition of antisocial peer groups, such as those involved in crime or violence. As Brown notes, "It does not appear that [antisocial peer groups] are composed of 'All-American kids' turned bad by peer influence" (1990, p. 193). Instead, aggressive children tend to gravitate toward one another and coalesce into cliques during preadolescence. Once in these groups, aggressive children find support and companionship for their antisocial activities. Similar processes are at work in positive peer groups as well, in which, for example, musically inclined teenagers seek each other out and reward each

other's interests. In other words, because adolescents select friends with similar interests, peer groups tend to strengthen preexisting patterns of behavior, rather than foster the development of new ones.

## POPULARITY, REJECTION, AND STATUS IN ADOLESCENT CLIQUES

Thus far, our discussion has focused on how and why crowds and cliques serve as the basis for adolescents' social activities. But what about the *internal* structure of peer groups? Within a clique, what determines which adolescents are the leaders and which the followers?

To answer this question we must first draw a distinction between popularity and status. **Popularity** refers to how well-liked someone is. The chief determinant of a youngster's popularity during adolescence is his or her social skill. Popular adolescents act appropriately in the eyes of their peers, are skilled at perceiving and meeting the needs of others, and are confident without being conceited. Additionally, popular adolescents are friendly, cheerful, good-natured, humorous, and, you may be surprised to learn, intelligent (Hartup, 1983; Hollingshead, 1949/1975). (Contrary to myth, popular adolescents are more intelligent than unpopular ones. This is because intelligent individuals are better at figuring out how to behave in ways that will get them liked. Remember also that being intelligent is not the same as being a "brain.") Interestingly, the determinants of popularity in adolescent peer groups are the same for boys and girls and are the same for older and younger individuals. People of all ages like to be around others who make them feel good, who know how to have a good time, and who are able to communicate well.

An interesting ethnographic study of early adolescent girls provides insight into the dynamics of popularity. Ethnographer Donna Eder (1985) spent two years observing interactions between early adolescent girls in various extracurricular and informal settings in their middle school (the cafeteria, the hallway, at school dances). In this school, the cheerleaders were considered the elite crowd, and girls who made the cheerleading squad were immediately accorded social status. Other girls then attempted to befriend the cheerleaders as a means of increasing their own status. This, in turn, increased the cheerleaders' popularity within school, since they became the most sought-after friends. The girls who were successful in cultivating friendships with the cheerleaders then became a part of this high-status group and themselves became more popular.

This popularity had a price, however, as one eighth-grader explained to the researcher:

A lot of times, people don't talk to the popular kids because they're kind of scared of them and they don't know their real personality. So that's kind of a bummer when you're considered to be popular because you don't usually meet a lot of other people because they just go, "Oh." (Eder, 1985, p. 162).

Paradoxically, popularity in many cases led to these girls being disliked. As Eder explains, "There are limits to the number of friendships that any one person can maintain. Because popular girls get a high number of affiliative offers, they have to reject more offers of friendship than other girls. Also, to maintain their higher status, girls who form the elite group must avoid associations with lower-status girls. . . . These girls are likely to ignore the affiliative attempts of many girls, leading to the impression that they are stuck-up. . . . Shortly after these girls reach their peak of popularity, they become increasingly disliked" (Eder, 1985, p. 163).

In general, the determinants of social rejection and isolation during adolescence are the opposite of those associated with popularity—in other words, unpopular adolescents are less socially adept than their peers. They may be timid, tactless, or conceited. They interfere with the group's having fun, either by being unenthusiastic or by constantly drawing attention to themselves.

Generally, social scientists believe that it is important to distinguish between adolescents who are actively rejected by their friends and those who are simply ignored or neglected. Rejected adolescents are more likely to behave in ways that are negative and that bother others—they may be tactless, conceited, aggressive, or egotistical. Neglected adolescents suffer more from problems of omission than commission. They may be overly timid, shy, or lacking in enthusiasm, or may find it difficult to socialize with their peers in appropriate ways (Coie and Dodge, 1983). Rejected adolescents are lonelier than neglected adolescents and more likely to develop psychological and emotional problems (Asher and Wheeler, 1985).

Many psychologists believe that rejected and neglected youngsters lack the social skills and social understanding necessary to be popular with peers. In recent years, several teams of psychologists have experimented with different sorts of interventions designed to improve the social skills of unpopular adolescents. These **social competence training** programs have focused on three different strategies. One type of program has been designed to teach conversational skills—self-expression, questioning others about themselves, and leadership (Kelly and de Armas, 1989). These social skills intervention programs have been shown to improve adolescents' abilities to get along with peers. A second approach has been to have unpopular adolescents participate in group activities with popular ones under the supervision of psychologists. Programs like this have been shown to improve adolescents' self-

conceptions and their acceptance by others (Bierman and Furman, 1984).

Finally, some social skills programs focus on a combination of behavioral and cognitive abilities, including social problem-solving. A number of studies (e.g., Dodge, 1986) have found that rejected children and adolescents are more likely to interpret the behavior of other children as hostile—even when it is not—and to respond with aggression. This leads other children to reject them, which only increases their hostility. In view of this, psychologist Roger Weissberg and his colleagues (Weissberg et al., 1989) developed a social problem-solving program designed to improve young adolescents' abilities to judge social situations and figure out acceptable ways of behaving. In Weissberg's program, for example, adolescents

In general, popularity in the adolescent peer group is associated with social competence—popular teenagers are friendly, cheerful, and humorous. Status in the peer group, in contrast, has more to do with leadership and capability in highly valued activities. *(Richard Hutchings/Photo Researchers)*

are taught to calm down and think before they react, decide what the problem is, figure out what their goal is, and think of positive approaches toward reaching that goal. Instead of lashing out at a classmate who grabbed the last basketball from a gym closet, for example, a hot-tempered youngster who had been through this sort of social skills program might calm himself down, tell himself that his goal is to play basketball rather than get into a fight, and approach another student to ask if he can get into a game.

The most popular adolescents are not always the leaders of their cliques. In contrast to popularity, an adolescent's **status**—that is, whether he or she is perceived as a leader—is associated with the ability to accomplish the things that the group wants done. For example, a girl may not be the most well-liked member of her clique, but she may be the group's leader because she is good at organizing parties and other social activities. A boy who is a good all-around athlete may be looked up to by his friends but may not be as popular as someone who is funnier and more good-natured.

Status in the peer group is highly related to the group's activities. Consequently, as adolescents' interests change, so do their cliques' status hierarchies—the arrangement of a group's members from highest status to lowest status. We all know people who were leaders during elementary school but somehow lost their prestige during high school. The reason is that unlike the determinants of popularity—which do not change much during childhood and adolescence—the determinants of status shift as peer activities change. For example, during early adolescence, boys who are physically mature and athletically talented may command a great deal of status, because sports are important activities at this age (Savin-Williams, 1976). As athletics become less important, however, athletic prowess is likely to be related to status, because being a talented athlete is less likely to help achieve the group's goals. During middle adolescence, when same-sex

cliques give way to mixed-sex crowds, competence in dating becomes a more important influence on the status hierarchies of adolescence (Dunphy, 1963).

## The Peer Group and Psychosocial Development

Regardless of the structure or norms of a particular peer group, peers play an extremely important role in the psychological development of adolescents. Problematic peer relationships are associated with a range of serious psychological and behavior problems during adolescence and adulthood. Individuals who are unpopular or who have poor peer relationships during adolescence are more likely than their socially accepted peers to be low achievers in school, to drop out of high school, to have a range of learning disabilities, to show higher rates of delinquent behavior, and to suffer from an array of emotional and mental health problems as adults (Savin-Williams and Berndt, 1990). Although it is likely that poorly adjusted individuals have difficulty making friends, there is now good evidence that psychological problems result from, as well as cause, problems with peers (Hartup, 1983).

Peers also play a crucial role in promoting (or hindering) normal psychosocial development. In the realm of *identity*, peers provide the sorts of models and feedback that adolescents cannot get from adults. In the context of the peer group, young people can try on different roles and personalities and experiment with different identities with greater ease than at home. And, as we saw earlier, the peer group may serve as a way station in the development of identity; as adolescents begin to develop a separate sense of self that is differentiated from the family (Brown et al., 1986a). Experience in the peer group also can be an important influence on adolescents' self-image.

Experience in the peer group also is vital for the development and expression of *auton-*

*omy.* The process of developing more mature and more independent relationships with parents is accompanied by the establishment of more mature relationships with peers. In addition, the peer group provides a context for adolescents to test out decision-making skills, in an arena where there are fewer adults present to monitor and control their choices (Hill and Holmbeck, 1986).

*Intimacy* and *sexuality,* of course, are much more common between peers than between adolescents and adults, for a variety of reasons. Perhaps most critical is that both intimacy and sexuality require interaction between two individuals who are relative equals. Moreover, sexual relationships and close intimacy within the family context would be likely to disrupt important functions of family relationships (Hartup, 1977). It is therefore the adolescent's peer group that generally plays the central role in socializing youngsters in appropriate sexual behavior and in developing the capacity for intimate friendship (Sullivan, 1953a).

Finally, peers are an important influence on *achievement*-related behavior. Although they may play a less influential role than parents or teachers, peers undoubtedly influence adolescents' educational and occupational plans (Epstein, 1983b).

The time adolescents spend with peers is one of the most enjoyable parts of the day (Csikszentmihalyi and Larson, 1984). One reason is that activities with friends are typically organized around having a good time, in contrast to activities with parents, which are more likely to be organized around household chores and the enforcement of parental rules (Larson, 1983; Montemayor, 1982). Rather than being competing institutions, the family and peer group seem to provide contrasting opportunities for adolescent activities and behaviors. The family is organized around work and other tasks, and may be important in the socialization of responsibility and achievement. The peer group provides more frequent op-

portunity for interaction and leisure, which contributes to the development of intimacy and enhances the adolescent's mood and psychological well-being.

## Summary

1. In contemporary society, adolescents spend a great deal of time with agemates, or peers. Many factors contributed to the rise of peer groups in the last century, including the spread of compulsory secondary education, changes in the workplace that segregated young from old, and changes in the family, especially the baby boom of the 1950s.

2. Social scientists have long debated whether the prominent role played by peer groups in the socialization of young people is cause for concern or celebration. On the one side are commentators who suggest that the rise of peer groups has contributed to the development of a separate "youth culture" that is hostile toward adult values. On the other side are those who point to the necessary and valuable educational role played by peer groups in quickly changing societies like ours.

3. The structure of peer groups changes as individuals move into adolescence. First, there is an increase in the amount of time individuals spend in the exclusive company of their peers. Second, peer groups function outside adult supervision more during adolescence than before. Third, during adolescence increasingly more time is spent with the opposite-sex peers. Finally, during adolescence larger collectives of peers, called "crowds," begin to emerge. These transformations are linked to the biological, cognitive, and social definitional changes characteristic of adolescence.

4. Social scientists distinguish between crowds and cliques. Crowds are larger and more vaguely defined groups that are based on reputation. Contrary to the stereotype of a homogeneous youth culture, research has indicated that the social world of adolescents is

composed of many distinct subcultures. In order to understand how peers influence adolescent development, it is essential to know which peer group a youngster is a part of.

5. Although the specific crowd names may differ from school to school, most high schools have relatively similar crowd structures with some version of "jocks," "populars," "brains," "nerds," and "toughs." Adolescents' crowds can be mapped on two distinct dimensions: how involved they are in adult institutions, like school; and how involved they are in the peer culture. Because they often serve as reference groups, crowds play an important role in the adolescent's identity development. Crowds appear to increase in importance during early adolescence and decline in importance during late adolescence.

6. Cliques are small groups of adolescents who are friends and who see each other regularly. For this reason, cliques play an important role in the development of social skills and intimacy. Although clique members influence each other's behavior and values, research has also shown that adolescents select their friends to begin with on the basis of similarity. Generally, adolescents form cliques with peers who are similar in background, orientation toward school, and orientation toward the peer culture.

7. Psychologists distinguish among popular, rejected, and neglected adolescents. Popular adolescents tend to be socially skilled, intelligent, humorous, and friendly. Rejected adolescents are likely to behave in ways that bother other adolescents: they may be tactless, aggressive, conceited, or egotistical. Neglected adolescents, in contrast, tend to suffer from errors of omission; more often than not, they are shy, timid, or socially awkward. Numerous interventions have been designed to improve adolescents' social competence, including those that focus on improving unpopular adolescents' social skills and their social understanding.

## Key Terms

cliques
cofigurative cultures
crowds
ethnography
participant observation
particularistic norms
peer groups
popularity
postfigurative cultures
prefigurative
    cultures

reference group
sex cleavage
significant others
social class
social competence
    training
social network
status
universalistic norms

## For Further Reading

BROWN, B. (1990). Peer groups. In S. Feldman and G. Elliott (Eds.), *At the threshold: The developing adolescent.* Cambridge: Harvard University Press. A thorough review of the literature on the structure and significance of peer groups in adolescence.

COLEMAN, J. (1961). *The adolescent society.* Glencoe, Ill.: Free Press. The classic study of ten midwestern high schools which provided evidence that adolescents had formed a separate "youth culture."

EDER, D. (1985). The cycle of popularity: Interpersonal relations among female adolescents. *Sociology of Education, 58,* 154–165. A fascinating ethnography of social interactions at the cheerleaders' table in a middle school cafeteria.

HOLLINGSHEAD, A. (1949/1975). *Elmtown's youth and Elmtown revisited.* New York: Wiley. Hollingshead's study of social class and social life among high school students in "Elmtown."

MEAD, M. (1978). *Culture and commitment.* Garden City, N.Y.: Anchor. A fascinating analysis of the important role played by peers in rapidly changing societies.

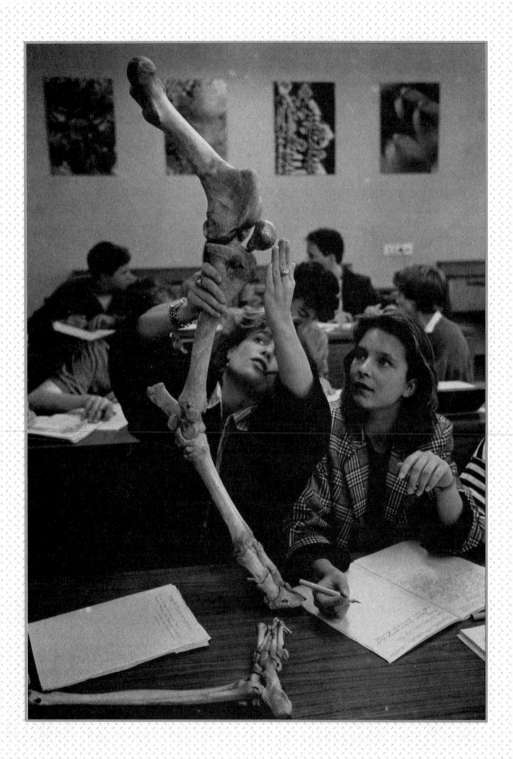

# 6

# SCHOOLS

The study of schools is important to social scientists and policymakers who are interested in influencing adolescent development, because it is through educational institutions that the greatest number of young people can most easily be reached. When, for example, politicians felt that the United States had lost its scientific edge of the Soviet Union—as they did in the 1950s—schools were called upon to see to it that students took more courses in math and science (Conant, 1959). When policymakers felt that society ought to do something to close the economic gap between the races—as they did in the 1960s—schools were called upon to implement desegregation programs so that all individuals would have equal schooling and equal economic opportunity (Coleman et al., 1966). When social scientists felt that adolescents were growing up unfamiliar with the world of work—as they did in the 1970s—schools were asked to provide opportunities for work-study and classes in career education (President's Science Advisory Committee, 1974). And when economists felt that America was losing its competitive edge in the world economy—as they did in the 1980s and 1990s—schools were called upon to return to the "basics" and become more academically demanding (National Committee on Excellence in Education, 1983; National Center on Education and the Economy, 1990).

Because of the important role it has come to play in modern society, the educational system has been the target of a remarkable amount of criticism, scrutiny, and social science research. Parents, teachers, educational administrators, and researchers debate what schools should teach, how schools should be organized, and how schools might best teach their students. They debate such issues as whether high schools should stick to instructing students in the basics—reading, writing, and arithmetic—or offer a more diverse range of classes designed to prepare young people for adulthood socially and emotionally as well as intellectually; whether students learn more in small schools and small classes or whether it is more efficient to consolidate resources into larger schools that can offer more varied courses and activities. They ask such questions as whether early adolescents be schooled in separate junior high schools; whether students should be grouped by ability ("tracked"); and whether certain classroom atmospheres are preferable to others.

These questions have proven difficult to answer. Nevertheless, they remain extremely important. Virtually all American adolescents under the age of 16 and the vast majority of 16- and 17-year-olds are enrolled in school. More than half of all youth now continue their education beyond high school graduation—in technical schools, colleges, and universities. During most of the year, the typical student spends more than one-third of his or her waking hours each week in school or in school-related activities. Not only are schools the chief educational arena for adolescents in America, they also play an extremely important role in defining the young person's social world and in shaping the adolescent's developing sense of identity and autonomy. It is therefore crucial that we understand how best to structure them.

## Secondary Education in America

Consider the data presented in Figure 6.1. Today, virtually all young people between the ages of 14 to 17 are enrolled in school Fifty years ago, only about half of this age group were students, and at the turn of the century, only one in ten (D. Tanner, 1972; W. T. Grant Foundation, 1988).

Not only are there considerably more youngsters enrolled in school today than there were 50 years ago; today's students also spend more days per year in school. In 1920, for

**FIGURE 6.1** The proportion of the 14- to 17-year-old population enrolled in school increased dramatically between 1910 and 1940. Today, nearly 95 percent of individuals this age are in school. (D. Tanner, 1972; William T. Grant Foundation, 1988)

example, the average school term was 162 days, and the average student attended only 121 days, or 75 percent of the term. By 1968, however, the school term had been lengthened to nearly 180 days, and the average student was attending over 160 days of school each year—about 90 percent of the days that school was open (President's Science Advisory Committee, 1974). In many European countries, the school year is even longer. In England, for example, high school students spend 220 days in school each year (National Commission on Excellence in Education, 1983). Although some critics of American schools have called for lengthening our school year (National Commission on Excellence in Education, 1983), others have pointed out that simply expanding the school year, without changing what takes place in school, may be misguided (Boyer, 1983).

Adolescents also remain in school longer

now than they did in past eras. In 1924, fewer than one-third of all youngsters entering the fifth grade eventually graduated from high school; today, about 75 percent of all fifth graders will eventually graduate on time, and a substantial number of those who do not graduate on schedule eventually get their diploma through equivalency programs or continuation schools. Over the course of the twentieth century, then, schools have become increasingly prominent settings in the life of the average American adolescent.

## THE ORIGINS OF COMPULSORY EDUCATION

The rise of secondary education in America was the result of several historical and social trends at the turn of the century. Most important were industrialization, urbanization, and immigration. Following widespread industrialization during the late nineteenth century, the role of children and young adolescents in the workplace changed dramatically. With the economy expanding, many families who at one time had needed their children in the labor force for financial reasons were able to make ends meet without the labor of their young. Furthermore, as the nature of the workplace changed, employers recognized that they needed workers who were more skilled and more reliable than youngsters. The few unskilled jobs that remained required strength beyond the capacity of many youth (Church, 1976). Social reformers also expressed concern over the dangers of children working in factories, and organized labor—an increasingly powerful force during the early 1900s—sought to protect not only the welfare of children but the security of their own employment. Child labor laws narrowed and limited the employment of minors (Bakan, 1972). Together, these changes in the workplace have kept many youngsters out of the labor force.

During this same period, the nature of life

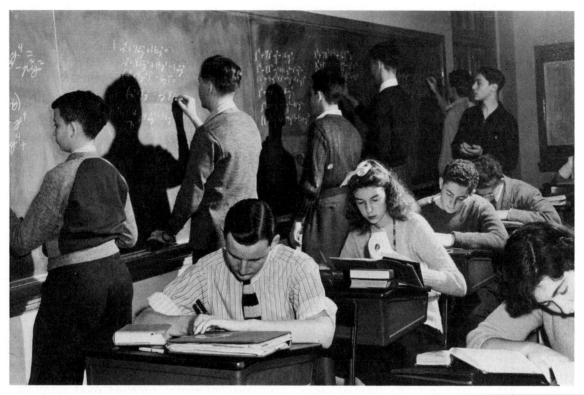

During the second quarter of this century, high schools began to play an increasingly important role in the lives of American adolescents. (Culver)

in American cities was also changing markedly. Industrialization brought with it urbanization and, along with the rising rate of immigration during the early twentieth century, new problems for urban centers. The effects of a rapidly expanding economy were seen in the tenements and slums of America's cities: poor housing, overcrowded neighborhoods, crime. Eager to improve living conditions for the urban masses, social reformers envisioned education as a means of improving the life circumstances of the poor and working classes. And eager to ensure that the problems of cities did not get out of hand, many saw compulsory secondary education as a means of social control. High schools would take thousands of idle young people off the streets, it was argued, and keep them in a social institution in which they could be supervised and kept out of trouble. Eager, too, to see that foreign-born immigrants were well socialized into the American way of life, reformers presented universal secondary education as a necessary part of the process of "Americanization": It was a way of homogenizing a population characterized by increasing—and to many, increasingly uncomfortable—ethnic and cultural diversity (Church, 1976; D. Tanner, 1972). By 1915, the idea of universal compulsory education for adolescents had gained widespread acceptance.

## THE RISE OF THE COMPREHENSIVE HIGH SCHOOL

Prior to the early twentieth century, before secondary education became compulsory, high schools were designed for the elite. In curriculum, staff, and student composition, they were similar to the colleges of the day (Church, 1976), the emphasis being for the most part on classical liberal-arts instruction (D. Tanner, 1972).

By 1920, however, educators saw a need for curricular reform. Compulsory secondary education had changed the social composition of the schools; many educators argued for a corresponding diversification in the secondary school curriculum. Now that secondary education was aimed at the masses, schooling was seen not merely as a means of intellectual training but as a way of preparing youth for life in modern society. It was argued that education, especially for the majority, should include preparation for work and citizenship roles.

The 1920s marked the birth of what came to be known as the **comprehensive high school,** an educational institution that would meet the needs of a diverse and growing population of young people. Classes in general education, college preparation, and vocational education were all housed under one roof. As can be seen in Figure 6.1, the proportion of high school-aged individuals enrolled in school jumped dramatically in the years between World War I and World War II—from 32 percent in 1920 to over 73 percent in 1940. This was also a time of tremendous change in the high school curriculum. During these years, new courses were added in music, art, family life, health, physical education, and other subjects designed to prepare adolescents for family and leisure as well as work roles.

The high school had come a long way from its exclusive focus on the intellectual development of the economic elite at the turn of the century. By the 1950s, its concern had broadened to include the social and intellectual development of all young people. And today, despite all the questioning and criticism that have been aimed at it over the years, the comprehensive high school remains the cornerstone of the American system of secondary education.

## *Debates Over the Curriculum*

Suppose you were asked to make a list of the things you think young people need to know in order to function as competent, responsible, and satisfied adults. Which items on your list should be the responsibility of high schools? Should high school curricula be limited to the traditional academic subjects, or should schools play a broader role in preparing young people for adulthood, by providing instruction more directly relevant to work, family, leisure, and citizenship? Should students receive instruction only in English, mathematics, science, and social studies, or should they take courses as well in "general education"—in subjects such as art, home economics, health, sex education, driver education, and personal finance? Which courses should be required, and which should be left as electives? If you were to discuss these questions with your classmates, you would probably find little consensus.

In recent years, politicians and parents have sounded the cry for schools to scale down their general education offerings and place greater emphasis on the traditional academic subjects: English, mathematics, science, social studies, and a new "basic"—computer science (National Commission on Excellence in Education, 1983). Several social commentators have argued that educators—in high schools and colleges alike—have lost sight of the common core of knowledge and values that serves as the intellectual foundation of our society (Bloom, 1987).

To observers who are unfamiliar with the history of America's high schools, this plea for limiting the high school curriculum to the "essentials" sounds like a fresh and timely idea. But while returning to the basics may indeed be seen as a welcome change, this is by no means the first time that educational critics have called for a more rigorous and more focused curriculum. When the question of high school curriculum is approached historically, we find that the pendulum has swung back and forth several times between calls for academic rigor and calls for real-world relevance.

During the early years of the comprehensive high school, for example, the pendulum swung away from a purely academic curriculum and toward more varied course offerings in vocational and general education. In response to the beginning of the Cold War and the launching of the first space satellite, Sputnik, by the former Soviet Union, however, educators called for a return to more rigorous academic preparation. At the time, many politicians and educators were concerned that America was losing ground because high schools were not spending enough time on math and science. They believed that the "watered-down" curriculum offered by comprehensive high schools had left American youth unprepared to face the challenge of communism (D. Tanner, 1972).

During the late 1960s, though, as the Cold War died down, the educational pendulum swung back toward relevance. Educational reformers claimed that schools were not preparing young people for the roles they would encounter as adults (Church, 1976). They felt that adolescents should spend less time in school and more time in community and work settings. Programs such as career education and experiential education were implemented in many school districts so that young people could receive "hands-on" experience in the

"real world" (President's Science Advisory Committee, 1974). During this time period, students also became more vocal and demanded more courses in relevant and practical subject areas. Schools began to offer an increasingly wide range of electives for students to choose among. By the late 1970s, over 40 percent of all high school students were taking a general, rather than college preparatory or vocational, course of study, and 25 percent of their educational credits came from work experience outside of school, remedial coursework, and courses aimed at personal growth and development (National Commission on Excellence in Education, 1983).

During the 1980s, the pendulum swung back again toward the "basics." Several proposals called for more demanding curricula (Adler, 1982; National Commission on Excellence in Education, 1983). One set of writers bemoaned what they called the "shopping-mall high school," where students were given too much freedom in choosing courses and schools were more concerned with keeping students happy than with seeing that genuine and important learning took place (Powell et al., 1985). The achievement test scores of American high school students had fallen steadily, and by 1981 they were lower than they had been when Sputnik was launched. This time, however, the prodding for academic rigor came not from a Soviet threat but to meet the threat of economic competition from Japan and Western Europe. Noting that America was losing its competitive edge in the world market, educational reformers called for more academic rigor in the schools as a means of preparing young people for the workplace of the future. One group, for example, called for schools to implement more demanding academic requirements, tougher standards for graduation, and longer school days (National Commission on Excellence in Education, 1983).

During the early 1990s, yet another curric-

During the 1990s, debates about the high school curriculum focused on how best to stimulate higher-order thinking. Higher-order thinking involves the interpretation, analysis, and evaluation of information, rather than rote memorization of facts and figures. *(Susan Lapides/Design Conceptions)*

ular "innovation" received widespread attention. This time, however, the focus shifted from the content of the curriculum to the process of learning. Educational reformers called for more emphasis in the classroom on **higher-order thinking**—whether in the teaching of "basics" or in the teaching of electives (Newmann, in press). Higher-order thinking is stimulated when students are encouraged to interpret, analyze, and evaluate information, rather than simply memorize or apply it in a routine way. In social studies, for example, asking students to discuss *why* political revolts occur may stimulate higher-order thinking, whereas asking them simply to memorize (and regurgitate) the dates of important political revolutions probably will not.

The stimulation of higher-order thinking sounds like an admirable goal. But as with all educational reforms, the reasons behind this goal are embedded in a particular historical and economic context. Why, in the 1990s, would educational reformers suddenly become interested in restructuring the curriculum toward the promotion of higher-order thinking? Because it became apparent during this time period that American adolescents were sorely deficient in skills requiring in-depth analysis, and that this did not bode well for our country's competitiveness in the international economy. Consider these grim conclusions of a blue-ribbon report issued by the National Assessment of Educational Progress in 1990 (Mullis, Owen, and Phillips, 1990):

> Students are learning facts and skills, but few show the capacity for complex reasoning and problem solving. ... Most of the gains [in achievement over the past two decades] appear to have occurred in lower-level skills and basic concepts. ... In contrast, most of the declines have occurred in the area of higher-level applications (p. 33).

For example, a national assessment found declines during the 1970s and 1980s in the proportion of 17-year-olds who could synthesize and learn from advanced reading materials, solve multi-step math problems, and use detailed scientific knowledge to draw conclusions. Improvements during this same time period were found among younger adolescents, but these improvements were limited to fairly basic skills, such as reading comprehension, addition, and subtraction, and to knowledge of everyday science facts.

In some regards, then, the movement "back to basics" characteristic of the early 1980s had been successful. But by the early 1990s, it had become evident to economists that merely training our students in "basics" was not going to help build a competitive work force for the next century (Jackson and Hornbeck, 1989; National Center on Education and the Economy, 1990). According to one commission, the world's workplace had become split into two markedly different sectors: one was composed of low-paying jobs that required little skill or training, while the other was composed of high-paying jobs that required advanced training and well-developed intellectual skills, including higher-order thinking abilities. Most industrialized countries have made a concerted effort to expand the high-skill sector of their workplace, because these jobs are more lucrative for their economy as well as their workers. But in order to maintain this expansion, it is necessary to develop a steady pool of highly skilled workers. In the words of this commission, America's choice was clear: "High skills or low wages" (National Center on Education and the Economy, 1990). This recognition fueled much of the educational reform's interest in the development of higher-order thinking.

You may well wonder why our ideas about the content of the high school curriculum have changed so often. Are we not able to make up our minds about the purpose and responsibilities of educational institutions? Why aren't we able to develop a high school curriculum that works and stick with it? One reason is that high schools, like other social institutions, are embedded in the broader society. As society changes, so does the sort of preparation young people need to develop into capable and competent adults. In all likelihood, the "higher-order thinking" movement of the 1990s will eventually give way to another approach, as social change once again makes educational reform necessary. The "fresh" educational proposals of the 1990s will seem as outmoded in the future as yesterday's do today.

## The Social Organization of Schools

In addition to debating the issue of curriculum, social scientists have also discussed the ways in which secondary schools should be organized. In this section we examine the research on five aspects of school organization: (1) school and classroom size; (2) different approaches to age grouping, in particular, how young adolescents should be grouped; (3) tracking, the grouping of students in classes according to their academic abilities; (4) school desegregation; and (5) public versus private schools.

### SCHOOL AND CLASS SIZE

When it comes to schools, is bigger better? The most extensive data on the effects of *school size* on adolescents come from a series of studies conducted by ecological psychologist Roger Barker and his colleagues (Barker and Gump, 1964). These researchers were interested in how the size of a school influences the variety of classes and extracurricular activities available to students and the students' participation in them.

Large schools offer more varied instruction than do small schools. But the variety of

"Relevance" was the catchword in discussions of secondary education during the 1970s. Here, a group of high school students interviews folk singer Pete Seeger for a student video project. *(Beringer-Dratch/Image Works)*

courses offered in a school increases substantially only when the size of the school increases dramatically. While a school with 2,000 students might offer 50 different classes, a school with 4,000 students might offer only 60.

Perhaps the most interesting findings, however, concern participation in nonacademic activities. One might expect that in addition to providing a more varied curriculum, large schools would be able to offer a more diverse selection of extracurricular activities to their students, and indeed they do. Large schools can afford to have more athletic teams, after-school clubs, and student organizations. In fact, Barker found that nearly four times the number of nonacademic activities were available to students attending very large high schools as were available to students in small schools.

But because the large schools also contained so many more students, actual participation in different activities was only half as high in the large schools as in the smaller schools. In Barker's terminology, the large schools were **overmanned**—they had many more students per activity than necessary. As a result, students tended more often to be observers than participants in school activities. For instance, during the fall, a small school and a large school might each field teams in football, soccer, and cross-country running, together requiring a total of 100 students. An individual's chances of being one of those 100 students are greater in a school that has only 500 students than in a school with an enrollment of 4,000.

Because students in small schools are more likely than students in large schools to be active in a wider range of activities, they are more likely to report doing things that help them develop their skills and abilities, allow them to work closely with others, and make them feel needed and important. In a small school, chances are that, sooner or later, most students will find themselves on a team, in the student government, or in an extracurricular organization. Students in small schools also are more likely to be placed in positions of leadership and responsibility, and they more often report having done things that made them feel confident and diligent. School size especially affects the participation of students whose grades are not very good. In large schools, academically marginal students often feel like outsiders; they rarely get involved in school activities. In small schools, however, these students feel a sense of involvement and obligation equal to that of more academically successful students.

Several recent studies of American high schools have echoed this sentiment (Boyer, 1983; Goodlad, 1984). Although large schools may be able to offer a more diverse curriculum or provide greater material resources to their students, the toll that school size may take on student learning and engagement appears to exceed the benefits of size. Experts now agree that the ideal size of a school for adolescents is between 500 and 1,000 students (Entwisle, 1990).

Between 1980 and 1990, numerous reports on American high schools appeared, all of them filled with suggestions for school reform (Boyer, 1983; Coleman and Hoffer, 1987; Goodlad, 1984; Lightfoot, 1983; Powell et al., 1985; Resnick, 1987; Sizer, 1984). Although the reports were not always consistent, several themes emerged that point to five general conclusions about good schools (Linney and Seidman, 1989).

First and foremost, good schools emphasize intellectual activities. They create this atmosphere in different ways, depending on the nature and size of the student body, but in these good schools, a common purpose—quality education—is valued and shared by students, teachers, administrators, and parents. Learning is more important to students than school athletics or social activities, and seeing that students learn is more important to teach-

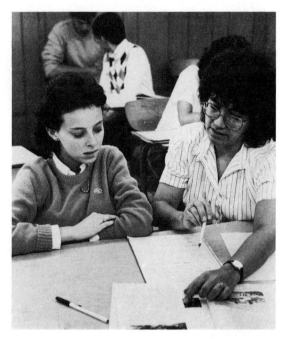

Generally speaking, research has shown that adolescents in large classes learn just as much as adolescents in small ones. An important exception, however, is remedial education: here, adolescents benefit from smaller classes and one-on-one instruction. *(Meri Houtchens-Kitchens/Picture Cube)*

ers and administrators than seeing that they graduate.

Second, good schools have teachers who are committed to their students and who are given a good deal of freedom and autonomy by the school administration in the way that this commitment is expressed in the classroom. In all schools, of course, teachers have curricular requirements that they must fulfill. But in good schools, teachers are given relatively more authority to decide how their lessons are planned and how their classes are conducted. When teachers are given this sort of say in school governance, they may find it easier to make a commitment to the shared values of the institution.

Third, good schools constantly monitor

themselves and their students in order to become even better. Rather than viewing questions and concerns about school policies and practices as threatening, principals and other administrators welcome opportunities for dialogue and discussion. When school personnel encourage flexibility, openness to change, and the exchange of ideas, they set a tone for the entire school that may even affect the classroom and result in more stimulating student-teacher interaction.

Fourth, good schools are well integrated into the communities they serve. Active attempts are made to involve parents in their youngsters' education. Links are forged between the high school and local colleges and universities, so that advanced students may take more challenging and stimulating courses for high school credit. Bridges are built between the high school and local employers, so that students begin to see the relevance of their high school education to their occupational futures.

Finally, and perhaps obviously, good schools are composed of good classrooms. In good classrooms, students are active participants in the process of education, not passive recipients of lecture material. The atmosphere is orderly, but not oppressive. Innovative projects replace rote memorization as a way of encouraging learning. Students are challenged to think critically and debate important issues, rather than asked simply to regurgitate yesterday's lessons.

There is no evidence that these goals can only be achieved in small classes, as one might think. In contrast to studies of school size, studies of *class size* indicate that variations within the typical range of classroom sizes—twenty to forty students—do not generally affect students' scholastic achievement (Rutter, 1983). Without changes in instruction, changes in class size alone are unlikely to have an effect on students (Bennett, 1987). Students in classes with forty students learn just as much as students in classes with twenty students.

However, in situations that call for highly individualized instruction or tutoring, smaller classes appear to be more effective. For example, in remedial education classes, where teachers must give a great deal of individual attention to each student, small classes are valuable. As Michael Rutter (1983) points out, one important implication of these findings is that it may be profitable for schools that maintain regular class sizes of twenty-five or thirty students to increase the sizes of these classes by a student or two in order to free instructors and trim the sizes of classes for students who need specialized, small-group instruction.

## APPROACHES TO AGE GROUPING

A second issue that social scientists have examined in the study of school structure and organization concerns the way in which schools group students of different ages. Early in this century, most school districts separated youngsters into an elementary school (which had either six or eight grades) and a secondary school (which had either four or six grades). However, many educators felt that the two-school system was unable to meet the special needs of young adolescents. During the early years of compulsory secondary education, the establishment of separate schools for young adolescents began, and the **junior high school** was born. In more recent years, the **middle school**—a three- or four-year school housing the seventh and eighth grades with one or more younger grades—has gained a certain popularity, replacing the junior high school in some districts. Proponents of middle schools point to the earlier maturation of young people today and the greater similarity of fifth- and sixth-graders to their older peers than to their younger ones.

What is known about the differential effects of these various arrangements? From the point of view of the developing adolescent, are some organizational schemes superior to others? One recent review suggests that the evidence, although sparse, favors the middle school arrangement (Entwisle, 1990). Middle schools are typically smaller and less departmentalized, which probably means that young adolescents are less likely to feel "lost" in them. In addition, teachers in middle schools are more likely to engage in team-teaching, to teach only one grade level, and to teach in their area of specialization. For these reasons, middle schools are likely to be better academic as well as social environments than are junior high schools.

Although most experts now agree that middle schools are preferable to junior high schools, there is still considerable room for improvement in existing middle schools. One well-publicized report on this subject was issued by the Carnegie Corporation's Council on Adolescent Development (1989). Among the most important recommendations made were to divide middle schools into units of between 200 and 500 students, in order to reduce students' feelings of anonymity; to hire teachers who have special training in adolescent development; and to strengthen ties between schools and the communities in which they are located.

Researchers also have compared school arrangements in which adolescents remain in elementary schools until eighth grade with those in which they move from elementary school, into a middle or junior high school, and later, from middle school into a high school. The most comprehensive study was conducted by sociologists Roberta Simmons and Dale Blyth (1987). These researchers studied youngsters in the Milwaukee public schools for a five-year period. Some of these students were in school districts organized around the 6-3-3 arrangement, while others were in schools using an 8-4 plan. The researchers were interested in the impact of having to change schools at different ages. They compared shifts in adolescents' self-esteem, grade-point averages, participation in extracurricular activities, and feelings of anonymity as the students moved through each of the two arrangements. In the 8-4 arrangement, students change schools only once, whereas in the 6-3-3 arrangement, they must make two transitions.

As shown in Figure 6.2, adolescent boys' and girls' self-esteem is affected quite differently by the different school arrangements. For boys, self-esteem rises throughout the years between sixth and tenth grades, with the exception of the year between ninth and tenth grades for those in a 6-3-3 arrangement, during which self-esteem remains essentially unchanged. For girls, self-esteem rises throughout the five years in the 8-4 arrangement—as with the boys in this arrangement. But the girls in the 6-3-3 arrangement show two dramatic drops in self-esteem, during each of the transitions into a new school (that is, between the sixth and seventh grades and between the ninth and tenth grades).

The data on youngsters' participation in extracurricular activities again favored the 8-4 arrangement, this time for both boys and girls. Over the five-year period, extracurricular participation decreased slightly for boys in the 6-3-3 plan, whereas it increased slightly for boys in the 8-4 plan. For girls, the differences were more striking. Although sixth graders in both types of schools participated in the same number of extracurricular activities, in the eighth grade, girls who were in the 8-4 arrangement participated in about twice as many activities as did girls in the 6-3-3 organization, and in the tenth grade, they participated in nearly three times as many. The findings concerning students' grade-point averages and feelings of anonymity paint a somewhat different picture. Students' grades declined *whenever* they had to change schools, regardless of the timing of the transition. Similarly, whenever students changed schools, their feelings of anonymity increased for a time.

The researchers concluded that, while all school transitions may have a temporary negative impact on adolescents' psychological well-

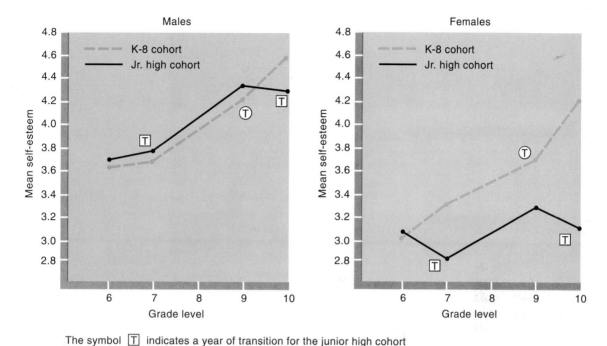

The symbol ⊤ indicates a year of transition for the junior high cohort

Ⓣ indicates a year of transition for the K-8 cohort

**FIGURE 6.2** For boys and girls, self-esteem is affected differently by different school arrangements.

being and social participation, changing schools may be harder—and consequently may have a more deleterious impact—the earlier it occurs during adolescence. This view is consistent with the authors' "developmental readiness" hypothesis, which we examined in Chapter 1. There we saw evidence that puberty, too, may be more disruptive if it occurs early. Simmons and Blyth also contend that the impact of several simultaneous changes is worse than the impact of any one change alone. Thus the early school transition is particularly hard for girls, because changing schools following the sixth grade often coincides with the onset of puberty and with their initiation into dating (Simmons et al., 1987). Although the effects for boys do not seem as severe, there is evidence that for them, too, the 8-4 arrangement may be preferable to the 6-3-3 plan.

An alternative explanation for these findings has been suggested by psychologist Jacquelynne Eccles and her colleagues (Eccles, Midgley, and Adler, 1984; Midgley, Feldlaufer, and Eccles, 1988). Eccles has argued that the classroom environment in the typical junior high school is quite different from that in the typical elementary school. Not only are junior high schools larger and less personal, junior high school teachers hold different beliefs about students than do elementary school teachers—even when they teach students of the same chronological age. For example, teachers in junior high schools are less likely to trust their students and more likely to emphasize control and discipline. They also tend to be more likely to believe that students' abilities are fixed and not easily modified through instruction. Eccles points out that it is little surprise that students

Despite the satisfied faces of these junior high school graduates, research has shown that changing schools often or early in early adolescence may affect school achievement and self-esteem negatively. A two-school arrangement, in which the separate junior high school is eliminated and adolescents make one school transition, from elementary school into high school after eighth-grade, may be preferable to the more widely-used three-school arrangement. *(Frederik D. Bodin/Stock, Boston)*

experience a drop in self-esteem and in achievement motivation when they enter junior high school, given the change in environments they experience. The issue, according to her, is not that the adolescents must make a transition; it is the *nature* of the transition they must make.

Why do junior high school teachers differ from those who teach elementary school? At this point, the answer is not clear-cut. It does not seem that the individuals who choose to become junior high teachers differ all that much from those who choose to teach younger grades. Rather, Eccles has suggested that the organization and anonymity of junior high schools has a negative effect on the teachers who work in them, which in turn affects the way they interact with students. This is consistent with a large body of evidence that students are more engaged in school when their teachers themselves are more engaged in their work (Louis and Smith, in press).

Eccles also points out that cultural stereo-

types about adolescence may have a negative influence on junior high school teachers' beliefs. As we saw in the introduction to this book, many adults believe that adolescence is an inevitably difficult time—not only for teenagers themselves, but for those who work with them. To the extent that teachers come into the classroom with negative images of adolescence as a stage in the life cycle—that teenagers are inherently unruly, or unteachable, or perplexing—their preconceptions may interfere with their work as educators (Midgley et al., 1988). As we shall see in a later section of this chapter, one of the most important influences on the adolescent's experience in school is the climate of the classroom.

One issue that school districts must consider when thinking about age grouping concerns the potential influence of older students on younger ones. In order to look at this phenomenon, an interesting study evaluated a school district's changeover from an organization in which ninth-graders were grouped with seventh- and eighth-graders (a 6-3-3 arrangement) to one in which ninth- and tenth-graders were housed in a school separate from older and younger students (a 6-2-2-2 arrangement; [Blyth, Hill, and Smyth, 1981]). Many parents in the school district had expressed concern that the ninth-graders exerted a negative influence on the younger adolescents, and they favored separating grades seven through twelve into three two-year schools. Parents felt, for example, that young adolescents were more likely to be exposed to drugs and alcohol when they attended school with older youngsters.

The researchers found that the presence of older students negatively affected younger students at all grade levels. Interestingly, the ninth-graders were more adversely affected by being placed with tenth-graders than were either seventh- or eighth-graders by being placed with ninth-graders. For example, the ninth-grade boys who were moved to schools with tenth-graders were less likely to participate in extracurricular activities, less likely to assume leadership positions, more likely to use marijuana and alcohol, more sexually active, more likely to feel anonymous, and more likely to be picked on. Ninth-grade girls in schools with tenth-graders also were less likely to participate in school activities, less likely to assume leadership positions, more likely to use drugs and alcohol, and more likely to feel anonymous. For seventh- and eighth-graders, the removal of the ninth-graders had positive effects: The transfer of older students to a different school increased the participation of younger students in school activities, decreased substance use, decreased feelings of anonymity, and decreased the likelihood of victimization.

These findings pose a dilemma for those hoping for simple solutions to problems in school organization. Removing ninth-graders from junior high schools and placing them with tenth-graders appears to benefit the younger students who remain in the junior high school. But doing so may place the ninth-graders at a disadvantage. As the authors suggest, different methods of school organization have different effects on students of different ages, and what may help some may harm others. Nevertheless, these studies indicate that early adolescents may benefit from changing schools less often and remaining somewhat separate from older peers.

Although some aspects of the transition into secondary school may be difficult for students to negotiate, not all students experience the same degree of stress during the transition. The Simmons and Blyth studies indicate that students experiencing the transition earlier in adolescence have more difficulty with it than those experiencing it later. Eccles' research shows that the environment that students move into makes a big difference. And other studies indicate that adolescents who have close friends before and during the transition into secondary school adapt more successfully to the new school environment (Berndt, 1987). Consistent with this, students who have more academic and psychosocial problems before the transition into middle or junior high school—that is, during elementary school—cope less successfully with the transition (Safer, 1986). Evidently, the transition into secondary school is not the sort of stressor that has uniform effects on all students. More vulnerable adolescents, adolescents with fewer sources of social support, and adolescents moving into more impersonal schools may be more susceptible to the adverse consequences of this stressor than their peers.

## TRACKING

In some schools, students with different academic abilities and interests do not attend classes together. Some classes are designated as more challenging and rigorous and are reserved for students identified as especially capable. Other classes in the same subject area are designated as average classes and are taken by most students. Still others are designated as remedial classes and are reserved for students having academic difficulties. The process of separating students into different levels of classes within the same school is called **tracking.** Not all high schools use tracking systems. In some schools, students with different abilities take all of their classes together.

Educators have debated the pros and cons of tracking for years (Rutter, 1983). On the positive side, tracking allows teachers to design class lessons that are more finely tuned to students' abilities. Tracking may be especially useful at the high school level, where students must master certain basic skills before they can learn such specialized subjects as science, math, or foreign languages.

Unfortunately, however, tracking creates problems of its own. Students who are placed in the remedial track are likely to be labeled by their peers as slow or stupid. Their self-esteem may suffer, and they may eventually come to see themselves as failures (Rutter, 1983). What is more, because schools play such an important role in influencing adolescents' friendships, when students are tracked they tend to socialize only with peers from the same academic group (Rosenbaum, 1976). Tracking can contribute to the polarization of the student body into different subcultures that feel hostile toward each other. The students in the advanced track may feel superior and look down on other students, and the students in the remedial track may feel angry and resentful. Finally, some critics of tracking point out that decisions about track placements often discriminate against poor and minority students and may hinder rather than enhance their academic progress (Rosenbaum, 1976). Some school counselors assume, for example, that minority or poor youngsters are not capable of handling the work in advanced classes and may assign them to average or remedial classes, where less material is covered and the work is less challenging (Vanfossen et al., 1987). Other studies, however, indicate that student ability is a stronger influence on track placement than

student background (Alexander and Cook, 1982).

Recent research on tracking in high schools indicates quite clearly that students in different tracks have markedly different opportunities to learn (Gamoran, 1987). Students in the more advanced tracks receive more challenging instruction and better teaching, and are more likely to engage in classroom activities that emphasize higher-order thinking rather than rote memorization. Being placed in a more advanced track has a positive influence on school achievement (how much is actually learned over time), on subsequent course selection (the curriculum to which a student is exposed), and on ultimate educational attainment (how many years of schooling a student completes) (Gamoran and Mare, 1989; Lee and Bryck, 1989; Natriello, Pallas, and Alexander, 1989).

In many respects, then, early track placements set in motion a sort of educational "trajectory" that is often difficult to change, once in place (Alexander and Cook, 1982). Junior high track placements, for example, determine which sorts of courses a student is eligible to take in high school, which in turn determine which colleges he or she may apply to. Moreover, because students are assigned to different tracks initially on the basis of test scores and other indicators of aptitude, the net effect of tracking over time is to increase preexisting differences between students. The students who need the most help are assigned to the tracks in which the quality of instruction is the poorest. In other words, in a school that uses tracking, the academically "rich get richer and the poor get poorer."

## SCHOOL DESEGREGATION

Since the landmark Supreme Court ruling in *Brown v. Board of Education* (1954), many of the nation's school districts have enacted changes aimed at desegregating their schools. Under-

# THE SEXES: ABILITY GROUPING AND SEX DIFFERENCES IN MATHEMATICS ACHIEVEMENT

According to most reviews, differences in the mathematics achievement of boys and girls, which favor boys, are well documented (Fennema and Peterson, 1985). Although in elementary school girls generally outscore boys on tests of math achievement, during junior and senior high school, boys are more likely to take math classes and are more likely to outperform girls. These sex differences are important, because students emerging from high school with little preparation in mathematics are unlikely to be able to enter college programs (such as engineering) and occupations (such as scientist) that require training in math. Decisions that young women make early in their educational careers therefore may have important long-term implications for their occupational and educational futures.

Many psychological explanations have been offered for the flipflop in math achievement during early adolescence, including (1) that girls come to see math achievement as part of the masculine role and develop negative attitudes toward math as a consequence, (2) that girls have fewer role models of successful mathematicians or scientists and, consequently, are less likely to aspire to enter these fields; and (3) that girls receive pressure from their male peers not to excel in math class (Hallinan and Sorensen, 1987). We examine some of these explanations in Chapter 12 as part of our discussion of adolescent achievement. As Hallinan and Sorensen point out, however, psychological explanations of sex differences in math achievement ignore organizational aspects of schools that may have important effects. In particular, they suggest that tracking biases in the math curriculum operate against the assignment of girls to high-ability math classes.

These researchers examined mathematics ability-group assignments in a large sample of fourth- through seventh-graders. They were interested in whether assignment to the high-ability group was influenced by the student's math ability, his or her sex, or a combination of both. They found, not surprisingly, that a student's ability weighed heavily in the assignment process, with more able students more likely to be assigned to the high-ability group. But they also found that high-ability girls were less likely to be assigned to the high-ability group than were boys of comparable talent (Hallinan and Sorensen, 1987).

Even within math classes, teachers interact differently with males and females. Teachers are more likely to communicate to girls who are having difficulty that their problem is related to a lack of ability, whereas they are more likely to communicate to boys who are having difficulty that their problem is due to a lack of effort. As a consequence, girls may be more likely than boys to develop feelings of helplessness when it comes to learning math, and may emerge with negative perceptions of their own abilities (Henderson and Dweck, 1990).

Moreover, the biased assortment of youngsters into math tracks has long-term implications for future course selection. An adolescent girl who is not assigned to a high-ability math class—despite her talent—may come to develop more negative attitudes toward math than she might have otherwise and miss opportunities to pursue certain careers that require advanced mathematics training.

lying the Court's ruling was the belief that segregation in schools impedes the academic and economic progress of students from racial minorities and, in addition, fosters hostility and misunderstanding between individuals of different backgrounds. Even if racially segregated schools appear equivalent on various indices of quality (for example, the amount of money spent on educational materials and programs), segregated schools are inherently unequal, the Court argued, because "to separate [black youngsters] from others solely because of their race generates a feeling of inferiority as to their status in the community that may affect their hearts and minds in a way unlikely ever to be undone" (*Brown v. Topeka Board of Education*, 1954). Since the Court's ruling, many school districts have adopted measures designed to create voluntary desegregation (for example, permitting families to choose among different schools within a large catchment area rather than assigning students to specific schools on the basis of their residence). Others have enacted policies aimed at mandatory desegregation (assigning students of different racial background to specific schools in order to create predetermined racial balances) (Bradley and Bradley, 1977).

Despite the considerable legal basis for desegregation, research on the effects of desegregation programs on high school students has not been overwhelmingly encouraging. Several sets of studies point to this disappointing conclusion. First, research indicates that desegregation has surprisingly little impact on the achievement levels of either minority or white youngsters (Entwisle, 1990). Second, there is some evidence that minority youngsters' self-esteem is higher when they attend schools in which they are in the majority—a phenomenon true not only for black youth, but for all youth (Rosenberg, 1975). Third, as we saw in the previous chapter, interracial contact, even in desegregated schools, is rare, largely because of the reluctance on the part of white students

to form cross-racial friendships (Hallinan and Teixeria, 1987). Fourth, studies indicate that immediately following the imposition of a desegregation program, white enrollment in a school declines as white families move or withdraw their child from the public school, although the high rate of "white flight" appears to be most pronounced during the first year of a desegregation program and slows shortly thereafter (Wilson, 1985).

As sociologist Jomills Braddock (1985) points out, however, focusing on the short-term impact of desegregation may provide only a very narrow means of assessing its costs and benefits. He notes that African-Americans who have attended desegregated high schools—especially boys—are more likely to graduate and to continue their education in desegregated institutions. Because African-Americans graduating from predominantly white colleges earn more when they enter the labor force than those who attend predominantly minority colleges, it seems that youngsters who attend desegregated high schools may reap advantages in the labor force later on, as young adults. Moreover, African-American graduates of predominantly white schools are more likely to work in integrated environments and live in integrated neighborhoods during adulthood. Taken together, these studies suggest that desegregated high school programs indeed benefit minority youth, but that these benefits may not be apparent until adulthood. Furthermore, these studies suggest that desegregation during high school does appear to help break down racial barriers in society at large.

It also may not be advisable to make sweeping generalizations about the impact of school desegregation without looking further at the processes inside the school and how they are affected (or not affected) by its racial composition. Segregation may be maintained in "desegregated" schools through tracking, seating assignments, and class scheduling (Entwisle,

Research on the presumed positive effects of school desegregation has not been encouraging. One reason is that many desegregated schools are integrated in theory but not in practice. In many so-called integrated schools, segregation continues through tracking and other structural arrangements. *(Peter Southwick/Stock, Boston)*

1990). One would need information on how school policies and procedures were changed and on how students, teachers, and administrators responded to the changes. All desegregated schools are not the same (Campbell, 1977). Consider, for example, the differences between two desegregated schools. Each has achieved a 50-50 racial balance. But in one school, the black and white students are taught in different classes; in the other, the classes themselves are all integrated. Obviously, it makes little sense to view these schools as having similar environments merely because they are both classified as "desegregated."

Finally, not all children and families respond in the same way to changes in the racial composition of their school. Some parents and students are enthusiastic about such changes, whereas others are apprehensive. Thus in any comprehensive study of the effects of school desegregation, it would be important to know how children of different ages are affected, how children from different racial and socioeconomic backgrounds are affected, how parents' attitudes toward desegregation affect the child's reacton, and so forth. These and other factors are likely to mediate the impact of desegregation on the adolescent (St. John, 1975).

## PUBLIC VERSUS PRIVATE SCHOOLS

While the vast majority of students attending secondary school in America are enrolled in public schools, a substantial minority attend private schools, either parochial (i.e., with a religious affiliation) or "independent." In the past, researchers cared little about studying differences between private and public schools. But during the late 1980s, many educational policy-makers suggested that one way to improve schools would be to give parents more of a choice in determining where their child was enrolled, in order to force schools to compete with each other for the best students. One concrete suggestion was that states should provide parents with vouchers that could be used to "purchase" education at the school of their choice—private or public. In light of these suggestions, researchers became interested in studying whether some types of schools produced more high-achieving students than others.

Initial investigations of this by sociologist James Coleman and his colleagues (e.g., Coleman, Hoffer, and Kilgore, 1982; Coleman and Hoffer, 1987) pointed to clear advantages for students attending private high schools, and especially for those attending Catholic schools. Even after taking into account preexisting differences between students from public and private schools that could explain their achievement differences (for example, we know that IQ scores are positively correlated with social class, and wealthier families can better afford private school; even within social classes, parents may be more likely to invest money in the education of more capable students), the studies found that students from private schools achieved more. This was especially true in comparisons of juniors and seniors (Entwisle, 1990).

Social scientists disagree about the interpretation of this finding. According to Coleman, the chief reason for the advantages enjoyed by Catholic school students has to do with the close links between their schools and families. He has argued that a Catholic school is a part of a **functional community**—a community in which parents, teachers, and students all share similar values and attitudes. Students profit from this because the lessons taught in Catholic school are reinforced at home, at church, and in the neighborhood. In addition, private schools are typically more orderly, more disciplined, and assign more homework (Coleman et al., 1982). Other researchers, however, have suggested that the curricula and tracking practices of private and public schools are very different (e.g., Lee and Bryk, 1988). Students at Catholic schools, for example, take more academic courses in school and are less likely to be tracked into general or vocational classes, even if their prior records are not strong. Given what we know about the negative effects of being placed in lower tracks, it makes sense that schools that have less tracking will have overall higher levels of achievement.

## The Importance of School Climate

Thus far we have seen that certain elements of the school's social organization—size, age grouping, tracking, and so forth—can affect student behavior and achievement. But these factors are important mainly because they influence what takes place in classrooms and in other school settings. Indeed, most social scientists and educators now agree that the school-related factors most important in influencing learning and psychosocial development during adolescence concern the more immediate environment of the school and classroom. As noted earlier, in good schools, the classroom environments encourage dialogue between teachers and students and among students, and learning is emphasized over memorization. According to Michael Rutter (1983), various aspects of the **school climate** have important effects on youngsters' learning and achievement. Specifically, the way teachers interact with students, the way classroom time is used, and the sorts of standards and expectations teachers hold for their students are all more important than the size of the school, the way that age groups are combined, or the racial composition of the school. One reason that tracking makes a difference, for example, is that it affects the school climate.

What sort of climate brings out the best in students? Considered together, the results of several studies indicate that the same factors which promote psychosocial development in the home—warmth, high standards, and moderate control—also promote positive behavior in the classroom. Students and teachers are more satisfied in innovative than control-oriented classes and in classes that combine a moderate degree of structure with high student involvement and high teacher support. In these classes, teachers encourage their students' participation but do not let the class get out of control. Classes that are too task-oriented, particularly when they also emphasize teacher control, tend to make students feel anxious, uninterested, and unhappy (Moos, 1978). The pattern of classroom variables associated with positive student behavior and attitudes, then, is reminiscent of the *authoritative* family environment. Similarly, an overemphasis on control in the classroom in the absence of support is reminiscent of the *authoritarian* family, while a lack of clarity and organization is reminiscent of the *indulgent* or the *indifferent* family—and these styles may affect adolescents detrimentally. Students do best when their teachers spend a high proportion of time on lessons (rather than on setting up equipment or dealing with discipline problems), begin and end their lessons on time, provide clear feedback to students on what is expected of them and on their performance, and give ample praise to students when they

perform well (Rutter, 1983). A good high school teacher, in other words, bears a striking resemblance to a good parent.

This general pattern of findings has been replicated in several other studies. In an extensive program of research on young adolescents in London schools, for example, Michael Rutter and his colleagues (Rutter et al., 1979) found that after controlling for differences in students' backgrounds and abilities before entering secondary school, school climate was significantly associated with student performance, attendance, and delinquency. Generally speaking, schools in which teachers were supportive but firm and maintained high, well-defined standards for behavior and academic work had fewer problems, higher rates of attendance, lower rates of delinquency, and higher scores on tests of achievement. This pattern is remarkably similar to that uncovered in studies comparing public and private high schools (Coleman, Hoffer, and Kilgore, 1982). In these studies, too, students' achievement was higher in schools that were somewhat more structured and demanding—no matter whether the school was public or private.

As Rutter (1983) explains, being an effective teacher entails two distinct processes: gaining and maintaining students' attention and instructing students in the subject matter. A teacher who is a good lecturer will not be an effective teacher if he or she lacks classroom management skills. Managing a classroom effectively entails more than merely knowing how to discipline students once they become unruly, however. In fact, teachers who spend too much time on disciplining the few students who misbehave run the risk of losing the interest of the rest of the class. Especially in junior high school classrooms, where young adolescents may not yet have developed a high level of self-control in the absence of guidelines from adults, maintaining students' attention depends on having well-organized lesson plans, teaching in a way that involves and en-

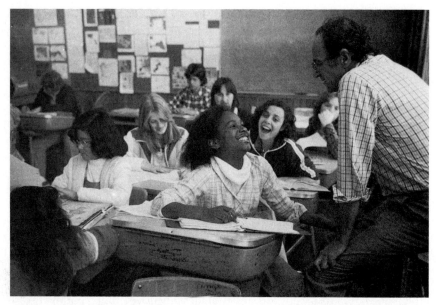

Students perform better when their teachers maintain well-defined, high standards for behavior and academic work and behave in a supportive but firm manner. *(Elizabeth Crews/Stock, Boston)*

gages the whole class, and using creative and innovative approaches to instruction. As most experienced teachers know, disorganized lesson plans and frequent interruptions for discipline can quickly lead to chaos in the classroom. The National Commission on Excellence in Education (1983), for example, recommended that schools adopt and enforce firm disciplinary codes and that continually disruptive students be removed from classrooms in order to permit teachers to spend more time on teaching and less on discipline.

Recently, educational researcher Fred Newmann (in press) has suggested that if we want to understand the impact of classroom climate on student achievement, we need to better understand how to enhance **student engagement** in school. Engagement refers to the extent to which students are psychologically committed to learning and mastering the material, and

not simply interested in completing the assigned work. Newmann believes that the makework, routinized, rigid structure of most classrooms, in which teachers lecture at students rather than engage them in discussion, alienates most students from school and undermines their desire to achieve. As one student explains:

> What do I like least about school? Basically, it's boring. Like English. What we do in there—we're supposed to read something, and then maybe do something in your notebook, when you could do everything at home. So I don't really have to show up. So, I'd say that class could be about 10 minutes long. (Cited in Brown, Lamborn, and Newmann, in press)

Think back to your own high school experience. What distinguished the good classes from the tedious ones? Newmann (in press) suggests a number of factors that contribute to engagement. First, teachers need to provide opportunities for students to genuinely display their competencies. Second, schools should try to facilitate students' feelings of belonging to their school. Finally, and most important, teachers should assign work that is "authentic." Authentic work is work that is interesting, fun, and relevant to the real world. There is nothing more alienating to a student than being asked to perform tasks that are boring, colorless, and irrelevant. Yet, this is what the typical student experiences in the classroom—especially outside the college prep track—and it is little surprise that so many students are disengaged from school.

Several studies also point to the importance of teachers' expectations of students. When teachers expect more of their students, they actually learn more; when teachers expect less, they learn less. This phenomenon is known as the **self-fulfilling prophecy** (Rosenthal and Jacobson, 1968). Unfortunately, research suggests that teachers are likely to base their expectations in part on students' ethnic and socioeconomic background. In much the same way that these factors may influence tracking decisions, as we saw earlier, they may consciously and unconsciously shape teachers' expectations, which, in turn, affect students' learning. Thus, for example, teachers may call on poor or minority students less often than on their affluent or white peers—conveying a not-so-subtle message about whose responses the teacher believes are more worthy of class attention (Good and Brophy, 1984). It is not difficult to see how years of exposure to this sort of treatment can adversely affect a student's self-concept and interest in school. Indeed, teacher biases against lower-class children may make it difficult for students from lower socioeconomic groups to attain a level of academic accomplishment that would permit upward mobility.

Teachers and school personnel, of course, are not the only influences on adolescents' behavior in school. Several writers have noted that the peer group's values and norms also exert an important influence. In *The Adolescent Society* (1961), for example, James Coleman found that high schools vary a great deal in the extent to which the prevailing peer culture emphasizes academic success as a route toward status and popularity. In schools in which academic success is not valued by the student body, students are less likely to achieve grades that are consonant with their tested ability. In other words, a bright student who attends a school in which getting good grades is frowned upon by other students will actually get lower grades than he or she would in a school in which scholastic success is generally admired.

As we noted in the previous chapter on peer groups, however, cliques and crowds differ enormously in the extent to which they encourage or discourage academic success (Clasen and Brown, 1985). It therefore is misleading to generalize about the impact of peer groups on adolescents' engagement in school without knowing more about the specific peer group in question. Some peer groups (e.g., the "brains") may place a great deal of pressure on their members to succeed in school and may engage in behaviors (e.g., studying together) that promote school success. Other groups, in contrast, may actively discourage school success. An especially telling example of this is seen in a recent ethnographic study of African-American male peer groups in an inner-city school (Fordham and Ogbu, 1986). In the peer groups studied, pressure was put on the group members *not* to achieve, because succeeding in school was seen as "acting white" and breaking from the group's ethnic identity. Thus those students with high aspirations found themselves having to choose between succeeding in school and keeping their friends, a position that few adolescents of any race would want to find themselves in.

On average, students whose parents are involved in school activities, such as attending parent-teacher conferences and "back-to-school" nights, perform better in school than their peers. In addition, parents can foster better school performance in their teenagers by being authoritative and by encouraging academic success. *(Susan Lapides/Design Conceptions)*

Other researchers have focused on adolescents' experiences outside of school—at home, at work, and in extracurricular activities—and on the impact of these experiences on their school achievement and engagement. This research demonstrates that the impact of school on adolescent achievement can not be understood in isolation. Studies show, for example, that students whose parents are involved in school activities (such as parent-teacher conferences and "back-to-school" nights), who encourage and emphasize academic success, and who use "authoritative" parenting practices (see Chapter 4) do better in secondary school than their peers (Dornbusch et al., 1987; Seginer, 1983; Steinberg, Lamborn, Dornbusch and Darling, 1992; Stevenson and Baker, 1987). In Chapter 7, we shall look more closely

at the effects of employment and extracurricular participation on school achievement—suffice it to say here that students who over-extend themselves on the job or the playing field may inadvertently jeopardize their school performance (Brown, Lamborn, and Newmann, in press; Steinberg and Dornbusch, 1991).

## Beyond High School

### THE COLLEGE BOUND

The early part of the twentieth century was an important time in the development not only of secondary schools but also of postsecondary educational institutions in the United States.

Although colleges and, to a lesser extent, universities had existed for some time previously, not until the latter part of the nineteenth century did diversity in institutions of higher education begin to develop. Early postsecondary institutions were typically small, private liberal arts colleges, often with a strong theological emphasis. But during a relatively brief period bridging the nineteenth and twentieth centuries, these colleges were joined by a host of other types of institutions, including large private universities, technical colleges, professional schools, publicly financed state universities, land-grant colleges, urban universities, and two-year community colleges (Brubacher and Rudy, 1976).

Although postsecondary educational institutions multiplied and became more varied during the early part of this century, enrollment in college was still a privilege enjoyed by very few young people. In 1900, only 4 percent of the 18- to 21-year-old population was enrolled in college; and by 1930, the proportion had grown to some 12 percent. Even as recently as 1950, fewer than one in five young people were enrolled in college (Church, 1976). During the first half of the twentieth century, then, colleges and universities were not prominent in the lives of most American youth.

How different the state of affairs is today. Paralleling the rise of secondary education between 1920 and 1940, postsecondary education grew dramatically between 1950 and 1970 (see Figure 6.3). By 1960, one-third of all young people were entering college directly after high school graduation. College enrollments, which numbered about 1 million in 1930, had risen to more than 3 million by 1960 and to nearly 8.5 million by 1970. Today, nearly half of the 18- to 19-year-old population is enrolled in college. Although there were large increases in the enrollment of minority youth during the 1970s, the proportion of mi-

**FIGURE 6.3** Between 1950 and 1970, U.S. college enrollments expanded markedly. They have remained reasonably stable since then.

nority youth enrolled in higher education fell during the early years of the 1980s (Wetzel, 1987).

If there are two dominant characteristics that distinguish the development of postsecondary education in contemporary America from that in other parts of the world, they are diversity and accessibility (Brubacher and Rudy, 1976). In countries other than the United States, postsecondary education is likely to be monopolized by monolithic public universities, and fewer adolescents continue their formal education beyond high school (President's Science Advisory Committee, 1974). Individuals are often separated into college- and noncollege-bound tracks early in adolescence, typically on the basis of standardized national examinations. In fact, rather than housing all high school students in comprehensive high schools such as those found in the United States, many European nations separate students during early adolescence into schools for college-bound youngsters and schools designed to provide vocational and technical education.

Although the accessibility and diversity of its postsecondary educational institutions have been commended by many, the American system of higher education has not been without its critics (Brubacher and Rudy, 1976). Some observers have suggested that educational diversity has been gained at the expense of quality. With so many different options and electives for young people to choose among, it has been hard for colleges to ensure that all students receive a high-quality education. Others have pointed out that it is difficult for many young people to obtain adequate information about the range of alternatives open to them and that students are often poorly matched with the colleges they enter (Boyer, 1986). The large enrollments of high schools make it difficult for school counselors to give each student individualized advice.

In some respects, the transition from high school to college parallels the transition from elementary to secondary school. For many students, going to college means entering an even larger, more formidable, and more impersonal environment. For some, the transition may coincide with other life changes, such as leaving home, breaking off or beginning an important relationship, or having to manage one's own residence or finances for the first time.

As a consequence of all of these factors, although many more young people enroll in college today than in previous years, a very large number do not graduate. Perhaps as a consequence of increasing accessibility, poor matching, and a lack of "consumer" knowledge among college applicants, rates of college attrition are high: Only four of every ten students who enter college in the United States graduate from the same college four years later. Of the 60 percent of students who leave the school they entered, about half eventually finish college, either returning to that particular college or transferring to another. Half, however, never obtain a college degree. Of the students who drop out of college, about half do so during their first year (Pantages and Creedon, 1978). In other words, while a great deal has been done to make college *entrance*

more likely, rates of college *graduation* lag far behind.

## THE "FORGOTTEN HALF"

The problems associated with moving from high school to college pale in comparison, however, with those associated with not going to college at all. In general, college graduates earn substantially more income over their lifetime than do individuals who attend college but do not graduate, and these individuals in turn earn much more than students who do not attend college at all (William T. Grant Commission on Work, Family, and Citizenship, 1988). Individuals who drop out of high school before graduation suffer a wide range of problems, which we examine in detail in Chapter 13.

One of the unfortunate by-products of our having made postsecondary education so accessible—and so expected—is that we have turned our backs on individuals who do not go to college, even though they comprise nearly half of the adolescent population—approximately 20 million individuals (William T. Grant Foundation Commission on Work, Family, and Citizenship, 1988). This so-called **Forgotten Half** was the subject of a lengthy and detailed study conducted in the late 1980s by a prestigious national commission.

The report concluded that our secondary schools are geared almost exclusively toward college-bound youngsters. We noted earlier that opportunities for learning and for higher-order thinking are much greater in college-prep classes than in the general or vocational tracks. In addition to this, the commission noted that students who are not headed for college—some by choice, others by unavoidable circumstance—find that their high schools have not prepared them at all for the world of work. Even those who complete school and earn a diploma—who have done what they

—will earn a 1/3 more $ for those who finish college.

were "supposed" to do as adolescents—may have a hard time finding employment and a nearly impossible time finding a satisfying, well-paying job. As a consequence, many individuals who make up the Forgotten Half spend their early adult years floundering between periods of part-time work, underemployment (working at a job that is less challenging than one would like), and unemployment. By the time they are 25 or so, most have found steady, if low-paying, employment. But they may have spent six or seven years living very close to the edge, if not in genuine poverty.

Noncollege-graduates have always fared worse economically than their peers who have continued their education past high school. But the gap between the "haves" and the "have-nots" widened considerably during the 1980s. For instance, in the United States, the "real" annual earnings (that is, earnings adjusted for changes in the cost of living) of young adult men fell between 1973 and 1986. But whereas the drop in income was about 6 percent for college graduates during this time period, the drop for high school graduates was more than 28 percent, and for high school dropouts, 42 percent. In other words, the typical high school graduate without college experience must survive on one-third less income today than his counterpart in the early 1970s (William T. Grant Commission on Work, Family, and Citizenship, 1988).

One important contributing factor to the declining fortunes of the Forgotten Half has been the change in the world of work mentioned earlier in this chapter: As manufacturing jobs began to be replaced by minimum-wage service jobs, the chances of making a decent living without college experience worsened appreciably. Today, young adults without college experience often must try to make ends meet on minimum-wage jobs—jobs that offer little in the way of promotion or advancement.

The economic problems faced by noncollege-bound youth have been compounded by the escalating costs of such essentials as housing and health care.

Given the high dropout rate already characteristic of most colleges, the answer to the problems of the Forgotten Half does not seem to be simply to encourage more individuals to continue their education past high school. Obviously, for those who want postsecondary education, we should make every attempt to see that they can obtain and afford it. But what about those adolescents who just are not interested in a college degree? How can these individuals be helped?

Experts believe that one potential answer involves strengthening the links between the worlds of school and work during high school. In most other industrialized countries, noncollege-bound youth begin apprenticeships during their last two years of compulsory school, so that by the time they have completed their formal schooling, they are well-trained to take on skilled jobs (Hamilton, 1990). Instead of just "dumping" these adolescents out into the labor force at graduation, as we do in America, schools and communities provide training, career counseling, and job placement services throughout high school. In most contemporary American high schools, counseling is geared toward helping college-bound students continue their education. Some critics have suggested that we should spend just as much time helping the other 50 percent of adolescents make their transition into adulthood as smooth as possible.

## Schools and Adolescent Development

Whatever the shortcomings of schools may be, staying in school is preferable to dropping out, not only in terms of earnings, but in terms of

Many critics of American secondary education have called for the development of formal apprenticeship programs, such as those presently in place in Europe, as a way of strengthening the link between school and work for noncollege-bound students. Here, a French adolescent is completing his apprenticeship with a master chef. *(Owen Franken/ Stock, Boston)*

cognitive development as well. One study contrasted the performance of dropouts and graduates on a battery of standardized tests of achievement administered during late adolescence (Alexander et al., 1985). The study took into account differences in achievement levels that existed before the dropouts had left school (two years before the assessment was conducted), because dropouts are more likely than graduates to show achievement problems early in their educational careers. Adolescents who stayed in school gained far more intellectually over the two-year interval than did the dropouts in a variety of content areas. More important, the results showed that the adverse effects of dropping out were most intense among socioeconomically disadvantaged students. Paradoxically, then, those students who are most likely to leave school prior to graduation may be most harmed by doing so.

One other way of assessing the contribution of schools to adolescents' intellectual development is by comparing early adolescents' intellectual gains during the school year with their gains during the summer. An ingenious study by Heyns (1982) did just this. Using information on the academic progress of students measured at three points in time—the beginning of the school year, the end of the school year, and the beginning of the next year—she was able to see how the academic progress of students during the summer compared with their academic progress during the school session. Her results were surprising and point once again to the importance of school for minority and disadvantaged youth. Among white students, rates of academic progress during the school year and during the summer were comparable. Among African-American students, however, the pattern was different. Although rates of progress during the school year were more or less equal to those of white students, during the summer months, African-American students' scores actually declined. In other words, if it were not for the effects of school on cognitive development, the discrepancy between white and African-American youngsters' achievement scores would be much greater than it currently is.

Far less is known about the impact of schools on the psychosocial development of adolescents. Some observers have noted that most schools are not structured to promote psychosocial development, with their excessive focus on conformity and obedience and their lack of encouragement for creativity, independence, and self-reliance (Friedenberg, 1967; Hill, 1980b). But there are very many good schools, in which students not only learn the academic material taught in classes, but learn about themselves, their relationships with others, and their society as well. Schools differ from each other, and it may be difficult to generalize about the impact of schools on adolescent development without knowing more about the particular school in question.

It is also important to recognize that, despite adults' intentions and objectives, students do not view school solely in terms of its academic agenda. In one study, the researchers asked a sample of 7th- through 12th-graders to list the best and worst things about school. The best things? "Being with my friends" and "Meeting new people." The worst? Homework, tests, and the restrictive atmosphere of the school (Brown, Lamborn and Newmann, in press). Adults may evaluate schools in terms of their contribution to adolescents' cognitive and ca-

reer development, but for the typical adolescent, school is the main setting for socializing. When we ask about the consequences of leaving school early, we must take into account the impact this would have on the individual's social, as well as cognitive, development.

Studies also show that students' experiences within a school can vary widely according to the track they are in, the peer group they belong to, and the extracurricular activities in which they participate. It seems safe to say that academically talented and economically advantaged students have a more positive experience in school than their less capable or less affluent counterparts—positive not only with respect to what they learn in class, but with respect to the impact of school on their feelings about themselves as individuals. Their teachers pay more attention to them, they are more likely to hold positions of leadership in extracurricular organizations, and they are more likely to experience classes that are engaging and challenging. In other words, the structure of a school—its size, its tracking policy, its curriculum—provides different intellectual and psychosocial opportunities for students who occupy different places within that structure. The best answer to the question, "How do schools affect adolescent development?" is another question: "Which schools, which adolescents, and in what respects?"

## Summary

1. Today, schools play an extremely important role in structuring the nature of adolescence in modern society. Virtually all individuals between 14 and 17 years old in the United States are enrolled in school. One hundred years ago, fewer than 10 percent of this age group were students.

2. A number of social forces combined to lead the development of compulsory education

for adolescents in America. Among the most important were industrialization, immigration, and urbanization. During the 1920s, the high school as we know it today—the comprehensive high school—was born.

3. Educators have long debated the nature of the high school curriculum. During the 1960s and 1970s, educators clamored for "relevance". During the 1980s, the pendulum swung "back to basics." During the 1990s, the fashion is "higher-order thinking." This is not because of indecisiveness: As society changes, so does the preparation young people need for adulthood.

4. Many features of the social organization of schools have been researched, including school and class size, various forms of age grouping, tracking, racial integration, and public versus private funding. In general, research indicates that adolescents fare best in smaller schools in which students are not tracked. They may also do better when they do not have to change schools as often.

5. Researchers agree that the climate of the school is more important than its organization or structure. Effective teachers are similar to effective parents: warm, firm, and fair. Students are also more likely to be engaged in school when they have opportunities for developing their competencies, feel attached to the school as an institution, and are engaged in authentic work, rather than make-work.

6. About half of all American adolescents go on to some form of education beyond high school, but only two-thirds of these students eventually receive a degree. Many social critics believe that high schools as they are presently structured do not serve noncollege-bound adolescents very well. As a result, half of the country's adolescents leave high school without adequate preparation for the world of work they hope to enter.

7. It is difficult to generalize about the role of schools in adolescent development. Research indicates, above all, that academically and economically advantaged adolescents have a more positive experience in school than their counterparts. One worrisome theme that has emerged from studies of high schools is that schools, as they are presently structured, seem to work best for those students who need the least help.

## Key Terms

comprehensive high
  school
Forgotten Half
functional
  community
higher-order thinking
junior high school
mainstreaming

middle school
overmanning
school climate
self-fulfilling
  prophecy
student engagement
tracking

## For Further Reading

CHURCH, R. (1976). *Education in the United States*. New York: Free Press. A comprehensive history of the development of schools in America.

ENTWISLE, D. (1990). Schools and the adolescent. In S. Feldman and G. Elliott (Eds.), *At the threshold: The developing adolescent*. Cambridge: Harvard University Press. A review of research on schools and adolescent development.

GAMORAN, A. (1987). The stratification of high school learning opportunities. *Sociology of Education, 60*, 135–155. How tracking affects students' opportunities to learn.

POWELL, A., FARRAR, E., AND COHEN, D. (1985). *The shopping mall high school*. Boston: Houghton Mifflin. An extensive critique of the nature and structure of contemporary high schools.

RESNICK, L. (1987). *Education and learning to think.* Washington: National Academy Press. Some proposals for improving schools' contribution to the development of higher order thinking.

WILLIAM T. GRANT FOUNDATION COMMISSION ON WORK, FAMILY, AND CITIZENSHIP. (1988). *The forgotten half: Non-college youth in America.* Washington: William T. Grant Foundation Commission on Work, Family, and Citizenship. A discussion of the special problems of noncollege-bound youth.

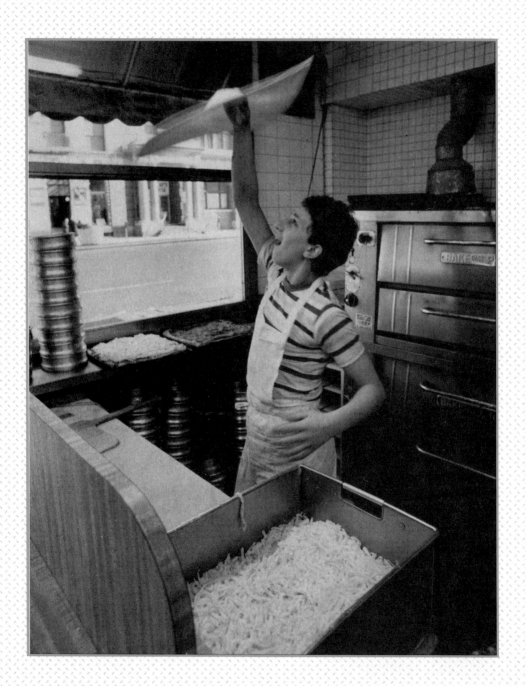

# WORK AND LEISURE

Most discussions of the contexts of adolescence are limited to those that we have looked at in the past three chapters: the family, the peer group, and the school. There is no question that these settings exert a profound influence on the development and behavior of the young person. Yet it may surprise you to learn that today's teenagers spend more time in leisure activities than they do in the "productive" activities of school, more time alone than with members of their family, about four times the number of hours each week on a part-time job as on homework, and considerably more time "wired" to music, videotapes, or television than "tuned into" the classroom (Csikszentmihalyi and Larson, 1984). In this chapter, we look at these other contexts of adolescence—the contexts of work and leisure.

Social scientists are just now beginning to study the ways in which work and leisure influence adolescent development (Fine, Mortimer, and Roberts, 1990). Perhaps because we historically have considered school to be the most important activity of adolescence in contemporary society, we have paid far less attention to what adolescents do in their "spare" time—even though their spare time occupies more of their waking hours than does their time in school. As you know, however, one of the hallmarks of life in industrialized society is that adolescents have considerable amounts of time and money to devote to activities of their choosing. Among the most popular are working at a part-time job, participating in an after-school extracurricular activity, shopping and hanging out with friends, and enjoying one or more of the mass media, including television, radio, recorded music, video, and movies.

## *Work and Leisure in Contemporary Society*

The tremendous significance of leisure in the lives of contemporary adolescents has had several origins. Ironically, one of the most important contributors was the development of compulsory schooling. Prior to this, adolescents were expected to work full-time, and most maintained schedules comparable to adults, working long hours each week. With the spread of high schools during the early decades of this century, however, adolescents were in effect barred from the labor force—the part-time jobs familiar to us today simply did not exist in large numbers, making after-school employment relatively rare. One indirect effect of compulsory high school, then, was to increase the amount of free time available to the young person—time that previously would have been occupied in work. Indeed, adults were so worried about the free time available to adolescents that they began to organize various youth clubs and activities, such as the Boy Scouts, or organized sports, for example, in order to occupy their "idle hands" (Modell and Goodman, 1990). In some respects, then, leisure became an institutionalized part of adolescence as a supplement to school and a replacement for full-time employment.

A second influence on the rise of adolescent leisure in contemporary society was the increased affluence of Americans following the second World War. As we noted in Chapter 3, the invention of the "teenager"—and, more important, the discovery of the teenager by those in advertising and marketing—changed the nature of adolescence in modern society. As adolescents gained more autonomy, they came to be recognized as consumers with plenty of discretionary income, an image that persists today. This week, notice the commercials and advertisements aimed at teenagers in popular television shows, teen magazines, or on rock stations. You'll see that much of the advertising aimed at young people concerns leisure expenditures: music, movies, eating out, athletic equipment, even, unfortunately, cigarettes and alcohol. The cultivation of adolescents as consumers has played an important role both in shaping their leisure tastes and in

In contemporary society, teenagers have a great deal of discretionary income, partly as a consequence of working in part-time jobs during the school year. Millions of dollars are spent each year cultivating teenagers' tastes for music, movies, and other leisure expenditures. *(Margot Granitsas/Image Works)*

studying; about 31 percent in "maintenance" activities, such as grooming, eating, or running errands; and about 40 percent in "leisure" activities, such as socializing, watching TV, or playing sports (Csikszentmihalyi and Larson, 1984) (see Figure 7.1). Interestingly, American adolescents spend far more time on leisure, and far less time on schoolwork, than do their counterparts in other countries. For instance, the average American high school student spends fewer than five hours per week on homework; in Japan, the average is close to five hours *per day* (Greenberger and Steinberg, 1986).

What is the effect of all this "free" time on adolescents' behavior and development? Are they learning about the "real world" from their part-time jobs? Are their extracurricular activities as "character-building" as adults believe they are? Are they being driven toward sex and violence by the mass media? Are teenagers really affected by the lyrics of rock music or the images of MTV? These are some of the questions we examine in this chapter. We begin with one of the most controversial issues in the study of contemporary adolescents: how teenagers are affected by after-school employment.

## Adolescents and Work

The participation of adolescents in the world of work has gone through a number of dramatic changes during the past 100 years. Today, it is commonplace to see teenagers working in restaurants and retail stores. Indeed, most youngsters who were enrolled in high school during the 1990s held part-time jobs at one time or another during the school year. More than 75 percent of today's high school students will have worked before graduating. But although working while attending high school may currently be the norm, only recently has part-time employment become prevalent among American adolescents. In fact, the

drawing them into the part-time labor force. As we shall see later in this chapter, today's adolescent can not afford such "necessities" as a personal stereo or inflatable sneakers without taking on an after-school job.

How much time do adolescents spend in various leisure activities? According to one study, in which adolescents were asked to monitor their time use with electronic pagers, the typical American adolescent spends about 29 percent of his or her waking hours in "productive" activities, such as attending class or

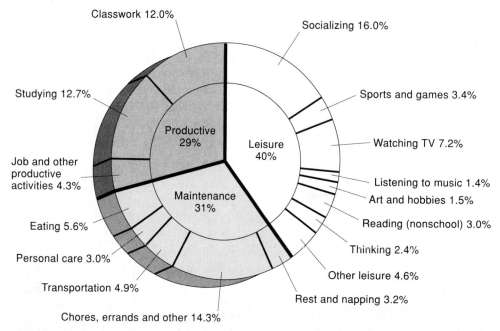

**FIGURE 7.1**   Adolescents spend more time in leisure activities (such as socializing) than in productive activities (such as studying) or "maintenance" activities (such as running errands). (Csikszentmihalyi and Larson, 1984)

widespread employment of students represents an important break from past eras, in which going to school and working were mutually exclusive activities. In order to understand how and why the state of affairs changed, we need to begin with a look at school and work early in this century.

## SCHOOL AND WORK IN THE EARLY TWENTIETH CENTURY

Before 1925—when continuing on in high school was the exception, not the rule—most teenagers entered the work force by the time they turned 15 years old. Teenagers from all but the most affluent families left school between the ages of 12 and 15 and became full-time workers (Modell, Furstenberg, and Hershberg, 1976). Adolescents were either students or workers, but not both.

During the second quarter of this century, however, the school began to replace the workplace as the setting in which most adolescents spent their weekdays. As secondary education grew and became more widespread among different social and economic segments of American society, more youngsters remained in school well into middle and late adolescence, and fewer elected to work. Compulsory education laws were passed in most states that required youngsters to remain in school until at least the age of 16, and part-time jobs were not plentiful. Furthermore, a variety of child labor laws were enacted to restrict youngsters' employment (Kett, 1977).

As a result of these social and legislative changes, the employment of American teenagers in the formal labor force declined steadily during the first four decades of this century. As labor force expert Beatrice Reubens points out,

In previous eras, adolescents played an important role in farming. Early work experience of this sort readied young people for the work they would perform during adulthood. *(Bettmann Archive)*

It is true that a tradition has long existed in the United States that it was respectable, even praiseworthy to work one's way through school, but [before 1940] the numbers [of students who worked] were not large. Prior to World War II, attending school and holding a . . . job were almost exclusive activities. (Reubens, Harrison, and Rupp, 1981, p. 296)

An incredible reversal has taken place in a period of about twenty-five years. Early in the century, most adolescents were workers, not students. By the middle of the century, most adolescents had become students, not workers. In 1940, only 5 percent of 16- and 17-year-old male high school students worked during the school year. Less than 2 percent of female stu-

dents of this age were employed (U.S. Department of Commerce, 1940).

## THE EMERGENCE OF THE STUDENT-WORKER

The situation began to change again between 1940 and 1950. The rise of a separate workplace, composed almost exclusively of adolescents, was under way. Examining this phenomenon in detail provides a nice example of how changes in society can transform the nature of adolescence.

Following the end of World War II, sectors of the American economy that needed large numbers of part-time employees expanded rapidly (Ginzberg, 1977). In particular, the postwar period was a time of tremendous growth in retail stores and restaurants. Between 1950 and 1976, the retail trade sector of the economy (which includes all jobs in which people sell finished products to consumers) expanded by 96 percent, and the service sector (which includes all jobs in which people provide services to others), by 172 percent. As economist Eli Ginzberg observed in 1977, "More than three out of every five new jobs created [since 1950] have been in retail trade or services, where many jobs are part-time and wages are traditionally low" (1977, p. 47). Employers, particularly in businesses such as fast-food restaurants, needed workers who were willing to work part-time for relatively low wages and for short work shifts. Many employers looked to teenagers to fill these jobs. Consequently, over the past twenty-five years or so, one out of every three new entrants into the labor force has been a young person (Ginzberg, 1977, p. 45).

Another reason for the phenomenal rise of the adolescent workplace is the dramatic increase during the last twenty years in the cost of living for the typical American teenager. Although inflation took its toll on people of all ages, it hit teenagers especially hard. For example, the cost of being a teenager rose more than 20 percent between 1975 and 1979, and more than 15 percent in 1979 alone. In both periods, the rate of inflation on typical teen items, such as records and movie tickets, rose considerably faster than the rate of inflation overall. But unlike many adults who receive cost-of-living salary increases commensurate with the rate of inflation, many adolescents rely on a weekly allowance from their parents, which usually does not rise as economic indicators change. As prices rose and allowances held steady, adolescents looking for spending money were drawn into the world of work (Rotbart, 1981).

As shown in Figure 7.2, the proportion of high school students holding part-time jobs

**FIGURE 7.2** More U.S. high school students are working during the school year now than at any other time in recent history.

rose dramatically from 1940 on. By 1980, according to a nationwide survey conducted for the National Center for Education Statistics (Lewin-Epstein, 1981), about two-thirds of all high school seniors and about half of all high school sophomores held part-time jobs during the week prior to the survey. More recent estimates indicate that the proportion of working high school students has not changed appreciably since this time (Bachman et al., 1986; Barton, 1989). By current estimates, at any one time during the school year, well over 6 million American high school students are working.

In less than half a century, adolescence had undergone a remarkable change. In 1940, it was virtually unheard-of for a high school student to hold a regular part-time job during the school year. Today, it is almost unheard-of for a high school student not to work.

In the past it was young people from less affluent families who were more likely to work;

today the opposite is true. Working during high school is more common among middle- and upper-middle-class teenagers, presumably because these youngsters have an easier time finding employment. Jobs in the adolescent workplace are more likely to be located in suburban areas, where the more affluent families reside. The national survey cited above revealed, for example, that the teenagers most likely to work came from families earning between $20,000 and $25,000 annually. Least likely to be employed were teenagers from families with annual incomes below $7,000 (Lewin-Epstein, 1981).

Not only are more high school students working today than ever before, but those who do work are working for considerably more hours than adolescents have in the past (Greenberger and Steinberg, 1986). The average high school sophomore put in close to 15 hours per week at a job, and the average senior, about 20 hours per week (Bachman et al., 1986; Barton, 1989; Lewin-Epstein, 1981; Steinberg and Dornbush, 1991). Considering that the average school day runs for about 6 hours, today's typical working adolescent is busy with school or work commitments for close to 50 hours a week.

Although youngsters in contemporary America do not enter the formal labor force until the age of 15 or 16, many individuals have worked on an informal basis during childhood. We can identify four phases in the transition of young people into adult work roles:

1. *Household work:* During childhood, most boys and girls are assigned chores around the house (White and Brinkerhoff, 1981). Typically, they help in the kitchen, help care for younger siblings, and help in such tasks as yardwork and cleaning. Families who own and operate a business such as a store or a farm may require children to work in the family enterprise. However,

Today, adolescents usually work in jobs that are unrelated to the careers they will pursue as adults. *(Sarah Putnam/Picture Cube)*

family businesses, once popular in America, are relatively rare today.

2. *Informal part-time employment:* By late childhood and during early adolescence, many youngsters begin to take on employment outside the home on an informal basis for other family members or neighbors. Baby-sitting is a common source of income for many young adolescents, as are gardening, house cleaning, and newspaper delivery (Greenberger and Steinberg, 1983).

3. *Formal part-time employment:* As adolescents reach the age required for formal employment in their home state, they generally enter the formal labor force as part-time employees in the adolescent workplace. Typically, this occurs between the ages of 14 and 16. Students take on jobs after school, in the evenings, and on weekends, with many working fifteen hours or more weekly on a regular schedule. Although most jobs open to teenagers pay only the minimum wage, they pay more than the informal jobs held by younger adolescents (Greenberger and Steinberg, 1986; Steinberg and Dornbusch, 1991).

4. *Full-time employment:* Full-time employment in the adult workplace usually begins shortly after an individual has completed his or her schooling.

## TEENAGE EMPLOYMENT IN AMERICA AND IN OTHER NATIONS

The extent and nature of teenage employment vary considerably from country to country. In most traditional societies, work life and family life are not as distinct as they are in contemporary America, and youngsters are typically integrated into the world of work before they reach adolescence (Whiting and Whiting, 1975). If the society subsists on farming, children are taught how to farm at an early age. If the society subsists on hunting, children are taught how to hunt. Although young people who are still acquiring work skills may be given tasks that are more elementary than those performed by their elders, adolescents and adults work side by side, and a distinct adolescent workplace—such as that in the United States—is not usually found. Whereas we draw a distinction between schooling and work in contemporary society, in many traditional societies, the two activities are essentially the same.

In developing nations, where industrialization is still in a relatively early stage and a large percentage of the population is poor, adolescents generally leave school early—at least by American standards. In these countries, most adolescents enter into full-time employment by the time they are 15 or 16, in jobs similar to those they will hold as adults. Very often, adolescents work for their families. The pattern in these countries closely resembles America at an earlier stage in its own industrialization: school for adolescents of the extremely affluent; work for the majority of teenagers.

The contrast with other comparably industrialized countries is the most interesting, for it reveals that the high school student-worker is a distinctively American phenomenon. In most highly industrialized countries other than the United States, adolescents are more likely to defer employment until their education is completed. As shown in Figure 7.3, for example, during 1979, over two-thirds of all American 16- and 17-year-old adolescents were working while attending school; but in Canada, only about 37 percent of this group was employed, in Sweden, only about 20 percent, and in Japan, less than 2 percent (Reubens, Harrison, and Rupp, 1983). More recent comparative figures are not available, but the consensus among experts is that U.S. students still work in larger numbers than their counterparts. In these countries and others in Western Europe, young people generally move from school directly into full-time employment without an intervening period of formal part-

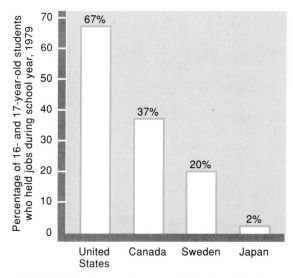

FIGURE 7.3 The employment of high school students is far more common in the United States than in other industrialized countries. (Reubens, Harrison, and Rupp, 1983)

education. In contrast, in Europe, students' work experience is much more continuous with the roles they will enter as adults.

How can we account for these differences between the United States and other industrialized countries? First, part-time employment opportunities are not as readily available elsewhere as they are in America. Fast-food restaurants, although increasingly popular in other countries, are not seen on every major street. Second, the scheduling of part-time jobs in other countries is not well suited to the daily routines of students. In Europe, for example, the school day lasts well into the late afternoon, and relatively few shops are open in the evenings. In the United States, many adolescents leave school early in the afternoon and go straight to their part-time jobs, where they work until nine or ten o'clock in the evening. Third, in most other industrialized countries,

time work. In the United States today, it is more common for youngsters to move from full-time school with no formal employment (during early adolescence), to a combination of school and part-time work (during middle and late dolescence), to full-time work (sometime during late adolescence or early adulthood).

Although European adolescents are less likely than their American counterparts to hold paying part-time jobs during the school year, they are *more* likely to work in school-sponsored or government-sponsored apprenticeships (Hamilton, 1990). In many countries, such as Germany, these apprenticeships play an extremely important role in preparing adolescents for the transition into adult employment, especially for students who are not bound for college. It is important to remember as you read this chapter that the studies of teen employment in the United States are typically studies of students who are working in part-time jobs that have little to do with the careers they hope to pursue after they complete their

The part-time employment of teenagers reached an all-time high in the early 1980s. Studies of the impact of employment on adolescent development, however, suggest that there may be costs associated with working more than fifteen or twenty hours per week during the school year. *(Rick Mansfield/Image Works)*

## THE SEXES: SEX DIFFERENCES IN THE ADOLESCENT WORKPLACE

One of the topics that social scientists interested in work have studied extensively concerns sex differences in the labor force. It is well documented that men and women typically work in different types of jobs and that men generally are paid higher wages—even when they do the same work as women. This disparity has been an important concern to many people who feel that such sex differences in patterns of work are unfair and serve to maintain economic inequities between the sexes. Are the same sorts of disparities found in teenagers' jobs? The answer seems to be yes (Greenberger and Steinberg, 1983; Lewin-Epstein, 1981).

Generally, boys are more likely to work as manual laborers, skilled laborers, gardeners, busboys, janitors, and newspaper deliverers. Girls are more likely to be employed as food servers, house cleaners, and babysitters. Moreover, boys almost never work as secretaries, receptionists, babysitters, nurse's aides, or house cleaners; and girls almost never as "busgirls," dishwashers, gardeners, manual laborers, janitors, or newspaper deliverers (see accompanying figure). A study of over 3,000 adolescents in southern California revealed that boys work longer hours than girls, and that "boys' " jobs pay better than "girls' " jobs. In fact, the average hourly wage for boys is about 15 percent higher than it is for girls (Greenberger and Steinberg, 1983).

These findings are important because they indicate that youngsters are exposed to the sort of sex differences characteristic of the adult workplace long before they reach adulthood. However, one question that cannot be answered is whether sex differences in adolescents' work experience are due to the different preferences of boys and girls (that is, whether boys and girls *choose* to work in different kinds of jobs) or to discrimination in the labor force (that is, whether employers choose boys for some jobs and girls for others). Could it be that sex differences in job preferences are established even *before* adolescence? In order to answer this question, one needs to look at patterns of work during childhood.

Were you given household chores when you were growing up? If you had a sibling of the opposite sex, were your chores the same, or were they different? Recent research suggests that in most families, the separation of "boys' " work and "girls' " work begins early in childhood, and that chores become even more sex-typed as children get older. Among young children, for example, boys and girls are equally likely to be given the chore of washing dishes. By the time children are a little older, however, this has become a "girls' " job. The opposite is true for various sorts of manual labor around the house, such as yardwork, which becomes more and more a "boys' " job as children get older (White and Brinkerhoff, 1981).

On the basis of these studies, it seems that young people learn lessons about the sex-appropriateness of various work roles at an early age. And these lessons have important implications for the subsequent occupational development of

*continued on next page*

the employment of children is associated with being poor, and there is a strong stigma attached to having one's children work. Many middle-class parents do not feel that it is appropriate for their children to have jobs while attending school. Fourth, schools demand much more out-of-school time in countries other than the United States; it is not uncom-

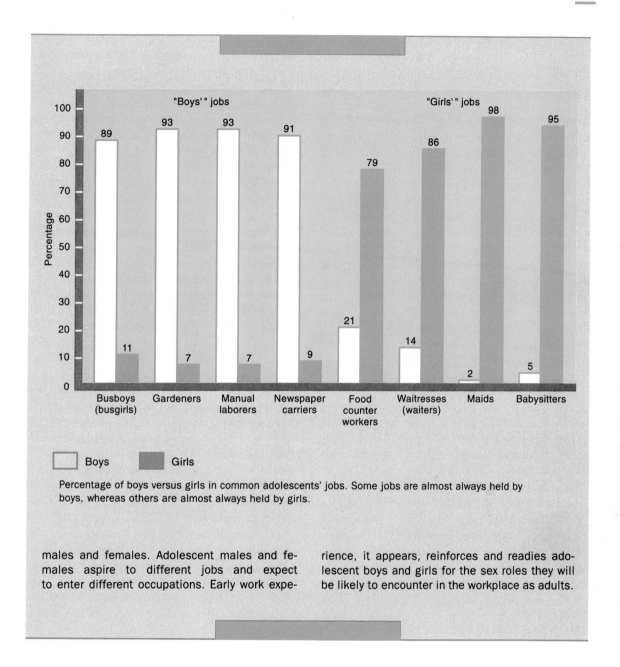

Percentage of boys versus girls in common adolescents' jobs. Some jobs are almost always held by boys, whereas others are almost always held by girls.

males and females. Adolescent males and females aspire to different jobs and expect to enter different occupations. Early work experience, it appears, reinforces and readies adolescent boys and girls for the sex roles they will be likely to encounter in the workplace as adults.

mon for a European high school student, for example, to be assigned four or five hours of homework nightly (Reubens, Harrison, and Rupp, 1981). Finally, as we noted in Chapter 6, American schools have not done a very good job of anticipating the needs of adolescents who do not intend to go on to college. As a result, formal apprenticeship programs, such as those found in most other industrialized countries, are quite rare in the United States.

## THE ADOLESCENT WORKPLACE TODAY

**Common adolescent jobs**  The range of jobs open to American adolescents who wish to work in the formal labor force is rather limited. Most surveys indicate that the proportion of adolescents who hold challenging or interesting jobs is very, very small. A substantial proportion of working high school students are employed in restaurants—staffing fast-food counters, preparing food, waiting on customers, clearing tables, seating guests, or washing dishes. About 17 percent of all working high school students work in these sorts of jobs. The remainder tend to work in other types of retail establishments—as cashiers or sales clerks (jobs that fall into these categories, outside of food service work, account for about 20 percent of working teenagers); in offices, as clerical assistants (10 percent); or as unskilled laborers (also about 10 percent). Unlike in previous eras, very few teenagers today are employed on farms or in factories (Charner and Fraser, 1987; Lewin-Epstein, 1981).

**The adolescent work environment**  In one series of studies of adolescents who work, the researchers examined teenagers' work environments. They were especially interested in collecting information about the degree to which adolescents had contact with adults on their jobs and about the sorts of tasks teenagers were given (Greenberger and Steinberg, 1981; Greenberger, Steinberg, and Ruggiero, 1982). If working is going to be a positive influence on youngsters' development, they reasoned, it is likely to be so only if the work environment provides opportunities for learning and self-reliance. Most of workers studied were employed in one of five types of work: food service (for example, fast-food counter worker); clerical (file clerk in an office); retail (cashier

in a store); manual labor (gardener); and skilled labor (assistant automobile mechanic). Using an elaborate coding system to record on-the-job activities, the researchers observed what went on in the work settings. They recorded the tasks adolescents performed (for example, cleans table), the things they said ("May I help you?"), and the people with whom they interacted (an adult customer). They also interviewed the adolescent workers and had them complete a series of questionnaires about their experiences at work.

The results were surprising. Unlike adolescents in traditional societies, whose work typically brings them into extensive contact with adults, the young people observed in the studies spent as much time on the job interacting with other adolescents as they did with their elders. In the typical fast-food restaurant, for example, nearly all of the workers were teenagers, the work supervisor was usually not much older, and the customers were often young people, too. Few of the teenage workers surveyed reported having formed close relationships with adults at work. They were unlikely to see their adult supervisors or co-workers outside of work, felt reluctant to go to the adults they knew at work with personal problems, and generally reported feeling less close to adults at work than to other people in their lives (Greenberger and Steinberg, 1981).

The studies also indicate that most teenagers' jobs are pretty dreary. Few jobs permit adolescents to behave independently or make decisions, they receive little instruction from their supervisors, and they are rarely required to use the skills they have been taught in school (Greenberger and Steinberg, 1986). As an illustration of this point, consider the following contrast: The average adolescent worker spends less than 6 percent of time on the job in such activities as reading, writing, or arithmetic; but he or she spends more than 25 percent of the time cleaning or carrying things.

With occasional exceptions, most teenagers'

# THE BURGER BLUES

The fast-food industry employs more American teenagers than does any other specific segment of the labor market. Given the results of the observational study described in the text, it is not surprising to learn that many adolescents who work in fast-food restaurants are unhappy with their jobs. Although nearly fifteen years old, the following newspaper excerpt still rings true today.

Low pay, distasteful working conditions, and autocratic bosses are hardly a new story to the millions of teenagers that the fast-food industry depends upon to peddle the billions of hamburgers, fries, and shakes it sells every year. But . . . few youngsters realize when they apply for a fast-food job that they will be doing better than average if they don't get disgusted and quit within four months. . . .

"I quit because I didn't like the way the managers treated us," says a 17-year-old who was a cashier at an Atlanta McDonald's last summer. "The managers," she says, "are real snotty. They yell at the workers in front of customers and call you stupid. At the end of August, fifteen of us quit because of one manager. Otherwise, most of us would have kept working after school." . . .

Low pay is a constant irritation. A 16-year-old who quit an Atlanta Wendy's last fall says he was "doing more work than I was getting paid for" at $2.65 an hour [the minimum wage at the time]. "Sometimes I'd have to work twelve hours a day. Other times there weren't enough of us for lunch-time crowds. One month we went through five assistant managers. When I get another job it won't be in fast foods."

To be sure . . . a number of fast-food employees . . . [feel] well-treated. "I like working here," says an Alabama fast-food worker. "It gives me a chance to meet new people." Another teen-ager, who makes $2.65 an hour as a Burger King food handler, says, "It's a lot of fun. The managers are nice to work for. I work pretty much the time I want to." And a young man working the counter in a Florida store says, "All the hard work is rewarding in the long run because the manager is a friend, parent, counselor, adviser, teacher, and boss."

More numerous, however, [are] comments such as [this] one from a counter employee in Texas who complained: "Management puts tremendous mental strain on the employees. We have all learned how to successfully steal enough money . . . to make working here with all the bull and pressure worthwhile."

*Source:* J. Montgomery, "Low Pay, Bossy Bosses Kill Kids' Enthusiasm for Food-Service Jobs," *Wall Street Journal*, March 15, 1979, pp. 1 ff.

jobs are repetitive, monotonous, and unlikely to be intellectually stimulating. Some are even highly stressful, requiring that youngsters work under intense time pressure without much letup (Greenberger and Steinberg, 1986).

## WORKING AND ADOLESCENT DEVELOPMENT

**The development of responsibility** Most people believe that working builds character, teaches adolescents about the "real" world, and helps young people prepare for adulthood. Like many of the widely held views of adolescence that have gone unquestioned over the years, these assumptions are not entirely supported by research on teenagers and work. Indeed, recent studies indicate that working during adolescence may even have some costs to young people's development.

One study examined the impact of employment on young people growing up during the Great Depression. The researchers found that boys who took on part-time jobs outside the home became more adultlike as a result: "Boys . . . who were employed showed a much greater interest in adults and spent more time with them . . . than other children. . . . Economic hardship and jobs increased their desire to associate with adults, to 'grow up' and become adult. This adult orientation is congruent with other behavioral correlates of roles in the household economy, including the responsible use of money . . . energetic or industrious behavior . . . and social independence" (Elder, 1974, pp. 81–82). Because very few girls worked outside the home during the Depression (most remained home and performed household labor so that their mothers could enter the labor force), the impact of employment on the development of responsibility among girls was not studied.

Studies of more contemporary youth also support the view that holding a job may help adolescents become more personally responsible (Steinberg, Greenberger, Garduque, Ruggiero, and Vaux, 1982). For example, in studies of southern California youngsters, standardized measures of responsibility were used to study adolescents before they entered their first part-time job and one year later. The study used a comparison group of nonworking teenagers, who were also studied at two times. The findings indicated that teenagers who work, compared with their peers who do not, are more likely to grow in self-reliance (the ability to manage themselves) and develop a more mature "work orientation" (the ability to complete work tasks and take pride in doing so). Not all studies have found this advantage, however (Mortimer et al., 1990; Steinberg and Dornbusch, 1991). There is no evidence that working enhances adolescents' self-esteem (Bachman et al., 1986).

These findings suggest that working may have a positive impact on some youngsters' development. But other findings, especially those pertaining to the issue of adolescents' sense of responsibility to others, are not as favorable. Generally, working does not enhance adolescents' feelings of social obligation, social tolerance, or social belongingness (Greenberger and Steinberg, 1986). It does not make adolescents feel more concern for the well-being of others. If anything, working seems to make youngsters more individualistic. Moreover, adolescents who have jobs are more likely to express cynical attitudes toward work and to endorse unethical business practices. For example, it has been found that workers are more likely to agree with such statements as, "Anyone who works harder than he or she has to is a little bit crazy" (an item from a scale designed to measure cynicism) and, "In my opinion, it's all right for workers who are paid a low salary to take little things from their jobs to make up for it" (an item from the scale measuring acceptance of unethical business practices; see Table 7.1 [Steinberg, Greenberger, Garduque, Ruggiero, and Vaux, 1982]. Another study found that adolescents who work long hours (twenty-plus hours weekly) are less satisfied with their lives than those who work fewer hours (Fine et al., 1990).

What can we make of these findings? Why would working make youngsters more self-reliant but at the same time more cynical about work, less concerned about the welfare of others and less satisfied with their lives? Perhaps the answer has something to do with the nature of the work most adolescents perform. Think for a moment about the job environ-

It is widely believed that working helps teenagers develop a greater sense of responsibility and healthier attitudes toward work. Recent research on the costs and benefits of adolescent employment, however, call this belief into question. *(Carolyn Hine/Picture Cube)*

ment of most teenagers. Their work is dull, monotonous, and often stressful. Even if you have never worked in such a job, you can certainly imagine that working under these conditions could make people feel cynical and protective of their own interests above all else.

**Money and its management** One specific aspect of responsibility that working is believed to affect is money management. Because the average working teenager earns between $250 and $300 each month, holding a job may provide many opportunities for learning how to budget, save, and use money responsibly. Although about half of all adolescents are given an allowance by their parents (most often, younger adolescents who are not employed), parents appear to exert more control over purchases made from allowances than they do over purchases made from job earnings (Greenberger and Steinberg, 1986; Miller and Yung, 1990). Research indicates, however, that few teenagers exercise a great deal of responsibility when it comes to managing their earnings. One national survey, for example, showed that the majority of working teenagers spent most of their earnings on their own needs and activities (Johnston et al., 1982). Few adolescents who work save a large percentage of their income for their education, and fewer still use their earnings to help their families with household expenses (see Table 7.2). Instead, the picture of the contemporary working teenager that emerges from these studies is one of self-indulgent materialism. Wages are spent on designer clothing, expensive stereo

## TABLE 7-1

### SCALES USED TO MEASURE "CYNICISM TOWARD WORK" AND "TOLERANCE OF UNETHICAL BUSINESS PRACTICES"

| Sample items from the "cynicism toward work" scale | Sample items from the "tolerance of unacceptable business practices" scale |
|---|---|
| People who work harder at their jobs than they have to are a little crazy. | People who break a few laws to make a profit aren't doing anything I wouldn't do in their position. |
| Most people today are stuck in dead-end, go-nowhere jobs. | Workers are entitled to "call in sick" when they don't feel like working. |
| Hard work really doesn't get you much of anything in this world. | It doesn't matter if a businessman bends the law a little to make a profit. |
| There's no such thing as a company that cares about its employees. | In my opinion, it's all right for workers who are paid a low salary to take little things. |
| If I had the chance, I'd go through life without ever working. | It's acceptable to me if a teenage worker cheats a little on the amount of income tax he or she pays the government. |
| People who take their work home with them probably don't have a very interesting home life. | |

Source: Steinberg et al., 1982.

equipment, movies, and eating out. A fair proportion of the earnings are spent on drugs and alcohol (Greenberger and Steinberg, 1986).

According to one social scientist, today's working teenagers may suffer from **premature affluence** (Bachman, 1983). As he put it, in an article entitled "Do High School Students Earn Too Much?":

A fairly popular assumption these days is that students should have a great deal of freedom in spending their part-time earnings, so that in making their own choices and occasionally their own mistakes they will get some reality experiences and "learn the value of a dollar." . . . The problem is that the "reality" faced by the typical high school student with substantial part-time earnings is just not very realistic. In the absence of payment for rent, utilities, groceries, and the many other necessities routinely provided by parents, the typical student is likely to find that most or all of his/her earnings are available for discretionary spending. . . . It seems likely that some

will experience what I've come to call "premature affluence"—affluence because $200 or more per month represents a lot of "spending money" for a high school student, and premature because many of these individuals will not be able to sustain that level of discretionary spending once they take on the burden of paying for their own necessities. (1983, p. 65)

What might be some of the effects of premature affluence? According to one team of researchers, some of the consequences may be increased cynicism about the value of hard work and a lack of interest in working harder than is absolutely necessary, increased interest in buying drugs and alcohol, and the tendency to develop more materialistic attitudes (Greenberger and Steinberg, 1986). The very experience that many adults believe builds "character" may, in reality, teach adolescents undesirable lessons about work and the meaning of money.

## TABLE 7-2

HIGH SCHOOL SENIORS IN 1982: WHERE THEIR EARNINGS WENT (Entries Are Percentages)

| | Males[1] | Females[1] | | Males[1] | Females[1] |
|---|---|---|---|---|---|
| *Please think about all the money you earned during the past year, including last summer. About how much of your past year's earnings have gone into:* | | | *D. Spending on your own needs and activities—things such as clothing, stereo, TV, records, other possessions, movies, eating out, other recreation, hobbies, gifts for others, and other personal expenses?* | | |
| *A. Savings for your future education?* | | | | | |
| None | 48 | 50 | None | 4 | 5 |
| A little | 23 | 21 | A little | 21 | 17 |
| Some[2] | 19 | 19 | Some[2] | 38 | 34 |
| Most[3] | 11 | 10 | Most[3] | 36 | 44 |
| *B. Savings or payments for a car or car expense?* | | | *E. Helping to pay family living expenses (groceries, housing, etc.)?* | | |
| None | 35 | 58 | None | 56 | 55 |
| A little | 19 | 16 | A little | 26 | 25 |
| Some[2] | 29 | 18 | Some[2] | 13 | 14 |
| Most[3] | 17 | 9 | Most[3] | 5 | 6 |
| *C. Other savings for long-range purposes?* | | | | | |
| None | 48 | 48 | | | |
| A little | 26 | 25 | | | |
| Some[2] | 18 | 20 | | | |
| Most[3] | 8 | 8 | | | |

[1] Number of cases are approximately 1500 for males and 1520 for females.
[2] Combines two categories: "Some" and "About half."
[3] Combines three categories: "Most," "About all," and "All."
*Source:* Bachman, 1983.

**Occupational deviance** It comes as no surprise to learn that some adolescents, like some adults, behave at work in ways that would certainly upset their employers—if their employers knew. Do adolescents who suffer from the "burger blues" actually do things at work to retaliate for their unpleasant working conditions? There is not a great deal of research on this question, but one study that has examined deviant behavior in the adolescent workplace revealed relatively high rates of misconduct among adolescent workers, even in the early months of their first jobs (Ruggiero, Greenberger, and Steinberg, 1982). Adolescent workers completed a questionnaire that examined several categories of **occupational deviance.** The workers, who were assured that their responses would remain confidential and anonymous, were asked to check whether and how often they had committed each of nine acts (see Figure 7.4). After nine months on the job, more than 60 percent had committed at least one "deviant" act. About 38 percent of working teenagers in the sample were "non-offenders," about 38 percent "occasional offenders," and about 24 percent "relatively frequent offenders."

Because comparisons between adolescent

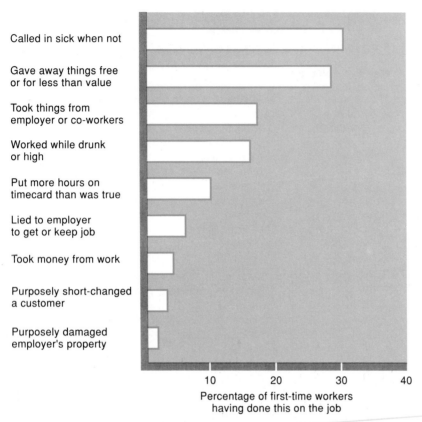

**FIGURE 7.4**  Some first-time workers do things on the job that their employers would not be pleased about. (Ruggiero, Greenberger, and Steinberg, 1982)

and adult workers were not made, it would be erroneous to conclude that adolescents necessarily made bad or untrustworthy workers. Furthermore, it is not clear from the study whether adolescents learned these deviant behaviors in the workplace or merely used the work setting as a context in which to display behaviors learned elsewhere. Nevertheless, the findings challenge the idea that the workplace is invariably a positive influence on the socialization of young people.

Some studies have also examined the time-honored belief that having a job deters youngsters from delinquent and criminal activity. Studies that have focused on youngsters

known to be more likely to get involved in delinquent behavior—inner-city youth, for example—do not show that working deters delinquency. In general, workers are no less likely to engage in delinquent behavior than nonworkers (Gottfredson, 1985). Studies of more representative samples of youngsters, however, suggest that employment during high school may be associated with *increased* delinquent behavior. In particular, workers—especially those who work long hours—are more likely than nonworkers to get into fights, commit vandalism and theft, and use, buy, and sell drugs (Bachman et al., 1986; Greenberger and Steinberg, 1986; Mortimer et al., 1990). It is

When teenagers work more than fifteen or twenty hours weekly, they are forced to cut back on other activities, including extracurricular activities that may be more psychologically, if not financially, rewarding. *(Joel Gordon)*

not clear from these studies, however, whether working actually leads to higher levels of delinquency or whether adolescents who are already involved in delinquent activities are more likely to choose to work long hours.

**The effects of long work hours** Many experts now believe that working more than twenty hours a week may jeopardize adolescents' schooling and psychological well-being. Youngsters who work long hours are absent from school more often, are less likely to participate in extracurricular activities, report enjoying school less, spend less time on their homework, and earn lower grades (Damico, 1984; Fine et al., 1990; Steinberg, Greenberger, Garduque, and McAuliffe, 1982; Steinberg and Dornbusch, 1991; Wirtz et al., 1987). Students who work long hours may miss out on family activities, such as eating dinner together or spending time together on weekends (Greenberger et al., 1980). Young people who spend more time at work report growing more distant from their parents and friends and being monitored less closely by their parents (Steinberg and Dornbusch, 1991; Steinberg, Greenberger, Garduque, Ruggiero, and Vaux, 1982). And working long hours is associated with higher rates of alcohol, marijuana, cocaine, and cigarette use (Bachman et al., 1986; Greenberger, Steinberg, and Vaux 1981; Steinberg and Dornbusch, 1991).

The adverse impact of working long hours on schooling is especially troublesome in light of studies pointing to achievement problems of American youngsters (see Chapter 12). Not only does working seem to lead to increased absenteeism and decreased time spent on homework and school activities, intensive involvement in a part-time job early in a student's education—during sophomore year in high school, for example—may actually increase the likelihood of dropping out of school (Damico, 1984). Moreover, students who work a good

**FIGURE 7.5** According to one recent study, students who work long hours are more likely to cut class and use drugs and alcohol, and are less closely monitored by their parents. (Steinberg and Dornbusch, 1991)

deal have less ambitious plans for further education while in high school and complete fewer years of college (Mortimer and Finch, 1986).

Although the size of the impact of working on students' grades and achievement test scores is small (Barton, 1989), several studies indicate that extensive employment during the school year may take its toll on school in ways that are not revealed by looking only at students' performance. One recent study, for example, found that students who work a great deal report paying attention in class less often, exerting less effort on their studies, and skipping class more frequently (Steinberg and Dornbusch, 1991). Additionally, when students work a great deal, they must develop strategies for protecting their grade point averages. These strategies include taking easier courses, cutting corners on their homework assignments, copying homework from friends, and cheating (Greenberger and Steinberg, 1986; McNeil, 1984; Steinberg and Dornbusch, 1991). Teachers respond by assigning less homework and by using class time for students to complete assignments that otherwise would be done outside of school (McNeil, 1984).

## EFFORTS TO COMBAT YOUTH UNEMPLOYMENT

Although the employment of teenagers has become commonplace in contemporary America, a sizable minority of young people who wish to work are nevertheless unable to find jobs. Much attention has been given to the problem of **youth unemployment** over the pst two decades, but there remains a good deal of controversy over the nature of the problem and possible solutions to it.

Most young people in this country ultimately find full-time employment after they graduate from high school or college. For example, one team of researchers, using data collected by the U.S. Department of Labor, found that more than 90 percent of all teenage boys were either in school, working, or both. Only 5 percent were out of school, unemployed, and looking for full-time work (Feldstein and Ellwood, 1982). Much of the unemployment of young people is attributable to their involvement in other productive activities, such as school, rather than to deficiencies in job skills or constraints in the labor force (Mare et al., 1984).

Moreover, those young people who are out of school and out of work are unemployed for only short periods of time. Nearly half of the unemployed youth in the survey mentioned above had been out of work for one month or less; only 10 percent had been unemployed for as long as six months. An important conclusion to keep in mind, therefore, is that long-term unemployment is a problem that afflicts a very small minority of young people.

It is also important to note that the majority of unemployed youth are high school dropouts. Minority youth are more likely to experience unemployment than white youth, and unemployment is more common among teenagers who come from low-income families and live in areas that have high overall unemployment rates and where competition for available employment is severe (Freeman and Wise, 1982). Their unemployment problems may have more to do with poverty and related factors than with youth or inexperience. Most studies show that unemployment during adolescence and young adulthood results primarily from a combination of economic and social factors, rather than from a lack of motivation on the part of unemployed individuals.

Finally, the consequences of unemployment during adolescence and young adulthood appear to be worse in the short term than in the long run. Unemployment is not a condition that stays with a person throughout his or her life. Researchers have found that most people who have been unemployed as teenagers are eventually able to secure stable full-time employment. Youth unemployment is a problem mostly because it is associated with higher rates of crime, drug abuse, and violence (Freeman and Wise, 1982).

Nevertheless, for the minority of youngsters who experience long-term difficulty in finding and holding a full-time job, chronic unemployment is an onerous condition filled with hopelessness. Because of the serious effects of chronic unemployment during young adulthood on individuals' later lives, many different approaches have been taken over the years in trying to solve the youth unemployment problem.

One set of proposals comes out of concern for the "Forgotten Half"—the nearly 50 percent of all adolescents who do not go on to college. As we have noted in this chapter and in Chapter 6, our secondary schools do little to prepare noncollege-bound youngsters for the work of work. These youngsters, of course, are far more likely to experience unemployment. Many experts therefore believe that the youth unemployment problem is attributable mainly to the lack of clear linkages between school and work. They point out that there are so many "cracks" in the transition that it is easy for students who are not in school—and carried along by inertia—to fall into periods of unemployment.

Several suggestions have been made to combat this problem (William T. Grant Foundation Commission on Work, Family, and Citizenship, 1988). As noted earlier, many commentators have argued that expanding opportunities for **community service** will help integrate adolescents into the community, enhance their feelings of confidence and responsibility, and put them in touch with adult role models. Some successful programs, like the Job Corps, have been shown to be effective in these regards. Participants in successful programs have an easier time securing full-time employment than do nonparticipants.

A second suggestion is that communities improve their services for young people and strengthen youth organizations. In Europe, for example, local communities provide much better employment services for youth—including job placement—than is the case in the United States. Such services would also help with career counseling, college counseling, summer employment, and placement in volunteer activities. In most high schools, guidance counselors are so busy counseling students for college that they rarely pay attention to the noncollege-bound.

Finally, it has been proposed that American schools experiment with apprenticeship programs modeled after those found in Europe (Hamilton, 1990). These programs would introduce young people to the world of work early in their high school careers and gradually move them from full-time school, into a mixture of school and work, and finally into full-time employment. Instead of working in the dead-end jobs of the adolescent workplace, teenagers would combine schooling and on-the-job training with employers likely to offer them full-time, career-oriented jobs after graduation.

## Adolescents and Leisure

Although adolescents devote considerable time each week to school, and many also commit a good number of hours to a part-time job, leisure occupies more of the typical adolescent's waking hours (about 40 percent) than school and work combined (about 30 percent) (Fine et al., 1990). Leisure activities include socializing with friends, playing sports and games, watching television and listening to music, working on hobbies, and just plain "kicking back." One important difference between leisure and other activities is that adolescents *choose* their leisure activities, whereas their time

at school and work is dictated by others (teachers, supervisors, etc.). Perhaps as a consequence, studies show that adolescents report being in a better mood during leisure activities than during school or work (Csikszentmihalyi and Larson, 1984).

Adults have very mixed feelings about adolescents' leisure. On the positive side, adults take pride in watching teenagers' organized sports and creative activities and believe that these "productive" uses of leisure help build character and teach important skills, such as teamwork and perseverance (consider, for example, the movie *Hoosiers*). On the other hand, adults view many adolescent leisure activities as wasted time, or worse, as preludes to trouble: They worry about groups of teenagers "cruising" the mall, poke fun at groups of girls sequestered in front of a mirror trying on an array of cosmetics, and cringe at the image of an adolescent plugged into his stereo, wildly playing an "air guitar" (*Fast Times at Ridgemont High*).

This mixed view of adolescent leisure reflects an interesting paradox about the nature of adolescence in modern society. Because industrialized society has "given" adolescents a good deal of free time, adults expect them to "use" it productively. But by definition, leisure is supposed to be time that can be used for purposes other than production. As you will read in Chapter 8, some theorists of adolescence believe that the existence of large blocks of uncommitted time is one feature of adolescence in modern society that has the potential to contribute in positive ways to young people's development (e.g., Erikson, 1968).

Nevertheless, it seems difficult for adults to resist the temptation to worry that leisure activities are displacing the more "important" tasks of adolescence, such as school. (This is generally referred to as the **displacement hypothesis.**). Interestingly, however, studies show that intensive involvement in the "productive" activity of part-time work has a more

Adults feel more positively about certain adolescent leisure activities than others. One favorite—"cruising the mall"—is not especially appreciated by adults. *(Eric Neurath/Stock, Boston)*

consistently negative impact on school performance than does comparable involvement in extracurricular activities (Lamborn et al., in press). And, although adults believe that television viewing has a negative effect on adolescents' academic performance, studies do not always support this conclusion. It is more likely that poor school performance leads to increased television viewing than the reverse. More often displaced by television viewing than schoolwork are more marginal activities, such as daydreaming or "goofing off" (Fine et al., 1990).

By valuing adolescent leisure only when it is "free" time that is used productively, however, adults may misunderstand the important functions that leisure serves in the psychosocial development of the young person. For example, studies show that a moderate amount of solitude (during which daydreaming is a central activity) is positively related to high school students' psychological well-being (Csikszentmihalyi and Larson, 1984). As we shall see in subsequent chapters, leisure plays an important role in helping young people develop a sense of themselves, explore their relationships with each other, and learn about the society around them.

## LEISURE ACTIVITIES AND SOCIALIZATION FOR ADULTHOOD

Despite adults' feelings to the contrary, leisure serves a number of important functions during adolescence. Many leisure activities—especially those organized and controlled by adults—are structured to socialize adolescents into adult roles, including, quite often, traditional sex roles. Donna Eder and Stephen Parker (1987), for example, have studied how high school extracurricular activities socialize males and females in different ways. In an extensive ethnographic study of a secondary school, the researchers examined how different extracurricular activities were viewed within the school and studied the values communicated to adolescents through these extracurriculars.

In the school they studied, as in many others, athletics was the chief route to popularity and status for boys. But which values were communicated through team sports? An analysis of interactions during practice and during other free periods (e.g., lunchtime) revealed that the culture of boys' athletics emphasizes achievement, toughness, dominance, and competition—all traits that society has traditionally valued in the socialization of adult males. Consider, for example, the following observation taken from the researchers' field notes during football practice:

> A player came up to a coach as practice was just beginning and complained that another player was starting a fight with him. The coach seemed aggravated at having to deal with this and told him to "knock his socks off in practice." This player was not particularly satisfied with the suggestion but realized that was all he could get from Coach James. (Eder and Parker, 1987, p. 205)

In contrast, although aggression and competitiveness were valued within girls' sports, athletics were not a route toward popularity or status for girls in the school, and, as a consequence, these traits were less likely to be socialized among girls. For instance, on days when "big" games were to be played by the boys' teams, team members wore their athletic jerseys to school, so that they would be recognized by their peers. On days when the girls' teams had "big" games, however, team members did not wear their jerseys. One reason was that being a member of an athletic team *detracted* from a girl's popularity.

The main route toward popularity for girls in this school was through cheerleading. Were the traits valued in this activity those traditionally stressed in the socialization of adult women? Consider the following observation recorded during cheerleading tryouts:

> At one point, Mrs. Tolson started to tell them what they were going to be judged on, saying they would get 10 points (out of 50) for a "sparkle," which was their smile, personality, bubbliness, appearance, attractiveness—not that all cheerleaders had to be attractive, but it was important to have a clean appearance, not to be sloppy, have messy or greasy hair, because that doesn't look like a cheerleader. (Eder and Parker, 1987, p. 207)

These traits—appearance, neatness, and bubbliness—are all characteristics traditionally socialized in women. In essence, the popularity accorded male athletes rewarded boys for behaving in ways stereotypic for men, while the popularity accorded female cheerleaders rewarded girls for behaving in ways stereotypic for women.

You may well be thinking that this difference in emphasis makes perfect sense, because football requires aggression and toughness and cheerleading requires "sparkle." But as the researchers point out, it is "interesting that neatly combed hair was emphasized [in cheerleading tryouts], given the physical nature of this activity, which includes cartwheels and backflips. It is also interesting to compare the focus on neatness during cheerleading with the absence of this concern during male and female athletics" (p. 207). According to these researchers, an important reason for the difference between the emphases of football and cheerleading concerns the role of extracurricular activities in the socialization of male and female gender roles.

Similar results emerged from an analysis of the content of leading magazines aimed at adolescent girls (Evans et al., 1990). The majority

Although regular television viewing declines during adolescence, it is replaced by time spent with other media, including listening to music, going to the movies, watching music videos, and viewing prerecorded movies on videocassettes. Today's adolescents spend between one-third and one-half of their waking hours with one or another of the mass media. *(Joseph Szabo/Photo Researchers)*

of articles in these magazines focused on dating and heterosexual relationships, and most emphasized the importance of physical attractiveness for young women. According to the researchers, the articles and advertisements contained in these magazines conveyed a clear message that attracting males by being physically beautiful was the road to true happiness. In contrast, little space was devoted to issues of education, self-improvement in other than physical ways, or matters of ethics or ideology. As in cheerleading, the emphasis in teen magazines aimed at girls is on cultivating that superficial "sparkle."

## LEISURE AND POPULAR CULTURE

Not all of the socialization that occurs in adolescents' leisure activities is aimed at traditional roles, however; indeed, if this were the case, adults would rarely complain about how adolescents spend their free time. Leisure activities also play an important role in exposing adolescents to elements of the popular culture in general, and elements of the youth culture in particular. It is in this respect that adolescent leisure activity has generated the most controversy.

Researchers estimate that adolescents spend between one-half and one-third of their waking hours with one or another of the mass media, including television, radio, and print. Sometimes the media are the focus of the teenager's activity; often, they are in the background. Contemporary adolescents view, on average, between two and four hours of television daily (not counting music video, which is typically grouped along with other types of music media in studies of adolescent media use, or prerecorded movies on VCR, which is typically considered along with other film viewing), although there is considerable variation within the adolescent population in the amount of time spent in front of the television (Fine et al., 1990). In general, TV viewing peaks during early adolescence, and then declines over the high school years.

One reason for the decline of television viewing during adolescence is that it is displaced by time spent with other media. By middle adolescence, the typical American teenager listens to music from four to six hours daily, either via radio, recorded music, or music video. As teenagers get older, more attend movies (about half of all teenagers report going to the movies at least monthly) and spend considerable time watching videocassettes—studies of VCR use report teenagers watching between five and ten hours weekly. Use of print media also increases during adolescence: between 60 percent and 80 percent of late adolescents report at least some daily newspaper reading, one third report daily magazine reading, and one-fifth report daily reading of nonschool books. According to a recent review, when time devoted to all media is combined—even figuring that some time is spent engaged in more than one activity simultaneously, such as reading while listening to music—it appears that the average adolescent spends about eight hours each day with some form of mass media (Fine et al., 1990).

Given the considerable amount of time adolescents spend in the presence of mass media, it is not surprising to find that the impact of the media on teenagers' behavior and development has been the subject of much debate. Unfortunately, little of the debate is grounded in scientific research. Although some adults have expressed worry that the sexually explicit lyrics of rock music or the aggressive images of MTV corrupt the values of young people (e.g., Gore, 1987), there is no scientific evidence that teenagers are influenced in any systematic way by what they listen to or watch (Fine et al., 1990).

For a number of reasons, it has been difficult to draw definitive conclusions about the impact of mass media on adolescent behavior. One major problem in studying the impact of media on teenagers' attitudes or behavior is separating cause and effect: Although it has been speculated that violent images provoke aggression, for example, it is just as, if not more, likely that aggressive adolescents are more prone to choose to watch violent images. If sexual behavior is correlated with listening to "sexy" music, it is impossible to say which causes which.

Researchers also have found that different media are used under different social circumstances. Television is often viewed with other members of the family, whereas radio is often listened to alone, while movies are typically viewed with other teenagers (Fine et al., 1990; Larson, Kubey, and Colletti, 1989). Whereas MTV is more attention-getting than audiotape, music videos provoke less imagination than audio recordings (Greenfield et al., 1987). It is quite difficult, in light of all this, to separate the effects of media *content* from those of media *context*.

Finally, and most important, we often fail to distinguish between what adolescents actually perceive and remember and what adults *believe* adolescents see and remember. After all, media are not simply viewed or heard—they are interpreted. Adolescents are not exposed to the mass media as blank slates; rather, they bring preexisting values, beliefs, and expectations to the experience of watching or listening, and these preexisting states influence what they perceive and remember (Leming, 1987). Ironically, adults read more sex and violence into the lyrics of rock music than adolescent listeners actually pick up (Prinsky and Rosenbaum, 1987).

## LEISURE AND THE ECONOMY

A final, and very important, function of adolescent leisure activity is economic. Both the size of the adolescent population and the fact that adolescents save less than any other age group make young people an attractive target for a variety of businesses (Fine et al., 1990). Not surprisingly, virtually all of adolescents' money is spent on purchases related to leisure activities.

One can certainly debate the merits of cultivating such strong consumer urges among the young and impressionable (see Greenberger and Steinberg, 1986). But it is important to recognize that the segments of our economy devoted to leisure and recreation depend on the adolescent market. Among the most important industries are those connected with movies, music, sports, and television. Teenagers make up a large, and therefore influential, segment of the consumers of these products—as a glance at the local movie or television listings or a trip through a music store will readily attest.

Students of adolescent consumerism have been quick to point out the strong influence teenagers have on each other when it comes to purchases. It is important to point out, however, that the influence of the adolescent market extends well beyond the youth cohort—as evidenced by the uncanny predictability with which adult tastes in clothing and music often follow those of teenagers, albeit in a toned-down fashion. Interestingly, the power of adolescents as consumers has increased in recent decades, owing to the growth in the proportion of single-parent and dual-worker households. In many such homes, adolescents influence both day-to-day and major purchases—in part because adolescents themselves may do a fair amount of the family's shopping (Graham, 1988).

## Summary

1. The rise of compulsory schooling and the affluence of the adolescent population have both contributed to the increased importance of both part-time employment and leisure in the lives of contemporary adolescents. Having large amounts of "free" time is one hallmark of adolescence in modern society.

2. Today, the majority of American teenagers hold part-time jobs during the school year. This is an important departure from the recent past, when it was unlikely for students to work. This is also a departure from the case in most other industrialized countries, where student employment is quite rare. Students in other countries are more likely to gain work experience through structured apprenticeship programs in career-related jobs.

3. Most employed U.S. adolescents work in retail jobs or in restaurants. Studies suggest that the work they do is highly routine and uninteresting, and that the main benefit of working is monetary. Perhaps as a consequence, studies show that student employment is unlikely to contribute to the psychological development or to the growth of healthy attitudes toward work. Rather, part-time employment is more likely to lead to cynicism and the development of "premature affluence."

4. Recent studies indicate that working long hours may take a toll on youngsters' schooling and behavior. Teenagers who work in excess of 15–20 hours weekly are less engaged in school, less closely monitored by their parents, and more likely to use drugs and alcohol. They are also more likely to "protect" their grades by taking easier classes and cutting corners on their schoolwork.

5. Although extensive part-time employment may be a problem, many social commentators have called for improving the transition between school and full-time work, especially among noncollege-bound students. Among the suggestions offered are increasing adolescents' opportunities for community service, strengthening counseling and career services for high school students, and encouraging the development of apprenticeship programs like those found in Europe.

6. Adolescents spend more time on leisure than they do in school and work combined. Although adults are prone to see leisure as

"wasted" time, leisure serves a number of important functions during adolescence. It socializes adolescents for adult roles, exposes them to elements of the popular culture, and helps support certain segments of the economy.

7. Much of adolescents' leisure time involves one or more of the mass media. Whereas television viewing declines during adolescence, use of music media, movies, and print media all increase. The average adolescent is exposed to the mass media about eight hours daily. Although adults have worried about the corrupting influence of media such as television or rock music, it has been difficult to document such alleged effects.

## Key Terms

community service
displacement hypothesis
occupational deviance
premature affluence
youth unemployment

## For Further Reading

EDER, D., AND PARKER, S. (1987). The cultural production and reproduction of gender: The effect of extracurricular activities on peer-group culture. *Sociology of Education, 60,* 200–213. An ethnographic look at sex-role socialization through organized extracurricular activities.

FINE, G., MORTIMER, J., AND ROBERTS, D. (1990). Leisure, work, and the mass media. In S. Feldman and G. Elliott (Eds.), *At the threshold: The developing adolescent.* Cambridge: Harvard University Press. A review of research on work and leisure in adolescence.

GREENBERGER, E., AND STEINBERG, L. (1986). *When teenagers work: The psychological and social costs of adolescent employment.* New York: Basic Books. A critical discussion of the nature and effects of school-year employment.

HAMILTON, S. (1990). *Apprenticeship for adulthood.* New York: Free Press. A thoughtful discussion of the school-to-work transition in the United States and abroad, with an emphasis on the European apprenticeship system.

LARSON, R., AND RICHARDS, M. (EDS.). The changing life space of early adolescence. *Journal of Youth and Adolescence, 18(6).* A special issue of the journal devoted to a series of studies of how adolescents spend their time.

# PSYCHOSOCIAL DEVELOPMENT DURING ADOLESCENCE

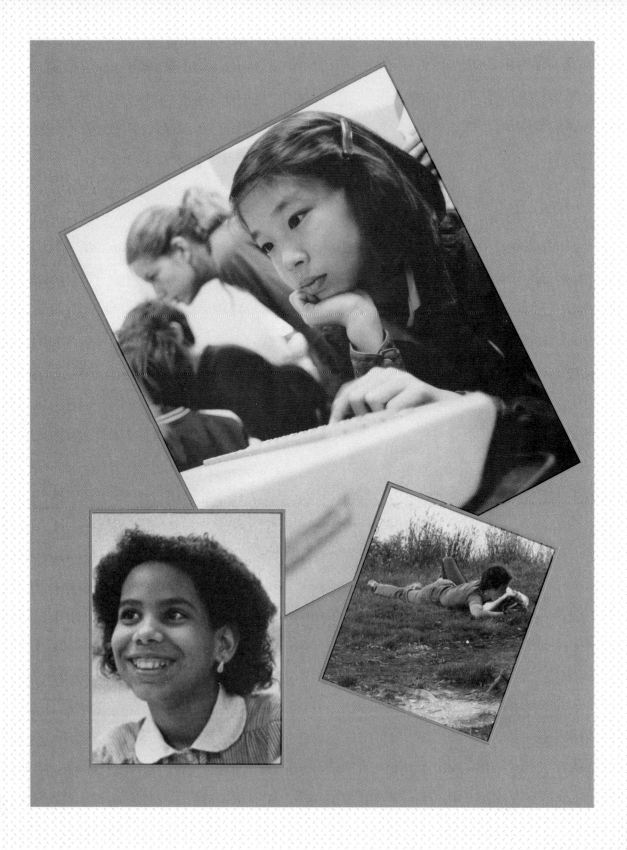

# Three

# PSYCHOSOCIAL DEVELOPMENT DURING ADOLESCENCE

# IDENTITY

What am I like as a person? Complicated! I'm sensitive, friendly, outgoing, popular, and tolerant, though I can also be shy, self-conscious, and even obnoxious. Obnoxious! I'd *like* to be friendly and tolerant all of the time. That's the kind of person I *want* to be, and I'm disappointed when I'm not. I'm responsible, even studious every now and then, but on the other hand I'm a goof-off too, because if you're too studious, you won't be popular. I don't usually do that well at school. I'm a pretty cheerful person, especially with my friends, where I can even get rowdy. At home I'm more likely to be anxious around my parents. They expect me to get all A's. It's not fair! I worry about how I probably *should* get better grades. But I'd be mortified in the eyes of my friends. So I'm usually pretty stressed-out at home, or sarcastic, since my parents are always on my case. But I really don't understand how I can switch so fast. I mean, how can I be cheerful one minute, anxious the next, and then be sarcastic? Which one is the *real* me? Sometimes I feel phony, especially around boys. Say I think some guy might be interested in asking me out. I try to act different, like Madonna. I'll be flirtatious and fun-loving. And then everybody, I mean *everybody* else is looking at me like they think I'm totally weird! Then I get self-conscious and embarrassed and become radically introverted, and I don't know who I really am! Am I just trying to impress them or what? But I don't really care what they think anyway. I don't *want* to care, that is. I just want to know what my close friends think. I can be my true self with my close friends. I can't be my real self with my parents. They don't understand me. What do *they* know about what it's like to be a teenager? They treat me like I'm still a kid. At least at school people treat you more like you're an adult. That gets confusing, though. I mean, which am I, a kid or an adult? It's scary, too, because I don't have any idea what I want to be when I grow up. I mean, I have lots of *ideas*. My friend Sheryl and I talk about whether we'll be stewardesses, or teachers, or nurses, veterinarians, maybe mothers, or actresses. I know I *don't* want to be a waitress or a secretary. But how do you decide all of this? I really don't know. I mean, I think about it a lot, but I can't resolve it. There are days when I wish

I could just become immune to myself! (Harter, 1990, pp. 352–353)

Some, but not all, adolescents share this 15-year-old's feelings of self-consciousness and confusion. For these young people, adolescence is a time of "identity crisis." For other adolescents, this period is one of more gradual and subtle change. As you may recall from your own adolescence, there are few experiences that can be as trying—or as exhilarating—as questioning who you really are and, more important, who you would like to be.

Because changes—whether gradual or abrupt—take place during adolescence in the way people view and feel about themselves, the study of identity development has been a major focus of research and theory on adolescents. In this chapter, we examine whether adolescence is indeed a time of major changes in identity and how the course of adolescent identity development is shaped by the nature of life in contemporary society.

## Identity as an Adolescent Issue

Changes in the way in which we see and feel about ourselves occur throughout the life cycle. You have probably heard and read about the so-called "midlife crisis," for example, an identity crisis thought to occur during middle age. And certainly, there are important changes in self-conceptions and in self-image throughout childhood. When a group of 4-year-olds and a group of 10-year-olds are asked to describe themselves, the older children display a far more complex view of themselves. While young children restrict their descriptions to lists of what they own or what they like to do, older children are more likely to tell you also about their personality.

If in fact changes in identity occur throughout the life cycle, why have researchers interested in identity development paid so much attention to adolescence? One reason is that the changes in identity which take place during adolescence involve the first substantial reorganization and restructuring of the individual's sense of self at a time when he or she has the intellectual capability to appreciate fully just how significant the changes are. Although important changes in identity certainly occur during childhood, the adolescent is far more self-conscious about these changes and feels them much more acutely.

Another reason for the attention that researchers and theorists have given the study of identity development during adolescence concerns the fundamental biological, cognitive,

and social changes characteristic of the period. Puberty, as we saw in Chapter 1, brings with it dramatic changes in physical appearance and alters the adolescent's self-conceptions and relationships with others. It is not hard to see why puberty plays an important role in provoking identity development during adolescence. When you change the way you look—when you have your hair cut in a different way, lose a great deal of weight, or get a new pair of glasses—you sometimes feel as if your personality has changed, too. During puberty, when adolescents are changing so dramatically on the outside, they understandably have questions about changes that are taking place on the inside. For the adolescent, undergoing the physical changes of puberty may prompt fluc-

Because adolescence is a time when career possibilities are seriously considered for the first time, volunteering in different work settings can provide useful information in the process of identity development. This young woman works as a volunteer in a New York City program for homeless children. *(Ursula Markus/Photo Researchers)*

tuations in the self-image and a reevaluation of who he or she really is.

The broadening of intellectual capabilities during early adolescence, just as it provides new ways of thinking about problems, values, and interpersonal relationships, also permits adolescents to think about themselves in new ways. We saw in Chapter 2 that it is not until adolescence that the young person is able to think in systematic ways about hypothetical and future events. For this reason, it is not until adolescence that individuals typically begin to wonder, "Who will I become?" "What possible identities are open to me?" or "What am I really like?" Because the preadolescent child's thinking is concrete, it is impossible for him or her to think seriously about being a different person. But the changes in thinking that take place during adolescence open up a whole new world of alternatives.

Finally, we saw in Chapter 3 that the changes in social roles that occur at adolescence open up a new array of choices and decisions for the young person that were not concerns previously. In contemporary society, adolescence is a time of important decisions about work, marriage, and the future. Facing these decisions about your place in society not only provokes questions about who you are and where you are headed—it necessitates them. At this point in the life cycle, young people must make important choices about their careers and their commitments to other people, and thinking about these questions prompts them to ask more questions about themselves: "What do I really want out of life?" "What things are important to me?" "What kind of person would I really like to be?" Questions about the future, which inevitably arise as the adolescent prepares for adulthood, raise questions about identity.

Identity development is complex and multifaceted. Actually, it is better understood as a series of interrelated developments—rather than one single development—that all involve changes in the way individuals view themselves in relation to others and in relation to the broader society in which they live. Generally speaking, researchers and theorists have taken three different approaches to the question of how the individual's sense of identity changes over the course of adolescence. Each approach focuses on a different aspect of identity development.

The first approach emphasizes changes in self-conceptions—the ideas that individuals have of themselves as regards various traits and attributes. An entirely different approach focuses on adolescents' self-esteem or self-image—how positively or negatively individuals feel about themselves. Finally, a third approach emphasizes changes in the sense of identity—the sense of who one is, where one has come from, and where one is going.

## Changes in Self-Conceptions

During adolescence, important shifts occur in the way individuals think about and characterize themselves—that is, in their **self-conceptions.** As individuals mature intellectually and undergo the sorts of cognitive changes described in Chapter 2, they come to conceive of themselves in more sophisticated and differentiated ways. As we saw in that chapter, adolescents are much more capable than children of thinking about abstract concepts. This intellectual advantage affects the way in which individuals characterize themselves. Compared with children, who tend to describe themselves in relatively simple, concrete terms, adolescents are more likely to employ complex, abstract, and psychological self-characterizations (Harter, 1990).

Self-conceptions change in structure as well as content during the transition from childhood into adolescence. Structurally, self-conceptions become more *differentiated* and better *organized* (Livesley and Bromley, 1973; Marsh,

1989; Montemayor and Eisen, 1977). Consider first the movement toward greater differentiation. In answer to the question, "Who am I?" adolescents are more likely than children to link traits and attributes describing themselves to specific situations, rather than using them as global characterizations. While a preadolescent child might say "I am nice" or "I am friendly" and not specify when or under what conditions, an adolescent is more likely to say "I am nice *if* I am in a good mood," or "I am friendly *when* I am with people I have met before." The realization that one's personality is expressed in different ways in different situations is one example of the increased differentiation that characterizes the self-conceptions of youngsters as they mature toward adulthood.

There is another way in which self-conceptions become more highly differentiated at adolescence. As opposed to characterizations provided by children, adolescents' self-descriptions take into account *who* is doing the describing (Livesley and Bromley, 1973). Teenagers differentiate between their own opinions of themselves and the views of others. Suppose you asked a group of youngsters to describe how they behaved when they were with other people. Instead of saying, "I am shy" or "I am outgoing," an adolescent would be more likely to say, "People think I'm not at all shy, but most of the time, I'm real nervous about meeting other kids for the first time." Adolescents also recognize that they may come across differently to different people, another type of differentiation in self-conceptions that does not appear until this point in time: "My parents think I'm quiet, but my friends know I really like to party a lot."

With this shift toward increased differentiation in self-conceptions comes better organization and integration (Harter, 1990; Marsh, 1989). When children are asked to describe themselves, the traits and attributes they list remain somewhat disparate, like items haphaz-

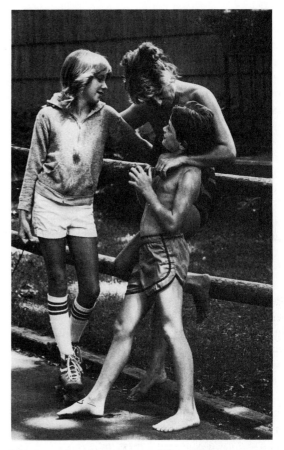

Self-conceptions become more differentiated during adolescence. Young people are able to see, for example, that they may be perceived differently by their parents and their siblings. *(Joel Gordon)*

ardly placed on a grocery list. Adolescents, however, are likely to organize and integrate different aspects of their self-image into a more logical, coherent whole. Whereas a younger child may list a sequence of several traits that appear to be contradictory ("I am friendly. I am shy."), an adolescent will attempt to organize apparently discrepant bits of information into more highly organized statements ("I am shy when I first meet people, but after I get to know them, I'm usually pretty friendly.")

Although it does not appear that self-conceptions become even more differentiated after early adolescence (Marsh, 1989), the movement toward more abstract and more psychological self-conceptions continues well into the high school years, as the 15-year-old's self-description at the beginning of this chapter clearly indicates. Interestingly, however, the increased abstraction and psychological complexity of self-conceptions may present some difficulties for middle adolescents, who may be able to recognize—but not yet quite understand or reconcile—inconsistencies and contradictions in their personality. Conflict and distress over such inconsistencies appear to increase during middle adolescence and then diminish, as individuals develop a more sophisticated understanding of themselves (Harter, 1990).

In one study, when asked to reflect on contradictions in their personalities, early, middle, and late adolescents responded in very different ways, as the following examples (cited in Harter, 1990, p. 358):

"I guess I just think about one thing about myself at a time and don't think about the other until the next day." (11–12 years old)

"I really think I am a happy person and I want to be that way with everyone, but I get depressed with my family and it really bugs me because that's not what I want to be like." (14–15 years old)

"You can be shy on a date, and then outgoing with friends because you are just different with different people; you can't always be the same person and probably shouldn't be." (17–18 years old)

Although the recognition that one's personality is multifaceted—even contradictory—may initially cause some distress, in the long run it probably has a number of advantages. One advantage is that the adolescent is now able to distinguish between his or her "actual" (who the adolescent really is) and "ideal" selves (whom the adolescent would like to be). According to one view, being able to make this distinction provides a motive for the adolescent to improve—to bring his or her actual self more into line with the ideal self (Markus and Nurius, 1986).

Another interesting consequence of adolescents' recognition that they are not always consistent in their personality concerns their ability to distinguish between their true (i.e., authentic) and false (i.e., inauthentic) selves. Adolescents are most likely to behave inauthentically in romantic and dating situations and with classmates, and least likely to put on a false front with close friends. Interestingly, false behavior with parents occurs less often than with dates, but more often than with close friends (Harter, 1990). Although adolescents sometimes say that they dislike false-self behavior, they also say that there are times in which it is acceptable, such as when one is trying to impress another person or trying to hide an aspect of his or her personality that others do not like. You can well imagine how the ability to put on a false front would come in handy on a date, at school, or with one's parents.

Understanding the way in which self-conceptions change during adolescence helps to explain why issues of identity begin to take on so much importance at this time in the life span. As individuals' self-conceptions become more abstract and as they become more able to see themselves in psychological terms, they become more interested in understanding their own personalities and why they behave the way they do. The distress caused by recognizing one's inconsistencies may spur identity development. You may recall having wondered as a teenager about your personality development, about the influences that shaped your character, about how your personality had changed over time. "Am I more like my father or like my mother? Why do my sister and I seem so different? Will I always be so shy?" Although these sorts of questions may seem commonplace to you now, in all likelihood, you did not think about these things until adolescence, when your own self-conceptions became more abstract and sophisticated.

## Changes in Self-Esteem

As noted in the introduction to this book, ever since G. Stanley Hall initially suggested that adolescence was a time of "storm and stress," researchers and theorists have asked whether adolescence is a more difficult time for the developing person than earlier or later periods in the life span. For many years, in fact, the idea that adolescence is inherently stressful for the individual was accepted without question. One of the manifestations assumed to result from the stress of adolescence involves problems in the adolescent's **self-esteem**—how the individual feels about himself or herself.

Research has not supported the view that adolescence is a time of tumultuous upheaval in self-image, however, nor is adolescence the time of "rebirth" philosophers once cast it as. As one team of researchers put it, in discussing their study of changes in adolescents' perceptions of themselves between ages 11 and 18, "The person who enters adolescence is basically the same as that who exits it" (Dusek and Flaherty, 1981, p. 39). There is also a good deal of evidence that many personality traits, such as aggressiveness, are quite stable between childhood and adolescence. Although the external manifestations of these traits may change with age (for example, anxiety may appear as bed-wetting in early childhood but as nervous talkativeness in adolescence), basic, underlying traits are quite stable over time. For example, studies show that individuals who have displayed relatively higher levels of aggression in preadolescence, temper tan-

trums during childhood, or negative emotions during infancy are more likely to behave aggressively as adolescents (Cairns et al., 1989; Caspi et al., 1987; Lerner et al., 1988).

Although adolescents' feelings about themselves may fluctuate somewhat, particularly during the very early adolescent years (late elementary school and junior high school), from about eighth grade on, self-esteem remains stable; individuals with high self-esteem as children are likely to have high self-esteem as adolescents. There is no apparent loss of self-esteem during adolescence. If anything, over the course of middle and late adolescence, self-esteem *increases* (Harter, 1990; Nottelmann, 1987; O'Malley and Bachman, 1983; Rosenberg, 1986; Savin-Williams and Demo, 1984). Just as the "storm and stress" view of adolescence is not supported in studies of family relations, neither does it appear to apply to adolescent self-esteem.

There is some evidence, however, that for a brief and temporary period during early adolescence, minor problems in self-image may arise. Roberta Simmons and her colleagues have completed a series of studies that shed light on when and why these problems in self-image are likely to occur. Simmons and her associates (Simmons, Rosenberg, and Rosenberg, 1973) employed an extensive questionnaire to assess three aspects of adolescents' self-image: their self-esteem (how positively or negatively they feel about themselves), their **self-consciousness** (how much they worry about their self-image), and the **stability of their self-image** (how much they feel that their self-image changes from day to day). They hypothesized that young adolescents would show the lowest levels of self-esteem, the highest levels of self-consciousness, and the shakiest self-image.

Consistent with their expectations, these researchers found that fluctuations in the self-image are most likely to occur between the ages of 12 and 14. Compared with older adolescents

(15 years and older) and with preadolescents (8 to 11 years old), early adolescents have lower self-esteem, are more self-conscious, and have a more unstable self-image than other youngsters. Generally speaking, the small but reliable differences between the preadolescents and the early adolescents are greater than those between the younger and older adolescents, which indicates that the most marked fluctuations occur during the transition into adolescence, rather than over the course of adolescence itself (Simmons, Rosenberg, and Rosenberg, 1973). How can we reconcile these findings about fluctuations in self-esteem with studies indicating that self-esteem is quite stable during adolescence?

According to sociologist Morris Rosenberg (1986), it is important to differentiate between two aspects of self-perceptions in looking at studies of self-esteem. **Barometric self-esteem** refers to the extent to which our feelings about ourselves shift and fluctuate rapidly, moment to moment. Perhaps you can remember times as a teenager—or even as an adult—when you entered a room full of people feeling confident and suddenly felt nervous and insecure, only to engage in a pleasant interaction with someone an hour later and feel confident once again. You were experiencing fluctuations in your barometric self-esteem.

Your **baseline self-esteem,** in contrast, is less transitory and less likely to fluctuate moment to moment. This aspect of self-image is relatively stable over time and unlikely to be easily shifted by immediate experiences. Even if you feel momentarily insecure when entering a room full of new people, your integral, or baseline, self-esteem has not shifted. Indeed, individuals with high baseline self-esteem would readily dismiss transient feelings of insecurity as having more to do with the situation than with themselves.

Studies that report very high stability in self-esteem over adolescence are likely tapping the individual's baseline self-esteem, which is un-

likely to change dramatically over time. This may be because the determinants of baseline self-esteem are themselves relatively stable factors such as social class (middle-class adolescents have higher self-esteem than their peers), sex (boys have higher self-esteem than girls), birth order (oldest or only children have higher self-esteem), and academic ability (more able adolescents have higher self-esteem [Bachman and O'Malley, 1986; Savin-Williams and Demo, 1983]). In contrast, studies that show fluctuation and volatility in self-image during early adolescence are probably focusing on the barometric self-image, which, by definition, is more likely to fluctuate. It seems safe to say, therefore, that although individuals' baseline self-image does not change markedly over adolescence, early adolescence is a time of increased volatility in the barometric self-image (Rosenberg, 1986). In other words, young adolescents are more likely than children or older adolescents to experience moment-to-moment shifts in self-esteem. Interestingly, the extent to which an individual's barometric self-esteem is volatile is itself a fairly stable trait—that is, young adolescents whose self-image fluctuates a lot moment to moment are likely to develop into older adolescents who experience the same thing (Savin-Williams and Demo, 1983).

Although an individual's baseline self-image is probably a better overall indicator of how a person feels about him- or herself, fluctuations in barometric self-image can be distressing and uncomfortable—as most of us know well (Rosenberg, 1986). Consistent with this, studies indicate that young adolescents report higher levels of depression than preadolescents or older teenagers (Simmons, Rosenberg, and Rosenberg, 1973). Moreover, young adolescents with the most volatile self-image report the highest levels of anxiety, tension, psychosomatic symptoms, and irritability (Rosenberg, 1986).

Volatility in barometric self-image during early adolescence probably is due to several interrelated factors. First, the sort of egocentrism common in early adolescence, discussed in Chapter 2, may make the young adolescent painfully aware of others' reactions to his or her behavior. Second, as individuals become more socially active, they begin to learn that people play games when they interact and, consequently, they learn that it is not always possible to tell what people are thinking on the basis of how they act or what they say. This ambiguity may leave the young adolescent, relatively unskilled at this sort of "impression management," puzzled and uncomfortable about how he or she is *really* viewed by others. Finally, because of the increased importance of peers in early adolescence, young adolescents are especially interested in their peers' opinions of them. For the first time, they may have to come to terms with contradictory messages that they get from their parents ("I think that hairstyle makes you even more beautiful") versus their peers ("You'd better wear a hat until your hair grows back!"). Hearing contradictory messages probably generates a certain degree of uncertainty about oneself (Rosenberg, 1986).

Some researchers have argued that the question of whether self-esteem is stable during adolescence is a poor one. According to one recent study (Hirsch and DuBois, 1991), some adolescents show very high stability in self-esteem over time while others do not. These researchers identified four dramatically different self-esteem trajectories followed by youngsters during the transition into junior high school (see Figure 8.1). Approximately one-third of the adolescents were classified as consistently high in self-esteem, and approximately one-sixth were classified as chronically low. Half the sample showed impressive patterns of change over just a two-year period, however: about one-fifth were categorized as steeply declining, and nearly one-third showed a small but significant increase in self-esteem. This pattern is reminiscent of one we encoun-

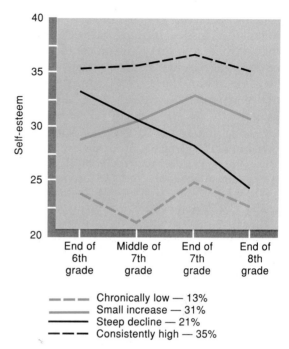

**FIGURE 8.1** Research indicates that individuals follow different self-esteem trajectories during early adolescence. (Adapted from Hirsch and DuBois, 1991)

tered in Chapter 2, in which we saw that while most youngsters demonstrated stability in IQ scores over time, a substantial minority showed marked fluctuations. These studies remind us that focusing only on general tendencies may mask important individual differences in developmental trajectories.

A second criticism of studies of the stability of self-esteem in adolescence questions the validity of examining self-esteem in such a global, or general, sense. Although most research on adolescent self-esteem has focused on teenagers' overall feelings about themselves, most researchers today believe that self-esteem is multidimensional, and that young people evaluate themselves along several different dimensions (Cauce, 1987; Harter, 1990; Lau, 1990). As a consequence, it is possible for an adolescent to have high self-esteem when it comes to his academic abilities, low self-esteem when it comes to athletics, and moderate self-esteem when it comes to his physical appearance. This passage, taken from a study of adolescent self-esteem by Susan Harter (1990, pp. 364–365), is fairly typical:

> How much do I *like* the kind of person I am? Well, I like some things about me, but I don't like others. I'm glad that I'm popular since it's really important to me to have friends. But in school I don't do as well as the really smart kids. That's OK, because if you're too smart you'll lose your friends. So being smart is just not that important. Except to my parents. I feel like I'm letting them down when I don't do as well as they want. But what's really important to me is how I look. If I like the way I look, then I really like the kind of person I am. Don't get me wrong. I mean, I don't exactly look like Madonna even though I try to act like her. But compared to the other girls in my school, I'm sort of good-looking. There's another thing about how much I like the kind of person I am. It matters what other people think, especially the other kids at school. It matters whether they like you. I care about what my parents think about me too. I've also changed. It started when I went to junior high school. I got really depressed. I thought it was going to be so great, like I'd feel so grown-up, and then I saw all of these new, older kids who really had it together and I didn't. So I felt terrible. There was this one day when I hated the way I looked, and I didn't get invited to this really important party, and then I got an awful report card, so for a couple of days I thought it would be best to just end it all. I mean, why bother getting up the next morning? What's the point? Who cares? I was letting my parents down, I wasn't good-looking anymore, and I wasn't that popular after all, and things were never going to get better. I talked to Sheryl, my best friend, and that helped some, but what does she really know? I mean, she's my best friend, so of course she likes me! I mean, her opinion doesn't really count. It's what all the other kids think and want that counts. It was a lot easier for my brother. He got involved in this gang and just decided that what they thought was what was really important, and he stopped caring about the kids in schol, or my parents, or even society. That's what he did, and he likes himself fine. But I really don't, not right now.

Do some aspects of self-esteem contribute more to an adolescent's overall self-image than others? The answer appears to be "yes." In general, a person's physical self-esteem—how she feels about her appearance—is the most important predictor of overall self-esteem, followed by self-esteem about acceptance by peers (Harter, 1990). Less important are self-esteem about academic ability, athletic ability, or moral conduct. It is important to note both that physical self-esteem is a more important influence on overall self-esteem among girls than boys (Harter, 1990), and that girls' physical self-esteem is, on average, lower than boys' (e.g., Wright, 1989). Taken together, these findings help to explain why there are sex differences in the extent to which adolescents' experience self-image difficulties and depression (see Chapter 13).

## VARIATIONS IN SELF-ESTEEM

Not all adolescents undergo the same degree of fluctuation in self-esteem, nor are all adolescents' levels of self-esteem comparable. Several studies have shown that early adolescent girls, especially white girls, are more vulnerable to disturbances in the self-image than any other group of youngsters. Specifically, their self-esteem is lower, their degree of self-consciousness higher, and their self-image shakier than is the case for boys (Rosenberg and Simmons, 1972; Simmons, Brown, Bush, and Blyth, 1978; Simmons and Rosenberg, 1975). They are more likely to say negative things about themselves, feel insecure about their abilities, and worry about whether other people like being with them.

Why would girls have greater difficulty dur-

Several recent studies have shown that white adolescent females may be more vulnerable to self-image problems than other teenagers. Many young women feel caught in a bind between pressures to be academically successful and pressures to be popular with peers. *(J. D. Sloan/Picture Cube)*

ing early adolescence than boys? The answer may be related to the special significance of physical self-esteem and self-esteem about acceptance by peers discussed earlier. Compared with other youngsters, young girls seem to worry a great deal about their looks and about dating and being popular in school. Yet they are also worried about doing well academically. Other adolescents care about these things, of course, but they have a more casual, less worried attitude. Adolescent girls may feel caught in a bind between pressures to do well academically and pressures to do well socially, especially as they move into secondary school. As we saw in Chapter 5, getting good grades in school is at the bottom of the list of attributes adolescent girls feel are important for being accepted into the leading crowd (Coleman, 1961). Several studies have shown that adoles-

cents who worry a lot about being popular are most likely to feel self-conscious and are most likely to have unstable views of themselves (Simmons and Rosenberg, 1975). Because young girls appear to be more concerned than boys about physical attractiveness, dating, and peer acceptance, they may experience a greater number of self-image problems.

Studies also indicate that an adolescent's **social class**—as indexed by his or her parents' occupations, education, or income—is an important determinant of self-esteem, especially as the individual moves into middle and later adolescence. In general, middle-class youngsters have higher self-esteem than their peers, and this discrepancy grows greater over the course of adolescence. One explanation for this is that middle-class youngsters do better in school than their peers, and this success leads to enhanced self-esteem (Demo and Savin-Williams, 1983). Although it once was believed that enhanced self-esteem leads to school success, there is no evidence for this, and a good deal of evidence for the reverse (Bachman and O'Malley, 1986; Bohrnstedt and Felson, 1983). That is, academic success leads to improvements in the way that adolescents feel about themselves. These findings cast doubt on the logic behind programs designed to raise teenagers' school performance by increasing their self-esteem.

Researchers are only now beginning to study ethnic variations in adolescent self-esteem. To date, most of this research has focused on African-American youngsters. Although early studies suggested that African-American children suffered from a poor self-image, more recent research indicates that the self-esteem of African-American adolescents is comparable to that of their majority peers (Harter, 1990). A number of researchers have asked why this is, given the prevalence of prejudice in American society and the generally disadvantaged position of African-Americans in the workplace and in school, two institutions where individuals' performance is believed to influence their self-image. Two main explanations for the surprisingly high self-esteem of African-American adolescents have been offered.

First, some writers have argued that, despite their encounters with racism and prejudice, African-American teenagers benefit from the support and positive feedback of adults in the African-American community, especially in the family (Barnes, 1980). This is not surprising, given the wealth of research showing that parents and "significant others" are especially powerful influences on adolescents' self-esteem (e.g., Felson and Zielinski, 1989). Second, other researchers suggest that all teenagers—minority and otherwise—tend to shift their priorities over time so that they come to value those activities at which they excel. In doing

so, adolescents are able to protect their self-esteem by focusing on areas of strength instead of weakness. For example, an outstanding artist who feels physically unattractive and who has not been doing well in school will likely derive positive self-esteem from his artwork and not restrict his self-evaluation to his looks or grades in school (Hunt and Hunt, 1977).

The context in which adolescents develop has a substantial impact on the self-image, however. Some research indicates, for example, that high school-aged youngsters who live in a social environment or go to a school in which their ethnic or socioeconomic group is in the minority are more likely to have self-image problems than those who are in the majority (Rosenberg, 1975). This seems to be true with regard to religion, socioeconomic status, race, and family structure (single-parent or two-parent home). African-American teenagers, for example, have a higher opinion of themselves when they go to schools in which African-American students are a majority than when they attend predominantly white schools, where they may feel out of place and pressured to play down their cultural heritage. By the same token, Jewish adolescents have higher self-esteem in schools in which there are many other Jewish students than in schools in which Jews comprise a small minority of the student body.

Research on changes in self-image during adolescence has helped paint a new picture of adolescence as a developmental period. In contrast to views that were popular even as recently as twenty-five years ago, adolescence is now viewed as a time of gradual rather than tumultuous change in the individual's self-image. Instead of adhering to the view that adolescence is an inevitably difficult time for *all* young people, researchers are coming to understand that certain factors seem to worsen stress during adolescence and that some youngsters are more susceptible to its adverse effects.

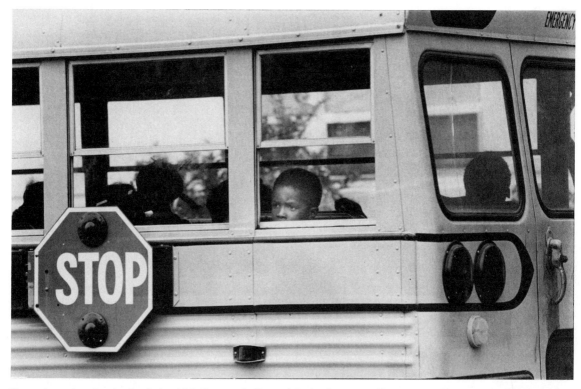

Youngsters who attend schools in which they are in the racial minority may suffer greater self-esteem problems than their peers who attend schools in which they are in the majority. Although desegregation may have a positive impact on minority youngsters' academic achievement, this benefit may be counterbalanced by the apparently negative impact of desegregation on minority youngsters' self-image. *(Rick Smolan/Stock, Boston)*

## The Adolescent Identity Crisis

If you were asked to talk about your own identity development, what sorts of things would you mention? Perhaps you would talk about the develpment of a sense of purpose, or the clarification of your long-term plans and values, or the growing feeling of knowing who you really are and where you are headed. If these are the sorts of things that come to mind when you think about identity development, you are thinking about an aspect of development that psychologists refer to as the **sense of identity.** The dominant view in the study of adolescent identity development emphasizes precisely these aspects of psychosocial development, and the theorist whose work has been most influential in this area is Erik Erikson.

### ERIKSON'S THEORETICAL FRAMEWORK

Erikson's (1959, 1963, 1968) theory developed out of his clinical and cross-cultural observations of young people at various stages of development. He views the developing person as moving through a series of eight psychosocial crises over the course of the life span. Each crisis, although present in one form or another at all ages, takes on special significance at a given period of the life cycle because biological and social forces interact to bring the crisis into prominence. Erikson believes that the establishment of a coherent sense of identity is the chief psychosocial crisis of adolescence.

In Erikson's model, each psychosocial crisis defines an "age" or "stage" of the life span (see Figure 8.2). Each crisis is a sort of challenge that the individual must resolve. The crises are *normative*, in the sense that they are an inevitable part of being alive and growing older.

Erikson describes each of the eight crises as a continuum with positive and negative poles. The crisis of infancy, for example, is labeled "trust versus mistrust." By this Erikson means that during infancy, the child must be able to establish a feeling of trust, or security, with its caregivers. Resolving each crisis, though, does not entail coming through the crisis either entirely positively or entirely negatively, nor does it mean resolving the issue once and for all. "It is instead a matter of tipping the balance more in one direction (i.e., toward one end of the continuum) than in another" (Gallatin, 1975,

**FIGURE 8.2** The eight stages of development and their corresponding psychosocial crises, according to Erikson (1959).

| Stage | 1 | 2 | 3 | 4 | 5 | 6 | 7 | 8 |
|---|---|---|---|---|---|---|---|---|
| I Infancy | Trust vs. mistrust | | | | | | | |
| II Early childhood | | Autonomy vs. shame, doubt | | | | | | |
| III Play age | | | Initiative vs. guilt | | | | | |
| IV School age | | | | Industry vs. inferiority | | | | |
| V Adolescence | | | | | Identity vs. identity diffusion | | | |
| VI Young adult | | | | | | Intimacy vs. isolation | | |
| VII Adulthood | | | | | | | Generativity vs. self-absorption | |
| VIII Mature age | | | | | | | | Integrity vs. disgust, despair |

p. 175). In other words, it is important that the infant come through the first stage of development feeling more secure than insecure.

In Erikson's view, each crisis builds on the previous ones. Specifically, the successful resolution of each challenge depends on the healthy resolution of the challenges that have preceded it. An infant who has not successfully resolved the crisis of trust versus mistrust, for example, will have a difficult time with the crises he encounters through the rest of the life cycle. He may be always somewhat hesitant about becoming close with other people because, deep down inside, he fears that others will let him down. With respect to adolescent identity development, then, Erikson believes that the successful resolution of the crisis of **identity versus identity diffusion** depends on how the individual has resolved the previous crises of childhood. Without a healthy sense of trust, autonomy, initiative, and industry, it is difficult to establish a coherent sense of identity. Moreover, the way in which the adolescent resolves the crisis of identity will have an im-

pact on his or her struggle with the crises of adulthood. Far from seeing adolescence as a separate period of the life cycle, Erikson believes that what takes place during adolescence is much intertwined with what has come before and what will follow.

## IDENTITY VERSUS IDENTITY DIFFUSION

Before adolescence, the child's identity is like patches of fabric that have not yet been sewn together. But by the end of adolescence, these patches will be woven into a patchwork quilt that is unique to the individual. This process of integration is at the center of the fifth psychosocial crisis described by Erikson: the crisis of identity versus identity diffusion. As Erikson describes it, "From among all possible and imaginable relations, [the young person] must make a series of ever-narrowing selections of personal, occupational, sexual, and ideological commitments" (1968, p. 245). The maturational and social forces that converge at ado-

One of the most important influences on the adolescent's sense of identity is the young person's interactions with peers. *(Martin Benjamin/Image Works)*

lescence force young people to reflect on their place in society, on the ways that others view them, and on their options for the future. Achieving a balanced and coherent sense of identity is an intellectually and emotionally taxing process. According to Erikson, it is not until adolescence that one even has the mental or psychological capacity to tackle this task.

The key to resolving the crisis of identity versus identity diffusion, argues Erikson, lies in the adolescent's interactions with others. Through responding to the reactions of people who matter, the adolescent selects and chooses from among the many elements that could conceivably become a part of his or her final identity. The other people with whom the young person interacts serve as a mirror that reflects back to the adolescent information about who he or she is and who he or she ought to be. As such, the responses of these important others shape and influence the adolescent's developing sense of identity. Through others' reactions, we learn whether we are competent or clumsy, attractive or ugly, socially adept or tactless. Perhaps more important, especially during periods when our sense of identity is still forming, we learn from others what it is we do that we ought to keep doing, and what it is we do that we ought not to do.

Forging an identity, therefore, is a social as well as mental process. Erikson places a great deal of weight on the role of the young person's society (and, especially, on those individuals who have influence over the adolescent) in shaping the adolescent's sense of self. The adolescent's final identity is the result of a mutual recognition between the young person and society: The adolescent forges an identity, but at the same time, society identifies the adolescent.

## THE SOCIAL CONTEXT OF IDENTITY DEVELOPMENT

The social context in which the adolescent attempts to establish a sense of identity exerts a tremendous impact on the nature and outcome of the process. Clearly, if adolescents' identities are forged out of a recognition on the part of society, society will play an important role in determining which sorts of identities are possible alternatives; and of those that are genuine options, which are desirable and which are not.

As a consequence, the course of identity development will vary in different cultures, among different subcultures within the same society, and over different historical eras. For example, the career options open to women in contemporary society have changed dramatically in the past twenty-five years, and, consequently, so has the nature of adolescent girls' identity development. In the past, most young women assumed that their adult identity would be exclusively tied to marriage and family life. But today, far more alternative identities are open to women. As a result, the process of choosing among different alternatives has become more complicated than it once was.

The social context in which an adolescent develops also determines to a large extent whether the youngster's search for self-definition will take the form of a full-blown crisis or whether it will be a more manageable challenge. Generally speaking, the more alternatives available to the young person and the more arenas in which decisions must be made, the more difficult establishing a sense of identity will be. Growing up in contemporary America, where adolescents have a range of careers to decide among, for example, is far more likely to provoke an occupational identity crisis than is growing up in a small agrarian community in which each young person continues farming the family's land. The rapid rate of social change has raised new and more complicated sets of questions for young people to consider—questions not only about occupational plans but about values, lifestyles, and commitments to other people. No longer are all young people expected to follow the same narrow path into adulthood: marriage and children for all, work for men, and homemaking for women. Today, male and female adolescents alike must ask themselves *if* they want to remain single, live with someone, or marry; *if* and *when* they want to have children; and *how* they plan to incorporate these choices into their career plans. Consequently, the likelihood of going through a prolonged and difficult identity crisis is probably greater today than it has ever been.

**The psychosocial moratorium** The complications inherent in identity development in modern society have created the need, Erikson argues, for a **psychosocial moratorium**—a time-out during adolescence from the sorts of excessive responsibilities and obligations that might restrict the young person's pursuit of self-discovery. Adolescents in contemporary America are given a moratorium of sorts by being encouraged to remain in school for a long time, where they can think seriously about their plans for the future without making irrevocable decisions.

During the psychosocial moratorium, the adolescent can experiment with different roles and identities, in a context that permits and encourages this sort of exploration. The experimentation involves trying on different postures, personalities, and ways of behaving— sometimes to the consternation of the adolescent's parents, who may wonder why their child's personality seems so changeable. One week, an adolescent girl will spend hours putting on make-up; the next week she will insist to her parents that she is tired of caring so much about the way she looks. An adolescent boy will come home one day wearing boots and a leather jacket and acting tough, and a few weeks later, he will discard the tough-guy image for that of a serious student. Sometimes, parents describe their teenage children as going through "phases." Much of this behavior is actually experimentation with roles and personalities.

Having the time to experiment with roles is an important prelude to establishing a coherent sense of identity. But role experimentation can take place only in an environment that allows and encourages it (Gallatin, 1975). Without a period of moratorium, a full and thorough exploration of the options and alternatives available to the young person cannot occur, and identity development will be somewhat impeded. In other words, according to Erikson, adolescents must grow into adulthood—they should not be forced into it prematurely.

It is clear, however, that the sort of moratorium Erikson describes is an ideal; indeed, some might even consider it to be a luxury of the affluent. Many young people—perhaps even most—do not have the economic freedom to enjoy a long delay before taking on the responsibilities of adult life. For many youngsters, alternatives are not open in any realistic sense, and introspection only interferes with the more pressing task of survival. Does the 17-year-old who must drop out of school to work a full-time factory job go through life without a sense of identity? Do youngsters who cannot afford a psychosocial moratorium fail to resolve the crisis of "identity versus identity diffusion"?

Certainly not. But from an Eriksonian point of view, the absence of a psychosocial moratorium in some adolescents' lives—owing either to restrictions they place on themselves or to restrictions placed on them by others or by their life circumstances—is truly lamentable. The price these youngsters pay is not in failing to develop a sense of identity but in lost potential. You may know people whose parents have forced them into prematurely choosing a certain career or who have had to drop out of college and take a job they really did not want because of financial pressures. According to Erikson, without a chance to explore, to experiment, and to choose among options for the future, these young people may not realize all that they are capable of becoming. In theory, these individuals should encounter difficulties in resolving the subsequent crises of intimacy, generativity, and integrity.

## RESOLVING THE IDENTITY CRISIS

Is establishing a sense of identity a consciously felt achievement? According to Erikson, it is. It is experienced as a sense of well-being, a feeling of "being at home in one's body," a sense of knowing where one is going, and an inner assuredness of recognition from those who count. It is a sense of sameness through time—a feeling of continuity between the past and the future.

Establishing a coherent sense of identity is a lengthy process. Most writers on adolescence and youth believe that identity exploration continues well into young adulthood. But rather than thinking of the adolescent as going through *an* identity crisis, it probably makes more sense to view the phenomenon as a series of crises that may concern different aspects of the young person's identity and that may surface—and resurface—at different points in time throughout the adolescent and young adult years. As Erikson writes, "A sense of identity is never gained nor maintained once and for all . . . it is constantly lost and regained, although more lasting and more economical methods of maintenance and restoration are evolved and fortified in late adolescence" (1959, p. 118). During adolescence, the feeling of well-being associated with establishing a sense of identity is somewhat fleeting. Ultimately, however, the identity crisis of adolescence, when successfully resolved, culminates in a series of basic life commitments: occupational, ideological, social, religious, ethical, and sexual (Bourne, 1978a).

## PROBLEMS IN IDENTITY DEVELOPMENT

Given the wide variations in developmental histories that individuals bring to adolescence and the wide variations in the environments in

Role experimentation during adolescence often involves trying on different looks, images, and patterns of behavior. According to theorists such as Erik Erikson, having time to experiment with roles is an important prelude to establishing a coherent sense of identity. *(M. B. Duda/ Photo Researchers)*

which adolescence is experienced, it is not surprising to find differences in the ways in which individuals approach and resolve the crisis of identity versus identity diffusion. Problems in identity development can result when an individual has not successfully resolved earlier crises or when the adolescent is in an environment that does not provide the necessary period of moratorium. Three sorts of problems have received special attention from Erikson. They are labeled identity diffusion, identity foreclosure, and negative identity, respectively.

**Identity diffusion** (sometimes called identity confusion) is characterized by an incoherent,

## FROM CARSON McCULLERS'S THE MEMBER OF THE WEDDING

One of the most wonderful and memorable stories of an adolescent's struggle to establish a sense of identity is told in Carson McCullers's novel *The Member of the Wedding*. Set in the South during the mid-1940s, the story revolves around the identity development of Frankie Addams, a 12-year-old girl who has her first encounter that summer with the sort of self-examination and introspection we have come to associate with the adolescent years. At one point during the summer, she changes her name to F. Jasmine Addams.

"Why is it against the law to change your name?"

Berenice sat in a chair against the pale white light of the window. She held the newspaper open before her, and her head was twisted down and to one side as she strained to see what was printed there. When F. Jasmine spoke, she folded the paper and put it away on the table.

"You can figure that out," she said. "Just because. Think of the confusion."

"I don't see why," F. Jasmine said.

"What is that on your neck?" said Berenice. "I thought it was a head you carried on that neck. Just think. Suppose I would suddenly up and call myself Mrs. Eleanor Roosevelt. And you would begin naming yourself

Joe Louis. And John Henry would try to pass off as Henry Ford. Now what kind of confusion do you think that would cause?"

"Don't talk childish," F. Jasmine said. "That is not the kind of changing I mean. I mean from a name that doesn't suit you to a name you prefer. Like I changed from Frankie to F. Jasmine."

"But it would still be a confusion," Berenice insisted. "Suppose we all suddenly changed to entirely different names. Nobody would ever know who anybody was talking about. The whole world would go crazy." . . .

"Listen," F. Jasmine said. "What I've been trying to say is this. Doesn't it strike you as strange that I am I, and you are you? I am F. Jasmine Addams. And you are Berenice Sadie Brown. And we can look at each other, and touch each other, and stay together year in and year out in the same room. Yet always I am I, and you are you. And I can't ever be anything else but me, and you can't ever be anything else but you. Have you ever thought of that? And doesn't it seem to you strange?"

*Source:* Carson McCullers, *The Member of the Wedding* (New York: Bantam, 1974; orig. pub. 1946), pp. 107–109.

disjointed, incomplete sense of self. Identity diffusion can vary in degree from a mild state of not quite knowing who you are while in the midst of an identity crisis to a more severe, psychopathological condition that persists beyond a normal period of exploration. It is marked by disruptions in the individual's sense of time (some things seem to happen much faster than they really do, while others seem to take forever); excessive self-consciousness, to the point that it is difficult to make decisions; problems in work and achievement-related activities; difficulties in forming intimate relationships with others; and concerns over sexuality. Identity confusion is reflected not just in problems of identity; it manifests itself in the areas of autonomy, intimacy, sexuality, and achievement as well.

A classic example of an adolescent in the throes of identity diffusion is Holden Caulfield in the novel *The Catcher in the Rye.* He has flunked out of several prep schools, has severed most of his friendships, and has no sense of where he is headed. At one point in the book, for example, walking up Fifth Avenue in New York City, Holden says, "Every time I came to the end of a block and stepped off the goddam curb, I had this feeling that I'd never get to the other side of the street. I thought I'd just go down, down, down, and nobody'd ever see me again. Boy, did it scare me" (Salinger, 1964, pp. 197–198).

**Identity foreclosure**  Some young people bypass—either willingly or unwillingly—the period of exploration and experimentation that precedes the establishment of a healthy sense of identity. Instead of considering a range of alternatives, these adolescents prematurely commit themselves to a role, or series of roles, and settle upon a certain identification as a final identity. In essence, these individuals are not given—or do not take advantage of—a psychosocial moratorium. For example, a college freshman who made up his mind about becoming a doctor at the age of 13 may enroll in a rigid pre-med curriculum without considering other career possibilities. The circumvention of the identity crisis is called **identity foreclosure.**

Typically, the roles adopted in the process of identity foreclosure revolve around the goals set for the young person by parents or other authority figures. The adolescent may be led into these roles directly or forced into them indirectly by being denied a true period of psychosocial moratorium. Perhaps the parents of the would-be doctor have arranged their child's school schedule and summer vacations so that all of his or her spare time is spent taking extra science courses. No time is left for

role experimentation or introspection. Individuals who have bypassed the identity crisis have made commitments, but they have not gone through a period of experimentation before making them. Identity foreclosure can be viewed, then, as a kind of interruption of the identity development process, an interruption that interferes with the individual's discovery of his or her full range of potentials.

**Negative identity**  Occasionally, adolescents appear to select identities that are obviously undesirable to their parents and their community. The examples are familiar: The daughter of the local police chief who repeatedly gets into trouble with the law; the son of prestigious and successful parents who refuses to go to college; the child of a devoutly religious family who insists that he or she is a confirmed atheist. Because the establishment of a healthy sense of identity is so intimately tied to the recognition of the adolescent by those who count in his or her life, the adoption of a so-called **negative identity** is a sign that problems in identity development have arisen. The adolescent who adopts a negative identity is indeed recognized by those around him or her but not in a way that fosters healthy development.

Usually, selecting a negative identity is an attempt to forge *some* sense of self-definition in an environment that has made it difficult for the young person to establish an acceptable identity. This appears to be especially likely when, after repeatedly trying and failing to receive positive recognition from those who are important in their lives, adolescents turn to a different, perhaps more successful, route to being noticed—adopting a negative identity. Consider this example: The son of successful parents is a good student but not quite good enough to please his excessively demanding parents. He feels he is a nobody in his parents' eyes. So the boy drops out of school to play guitar in a band—something his parents ve-

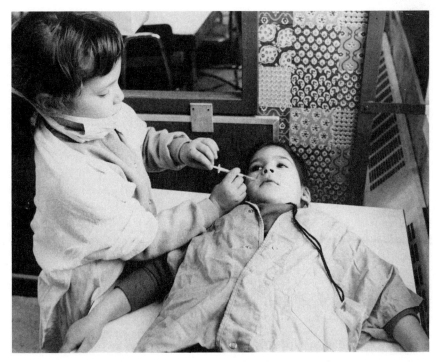

It is perfectly fine for young children to play at different jobs, but when parents encourage their adolescents to make early career choices, they may deny them opportunities to experiment with different occupational identities and discover their full range of potential. *(Alice Kandell/Photo Researchers)*

hemently oppose. To paraphrase Erikson, this adolescent, like most youngsters, would rather be somebody "bad" than nobody at all.

## Research on Identity Development

### DETERMINING AN ADOLESCENT'S IDENTITY STATUS

In order to determine an individual's identity status, researchers have used an approach developed by James Marcia (1966, 1976), which focuses on identity exploration in three areas—occupation, ideology, and interpersonal relations. Based on responses to an interview or questionnaire, individuals are rated on two dimensions: (1) the degree to which they have made commitments and (2) the degree to which they engaged in a sustained search in the process (see Figure 8.3). On the basis of these ratings, the researchers assign young people to one of four categories: *identity achievement* (the individual has established a coherent sense of identity, that is, has made commitments after a period of crisis and experimentation); *moratorium* (the individual is in the midst of a period of crisis and experimentation); *foreclosure* (the individual has made commitments but without a period of crisis or experimentation); and *identity diffusion* (the individual does not have firm commitments and is not currently trying to make them).

|  | **Commitment** | |
|---|---|---|
|  | Present | Absent |
| **Exploration** Present | Identity achievement | Moratorium |
| Absent | Identity foreclosure | Identity diffusion |

**FIGURE 8.3**  Identity status categories derived from Marcia's measure.

Generally speaking, research employing this approach has supported Erikson's theory. For example, identity achievers are psychologically healthier than other individuals on a variety of measures: They score highest on measures of achievement motivation, moral reasoning, intimacy with peers, and reflectiveness. Individuals in the moratorium category score highest on measures of anxiety, show the highest levels of conflict over issues of authority, and are themselves the least rigid and authoritarian. Individuals classified as being in the foreclosure group have been shown to be the most authoritarian and to have the highest need for social approval, the lowest level of autonomy, and the greatest closeness to their parents. Individuals in a state of identity diffusion display the highest level of psychological and interpersonal problems: They are the most socially withdrawn and show the lowest level of intimacy with peers (Bourne, 1978b).

What sorts of parenting practices are associated with these different identity statuses? Generally speaking, individuals whose identity development is healthy are more likely to come from homes characterized by warm, not excessively constraining relations (Grotevant and Cooper, 1986). As we saw in Chapter 4, individuals who grow up in these environments are encouraged to assert their individuality but to remain connected to their families at the same time. Typically, the absence of parental warmth is associated with problems in making commitments—the most extreme case being

identity diffusion—whereas the absence of parental encouragement of individuality is associated with problems in engaging in extensive exploration (Campbell, Adams, and Dobson, 1985).

## STUDYING IDENTITY DEVELOPMENT OVER TIME

In order to examine the development of a sense of identity, researchers have done both cross-sectional studies (comparing individuals of different ages) and longitudinal studies (following the same individuals over a period of time). Perhaps the most significant finding to emerge from this line of research is that establishing a coherent sense of identity generally does not occur much before age 18 (Marcia, 1980). In general, when comparisons are made among groups of youngsters of different ages over the span from ages 12 to 24, differences in identity status are most frequently observed between groups in the 18- to 21-year-old range. Few consistent differences emerge in comparisons of teenagers in the middle adolescent years, suggesting that, although self-examination may take place throughout adolescence, the consolidation of a coherent sense of identity does not begin until very late in the period (Adams and Jones, 1983; Archer, 1982). The late teens and early twenties appear to be the critical times for the crystallization of a sense of identity.

The movement toward identity achievement that occurs between ages 18 and 21 among college students appears to be primarily in the area of occupational commitments. Alan Waterman and his associates (Waterman, Geary, and Waterman, 1974; Waterman and Goldman, 1976; Waterman and Waterman, 1971), who followed samples of college students for several years, found that during the college years, vocational plans solidify, but religious and political commitments are not as clearly established. More specifically, individuals emerge from college with more clearly defined occupational plans but no firm religious or political commitments (Waterman, 1982). In fact, college seems to undermine students' "traditional" religious beliefs—the beliefs that they acquired from their parents—without replacing them with others. Students who enter college as devout Catholics, for example, may graduate having lost some of their commitment to Catholicism but without having developed any new religious commitments instead.

A study by Raymond Montemayor and his colleagues supports the idea that the freshman year of college may be an important time in the process of identity development. A group of students were assessed before entering college and again toward the end of their freshman year. Before entering college, half of the adolescents were judged to be in a state of identity diffusion and 40 percent in a state of moratorium—consistent with the notion that the identity crisis is unlikely to be resolved during high school. Eight percent were in the identity achievement status, and the rest were judged to be foreclosed. What happened to these individuals as college freshmen? Over the first year of college, the most common pathway was either remaining diffused or in a state of moratorium or moving from one of the "committed" statuses (identity achievement or identity foreclosure) to one of the "noncommitted" statuses (diffusion or moratorium). In other words, while freshman year may "shake up some students and cause them to reexamine previously held commitments, students who are uncertain to begin with . . . remain so. . . . The freshman year appears to produce uncertainty in many students but does not help to

During the college years, many individuals begin to develop clearer vocational identities. Many colleges sponsor career days and offer job counseling services. *(Stu Rosner/Stock, Boston)*

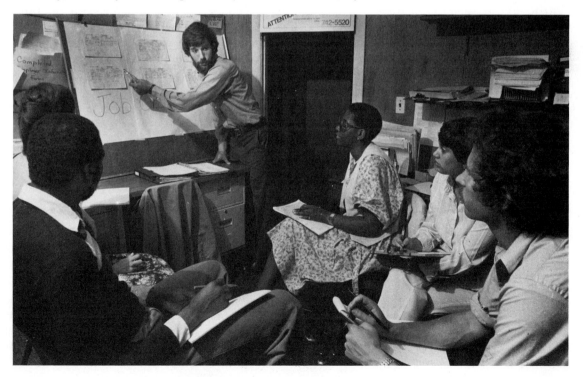

resolve it" (Montemayor, Brown, and Adams, 1985, p. 7).

Do young people need to go to college in order to develop a clear sense of identity? Unfortunately, because there are so few developmental studies among noncollege youth, we have little way of answering this question. But the results of one study comparing identity development in college and noncollege youth are quite interesting. Gordon Munro and Gerald Adams (1977) compared a sample of college students with a same-aged (18–21) sample of noncollege working youths. The working youths were actually *more* likely to have established a sense of identity—more in the area of ideological commitments than in vocational commitments. This finding suggests that for many young people, college may prolong the psychosocial moratorium, especially in matters of political and religious belief.

## SHIFTS IN IDENTITY STATUS

As you will recall, Erikson theorizes that the sense of identity developed during adolescence is constantly lost and regained, that the challenge is not resolved once and for all at one point in time. If, according to Erikson's model, identity crises surface and resurface throughout the life cycle, we ought to find that individuals move from one identity status to another, particularly during the adolescent and young adult years.

This appears to be precisely the case. In one study that followed students over a one-year period (Adams and Fitch, 1982), nearly 60 percent of the students classified as experiencing identity diffusion at the beginning of the study were no longer in this category one year later. Changes in status also occurred for half of the students initially placed in the moratorium category. In two other longitudinal studies, each spanning a four-year period (Waterman, Geary, and Waterman, 1974; Waterman and Goldman, 1976), the degree of shifting was 50 percent in one study and 33 percent in the

other for students classified as experiencing identity diffusion, and 91 percent and 100 percent for students initially classified as being in the midst of a moratorium.

These sorts of shifts are not surprising, of course, since both the diffusion and moratorium categories are, theoretically, unstable ones. But in these same longitudinal studies, about one-third of each of the identity achievement and foreclosure groups *also* shifted status over the course of one year; and, over the course of four years, more than half of the students initially classified as foreclosures and one-third of those initially classified as identity achievers moved into a different group. In other words, some individuals who at one point had apparently resolved the identity crisis (had been classified as identity achievers) actually had not resolved it—at least, in any final sense. The weight of the evidence collected to date, therefore, suggests that identity status classifications made during adolescence and young adulthood probably represent short-term, temporary states, rather than long-term, enduring traits. As Erikson has suggested, revising and maintaining one's sense of self-definition is a challenge that continues beyond adolescence.

## The Development of Ethnic Identity

In recent years, researchers have begun to study more intensively American adolescents from minority groups. This research has tended to focus more on problematic aspects of development, however, such as unemployment, teenage pregnancy, or delinquency, rather than on more normative aspects of adolescence, such as the development of identity or intimacy. Studies of problem behavior among minority adolescents are important when they shed light on the dimensions, causes, and consequences of these problems and provide information with which to compare the behavior of white adolescents. Nonetheless, it is misleading and disparaging to limit our research on minority adolescents to the study of problem behavior, because there is reason to believe that most minority youngsters—like most white youngsters—progress through adolescence without major difficulty. We do not know, however, whether the progression through the developmental challenges of adolescence follows the pattern described in most theories and research, because virtually all of our knowledge about *normative* aspects of adolescent development derives from studies of white youth—white, middle-class youth, to be precise. Consequently, we must be cautious about generalizing these results to nonwhite populations. Furthermore, as studies of normative aspects of development among minority youth begin to appear, we must be cautious about generalizing the findings from one minority group to another: African-American, Hispanic-American, Asian-American, and Native American adolescents may share the fact that they are members of ethnic minorities, but their similarities may end there. Even within these broad ethnic categories there are substantial differences in adolescents' experiences between Mexican-American and Puerto Rican adolescents, for instance, or between Japanese-American and Chinese-American adolescents.

For all individuals, but especially for those who are not part of the white majority, integrating a sense of **ethnic identity** into their overall sense of personal identity is likely to be an important task of late adolescence, perhaps as important as establishing a coherent occupational, ideological, or interpersonal identity (Phinney and Alipuria, 1987). According to several writers (Cross, 1978; Kim, 1981, cited in Phinney and Alipuria, 1987), the process of ethnic-identity development follows in some respects the process of identity development in general, with an unquestioning view of oneself being displaced or upset by a crisis. Following the crisis, the individual may become im-

mersed in his or her own ethnic group and turn against the white majority culture. Eventually, as the value and importance of having a strong ethnic identity become clear, the individual establishes a more coherent sense of personal identity that includes this ethnic identity and, with growing confidence, attempts to help others deal with their own struggles with ethnic identity.

Do members of ethnic minorities have more difficulty than white adolescents in resolving the identity crisis, however? Researchers are just now beginning to examine this question, and the answer is still not known. The little research that has been done suggests more similarities than differences in the *process* through which identity development occurs. One difference, though, appears to be quite important, if perhaps not very surprising: Having a strong ethnic identity is associated with higher self-esteem among minority youngsters, especially among African-American and Hispanic-American youth, but this is not the case among white youth (Phinney and Alipuria, 1987). It would seem, therefore, that establishing a sense of ethnic identity is more important to individuals who are part of an ethnic minority than for those who are part of a majority.

As one recent review of research on minority adolescent development noted, the task of developing a coherent sense of identity is much more complicated for minority adolescents than for their majority counterparts (Spencer and Dornbusch, 1990). Because identity development is profoundly influenced by the social context in which the adolescent lives, the development of the minority adolescent must be understood in relation to the specific context that nonwhite youngsters face in contemporary society. All too often, this context includes racial stereotypes, a limited number of role models, and mixed messages about the costs and benefits of identifying too closely with the majority culture. Not surprisingly, a number of studies suggest that the prevalence of iden-

## THE SEXES: ARE THERE SEX DIFFERENCES IN THE ROUTE TO A SENSE OF IDENTITY?

Many writers have argued that male and female adolescents approach the crisis of identity from different perspectives and resolve it through different means. Some theorists have gone so far as to say that although Erikson's framework, which places the crisis of identity developmentally earlier than the crisis of intimacy, is a reasonable model of psychosocial development for males, it does not adequately account for development among girls (Gallatin, 1975). They argue that girls are much more interpersonally oriented than boys and that as a consequence, girls are likely to face the challenge of intimacy before they deal with the crisis of identity—or at the very least, that girls pursue their sense of identity *through* their relationships with others. Girls learn about themselves, it is argued, in the context of friendships and close relationships, whereas boys forge a sense of identity by being autonomous and independent (Douvan and Adelson, 1966).

There is undoubtedly some truth to the idea that males and females approach and resolve the psychosocial issues of adolescence differently; how could they help but do so, given the strong pressures on them to adhere to two different sets of behavioral standards? But linking male identity development to autonomy and independence and female identity development to intimacy and other interpersonal pursuits is no longer as useful as it once was. Although one classic study of adolescents conducted during the early 1960s (Douvan and Adelson, 1966) concluded that "there is not one adolescent crisis, but two major and clearly distinctive ones—the masculine and the feminine" (p. 350), research carried out during the 1980s has pointed to similarities rather than differences in the ways in which males and females struggle with the task of self-definition (Adams and Fitch, 1982; Archer, 1989; Grotevant and Thorbecke, 1982). Were the early descriptions of sex differences in identity development erroneous, or are these recent studies off the mark?

In answering this question, we must bear in mind that sex differences—or for that matter similarities—in identity development can be understood only against the backdrop of the social context in which development takes place. Assessing the studies in a historical context sheds some light on the controversy. For many adolescent girls, particularly twenty or thirty years ago,

*continued on next page*

tity foreclosure is higher among minority youth (e.g., Hauser and Kasendorf, 1983).

According to Phinney and her colleagues (Phinney et al., in press), minority youth have four possibilities open to them for dealing with their ethnicity: assimilation (i.e., trying to adopt the majority culture's norms and standards while rejecting those of one's own group), alienation (i.e., living within majority culture but feeling estranged and outcast), separation (i.e., associating only with members of one's own culture and rejecting majority culture), and biculturalism (i.e., maintaining ties to both the majority and minority cultures). In the past, minority youth were encouraged by majority society to assimilate as much as possible. Assimilation, however, has not proven to be as simple as many nonminority individuals imagine. First, although minority youth are told to assimilate, they may be tacitly excluded from majority society on the basis of their physical appearance or language. This leads to the roles of adulthood open to them *were* primarily interpersonal in nature, so that it comes as no surprise that the crisis of identity manifested itself for these young women through their relationships with others. After all, in Erikson's model, identity is pursued with one eye toward the future. But today, as new generations of adolescent girls face a society that presents them with greater and more diverse options for the future, especially in terms of occupation, their identity explorations are likely to extend further into the realms of autonomy and independence than they have in the past.

In this regard, it is interesting to note that some studies show that adolescent males move through the process of identity development faster than females (Marcia, 1980), although this is not always the case (Archer, 1989). If young women appear to take more time resolving the crisis of identity than young men do, perhaps it is because the options and alternatives open to women in contemporary society are more confusing, more complicated, and more rapidly changing than they are for men. As noted earlier, the length of a moratorium needed to experiment with enough roles is linked to the complexity of the choices the young person faces.

This is not to say that the outcomes of the identity development process are the same for males and females, however, or that the similarities that may characterize identity development during adolescence persist into adulthood. Society has still not fully come to terms with women's interest in careers, and, consequently, the task of integrating occupational and interpersonal commitments into a coherent and satisfying sense of self is likely to be more difficult for women than men (Chile, 1989). Accordingly, even though boys and girls may go through similar struggles in establishing a sense of identity in adolescence, the consequences of resolving the crisis may have clearer and more immediate advantages for men than women. Thus, for example, achieving a coherent sense of identity during adolescence is a strong predictor of life satisfaction and of becoming married as an adult for men, but for women, it predicts neither (Kahn et al., 1985). Whatever similarities exist between boys and girls in their search for identity as adolescents, the structure of adult experience introduces important differences into the process—and, consequently, the outcome.

a situation of **marginality,** in which the minority youth is on the edge of majority society but never really accepted as a full status member.

Second, minority youth who do attempt to assimilate are often scorned by their own communities for trying to "act white"—as captured in the array of pejorative terms minority youth have for their friends who have tried too hard to assimilate: Asian-Americans who act white are "bananas"; Hispanic-Americans are "coconuts"; African-Americans are "Oreos"

(Spencer and Dornbusch, 1990, p. 132). Partly in reaction to this, many minority youth are adopting a strategy of separation.

Some writers argue that a more viable alternative to assimilation or separaton is **biculturalism.** Bicultural adolescents "shuttle successfully between their primary or familial culture and the dominant culture" (Spencer and Dornbusch, 1990, p. 133). One writer has proposed a flexibility model, in which minority youth have open to them the norms of both cultures and select between them depending on the situation. At a majority-controlled school, for example, it may be more adaptive to "act white" when being evaluated by white teachers, but more adaptive to conform with the minority group's own norms and standards when in one's neighborhood. Research that compares biculturalism with other strategies, such as assimilation or separation, is sorely needed.

## Sex-Role Development

Gender is a critical component of one's identity. From birth, boys and girls are socialized to behave in "sex-appropriate" ways—that is, to conform to society's standards for acceptable masculine and acceptable feminine behavior. In American society, strong sex-role stereotypes prevail among children, adolescents, and adults. Traits such as logical, independent, ambitious, and aggressive are considered masculine; and traits such as gentle, sociable, empathic, and tender are considered feminine (Broverman et al., 1972).

Individuals vary in their degrees of masculinity and femininity. Some are decidedly more masculine than feminine, and others are decidedly more feminine than masculine. But some people have a high degree of both masculinity and femininity. For instance, some people are both highly ambitious (a trait usually considered masculine) and highly sensitive (a trait usually considered feminine). Individuals who are both highly masculine and highly feminine are said to be **androgynous** (Bem, 1975).

Researchers have begun to take an interest in the relation between sex-role stereotypes and adolescent identity development. Are teenagers, for example, pressured more than children to behave in stereotypically masculine or feminine ways? If so, to what extent does a person's compliance with prevailing sex-role stereotypes affect his or her self-image?

## SEX-ROLE SOCIALIZATION DURING ADOLESCENCE

There is some thought that pressures to behave in "sex-appropriate" ways intensify during adolescence, especially for girls (Huston and Alvarez, 1990). This idea, called the **gender intensification hypothesis** (Hill and Lynch, 1983), is that many of the sex differences observed between adolescent boys and girls are due not to biological differences but to an acceleration in their socialization to act in stereotypically masculine and feminine ways.

Psychologists John Hill and Mary Ellen Lynch (1983) have summarized some of the research that bears on this issue. They note that at adolescence, girls become more self-conscious and experience more disruptions in self-image than boys; that achievement behavior becomes more sex-stereotyped, with girls beginning to disengage from math and science; and that girls become more invested in and more competent at forming intimate friendships. One study has found that sex differences in sex-role attitudes and in masculinity do, in fact, increase in early adolescence (Galambos et al., in press). As we saw in the chapter on cognitive development, it is impossible to rule out totally the biological explanations for some of these sex differences, because patterns of hormonal change at puberty differ markedly for boys and girls. Nonetheless, according to Hill and Lynch, it seems reasonable to conclude that at least in some areas, sex-role socialization does intensify during adolescence. As teenagers begin to date, for example, it may become more important for them to act in ways that are consistent with sex-role expectations and that meet with approval in the peer group. Boys who do not act masculine enough and girls who do not act feminine enough may be less popular and may be less accepted by their same- and opposite-sex peers.

In many respects, sex-role identity, already

an important part of the self-concept during childhood, may become an even more important aspect of identity during adolescence. As we shall see in the chapters on intimacy, sexuality, and achievement, the intensification of sex-role socialization during adolescence has important implications for understanding sex differences in a range of different issues. For example, girls' achievement in high school may be lower than boys' because doing well in school is not perceived as appropriately feminine, and girls who earn high grades may pay a price in popularity.

## MASCULINITY, FEMININITY, ANDROGYNY, AND SEX-ROLE TRANSCENDENCE

If sex-role socialization becomes more intense during adolescence, we would expect to find that conformity to sex-role expectations is an important influence on the adolescent's self-image. Do more feminine girls and more masculine boys feel better about themselves than do their peers, or are boys and girls both better off being somewhat androgynous—as some psychologists suggest (Bem, 1975; Spence and Helmreich, 1978)?

Recent research on sex-role identity during adolescence suggests that the answer to this question may differ for males and females. The benefits of androgyny to youngsters' self-image are greater for girls than for boys. Although androgynous girls feel better about themselves than either very masculine or very feminine girls, masculine boys (not androgynous boys) show the highest levels of self-acceptance. This may be due to the fact that peer acceptance during adolescence is also highest for androgynous girls and masculine boys (Massad, 1981). These findings suggest that it is easier for girls to behave sometimes in masculine ways during adolescence than it is for boys to act occasionally in feminine ways. Consistent with research on younger children (Lynn,

1966), during adolescence—at least in contemporary American society—males who do not conform to traditionally masculine sex-role norms are judged more deviant than females whose behavior departs from exclusively feminine roles.

At first glance, this finding may seem to contradict something we noted earlier—that during adolescence, pressures to conform with sex-role norms increase more for girls than for boys. If this is so, why is it that boys suffer greater self-image problems when they deviate from what is viewed as appropriate for their gender?

The answer is that although girls may be pressured to adopt (or maintain) certain feminine traits during adolescence, they are not necessarily pressured to relinquish all elements of masculinity. In contrast, boys are socialized from a very early age not to adopt feminine traits and are judged deviant if they show signs of femininity. In other words, girls can be highly pressured during adolescence to behave in feminine ways without necessarily being punished or labeled deviant for exhibiting some masculine traits at the same time; thus for girls, androgyny is a viable alternative to exclusive femininity. Girls may feel increasingly pressured to dress nicely and wear makeup when they reach adolescence; but they are not pressured to give up athletics or other typically masculine interests. But boys, from childhood on, are pressured not to behave in feminine ways—even if the femininity is in the context of androgyny. Their gender-role socialization does not intensify during adolescence as much as it does for girls because it is so intense to begin with.

Several theorists have proposed alternatives to the models of gender roles that emphasize individual differences in masculinity, femininity, and androgyny. Instead, these writers suggest that, with development, individuals move toward an endpoint that ultimately "transcends" sex-roles (Katz, 1979; Rebecca et al.,

Androgynous girls—girls who have a mix of masculine and feminine traits—have a more positive self-image and are more accepted by their peers than are extremely feminine or extremely masculine girls. *(Barbara Alper)*

1976). Rather than viewing androgyny—a mixture of traditionally masculine and traditionally feminine characteristics—as the pinnacle of mature sex-role development, these theorists argue that the most psychologically mature individuals have the capacity to look beyond sex-roles entirely and permit one another to take advantage of their unique strengths and talents, regardless of their biological sex. This is what is meant by **"sex-role transcendence."**

## *Summary*

1. Although changes in the way we see and feel ourselves occur throughout the life cycle, the study of identity development has been a prominent issue in the field of adolescent development in particular. One reason for this attention concerns the impact that the biological, cognitive, and social definitional changes of adolescence have on the young person's ability to engage, and interest in engaging, in self-examination.

2. Identity development is complex and multifaceted. Researchers have traditionally distinguished among three aspects of identity development in adolescence: changes in self-conceptions (the ideas people have about themselves), changes in self-esteem (how positively or negatively people feel about themselves), and changes in the sense of identity (how coherent their sense of self is).

3. During the transition into adolescence, self-conceptions become more complex, abstract, and psychological. In addition, adolescents' self-conceptions are more differentiated and better organized than those of children. Although having more complex self-conceptions initially may be unsettling to the adolescent, it ultimately provides for a more sophisticated and more accurate view of oneself.

4. Researchers have differed in their approach to the study of self-esteem. While some

have studied adolescents' general, or global, feelings about themselves, others have stressed the multidimensional nature of self-esteem. In general, global self-esteem during adolescence is quite stable and, contrary to popular belief, increases slightly during adolescence. During early adolescence, however, individuals' self-image may fluctuate more than during other periods.

5. The predominant influence on the study of identity development in adolescence comes from the work of Erik Erikson. Erikson suggested that the major psychosocial issue of adolescence revolves around the "identity crisis"—coming to terms with who one is and where one is headed. In order to resolve this crisis successfully, the young person needs some time out from excessive responsibilities in order to engage in identity exploration and experimentation.

6. Research on identity development from Erikson's theoretical perspective has generally supported his model. Most studies indicate, however, that the major developments in this domain occur in late adolescence and young adulthood, rather than earlier during the adolescent decade.

7. Two important aspects of identity development in adolescence are ethnic identity development and gender-role development. For minority youth in particular, developing a strong sense of ethnic identity is a complicated and often difficult process. And for all adolescents, developing a healthy sense of gender identity is a major task of the period.

## Key Terms

| | |
|---|---|
| androgynous | identity diffusion |
| barometric self-esteem | identity fore- |
| baseline self-esteem | closure |
| biculturalism | identity versus iden- |
| ethnic identity | tity diffusion |
| gender intensification | marginality |
| hypothesis | negative identity |

| | |
|---|---|
| psychosocial mora- | self-image stability |
| torium | sense of identity |
| self-conceptions | sex-role transcend- |
| self-consciousness | ence |
| self-esteem | social class |

## For Further Reading

ERIKSON, E. (1968). *Identity: Youth and Crisis.* New York: Norton. In this book, Erikson presents his theory of identity development during adolescence.

BAUMEISTER, R., AND TICE, D. (1986). How adolescence became the struggle for self: A historical transformation of psychological development. In J. Suls and A. Greenwald (Eds.), *Psychological perspectives on the self,* Vol. 3. Hillsdale, N.J.: Erlbaum. A thoughtful discussion of the social and historical factors that have made identity development such a salient issue in the study of adolescent development.

PHINNEY, J., LOCHNER, B., AND MURPHY, R. (in press). Ethnic identity development and psychological adjustment in adolescence. In A. Stiffman and L. Davis (Eds.), *Advances in adolescent mental health*, Vol. 5: *Ethnic issues.* Greenwich, Conn.: JAI Press. A review of the literature on ethnic identity development.

HARTER, S. (1990). Identity and self development. In S. Feldman and G. Elliott (Eds.), *At the threshold: The developing adolescent.* Cambridge: Harvard University Press. An extensive review of the literatures on self-conceptions, self-esteem, and identity development in adolescence.

WATERMAN, A. (1982). Identity development from adolescence to adulthood: An extension of theory and a review of research. *Developmental Pscyhology, 18,* 341–358. An extensive review of research on Erikson's ideas about identity development during adolescence.

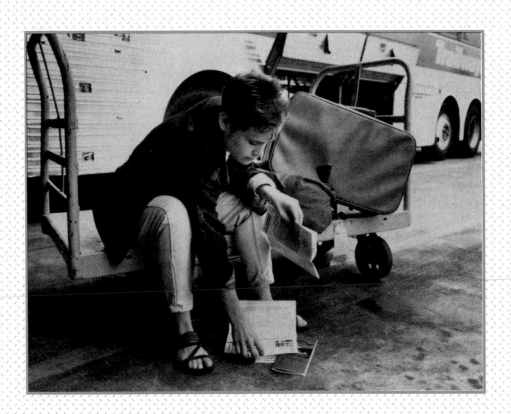

# AUTONOMY

You are about to leave the house:

"Where are you going?"

"Out."

"Out where?"

"Just out."

"Who are you going with?"

"A friend."

"Which friend?"

"Mom, just a friend, okay? Do you have to know everything?"

"I don't have to know everything. I just want to know who you're going out with."

"Debby, okay?"

"Do I know Debby?"

"She's just a friend, okay?"

"Well, where are going?"

"Out."

—Delia Ephron, *Teenage Romance*

*F*or most adolescents, establishing a sense of **autonomy** is as important a part of becoming an adult as is establishing a sense of identity. Becoming an autonomous person—a self-governing person—is one of the fundamental developmental tasks of the adolescent years.

Although we often use the words *autonomy* and *independence* interchangeably, in the study of adolescence, *autonomy* means something slightly different from *independence*. Independence generally refers to individuals' capacity to behave on their own. The growth of independence is surely a part of becoming autonomous during adolescence, but, as you will see in this chapter, autonomy has emotional and cognitive as well as behavioral components.

During adolescence, there is a movement away from the dependency typical of childhood toward the autonomy typical of adulthood. But the growth of autonomy during adolescence is often misunderstood. Autonomy is often confused with rebellion, and becoming an independent person is often equated with breaking away from the family. This perspective on autonomy goes hand in hand with the idea that adolescence is inevitably a time of stress and turmoil. But as we saw in the last chapter, the view that adolescence is a period of "storm and stress" has been questioned repeatedly by recent research. The same sort of rethinking has taken place with regard to the development of autonomy. Rather than viewing adolescence as a time of spectacular and active rebellion, researchers now see the growth of autonomy during adolescence as gradual, progessive, and although important, relatively undramatic.

Because today's adolescents spend so much time away from the direct supervision of adults, either by themselves or with their peers, learning how to govern their own behavior in a responsible fashion is a crucial task for contemporary youth. As we saw in earlier chapters, with increasing numbers of single-parent and two-career households, more young people are expected to supervise themselves for a good part of the day (Steinberg, 1986). Many young people feel pressured—by parents, by friends, and by the media—to grow up quickly and to act like adults at an earlier age (Elkind, 1982). One 13-year-old must make plane reservations to fly back and forth between his separated parents' homes. Another is pregnant and, afraid to tell her parents, must seek counseling on her own. A third is expected to take care of his younger siblings each afternoon because both of his parents work. In many regards, the demands on young people to behave independently are greater today than ever before.

There is a curious paradox to all of this, however. At the same time that adolescents have been asked to become more autonomous psychologically and socially, they have become less autonomous economically. Because of the extension of schooling well into the young adult years for most individuals, financial independence may not come until long after psychological independence has been established. Many young people who are emotionally independent find it frustrating to discover that they have to abide by their parents' rules as long as they are being supported economically. They may feel that the ability to make their own decisions has nothing to do with financial dependence. A 16-year-old who drives, has a part-time job, and has a serious relationship with his girlfriend, for example, may be independent in these respects, but he is nonetheless still dependent on his parents for food and shelter. His parents may feel that as long as their son lives in their home, they should decide how late he can stay out at night. The adolescent may feel that his parents have no right to tell him when he can come and go. This sort of difference of opinion can be a real source of problems and confusion for teenagers and their parents, particularly when they have difficulty agreeing on a level of independence for the adolescent. Disagreements over autonomy-related concerns are at the top of the list of quarrel-provokers between adolescents and parents (Holmbeck and O'Donnell, in press; Montemayor, 1986).

## Autonomy as an Adolescent Issue

Like identity, autonomy is a psychosocial concern that surfaces and resurfaces during the entire life cycle. The development of independent behavior begins long before puberty. Erik Erikson (1963), whose ideas we examined in the previous chapter, believes that autonomy is the central issue of toddlerhood, just as identity is the central issue of adolescence. Young children, he observes, try to establish an initial sense of autonomy when they begin to explore their surroundings on their own and assert their desire to do as they please. If you spend any time with 3-year-olds, you know that one of their favorite expressions is "No!" In some regards, the early adolescent's behavior captured in the excerpt that began this chapter is quite similar. The toddler who insists on saying

"no" and the young adolescent who insists on keeping her whereabouts secret are both demonstrating their growing sense of independence and autonomy.

Although childhood and adolescence are important periods for the development of autonomy, it is a mistake to suggest that issues of autonomy are resolved once and for all by young adulthood. Questions about our ability to function independently arise whenever we find ourselves in positions that demand a new degree of self-reliance. Following a divorce, for example, someone who has depended on a spouse over the years for economic support, guidance, or nurturance must find a way to function more autonomously and independently. During late adulthood, autonomy may become a significant concern of the individual who suddenly finds it necessary to depend on others for assistance and support.

If establishing and maintaining a healthy sense of autonomy is a lifelong concern, why has it attracted so much attention among scholars interested in adolescence? When we look at the development of autonomy in relation to the biological, cognitive, and social changes of adolescence, it is easy to see why. Consider first the impact of puberty. Some theorists (for example, A. Freud, 1958) have suggested that the physical changes of early adolescence trigger changes in the young person's emotional relationships at home (Holmbeck and Hill, in press). Adolescents' interest in turning away from parents and toward peers for emotional support—a development that is part of establishing adult independence—may be sparked by their emerging interest in sexual relationships and their concerns over such things as dating and intimate friendships. In some senses, puberty drives the adolescent away from exclusive emotional dependence on the family. Furthermore, the changes in stature and physical appearance occurring at puberty may provoke changes in how much autonomy the young person is granted by parents and teach-

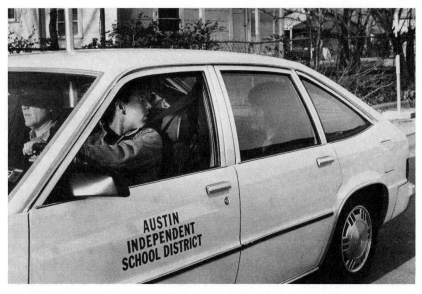

The development of autonomy becomes an especially salient issue during adolescence as young people find themselves moving into positions that demand independent and responsible behavior. *(Bob Daemmrich/Image Works)*

ers. Youngsters who simply *look* more mature may be given more responsibility by adults around them.

The cognitive changes of adolescence also play an important role in the development of autonomy. Part of being autonomous involves being able to make our own decisions. When we turn to others for advice, we often receive conflicting opinions. If you are deciding between staying home to study for an exam and going out to a party, your professor and the person throwing the party would probably give you different advice. As an adult, you are able to see that each individual's perspective influences his or her advice. The ability to see this, however, calls for a level of intellectual abstraction not available until adolescence. Being able to take other people's perspectives into account, reason in more sophisticated ways, and foresee the future consequences of alternative courses of action all help the young person to weigh more effectively the opinions and sug-

gestions of others and reach his or her own independent decisions. The cognitive changes of adolescence also provide the logical foundation for changes in the young person's thinking about social, moral, and ethical problems. These changes in thinking are important prerequisites to the development of a system of values that is based on the individual's own sense of right and wrong and not merely on rules and regulations handed down by parents or other authority figures (Mazor et al., 1990; Mazor and Enright, 1988).

Finally, changes in social roles and activities during adolescence are bound to raise concerns related to independence, as the adolescent moves into new positions that demand increasing degrees of responsibility and self-reliance. Being able to work, to marry, to drive, to drink, and to vote, to name just a few activities that are first permitted during adolescence, all require a certain degree of autonomy—the ability to manage oneself responsibly in the absence of monitoring by parents or teachers. Becoming involved in new roles and taking on new responsibilities place the adolescent in situations that require and stimulate the development of independent decision-making abilities and the clarification of personal values. A teenager might not really think much about the responsibilities associated with taking a job, for example, until he or she actually ends up in one. Choosing whether to drink does not become an important question until the adolescent begins to approach the legal drinking age. And deciding what one's political leanings are becomes a more pressing concern when the young person realizes that he or she has the right to vote.

## Three Types of Autonomy

We have talked a great deal thus far about the need to develop a sense of autonomy during adolescence. But what does it really mean to be an autonomous or independent person? One way to approach this question is to begin by thinking of people whom you would describe as independent. Why did you pick them? Is it because they seem to be able to rely on themselves rather than depending excessively on others for support or guidance? Is it because they can make their own decisions and follow them through, withstanding pressures to go against what they really know is right? Or it is perhaps because they are independent thinkers—people who have strong principles and values that they won't compromise?

Each of these characterizations is a reasonable enough description of what it means to be independent, yet each describes a different sort of independence. The first involves what psychologists call **emotional autonomy**—that aspect of independence related to changes in the individual's close relationships, especially with parents. The second characterization corresponds to what is sometimes called **behavioral autonomy**—the capacity to make independent decisions and follow through with them. The third characterization involves an aspect of independence referred to as **value autonomy**—which is more than simply being able to resist pressures to go along with the demands of others; it means having a set of principles about right and wrong, about what is important and what is not. We will examine each of these three aspects of autonomy in turn.

## The Development of Emotional Autonomy

The relationship between children and their parents changes repeatedly over the course of the life cycle. Changes in the expression of affection, the distribution of power, and patterns of verbal interaction, to give a few examples, are likely to occur whenever important transformations take place in the child's or the parents' competencies, concerns, and social roles. By the end of adolescence, individuals are far less emotionally dependent on their parents than they were as children. One can see this in several ways. First, older adolescents do not generally rush to their parents whenever they are upset, worried, or in need of assistance. Second, they do not see their parents as all-knowing or all-powerful. Third, adolescents often have a great deal of emotional energy wrapped up in relationships outside the family; in fact, they may feel more attached to a boyfriend or a girlfriend than to their parents. And finally, older adolescents are able to see and interact with their parents as people—not just as their parents. Many parents find, for example, that they can confide in their adolescent children, something that was not possible when their children were younger, or that their adolescent children can easily sympathize with them when they have had a hard day at work. These sorts of changes in the adolescent-parent relationship all reflect the development of emotional autonomy (Steinberg, 1990).

## EMOTIONAL AUTONOMY AND DETACHMENT

Early writings on emotional autonomy were influenced by psychoanalytic thinkers such as Anna Freud (1958), who argued that the physical changes of puberty cause substantial disruption and conflict inside the family system. The reason, Freud believed, is that intrapsychic conflicts that have been repressed since early childhood are reawakened at early adolescence by the resurgence of sexual impulses. (These conflicts revolved around the young child's unconscious attraction toward the parent of the opposite sex and ambivalent feelings toward the parent of the same sex.) The reawakened conflicts are expressed as increased tension among family members, arguments, and a certain degree of discomfort around the house. As a consequence of this tension, early adolescents are driven to separate themselves, at least emotionally, from their parents and turn their emotional energies to relationships with peers—in particular, peers of the opposite sex. Psychoanalytic theorists call this process of separation **detachment,** because it appeared as if the early adolescent were attempting to sever the *attachments* that had been formed during infancy and strengthened throughout childhood.

Detachment, and the accompanying storm and stress inside the family, were viewed by Freud and her followers as normal, healthy, and inevitable aspects of emotional development during adolescence. In fact, Freud believed that the absence of conflict between an adolescent and his or her parents signified that the young person was having problems growing up. This view was compatible with the idea that adolescence was an inherently tumultuous time, a perspective that, as you know, dominated ideas about adolescence for many, many years.

Studies of adolescents' family relationships have not supported Freud's idea, however. In contrast to predictions that high levels of adolescent-parent tension are the norm, that adolescents detach themselves from relationships with their parents, and that adolescents are driven out of the household by unbearable levels of family conflict, every major study done to date of teenagers' relations with their parents has shown that most families get along quite well during the adolescent years (Steinberg, 1990). Although parents and adolescents may bicker more often than they did during earlier periods of development, there is no evidence that this bickering significantly diminishes closeness between parents and teenagers (Hill and Holmbeck, 1986). One team of researchers, for example, who asked adolescents and children of different ages to rate how close they were to their parents, found that 19-year-old college students reported being just as close as fourth graders (Hunter and Youniss, 1982).

The psychic and interpersonal tension believed to arise at puberty does not show up in markedly strained family relationships. Although adolescents and their parents undoubtedly modify their relationships during adolescence, their emotional bonds are by no means severed. This is an important distinction, for it means that emotional autonomy during adolescence involves a *transformation*, not a breaking off of family relationships. Adolescents can become emotionally autonomous from their parents *without* becoming detached from them (Collins, 1990; Hill and Holmbeck, 1986; Steinberg, 1990).

## EMOTIONAL AUTONOMY AND INDIVIDUATION

As an alternative to the classic psychoanalytic perspective on adolescent detachment, some theorists have suggested that the development of emotional autonomy be looked at in terms of the adolescent's developing sense of **individuation.** One such theorist is the noted psy-

Every major study conducted to date of teenagers' family relations has shown that young people and their parents feel quite close to one another. Contrary to stereotypes, there is no evidence that family relations are any more strained during adolescence than during other periods of life. *(Richard Kalvar/Magnum)*

choanalyst Peter Blos. "Individuation," writes Blos, "implies that the growing person takes increasing responsibility for what he does and what he is, rather than depositing this responsibility on the shoulders of those under whose influence and tutelage he has grown up" (1967, p. 168). The process of individuation, which begins during infancy and continues well into late adolescence, involves a gradual, progressive sharpening of one's sense of self as autonomous, as competent, and as separate from one's parents. Individuation, therefore, has a great deal to do with the development of a sense of identity, in that it involves changes in how we come to see and feel about ourselves. The process does not involve stress and turmoil. Rather, individuation entails relinquishing childish dependencies on parents in favor of more mature, more responsible, and less dependent relationships. Adolescents who have been successful in establishing a sense of

individuation can accept responsibility for their choices and actions instead of looking to their parents to do it for them (Josselson, 1980). For example, rather than rebelling against her parents' midnight curfew by deliberately staying out later, a girl who has a healthy sense of individuation might take her parents aside before going out and say, "This party tonight may last longer than midnight. If it does, I'd like to stay a bit longer. Suppose I call you at eleven o'clock and let you know when I'll be home. That way, you won't worry as much if I come home a little later."

Several studies of the growth of emotional autonomy have appeared in recent years. These studies indicate that the development of emotional autonomy is a long process, beginning early in adolescence and continuing well into young adulthood. In one (Steinberg and Silverberg, 1986), a questionnaire measuring four aspects of emotional autonomy was administered to a sample of 10- to 15-year-olds. The four components were (1) the extent to which adolescents' *de-idealized* their parents ("My parents sometimes make mistakes"); (2) the extent to which adolescents were able to see their *parents as people* ("My parents act differently with their own friends than they do with me"); (3) *nondependency*, or the degree to which adolescents depended on themselves, rather than their parents, for assistance ("When I've done something wrong, I don't always depend on my parents to straighten things out"); and (4) the degree to which the adolescent felt *individuated* within the relationship with his or her parents ("There are some things about me that my parents do not know"). As you can see in Figure 9.1, scores on three of the four scales—all except "perceives parents as people"—increased over the age period studied.

In another study, in which adolescents were interviewed about their family relationships, similar findings emerged. The researchers also found that older adolescents were more likely to de-idealize their parents. For example, one adolescent said about his father, "I used to listen to everything. I thought he was always

right. Now I have my own opinions. They may be wrong, but they're mine and I like to say them" (Smoller and Youniss, 1985, p. 8).

De-idealization may be one of the first aspects of emotional autonomy to develop, because adolescents may shed their childish images of their parents before replacing them with more mature ones. Although middle adolescents are less likely than young adolescents to hold on to idealized pictures of their parents, when it comes to seeing their parents as individuals, 15-year-olds are no more emotionally autonomous than 10-year-olds. Even during the high school years, adolescents appear to have some difficulty in seeing their parents as individuals beyond their roles as parents. This aspect of emotional autonomy may not develop until much later—perhaps not until young adulthood (Smollar and Youniss, 1985; White, Speisman, and Costos, 1983). This aspect of emotional autonomy appears to develop later in adolescents' relations with their fathers than with their mothers, because fathers seem to interact less often with their adolescents in ways that permit them to be seen as individuals (Youniss and Smollar, 1985).

Several writers have explored the ways in which the process of developing autonomy may differ for adolescents whose parents have divorced (Feldman and Quatman, 1988; Sessa and Steinberg, 1991; Wallerstein and Kelly, 1974; Weiss, 1979). These writers argue that having divorced parents prompts the adolescent to grow up "faster"—to de-idealize parents at an earlier age. As a consequence, adolescents from divorced homes may begin the process of individuation somewhat earlier than their peers. Whether this has positive or negative consequences, however, is not known.

What triggers the process of individuation? Two different models have been suggested. According to several researchers, puberty is the main catalyst (e.g., Bulcroft, 1991; Holmbeck and Hill, in press; Steinberg, 1989). Changes in the adolescent's physical appearance provoke changes in the way that adoles-

**FIGURE 9.1** Age differences in four aspects of emotional autonomy. (Steinberg and Silverberg, 1986)

cents are viewed—by themselves and by their parents—which in turn provoke changes in parent-child interaction. As we saw in Chapter 4, shortly after puberty most families experience an increase in bickering and squabbling. Some writers have suggested that this increase in conflict helps adolescents to see their parents in a different light and to develop a sense of individuation (Cooper, 1988; Holmbeck and Hill, in press; Steinberg, 1990).

Other authors believe that adolescents' movement toward higher levels of individuation is stimulated by their social-cognitive development (Collins, 1990; Smetana, 1988). As you read in Chapter 2, *social cognition* refers to the thinking we do about ourselves and our relationships with others. The development of emotional autonomy in adolescence may be provoked by young people's development of more sophisticated understandings of themselves and their parents. Prior to adolescence, individuals accept their parents' views of themselves as accurate (e.g., "My parents think I am a good girl, so I must be"). But as individuals develop more differentiated self-conceptions in early and middle adolescence (recall the discussion of this in Chapter 8), they come to see that their parents' view is but one of many—and one that may not be entirely accurate ("My parents think I am a good girl, but they don't know what I am really like"). By late adolescence, individuals are able to see that these apparent discrepancies between their self-conceptions and the views of their parents are perfectly understandable ("There are sides of me that have been influenced by my parents and sides of me that have not") (see Mazor and Enright, 1988).

This is not to suggest that the process of individuation is always a smooth one. Some writers have suggested that as adolescents begin to de-idealize their parents, they may begin to feel both more autonomous and more insecure—what one research team labelled a "double-edged" sword (Frank et al., 1990). That is, even though our childish images of

our parents as being all-knowing and all-powerful may be inaccurate, they still provide a certain degree of emotional comfort. Leaving such images behind can be both liberating and frightening. Indeed, some researchers have found that emotional autonomy is associated not only with insecurity for the adolescent, but with increased feelings of parental rejection (Ryan and Lynch, 1989).

Whether provoked by puberty or the development of more advanced cognitive skills, and whether approached with confidence or trepidation, most theorists believe that healthy individuation is fostered by close, not distant, family relationships (Grotevant and Cooper, 1986). Tense family relationships during adolescence indicate problems, not positive development. Researchers have found, for example, that adolescents who feel the most autonomous—that is, those who are most likely to feel that they have been granted "enough" freedom by their parents—are not the ones who have severed relationships at home. In fact, just the opposite is the case: Autonomous adolescents report that they are quite close to their parents, enjoy doing things with their families, have few conflicts with their mothers and fathers, feel free to turn to their parents for advice, and say they would like to be like their parents (Kandel and Lesser, 1972). Rebellion, negativism, and excessive involvement in the peer group are more common among psychologically immature than mature adolescents (Josselson, Greenberger, and McConochie, 1977a, 1977b). Even during the college years, students who live away from home (which is in its own way a type of autonomy), as opposed to remaining in their parents' home and commuting to school, report more affection for their parents, better communication, and higher levels of satisfaction in the relationship (Sullivan and Sullivan, 1980). Strained family relationships appear to be associated with a lack of autonomy during adolescence, rather than with its presence.

Emotional autonomy develops best under

conditions that encourage both individuation and emotional closeness. This can be seen quite clearly in the work of Stuart Hauser and his colleagues, who have studied videotapes of parents and adolescents in discussion and have examined whether certain types of interaction are more or less facilitative of healthy adolescent development (Hauser et al., 1991). The tapes were coded for two specific types of behavior: *enabling behavior* and *constraining behavior*. Parents who use a lot of enabling behavior accept their adolescent while at the same time helping the teenager to develop and state his or her own ideas, through questions, explanations, and the tolerance of differences of opinion. In contrast, constraining parents have difficulty accepting their child's individuality and react to expressions of independent thinking with remarks that are distracting, judgmental, or devaluing. After hearing an adolescent's opinion that differs from his own, for example, an enabling father might ask for more clarification or genuinely probe the adolescent's logic, whereas a constraining father might cut off further discussion by telling the adolescent that she was wrong or ignorant.

Not surprisingly, Hauser has found that adolescents whose parents use a great deal of enabling and relatively little constraining are more likely to develop in healthy ways: They are more individuated and score higher on measures of ego development and psychosocial competence. This is in line with other research showing that healthy identity development is more likely to occur within families in which adolescents are encouraged to be both "connected" to their parents and to express their own individuality (Cooper et al., 1983; Grotevant and Cooper, 1986).

## EMOTIONAL AUTONOMY AND PARENTING PRACTICES

As we saw in Chapter 4, adolescents' development is affected differently by different styles of parenting. In particular, independence, responsibility, and self-esteem are all fostered by parents who are authoritative (friendly, fair, and firm), rather than authoritarian (excessively harsh), indulgent (excessively lenient), or neglectful (excessively aloof). Let us now look more closely at these findings in light of what we know about the development of emotional autonomy.

In authoritative families, guidelines are established for the adolescent's behavior and standards are upheld, but they are flexible and open to discussion. Moreover, these standards and guidelines are explained and implemented in an atmosphere of closeness, concern, and fairness. Although parents may have the final say when it comes to their child's behavior, the decision that is reached usually comes after consultation and discussion—with the child included. In discussing an adolescent's curfew, for example, authoritative parents would sit down with their child and explain how they arrived at their decision and why they picked the hour they did. They would also ask the adolescent for his or her suggestions and consider them carefully in making a final decision.

It is not difficult to see why the sort of give and take found in authoritative families is well suited to the child's transition into adolescence. Because standards and guidelines are flexible and adequately explained, it is not hard for the family to adjust and modify them as the child matures emotionally and intellectually. At some point, for example, a teenager may ask his or her parents to consider establishing a later curfew, and authoritative parents would think about the request seriously and discuss it openly. Gradual changes in family relations that permit the young person more independence and encourage more responsibility but that do not threaten the emotional bond between parent and child—in other words, changes that promote increasing emotional autonomy—are relatively easy to make for a family that has been flexible and has been making these sorts of modifications in family relationships all along (Baumrind, 1978).

In authoritarian households, where rules are rigidly enforced and seldom explained to the child, adjusting to adolescence is more difficult for the family. Authoritarian parents may see the child's increasing emotional independence as rebellious or disrespectful, and they may resist their adolescent's growing need for independence, rather than react to it openly. Authoritarian parents, on seeing that their daughter is becoming interested in boys, may implement a rigid curfew in order to restrict her social life. Instead of encouraging autonomy, authoritarian parents may inadvertently maintain the dependencies of childhood by failing to give their child sufficient practice in making decisions and taking responsibility for his or her actions. In essence, authoritarian parenting may interfere with adolescent individuation.

When closeness is absent as well, the problems are compounded. In families in which excessive parental control is accompanied by extreme coldness and punitiveness, the adolescent may rebel against parents' standards explicitly, in an attempt to assert his or her independence in a visible and demonstrable fashion (Hill and Holmbeck, 1986). Adolescents whose parents refuse to grant reasonable curfews are the ones who typically stay out the latest. Such rebellion is not indicative of genuine emotional autonomy, though; it is more likely to be a demonstration of the adolescent's frustration with his or her parents' rigidity and lack of understanding.

In indulgent and neglectful families, a different sort of problem arises. These parents do not provide sufficient guidance for their children, and as a result, youngsters who are raised permissively do not acquire adequate standards for behavior. Someone who has never had to abide by his parents' rules as a child faces tremendous difficulty learning how to comply with rules as an adult. In the absence of parents' guidance and rules, permissively reared teenagers often turn to their peers for advice and emotional support—a practice that can be problematic when the peers are themselves still relatively young and inexperienced. Not surprisingly, adolescents whose parents have failed to provide sufficient guidance are likely to become psychologically dependent on their friends—emotionally detached from their parents, perhaps, but not genuinely autonomous. The problems of parental permissiveness are exacerbated by a lack of closeness, as is the case in neglectful families.

Some parents who have raised their children permissively until adolescence are caught by surprise by the consequences of not having been stricter earlier on. The greater orientation toward the peer group of permissively raised adolescents may involve the young person in behavior that his or her parents disapprove of. As a consequence, some parents who have been permissive throughout childhood shift gears at adolescence and become autocratic, as a means of controlling a youngster over whom they feel they have lost control. For instance, parents who have never placed any restrictions on their child's afternoon activities during elementary school suddenly begin monitoring their teenager's social life once she enters junior high school. Shifts like these are extremely hard on adolescents—just at the time when they are seeking greater autonomy, their parents become more restrictive. Having become accustomed to relative leniency, adolescents whose parents change the rules in the middle of the game may find it difficult to accept standards that are being strictly enforced for the first time.

## The Development of Behavioral Autonomy

One of the most popular misconceptions about adolescent development is that adolescents demonstrate autonomy by rebelling against the wishes of their parents. But in many instances, rebelling against one's parents or other authorities is done not out of independence but

Parents who have been extremely lenient before adolescence may face the consequences of not having been stricter when they discover that their children are involved in behavior of which they disapprove. *(Joseph Koudelka/Magnum)*

in the service of conforming to one's peers. One recent study indicated, in fact, that during early adolescence individuals become more emotionally autonomous from their parents but *less* autonomous from their friends (Steinberg and Silverberg, 1986). Merely substituting one source of influence (the peer group) for another (the family), though, is hardly evidence of growth toward independence. Excessive adherence to the pressures of one's friends is not more autonomous than is excessive adherence to the pressures of one's parents. Moreover, as we saw earlier in this chapter, rebellion is associated with *immaturity*, not healthy development. Just what is meant, then, by behavioral autonomy?

All individuals—at any age—are susceptible to the pressures of those around them. The opinions and advice of others, especially peo-ple whose knowledge and judgment we respect, are, and should be, important influences on our choices and decisions. Surely, then, we would not want to say that the behaviorally autonomous adolescent is entirely free from the influence of others. Rather, an individual who is behaviorally autonomous is able to turn to others for advice when it is appropriate, weigh alternative courses of action based on his or her own judgment and the suggestions of others, and reach an independent conclusion about how to behave (Hill and Holmbeck, 1986). Let's look more closely at why and how changes in behavioral autonomy occur during adolescence. Researchers have looked at this in three domains: changes in decision-making abilities, changes in susceptibility to the influence of others, and changes in feelings of self-reliance.

## CHANGES IN DECISION-MAKING ABILITIES

The more sophisticated reasoning processes employed by the adolescent permit him or her to hold multiple viewpoints in mind simultaneously, allowing comparisons among them to be drawn—an ability that is crucial for weighing the opinions and advice of others. In addition, because adolescents are better able to think in hypothetical terms, they are more likely to consider the possible long-term consequences of choosing one course of action over another. And the enhanced role-taking capabilities of adolescence permit the teenager to consider another person's opinion while taking into account that person's perspective. This is important in determining whether someone who gives advice has special areas of expertise, particular biases, or vested interests that one should keep in mind. Taken together, these cognitive changes result in improved decision-making skills and, consequently, in the individual's greater ability to behave independently.

A study by Catherine Lewis (1981b) sheds a good deal of light on these issues. She presented over 100 adolescents ranging in age from 12 to 18 with a series of "problems" that they were to help another teenager solve. The problem concerned becoming involved in different sorts of risky situations, revising an opinion of someone who had previously been respected, or reconciling different pieces of advice from two "experts." One of the problems, for example, focused on a teenager's indecision about whether to have cosmetic surgery.

Lewis looked at adolescents' responses along five dimensions: whether they were aware of risks; whether they were aware of likely future consequences; whether parents, peers, or outside specialists were recommended as consultants; whether attitudes were revised in light of new information; and whether the adolescent recognized and cautioned against the vested interests of people giving advice. The adolescents were grouped by grade level, with seventh and eighth graders forming one group, tenth graders a second group, and twelfth graders a third group. The results of the study are shown in Figure 9.2.

The age groups differed along four of the five dimensions studied, with older adolescents demonstrating more sophisticated decision-making abilities. The older adolescents were more likely to be aware of risks; more likely to consider future consequences; more likely to turn to an independent specialist as a consultant; and more likely to realize when vested interests existed and to raise cautions about accepting advice from people who might be biased.

Decision-making abilities improve over the course of the adolescent years, with gains continuing well into the later years of high school. These developments provide the cognitive tools for behavioral autonomy: being able to look ahead and assess risks and likely outcomes of alternative choices, being able to recognize the value of turning to an independent "expert," and being able to see that someone's advice may be tainted by his or her own interests. Whether these changes in decision-making abilities translate into changes in actual behavior, however, is a different matter. Older adolescents may be more *intellectually* skilled when it comes to decision making, but are they actually more able to resist pressures to conform? It is to this question that we now turn.

## CHANGES IN CONFORMITY AND SUSCEPTIBILITY TO INFLUENCE

As the adolescent comes to spend more time outside the family, the opinions and advice of others—not only peers but adults as well—become more important. At a certain point, for example, adolescents seek their friends' advice, rather than their parents', on how to dress. They may turn to a teacher or guidance counselor for advice on what courses to take in

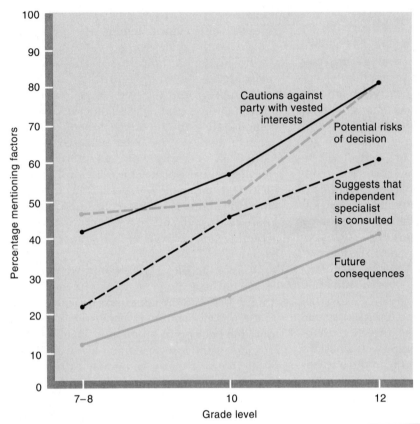

**FIGURE 9.2**   Decision-making abilities improve during adolescence. (Derived from Lewis, 1981b)

school, instead of bringing such questions home. Understandably, a variety of situations arise in which adolescents may feel that their parents' advice may be less valid than the opinions of others.

And there are issues that might be talked over with more than one party. For example, a teenager trying to decide whether to take on a part-time job after school might discuss the problem with her parents, but she might also turn to friends and ask their advice on the same question. When friends and parents disagree, adolescents must reconcile the differences of opinion and reach their own, independent conclusions.

In situations in which parents and peers give conflicting advice, do teenagers tend to follow one group more often than the other? Adolescents are often portrayed as being extremely susceptible to the influence of **peer pressure**— more so than children or young adults—and as stubbornly resistant to the influence of their parents. But is peer pressure really more potent during adolescence than during other times in the life cycle?

Researchers have studied conformity and peer pressure during adolescence by putting adolescents in situations in which they must choose between the pressures of their parents and the pressures of their peers or between

By the time young people reach late adolescence, they have developed fairly sophisticated decision-making abilities. Compared with younger teenagers, for example, high school seniors are better able to anticipate the long-term consequences of their decisions and more likely to understand the personal biases that advice givers sometimes have. *(Joel Gordon)*

their own wishes and those of others—typically, parents or friends. For example, an adolescent might be told to imagine that he and his friends discover something on the way home from school that looks suspicious. His friends tell him that they should keep it a secret. But the adolescent tells his mother about it, and she advises him to report it to the police. He then would be asked by the researcher to say what he would do.

In general, studies that contrast parents' and peers' influences indicate that in some situations, peers' opinions are more influential, while in others, parents' are more influential. Specifically, adolescents are more likely to conform to their peers' opinions when it comes to short-term, day-to-day, and social matters— styles of dress, tastes in music, choices among leisure activities, and so on. This is particularly true during junior high school and the early

years of high school. When it comes to long-term questions concerning educational or occupational plans, however, or questions of values, religious beliefs, or ethics, teenagers are primarily influenced by their parents (Brittain, 1963; Young and Ferguson, 1979). Some studies also have looked at adolescents' willingness to seek advice from adults outside their family. These studies indicate that in situations calling for objective information (the facts about getting admitted to a particular college) rather than opinion (whether the college is supposed to be a friendly place), teenagers are likely to turn to outside experts such as their teachers (Young and Ferguson, 1979).

Similar findings emerge from studies of the consultants adolescents turn to when they have problems (Wintre, Hicks, McVee and Fox, 1988). In general, when the adolescent's problem centers around a relationship with a

Adolescents are more likely to conform to their peers' opinions when it comes to short-term, day-to-day, and social matters such as styles of dress. But when it comes to long-term questions or issues concerning basic values, parents remain more influential than peers. *(Shirley Zeiberg)*

friend, he or she chooses to turn to a peer, and this preference becomes stronger with age. But adolescents' willingness to turn to an adult for advice with problems—especially problems that involve adolescents and their parents—remains very strong and increases as individuals move toward late adolescence. This suggests that older adolescents are quite willing to turn to adult experts whose advice they consider valuable.

Considered together, these findings are consistent with some of the findings we looked at earlier on changes in adolescents' decision-making abilities. With age, adolescents become increasingly likely to turn to "experts" for advice. On social matters, the "experts" are

friends; on issues requiring specific objective information, teachers and other adults likely to have the necessary knowledge are the authorities; and on questions of values, ethics, and plans, parents remain the advisers of choice. More important, the results of these studies indicate that peer pressure—or, for that matter, parental pressure—is likely to be ineffective in some situations and powerful in others.

Studies that contrast the influence of peers and adults do not really get to the heart of peer pressure, however, because most peer pressure operates when adults are absent from the scene—at a party, on the way home from school, on a date. In order to get closer to this issue, researchers have studied how adolescents respond when placed between the pressure of their friends and their own opinions of what to do. For example, an adolescent might be asked whether he would go along with his friends' pressure to vandalize some property even though he did not want to do so (Berndt, 1979).

In general, most studies using this approach show that conformity to peers is higher during early and middle adolescence than during preadolescence or later adolescence (Berndt, 1979; Brown, 1990; Krosnick and Judd, 1982; Steinberg and Silverberg, 1986). This is especially true when the behavior in question is antisocial, such as cheating, stealing, or trespassing, and especially true for boys. These findings are in line with studies of delinquency, which is often committed by boys in groups and is more common during middle adolescence (Berndt, 1979). Several studies indicate that adolescents who are more susceptible to peer pressure to engage in delinquent activity actually are more likely to misbehave than their more autonomous friends (Brown, Clasen, and Eicher, 1986).

Although we know that conformity to peer pressure is greater during early adolescence than before or after, it is not exactly clear just why this is so. One interpretation is that adolescents are more susceptible to peer influence during this time because of their heightened orientation toward the peer group. Because they care more about what their friends think of them, they are more likely to go along with the crowd to avoid being rejected (Brown, Clasen, and Eicher, 1986). It is possible that this heightened conformity to peer pressure during early adolescence is a sign of a sort of emotional "way station" between becoming emotionally autonomous from parents and becoming a genuinely autonomous person (Steinberg and Silverberg, 1986). In other words, the adolescent may become emotionally autonomous from parents before he or she is emotionally ready for this degree of independence and may turn to peers to fill this void. Each of these accounts suggests that *susceptibility to peer pressure* increases as youngsters move into early adolescence, peaks at around age 14, and declines thereafter (Brown, Clasen, and Eicher, 1986; Steinberg and Silverberg, 1986).

A different version of the same story focuses on the *strength of peer pressure*. It may be, for instance, that individuals' susceptibility to peer pressure remains constant over adolescence but that the peer pressure itself increases and then decreases over the period. Early adolescent peer groups may exert more pressure on their members to conform than groups of younger or older individuals, and the pressure may be strong enough to make even the most autonomous teenagers comply. Although this is an appealing alternative explanation—particularly to adolescents who appeal to their parents by saying, "No one will talk to me if I don't do it!"—studies have not borne it out. In fact, it appears that peer pressure to misbehave increases steadily throughout adolescence, beyond the age at which it would be expected to diminish (Brown, Clasen, and Eicher, 1986).

When we put the findings on peer pressure, peer conformity, and parental conformity together, then, the following picture emerges. During childhood, boys and girls are highly oriented toward their parents and far less so toward their peers. Peer pressure is not especially strong. As they approach adolescence, children become somewhat less oriented toward their parents and more oriented toward their peers, and peer pressure begins to escalate. As a result, during preadolescence, there is little net gain in behavioral autonomy—overall levels of conformity do not change, but the source of influence shifts. During early adolescence, conformity to parents continues to decline and both conformity to peers and peer pressure continue to rise—again, little change in overall behavioral autonomy. It is not until middle and late adolescence, therefore, that genuine increases in behavioral autonomy occur, for it is during this time period (between the ninth and twelfth grades) that conformity both to parents *and* to peers declines even though peer pressure continues to increase (see Figure 9.3).

Within a group of teenagers of the same age, of course, there are some who are highly autonomous, others who are easily influenced by their peers, others who are oriented toward their parents, and still others who are swayed by both peers and parents, depending on the situation. In general, autonomous youngsters and adult-oriented youngsters are likely to have come from homes in which their parents were warm and moderately controlling—the typical authoritative household. Peer-oriented children are likely to have parents who were less nurturant and either extremely controlling or extremely permissive. Like emotional autonomy, then, behavioral autonomy appears to be associated with authoritative, rather than with permissive, autocratic, or neglectful, parenting (Devereux, 1970).

Although it is tempting to conclude from these and other studies that authoritative parenting *fosters* the development of autonomy, we must be careful about drawing this conclusion,

**FIGURE 9.3** During adolescence, susceptibility to peer pressure increases and then falls, while susceptibility to parental pressure decreases. Perceptions of the strength of peer pressure increase throughout the period.

since the direction of effects could work just as plausibly the other way around. Perhaps responsible, independent children elicit warm and democratic behavior from their parents, whereas less autonomous youngsters invoke harsher discipline or parental nonchalance. In all likelihood, both processes are at work—children are affected by their parents, and parents are affected by their children. Authoritative parenting probably leads to adolescent autonomy, which in turn leads to more authoritative parenting.

Interestingly, the development of behavioral autonomy varies across cultures because of differences in the age expectations adolescents and parents have for independent behavior. Psychologist Shirley Feldman and her colleagues have examined this issue by asking parents and adolescents from both Asian and Anglo cultural groups to fill out a "teen timetable"—a questionnaire that asks at what age one would expect an adolescent to be permitted to engage in various behaviors that signal autonomy (e.g., "spend money however you want," "go out on dates," "go to rock concerts with friends"). In general, she has found that Anglo adolescents and their parents living in America, Australia, or Hong Kong have earlier expectations for adolescent autonomy than do Asian adolescents and parents from these same countries (Feldman and Quatman, 1988; Rosenthal and Feldman, 1991). Because of this, adolescents from Asian families may be less likely to seek autonomy from their parents than are their Anglo counterparts. Surprisingly, in these studies there were neither sex nor birth-order differences in age expectations for autonomy—contrary to popular belief that boys expect more autonomy than girls or that later-born adolescents are granted earlier freedom because their older siblings have paved the way.

## CHANGES IN FEELINGS OF SELF-RELIANCE

A third approach to the study of behavioral autonomy focuses on adolescents' own judgments of how autonomous they are. When adolescents of different ages are asked to complete standardized tests of *self-reliance*, for example, the results show that subjective feelings of autonomy increase steadily over the adolescent years and, contrary to stereotypes, that adolescent girls report feeling more self-reliant than adolescent boys (Greenberger, 1982; Steinberg and Silverberg, 1986). This is especially interesting in light of the findings concerning susceptibility to peer pressure, discussed earlier, since it indicates that adolescents may describe themselves as gaining in self-reliance during a period when their susceptibility to peer pressure may be increasing

Conformity to peers—especially in situations involving antisocial or delinquent behavior—is higher during early and middle adolescence than during other points in the lifespan. According to some theorists, some forms of delinquency may result from youngsters' heightened susceptibility to the influence of their friends. *(Joel Gordon)*

(see Figure 9.4). Although adults may view giving in to peer pressure as a sign of diminished autonomy, adolescents may not see their own behavior in this light.

## The Development of Value Autonomy

The development of value autonomy entails changes in the adolescent's conceptions of moral, political, ideological, and religious issues. Three aspects of the development of value autonomy during adolescence are especially interesting. First, adolescents become increasingly abstract in the way they think about things. Take the example of an 18-year-old who is deciding whether to participate in a disruptive demonstration at his state capital against policies that indirectly support apartheid. Instead of looking at the situation only in terms of the specifics of apartheid, he might think about the implications of knowingly violating the law in general. Second, during adolescence, beliefs become increasingly rooted in general principles that have some ideological basis. So an 18-year-old might say that demonstrating against apartheid is acceptable because promoting racial equality is more important than living in accord with the law,

Peer resistance   ———— Emotional autonomy
········ Self-reliance

**FIGURE 9.4**   Age differences in three types of autonomy. (Steinberg and Silverberg, 1986)

and breaking a law is legitimate when the status quo maintains racial discrimination. Finally, beliefs become increasingly founded in the young person's own values and not merely in a system of values passed on by parents or other authority figures. Thus an 18-year-old may look at the issue of apartheid in terms of what he himself believes, rather than in terms of what his parents have told him to do.

Much of the growth in value autonomy can be traced to the cognitive changes characteristic of the period. With the adolescent's enhanced reasoning capabilities and the further development of hypothetical thinking comes a heightened interest in ideological and philosophical matters and a more sophisticated way of looking at them. The ability to consider alternative possibilities and to engage in thinking about thinking allows for the exploration of differing value systems, political ideologies, personal ethics, and religious beliefs.

But the growth of value autonomy is encouraged by the development of emotional and behavioral independence as well. As we shall see in a moment, there is some evidence that the development of value autonomy occurs later (between ages 18 and 20) than does

the development of emotional or behavioral autonomy, which takes place during early and middle adolescence. As young people gain increasing distance from the emotional dependencies of childhood, they rely less on their parents' beliefs and values. The establishment of emotional autonomy provides the adolescent with the ability to look at his or her parents' views more objectively. When young people no longer see their parents as omnipotent and infallible authorities, they may seriously reevaluate the ideas and values that they accepted without question as children.

And as adolescents begin to test the waters of independence behaviorally, they may experience a variety of cognitive conflicts caused by having to compare the advice of parents and friends and having to deal with competing pressures to behave in given ways. These conflicts may prompt the young person to consider, in more serious and thoughtful terms, what it is that he or she really believes. This struggle to clarify values, provoked in part by the exercise of behavioral autonomy, is a large part of the process of developing a sense of value autonomy.

## MORAL DEVELOPMENT DURING ADOLESCENCE

Moral development has been the most widely studied aspect of value autonomy during adolescence. The dominant theoretical viewpoint for some time now has been a perspective that is grounded in Piaget's theory of cognitive development. As you will recall from the discussion in Chapter 2 of changes in thinking processes during adolescence, the emphasis within the Piagetian, or **cognitive-developmental,** perspective is on changes in the structure and organization of thought rather than on changes in its content. Theories of morality that stem from the cognitive-developmental viewpoint similarly emphasize shifts in the type of reasoning that individuals use in making moral decisions and not changes in the content

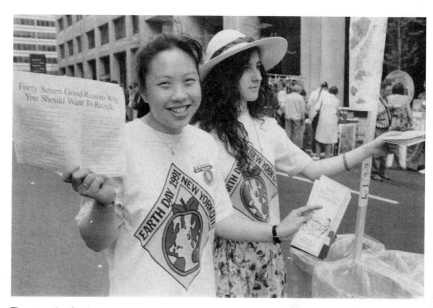

The growth of value autonomy during adolescence is often reflected in increased interest in political and social issues. *(Joel Gordon)*

of the decisions they reach or the action they take as a result. Although the initial formulation of the cognitive-developmental perspective on morality was presented by Piaget himself, the theory was subsequently expanded by Lawrence Kohlberg, and it is Kohlberg's work that is more relevant to the study of value autonomy during adolescence.

**Moral reasoning**  Consider the following dilemma:

In Europe, a woman was near death from a very bad disease, a special kind of cancer. There was one drug that the doctors thought might save her. It was a form of radium that a druggist in the same town had recently discovered. The drug was expensive to make, but the druggist was charging ten times what the drug cost him to make. He paid $200 for the radium and charged $2,000 for a small dose of the drug. The sick woman's husband, Heinz, went to everyone he knew to borrow the money, but he could only get together about $1,000, which was half of what

it cost. He told the druggist that his wife was dying, and asked him to sell it cheaper or let him pay later. But the druggist said, "No, I discovered the drug and I'm going to make money from it." Heinz got desperate and broke into the man's store to steal the drug for his wife.

Should the husband have done that? Was it right or wrong? (Kohlberg and Gilligan, 1972)

According to Kohlberg, whether you think that Heinz should steal the drug is less important than the reasoning behind your answer. Kohlberg suggested that there are three levels of moral reasoning—the **preconventional** level, which is dominant during most of childhood; the **conventional** level, which is usually dominant during late chldhood and early adolescence; and the **principled** (or postconventional) level, which emerges sometime during the adolescent or young adult years. Although Kohlberg initially proposed that each level was further divided into two stages, research has not supported this contention.

Researchers  assess  individuals'  levels  of

moral thinking by examining their responses to a series of moral dilemmas, such as the story about Heinz and the drug. These dilemmas are presented either in an interview, in which case the adolescents' responses are recorded, transcribed, and coded (Kohlberg and Gilligan, 1972), or in a questionnaire, in which adolescents respond to the dilemmas in a sort of multiple-choice format (Rest, Davison, and Robbins, 1978). The responses of individuals are classified as falling into one of the three levels described above.

Preconventional thinking is characterized by reference to external and physical events. Preconventional moral decisions are not based on society's standards, rules, or conventions (hence the label, *pre*conventional). Children at this stage approach moral dilemmas in ways that focus on the rewards and punishments associated with different courses of action. One preconventional child might say that Heinz should not have stolen the drug because he could have gotten caught and sent to jail. Another might say that Heinz was right to steal the drug because people would have been angry with him if he had let his wife die.

Conventional thinking about moral issues focuses not so much on tangible rewards and punishments but on how an individual will be judged by others for behaving in a certain way. In conventional moral reasoning, special importance is given to the roles people are expected to play and to society's rules, social institutions, and conventions. One behaves properly because, in so doing, one receives the approval of others and helps to maintain the social order. The correctness of society's rules is not questioned, however—one "does one's duty" by upholding and respecting the social order. A conventional thinker might say that Heinz should not have stolen the drug because stealing is against the law. But another might counter that Heinz was right to steal the drug because it is what a good husband is expected to do. According to most studies of moral rea-

soning, the majority of adolescents and adults think primarily in conventional terms.

Principled thinking is relatively rare. At this level of reasoning, society's rules and conventions are seen as relative and subjective rather than as authoritative. One may have a moral duty to abide by society's standards for behavior—but only insofar as those standards support and serve human ends. Thus occasions arise in which conventions ought to be questioned and when more important principles—such as justice, fairness, or the sanctity of human life—take precedence over established social norms. For instance, a principled response might be that Heinz should not have stolen the drug because in doing so he violated an implicit agreement among members of society—an agreement that gives each person the freedom to pursue his or her livelihood. However, another principled thinker might respond that Heinz was right to steal the drug because someone's life was at stake, and preserving human life is more important than preserving individual freedoms. Whereas conventional thinking is oriented toward society's rules, principled thinking is founded on more broadly based moral principles and is oriented toward the individual's personal conscience. For this reason, it is the development of principled reasoning that is especially relevant to the discussion of value autonomy.

Kohlberg's theory and its derivatives (for example, Gilligan, 1982) have generated a wealth of research and have for the past twenty-five years dominated the study of moral development during adolescence. An important alternative to Kohlberg's model was proposed in the late 1970s by psychologist Carol Gilligan (1977, 1982), who argued that Kohlberg's view of morality placed too much emphasis on a type of moral orientation characteristically employed by men. Gilligan's perspective is discussed in the box on pages 308–309.

Studies have confirmed Kohlberg's suggestion that moral reasoning becomes more principled over the course of childhood and adolescence (Hoffman, 1980). Moreover, development appears to proceed through the sequence described in Kohlberg's theory (Colby et al., 1983). Preconventional reasoning dominates the responses of children; conventional responses begin to appear during preadolescence, and continue into middle adolescence; and principled reasoning does not appear until late adolescence. Researchers have found also that advanced levels of moral reasoning are more common among children raised in families in which parents encourage their children to participate in family discussions and in which the level of conflict in family discussions is neither extremely low nor extremely high (Haan, Smith, and Block, 1968; Holstein, 1972).

Kohlberg's idea that individuals become more principled in their thinking during adolescence is especially relevant to our discussion of value autonomy. Although individuals may not enter a stage of principled thinking during adolescence, they do begin to place greater emphasis on abstract values and moral principles during the adolescent years. Studies by James Rest and his colleagues (Rest, Davison, and Robbins, 1978) have shown this to be true. Their studies indicate that the appeal of principled moral reasoning increases over the course of adolescence, while the appeals of preconventional and of conventional reasoning both decline. During the high school years, the proportion of principled responses given by individuals increases from about 25 percent to about 33 percent. Over the course of late adolescence and early adulthood, the proportion increases further, to about 45 percent. (The appeal of principled thinking appears to increase both with age and with schooling, with most adults reaching a plateau after completing their formal education.) Thus Rest's studies provide support for the idea that value autonomy grows during adolescence, particularly during the late adolescent years.

**Moral reasoning and moral behavior**   It is one thing to reason about moral problems in an advanced way, but it is another thing to *behave* consistently with one's reasoning. Some critics have argued that although Kohlberg's theory may provide a window on how people think about abstract and hypothetical dilemmas of life and death, it does not tell us very much about the ways people reason about day-to-day problems or the ways people behave when they find themselves in situations that might evoke moral considerations. As for the first of these concerns, research indicates that people reason about life-and-death dilemmas in ways parallel to their reasoning about moral dilemmas that they actually encounter in their everyday life (Walker, de Vries, and Trevethan, 1987). As for the second of these concerns, many studies indicate that individuals' behavior is related to the way in which they reason about hypothetical moral dilemmas. For example, individuals who are capable of reasoning at higher stages of moral thought are less likely to commit antisocial acts, less likely to cheat, less likely to conform to the pressures of others, more likely to engage in political protests, and more likely to assist others in need of help (Rest, 1983).

Of course, moral behavior and moral reasoning do not always go hand in hand. Most of us have found ourselves in situations where we have behaved less morally than we would have liked to act. According to one writer, however, we would not expect that moral behavior would follow exactly from moral reasoning, because other factors enter into moral decision making that complicate matters (Rest, 1983). In tests measuring moral reasoning, assessments are made in a social vacuum, but such vacuums rarely exist in the real world. For example, you may realize in the abstract that complying with highway speed limits is important because such limits prevent accidents, and you may obey these limits most of the time when you drive. But you may have found your-

# THE SEXES: DO A MAN AND A WOMAN SPEAK ABOUT MORAL PROBLEMS "IN A DIFFERENT VOICE"?

Few theories have generated as much controversy among psychologists as Lawrence Kohlberg's theory of the development of moral reasoning. In particular, critics have argued that his view of what constitutes "more advanced" moral reasoning is oriented to how men typically view moral problems and underrepresents an equally valid approach to morality that women happen to use more often. The most compelling argument in this spirit was made by psychologist Carol Gilligan in her book, *In a Different Voice* (1982).

Essentially, Gilligan argues that Kohlberg's scheme places great weight on what she calls a **justice orientation.** This is an orientation toward problems of inequality or oppression that holds out as its ideal a morality of reciprocity and equal respect. From this perspective—or "voice," as Gilligan would call it—the most important consideration in making a moral decision would be whether the individuals involved were treated "fairly" by the ultimate decision.

An equally valid alternative to the justice orientation, says Gilligan, is a **care orientation.** From this perspective, the focus is on problems of abandonment and detachment, and the ideal is a morality of attention to others and responsiveness to human need. As opposed to the justice orientation, which is rooted in the premise that moral decisions are best made from a detached position of "objectivity" ("rules are rules," "fair is fair"), the caring orientation is rooted in the belief that our moral decisions should be shaped by our attachments and our responsiveness to others.

An example may help to clarify the distinction. In responding to the Heinz dilemma, discussed on page 305, individuals with a justice orientation cast the problem as a conflict between Heinz's desire to save his wife and the druggist's right to engage in his business—a conflict between the abstract values of life and property. Individuals with a caring orientation, in contrast, see the dilemma in entirely different terms: as a dilemma of responsiveness. The question is not whether the druggist has a right to property that outweighs other rights but rather why the druggist is not being responsive to the needs of another person. Rather than seeing society as functioning with a system of rules or abstract principles, individuals with a caring orientation view society as functioning through the interconnection of human relationships.

Theories of morality and of human development in general, argues Gilligan, have emphasized the sort of intellectual, individualistic, and detached reasoning characteristic of the justice orientation as the index of mental health and have given short shrift to emotional, interpersonal, and attachment concerns. The pinnacle of psychological health in most theories is the individual who can function independently, argues Gilligan, rather than the person who can function *interdependently.* We see this not only in abstract theories of development, but in the way in which our children are socialized to emphasize competition over cooperation, and assertiveness over concern for others. In Kohlberg's theory, this bias toward detached individualism is reflected in the

*continued on next page*

elevation to the highest level of morality of a view that places abstract principles of individual rights over all other considerations. In her book, Gilligan presented evidence that women are likely to approach moral problems from a caring orientation, rather than from the justice orientation idealized in Kohlberg's theory.

In more recent studies, Gilligan and others have found that both men and women are capable of approaching moral problems from the perspectives of justice and caring but that women may be more likely to give caring-oriented responses before justice-oriented ones, whereas men are more likely to follow the opposite pattern (Ford and Lowery, 1986; Galotti, 1989; Galotti et al., 1991; Gilligan, 1986; Walker, de Vries, and Trevethan, 1987). When individuals are prompted to hear a moral problem in a different voice, they appear to be able to do so—regardless of their sex. In other words, men are capable of viewing a moral problem from a caring orientation and women are capable of viewing a problem from a justice orientation.

Although men and women are more similar than different in the types of responses they give to moral dilemmas, at least one study indicates that the *process* of moral development may differ between the sexes (Boldizar, Wison, and Deemer, 1989). In a longitudinal study that followed individuals from high school into young adulthood, these researchers found that both men's and women's moral development was correlated with the amount of education they had completed, but that the relation between moral development and both work and marriage differed for males and females. The moral development of males, but not females, was associated with their feelings of career fulfillment, with more satisfied men scoring higher on the test of moral reasoning. In contrast, moral development among females, but not males, was associated with marriage, with young adult married women scoring lower on the test of moral reasoning than their single counterparts. Of course, we must be careful not to infer a causal connection between moral reasoning and work or marriage: it could simply be the case that more advanced moral thinkers were able to find satisfying careers (in the case of men) or chose to delay marriage (in the case of women). But this study suggests that even though men and women may reach similar moral endpoints, they may follow different routes in getting there.

Gilligan's work suggests that there are two distinct voices to be heard in moral debates and that society—especially a society governed primarily by men—may be more inclined to listen to one voice than another. The fact that most of the major theories of human development have been constructed by men—Freud, Piaget, Erikson—also has biased our views of what mental health is. But while Gilligan's studies suggest that there may be sex differences in our tendencies to *prefer* one orientation, her work also indicates that men and women can adopt both perspectives. By helping children to hear and speak with *both* voices, we may encourage the development of more complete—and more moral—people.

self in a situation in which you weighed your need to get somewhere in a hurry (perhaps you were late for an important job interview) against your moral belief in the importance of obeying speeding laws and decided that in this instance you would behave in a way inconsistent with your belief. Situational factors influence moral choices, and they also influence moral reasoning. When individuals perceive that they will be severely hurt by behaving in a morally advanced way (for example, if standing up for someone will lead to severe punishment), they are less likely to reason at a higher moral level (Sobesky, 1983). Moral reasoning is an important influence on moral behavior, but neither can be considered out of context.

## POLITICAL AND RELIGIOUS THINKING DURING ADOLESCENCE

Less is known about the development of political or religious thinking during adolescence than about moral development, but research in these areas is generally consistent with the view that beliefs become more principled, more abstract, and more independent during the adolescent years. Let us look first at changes in youngsters' political beliefs.

**Political thinking during adolescence** Between the sixth and twelfth grades, political thinking becomes more conceptual and principled and less simplistic and pragmatic (Torney-Purta, 1990). One researcher who has studied the development of political ideology during adolescence extensively is Joseph Adelson (1972). He suggests that political thinking changes during adolescence in several important ways. First, it becomes more abstract. In response to the question, "What is the purpose of laws?" for example, 12- and 13-year-olds are likely to reply with concrete answers—"So people don't kill or steal," "So people don't get hurt," and so on. Older adolescents, in contrast, are likely to respond with more abstract

and more general statements—"To ensure safety and enforce the government," and "They are basically guidelines for people. I mean, like this is wrong and this is right and to help them understand" (Adelson, 1972, p. 108).

Second, political thinking during adolescence becomes increasingly less authoritarian and rigid. Young adolescents are inclined toward obedience, toward authority, and toward an uncritical, trusting, and acquiescent stance toward government. For example, when asked what might be done in response to a law that is not working out as planned, the young adolescent will "propose that it be enforced more rigorously." An older teenager may suggest, instead, that the law needs reexamination and perhaps amendment. In contrast to older adolescents, younger adolescents are "more likely to favor one-man rule as [opposed to] representative democracy; . . . [show] little sensitivity to individual or minority rights; [and are] indifferent to the claims of personal freedom" (Adelson, 1972, p. 108). Although we often complain about the political leaders we elect to office, we can be thankful that we don't have to live under the autocratic thumbs of young adolescents!

Of special significance is the development during middle and late adolescence of a roughly coherent and consistent set of attitudes—a sort of ideology—which does not appear before this point. This ideology is, in Adelson's words, "more or less organized in reference to a more encompassing . . . set of political principles" (1972, p. 121).

Shifts in all three of these directions—increasing abstraction, decreasing authoritarianism, and increasing use of principles—are similar to those observed in studies of moral development, and they support the idea that value autonomy begins to emerge during the late adolescent years. The movement away from authoritarianism, obedience, and unquestioning acceptance of the rulings of au-

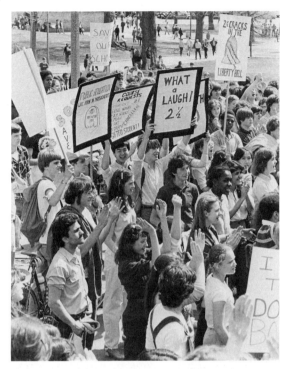

Whereas younger adolescents believe in autocratic rule and support existing laws, older adolescents are more likely to challenge authority and argue that laws should be reexamined. These Massachusetts students are protesting against an initiative that would lower property taxes and cut school budgets. (Sandra Johnson/Picture Cube)

thority is especially interesting because it suggests, further, that an important psychological concern for adolescents revolves around questioning the values and beliefs emanating from parents and other authority figures and trying to establish their own priorities.

As is the case with moral development, there may be gaps between adolescents' political thinking in hypothetical situations and their political attitudes and behavior. In general, the most important influences on the political behavior of young people tends to be the social context in which they come of age (Torney-Purta, 1990). This context includes the adoles-

cent's immediate community as well as the larger social and historical environment. Thus, for example, minority adolescents, especially those living in environments in which there are limited economic opportunities, tend to be more cynical about politics than their white counterparts. Along similar lines, studies of adolescents' political attitudes over historical periods show quite clearly that young people's political attitudes and level of political participation (voting, demonstrating, letter-writing, etc.)—like those of adults—fluctuate and change in relation to current events (Torney-Purta, 1990).

**Religious beliefs during adolescence**   Religious beliefs, like political beliefs, also become more abstract and principled during the adolescent years. Specifically, adolescents' beliefs become more oriented toward spiritual and ideological matters and less oriented toward rituals, practices, and the strict observance of religious customs (Wuthnow and Glock, 1973). For example, while 87 percent of all adolescents pray, and 95 percent believe in God, 60 percent of all young people feel that organized religion does not play a very important role in their lives (Farel, 1982). Compared with children, adolescents place more emphasis on the internal aspects of religious commitment (such as what an individual believes) and less on the external manifestations (such as whether an individual goes to church [Elkind, 1978]).

Generally speaking, the stated importance of religion—and especially of participation in an organized religion—declines somewhat during the adolescent years. More high school students than older adolescents attend church regularly, and not surprisingly, more of the younger adolescents state that religion is important to them (Benson et al., 1989; Johnston et al., 1986). Interestingly, several studies have indicated that the decline in the importance of religion during late adolescence appears to be more noteworthy among college than noncol-

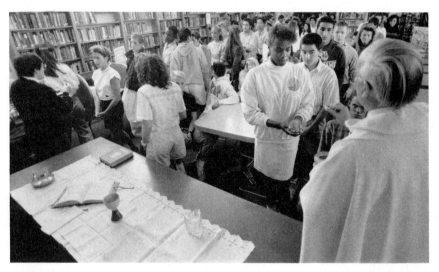

More than one-third of high school seniors attend religious services weekly. Another 30 percent report that religion is very important to them, even though they do not worship regularly. (Spencer Grant/Photo Researchers)

lege youth (Yankelovich, 1974), suggesting that college attendance may play some part in shaping (or, as the case may be, unshaping) young people's religious beliefs. As we saw in Chapter 8, studies of identity development during the college years have indicated that over the course of college, students' traditional religious commitments are shaken but are not replaced with alternative beliefs (Waterman, 1982). Late adolescence appears to be a time when individuals reexamine and reevaluate many of the beliefs and values they have grown up with.

Although individuals generally become less involved in formal religion during the adolescent years, there are differences among adolescents in their degree of religiosity. Approximately 35 percent of high school seniors report weekly attendance at religious services; another 30 percent report that religion is "very important to them," even though they do not worship regularly; and about 10 percent of high school seniors report no religious pref-

erence at all. The remaining 25 percent report having a religious preference but do not feel that religion is very important to them (Johnston et al., 1986). Some, but not all, research suggests that religious adolescents are significantly less likely than their peers to engage in premarital sexual intercourse and somewhat less likely to engage in deviant or delinquent behavior, such as drug use (Benson et al., 1989).

All in all, studies of the development of religious beliefs during adolescence indicate many parallels with the development of moral and political reasoning. According to a widely cited stage theory of religious development, during late adolescence individuals enter into a stage in which they begin to form a system of personal religious beliefs, rather than relying solely on the teachings of their parents (Fowler, 1981). This is reminiscent, of course, of the adolescent's transition to principled moral reasoning or to the development in middle to late adolescence of a coherent political ideology. In all likelihood, developments in all three domains—moral, political, and religious—probably reflect the underlying growth of cognitive abilities and the shift from concrete to abstract reasoning characteristic of the adolescent transition. As you now understand, this fundamental shift in cognitive ability affects adolescents' thinking across a wide variety of topics.

## A CONCLUDING NOTE

Theories of adolescent development popular in Western societies have tended to emphasize the goals of self-definition (i.e., identity) and independent functioning (i.e., autonomy) (Baumeister and Tice, 1986). It is important to keep in mind, however, that healthy adolescent development involves not only the ability to be a successful individual, but also the ability to maintain healthy and satisfying attachments with others. Put another way, experts think of positive psychosocial development in terms of the adolescent's capacity to function both independently and *inter*dependently (Ford, 1987; Greenberger and Sorensen, 1974).

These dual goals—what some writers have called *agency* and *communion* (e.g., Bakan, 1972)—define the psychosocial agenda in adolescence. In this chapter, on autonomy, and in the previous chapter, on identity, we emphasized the development of agency. In the next two chapters, on intimacy and sexuality, we turn our focus to communion.

## *Summary*

1. Although the development of autonomy is an important psychosocial issue throughout the life span, it is especially salient during adolescence because of the physical, cognitive, and social changes of the period. Psychologists generally differentiate among three types of autonomy in adolescence: emotional autonomy, which refers to emotional independence in relationships with others; behavioral autonomy, which refers to the development of independent decision-making abilities; and value autonomy, which concerns the development of independent beliefs.

2. Formerly, adolescence was viewed as a time during which individuals break away from and rebel against their parents. More recent research indicates, however, that the growth of emotional autonomy is typically more peaceful and less tumultuous. Instead of writing about the young person's "detachment" from parents, therefore, contemporary psychologists emphasize a process called "individuation." Research indicates that the process of individuation is set in motion by the physical and cognitive changes of early adolescence.

3. Healthy individuation is fostered by close, not distant, family relationships. Adolescents who are raised in authoritative homes in which their parents are both accepting and tolerant of the young person's individuality enjoy many psychological advantages over their peers.

4. Adolescence is also a time of important changes in decision-making, or behavioral autonomy. As individuals develop, they become better able to seek out and weigh the advice of different "experts" and use this information to make decisions. In this regard, they are becoming more behaviorally autonomous. For a short time during early adolescence, however, it appears that adolescents are especially susceptible to the advice of their peers, especially on issues concerning day-to-day behavior. Susceptibility to peer pressure increases from preadolescence to early adolescence, and then begins to decline as adolescents enter high school.

5. Research on value autonomy—the development of independent beliefs and attitudes—has focused mainly on moral development. According to Kohlberg's theory, the most influential model of moral development, adolescents' reasoning about moral problems

becomes less tied to whether actions violate concrete rules and regulations and more grounded in basic moral principles. So-called principled reasoning does not appear until relatively late in adolescence, however.

6. Although less studied than moral development, political and religious thinking also grow during the adolescent years. As with moral development, during late adolescence beliefs in these domains become more abstract, more principled, and more independent.

## Key Terms

autonomy

behavioral autonomy

care orientation

cognitive-developmental perspective

conventional moral reasoning

detachment

emotional autonomy

individuation

justice orientation

peer pressure

preconventional moral reasoning

principled moral reasoning

self-reliance

value autonomy

## For Further Reading

BERNDT, T. (1979). Developmental changes in conformity to peers and parents. *Developmental Psychology, 15,* 608–616. A study of age differences in youngsters' susceptibility to the influence of parents and peers.

FOWLER, J. (1981). *Stages of faith.* New York: Harper & Row. The dominant theoretical view on the development of religious belief from childhood through adulthood.

GILLIGAN, C. (1982). *In a different voice.* Cambridge: Harvard University Press. A discussion of gender differences in moral reasoning, written by one of Kohlberg's most provocative critics.

HAUSER, S., POWERS, S., AND NOAM, G. (1991). *Adolescents and their families.* New York: Free Press. A fascinating study of parent-child interaction, emotional autonomy, and adolescent ego development.

STEINBERG, L. (1990). Autonomy, conflict, and harmony in the family relationship. In S. Feldman and G. Elliot (Eds.), *At the threshold: The developing adolescent.* Cambridge: Harvard University Press. A comprehensive review of the literature on changes in the parent-child relationship at adolescence, with special emphasis on autonomy.

# INTIMACY

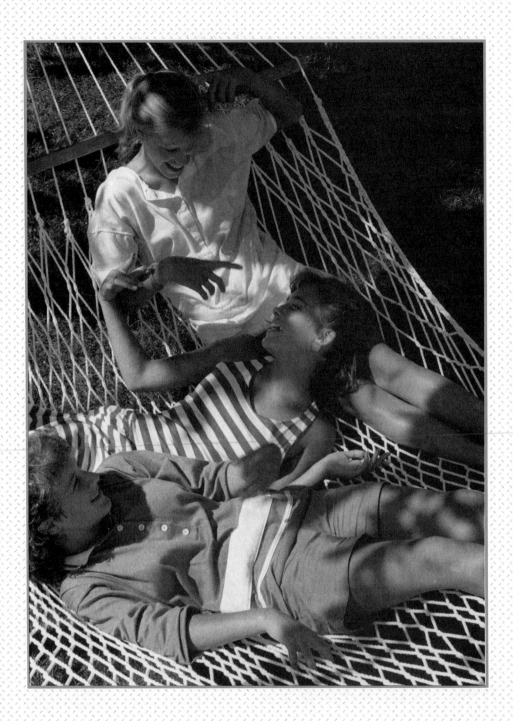

# INTIMACY

$O$ ne of the most remarkable things about adolescence is the way in which close relationships change during these years. Think about the friendships you had as a child and compare them with those you had as a teenager. Think about the boyfriends or girlfriends that children have and the boyfriends or girlfriends of adolescents. And think about relationships between parents and their children, and how these relationships change during adolescence. In all three cases, adolescents' relationships are closer, more personal, more involved, and more emotionally charged. During adolescence, in short, relationships become more intimate.

At the outset, it is necessary to draw a distinction between *intimacy* and *sexuality*. The word **intimacy**—at least as it is used in the study of adolescence—does not have a sexual or physical connotation. Rather, an intimate relationship is an emotional attachment between two people characterized by concern for each other's well-being; a willingness to disclose private, and occasionally sensitive, topics; and a sharing of common interests and activities. Two individuals can therefore have an intimate relationship without having a sexual one. And by the same token, two people can have a sexual relationship without being especially intimate.

The development of intimacy during adolescence involves changes in the adolescent's *need* for intimacy, changes in the *capacity* to have intimate relationships, and changes in the extent to which and the way in which this capacity to be intimate is *expressed*. Although the development of intimacy during adolescence is almost always studied in relation to friendships with peers, adolescents' intimate relationships are by no means limited to other teenagers. Parents often have intimate relationships with their adolescents, especially when their children have reached a sufficient level of maturity. Siblings, even with many years between them, are often close confidants. Sometimes young people even form intimate relationships with adults who are not in their immediate family.

Obviously, one of the central issues in the study of intimacy during adolescence is the onset of dating. Although the young person's initiation into opposite-sex relationships is undoubtedly important, it is not the only noteworthy change that occurs in close relationships during adolescence. Adolescence is also an important time for changes in what we look for in friends, in our capacity to be intimate with people of *both* sexes, and in the way we express our closeness with friends.

## Intimacy as an Adolescent Issue

Intimacy is an important concern throughout most of the life span. Friends and confidants provide support when we are feeling emotionally vulnerable, assistance when we need it, and compansionship in a variety of activities and contexts (Weiss, 1974). During childhood, not having friends is associated with a range of psychological and social problems (Hartup, 1983). And in adulthood, having at least one intimate friendship is beneficial to your health: People who have others to turn to for emotional support are less likely to suffer from psychological and physical disorders (Myers, Lindentthal, and Pepper, 1975). Without question, close relationships are extremely important to people of all ages. Why, then, is the development of intimacy especially important during adolescence?

One reason is that it is not until adolescence that truly intimate relationships—relationships characterized by openness, honesty, self-disclosure, and trust—first emerge. Although children certainly have important friendships, their relationships are different from those formed during adolescence. Children's friendships are activity-oriented, for example, built around games and shared pastimes. To a child, a friend is someone who likes to do the same

Children's friendships center around shared activities. Not until adolescence are friendships based on the sorts of bonds that are formed between individuals who care about, know, and understand each other in a special way. *(David Wells/Image Works)*

things he or she does. But teenagers' close friendships are more likely to have a strong emotional foundation; they are built on the sorts of bonds that form between people who care about and know and understand each-other in a special way.

Another reason for the importance of intimacy during adolescence concerns the changing nature of the adolescent's social world: during early adolescence, the increasing importance of peers and, during late adolescence, the increasing importance of opposite-sex peers. In the previous chapter, we looked at the young person's growing orientation toward peers as part of the development of emotional autonomy. In this chapter, we look at changes in adolescent peer relations again but in a different light—as part of the development of intimacy.

Why do such important changes take place in close relationships during adolescence? Several theorists have answered this question by pointing to significant links between the development of intimacy during adolescence and the biological, cognitive, and social changes of the period (Berndt, 1982; Savin-Williams and Berndt, 1990). Puberty and its attendant changes in sexual impulses often raise new issues and concerns requiring serious, intimate discussion. Some young people feel hesitant to discuss sex and dating with their parents and turn instead to relationships outside the family. Sexual maturation may also provoke intimacy between adolescents and their parents, when young people turn to their mothers or fathers for advice, information, and guidance (Kandel and Lesser, 1972).

Advances in thinking—especially in the realm of *social cognition*—are also related to the development of intimacy during adolescence (Hill and Palmquist, 1978). The growth of social cognition during adolescence, as we saw in Chapter 2, is reflected in the young person's more sophisticated conceptions of social relationships and in improvements in interpersonal understanding and communication. These changes permit adolescents to establish and maintain far more mature relationships, characterized by higher levels of empathy, self-disclosure, and responsiveness to each other's thoughts and feelings. The limitations in pre-adolescents' ability to look at things from another person's point of view may make intimate interpersonal relationships a cognitive impossibility (Beardslee, Schultz, and Selman, 1987, Selman, 1980). It is hard to be an intimate friend to someone when you are unable to empathize with that person. Improvements in social competence and gains in intimacy during adolescence, therefore, are partly attributable to improvements in social cognition (Ford, 1982).

We can also point to changes in the adolescent's social roles as potentially affecting the development of intimacy. Perhaps most simply, the behavioral independence that often accompanies the transition from childhood into adolescence provides greater opportunities for adolescents to be alone with their friends, engaged in intimate discussion. Adolescents spend more time talking to their friends than in any other activity (Csikszentmihalyi and Larson, 1984). Moreover, the recognition of adolescents as "near adults" may prompt their parents and other adults to confide in them and turn to them for support. Shared experiences, such as working, as well as the development of emotional autonomy, may help give young people and their parents more of a basis for friendship and communication (Youniss and Smollar, 1985). Finally, changes in the structure of schools during early adolescence, often giving younger teenagers more contact with older ones, may promote new types of peer relationships (Blyth, Hill, and Smyth, 1981).

During the course of preadolescence and adolescence, relationships are gradually transformed—from the friendly but activity-oriented friendships of childhood to the more self-conscious, more analytical, and more intimate relationships of adulthood. In the next section, we examine why and how this transformation occurs.

## Theoretical Perspectives on Adolescent Intimacy

The most important theoretical perspectives on the development of intimacy during adolescence are those of Harry Stack Sullivan (1953a), Erik Erikson (1968), and, more recently, a group of writers who have studied

**attachment** relationships in adolescence, using models that initially had been developed for the study of attachment in infancy (e.g., Greenberg, Siegel, and Leitch, 1983; Kobak and Sceery, 1988; Rice, 1990). Let's look at each of these views in turn.

### SULLIVAN'S THEORY OF INTERPERSONAL DEVELOPMENT

Like Erikson, whose theory of adolescent identity development was discussed at length in Chapter 8, Sullivan took a far less biological view of development than other psychoanalytic thinkers, such as Anna Freud, had taken. Instead, Sullivan emphasized the social aspects of growth, suggesting that psychological development can be best understood when looked at in interpersonal terms. Specifically, Sullivan's theory focuses on transformations in the adolescent's relationships with others. In particular, the challenges of adolescence (and, indeed, according to Sullivan, of the entire life cycle) revolve around trying to satisfy our changing interpersonal needs.

As the child develops, different interpersonal needs surface that lead either to feelings of security (when the needs are satisfied) or to feelings of anxiety (when the needs are frustrated). Sullivan charted a developmental progression of needs, beginning in infancy and continuing through adolescence (see Table 10.1): the *needs for contact and for tenderness* (infancy), the *need for adult participation* (early childhood), the *needs for peers and for peer acceptance* (middle childhood), the **need for intimacy** (preadolescence), the **needs for sexual contact and for intimacy with a peer of the opposite sex** (early adolescence), and the **need for integration into adult society** (late adolescence [Sullivan, 1953b]). These changing interpersonal needs define the course of interpersonal development through different phases of the life span. During middle childhood, for example, youngsters need to be ac-

## TABLE 10.1

INTERPERSONAL NEEDS ASSOCIATED WITH
DIFFERENT DEVELOPMENTAL ERAS:
SULLIVAN'S THEORY

| Developmental epochs | Interpersonal needs |
| --- | --- |
| Infancy (0 to 2–3 yrs.) | Need for contact with people<br>Need for tenderness from the mothering one |
| Childhood (2–3 to 6–7 yrs.) | Need for adult participation in the child's play |
| Juvenile era (6–7 to 8–10 yrs.) | Need for peer playmates<br>Need for acceptance into peer society groups |
| Preadolescence (8–10 to 12–14 yrs.) | Need for intimacy and consensual validation in same-sex chumships |
| Early adolescence (12–14 to 17–18 yrs.) | Need for sexual contact<br>Need for intimacy with an opposite-sex peer |
| Late adolescence (17–18 yrs. to adult) | Need for integration into adult society |

*Source:* Sullivan, 1953b.

cepted into peer groups, or else they feel rejected and ostracized.

In Sullivan's view, the security derived from having satisfying relationships with others is the "glue" that holds together a sense of self. Identity and self-esteem are gradually built up through interpersonal relationships. Like Erikson, Sullivan viewed psychosocial development as cumulative: The frustrations and satisfactions we experience during earlier periods affect our later relationships and developing sense of identity. The child who as an infant has his or her need for contact or tenderness frustrated will approach interpersonal relationships in subsequent eras with greater anxiety, a more intense need for security, and a shakier sense of self.

When important interpersonal transitions arise (for example, during childhood, when the social world is broadened to include significant relationships with peers), having a solid foundation of security in past relationships will aid in the successful negotiation of the transition. An individual who is very anxious about forming relationships with others is likely to have trouble forming new types of relationships, because they threaten an already shaky sense of security. A child who does not have a strong sense of security may have many friends in elementary school but may be too afraid to form intimate friendships when she reaches preadolescence. She may try to continue having the sorts of friendships she had as a child—friendships that focus on playing games, for example, rather than talking—long after her friends have outgrown getting together to "play." As a result, she may be rejected by her peers and feel lonely and isolated.

**Sullivan's view of interpersonal development during adolescence** Looking back at the progression of interpersonal needs that Sullivan mapped out, we see that he distinguished between intimacy and sexuality and, perhaps more important, that he suggested that the need for intimacy—which surfaces during preadolescence—precedes the development of heterosexual relationships—which do not emerge until adolescence. In other words, Sullivan believed that the capacity for intimacy first develops before adolescence and in the context of same-sex, not opposite-sex, relationships. One of the main challenges of adolescence, according to Sullivan, is making the transition from the nonsexual, intimate, same-sex friendships of preadolescence to the sexual, intimate, opposite-sex friendships of late adolescence.

Sullivan divided the years between childhood and adulthood into three periods: *prea-*

*dolescence, early adolescence,* and *late adolescence.* During preadolescence, children begin to focus their attention on relationships with a few close friends, generally of the same sex. It is through these friendships—"chumships," as Sullivan called them—that the need for intimacy is first satisfied. With chums, the young person learns to disclose and receive intimate, private information and to build a close, mutual friendship that is based on honesty, loyalty, and trust. Sullivan believed that these relationships could even have a corrective influence, helping to repair interpersonal problems that might have developed during childhood. A good preadolescent friend, for example, can help overcome feelings of insecurity that have developed as a result of poor family relationships.

Not all youngsters feel secure enough as preadolescents to forge these more mature, intimate friendships, however. The feelings of insecurity are so strong for some that anxiety holds them back. As a result, some youngsters never fully develop the capacity to be intimate with others, a limitation that takes its toll on relationships throughout adolescence and adulthood. In other words, Sullivan felt that forming intimate friendships during preadolescence is a prerequisite to forming close relationships as an adolescent or young adult.

According to Sullivan, the preadolescent era comes to an end with the onset of puberty. Early adolescence is marked by the emergence of sexuality, in the form of a biologically based, powerful sex drive. As a consequence of this development, a change in the preferred "target" of the adolescent's need for intimacy takes place. He or she must begin to make a shift from intimate relationships with members of the same sex to intimate relationships with members of the opposite sex.

Like all interpersonal transitions, the movement from same-sex into opposite-sex relation-

For many adolescents, middle adolescence marks an important transition into opposite-sex friendships. *(Richard Hutchings/Photo Researchers)*

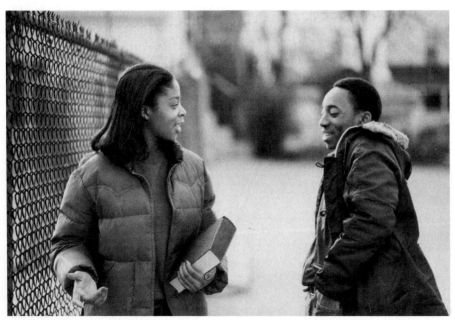

ships can be fraught with anxiety. For adolescents who do not have a healthy sense of security, it can be scary to leave the safety of nonsexual same-sex friendships and venture into the world of opposite-sex relationships, dating, and sexuality.

The chief challenge of adolescence, according to Sullivan, is to integrate the individual's established need for intimacy with the emerging need for sexual contact in a way that does not engender an excessive degree of anxiety. Just as Erikson views adolescence as a time of experimentation with different identities, Sullivan saw adolescence as a time of experimentation with different types of interpersonal relationships. Some adolescents choose to date many different people to try to find out what they are looking for in a relationship with someone else. Others get involved very deeply with a boyfriend or girlfriend in a relationship that lasts throughout their entire adolescence. Others may have a series of serious relationships. And still others keep intimacy and sexuality separate. They may develop close platonic relationships with opposite-sex peers, for example, or they may have sexual relationships without getting very intimate with the people they have sex with. And just as Erikson views role experimentation as a healthy part of the adolescent's search for identity, Sullivan viewed the adolescent's experimentation with different types of relationships as a normal way of handling new feelings, new fears, and new interpersonal needs. For many young people, experimentation with sex and intimacy continues well into late adolescence.

If the interpersonal tasks of adolescence have been negotiated successfully, the young person enters late adolescence able to be intimate, able to enjoy sex, and most critical, able to experience intimacy and sexuality in the same relationship. This accomplished, the adolescent turns to the interpersonal needs of late adolescence: carving his or her niche in adult society. This latter task, in some senses, is reminiscent of the adolescent identity crisis described by Erikson.

## ERIKSON'S VIEW OF INTIMACY

Erik Erikson believes that development during the adolescent and young adult years revolves around two psychosocial crises: the crisis of identity versus identity diffusion, prominent during adolescence, and the crisis of **intimacy versus isolation,** prominent during early adulthood (1968). Erikson's ideas on the subject of intimacy are far less developed than his ideas on the issue of identity. Nonetheless, his view of the relationship *between* intimacy and identity is important to understand and provides something of a contrast to Sullivan's perspective.

Erikson feels that in a truly intimate relationship, two individuals' identities become fused in such a way that neither person's identity is lost. Together, two people who are in love form a couple that has its own life, its own future, and its own identity. Yet the partners do not lose their own sense of individuality. When two people marry, for example, becoming a part of a couple becomes an important part of each person's identity, but it doesn't erase the sense of self that each person had before the marriage.

It follows, Erikson reasons, that adolescents must establish a sense of identity before they are capable of real intimacy. Without a secure sense of identity, people are afraid and unwilling to make serious commitments to others: They fear that they will lose their identity in the relationship. A young woman who is struggling to establish an occupational identity, for example, may feel that getting seriously involved with someone may impede her progress toward discovering who *she* really is as an individual.

Relationships between individuals who have not yet established a sense of identity may look intimate, but generally they are not. Adolescents who throw themselves into going steady often display a sort of "pseudointimacy." On the surface, their relationship may seem to be close, but a more careful examination usually reveals a sort of shallow, superficial intimacy. The couple may proclaim their faith in each other, for instance, but deep down they may be mistrustful or afraid to voice their fears. They may say that they are open with each other, but they may not disclose what they are really feeling, for fear of losing the relationship. They may say that they will stay together forever, but they have trouble making any concrete plans for the future that include each other. According to Erikson, this type of pseudointimacy is to be expected during adolescence. After all, it is difficult to commit yourself to someone else before you yourself know who you are.

**Erikson and Sullivan: Conflicting views?**   It may appear that there is a disagreement between Erikson and Sullivan on the relation between intimacy and identity. Sullivan viewed the development of intimacy as occurring primarily in *preadolescence*. He suggested that the development of the capacity for intimacy is a precedent to the development of a coherent sense of identity, which does not occur until late adolescence. Erikson, on the other hand, argues that the establishment of a coherent sense of identity necessarily occurs prior to the development of intimacy, since one must have a clear sense of who one is in order to avoid becoming lost in a relationship with someone else. What are we to make of this difference? Which comes first, the development of identity or the development of intimacy?

A number of studies have attempted to answer this question by assessing individuals on separate measures of identity and intimacy and examining the relation between the two scores (e.g., Dyk and Adams, 1990; Levitz-Jones and Orlofsky, 1985; Orlofsky, Marcia, and Lesser, 1973). If Erikson's view is correct, only individuals who have achieved a sense of identity should score high in intimacy and no individuals high in intimacy should be low in identity. If Sullivan's view is correct, only individuals who have achieved intimacy in their relationships should score high in identity, and no individuals who score high in identity should score low in intimacy.

Unfortunately, none of the studies of the relation between identity and intimacy provide clear support for one theory over the other. While scores on measures of identity and intimacy are generally correlated (that is, individuals who have a coherent sense of identity are more likely to have intimate interpersonal relationships, and vice versa), it has been difficult to determine whether development in one domain actually *leads to* development in another. Rather, it seems that individuals follow different developmental routes, with some establishing a sense of identity first and then advancing in the realm of intimacy, and others following the reverse pattern.

One hypothesis along these lines concerns sex differences in patterns of psychological development. As we shall see later in this chapter, many theorists have argued that intimacy is a far more fundamental concern for the adolescent girl than for the adolescent boy, and that the psychosocial "crises" of identity and intimacy may even be merged for female adolescents (Josselson, Greenberger, and McConochie, 1977). For the adolescent boy—actually, for males at all ages—intimacy is perhaps a more distant concern that is less important in the process of self-definition (Maccoby, 1990). In essence, Sullivan's view may be more applicable to girls, whereas Erikson's may be more applicable to boys (Dyk and Adams, 1990).

Rather than debating which comes first—identity or intimacy—it seems more sensible to suggest that the development of intimacy and the development of identity go hand-in-hand throughout adolescence, with changes in one realm of psychosocial development affecting changes in the other. One reason for the apparent disagreement between Erikson and Sullivan is that the two theorists focus on different aspects of intimacy. Whereas Sullivan's concern was primarily with the adolescent's *need* and *capacity* for intimacy (hence, his focus on early adolescence), Erikson's has been with the *expression* of intimacy and commitment (hence, his focus on late adolescence). Close relationships are used as a safe context in which adolescents confront difficult questions of identity; yet at the same time, the development of an increasingly coherent and secure sense of self provides the foundation upon which adolescents build and strengthen intimate relationships with others. Although we may speak of them as though they are independent processes, the development of intimacy and identity—along with the development of autonomy, sexuality, and achievement—are highly interrelated.

## ATTACHMENT IN ADOLESCENCE

In recent years, a new perspective on intimacy in adolescence has emerged, one that draws on theories of the development of the **attachment** relationship in infancy (e.g., Ainsworth et al., 1978; Bowlby, 1969; Sroufe, 1977). In these theories of infant development, an attachment is defined as a strong affectional bond that is enduring and persistent. Virtually all infants form attachment relationships with their mothers (and most do with their fathers and other caregivers, as well), but not all infants have attachment relationships of the same quality. Psychologists differentiate among three types of attachment: **secure attachment, anxious-avoidant attachment,** and **anxious-resistant attachment.** The security of the early attachment relationship is important, because studies show that infants who have had a secure attachment are more likely to grow into psychologically and socially skilled children (Matas, Arend, and Sroufe, 1978).

Many theorists who study adolescent development believe that the nature of the individual's attachment relationships in infancy continues to have an influence on his or her capacity to form satisfying intimate relationships in adolescence and adulthood, for two reasons. First, some theorists have argued that the initial attachment relationship forms the basis for a more general model of interpersonal relationships that we employ throughout life. This so-called **internal working model** determines to large measure whether we feel trusting or apprehensive in relationships with others and whether we see ourselves as worthy of others' affection. According to the theory, individuals who had enjoyed a secure attachment relationship in infancy will have a more positive and healthy "working model" of relationships in adolescence, whereas individuals who had been anxiously attached as infants will not (e.g., Kobak and Sceery, 1988).

A second reason for the continued importance of early attachment relationships in adolescence is cumulative. Although few longitudinal studies of infant attachment have followed individuals into and through adolescence, a number of studies have followed infants well into the childhood years (e.g., Erickson, Sroufe and Egeland, 1985; Lewis, Feiring, McGuffog, and Jaskir, 1984; Renken et al., 1989). These studies quite convincingly show that anxiously attached infants are more likely to develop psychological and social problems in childhood, including poor peer relationships. These problems in peer relations in childhood, in turn, likely affect the development of social competence in adolescence, forming a link between early experience and later social relations. Interestingly, several studies indicate that the benefits of positive relations with peers extend beyond adolescence: individuals who establish healthy intimate relationships with agemates in adolescence are more psychologically healthy and and more satisfied with their lives as middle-aged adults (Hightower, 1990; Willits, 1988). Taken together, these studies suggest an orientation toward the study of intimate relation-

insecure attachment

ships that examines the development of close relationships over the entire life span, as emphasized in the theoretical models of both Erikson and Sullivan.

In addition to employing the three-way attachment classification scheme to study the links between infancy, childhood, and adolescence, attachment theorists have also applied this model to the study of so-called adolescent attachments (e.g., Armsden and Greenberg, 1987; Greenberg et al., 1983; Kenny, 1987; Kobak and Sceery, 1988). In some of these studies, adolescents' *current* relationships with parents and peers are assessed, whereas in others, adolescents are asked to recount their childhood experiences. In general, individuals who have secure attachments in adolescence (or who describe their earlier attachments as having been secure) are more socially competent and better adjusted than their anxiously-attached peers (Rice, 1990).

## *Research on the Developmental Course of Intimacy*

### CHANGES IN THE NATURE OF FRIENDSHIP

"How do you know that someone is your best friend?" When this question is posed to children and adolescents of different ages, younger and older respondents give different sorts of answers. Consider, for example, the following two responses—the first from a kindergarten child, the second from a sixth grader (from Berndt, 1981, p. 180):

> "I sleep over at his house sometimes. When he's playing ball with his friends, he'll let me play. When I slept over, he let me get in front of him in four-squares [a playground game]. He likes me."

> "If you can tell each other things that you don't like about each other. If you get into a fight with

someone else, they'd stick up for you. If you can tell them your phone number and they don't give you crank calls. If they don't act mean to you when other kids are around."

These two examples illustrate the most important trend in the development of children's conceptions of friendship: it is not until early adolescence that such features as self-disclosure and loyalty are mentioned as important dimensions of friendship. Thomas Berndt (1981), for example, compared the responses of kindergarten children, third-graders, and sixth-graders to questions about their conceptions of close friendship. The children's responses were classified into one of eight categories, including *play or association* ("He calls me all the time"), *prosocial behavior* ("She helps me do things"), *intimacy or trust* ("I can tell her secrets"), and *loyal support* ("He'll stick up for me when I'm in a fight"). In general, responses mentioning prosocial behavior and association were equally frequent across all age groups—in fact, they were among the most frequent types of responses at all ages. But answers mentioning intimacy and loyalty, which were virtually absent among the kindergarten students, increased dramatically between the third and sixth grades.

A similar study revealed comparable results (Bigelow and LaGaipa, 1975). Not until seventh grade did individuals mention intimacy, and not until this time did children mention "common interests" or "similar attitudes and values" (see Figure 10.1). As in Berndt's study, the researchers found that responses mentioning prosocial behavior and common activities were high in all age levels. One team of writers suggest that it may be important to differentiate between companionship, which appears much before adolescence, and intimacy, which may not emerge until considerably later (Buhrmester and Furman, 1987).

That conceptions of friendship come to place greater weight on such dimensions as

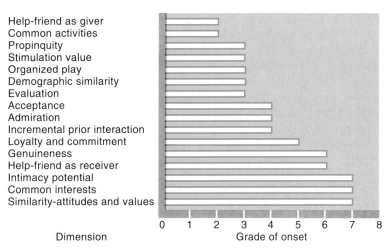

**FIGURE 10.1**  Children and adolescents have different conceptions of "friendship." Some sorts of conceptions do not appear until the fifth or sixth grade. (Derived from Bigelow and LaGaipa, 1975)

intimacy, loyalty, and shared values and attitudes during early adolescence is consistent with Sullivan's theory (Savin-Williams and Berndt, 1990). As adolescents' needs for intimacy increase, so might the emphasis that they place on intimacy as an important component of friendship. The findings are also consistent with what we know about other cognitive changes characteristic of early adolescence. As you will recall from Chapter 2, adolescents have greater facility than children in thinking about abstract concepts, such as intimacy and loyalty. And adolescents' judgments of others are more sophisticated, more psychological, and less tied to concrete attributes than are those of children.

Several studies indicate that the importance of intimacy continues to increase throughout early and middle adolescence (Berndt and Perry, 1990). But an interesting pattern of change occurs around age 14. During middle adolescence (between ages 13 and 15), particularly for girls, concerns about loyalty and anxieties over rejection become more pronounced and may temporarily overshadow concerns

about intimate self-disclosure (Berndt and Perry, 1990; Douvan and Adelson, 1966). As Elizabeth Douvan and Joseph Adelson explain:

> The girls in this age group [14–16] are unique in some respects, that is, different from both older and younger girls. What stands out in their interviews is the stress placed on security in friendships. They want the friend to be loyal, trustworthy, and a reliable source of support in any emotional crisis. She should not be the sort of person who will abandon you or who gossips about you behind your back. . . . With so much invested in the friendship, it is no wonder that the girl is so dependent on it. . . . The girl is likely to feel like the [patient] in that famous *New Yorker* cartoon, who, getting up from the couch, takes a pistol from her purse, and says [to her psychoanalyst]: "You've done me a world of good, Doctor, but you know too much." (1966, pp. 188–189)

How might Sullivan have explained this pattern? Why might loyalty become such a pressing concern for girls during the middle adolescent years? One possible answer is that at this age, girls may feel more anxious about their relationships because they are beginning to make the transition into opposite-sex relationships. These transitions, as Sullivan noted, can sometimes make us feel insecure. Perhaps it is anxiety over dating and heightened feelings of insecurity that cause adolescent girls temporarily to place a great deal of emphasis on the trust and loyalty of their close friends.

## CHANGES IN THE DISPLAY OF INTIMACY

In addition to placing greater emphasis on intimacy and loyalty in defining friendship than children do, teenagers are also more likely actually to display intimacy in their relationships. For example, one team of researchers examined age differences in the degree to which youngsters had intimate knowledge about their best friends (Diaz and Berndt, 1982). Although fourth- and eighth-graders had comparable degrees of knowledge about *nonintimate* characteristics of their best friends (such as the friend's telephone number or birth date), eighth graders knew significantly more things about their friends that could be classified as *intimate* (such as what their friends worry about or what they are proud of). Along similar lines, another study showed that, between the fifth and eleventh grades, increasingly more adolescents agree with such statements as, "I know how [my friend] feels about things without his [or her] telling me," and "I feel free to talk to [my friend] about almost everything" (Sharabany, Gershoni, and Hofman, 1981). Consistent with Sullivan's viewpoint, then, during preadolescence and early adolescence, youngsters' friendships become more personal.

Individuals also become more responsive to-

The development of intimacy generally surfaces first in same-sex friendships. Research suggests that intimate friendships develop earlier among girls than boys. *(Rae Russel)*

ward close friends during adolescence (Berndt, 1982; Berndt and Perry, 1990). This can be interpreted as another indicator of their increased capacity for intimacy. Before preadolescence, for example, children are actually *less* likely to help and share with their friends than with other classmates (perhaps because children are more competitive with their friends than with other youngsters and do not want to feel inferior). By about fourth grade, children treat their friends and other classmates similarly when it comes to sharing and cooperation. But by the time they have reached eighth grade, one team of researchers found, friends are "more generous and more helpful toward each other than toward other classmates" (Berndt, 1982, p. 1452).

Finally, during the course of adolescence, individuals become more interpersonally sen-

sitive—they show greater levels of empathy and social understanding—in situations in which they are helping or comforting others. Compared with children, adolescents are more likely to understand and acknowledge how their friends feel when those friends are having problems. For instance, one researcher asked children and adolescents how they would help a younger friend who had been scared by a horror movie on television. The children were more likely to deny their friend's feelings ("You're getting to be a big kid now. . . . There's no reason to be upset. Don't make it so big"); but the adolescents were more likely to respond sensitively and supportively ("The movie *was* scary, and I know 'cause it scared me too. . . . Just remember the picture isn't true—it's all camera angles and stuff") (Burleson, 1982).

Although intimate, opposite-sex relationships begin to develop during middle adolescence, they do not replace friendships with same-sex peers. Rather, new types of relationships appear to be added to old ones. *(Joel Gordon)*

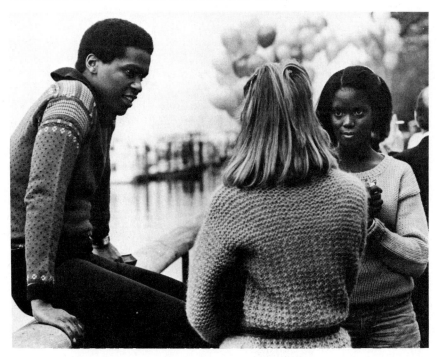

# CHANGES IN THE "TARGETS" OF INTIMACY

According to Sullivan, adolescence is a time of noteworthy changes in the "targets" of intimate behavior. During preadolescence and early adolescence, intimacy with peers is hypothesized to replace intimacy with parents, and during late adolescence, intimacy with peers of the opposite sex is thought to take the place of intimacy with same-sex friends. Actually, this view appears to be only somewhat accurate. As we shall see, new "targets" of intimacy do not *replace* old ones. Rather, new targets are *added to* old ones.

**Parents and peers as targets of intimacy** The increasing intimacy between teenagers and their friends during the course of adolescence is generally not accompanied by a decrease in intimacy toward parents. Declines in intimacy between adolescents and their parents, which appear to occur during early adolescence, are temporary. By the end of adolescence, young people and their parents are quite close. One study, for example, compared levels of intimacy between adolescents and their best friends, their mothers, and their fathers (Hunter and Youniss, 1982). Thirty adolescents in each of four different age groups—9, 12, 15, and 19—were asked to rate the three relationships along four measures of intimacy: (1) their willingness to discuss problems with the other person, (2) their ability to talk through disagreements, (3) feelings of companionship, and (4) the degree of intimate knowledge possessed by the other person. Ratings across these measures were summed to form overall intimacy scores for each of the three relationships (see Figure 10.2).

As expected, intimacy between adolescents and their best friends increased across the four groups. And from age 12 on, adolescents described their relationships with their best friends as more intimate than those with their

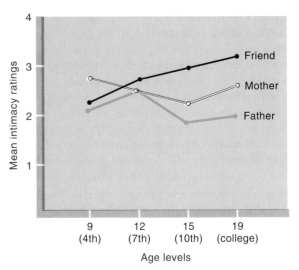

**FIGURE 10.2** Age differences in intimacy in three relationships. (Adapted from Hunter and Youniss, 1982)

mothers or fathers. But this difference between parent and peer intimacy was due to increases in intimacy with peers, not to decreases in intimacy with parents. Intimacy between adolescents and their mothers was equal across the four groups, and intimacy between adolescents and their fathers appeared to increase slightly between ages 9 and 12, to decrease slightly between ages 12 and 15 (returning to the level at 9 years of age), and to remain steady between ages 15 and 19.

Findings consistent with these were obtained when nearly 2,500 students in a large midwestern school district were asked to list the important people in their lives—people they cared about, went to for advice, or did things with (Blyth, Hill, and Thiel, 1982). The number of peers listed increased over the course of the age range studied (from grades seven through ten). But no changes were found across this same age range in the percentage of adolescents listing their mothers or fathers—in each grade, for both boys and girls, about 93 percent of the adolescents sampled listed their parents. Similarly, studies of adolescents' preferences for social support show that the likelihood of turning to a peer during a time of trouble increases during adolescence but that the likelihood of turning to a parent remains constant (Kneisel, 1987). In other words, even though adolescents begin to see their friends as increasingly important sources of emotional support, they do not cease needing or using their parents for the same purpose.

There are important differences between adolescents' relationships with their mothers and fathers, however. In general, adolescents interact much more often with their mother than with their father, and this is true for males as well as females. Compared to their fathers, adolescents see their mothers as more understanding, accepting, and willing to negotiate, and less judgmental, guarded, and defensive. The difference between perceptions of mothers and fathers is especially large for girls: As a rule, the mother-daughter relationship tends to be the closest and the father-daughter relationship the least intimate, with mother-son and father-son relationships falling in between (Noller and Callan, 1990; Steinberg, 1987; Youniss and Smollar, 1985).

An important transition in intimate relationships appears to take place sometime between the fifth and eighth grades, however. During this period, peers become the most important source of companionship and intimate self-disclosure, surpassing parents and, interestingly, other family members, such as siblings, as well (Buhrmester and Furman, 1987). Peers may become increasingly important as targets of intimacy not simply because of their similar age, but because they do not share the same family with the adolescent. As adolescents begin the process of individuation, they may need to seek intimacy outside the family as a means of establishing an identity beyond their family role.

Adolescents also have very different sorts of intimate relationships with parents and peers, and these differences point to different ways

in which mothers, fathers, and friends may contribute to the social development of the young person. Even in close families, parent-adolescent relations are characterized by an imbalance of power, with parents as nurturers, advice givers, and explainers whom adolescents turn to because of their experience and expertise. Adolescents' interactions with their friends, in contrast, are more mutual and balanced and are more likely to provide adolescents with opportunities to express alternative views and engage in an equal exchange of feelings and beliefs (Hunter, 1984). Rather than viewing one type of relationship as more or less intimate than the other, it seems wiser to say that both types of intimacy are important, for each influences a different aspect of the adolescent's developing character in important ways. Intimacy with parents provides opportunities to learn from someone older and wiser; intimacy with friends provides opportunities to share experiences with someone who has a similar perspective and degree of expertise.

The different functions of intimacy with parents and peers are illustrated in a study of **social support** during a transition into a new school (Dunn et al., 1987). As you recall from Chapter 6, changing schools during adolescence can sometimes be stressful, and social support—emotional assistance from others—can help buffer adolescents against the potential negative effects of stress (Hauser and Bowlds, 1990). The study found that support from family members was more predictive of adaptation to the demands of the new school, as indexed by grades and attendance, but that support from peers was more predictive of low psychological distress, as indexed by measures of depression and anxiety. The absence of peer support was especially critical for boys. One reason: Girls may be more likely than boys to seek out other sources of support when their peers do not provide it.

In general, these findings on age changes in

intimacy with parents and peers are similar to the findings discussed in the chapter on autonomy: Although the importance of peer relationships undoubtedly increases during adolescence, the significance of family relationships does not decline. Contrary to widely held stereotypes about adolescents' social relationships, then, parents do not cease to be important sources of influence or, as we see here, targets of intimacy. Throughout adolescence, parents and adolescents remain close; parents—especially mothers—remain important confidants; and both mothers and fathers continue to be significant influences on the young person's behavior and decisions. Indeed, even in adolescence being close to one's parents has a more positive impact on psychological health than being close to one's friends (Greenberg, Siegel, and Leitch, 1983), and studies show that the quality of the relationship adolescents have with their parents may have an influence on the quality of the relationship they have with close friends (Gold and Yanof, 1985). Increasingly, psychologists are coming to see family relationships and peer relationships as influencing each other, rather than competing with each other. Nevertheless, it seems clear that peers take on an increasingly important role in the individual's social life over the course of adolescence. Although peers do not *replace* parents, they clearly contribute to the adolescent's social development in a unique and beneficial way.

## SAME-SEX VERSUS OPPOSITE-SEX FRIENDSHIPS

It is not until middle or even late adolescence that intimate relationships with opposite-sex peers begin to be important. Consistent with Sullivan's theory, studies of preadolescents and young teenagers point to a very strong sex cleavage in adolescents' friendships, with boys rarely reporting friendships with girls, and girls rarely reporting friendships with boys

(Hallinan, 1981). Indeed, gender is the single most important determinant of friendship during preadolescence, playing a considerably more powerful role than, for example, race or socioeconomic background (Schofield, 1981). (Age is also an important determinant of preadolescents' friendships, but it is difficult to study, since the structure of most elementary schools—at least in America—makes it hard for children to develop friendships with older or younger peers.)

The schism between boys and girls during early adolescence is due to a variety of factors. First, despite whatever changes may have taken place in American society with regard to sex-role socialization during the past twenty years, it is still the case that preadolescent and early adolescent boys and girls have different interests, engage in different sorts of peer activities, and perceive themselves to be different from each other (Schofield, 1981). In one study, for example, an interviewer asked a young adolescent boy why boys and girls sit separately in the school lunchroom. "So they can talk," the boy replied. "The boys talk about football and sports and the girls talk about whatever they talk about" (Schofield, 1981, p. 68).

But perhaps a more interesting reason for the low frequency of cross-sex friendships during early adolescence is the concern of some adolescents that contact with members of the opposite sex will be interpreted as a sign of romantic involvement (Schofield, 1981). As one girl put it, "If you talk with boys they [other girls] say that you're almost going with him." Another girl from the same class remarked that boys and girls rarely work together on class projects, "because people like to work with their friends. . . . When you're working on a project . . . your friend has to call and come over to your house. If it's a boy, it can be complicated" (Schofield, 1981, p. 69).

The discomfort that younger adolescents feel about cross-sex relationships is vividly il-

Despite supposed changes in sex-role socialization, early adolescents tend to have exclusively same-sex friendships because—quite simply—boys and girls have different, sex-stereotyped interests. *(Frank Sitemen/Picture Cube)*

lustrated in the following observation of three preadolescent boys in an amusement park:

> The boys seem very interested in the girls they see, and there is considerable whispering and teasing about them. Tom had received a small coin bank as a prize which he decides that he no longer wishes to keep. At this time we are standing in line for a roller coaster directly behind three girls—apparently a year or two older than these twelve-year-olds—one of whom is wearing a hooded jacket. Frank tells Tom to take the bank and "stuff it in her hood," which Tom does to the annoyance of his victim. When she turns around, Tom and Hardy tell her that Frank did it, and of course Frank denies this, blaming Tom. The girls tell the boys to shut up and leave them alone. As things work out, Hardy has to sit with one of these girls on the ride and he clearly appears embarrassed, while Tom and Frank are vastly amused. After the ride Tom and Frank claim that they saw Hardy holding her. Frank said that he saw them holding hands, and Tom said: "He was trying to go up her shirt." Hardy vehemently denies these claims. A short while later we meet these girls again, and Frank turns to Hardy, saying "Here's your honey." The girl retorts as she walks away, "Oh, stifle it." (Fine, 1981, p. 43)

Friendly interactions between early adolescent boys and girls, when they do occur, typically involve "overacting attraction or romantic interest in such a pronounced or playful way that the indication of interest can be written off as teasing or fooling around" (Schofield, 1981, p. 71).

The transitional period—between same-sex nonsexual relationships and opposite-sex sexual ones—appears to be a somewhat trying time for adolescents. This period usually coincides with the peer group's shift from same-sex cliques to mixed-sex crowds, which we examined in Chapter 5. The interpersonal strains and anxieties inherent in the transition show up in the high levels of teasing, joking around, and overt discomfort young adolescents so often display in situations that are a little too close to being romantic or sexual. As one researcher put it, intimacy between boys and girls before middle adolescence appears to be "impeded at least partly because . . . children are aware that they are approaching the age when they may begin to become deeply involved with each other in a romantic or sexual way" (Schofield, 1981, pp. 69–71).

These observations support Sullivan's claim that intimacy between adolescent boys and girls is relatively slow to develop and generally tinged with an air of sexuality. Contrary to his notion that cross-sex intimacy comes to *replace* intimacy with peers of the same sex, however, researchers have found that intimate relationships between adolescents of the same sex continue to develop throughout adolescence. They clearly are not displaced by the eventual emergence of intimacy between adolescent males and females (Sharabany, Gershoni, and Hofman, 1981). Although researchers find that the likelihood of opposite-sex peers appearing on adolescents' lists of people who are important to them increases between the seventh and tenth grades, the number of same-sex peers listed remains constant, at around five (Blyth, Hill, and Thiel, 1982).

Actually, intimacy between the sexes increases during early adolescence (Buhrmester and Furman, 1987), but many adolescents in grades seven through ten—half of all males and about one quarter of all females—do not list a single opposite-sex peer as a significant person in their lives (see Figure 10.3). When females do include opposite-sex peers, the boys they list are often older and often from another school, suggesting that opposite-sex intimacy occurs primarily in the context of dating—again, consistent with predictions derived from Sullivan's theory. Similarly, when boys list girls as important friends, they generally are of the same age or younger (Blyth, Hill, and Thiel, 1982). Interestingly, having an intimate relationship with an opposite-sex peer is more strongly related to boys' general level of interpersonal intimacy than it is to girls' (Buhrmester and Furman, 1987). This suggests that opposite-sex relationships may play a more important role in the development of intimacy among adolescent boys than girls.

## Intimacy and Psychosocial Development

### THE FUNCTION OF CLOSE RELATIONSHIPS

Intimate friendships during adolescence play an important role in the young person's overall psychological development, particularly in the realms of identity and sexuality. Both Sullivan and Erikson have stressed the role of friendship in helping the adolescent establish a coherent sense of identity. Close friends serve as a sounding board for adolescents' fantasies and questions about the future. Adolescents often talk to their friends about the careers they hope to follow, the people they hope to get involved with, and the life they expect to lead after they leave home. Friends provide advice on a range of identity-related matters—from how to act in different situations to what sorts of occupational and educational paths to pursue. Not surprisingly, adolescents who report having at least one close friendship report higher levels of self-esteem than their peers who do not. However, it is not clear whether intimacy leads to self-esteem or whether adolescents with already high self-esteem are more likely to develop close friendships (Savin-Williams and Berndt, 1990).

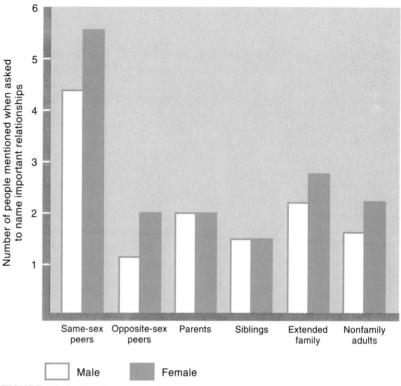

**FIGURE 10.3** The frequency of adolescents' important relationships with others. (Derived from Blyth, Hill, and Thiel, 1982)

Peers also play an extremely important part in socializing adolescents into the roles of adulthood. This is especially the case when it comes to sex roles. The pressure that adolescents exert on each other to behave in what they deem as sex-appropriate ways is often remarkably strong (Fine, 1981, 1987; Schofield, 1981).

As we shall see in the next chapter, friends are also important agents of sexual socialization during adolescence: Teenagers are far more likely to discuss sex with their friends than with their parents. Through close friendships, adolescents learn a great deal about sex and about ways of dealing with members of the opposite sex—lessons that are less likely to be learned from parents or other adults.

These positive aspects of close relationships notwithstanding, it is important to recognize that intimate relationships can have negative as well as beneficial effects on the young person's development. According to one theorist, frequent conversations with friends about personal problems and difficulties may lead to too much introspection and self-consciousness in the young person (Mechanic, 1983). Adolescent friendships may be beneficial precisely because they are *not* like those envisioned by Sullivan, but because they involve young people in exciting activities that distract them from being preoccupied with themselves (Savin-Williams and Berndt, 1990).

We should also keep in mind that the effects of being an intimate friend of someone depend

# THE SEXES: ARE THERE SEX DIFFERENCES IN INTIMACY?

It is often noted that intimacy develops earlier in girls than in boys, that intimate relationships are more common among girls throughout adolescence, and that girls experience more intimacy in their relationships than boys do (Maccoby, 1990). In most respects, as we shall see, these observations are absolutely true.

When asked to name the people who are most important to them, adolescent girls—particularly in the middle adolescent years—list more friends than boys do, and girls are more likely to mention intimacy as a defining aspect of close friendship. In interviews, adolescent girls express greater interest in their close friendships, talk more frequently about their intimate conversations with friends, and express greater concern about their friends' faithfulness and greater anxiety over rejection. Girls are more likely than boys to make distinctions in the way they treat intimate and nonintimate friends, and girls appear to prefer to keep their friendships more exclusive, being less willing to include other classmates in their cliques' activities. Intimacy with same-sex friends increases markedly between childhood and early adolescence among girls but does not show a similar increase among boys. Indeed, when self-disclosure is taken as the measure of intimacy, it is clear that boys' friendships with other boys do not approach girls' friendships with other girls until late in adolescence, if at all (Buhrmester and Furman, 1987; Savin-Williams and Berndt, 1990). Girls also appear to develop intimate relationships with boys earlier than boys do with girls (see figure). And girls appear to be more sensitive than boys and more empathic when comforting friends who are distressed (Berndt, 1981, 1982; Blyth, Hill, and Thiel, 1982; Burleson, 1982; Coleman, 1980; Douvan and Adelson, 1966; Sharabany, Gershoni, and Hofman, 1981). In these very numerous—and very important—respects, the expression of intimacy therefore appears to be more advanced among adolescent girls than boys.

Yet on some measures, adolescent boys and girls show similar degrees of intimacy in their interpersonal relationships. Although girls are more likely to mention self-disclosure when asked to define close friendship, boys and girls report similar levels of actual self-disclosure in their same-sex friendships and have equivalent degrees of intimate knowledge about their best friends (Diaz and Berndt, 1982; Sharabany, Gershoni, and Hofman, 1981). In group situations, boys and girls are equally likely to help their friends (Zeldin, Small, and Savin-Williams, 1982). Boys and girls report comparable levels of intimacy with their mothers, with the majority of adolescents feeling closer to their mothers than to their fathers, but boys report greater intimacy with fathers than girls do (Blyth and Foster-Clark, in press; Kandel and Lesser, 1972; Youniss and Smollar, 1985). As we noted in Chapter 4, the father-daughter relationship is generally more distant than other parent-child relationships in adolescence.

On the face of it, it appears that intimacy is a more *conscious* concern for adolescent girls than for boys. But this does not mean that intimacy is absent from boys' relationships. "Boys may spend less time in conversations about their emotions and ideas than girls, but they may [nevertheless] acquire a deep understanding of each other by spending time together" (Berndt, 1982, p. 1450). It is important to recognize, therefore, that boys and girls have different *types* of friendships. Consequently, they express intimacy in somewhat different ways. Observations of youngsters on a camping trip, for example, showed that although boys and girls are equally helpful when their friends are in need, boys were more likely to help *physically* (perhaps by helping someone set up a tent), but girls were more likely to help *verbally* (by explaining to someone how to put up a tent) (Zeldin, Small, and Savin-Williams, 1982). In general, boys' friendships are more oriented toward shared activities than toward the

*continued on next page*

explicit satisfaction of emotional needs—as is often the case of girls; and the development of intimacy between adolescent males may be a quieter, more subtle phenomenon.

Many theorists have suggested that these sex differences in intimacy are the result of different patterns of socialization, with females more strongly encouraged to develop and express intimacy—especially verbal intimacy—than males. Other factors could be at work, however, that lead to the greater expression of certain types of intimacy in females' than in males' relationships. Social pressures on males and females *during* adolescence are quite different and may lead to differences in expressions of intimacy in certain types of relationships. For instance, theorists have noted that **homophobia**—the fear of homosexuality—is stronger among adolescent males than adolescent females and leads to suppressed intimacy in relationships between adolescent boys (Kite, 1984). One reason adolescent boys may not be as intimate in their friendships as adolescent girls may be that adolescent boys are nervous that expressions of intimacy—even without sexual contact—will be taken as a sign of their sexual orientation.

Age differences in reported intimacy in same- and opposite-sex relationships. Intimacy is reported by girls before boys. (Adapted from Sharabany, Gershoni, and Hofman, 1981)

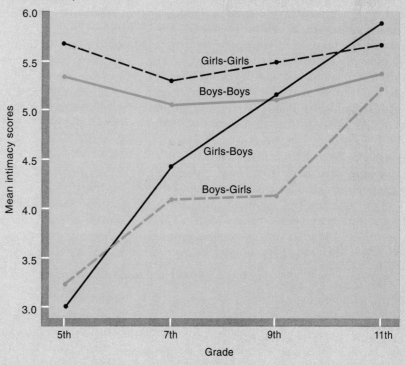

at least in part on who that someone is and what takes place in the relationship. Friendships often provide for positive things like self-disclosure, intimacy, and companionship, but they also may give rise to insecurity, jealousy, and mistrust (Rubin, 1980). And, as we saw in Chapter 5, adolescents who are intimate with peers with antisocial values or habits are themselves more likely to develop similar patterns of behavior. It is easy to forget, but it goes without saying, that not all close relationships foster positive developmental outcomes.

## ADOLESCENT LONELINESS

According to several surveys of high school and college students, late adolescence is one of the loneliest times in the life span. Although we often think of the elderly as being lonely, most studies show that the highest levels of loneliness are reported not by older adults but by adolescents and youth (Cutrona, 1982). Because adolescents may have developed strong needs for intimacy but may not yet have forged the social relationships necessary to satisfy these needs, they may be especially prone to feelings of social isolation. Being with other people who have active social lives can also be hard. Feelings of loneliness are intensified when we feel that the people around us are happier and more socially active than we are. The college student who remains back in his room while the rest of his suitemates are out on a weekend evening is likely to feel lonelier than the student who is in his room but knows that the student next door is having an equally miserable night.

The potential for feeling lonely increases over the adolescent years, as the large cliques and crowds common to early and middle adolescence begin to break down. In addition, changing conditions in the school setting over the adolescent years—having to change

schools, or having a daily schedule of classes that is different from one's friends—makes it difficult for high school students to maintain as many close friends as had been the case in junior high school or elementary school (Berndt and Perry, 1990). In surveys on friendship, the number of best friends named by individuals typically peaks in early adolescence at about four to six and then begins to decline. By adulthood, most individuals name only one best friend, a few close friends, and numerous acquaintances (Savin-Williams and Berndt, 1990).

If the transition from junior high school to high school can take a toll on the adolescent's intimate social network, the transition from high school to college can be absolutely devastating. Most young people report a steep decline in their satisfaction with their high school friendships over the course of the transition into college (Shaver, Furman, and Buhrmester, 1985). And unfortunately, many students in their first year of college do not immediately find replacements for this loss of intimacy.

According to an extensive study of loneliness among students at UCLA (Cutrona, 1982), nearly half of all students experience great loneliness during the first months of college. Leaving behind the familiarity of one's family, high school friends, and a hometown boyfriend or girlfriend, and entering a large, impersonal institution can be a very difficult transition. In an earlier chapter, we noted that half of all students who drop out of college do so during their first year. Loneliness is a contributing factor in many cases. Researchers find that loneliness is equally likely to be experienced by male and female students, by students from different ethnic groups, and by students living in dormitories and in off-campus housing (Cutrona, 1982). Although many students experience severe loneliness during their first year in college, these feelings subside somewhat for most people by the end of the year.

# Opposite-Sex Relationships

## DATING AND ROMANTIC RELATIONSHIPS

Opposite-sex relationships during middle and late adolescence may play an important role in furthering the development of intimacy, although there are surprisingly few studies of how adolescents are affected by their boyfriends or girlfriends. Sullivan believed that establishing intimate relationships with peers of the opposite sex was the chief developmental task of middle and late adolescence. The capacity for intimacy, which initially develops out of same-sex friendships, eventually is brought into cross-sex relationships. In some senses, then, Sullivan viewed relationships between boyfriends and girlfriends as a context in which intimacy is *expressed* rather than learned.

Some theorists have speculated that this view may be more accurate for females than for males. In American society, boys are not encouraged to develop the capacity to be emotionally expressive, particularly in their relationships with other males. During middle adolescence, as we have seen, girls may be better than boys at certain types of intimacy—self-disclosure and interpersonal understanding, for example. Girls, therefore, are more likely than boys to enter into relationships capable of being intimate and eager for emotional closeness. Some studies of early sexual relationships confirm this idea: For adolescent girls, early sexual relationships are far more likely to involve love, emotional involvement, and intimacy. For this reason, some writers have suggested that girls play an important role in teaching boys how to be more open, more sensitive, and more caring (Simon and Gagnon, 1969). In other words, whereas for girls cross-sex relationships may provide a context for further *expression* of intimacy, for boys they may provide a context for the further

*development* of intimacy. This notion is consistent with the finding, discussed earlier, that opposite-sex relationships may play a more important role in the development of intimacy among boys than among girls, who may develop and experience intimacy earlier with same-sex friends (Buhrmester and Furman, 1987).

There is a big difference between the sort of learning that takes place in a long-term, intimate relationship between two people and the lessons that are learned through casual dating. Dating is a well-established social institution in American adolescent life. Today, adolescent girls begin dating around age 12 or 13, and most boys between ages 13 and 14, earlier than was the case in previous decades (McCabe, 1984). Although early maturers begin dating somewhat earlier than late maturers (Simmons and Blyth, 1987), age norms within the adolescents' school are more important in determining the age at which dating begins than is the adolescent's level of physical development. In other words, a physically immature 14-year-old who goes to school where it is expected that 14-year-olds date is more likely to date than a physically mature 14-year-old who lives in a community where dating is typically delayed until 16 (Dornbusch et al., 1981). *Sexual* behavior, however, as we shall see in the next chapter, is more strongly influenced by biological development (Udry et al., 1985). By the age of 16, more than 90 percent of adolescents of both sexes have had at least one date, and during the later years of high school, more than half of all students average one or more dates weekly. Only 15 percent of high school students date less than once a month. About 75 percent of high school students have been steadily involved with someone else by the end of high school (Dickenson, 1975).

Given the prevalence of dating among contemporary adolescents, it is almost embarrassing to say that we know virtually nothing about the impact or significance of dating relation-

The role of dating in the development of intimacy is not entirely clear. Recent studies indicate that boys may learn more about being intimate from girls than vice versa. *(Hazel Hankin)*

ships for adolescent development (Savin-Williams and Berndt, 1990). In particular, the role of *dating* in the development of intimacy is not at all clear. Some young people—especially boys—may learn how to be more intimate through dating. But for the majority of young people, dating appears more likely to foster superficiality, rather than self-disclosure; shallow sociability, rather than genuineness; and the avoidance of real closeness (Douvan and Adelson, 1966). All in all, "pseudointimacy" is as likely an outcome of dating as is intimacy.

It is not until late adolescence that dating relationships begin to be characterized by a level of emotional depth and maturity that can be described as intimate (Douvan and Adelson, 1966). But even among college juniors and seniors, intimate dating relationships may be fairly rare. Less than one quarter of the male or female students interviewed in studies of psychosocial development were judged as having relationships that were truly intimate. More than half either had relationships that were stereotyped and shallow, excessively (and unhealthily) dependent, or they had no close relationships at all (Levitz-Jones and Orlofsky, 1985; Orlofsky, Marcia, and Lesser, 1973).

"Dating" during adolescence can mean a variety of different things, of course, from group activities that bring males and females together (without much actual contact between the sexes); to group dates, in which a group of boys and girls go out jointly (and spend part of the time in couples and part of the time in large groups); to casual dating in couples; to serious involvement with a steady boyfriend or girlfriend. More adolescents have experience in mixed-sex group activities like parties or dances than dating, and more have experience in dating than in having a serious boyfriend or girlfriend (Tobin-Richards, 1985).

One reason that we may not know very much about the impact of dating on adolescent development is that researchers have not paid enough attention to differences among various types of dating activities. There is some evi-

## HOW TO GO ON A DATE

Intimacy between adolescent males and females is slow to develop, and early dating experiences can be tortuous for tongue-tied teenagers, as Delia Ephron illustrates:

GIRL: Look around the restaurant at the other couples. Wonder if people are looking at the two of you as a couple. Hope that they are.

BOY: Out of sight, under the table, wipe finger on pants. Did anything come off? Look down, then look up quickly to see if your date had any idea what you were doing. Smile at her.

GIRL: Stop meeting his eye: Look down at your paper placemat and fold the edge of it over and over.

BOY: Bang the bowl of a spoon with your fork to try to flip it into the air. Notice what you are doing and stop. Put down fork and try desperately to think of something to say.

GIRL: Run your finger along the edge of the placemat, tracing its rim. Appear to be fascinated by the rim. Appear to study its every curve and turn while you worry—I can't think of anything to say. I knew this would happen. I knew it, I knew it, I knew it!

BOY: You know you heard a joke last week in school—now what was it? Who told it to you? Oh yeah, him. What was it? Put fork down. Try to remember. Pick it up, you can't remember, put it down, put hands in lap, put hands back on table, pick up knife and twirl it. What was it?

GIRL: Stop studying the placemat and instead look curiously and intently around the restaurant. Scrutinize the people at the next table. Scrutinize the pictures on the walls. Pray: Please God, let me think of something to say. Please, I'll do anything, just let me think of something. Oh, this is unreal! I knew that this would happen. I knew it and I was right! Oh God, please!!! I'll never ask for anything else, just let me have this, please. This is awful. This is the worst! Suppose the entire rest of the date goes by and I can't think of anything. Suppose I have to sit here in silence. I'll die, I'll absolutely die. Oh God, please!!!!!!

*Source:* Delia Ephron, *Teenage Romance* (New York: Viking, 1981), pp. 79–81.

dence, for example, that especially for girls, it may be important to differentiate between group versus couple activities in examining the impact of dating on psychological development. Evidently, participating in mixed-sex activity in group situations—going to parties or dances, for example—may have a positive impact on the psychological well-being of young adolescent girls, while serious dating in couples may have a more negative effect (Tobin-Rich-

ards, 1985). The reasons for this are not entirely clear, but researchers believe that pressures on girls to engage in sexual activity when they are out alone on dates or involved with a steady boyfriend may have a negative impact on their mental health (Simmons and Blyth, 1987). Although boys may feel peer pressure to become sexually active, this may be a very different sort of pressure—with very different consequences—from what girls feel. Because boys generally begin dating at a later age than girls—and date people who are younger rather than older—beginning to date in couples may be less anxiety-provoking for the adolescent boy, who has the advantage of a few additional years of "maturity," than for the adolescent girl.

Given the generally high level of superficiality operating in most adolescents' dating relationships, it comes as no surprise that early and intensive dating—for example, becoming "seriously involved" before age 15—has a somewhat stunting effect on interpersonal development. This is probably true for both sexes, but researchers have focused primarily on girls, because boys are less likely to begin serious dating quite so early. Compared with their peers, girls who begin serious dating early are more socially immature, more superficial, and less imaginative (Douvan and Adelson, 1966). In addition, adolescents of different ages date for different reasons—younger adolescents are more likely than older ones to date because it enhances their own status (Roscoe et al., 1987).

This is not to say that dating is not a valuable source of interpersonal experience for the adolescent. Adolescent girls who do not date at all show signs of retarded social development, excessive dependency on their parents, and feelings of insecurity (Douvan and Adelson, 1966), and adolescents who date and go to parties regularly have a stronger self-image and report greater acceptance by their friends (Long, 1989; Tobin-Richards, 1985). It is not clear, of course, whether a moderate degree of dating *leads to* higher levels of social development or whether more socially advanced and confident adolescents are simply more likely to date and go to parties. Nonetheless, it does seem that for girls in particular, *early* and *intensive* involvement with a boyfriend may do more harm than good. All in all, a moderate degree of dating, with serious involvement delayed until middle adolescence, appears to be the most potentially valuable pattern. Perhaps adolescents need more time to develop the capacity to be intimate through same-sex friendships and less pressured group activities before they enter intensively into the higher ritualized and not very intimate relationships encouraged through dating.

We also know that adolescents behave in different ways within dating relationships, and that these patterns of behavior may be learned at home. One recent study, for example, looked at the relationship between the type of conflict behavior that adolescents saw their parents engage in, the level of conflict they experienced with their parents, and the type of conflict behavior the adolescents engaged in with their dating partners (Martin, 1990). In general, adolescents' ways of dealing with conflict in their romantic relationships were linked to the models they had been exposed to at home, especially for daughters. For example, girls who had witnessed a great deal of conflict between their parents reported higher levels of verbal aggression, physical aggression, and relationship difficulties with their boyfriends. This study, along with those discussed earlier, on adolescent attachment, suggest that variations in adolescents' romantic relationships may have their origins—at least in part—in the adolescents' family experiences.

One of the reasons that we know so little about dating and the impact of romantic relationships on young people's development is that research has not kept pace with the changing nature and function of dating (Gordon and Miller, 1984). In earlier eras, dating during adolescence was a part of the process of courtship and mate selection—individuals would date in order to ready themselves for marriage and "play the field" before settling down. As you will see in the next section, during the mid-1950s, the *average* age at first marriage in the United States was 20 among women and 22 among men—which means that substantial numbers of individuals were marrying during

Most adolescents begin dating by the age of 13 or 14. There are differences in the ways in which adolescents behave within romantic relationships, however, which can be traced, in part, to their family experiences. *(Owen Franken/Stock, Boston)*

their late adolescent years. Because of this, the dating that individuals engaged in during their high school years was clearly a prelude to settling down.

Now, however, the average age at which people marry is considerably later—24 for women and 26 for men (Barringer, 1990). This, of course, gives high school dating a whole new meaning, since it is clearly divorced from its courtship function. One sign of this is that over the past decade, dating appears to have become more informal, less competitive, and less rigidly structured by traditional sex-role stereotypes (Miller and Gordon, 1986). Adolescent dating is now an end in itself, especially for the majority of young people who are headed toward college (Long, 1989; McCabe, 1984). All in all, most adolescents date because it is fun—although what constitutes "fun" varies from one adolescent to the next:

In one high school newspaper, one girl was quoted as saying that her "favorite way to have a good time is going to church or to Bible study and praising the Lord," while a male classmate of hers said that one of his "favorite ways to have a good time is to go out to eat with my girlfriend, stop at the store to get a couple of beers, and go back to my house to make sweet, beautiful love when nobody is there" (Glenbard East *Echo*, 1984, pp. 90–91, cited in Nielsen, 1991).

## BREAKING UP

As is the case with friendships during the move from high school to college, young people are likely to report dissatisfaction with their high school romances over this transition as well. In one study, which followed a sample of students from the summer before their first year in college through the first three semesters of college, about one-half of all high school romances ended, and those that did not end became much less satisfying when one of the partners began college. Males were far more likely than females to report feeling lonely and dissatisfied with their older relationships (Shaver et al., 1985).

The evidence, then, suggests that high school romances are not especially durable. Are the prospects any better for dating relationships formed during college? Athough it is now nearly 15 years old, the best data on this issue come from a study that followed 231 college couples in the Boston area over a period of two years (Hill, Rubin, and Peplau, 1979). Questionnaires covering a wide range of psychological and social topics were completed by both members of each couple several times over the course of the study. By the end of the two-year period, 103 couples (45 percent of the original group) had broken up; the average amount of time that these relationships had lasted was 16 months.

On the basis of the questionnaires completed at the beginning of the study, could the breakups have been predicted in advance? According to the results of this study, a variety of factors considered together could significantly predict which relationships would eventually break up and which ones would remain intact. Couples who remained together reported higher levels of intimacy and love to begin with, were equally committed to each other (rather than one person being significantly more involved than the other), and were highly similar on such characteristics as age, educational plans, SAT scores, and physical attractiveness. Similarity of attitudes, religion, and social class (as assessed by parents' education levels) were *not* good predictors of staying together.

Breakups were most likely to occur at three times of the year, reflecting the sensitivity of students' social relationships to the school calendar: May–June, September, and December–January. Evidently, having to make vacation plans, changes in living arrangements, and changes in school plans prompt many couples to reevaluate the status of their relationship.

As the authors point out, there are two sides to every breakup. Although, in the majority of cases, it was possible to identify a "breaker-upper" and a "broken-up-with"—in the sense of who was primarily responsible for ending things—couples did not always agree on who *wanted* to end the relationship: Respondents were biased toward saying that "they themselves, rather than their partners, were the ones who wanted to break up." Moreover, members of a couple often had different perceptions of why the relationship ended. The factors typically mentioned were boredom, differences in interests, and the woman's desire to be independent. Less often mentioned was one of the partners having a romantic interest in someone else.

Contrary to beliefs about women being more romantic than men, this and previous studies provide some evidence that men fall in love more readily than women and that women fall out of love more easily than men. For example, it was more often the woman who ended the relationship, frequently because she had become the less involved partner. And rejected men took breaking up harder than did rejected women—they often could not reconcile themselves to the fact that they were no longer loved and that the relationship had ended. Men also found it more difficult than women to stay friends after the relationship ended.

Why the sex differences? The authors give two interpretations, one economic, the other interpersonal. First, women may take a more practical stance toward relationships, because, "in most marriages, the wife's status, income, and life chances are far more dependent on

Fewer individuals are marrying during adolescence or early adulthood today than has been the case in the past. This is probably for the better, since the divorce rate is very high among couples who marry young. *(Harriet Gans/Image Works)*

her husband's than vice versa . . . For this reason . . . the woman cannot allow herself to fall in love too quickly, nor can she allow herself to stay in love too long with the wrong person. Men, on the other hand, can afford the luxury of being romantic." Second, "the emphasis upon social-emotional matters in women's socialization may lead women to be more sensitive than men to the quality of their interpersonal relationships, both in the present and projecting into the future. . . . Because of greater interpersonal sensitivity and discrimination, it may also be more important for women than for men that the quality of a relationship remain high."

Incidentally, although the song says that "breaking up is hard to do," it is harder on the person being broken up with: "Breaker-uppers" feel considerably less depressed, less lonely, and happier—albeit guiltier—even one year after the breakup.

## ADOLESCENT MARRIAGE AND DIVORCE

Most Americans marry for the first time in their middle twenties, with men, on the average, marrying at a somewhat later age than women. In 1990, the median age at first marriage was 26.1 for men and 23.9 for women, the latest it has been in 100 years (Barringer, 1991). Generally, from the late 1950s on and particularly during the past fifteen years, the average age at which American men and women first marry has risen steadily, no doubt due to the increasing labor force involvement of young women, the increasing acceptance of cohabitation, higher rates of college enroll-

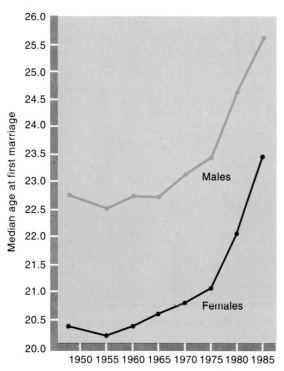

**FIGURE 10.4** First marriage occurs at a much later age today than it did forty years ago.

differences in teenage divorce rates, however. Proportionately more black 18- and 19-year-olds are divorced or separated than Hispanic youths of this age, and more Hispanic youths are divorced or separated than white youths (U.S. Bureau of the Census, 1982).

The higher rate of marital instability among the young is not surprising, given the array of other factors often characteristic of early marriage. Teenagers are more likely than adults to marry because of premarital pregnancy (the most common reason for marriage during adolescence), they are more likely to be under economic stress, and they are more likely to have low levels of education and, therefore, poor job prospects. (Teti et al., 1987). On several counts, teenagers who marry are likely to begin married life with problems that require a tremendous degree of coping and that, consequently, do not bode well for marital success. Premarital pregnancy, economic stress, and low levels of education are associated with higher divorce rates at *all* ages. In other words, teenagers' marriages are more likely to end in divorce because teenagers who marry are more likely to have the problems that lead to divorce among couples of all ages.

Not all adolescents who marry get divorced, of course. Adequate financial resources, a long-standing relationship before marriage, having completed high school, and delaying pregnancy until at least one year into married life are among the factors most predictive of marital success (Burchinal, 1965). Not surprisingly, these same factors—education, income, long engagement, and delayed childbearing—are also highly predictive of marital success among adults.

ment among women, and the increasing availability of contraception (see Figure 10.4). As a consequence, the percentage of married teenagers has diminished substantially in recent decades. In 1960 and 1970, one in ten teenage women was married. In 1986, this had declined to one in twenty (Wetzel, 1987).

The trend toward delayed marriage is probably for the better. The younger people are when they marry, the greater their chances of experiencing marital problems and divorce (Teti et al., 1987). Indeed, the divorce rate among men who marry in their teens is three times that of men who marry in their late twenties, and the divorce rate of women who marry before turning 18 is four times that of women who marry in their late twenties (Lewis and Spanier, 1979). There are considerable ethnic

## Summary

1. Most writers draw a distinction between intimacy and sexuality. In adolescence, the de-

velopment of intimacy refers to the development of relationships that are characterized by self-disclosure, trust, and concern. There are a number of reasons that intimacy becomes an important psychosocial concern in adolescence. Chief among them are the changes of puberty, which draw young people together around common concerns; the cognitive changes of the period, which allow for a more sophisticated understanding of relationships; and the social changes of the period, which provide more opportunities for adolescents to be alone with each other.

2. The three main theoretical approaches to the study of intimacy in adolescence are those of Sullivan, Erikson, and the attachment theorists. According to Sullivan, the need for intimacy emerges in preadolescence and is typically satisfied through same-sex friendships. During adolescence, this need is integrated with sexual impulses and desires and the focus of the adolescent's interpersonal concerns are redirected toward opposite-sex peers.

3. In Erikson's theory, the psychosocial crisis of late adolescence is labelled "intimacy versus isolation." According to this viewpoint, individuals must first develop a coherent sense of identity before they are able to develop genuinely intimate relationships with others. This position contrasts somewhat with that of Sullivan, who argues that the development of intimacy precedes the development of a coherent sense of self. There is some evidence that Erikson's model may be more true for males than females and that for females, the tasks of identity and intimacy may be somewhat merged.

4. According to attachment theorists, intimacy during adolescence must be examined in relation to the individual's history of close relationships, and in particular, the individual's infant attachments. There is evidence that individuals who enjoyed a secure attachment to their caregiver during infancy develop more healthy ideas about relationships and more advanced social competencies. Together, these permit the individual to enter into more satisfying intimate relationships in adolescence and adulthood.

5. Research on the development of intimacy in adolescence points to changes in individuals' conceptions about friendship, changes in the display of intimacy, and changes in the "targets" of intimacy. With development, adolescents place more emphasis on trust and loyalty as defining features of friendship, become more self-disclosing in their relationships, and broaden their circle of confidants to include peers as well as family members. It is not until relatively late in adolescence, however, that intimacy with opposite-sex peers develops.

6. Studies show that adolescents who have intimate friendships typically have better mental health than their peers. We do not know which comes first, however, intimacy or psychological health: Although it seems likely that intimacy, and the social support it provides, enhances adolescents' well-being, it is also likely that psychologically healthy adolescents are better able to make and maintain close relationships with others.

7. Transitions between schools often disrupt adolescents' intimate social networks. As a result, loneliness tends to increase during the adolescent years and is quite common in the early years of college. Research indicates that relatively few high school friendships and romances survive the transition into college.

8. Because the age at which individuals marry has become considerably later over the past forty years, dating during adolescence—although still quite common—has lost its significance for courtship. Once viewed as a prelude to marriage, the role of dating in adolescent psychosocial development today is not known. Although dating may provide a context for the further development of intimacy, most studies indicate that the majority of dating relationships are not especially intimate.

## Key Terms

anxious-avoidant
  attachment
anxious-resistant
  attachment
attachment
homophobia
internal working
  model
intimacy
intimacy versus iso-
  lation

need for integration
  into adult society
need for intimacy
needs for sexual con-
  tact and for a loving
  relationship with a
  peer of the other
  sex
secure attachment
social support

## For Further Reading

BUHRMESTER, D., AND FURMAN, W. (1987). The development of companionship and intimacy. *Child Development, 58,* 1101–1113. A study of relationships among children and young adolescents.

SAVIN-WILLIAMS, R., AND BERNDT, T. (1990). Friendship and peer relations. In S. Feldman and G. Elliott (Eds.), *At the threshold: The developing adolescent.* Cambridge: Harvard University Press. A review of the literature on friendship and intimacy during adolescence.

SULLIVAN, H. S. (1953). *The interpersonal theory of psychiatry.* New York: Norton. Sullivan's most extensive statement of his theory of interpersonal development.

YOUNISS, J., AND SMOLLAR, J. (1985). *Adolescent relations with mothers, fathers, and friends.* Chicago: University of Chicago Press. A study of the different roles played by mothers, fathers, and friends in the development of the adolescent.

# SEXUALITY

# SEXUALITY

How have teenagers' attitudes towards sex changed in recent decades? Should society be worried about sexual activity among young adolescents, or is teenage sex no more troublesome than many of the other new and adultlike activities that young people engage in? Does sex education prevent unwanted pregnancies, or does it encourage young people to begin sexual activity earlier? Should adolescents have access to contraceptives, and if so, should their parents be told? To what extent is interest in sex at adolescence driven by the hormonal changes of puberty and to what extent is it culturally conditioned? How have adolescents changed their sexual behavior in response to the epidemic of AIDS?

In this chapter, we examine adolescent sexuality in contemporary society with an eye toward dedramatizing and demystifying an aspect of adolescent behavior that has received a great deal more media attention than systematic research investigation. In order to present a more accurate picture of adolescent sexuality, we will need to step back and look at sexual behavior and development during adolescence in context—in the context of society and how it has changed and in the context of adolescence as a period in the life cycle and how it has changed.

## Sexuality as an Adolescent Issue

Like other aspects of psychosocial development, sexuality is not an entirely new issue that surfaces for the first time during adolescence. Children, of course, are known to be curious about their sex organs and at a very early age derive pleasure (if not what adults would label orgasm) from genital stimulation—as the famous sex researcher Alfred Kinsey pointed out many years ago (Kinsey, Pomeroy, and Martin, 1948). And of course, sexual activity and sexual development continue after adolescence.

While sexual development may be more dramatic and, for this reason, more obvious before adulthood, it by no means ceases at the end of adolescence.

Nonetheless, most of us would agree that adolescence is a fundamentally important time—if not the most important time in the life cycle—for the development of sexuality. There are several reasons for this. Perhaps most obvious is the link between adolescent sexuality and puberty. There is an increase in the sex drive in early adolescence as a result of hormonal changes (Udry, 1987). Moreover, it is not until puberty that individuals become capable of sexual reproduction. Before puberty, children are certainly capable of kissing, petting, masturbating, or even having sexual intercourse. But it is not until puberty that males can ejaculate semen or females begin to ovulate, and the fact that pregnancy is a possible outcome of sexual activity changes the nature and meaning of sexual behavior markedly—for the adolescent and for others. What had previously been innocuous sex play becomes serious business when pregnancy is a genuine possibility. Finally, as we saw in Chapter 1, not until puberty do individuals develop the secondary sex characteristics that serve as a basis for sexual attraction and as dramatic indicators that the young person is no longer physically a child.

But the increased importance of sexuality at adolescence is not due solely to puberty. The cognitive changes of adolescence play a part in the changed nature of sexuality as well. One of the obvious differences between the sexual play of children and the sexual activity of adolescents is that children are not especially introspective or reflective about sexual behavior. Sex during adolescence is the subject of sometimes painful conjecture ("Will she or won't she?"), decision making ("Should I or shouldn't I?"), hypothetical thinking ("What if he wants to do it tonight?"), and self-conscious concern ("Am I good-looking enough?"). As we saw in

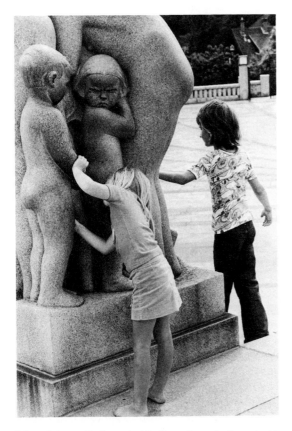

Although sexuality is undoubtedly an important psychosocial issue during adolescence, sexual concerns do not surface for the first time at this stage in the life span. It is normal for children to be curious about sex and about their sex organs at an early age. (*Fredrik D. Bodin/Stock, Boston*)

the previous chapter, one of the chief tasks of adolescence is to figure out how to deal with sexual desires and how to incorporate sex successfully and appropriately into social relationships (Sullivan, 1953a). Much of this task is cognitive in nature, and much of it is made possible by the expansion of intellectual abilities that takes place during the period.

In addition to the influence of the physical changes of puberty and the growth of sophisticated thinking capabilities on sexuality in adolescence, the new social meaning given to sex-

ual and dating behavior at this time in the life cycle makes sexuality an especially important psychosocial concern. As we shall see, the main influences on adolescents' sexual behavior are social, not biological.

You may have played "doctor" with your friends when you were a little child, but—as you well know—the game meant something quite different then from what it would if you were to play it now. Although younger children may engage in sex play, and although even infants may experience sexual arousal, it is not until adolescence that sexual activity begins to take on the social meaning it will continue to have throughout adulthood. With all due respect to Freud and Kinsey, one must place the sex play of children in proper perspective. Sullivan, for example, despite his psychoanalytic orientation, believed that sex play before adolescence had more to do with simple curiosity than with true sexuality (1953a). Adolescence is a turning point in the development of sexuality because it marks the onset of deliberate sexually motivated behavior that is recognized, both by oneself and by others, as primarily and explicitly sexual in nature.

## How Sexually Permissive Is America?

It is impossible to understand sexuality as a psychosocial phenomenon without taking into account the social milieu in which adolescents learn about and first experience sexual activity. Although we tend to think of sex as something that adolescents are inevitably anxious or concerned about, it is no more true to suggest that sexuality is always riddled with problems during adolescence than it is to say that all adolescents have problems in establishing a sense of identity or in developing a sense of autonomy. Like any other aspect of psychosocial growth, the development of sexuality is determined largely by its context. Of particular importance is the way in which adolescents and children are exposed to and educated about sexuality—a process called **sexual socialization.**

When did you first learn about sex? How much were you exposed to as a child? Was it something that was treated casually around your house or something that had an air of mystery to it? Was your transition into adult sexual activity gradual or abrupt?

As you know from previous chapters, the passage of adolescents into adulthood is believed to be easier and less stressful when transitions between the two eras are gradual, or continuous (Benedict, 1934). One aspect of the adolescent passage that anthropologists have examined extensively from this perspective is the transition of young people into adult sexual roles. In *Patterns of Culture* (1934), Ruth Benedict observed that anxiety over sex—thought to be common among teenagers in contemporary society—was absent in many traditional cultures. Margaret Mead's observations of young people in Samoa and New Guinea (1928) provided evidence that sexual development at adolescence was placid, not tumultuous—calm, not stressful—in societies where sexual experimentation was treated openly and casually during childhood and where special attention was not drawn to the adolescent's changed sexual status.

Think about some of the things you learned gradually and casually as a child—learning your way around the kitchen, for example—and imagine how different things would have been had this learning been handled the way most families handle sexual socialization. Suppose from an early age your parents had treated cooking food as if the activity had special, mysterious significance. Suppose you had never been permitted to see anyone actually cooking food, that you had been prohibited from seeing movies in which people cooked food, and that you had been excluded from any discussions of cooking. Nevertheless, imagine that you knew that *something* went on in the kitchen and that there was some special activity that adults did there which you would be permitted, and expected, to do when you grew up. Perhaps you even overheard other kids at school talking about cooking, but you still weren't sure just what the activity was or what one was supposed to do (or not do). Imagine how confused and ambivalent and anxious you would feel.

In many respects, this is how families in contemporary society handle sexual socialization. By being so secretive about sex when children are young and so worried about it when they are adolescents, Mead and Benedict argued, contemporary societies have turned sexuality into a problem for young people. Adolescents today are understandably confused and concerned about sex because their sexual socialization is so discontinuous.

Mead's and Benedict's observations of sexual socialization in traditional societies also indicated that cultures vary considerably in the ways in which they handle the sexual development of children and adolescents. Their observations were further borne out in *Patterns of Sexual Behavior* (1951), perhaps the most extensive study to date of sexual behavior in different cultural contexts. In this enormous undertaking, Clellan Ford and Frank Beach catalogued the sexual socialization and activity of children and adolescents in over 200 societies. The diversity in attitudes and behaviors uncovered by Ford and Beach is quite remarkable. Moreover, it helps to place debates over the sexual "permissiveness" of contemporary America in a somewhat sobering perspective. Drawing on hundreds of studies undertaken by cultural anthropologists over the years, Ford and Beach categorized societies into three groups: restrictive societies, semirestrictive societies, and permissive societies. As we shall see, present-day America is anything but permissive.

## SEXUAL SOCIALIZATION IN RESTRICTIVE SOCIETIES

*[handwritten: MORAL MAJORITY THINK WE ARE THIS]*

In **restrictive societies,** the adolescent's transition into adult sexual activity is highly discontinuous. Pressure is exerted on youngsters to refrain from sexual activity until they either have undergone a formal rite of passage or have married. In many restrictive societies, adolescents are forced to pursue sex in secrecy. Within the broad category of restrictive societies, of course, there are wide variations in the degree of restrictiveness and in the methods used to discourage sexual activity before marriage. For example, in some societies, such as the Cheyenne of Colorado and Montana, the sexual activity of young people is controlled by separating the sexes throughout childhood and adolescence. Boys and girls are not permitted to play together and never associate with each other before marriage in the absence of chaperones. In other societies, such as the Ashanti of the Guinea coast in Africa, sexual activity before the attainment of adult status is restricted through the physical punishment and public shaming of sexually active youngsters (Ford and Beach, 1951).

## SEXUAL SOCIALIZATION IN SEMIRESTRICTIVE SOCIETIES

*[handwritten: OUR SOCIETY IS SEMI-RESTRICTIVE]*

In **semirestrictive societies,** "adult attitudes toward . . . premarital affairs in adolescents are characterized by formal prohibitions that are . . . not very serious and in fact are not enforced" (Ford and Beach, 1951, p. 187). For example, among the Alorese of Indonesia, sexual activity among youngsters is formally prohibited; but children playing together often imitate the sexual behavior of their elders, and unless this play is brought explicitly to the attention of adults, little is done about it. Similarly, among the Andamanese (Southeast Asia), "premarital promiscuity is common, and the parents do not object as long as the love affairs are kept secret" (Ford and Beach, 1951, p. 187). In many semirestrictive societies, it is premarital pregnancy, rather than premarital sex, that is objectionable, and unmarried adolescents whose sexual activity has resulted in pregnancy are often forced to marry.

Generally speaking, the sexual socialization of children and adolescents in America has followed either a restrictive or a semirestrictive pattern, depending on the particular historical period and social group in question. At the time of the publication of *Patterns of Sexual Behavior* almost forty years ago, Ford and Beach classified America as restrictive. And some would argue that this classification is still valid today. For the most part, for example, American children are likely to be discouraged from (or even punished for) masturbation, sexual exploration is frowned upon, and sex play is discouraged. Adults rarely mention sexual matters in the presence of children; there even are laws prohibiting children from being exposed to sexual activity on television or in the movies. During adolescence, sexual activity—and in particular, sexual intercourse—between unmarried youth is discouraged. Adults openly try to discourage young people—especially young women—from becoming sexually active by lecturing them on the virtues of virginity, by not openly discussing matters of sex and pregnancy, and by making it difficult for young people to obtain contraception.

At the same time, however, some aspects of sexual socialization appear to place contemporary America more in the semirestrictive category. Adolescent boys and girls are not typically segregated; boys and girls often date without chaperones present; and premarital sex is not generally punished with public humiliation. Adolescents are encouraged to date, although adults know that dating provides a context for sexual activity. And it does seem at times as if we attempt only halfheartedly to enforce prohibitions against premarital sexual activity. Many parents are well aware that young people are sexually active, and they prefer to look the other way rather than restrict children's activities.

## SEXUAL SOCIALIZATION IN PERMISSIVE SOCIETIES

In **permissive societies,** the transition of young people into adult sexual activity is highly continuous and usually begins in childhood. Whether contemporary America is restrictive or semirestrictive may be subject to debate, but by no stretch of the imagination is it a permissive society—at least in comparison with many of the cultures described by Ford and Beach. Consider, for example, these descriptions of sexual socialization in some of the societies they categorized as permissive:

Among the Pukapukans of Polynesia, where parents simply ignore the sexual activities of young children, boys and girls masturbate freely and openly in public.... Young Trobriand [Melanesia] children engage in a variety of sexual activities. In the absence of adult control, typical forms of amusement for Trobriand girls and boys include manual and oral stimulation of the genitals and simulated coitus. Young Seniang [New Hebrides] children publicly simulate adult copulation without being reproved.... Lesu [New Ireland] children playing on the beach give imitations of adult sexual intercourse, and adults in this society regard this to be a natural and normal game....

Most of the societies that permit children free sex play ... also allow them opportunity to observe adult sexual behavior and to participate in discussions of sexual matters.... On Ponape [Caroline Islands] children are given careful instruction in sexual intercourse from the fourth or fifth year. Trukese [Caroline Islands] children receive no formal tutelage, but they learn a great deal by watching adults at night and by asking their elders about sexual matters....

Sexual life begins in earnest among the Trobrianders at six to eight years for girls, ten to twelve for boys. Both sexes receive explicit instruction from older companions whom they imitate in sex activities.... At any time a couple may retire to the bush, the bachelor's hut, an isolated yam house, or any other convenient place and there engage in prolonged sexual play with full approval of their parents. (Ford and Beach, 1951, pp. 188–191)

# Adolescents' Sexual Attitudes and Behavior

## ATTITUDES TOWARD SEX

Most social scientists agree that adolescents' attitudes toward sex—and toward premarital sex in particular—became more liberal during the late 1960s and 1970s and have become only slightly more conservative since then (Chilman, 1986). But the meaning of this change in attitudes is often misunderstood. Three points must be kept in mind. First, while it is certainly true that teenagers became more tolerant of sexual relations before marriage, it is also true that adults themselves became more permissive of premarital sex during this same time period (Clayton and Bokemeier, 1980). In other words, society as a whole, not simply young people, changed its views toward sex. Second, the changes in attitudes toward premarital sex among adolescents during the late 1960s and early 1970s and the trend toward greater conservatism during the 1980s cannot be understood apart from many other attitudinal changes that took place during this historical era. Although attitudes toward premarital sex changed, many other attitudes shifted in the same direction (for example, attitudes toward racial equality and women's rights). Thus trends in sexual attitudes are best understood as a part of a larger attitudinal shift. Finally, although adolescents become more permissive of premarital intercourse, they did not become proponents of promiscuity, "free love," or casual sex. Being emotionally in-

Although adolescents became more sexually permissive during the 1970s, they did not become promiscuous. Most sexually active teenagers today are likely to be monogamous. *(Barbara Alper/Stock, Boston)*

volved, rather than being legally married, became the important criterion for judging the acceptability of sexual involvement.

Although young people have become more permissive over the past three decades, adolescents clearly do not favor sexual promiscuity or sexual exploitation. Surveys indicate that the majority of adolescents believe that openness, honesty, and fidelity are important elements of a sexual relationship. Although an adolescent may have a series of sexual partners over a period of time, he or she is likely to be monogamous within each relationship, a pattern known as **serial monogamy.** And most young people oppose "exploitation, pressure, or force in sex; sex solely for the sake of physical enjoyment without a personal relationship; and sex between people too young to understand what they are getting into" (Conger, 1977a, p. 283).

Another important trend in young people's changing attitudes toward sex has been the decline in popularity of the double standard. In past eras, many people believed that premarital sex was permissible for men but not for women. But most adolescents today believe that males and females should follow the same standards for premarital sexual behavior (Ferrell, Tolone, and Walsh, 1977; King, Balswick, and Robinson, 1977). This shift toward a single standard of sexual conduct, which began during the late 1960s and accelerated during the early 1970s, was related, no doubt, to other large-scale attitudinal shifts in matters related to women's rights and sexual equality. Although the double standard has waned, it has not disappeared: Aggressive sexual behavior is still more accepted among adolescent males than females (Goodchilds and Zellman, 1984).

It appears, then, that what has taken place—

not only in sexual values and attitudes but across a range of topics—has been a shift away from conformity to institutionalized norms and toward a perspective that places greater emphasis on the individual's personal judgment and values (Conger, 1975). Today, despite stereotypes and parents' concerns to the contrary, most adolescents are neither preoccupied with sex nor anxious about it. Indeed, as we shall see, being sexually active during adolescence—and being comfortable about it—has become part of the normal adolescent experience.

## SEXUAL BEHAVIOR

Because of the controversies surrounding premarital intercourse, most of the research conducted on the sexual behavior of adolescents has focused on this single activity. While this is undoubtedly an important topic of concern, it is also wise to remember that a good deal of the sexual activity of adolescents—even sexually experienced adolescents—involves activities other than sexual intercourse, such as necking and petting. Moreover, because most individuals do not begin their sexual careers with intercourse but progress toward it through stages of gradually increasing intimacy, it is important to view intercourse as one activity in a long progression, rather than as an isolated behavior.

**The stages of sexual activity**   When do individuals first begin experimenting with sex, and is there a fairly common order of activities in which adolescents proceed toward intercourse? Most adolescents' first experience with sex falls into the category of **autoerotic behavior**—sexual behavior that is experienced alone (Katchadourian, 1990). The most common autoerotic activities reported by adolescents are having erotic fantasies (about three-quarters of all teenagers report having sexual fantasies,

mainly about television figure or movie stars) and masturbation (reported by about half of all adolescent boys and one-fourth of all adolescent girls). According to one study (Sorensen, 1973), most girls who masturbated began at around age 12, whereas most boys began at around age 14. This sex difference parallels differences in the age of puberty, with girls maturing, on average, about two years earlier than boys.

By the time most adolescents have reached high school, they have "crossed the line from autoerotic to **sociosexual behaviors**" (Katchadourian, 1990, p. 335). (Sociosexual behaviors are those involving another person.) Most studies indicate that the developmental progression of sexual behaviors, from less intimate to more intimate, has not changed very much over the past 30 years and that the sequence in which males and females engage in various sexual activities is remarkably similar. Necking and petting are more common activities and occur earlier than genital contact or intercourse, which in turn occur earlier than oral sex, although there is some evidence that teenagers are engaging in oral sex at an earlier age today than in the past (Newcomer and Udry, 1985). Although boys engage in these activities at a somewhat earlier age than girls, the similarities in age of first experience and in prevalence are far more striking than the differences.

### Adolescent premarital intercourse

*The prevalence of premarital intercourse among contemporary American youth.*   Estimates of the prevalence of premarital intercourse among American adolescents vary considerably from study to study, depending on the nature of the sample surveyed and the year and region in which the study was undertaken. Only a few studies have examined premarital intercourse among adolescents younger than age 15. These indicate that, overall, about 12 percent of boys and 6 percent of girls report having intercourse by age 13 (Katchadourian, 1990). There are vast regional and ethnic differences in the prevalence of sexual activity during the junior high school years, however (Dreyer, 1982; Miller and Simon, 1980). Thus, while only 12 percent of white males are sexually active by this age, 19 percent of Hispanic males and 42 percent of African-American males are (Hayes, 1987). The comparable figures for girls are 5 percent, 4 percent, and 10 percent, respectively. There are also large regional differences in the prevalence of early sexual intercourse, with sexual activity occurring earlier in rural and inner-city communities than in the suburbs. One recent study, for example, found that more than half of all eighth-graders living in rural Maryland reported having had sexual intercourse—about twice the rate found in studies of nationwide samples of adolescents from this age group (Alexander et al., 1989). In this study of rural youth, and in studies of inner-city Baltimore teenagers (e.g., Zabin et al., 1986b), about 85 percent of African-American male 14 year-olds surveyed report having had intercourse. As noted earlier, the prevalence of early sexual activity is extremely culturally variable, and such variability is apparent even within American society.

Although these regional and ethnic variations make it difficult—if not misleading—to generalize about the "average" age at which American adolescents initiate sexual intercourse, national surveys of young people indicate that more adolescents are sexually active at an earlier age today than in the recent past. The best estimates we have are that by age 15, about 17 percent of boys and 6 percent of girls have had intercourse; by age 18, about 67 percent of boys and 44 percent of girls are no longer virgins; and by age 20, the percentages of sexually experienced young are 80 percent among boys and 70 percent among girls (see Fig. 11.1) (Katchadourian, 1990). Whatever one feels about these figures, one conclusion

**FIGURE 11.1**  About half of all American teenagers have had sexual intercourse by high school graduation. At all ages, intercourse is more common among boys.

is inescapable: Sexual intercourse during high school is now a part of the normative experience of adolescence in America.

As you can see from Figure 11.2 (page 360), however, there are substantial ethnic differences in age of sexual initiation. African-American adolescents are more likely to begin sexual activity earlier than other adolescents and to progress toward intercourse more quickly. This is readily apparent from Figure 11.2, which shows the cumulative percentage of sexually active adolescents at each age, separately for white, African-American, and Hispanic youth. These data indicate that African-American adolescents are much more likely to have had sexual intercourse at each age and that ethnic differences in the ages at which sex begins are most dramatic early in adolescence. Studies also indicate that rates of sexual activity are higher among economically disadvantaged

**FIGURE 11.2**  This chart shows the cumulative percentage of sexually active adolescents at various ages, by sex and ethnicity. (Hayes, 1987)

youth, in all ethnic groups. Interestingly, early sexual activity is more common among African-American youth attending all-black schools than among their peers in integrated schools (Furstenberg et al., 1987), indicating the importance of the social context in which teenagers live as an influence on their sexual behavior.

There is a large difference, of course, between having intercourse once and being sexually active on a regular basis—a distinction that seems to get lost in discussions of sexual activity among youth. How frequently do teenagers have intercourse? The average sexually experienced high school girl has sexual inter-

course between two and three times each month. However, about 15 percent of the high school–aged girls who report having had sexual intercourse have done so only once (Zelnick, Kantner, and Ford, 1981). Interestingly, although African-American youngsters generally begin sexual activity at an earlier age than their peers, sexually active African-American teenagers have intercourse less frequently than other sexually active adolescents (Hayes, 1987). There also is little evidence that young people are sexually promiscuous: The majority of teenage respondents who have engaged in premarital intercourse have had only one sexual partner, and fewer than 10 percent had had more than three (Zelnick, Kantner, and Ford, 1981). Consistent with their attitudes toward premarital sex, teenagers' sexual behavior is not promiscuous.

**Rape and sexual abuse during adolescence**
Although most research on adolescent sexual activity has focused on voluntary sexual behavior between consenting individuals, there is growing public awareness that a significant minority of teenagers are forced to have sex against their will (Moore et al., 1989). This includes adolescents who have been the victims of forcible rape by a stranger, sexual abuse within the family, or **date rape**—when a young person, typically a woman, is forced by a date to have sex against her will (Carlson, 1987). Date rape continues to be a serious problem on college campuses as well as within the younger adolescent population.

Because both perpetrators and victims of sexual assaults are often reluctant to admit their experience, it is difficult to obtain accurate estimates of the numbers of adolescents who have been sexually victimized. According to one team of researchers, however, more than 10 percent of white females, and more than 5 percent of African-American females, report having had nonvoluntary sexual intercourse before age 18 (Moore et al., 1989). Women who were most likely to have been raped during adolescence were those who lived apart from their parents before age 16; who were physically, emotionally, or mentally limited; who were raised at or below the poverty level; or whose parents abused alcohol or used other drugs. Indeed, two-thirds of all women who had three or more of these risk factors were raped as adolescents.

These figures do not include adolescents who have been forced to engage in sexual activity other than intercourse, and as such, clearly underestimate the proportion of teenagers who have been sexually abused. Other estimates, which include all forms of nonvoluntary sex, however, suggest that between 15 and 25 percent of all women, and between 5 and 15 percent of all men, have been abused sexually before reaching adulthood. About one in ten women is the victim of incest before reaching 16 (Hogue, 1991).

*Changes in patterns of adolescent premarital intercourse.* We noted earlier that attitudes toward premarital intercourse during adolescence have become increasingly liberal since the mid-1960s and became especially so during the early 1970s. Not surprisingly, accompanying this shift in attitudes has been an equally noteworthy shift in the actual prevalence of adolescent premarital sex. The major changes have not been in behaviors such as necking and petting, but in the incidence and prevalence of intercourse among teenagers (Vener and Stewart, 1974). Presumably, teenagers have long distinguished between intercourse and other sexual activities in their values and actions, and what has shifted during the past three decades has been their stance specifically toward intercourse.

Three trends are of special interest. First, the overall percentage of American adolescents—of all ages—who have engaged in premarital sex accelerated markedly during the early 1970s but stabilized somewhat during the 1980s (Hayes, 1987; Ventura, 1984). For example, the proportion of high school youth who have had premarital intercourse rose from about 20 percent before the mid-1960s, to about 35 percent during the early 1970s, to approximately 50 percent in the late 1970s, and is still about 50 percent today (Hayes, 1987; Katchadourian, 1990). Among college students, the increase has been equally notable, but it occurred primarily during the period 1966–1973, when the prevalence rate rose from about 40 percent to about 75 percent; changes in the prevalence of premarital sex

## THE SEXES: THE INFLUENCES OF HORMONES AND FRIENDS ON ADOLESCENT SEXUAL BEHAVIOR

We noted earlier that increased interest in sex at adolescence is likely to have both biological and social causes. Specifically, adolescents are thought to become interested in sex in part because of increases in sex hormones at puberty and in part because sexual activity becomes accepted—even encouraged—in their peer group. But is one set of factors more important than the other? One recent series of studies, by J. Richard Udry and his colleagues (Smith, Udry, and Morris, 1985; Udry, 1987; Udry, Talbert, and Morris, 1986) suggests that a fuller understanding of adolescent sexual behavior comes from looking at biological and social influences *in interaction* rather than at either set of influences alone. However, the way in which hormones and friends influence sexual behavior at adolescence appears to be different for males than females.

According to Udry's studies, boys' and girls' initial interest in sex is influenced primarily by the surge in certain hormones—**testosterone,** to be specific—at puberty. Adolescents with higher levels of androgens (testosterone is an androgen) are more likely than their peers to report masturbating, thinking about sex, and planning to have sexual intercourse within the next year. This hormonal change therefore appears to increase adolescents' interest in sex and in their arousal when exposed to sexual stimuli.

Motivation to have sex is one thing; becoming sexually active is another. How important is the rise in testosterone levels at puberty in determining the onset of sexual intercourse? The answer appears to differ in boys and girls. Among boys, but not girls, the increased level of androgens is directly related to the likelihood of their being sexually active. Younger boys who were more mature biologically were more likely to be sexually active than older boys whose hormone levels were lower. Boys' sexual behavior is not *entirely* dependent on their hormone levels, however. The studies also found that boys who are more popular with girls in their school are more likely to initiate sex early than are boys who are less popular with girls. Although there is also some evidence that boys whose friends are sexually active are themselves more likely to be involved in sex, this seems more to do with hormones' influences than with friends' influence. Boys tend to have friends who are at a similar level of pubertal development and therefore may be more likely to have high testosterone levels and be sexually active. All in all, the evidence provided in these studies indicates a very strong biological influence on the sexual behavior of adolescent boys.

As you know from the earlier chapter on biological development during adolescence, androgens, including testosterone, contribute to in-

*continued on next page*

among college students since then have been less dramatic (Dreyer, 1982).

Second, the median age at which adolescents first engage in intercourse declined during this same time period (see Figure 11.3). For example, in 1971, the average age at first intercourse was 16.4 years. By 1976, this had declined to 16.1 years, and is slightly lower today. As we shall see in a later section, these figures are important to consider in discussions of sex education, because they indicate that programs which do not begin until the later creases in boys' sex drive as well as to the development of secondary sex characteristics like facial hair. Because of this, it is difficult to determine whether increases in androgens lead to increased sexual activity because of the increased sex drive (which may make boys with higher testosterone levels *want* to have sex more) or because of changes in their physical appearance (which may make them more attractive to girls). In girls, however, although androgens are responsible for increases in the sex drive, a different set of hormones—estrogens—are primarily responsible for changes in appearance, including breast development. Because of this, it is possible to study whether increased interest in sex among adolescent girls is more influenced by increases in sex drive or by changes in physical appearance (and, presumably, their sexual attractiveness to boys). Thus far, the answer appears to be both, although the effects of high androgen levels in girls seem to be stronger than the effects of changes in physical appearance.

Despite the effects of hormones on girls' sex drive, though, Udry's studies show that social factors are far more important in influencing girls' involvement in sexual intercourse than boys', especially among white girls (Udry and Billy, 1987). Although increases in androgens lead to increased interest in sex among girls, whether this interest is translated into behavior depends on their social environment. Among girls with high levels of androgens, those who have sexually permissive attitudes and friends who are sexually active are likely to engage in intercourse. But girls whose social environment is less encouraging of sex—even girls with high levels of androgens—are unlikely to be sexually active. In other words, whereas hormones seem to have a direct and powerful effect on the sexual behavior of boys, the impact of hormones on the sexual behavior of girls seems to depend on the social context in which they live.

To what can we attribute this sex difference? Udry hypothesizes that boys develop in an environment that is more uniformly tolerant and encouraging of sexual behavior than girls do. In this environment, all boys need is the jolt that the increase in androgens provides in order to become sexually active. For girls, however, the environment is more varied. Some girls develop within a context that permits or even encourages sexual activity; others do not. Although the increase in androgens also provides a jolt to the sexual motivation of the adolescent girl, if she develops within a context that places social controls on sexual activity, this hormonal awakening will not be translated into sexual experience.

years of high school may be too late for a substantial number of young people. Indeed, as of 1987, well over half of adolescent girls living in metropolitan areas had had sexual intercourse before turning 16 (Hayes, 1987).

Finally, the greatest recent increases in prevalence of premarital intercourse have been among white females. Before 1966, there were substantial gaps between boys and girls and between African-American females and white females. As Figure 11.4 shows, since about 1965 the proportion of sexually experienced

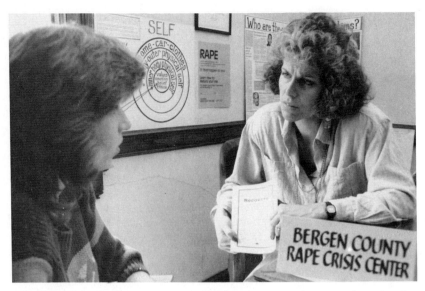

Precise estimates of the percentage of adolescents who have been raped or otherwise sexually abused are difficult to obtain. Some studies suggest that between 15 and 25 percent of all women have been sexually abused before reaching adulthood. *(Rhoda Sidney/Image Works)*

**FIGURE 11.3** The proportion of girls who are sexually active at an early age rose dramatically during the 1960s and 1970s. (Gans, 1990)

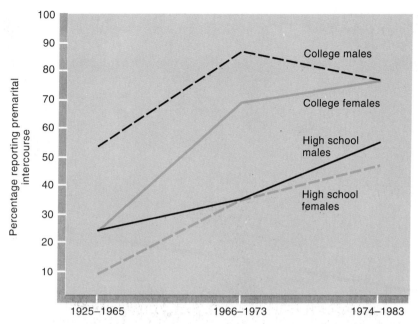

**FIGURE 11.4** Changes in the percentage of high school and college males and females who have experienced sexual intercourse in three historical eras. (Derived from Dreyer, 1982; Hayes, 1987; and Vrazzo, 1990)

high school males has doubled, but the proportion of sexually experienced high school females has *more than quadrupled.* Among college students, the proportion of boys who have had premarital intercourse has increased by 36 percent since 1965; for girls, the increase has been a remarkable 300 percent (Dreyer, 1982). As noted earlier, sex differences in rates of premarital intercourse today are minimal.

A similar, though less dramatic, picture of change emerges when we look at the prevalence of premarital intercourse among African-American and white teenage women. Between 1971 and 1976, the prevalence of premarital intercourse among African-American 15- to 19-year-old females increased by 19 percent. But during this same time period, there was a *41 percent increase* in the proportion of sexually experienced white girls of the same age (Zelnick, Kantner, and Ford, 1981). Be-

tween 1976 and 1982, however, the percentage of African-American 15- to 19-year-olds who were sexually experienced declined, while the comparable percentage among white teenagers continued to increase. Thus rates of premarital intercourse in different subgroups of American adolescents have converged with the passing of time.

**Adolescent sexual behavior in perspective** Whether adults approve or not, sexual activity has become a part of the *normal* American teenager's life. Nevertheless, it is important to understand these trends for what they really are. Although many parents, educators, and other adults are alarmed and concerned about sexual activity among the young, it is clear that for most adolescents, sexual involvement is accompanied by affection, emotional involvement, and commitment to a relationship and

Well over half of all American adolescents have had sexual intercourse by the time they graduate from high school. By the end of college, about 80% are sexually experienced. *(Bob Daemmrich/Image Works)*

that by no stretch of the imagination can the majority of today's young people be described as promiscuous or morally lax in matters of sex.

Although it is interesting to speculate on the causes of these changes in adolescents' sexual behavior—the increased availability of the birth control pill, the overall liberalization of social attitudes, and the earlier age of puberty have all been suggested—the more pressing issue is how society ought to react to the changed nature of sex during adolescence. Premarital sex is not limited to males, to minority youngsters, or to adolescents with emotional problems. It is a part of life for the av-

erage teenager. The longer we ignore this—by failing to provide adequate sex education, by limiting the accessibility of effective contraception, and by not dealing with the issue squarely—the more difficulties society, and young people in particular, will face.

## PSYCHOLOGICAL AND SOCIAL CHARACTERISTICS OF SEXUALLY ACTIVE ADOLESCENTS

For many years, researchers studied the psychological and social characteristics of adolescents who engaged in premarital sex, assuming that sexually active teenagers were more trou-

The percentage of younger American adolescents having premarital sex increased dramatically during the 1970s and 1980s. Adolescents become sexually active at a much earlier age today than was the case previously. *(Monique Manceau/Photo Researchers)*

bled than their peers. This view has been replaced as sexual activity has become more prevalent.

Indeed, several recent studies show that sexual activity during adolescence is decidedly *not* associated with psychological disturbance. Two studies, for example, showed that adolescents who became sexually active earlier than their peers had levels of self-esteem and life satisfaction similar to that of other adolescents (Billy et al., 1988; Jessor et al., 1983). Another study indicated that unmarried girls who became pregnant were more likely to have high self-esteem and strong feelings of efficacy than the reverse (Robbins, Kaplan, and Martin, 1985). It does seem to be the case, however, that early sexual activity is associated with being from a lower socioeconomic class and with a more general attitude and behavioral profile that includes involvement with drugs

and alcohol, a low level of religious involvement, tolerance of deviant behavior, a lower value on academic achievement, and a higher orientation toward independence (Jessor et al., 1983). In general, though, studies indicate that these characteristics are likely to *lead to,* rather than result from, earlier sexual activity (Elliott and Morse, 1989).

Researchers also have asked whether adolescents who become sexually active earlier than their peers have different family histories than other adolescents. In general, studies have not supported the widely held view that monitoring by parents and communication between parents and children have a strong impact on adolescent sexual behavior (Casper, 1990; Moore et al., 1986; Newcomer and Udry, 1984). That is, in general, adolescents whose parents keep close tabs on them or who discuss sex with them are neither more nor less likely to be sexually active. Not surprisingly, the effect of parent-child communication about sex on adolescent sexual behavior depends on who is doing the communicating and what is being communicated. In general, communication between adolescents (both boys and girls) and their mothers about sex is associated with less sexual activity, but communication between fathers and sons about sex is associated with increased sexual activity—presumably because fathers tacitly encourage their sons to become sexually active (Brooks-Gunn and Furstenberg, Jr., 1989). Not surprisingly, parental attitudes may make a difference, especially for girls: Among girls with liberal parents, talking about sex is associated with more sexual activity; this is not true among girls with conservative parents, however (Fisher, 1989).

Overall, however, most studies find that the impact of parent-adolescent communication on adolescent's sexual behavior is very small, especially compared with other factors (Casper, 1990). One family factor that does appear to make a difference, however—especially for girls—is household composition. In general, adolescents whose parents are in the process of divorcing as well as girls who live in single-parent households—regardless of when (or if) a divorce took place—are more likely to be sexually active than their peers (Miller and Bingham, 1989; Newcomer and Udry, 1987). One hypothesis, consistent with what we saw in the earlier chapter on the adolescent's family, is that parental divorce temporarily disrupts the adolescent's behavior, leading him or her into early involvement with drugs, alcohol, and minor delinquency, which increases the likelihood of sex.

Why should growing up in a single-parent home affect girls' sexual behavior more than that of boys, however? At least two possibilities exist. One possibility, which we encountered earlier in this chapter, is that social influences on girls' sexual behavior are in general more varied than those of boys. Boys' parents may

not attempt to exert great control over their sexual activity regardless of whether the household has one parent or two. Consequently, boys from one- and two-parent homes may be equally likely to be sexually active. Girls' sexual behavior, in contrast, may be more subject to parents' controls. Single-parent homes are typically more permissive than two-parent homes (Dornbusch et al., 1985), and this difference in control may be enough to make a difference in girls' sexual activity. Because monitoring appears to have little impact on adolescent sexual activity, however, this explanation is not sufficient. An alternative possibility is that single-parent mothers are more likely to be dating than married mothers and in so doing, may inadvertently be role models of sexual activity to their adolescents. To the extent that this modeling effect is stronger between parents and children of the same sex, we would expect to find a more powerful effect of growing up in a single-parent home on the sexual behavior of daughters than sons.

Less is known about the influence of people other than parents on adolescents' sexual behavior. It does seem to be the case, however, that adolescents are more likely to be having sexual intercourse when their peers are sexually active (Udry, 1987), when they *believe* that their friends are sexually active (whether or not their friends actually are) (Brooks-Gunn and Furstenberg, Jr., 1989), and when they have older siblings, who, presumably, model more sexually advanced behavior (Rodgers and Rowe, 1989). There are age, sex, and ethnic differences in the relative importance of parental and peer influence, however. As one would expect, peers become increasingly more influential with age (Treboux and Busch-Rossnagel, 1990a), and peer influences appear to be somewhat greater for females than males (Treboux and Busch-Rossnagel, 1990b). As well, African-American adolescents report relatively less familial influence over their sexual behavior than do white adolescents, whereas

Hispanic adolescents report relatively more (Scott and Owen, 1990).

## SEX DIFFERENCES IN THE MEANING OF SEX

Any discussion of the psychosocial significance of sexual experience during adolescence must be sensitive to the very substantial sex differences in the way in which early sexual activity is experienced. Despite the convergence of males' and females' *rates* of sexual activity, the early sexual experiences of adolescent boys and girls are usually very different in nature and, as a consequence, are imbued with very different *meanings*. In other words, the sexual behavior of males and females may be similar, but the sexual socialization of males and females is quite different—although not as much as has been the case previously.

As noted earlier, the typical adolescent boy's first sexual experience is in early adolescence, through masturbation (Gagnon, 1972). At the outset, then, the sexual socialization of the adolescent boy typically places sex outside of an interpersonal context. Before adolescent boys begin dating, they have generally already experienced orgasm and know how to arouse themselves sexually. For males, the development of sexuality during adolescence revolves around efforts to integrate the capacity to form close relationships into an already existing sense of sexual capability.

Yet at the time of first intercourse, boys are likely to keep matters of sex and intimacy separate. Boys often have as their first partner someone they describe as a "casual date" or "pickup" (Carns, 1973). Indeed, in one-third of the cases, boys never sleep with their first sexual partner again, and fewer than 25 percent of adolescent boys sleep with their first partner more than five times after their first time together (Simon, Berger, and Gagnon, 1972). Generally, it is the male member of a couple who is likely to initiate sex, and inter-

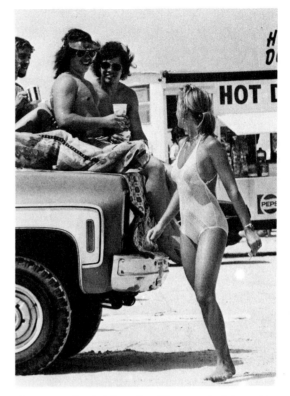

There are substantial gender differences in the way in which early sexual activity is experienced psychologically. For adolescent boys, early sexual relationships are often brief, impersonal, and associated with a sense of achievement *(Rick Smolan/Stock, Boston)*

estingly, the typical male reports more love for a woman who lost her virginity with him than for a woman who lost her virginity with a previous partner. His own loss of virginity, however, has no impact on his feelings of affection in a relationship (Peplau, Rubin, and Hill, 1977). These findings suggest that the early sexual experiences of males are often interpreted not in terms of intimacy and emotional involvement but in terms of achievement, or "scoring." And males typically report that the people to whom they describe their first sexual liaison—generally, male peers—are overwhelmingly approving (Carns, 1973; Miller and Simon, 1980). It is little surprise, when looked at in light of these findings, that the most common immediate reactions among adolescent males to having intercourse for the first time are "excitement" (46 percent), "satisfaction" (43 percent), exhilaration (43 percent), or "happiness" (43 percent) (Sorensen, 1973).

The typical girl's first experience is likely to be very different and likely to leave her feeling very differently as well. Although the majority of adolescent girls masturbate, masturbation is a far less prevalent activity among girls than among boys, and it is far less regularly practiced. Thus the typical adolescent girl, in contrast to the typical boy, is more likely to experience sex for the first time in an interpersonal relationship. Unlike her male counterpart, then, the adolescent girl begins her sexual career not alone but with someone else. For her, the development of sexuality involves the integration of sexual activity into an existing capacity for intimacy and emotional involvement. The girl's sexual script is one that, from the outset, tinges sex with romance, love, and intimacy.

Boys and girls also encounter a set of social attitudes that differ in a very important way: Society still is much more discouraging of sexual activity outside the context of emotional involvement among adolescent girls than boys (Carns, 1973; Goodchilds and Zellman, 1984). Because of the possibility of pregnancy, the potential adverse consequences of premarital sexual activity are far more serious for girls than for boys. For this reason, society monitors the sexual activity of girls more carefully, and girls are more likely to be encouraged to take a cautious approach in matters of sex.

Not surprisingly, then, at the time of first intercourse, the adolescent girl's first sexual partner is likely to be a person she describes as someone she was "planning to marry" or was "in love with" at the time (Carns, 1973; Kallen

and Stephenson, 1982). In contrast with men, nearly two-thirds of all young women have sex with their first partner many times thereafter (Simon, Berger, and Gagnon, 1972). There is a social meaning to losing one's virginity that is still today very different for young women and for young men, and women typically report feeling more love for a man if he was their first sexual partner (Peplau, Rubin, and Hill, 1977). After having intercourse for the first time, the typical adolescent girl is more likely to encounter disapproval or mixed feelings on the part of others in whom she confides (generally speaking, peers) than is the typical boy (Carns, 1973). And she is more likely to report feeling "afraid" (63 percent), "guilty" (36 percent), "worried" (35 percent), and "embarrassed" (31 percent) than happy, excited, or exhilarated (Sorensen, 1973). Thus for the adolescent girl, early sexual experience is nearly always tied to emotional involvement and an enduring relationship and, more often than not, complicated by fears of becoming pregnant. Although young women are more likely today than they were fifteen years ago to admit to their friends that they have lost their virginity soon after the event has occurred, boys still are more likely than women to tell their friends soon after having intercourse for the first time because it is easier to do so when the act has not been accompanied by emotional involvement (Kallen and Stephenson, 1982).

## HOMOSEXUALITY DURING ADOLESCENCE

Much discussion about homosexuality during adolescence is muddied with confusion and misinformation about the nature and antecedents of homosexuality. In attempting to separate fact from myth, we need to keep in mind several important distinctions.

First, there is an important distinction between engaging in homosexual activity or having homosexual feelings, on the one hand, and having an exclusive and enduring preference for sexual activity with people of the same sex, on the other. It is not uncommon, for example, for young adolescents to engage in sex play with members of the same sex or to have questions about the nature of their feelings for same-sex peers. Indeed, one study indicated that by age 16, over 20 percent of adolescent boys had engaged in homosexual activity to the point of orgasm (Kinsey, Pomeroy, and Martin, 1984). But even though many adolescents have such homosexual experiences, nearly all young people—over 90 percent, in fact—develop an exclusive preference for heterosexual relationships by the end of adolescence. And contrary to myths about the increasing prevalence of homosexuality in contemporary American society, the proportion has remained at or near this level since the mid-1940s, when researchers began studying the phenomenon (Hunt, 1974).

A second distinction is that between homosexuality as an exclusive preference and homosexuality as an interest that may exist simultaneously with strong heterosexual interests. Many people mistakenly view sexual preference as an "either-or" attribute, with individuals being either exclusively heterosexual or exclusively homosexual. In fact, of the 8 percent of Americans who do not develop an exclusive preference for heterosexual relationships, only one-third are exclusively homosexual in their orientation. Nearly twice as many describe themselves as having *both* heterosexual and homosexual interests (Conger, 1977a).

Finally, a great deal of confusion about homosexuality results because people tend to confuse sexual preference (the extent to which someone prefers heterosexual activity, homosexual activity, or both), sex-role behavior (the extent to which an individual behaves in traditionally "masculine" or "feminine" ways), and gender identity (which gender an individual believes he or she is psychologically). There is no simple connection between an adolescent's sexual preference and his or her sex-role behavior. Thus individuals with strong or even exclusive preferences for homosexual relationships exhibit the same range of masculine and feminine behaviors characteristic of individuals with strong or exclusive heterosexual interests. In other words, exclusively gay men (like exclusively heterosexual men) may act in very masculine, very feminine, or both masculine and feminine ways; and the same holds true for exclusively lesbian and exclusively heterosexual women. Along similar lines, individuals with homosexual interests are generally not confused about their gender identity—at least, no more confused than are individuals with heterosexual interests.

Studies of the antecedents of homosexuality generally have focused on two sets of factors: biological influences, such as hormones, and social influences, including the parent-child relationship and early patterns of play. More is known about the development of homosexuality among men than women—the prevalence of homosexuality is much greater among men than women—but the weight of the evidence thus far suggests that an adolescent's sexual preference is likely to be shaped by a complex interaction of social and biological influences (Green, 1980, 1987; Savin-Williams, 1988).

Support for the contention that homosexuality is at least partly biologically determined comes from several sources. You may recall that in Chapter 1, a distinction was made between the organizational and activational roles of hormones on behavior. The hormonal changes of puberty activate sexual behavior, but the particular pattern of sexual behavior that is activated may depend on the way in which certain hormonal pathways in the brain were organized early in life. There is suggestive, albeit indirect, evidence that gay and lesbian adults may have been exposed prenatally to certain hormones that in theory could affect sexual orientation through their effect on early brain organization (Savin-Williams, 1988). Second, there is some evidence that homosexuality has a strong genetic component, since sexual orientation is more likely to be shared among close than distant relatives and between identical than fraternal twins (Savin-Williams, 1988). Although environmental explanations for this similarity cannot be ruled out, chances are that at least some of the predisposition to develop a homosexual orientation is inherited.

One popular theory of biological-environmental interaction is that *early* biological predispositions may channel some youngsters into patterns of play and social relationships that can lead to the development of homosexuality. Studies suggest that sex hormones may influence preferences for aggressive activities, which, consequently, may be related to preferences for stereotypically masculine or feminine behavior. Thus, for example, boys who are biologically predisposed toward timidity may avoid rough play as young children and gradually come to prefer activities that are more typical of young girls.

These early behavioral preferences may come to affect the parent-child relationship in ways that increase the likelihood of an individual developing a homosexual orientation. Several studies suggest that a higher proportion of homosexuals than heterosexuals report having had problems in their early family relationships and, specifically, in their relationships with their father. The stereotype of the homosexual's father as cold and distant once was rejected as an artifact of poor research designs, which focused exclusively on unhappy or psychologically distressed homosexuals (who, given their psychological distress, might be expected to report disrupted family relationships). But more carefully designed studies have offered at least partial confirmation of this notion. Both gay and lesbian adults are more likely than heterosexuals to describe their fathers as distant and rejecting. Whereas gay men are more likely than heterosexuals to report having had close and generally positive relationships with their mothers, lesbians are more likely than heterosexuals to describe their mothers as cold and unpleasant (Bell et al., 1981).

It is difficult to conclude that these disruptions in the parent-child relationship are the primary cause of homosexuality, however. Researchers now believe that, at least for many gay men, early, biologically-influenced preferences for feminine behavior may have alienated these boys from their fathers and from other boys, and these youngsters may have grown up seeking the affection from males that they did not receive as children. One recent study, for example, showed that the majority of young boys who behave like girls grow up to be gay adults (Green, 1987). Several other studies also suggest that nonconformity with gender roles during early childhood is an important predictor of adult homosexuality (Bell et al., 1981).

Although these studies point to certain factors that appear more often than not in the early histories of homosexuals, the research evidence does not indicate that *all* individuals who show patterns of gender nonconformity or who have distant relations with their fathers inevitably become homosexual. Nor does research show that all homosexuals have identical developmental histories. For example, while it is true that homosexuals are more likely than heterosexuals to describe their parents in negative terms, not all gay and lesbian individuals feel this way. Indeed, only about half do, suggesting that a large number of homosexuals had quite positive family relationships growing up. And, of course, many heterosexuals describe their parents in exceedingly negative terms. Similarly, although the majority of boys with persistently feminine behavior preferences may grow up to be gay, a substantial number of boys with this preference do not.

It is important to bear in mind that homosexuality is not considered by mental health experts to be a form of psychopathology, an indicator of an underlying psychological disturbance, or a condition warranting psychological treatment. Perhaps as we begin to understand more about the interplay among biological and social factors that contribute to the development of a homosexual orientation, our attitudes toward homosexuality will change for the better. Indeed, as one expert noted, "Society tends to treat . . . homosexuals as if they had a choice about their sexual orientation, when in fact they have no more choice about how they develop than heterosexuals do" (Marmor, quoted in Brody, 1986, p. 17).

Indeed, prejudice and ignorance about homosexuality may cause significant psychological distress for gay and lesbian adolescents, especially if they encounter hostility from those around them. As you know by now, the developmental tasks in the domains of identity, intimacy, and sexuality present formidable challenges for many teenagers. These challenges may be exacerbated for gay and lesbian adolescents, who may be forced to resolve these issues without the same degree of social support as their heterosexual peers.

## CONTRACEPTIVE USE

One of the reasons for the great concern of adults over the sexual activity of adolescents is the failure of many sexually active young people to use birth control measures regularly. Only half of all young women reported having used some method of birth control the first time they had intercourse, and nearly one-sixth of all 15- to 19-year-old sexually active women report *never* having used any contraception. About 40 percent of sexually active teenagers use birth control sporadically. Only one-third of sexually active adolescents always use birth control. While these figures are still worrisome, they show a clear improvement in adolescent contraceptive behavior during the last decade.

In 1976, for example, nearly two-thirds of sexually active young women reported that they had not used contraception during their first intercourse, and more than 35 percent reported never using birth control. In general, older adolescents are more likely to use contraception than younger ones, and adolescents are more likely to use contraception when they plan in advance to have sex than when intercourse is unplanned (Hayes, 1987).

Among adolescents who do use contraception, the most popular method is by far the birth control pill, which is used by approximately 60 percent of sexually active teenage girls. About 20 percent of girls report that their partner uses condoms, and an additional 5 percent report using a diaphragm. Withdrawal, a highly ineffective method of preventing pregnancy, unfortunately is still used by a large number of teenagers, as is the rhythm method—a method of birth control that requires more regular menstrual cycling than many teenagers have and more careful monitoring of menstrual cycling than most teenagers are capable of. Other methods, such as the intrauterine device (IUD), are not widely used by teenagers (Hayes, 1987).

Why do so few adolescents use contraception regularly? Social scientists point to several factors. First, for a sizeable minority of adolescents, contraceptives are not readily available— or if they are, young people may not know where to get them. Approximately 15 percent of adolescent girls and 25 percent of adolescent boys report that they did not use contraceptives when they had sex for the first time because they could not get them (Hayes, 1987). This is likely to be an especially important barrier among younger adolescents, who may feel uncomfortable discussing their sexual activity with parents or other adults whose help or consent may be necessary in order to obtain birth control. Having ready access to a free, confidential family planning service that does not require parents' consent is a strong predictor of whether adolescents will use contraceptives at all or use them consistently (Brooks-Gunn and Furstenberg, 1989; Chilman, 1980).

Second, many young people are insufficiently educated about sex, contraception, and pregnancy (Trussell, 1989). Many young people do not fully understand that the likelihood of pregnancy varies over the course of a woman's menstrual cycle, and more than half mistakenly believe that it is during menstruation that the risk of pregnancy is greatest (Zelnick and Kantner, 1973). At the time of first intercourse, about one-third of all teenagers who do not use contraception fail to do so because they don't know about contraception or didn't think about using contraceptives (Hayes, 1987). Among sexually active teenagers, 20 percent of all girls and more than 40 percent of all boys usually "just trust to luck" that pregnancy will not result from intercourse (Sorensen, 1973). Unfortunately, few sexually active adolescents who fail to use contraception remain lucky for very long.

Psychological factors also play a role in adolescents' failure to use contraception. Although it certainly is a misconception that many young women unconsciously want to become pregnant, many young people nevertheless do not recognize the seriousness of pregnancy and take the possibility lightly (Hayes, 1987). More than 25 percent of non-users report that they or their partners simply did not want to use birth control. From a cognitive perspective, the limited ability of young adolescents to engage in long-term, hypothetical thinking, and their occasionally egocentric tendency to believe that they are immune from the forces that affect others may impede their consideration of pregnancy as a likely outcome of sexual activity. Perhaps most important, many adolescents fail to use birth control because doing so would be tantamount to admitting that they are planfully and willingly sexually active (Cvetkovich et al., 1975). Going on

the pill or purchasing a condom requires an adolescent to acknowledge that he or she is having sexual relations. For many young people, this is an extremely difficult admission to make. This may be especially true for young women who feel ambivalent and guilty about sleeping with someone for the first time. And many teenagers do not anticipate having intercourse (Trussell, 1989).

One recent study of "sex guilt" documented the role that emotional factors play in influencing contraceptive use. Individuals who feel very guilty about having sex are less inclined to be sexually active, but when they are, they are also less inclined to use effective contraception—perhaps because their guilt inhibits their ability to plan for sex (Gerrard, 1987). When sexual standards become more permissive, many individuals who would otherwise feel guilty about having sex are drawn into sexual relationships. Unfortunately, their feelings of guilt are not changed by the aura of permissiveness, and as a consequence, they have sex without using effective contraception. As attitudes become more conservative, fewer individuals are sexually active, but those who are use contraception more effectively. Presumably, during more conservative times individuals who feel guilty about sex have enough support to abstain from sexual activity. One lesson from these studies is that inducing feelings of guilt about sex may have different consequences for sexual behavior depending on the prevailing social norms. During conservative periods, the guilt may inhibit sexual activity; during times of liberal attitudes, however, sex guilt may actually increase careless sex. Along these lines, studies indicate that religious adolescents are less likely to be sexually active, but also less likely to use birth control if they are having sex (Studer and Thornton, 1987).

More interesting, perhaps, is research indicating that the rate of adolescent pregnancy is substantially higher in the United States than in other industrialized countries—despite the fact the rate of teenage sexual activity in the United States is comparable to that in other countries (Jones et al., 1987). For numerous reasons, American teenagers are less likely than their counterparts in other industrialized countries to use contraception regularly and effectively. According to one widely-cited study, this is because nonmarital sex is portrayed in the United States as "romantic, exciting, and titillating . . . [while] at the same time, young people get the message that good girls should say no" (Jones et al., 1987, p. 239). As yet another expert wrote, "Sex saturates American life—in television programs, movies, and advertisements—yet the media generally fail to communicate responsible attitudes toward sex, with birth control remaining a taboo subject" (Westoff, 1988, p. 254). One result of this set of mixed messages is that the rates of both teenage childbearing and teenage abortion are substantially higher here than in many industrialized nations (Westoff, 1988).

Taken together, this evidence suggests that there is a great deal that adults can do to improve the contraceptive behavior of adolescents. First, adults can see that contraceptives are made accessible to the young people who feel they need them. In many large cities, for example, condoms are now distributed to teenagers at school. Second, adults can provide sex education at an early enough age to instruct young people in the fundamentals of pregnancy and birth control before, rather than after, the adolescents have become sexually active. Third, parents and teachers can make adolescents feel more free to talk about their sexual interests and concerns, so that young people will be more apt to look at their own behavior seriously and thoughtfully. Finally, the mass media need to portray sex in a more responsible fashion, showing contraception use along with sexual activity. When, for instance, was the last time you saw a couple in a film or on television interrupt sex in order to discuss birth control?

## Teenage Pregnancy and Childbearing

### THE NATURE AND EXTENT OF THE PROBLEM

Given the high rate of sexual activity and poor record of contraceptive use among contemporary adolescents, it comes as little surprise to learn that many young women become

Nearly one-fourth of American young women become pregnant before their 18th birthday. About half of these pregnancies result in the birth of a baby. *(Gale Zucker/Stock, Boston)*

pregnant before the end of adolescence. Recent statistics indicate that nearly one-fourth of American young women experience pregnancy before the age of 18 and about 45 percent before their twenty-first birthday. Among black youth, over 40 percent experience pregnancy by age 18 and nearly two-thirds by age 21. These rates are actually slightly lower than they were in the 1970s, not because rates of sexual activity have declined, but primarily because of more effective contraceptive use among sexually active teenagers (Furstenberg et al., 1989; Hayes, 1987). In 1988, however, the rate of teenage childbearing increased, either because of increased sexual activity, decreased use of contraceptives, decreased access to abortion, or some combination of these factors (Barringer, 1990).

It is important to keep in mind that not all adolescent pregnancies result in childbirth. About 40 percent of all teenage pregnancies are aborted, and slightly more than 10 percent end in miscarriage. Among women who carry their pregnancy full term, the vast majority—over 90 percent—keep and raise the infant, while one in ten chooses to have the child adopted. Thus, of the approximately 1 million pregnancies recorded among teenage women each year, approximately half end in abortion or miscarriage, about 45 percent result in the birth of an infant who would be raised by his or her mother (with or without the help of a spouse or other family members), and about 5 percent result in the birth of an infant put up for adoption (Hayes, 1987) (see Figure 11.5).

It is important to distinguish between pregnancies and actual births—a distinction that seems often to get lost in debates over the consequences of teenage pregnancy. Because of the many pregnant adolescents choosing abortion, the *birth rate* among teenage women is far lower than it would otherwise be, and it may surprise you to learn that the birth rate among adolescent women today is considerably lower than it was in previous eras. Contrary to the popular idea that teenage childbearing has reached epidemic proportions in this country is the truth of the matter: Relatively more women gave birth to an infant before reaching adulthood in previous decades than is the case today—by a large margin. For example, in 1955 the rate of childbearing among women between the ages of 15 and 19 was ninety births per 1,000 women. Today, by contrast, it is less than fifty births per 1,000 women (Furstenberg et al., 1987).

If teenage childbearing is less prevalent today than in earlier eras, why does the issue receive so much attention in the popular press? First, while the rate of childbearing may be lower today than before, the proportion of teenage childbearing that occurs *out of wedlock* is much higher. In earlier eras, adolescents who became pregnant were much more likely to marry before the child was born. Their pregnancy and childbearing did not cause as much concern, because they were "legitimized" by marriage. One source estimates that about half of all adolescent women who married during the late 1950s were pregnant at the time of marriage (Furstenberg et al., 1987). As recently as 1955, out-of-wedlock births accounted for only about 14 percent of all births to young women. But by 1984, this had skyrocketed to more than 55 percent, and by 1988, to 66 percent (Furstenberg, 1991; Furstenberg et al., 1987). Clearly, society is more tolerant of single parenthood and of nonmarital pregnancy, and many more women choose this option today than did so in the past. Nonetheless, one reason for the special concern about teenage childbearing in the popular press is that such a high proportion of it occurs outside of marriage. Whether this *should* be a concern, however—questions of morals aside for the moment—is still hotly debated, as we shall see in a moment. Indeed, there is some evidence that the fates of a large group of adolescent mothers are *worsened*, not bettered, by marrying the father of their child.

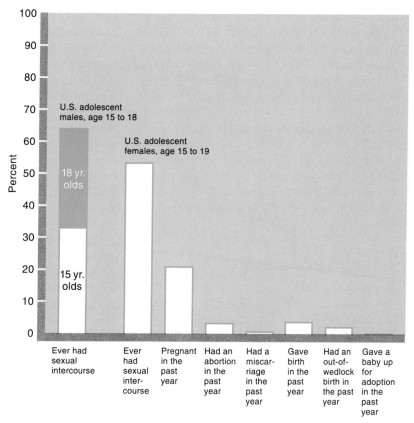

Percentage of sexual intercourse, pregnancies, and out-of-wedlock births were tabulated from 1988 data. Percentage of abortions, miscarriages, and births were tabulated from 1984 data. Percentage of adoptions were tabulated from 1982 data.

**FIGURE 11.5** An overview of adolescent pregnancy and parenting in the United States. (Office of Technology Assessment, 1991)

A second reason for widespread concern is that rates of teenage childbearing vary markedly across ethnic and socioeconomic groups. White and middle-class women are more likely to abort their pregnancies than are non-white and poor women, and, as a consequence, the problem of teenage childbearing is densely concentrated among economically disadvantaged youth. Among white young women, 54 percent of all births occur outside of marriage; among African-American women of the same age, the figure is more than 90 percent (Furstenberg, 1991). The rate for Hispanic women falls somewhere in between; interestingly, young Mexican-American women are more likely to bear their first child within marriage (the pattern similar to whites'), whereas young Puerto Rican women are more likely to bear children out of wedlock (the pattern similar to blacks') (Darabi et al., 1987). Because minority youth are likely to experience other problems as well, such as school failure or substance abuse, early childbearing is likely to take place in the context of limited social and economic resources. One problem that researchers have in studying adolescent childbearing is to disentangle the effects of childbearing itself from those of factors like economic stress. At least one analysis shows that the main reason for the high rate of nonmarital childbearing among African-Americans is the higher proportion of single-parent homes (Bumpass and McLanahan, 1987), which experience more stress.

## CONTRIBUTING FACTORS

Many myths permeate discussions of the causes of adolescent pregnancy and complicate what is actually a fairly simple matter. The most important difference between young women who do and do not become pregnant during adolescence is effective contraceptive use. We have seen in previous chapters that sexual activity among American young people is high and contraceptive use sporadic and inadequate. Studies of adolescent contraceptive use, as we have seen, suggest that misinformation about sex and pregnancy, a lack of access to contraceptives, and adherence to the "personal fable" that unprotected intercourse is not going to result in conception all contribute to teenage pregnancy. No scientific evidence exists indicating that most—or even many—teenagers who become pregnant consciously or unconsciously want to have a baby.

There are, however, important differences between pregnant teenagers who do, and do not, seek abortion. Although studies show that teenagers can make well-reasoned decisions about abortion, this option is not chosen equally often within all segments of the adolescent population: Unplanned pregnancies are much more likely to be terminated by abortion among young women who are academi-

cally successful, ambitious, from middle- or upper-class families, and whose parents are well-educated (Hayes, 1987). An important factor accounting for the racial and socioeconomic differences in adolescent childbearing, therefore, is that white and middle-class adolescent women perceive themselves as having more to lose—economically and careerwise—by having a child so early in life than do their minority and poor counterparts. By expanding educational and occupational opportunities for poor and minority women, a greater number may realize that delaying childbearing may be preferable (Hayes, 1987).

Several studies have examined whether teenagers who choose to abort an unwanted pregnancy are harmed psychologically by the experience. The consensus among experts is that they are not (Hayes, 1987). Indeed, one recent study indicates that pregnant teenage women who abort their pregnancy are significantly better off two years later, psychologically as well as socially and economically, than comparable women who choose to give birth to their child (Zabin, Hirsch, and Emerson, 1989). Among the most important differences between the groups was that the women who had terminated their pregnancy by abortion were less likely over the next two years to experience a subsequent pregnancy and more likely to practice contraception. Given the apparent psychological and economic benefits of terminating an unwanted adolescent pregnancy, it is easy to understand why many social scientists have questioned the wisdom of recent court decisions designed to restrict adolescents' access to abortion services (Blum et al., 1990).

## THE ROLE OF THE FATHER

Relatively little is known about the male partners of pregnant adolescents. Research indicates, however, that this group of males may share a number of distinguishing characteristics that differentiate them from their peers who do not impregnate adolescent women. Most important has been the discovery that the sexual partners of adolescent girls are less likely to be adolescents themselves than to be young adults and more likely than their peers to have had problems with school, with work, with drugs and alcohol, and with the law and to have fathered a child previously (Elster et al., 1987; Hardy et al., 1989; Marsiglio, 1987; Rivara et al., 1987). These higher rates of problem behavior among the male partners of pregnant adolescents help to explain why marriage may not be the best response to teenage pregnancy for the woman, as we shall see in a few pages.

The problematic profiles of teenage fathers notwithstanding, research indicates that young men's educational development and mental health is hurt by fathering a child early in life, even if they do not marry the child's mother (Buchanan and Robbins, 1990; Furstenberg et al., 1989). Men who impregnate adolescent women are more likely to drop out of school and to report feeling anxious and depressed as young adults than their peers. The adverse effects of teenage fatherhood appear to be greater among white and Hispanic men than among African-American men, however, perhaps because teenage fatherhood is more disruptive and seen as less acceptable within the white and Hispanic communities (Buchanan and Robbins, 1990).

## CONSEQUENCES FOR MOTHER AND CHILD

Because teenage childbearing tends to go hand in hand with a variety of other problems—the most critical of which is poverty—it is extremely difficult to know whether any problems of teenage mothers or their children are due to the mother's young age or to other, correlated factors. Separating the effects of early childbearing from poverty is a matter of more than theoretical importance: If early

childbearing is in fact a problem in and of itself, it would be important to direct preventive programs at deterring adolescent pregnancy (either by discouraging sexual activity or by encouraging effective contraceptive use) and childbearing (by encouraging adoption and abortion). But if *poverty,* not the mother's age, is the key, an entirely different set of strategies would be called for, aimed not at youngsters' sexual behavior but at all individuals' economic circumstances. It is extremely important, therefore, to ask whether and in what ways a mother's age at the time she gives birth affects her and her child's well-being.

The prevailing wisdom until recently was that children born to teenage mothers were at great risk for a range of health and behavioral problems in the short and long term, including low birth weight, conduct problems, hyperactivity, and achievement difficulties. New and more sophisticated studies, however, temper this conclusion. These new studies indicate that many of the problems believed to plague children born to adolescent mothers are due primarily to the environment of poverty and single parenthood these children grow up in, rather than to the mother's age. In general, children born to middle-class adolescents differ little from their counterparts born to older mothers, and children born to poor adolescents are similar to children born to equally poor adults. One important exception to this general similarity between the children of adolescent and adult mothers is that adolescent mothers—even of similar socioeconomic origin—interact with their infants less often in ways that are known to be beneficial to the child's cognitive and social development (Coll et al., 1987; Furstenberg et al., 1989). To what extent this actually jeopardizes the child's development, however, is not known with any certainty, although studies suggest that children born to adolescent mothers are more likely to have school problems, more likely to be involved in misbehavior and delinquent activity, and more likely themselves to be sexually active at an early age (Furstenberg et al., 1987).

We know from other studies that many of the problem behaviors seen among children of adolescent mothers are prevalent among poor children growing up in single-parent homes. Because adolescent mothers are more likely than adult mothers to be both unmarried and poor, their children are at greater risk of developing a variety of psychological and social problems. In other words, the greater incidence of problems among offspring of adolescent mothers may be due to the overall environment in which their children grow up, rather than to the ways in which they are raised by their mothers.

Studies of the long-term consequences of adolescent parenthood indicate that serious problems associated with it directly involve the teenage mother, however (Furstenberg et al., 1989). In general, women who bear children early are likely to suffer disruptions in their educational and occupational careers, and these disruptions can have dire long-term consequences (Hayes, 1987). Not only are adolescent mothers more likely to come from a poor background, but they are also more likely to remain poor than their equally disadvantaged peers who delay childbearing until after their schooling is completed. Adolescent childbearing, then, can contribute to a vicious cycle of welfare dependency: Individuals who grow up in families dependent on welfare are more likely to have children early in life, which generally means that their economic opportunities will be limited by having to change educational and occupational plans. The result often is continued dependence on public assistance by the adolescent mother and, therefore, her child—who, like his or her mother, grows up with welfare as a part of life. Although we can *in theory* separate the effects of poverty on children from the effects of adolescent childbearing, *in reality* the two usually go together, and the end result is that children born to adoles-

cent mothers are more likely than other children to suffer the effects of malnutrition—in the womb as well as in the world—and environmental deprivation.

Yet the news is not always bad, and having a child early in life does not cast in concrete a life of poverty and misery for the mother and her youngster. Studies show that there is considerable diversity among teenage mothers in the routes that their adult lives take. As Furstenberg and his colleagues point out (1987), women who remained in high school and delayed subsequent childbearing fared a great deal better over the long run—as did their children—than their counterparts who dropped out of school or had more children relatively early on. Marriage tends to be a "high-risk" strategy (Furstenberg et al., 1987). In some cases, when a stable relationship is formed and economic resources are available, marriage improves the mother's and the child's chances for life success; this seems to be especially true for women who marry somewhat later. In other cases, however, a hasty decision to marry in the absence of a stable relationship and economic security actually worsens many other problems (Teti and Lamb, 1989).

## PREVENTION AND PROGRAMS

Although there are stories of young women whose lives are not devastated by early childbearing, in general, studies suggest that there are not many such successes. The statement, some twenty-five years ago, that "the girl who has an illegitimate child at the age of 16 suddenly has 90 percent of her life's script written for her" (Campbell, 1968, p. 238) is still more often than not true today. In general, the "successes" are women who have avoided dire poverty, rather than women who have achieved great economic success. Although the picture of adolescent parenthood appears less uniform or dire than typically painted in the popular press, there is still consensus among experts that it is important to try to prevent teenage pregnancy and childbearing. Unfortunately, this task is more easily said than done. To date, few strategies have proven effective on a large scale. One approach that we can be cautiously optimistic about involves a combination of school-based sex education and school-based health clinics through which adolescents can receive information about sex and pregnancy as well as contraception. Evaluations indicate that this combination of sex education and clinic actually diminishes the rate of teen pregnancy, even within inner-city communities characterized by high rates of adolescent pregnancy and childbearing (Zabin et al., 1986). Unfortunately, as you might suspect, many parents have objected to such programs in their community, fearing that they will stimulate teenage sexual activity. However, most studies indicate that these fears—however intuitively reasonable—are unwarranted (Furstenberg et al., 1987).

Research on the consequences of adolescent childbearing also suggests that many of the negative effects of having children early could be prevented or at least minimized by lessening the disruptive economic impact of teenage parenthood on young women's lives. What do we know about the factors that work toward this end? First, it is clear that marrying the father of the child may place the adolescent mother at greater risk if the father is not capable of supporting himself economically, much less his family. Studies show, in contrast, that if the father is able to find a good job and remain employed, he can be an important source of psychological and economic support and a healthy influence on the mother and child. Given the problems characteristic of male partners of adolescent mothers discussed earlier, however, it is all too likely that marriage may diminish, rather than enhance, an adolescent mother's economic circumstances. In addition, marriage places the adolescent mother at greater risk of having another child relatively

soon, which further jeopardizes her already precarious economic situation. One of the factors most likely to worsen the problems of teenage mothers is having yet another child (Furstenberg et al., 1987). Moreover, teenage marriage, as you know, is very likely to end in divorce (see Chapter 10), which itself is an additional stressor on the mother and child.

Adolescent mothers therefore cannot always look to the father of the child to help break the cycle of poverty that afflicts young parents. However, they can, in many cases, look to their own parents for support, and this seems to be an effective strategy (Stevens, 1988). Teenage mothers who move in with their own family for a short time are more likely to enjoy educational and occupational success than their counterparts who live on their own, studies show. The family's help allows the young mother to return to school or find employment. Without this help, many young mothers must drop out of school and find and pay for child care, which often is more costly than the income their low-paying jobs generate. Without a high school diploma, these women have little chance of improving their economic situation and, consequently, improving the opportunities for their child.

Because it is so important for young mothers to have adequate incomes and the chance for adequate employment, many policymakers have called for changes in the ways that schools treat pregnant students and for changes in the provision of day care. Among the most important are adaptations in school schedules and the development of school-based child-care centers, so that pregnant students can remain in school after the birth of their child; the expansion of subsidized child care for young mothers who are out of school, so that the economic benefits of having a job are not outweighed by the costs of suitable child care during the workday; and the expansion of family planning services to adolescent mothers so that they can prevent yet another pregnancy.

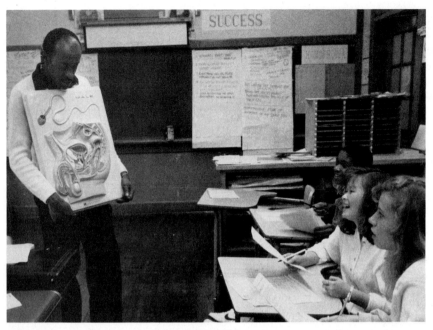

Many young people receive sex education through a school-based program. Experts recommend that sex education begin early, include units on decision-making and interpersonal assertiveness, and be accompanied by access to contraceptive services. *(Elizabeth Crews/Stock, Boston)*

## Sex Education

Many adolescents receive some sort of classroom instruction on sexual matters—whether through high school health classes, biology classes, classes designated exclusively for the purpose of sex education, or educational programs administered through youth or religious organizations. Such classes and programs, if they are available, are likely to be targeted toward adolescents rather than toward children and preadolescents (Kirkendall, 1981).

Until recently, most evaluations of formal sex education programs administered through schools rated them remarkably disappointing (Spanier, 1976). The consensus among experts was that most sex education programs failed because they emphasized the biological over the emotional aspects of sex (and thus did not prepare adolescents for making decisions about sexual involvement), because they came too late in high school (and thus did not reach adolescents before they became sexually active), and because they focused primarily on changing students' knowledge rather than their behavior (and thus did not directly affect patterns of sexual activity or contraceptive use).

A new wave of sex education programs has been developed, and initial evaluations of these programs have been more encouraging, however. According to a recent review of these programs by a panel of the National Academy of Sciences, sex education courses that focus on increasing youngsters' knowledge about sex, contraception, and pregnancy should begin early and should be combined with courses designed to teach decision-making skills and interpersonal assertiveness. They should teach adolescents the skills they need to resist peer pressure to become sexually active. In addition, the panel recommended that the media take a more socially responsible position and portray sexual relationships and the responsibilities of parenthood more accurately on television and in movies (Hayes, 1987).

The panel also recommended that contraceptive services be expanded for teenagers. Noting that adolescents are often reluctant to seek contraceptives from their physicians and more inclined to use the services of clinics, the experts recommended that sex education programs include clear information on how to use and obtain contraceptives and that communities consider developing school-based clinics in which adolescents can receive information about contraception and obtain contraceptives. Research suggests that the combination of sex education and school-based clinics is more effective in deterring adolescent pregnancy than sex education programs alone (Zabin et al., 1986). Indeed, studies show that increasing adolescents' knowledge about sex has little impact—positive or negative—on their sexual behavior (Hanson et al., 1987; Kirby et al., 1989).

During the mid-1980s, the emphasis in sex education shifted from encouraging "responsible" sex to encouraging sexual abstinence. In addition to sessions on sexual decision making and values and exercises designed to enhance students' self-esteem, adolescents enrolled in such programs were taught to "just say no" to sexual intercourse. It was hoped that by encouraging sexual abstinence, these programs would also have the effect of reducing teenage pregnancy. Unfortunately, careful evaluations of these programs have shown that they are not at all successful, either in changing adolescents' sexual behavior or in reducing rates of nonmarital pregnancy (Christopher and Roosa, 1990; Roosa and Christopher, in press).

To date, the only clear successes in decreasing the rate of adolescent pregnancy are programs that combine education about sexuality and contraception with referrals for contraceptive services (e.g., Zabin et al., 1986).

## AIDS and Other Sexually Transmitted Diseases

Helping youngsters understand sex, pregnancy, and contraception is an important goal of sex education programs for adolescents. Helping them avoid the risks of **sexually transmitted diseases,** or STDs, is another. STDs—once called "venereal diseases"—are caused by viruses, bacteria, or parasites that are transmitted through sexual contact (Mahoney, 1983).

According to the American Medical Association, 2.5 million adolescents contract a sexually transmitted disease each year, and one in four teenagers contracts a sexually transmitted disease before graduating from high school (Gans, 1990). The most common STDs among adolescents are **gonorrhea** (caused by a bacterium), **chlamydia** (caused by a parasite), and **herpes** (caused by a virus). In the cases of gonorrhea and chlamydia, the main symptoms are painful urination and a discharge from the penis, vagina, or urethra. If untreated, either disease can lead to disorders of the reproductive system and sterility. Antibiotic treatment of gonorrhea and chlamydia is relatively simple, but, unfortunately, many individuals who have these diseases do not have the symptoms, which makes it less likely that they will seek treatment.

The symptoms of herpes are tiny, itching blisters that turn into open sores on the penis, vulva, or cervix. These symptoms are sometimes accompanied by headaches, fever, and pelvic pain. The signs of herpes may appear and then disappear, only to reappear again.

Herpes is transmitted through direct contact with open sores and can therefore be transmitted only when symptoms are present. Although there are medications that can be used to relieve the symptoms of herpes, to date there is no cure. The main risks of herpes are increased likelihood of cervical cancer in women, and, during pregnancy, the increased likelihood of miscarriage or damage to the newborn's central nervous system.

During the 1980s, a new and far more serious STD commanded the world's attention: **AIDS** or **Acquired Immune Deficiency Syndrome.** AIDS is transmitted through bodily fluids, especially semen, during sexual intercourse, or blood when drug users share needles. Before information was available about the transmission of AIDS, some individuals were infected through blood transfusions in hospitals. Now hospitals routinely screen blood for the AIDS virus, **HIV,** or **human immunodeficiency virus,** and this means of transmission is extremely rare today.

AIDS itself has no symptoms, but HIV attacks the body's immune system, interfering with the body's ability to defend itself against life-threatening diseases like pneumonia or cancer. About 25 percent of all individuals who are infected with the virus develop complications within five years; about half of all people in the United States known to have AIDS have died as a result.

Although the incidence of AIDS in the United States was initially concentrated within two groups, gay men and drug users who use needles, recent surveys indicate that the transmission of AIDS through heterosexual activity is a clear danger within the adolescent community, particularly among inner-city minority youngsters. In one inner-city clinic, for example, between 2 and 3 percent of adolescents between the ages of 15 and 19 tested positive for the presence of HIV (DiClemente, 1990). Becauase there is a long period of time between HIV infection and the actual manifes-

tation of illness, however—sometimes, as long as 10 years—many more adolescents are likely to be asymptomatic carriers of the HIV virus who may develop AIDS in young adulthood (Hein, 1988).

The chances of contracting HIV are greatest among individuals who use intravenous drugs, have unprotected sex, have many sexual partners, and already have another sexually transmitted disease (such as gonorrhea). Because these risk factors are more common among young people than adults, the risk of HIV infection among adolescents is substantial. Accordingly, in recent years numerous efforts have been made to develop AIDS education programs specifically aimed at teenagers (Shayne and Kaplan, 1988).

Unfortunately, despite numerous attempts at programs designed to reduce the prevalence of HIV infection among adolescents, many young people, especially minority youth, remain confused and misinformed about AIDS (DiClemente et al., 1988). Educating young people about the risk factors associated with AIDS is important, because adolescents who believe that they are at risk are more likely to take precautions during intercourse (Brooks-Gunn et al., 1988). Unfortunately, public education about AIDS has been least successful in reaching those adolescents at greatest risk.

Most experts believe that, short of abstinence, the best way for teenagers to protect themselves against contracting HIV is by using condoms during sexual intercourse. Unfortunately, while most adolescents now recognize this—largely through public-health education efforts—it has been difficult to convince teenagers to translate this knowledge into safer behavior (Kegelles et al., 1988). As one team of authors concluded, "dissemination of information, in and of itself, is unlikely to deter the spread of AIDS significantly" (Shayne and Kaplan, 1988, p. 199). For this reason, sex education programs that combine AIDS information with the distribution of condoms hold the most promise. Contrary to widespread public opinion, such programs do *not* increase the likelihood of adolescents becoming sexually active (Furstenberg et al., 1985; Hanson et al., 1987).

## *Summary*

1. Adolescence is a fundamentally important time in the life cycle for the development of sexuality, due to the physical and hormonal changes of puberty, the increased capacity for the individual to understand and think about sexual feelings, and the new social meaning given to sexual behavior by society and its institutions.

2. Although we tend to think of the United States as being sexually permissive, there are many societies around the world that are more lenient about sex. By most indications, Americans' attitudes toward adolescent sex are neither restrictive nor permissive—but ambivalent. Many experts believe that the mixed messages adolescents receive about sexuality in the United States contribute to the high incidence of problems such as teenage pregnancy.

3. Important changes in attitudes toward nonmarital sex occurred during the 1970s, which have resulted in a view that has been labeled "permissiveness with affection." Most teenagers today believe that it is acceptable to have intercourse before marriage as long as it takes place within the context of a loving, intimate relationship.

4. Sexual intercourse, once delayed until early adulthood, is clearly now a part of the typical adolescent's experience. More than half of all teenagers have sexual intercourse before graduating from high school, although there are wide ethnic and regional differences in the age of onset of sexual activity. Despite the decline of the double standard, there are still important sex differences in the psychological meaning of sexual intercourse among adolescents.

5. Early sexual activity does not carry the psychological risks that many adults associate with it. In general, adolescents who are sexually active have psychological profiles that are similar to, rather than different from, their peers. There is evidence, however, that early sexual activity is more common among teenagers growing up in single-parent households.

6. Approximately 8 percent of the adolescent and young adult population is either partially or exclusively gay or lesbian. Current theories of the origins of homosexuality suggest a complex interaction of genetic and environmental influence.

7. Adolescents are infamously poor users of contraception, especially in the United States. Most experts agree that the reasons so few adolescents use birth control regularly are that contraceptives are not as accessible as they might be, that adolescents are insufficiently educated about pregnancy and contraception, that adolescents seldom anticipate having intercourse until they become sexually active on a regular basis, and that using birth control requires the sort of long-term planning that many young people are reluctant to engage in.

8. There are approximately 1 million teenage pregnancies each year in the United States, about half of which are carried full term. Research on the consequences of teenage childbearing indicates that the problems for the teenage mother are typically much greater than are those for her child. Although there are occasional success stories, teenage parents are more likely than their peers to experience disruptions in their educational and occupational development.

9. Sex education programs that combine information with contraceptive services appear to hold the most promise in reducing unintended pregnancy and the prevalence of sexually transmitted disease, including AIDS—a growing problem in the adolescent population.

Programs that simply advocate abstinence have not been successful, and information alone appears to do little to change adolescents' sexual behavior.

## Key Terms

Acquired Immune Deficiency Syndrome (AIDS)
autoerotic behavior
chlamydia
date rape
gonorrhea
herpes
Human Immuno deficiency Virus (HIV)
permissive societies
restrictive societies
semirestrictive societies
serial monogamy
sexual socialization
sexually transmitted disease (STD)
sociosexual behavior
testosterone

## For Further Reading

DICLEMENTE, R. (1990). The emergence of adolescents as a risk group for Human Immunodeficiency Virus infection. *Journal of Adolescent Research, 5*, 7–17. A recent review of the literature on adolescents and AIDS.

FURSTENBERG, F., JR. (1991). As the pendulum swings: Teenage childbearing and social concern. *Family Relations, 40*, 127–138. A prominent social scientist examines facts and fallacies about the teenage pregnancy problem.

HAYES, C. (ED.). (1987). *Risking the future: Adolescent sexuality, pregnancy, and childbearing.* Washington: National Academy Press. The comprehensive report of the National Academy of Sciences on sexuality and pregnancy among American youth.

KATCHADOURIAN, H. (1990). Sexuality. In S. Feldman and G. Elliot (Eds.), *At the threshold: The developing adolescent.* Cambridge: Harvard University Press. A review of the literature on adolescent sexual behavior.

MILLER, P., AND SIMON, W. (1980). The development of sexuality in adolescence. In J. Adelson (Ed.), *Handbook of adolescent psychology.* New York: Wiley. An extensive discussion of the psychological aspects of sexual development during adolescence.

# ACHIEVEMENT

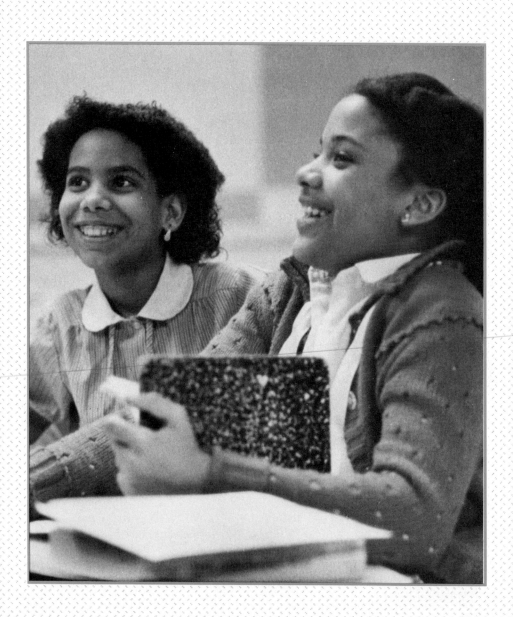

# ACHIEVEMENT

*B*ecause adolescence typically is a time of preparation for the roles of adulthood, considerable attention has been paid to the development and expression of achievement during these years. Broadly defined, achievement concerns the development of motives, capabilities, interests, and behavior that have to do with performance in evaluative situations. More specifically, the study of achievement during adolescence has focused on young people's performance in educational settings and on their hopes and plans for future scholastic and occupational careers. Since most young people form their first realistic educational and vocational plans during adolescence, researchers have long been interested in the factors that appear to play the greatest role in influencing individuals' futures.

Achievement is a particularly important consideration in the study of adolescence in contemporary society. Industrialized societies place an extraordinary emphasis on achievement, competition, and success—more so than on cooperation, for example, or the development of satisfying interpersonal relationships (McClelland, 1961). During childhood and adolescence, youngsters are continually tested to determine how they stand scholastically in relation to their peers. In most industrialized societies, the amount of education a person has completed and the job he or she holds—two of the most important indicators of achievement—provide a basis for individuals' self-conceptions and their image in the eyes of others (Featherman, 1980).

A second reason for the importance of achievement in the study of adolescence in contemporary society concerns the range and rapidly changing nature of the choices faced by today's young people. Unlike youth in most traditional cultures, adolescents in modern societies are confronted with a phenomenally wide array of difficult occupational and educational decisions before they turn 25. Beyond such fundamental questions as what type of career to follow and whether to continue with schooling after high school, there are other difficult issues to ponder: what specific sorts of jobs should be pursued within a particular career path, what kind of educational preparation would be most appropriate, and how entry into the labor force is best negotiated. For the college student contemplating a career in business, for instance, is it better to major in business administration or is it better to follow a liberal arts course of study? How early is it necessary to decide which aspects of business to specialize in? Is it necessary to go to graduate school, or do employers prefer applicants with work experience in place of an advanced degree? These are all difficult questions to answer. And they are made more difficult because the nature of education and work changes so rapidly in contemporary society.

Finally, achievement is a particularly important issue in the study of adolescence in contemporary society because of wide variation in levels of educational and occupational success. By the end of high school, many adolescents demonstrate a high enough level of academic achievement to enter selective colleges and universities; yet a sizable number of their peers enter adulthood unable even to read a newspaper or understand a bus schedule. Although the majority of adolescents today complete high school and go on to college, a substantial number leave high school before graduating. Similar disparities exist in the occupational achievements of young people: Most youth make the transition from school to work without a great deal of difficulty, but a significant number experience long bouts of unemployment. Even within the population of young people who enter the labor force, there is considerable variation in earnings and in occupational status. Many important questions in the study of adolescent achievement, therefore, concern factors that distinguish between young people who are successful—however success is defined—and those who are not.

390

## Achievement as an Adolescent Issue

As noted above, in contemporary society, achievement is a lifelong concern. Educational institutions—even for young children—stress performance, competition, and success on tests of knowledge and ability. Concerns over achievement continue throughout adulthood as well. Like their younger counterparts, adults for the most part place a premium on success. Work and occupational attainment play an important role in shaping the adult's values, self-concept, and self-esteem (Featherman, 1980). Development in the realm of achievement neither begins nor ends during adolescence.

Achievement during the adolescent years, though, merits special attention for several reasons. First, the fact that adolescence is a time of preparation for adult work roles raises questions about the nature of the preparation that young people receive and the processes through which they sort themselves (or are sorted) into the occupational roles that may influence the remainder of their lives. Many of the factors that narrow an individual's educational options and vocational alternatives are prominent during the high school and college years, and it is important to ask how such options are defined and how early educational and occupational decisions are made.

Second, although differences in school performance and achievement are apparent as early as the first grade, not until adolescence do individuals begin to appreciate fully the implications of these differences for immediate and future success. During childhood, for example, children's occupational plans are made to a large extent on the basis of fantasy and passing interests, without any realistic assessment of their practicality or feasibility. Not until adolescence do individuals begin to evaluate their occupational choices in light of their talents, abilities, and opportunities.

Third, it is clear that the educational and occupational decisions made during adolescence are more numerous, and the consequences more serious, than those characteristic of childhood. For example, in most elementary schools, although children may be grouped by ability—groupings that have implications for subsequent achievement—they generally are all exposed to fairly similar curricula and have few opportunities to veer from the educational program established by their school system. In high school, however, students can select how much science and math they want to take, whether they wish to study a foreign language, whether they want to pursue an academic or vocational track—even whether they want to remain in school once they have reached the legal school-leaving age. Moreover, it is during adolescence that most individuals decide whether they want to pursue post-secondary education or enter a full-time job directly from high school. All of these decisions have important implications for the sort of choices and plans the adolescent will make in the future, which in turn will influence his or her earnings, lifestyle, identity, and subsequent psychosocial development.

It is neither surprising nor coincidental that many achievement-related issues surface for the first time during adolescence rather than during early or later periods of development. One reason concerns the social transition of adolescence. In virtually all societies, adolescence is the period when important educational and occupational decisions are made, and society has structured its educational and work institutions accordingly. In America, for example, it is not until adolescence that individuals attain the status necessary to decide whether they will continue or end their formal education. And it is not until adolescence that people are allowed to enter the labor force in an official capacity, since child labor regulations typically prohibit the employment of youngsters under the age of 14 or so. The

Achievement-related issues take on increased prominence during adolescence because it is during this time that individuals must begin to make important decisions about their educational and occupational futures. Volunteer experiences can help adolescents clarify their future plans. *(David M. Grossman/Photo Researchers)*

transition from school to work—one of the central issues in the study of achievement during adolescence—is a *socially* defined transition and one that is determined by society as a passage to be negotiated during adolescence.

Not until adolescence are individuals cognitively capable of seeing the long-term consequences of educational and occupational choices or of realistically considering the range of scholastic and work possibilities open to them. Thus a second reason for the prominence of achievement-related issues at adolescence concerns the advent of more sophisticated forms of thinking. The ability to think in hypothetical terms, for example, raises new achievement concerns for the individual (Should I go to college after I graduate or work for a while?) and at the same time permits the young person to think through these concerns in a logical and systematic fashion (If I decide to go onto college, then . . .).

Finally, the emergence of many achievement concerns at adolescence is tied to the biological changes of puberty. As noted in Chapter 2, not until early adolescence do sex differences in achievement test performance begin to emerge, with boys scoring higher on tests of mathematics and girls outscoring boys on tests of verbal skills. As we shall see, sex differences in achievement-related motives and beliefs appear around puberty as well. These sex differences are related primarily to the differential responses that boys and girls receive from others following changes in their appearance at puberty and to differences in the ways that adolescent boys and girls view themselves. Boys may be encouraged to pursue course work (and, by implication, careers) in math and science, girls in the arts and humanities. This differential treatment may have important implications for sex differences in educational and occupational attainment.

In this chapter, we look at the nature of achievement during the adolescent years. As you will see, the extent to which an adolescent is successful in school and in preparing for work is influenced by a complex array of personal and environmental factors. In addition, we shall find that development in the realm of achievement is cumulative, in that youngsters who are successful early are likely to reap the benefits of the educational system, continue to succeed in school, and to complete more years of education than their peers. This success, in turn, gives them an advantage in the labor market, since the prestige and status of individuals' entry-level jobs are largely dependent on their educational background.

If there is a theme to this chapter, it is that at least with respect to achievement during adolescence, the rich get richer and the poor get poorer. More often than not, personal and environmental influences on achievement complement rather than correct each other, in the sense that individuals who bring personal advantages to the world of achievement—talent, a motive to succeed, high aspirations for the future—are also likely to grow up in an environment that supports and maintains achievement success. We begin with a look at one set of factors that may differentiate the "rich" from the "poor" early in their schooling—long before adolescence, in fact: their motives to succeed and their beliefs about the causes of their successes and failures.

## *Achievement Motives and Beliefs*

### EARLY THEORIES OF ACHIEVEMENT MOTIVATION

One of the longest-standing notions in the study of achievement is that individuals differ in the extent to which they strive for success and that this differential striving—which can be measured independently of sheer ability—helps to account for different degrees of actual achievement. Two students may both score 100 on an intelligence test, but if one student tries much harder than the other to do well in school, their actual grades may differ. The extent to which an individual strives for success is referred to as his or her **need for achievement** (McClelland et al., 1953).

Generally, researchers have found that adolescents who have a strong need for achievement come from families where parents have set high performance standards, have rewarded achievement success during childhood, and have encouraged autonomy and independence (Rosen and D'Andrade, 1959; Winterbottom, 1958). Equally important, however, this training for achievement and independence generally takes place in the context of warm parent-child relationships in which the child forms close identifications with his or her parents (Shaw and White, 1965). Put most succinctly, *authoritative* parenting, coupled with parents' encouragement of success, is likely to lead to the development of a strong need for achievement.

### THE IMPORTANCE OF BELIEFS

More recently, researchers have questioned the usefulness of asserting the existence of global achievement-related motives that are expressed equally in a variety of situations. The relation between an individual's internal needs and his or her actual effort and performance varies in different situations. Someone who has a strong need for achievement might express this need to different degrees in academic and in social situations—or even in different sorts of academic and different sorts of social situations—depending on her past experiences and her perception of the specific situation. Because of this, individuals' actual performance in achievement situations may not be strongly related to their general achievement motives. Some students who want very much to succeed are susceptible to feelings of anxiety and helplessness in performance settings.

## THE SEXES: PATTERNS OF ACHIEVEMENT IN ADOLESCENT BOYS AND GIRLS

We noted in an earlier chapter on cognitive development that sex differences in cognitive skills during adolescence are trivial. On standardized tests of intellectual abilities, girls and boys perform at about the same level, and when sex differences are observed, they are small—too small, indeed, to make a meaningful difference in adolescents' school performance. Despite this absence of sex differences in ability, girls in general are less likely than boys to pursue advanced courses in math and science, and those girls who do are more likely to drop out before finishing (Kavrell and Petersen, 1984). Studies of college students show that women are exceedingly underrepresented among graduates whose degrees are in math, engineering, and the physical science but overrepresented among graduates whose degrees are in the humanities and education (Eccles, Adler, and Meece, 1984). Because high school preparation undoubtedly influences college course choices, which in turn affect career choices, educators have been interested in understanding why sex differences in math achievement emerge in adolescence. In essence, if adolescent girls and adolescent boys have equal math ability, why do they show different patterns of math and science achievement during high school?

Psychologists have offered several explanations. The first concerns sex differences in the social consequences of succeeding in school, and in math classes in particular. Fear of success may be more prevalent among women than men during early and middle adolescence than during childhood or adulthood (Butler and Nissan, 1975; Hoffman, 1977; Ishiyama and Chabassol, 1985). This finding and other research on achievement-related conflicts among adolescent girls (Rosen and Aneshensel, 1975) suggest that the social world of adolescent peer groups may make it difficult for adolescent girls to integrate positive feelings toward achievement—especially toward achievement in stereotypically masculine subject areas—into their sense of identity (Douvan and Adelson, 1966).

Of special importance for girls is the relation between academic achievement, the development of a feminine identity, and social relations with boys. As psychologists Judith Bardwick and Elizabeth Douvan (1971) explain: "Until adolescence the idea of equal capacity, opportunity, and life style [for men and women] is held out to [girls]. But sometime in adolescence the message becomes clear that one had better not do too well, that competition is aggressive and unfeminine, that deviation threatens the heterosexual relationship" (p. 152).

In other words, adolescent girls may not fear "success" per se, but they may be wary of other consequences—not necessarily negative consequences, but often merely complicated consequences—that may befall them as a result of their achievement. Girls are more likely to have been socialized to believe that their achievement is out of their control, and they are consequently more likely to feel helpless in response to failure (Dweck and Light, 1980). During adolescence, when concerns over dating and socializing may

*continued on next page*

be paramount, and when the sense of self is shaky and the view of the future cloudy, achievement may carry a different connotation for girls than it does for boys. Actually, one study indicated that *both* men and women had negative feelings about women's occupational success, suggesting that women's fear of success may be just as much due to a cultural bias against women succeeding as to an achievement-related motive prevalent among females (Monahan, Kuhn, and Shaver, 1974).

A second account focuses on sex differences in attitudes toward mathematics. Although girls and boys are equally likely to report liking math, girls are less likely than boys to believe that taking math classes will be useful to their future careers (Kavrell and Petersen, 1984). As a result, girls may place less value on achievement in math classes and may be less inclined to continue a math curriculum and more inclined to drop out of advanced math classes (Eccles et al., 1984). Thus, it appears that sex differences in career expectations may influence early attitudes toward math classes, which in turn influence math attainment. As we shall see later in this chapter, sex differences in adolescents' occupational ambitions are still quite marked. Unfortunately, to the extent that young adolescent girls opt out of advanced math classes, they limit their chances of moving into occupations that require preparation in math and only perpetuate occupational sex stereotypes.

Psychologist Jacqueline Eccles and her colleagues have argued that these sex differences in course selection may be related to sex differences in achievement attributions and beliefs. Parents, in particular, may pass on different expectations to sons and daughters, regardless of similarities in sons' and daughters' actual achievement. Parents of sons are more likely to believe that their child's success in math is due to his intrinsic math ability, whereas parents of daughters are more likely to attribute their child's math success to hard work. Parents of sons are also more likely than parents of daughters to think that taking advanced math courses is important (Parsons [Eccles], Adler, and Kaczala, 1982). To make matters worse, studies also indicate that school counselors and teachers also endorse views that support math achievement among boys but discourage it among girls (Kavrell and Petersen, 1984).

Studies show that grades in school decline during early adolescence, for both boys and girls. This decline has been attributed to harder grading practices by teachers (Kavrell and Petersen, 1984) and to the declining importance of achievement to adolescents as they approach high school. (Elmen, 1991). But the decline in grades in math and science may evoke very different responses in boys and girls. Boys, who have been told that they are good at math and that math is important, may simply try harder to do better. Girls, who receive less support for achievement in math from both adults (who may inadvertently socialize them to believe that math is difficult and not very useful) and peers (who may convey the message that success in math is not attractive), may respond by avoiding math entirely. This response is easy to understand: By the time an adolescent girl has reached the point in her high school career that she is able to choose among electives, she has been socialized to believe that math is difficult, that math classes are not especially worthwhile, and that success in math is inconsistent with being popular and attractive.

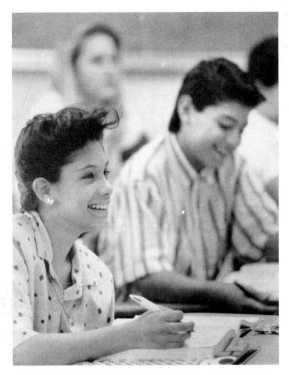

Individuals who are intrinsically motivated strive to achieve because of the pleasure they get out of mastering the material. *(Spencer Grant/Stock, Boston)*

Adolescents make judgments about their likelihood of succeeding or failing and exert different degrees of effort accordingly. Consider, for instance, the different ways that two individuals might approach a card game. Someone who believes that the outcome of the game is based on luck rather than skill will not try as hard as someone who feels that how he or she plays the game makes a difference.

A number of studies indicate that students' beliefs about their abilities exert a strong influence on their motivation, which in turn influences their scholastic performance (Harter et al., 1991). In order to understand this process, it is necessary to draw a distinction between **intrinsic motivation** and **extrinsic motivation.** Individuals who are intrinsically motivated strive to achieve because of the pleasure they get out of learning and mastering the material. Individuals who are extrinsically motivated strive to achieve because of the rewards they get for performing well. Early theories of achievement motivation did not draw this distinction, and as a consequence, may have grouped together students who, while highly motivated to do well in achievement situations, may have been motivated for very different reasons.

We all know individuals who are genuinely interested in what they learn in school, and we know others whose main concern is their grade point average. These two approaches to achievement have very different psychological consequences for the individual adolescent. Adolescents who believe that they are competent are more likely to be intrinsically motivated and are more likely to maintain their efforts to do well in school. In contrast, adolescents who have doubts about their abilities are more likely to be extrinsically motivated and more susceptible to feelings of anxiety and hesitation in the face of challenge. That is, although extrinsically motivated adolescents want to do well in school, the source of their motivation puts them on shaky ground.

Other studies suggest that the way in which adolescents view intelligence in general enters into the achievement equation. According to the **motivational process model** (Henderson and Dweck, 1990), three factors interact to predict student behavior: whether the student believes that intelligence is fixed or malleable; whether the student is oriented more toward extrinsic rewards (performance) or more toward intrinsic rewards (mastery); and whether the student is confident about his or her abilities (see also Ames and Archer, 1988).

Students who believe that intelligence is fixed tend to be oriented toward their performance and are greatly affected by their degree of confidence. If they are confident about their abilities, they tend to work hard and seek out challenges. If they are insecure, however, they tend to give up easily and feel helpless.

Students who believe that intelligence is malleable, in contrast, approach achievement situations from a different perspective. These students are more likely to have learning goals than performance goals; for them, satisfaction comes from mastering the material, not simply from gaining a good evaluation. Students who have this orientation are far less affected by their level of confidence, because they are less concerned about their performance. Whether assured or insecure, these students exert effort and seek out challenges, because they are motivated by learning rather than performing.

When conditions change such that performance becomes more important than learning, students' motives and beliefs change as a result. You have probably experienced this when you have enrolled in a course in which the instructor stressed grades, rather than mastery of the material. This sort of emphasis brings out the worst in students—literally. Performance goals make students more extrinsically motivated, insecure about their abilities, and hesitant to challenge themselves.

One of the most interesting applications of this viewpoint has been in studies of changes in adolescents' academic motivation during the transition from elementary school to junior high school (Eccles and Midgley, 1990). It has been widely reported that students' motivation and school performance decline when they move into secondary school (Elmen, 1991). Why might this be? Among the other important changes that take place during this school transition (see Chapter 6) is a shift, on the part of teachers, toward a more performance-oriented style of instruction and evaluation. During secondary school, students discover that more of an emphasis is placed on grades than had been the case in elementary school. This shift in emphasis undermines many students' intrinsic motivation and their self-confidence, which diminishes their performance.

These newer models of the psychological aspects of achievement in adolescence suggest that students' beliefs (about the nature of ability in general and the nature of *their* ability in particular) influence their motivation, which in turn influences their performance. One additional factor involves the way in which students interpret their successes and failures. Researchers interested in **achievement attributions** (Dweck and Wortman, 1980) have studied how the attributions individuals make for their success or failure influence their performance. According to these theorists, individuals attribute their performance to a combination of four factors: ability, effort, task difficulty, and luck. When individuals succeed and attribute their success to "internal" causes, such as their ability or effort, they are more likely to approach future tasks confidently and with self-assurance. If, however, individuals attribute their success to "external" factors outside their own control, such as luck or having an easy task, they are more likely to remain unsure of their abilities. Not surprisingly, individuals high in achievement motivation are likely to attribute their successes to internal causes (Powers and Wagner, 1984).

How youngsters interpret their failures is also important in influencing their subsequent behavior. Some youngsters try harder in the face of failure, whereas others withdraw and exert less effort. According to psychologist Carol Dweck (Dweck and Light, 1980), when individuals attribute their failures to a lack of effort, they are more likely to try harder on future tasks. Individuals who attribute their failure to factors that they feel cannot be changed (bad luck, lack of intelligence, task difficulty) are more likely to feel helpless and exert less effort in subsequent situations.

Suppose, for instance, a student takes the SAT examination and receives a score of 500. He then is told by his guidance counselor that the SAT is a measure of intelligence and that his score reflects how smart he is. The counselor tells the student that he can retake the test if he wants to but that he should not expect to score much higher than 500. Now imagine a different student, who also scored 500 on the test. She is told by her guidance counselor that effort has a great deal to do with scores on the SAT and that she can raise her score by trying harder. In all likelihood, the first student would not try as hard the next time he takes the test as the second student would, because the first student is more likely to feel helpless.

Students who are led to believe that their efforts do not make a difference—by being told, for example, that they are stupid or that the work is too difficult for them—develop **learned helplessness:** the belief that their failure is inevitable (Dweck and Light, 1980). As a result, these students try less hard than their peers and do not do as well. Research on adolescents' attributions for success and failure suggests that instead of dismissing low-achieving students as having "low needs for achievement" or "low intelligence," teachers and other school personnel can help students achieve more by helping them learn to attribute their performance to factors that are under their own control (Wilson and Linville, 1985).

## Environmental Influences on Achievement

Ability, beliefs, and motivation may play a large role in influencing individual performance, but opportunity and situational factors also have a great deal to do with achievement (Featherman, 1980). Many of the differences in academic or occupational achievement observed among adolescents are due not to differences in adolescents' abilities, motives, or beliefs, but to differences in the environments in which these abilities and motives are expressed.

School environments differ markedly—in physical facilities, in opportunities for pursuing academically enriched programs, and in classroom atmosphere, for example. Many school districts, plagued with shrinking tax bases, are characterized by decaying school buildings, outdated equipment, and textbook shortages. In some schools, problems of crime and discipline have grown so overwhelming that attention to these matters has taken precedence over learning and instruction. Many young people who genuinely want to succeed are impeded not by a lack of talent or motivation but by a school environment that makes academic success virtually impossible.

The school, of course, is not the only environment that makes a difference in adolescent achievement, and few would argue that schools should accept full responsibility for adolescents who do not succeed at a level consonant with their ability. If anything, the evidence suggests that important aspects of the *home* environment are better predictors of adolescents' academic achievement tham important aspects of the school environment (Coleman et al., 1966).

Researchers have focused on three ways in which the adolescent's home may influence his or her level of achievement. First, studies have shown that authoritative parenting is linked to school success during adolescence. In one recent study, sociologist Sanford Dornbusch and his colleagues (Dornbusch et al., 1987) demonstrated that adolescents whose parents were authoritative consistently performed better in school than their peers whose parents were permissive or autocratic. Interestingly, the poorest school performance was observed among adolescents whose parents were inconsistent in their child rearing. That is, even though adolescents whose parents were autocratic received lower grades than students whose parents were authoritative, adolescents whose parents used a mixture of autocratic and permissive techniques performed even worse. Other studies suggest that authoritative parenting promotes the development of a healthy achievement orientation—including an emphasis on intrinsic motivation—which in turn facilitates adolescent school performance

(Lamborn et al., 1991; Steinberg et al., 1989). Having a strong work orientation enhances achievement both directly, as we saw earlier, and indirectly, through the positive impression it makes on teachers (Farkas et al., 1990). In general, these findings are in line with a good deal of research suggesting that consistent, authoritative parenting is associated with a wide array of benefits to the adolescent, including higher achievement motivation, greater self-esteem, and enhanced competence (Maccoby and Martin, 1983).

A second way in which the family influences adolescent achievement is through parents' encouragement. Studies have shown that adolescents' achievement is directly related to the level of achievement their parents expect them to attain. Adolescents whose parents expect them to go on to college are more likely to do so than adolescents of equal ability whose parents expect less of them (Featherman, 1980).

Parental encouragement of academic success may be manifested in a number of ways, all of which have been shown to be beneficial to adolescents' school performance. First, parents who encourage school success set higher standards for their child's school performance and homework completion, which in turn contribute to school success (Entwisle and Hayduk, 1988; Natriello and McDill, 1986). Second, parents who encourage school success support values that are consistent with doing well in school and structure the home environment to support academic pursuits, so that the messages children receive from their teachers are echoed at home (Hanson and Ginsberg, 1988; Kurdek and Sinclair, 1988). Finally, parents who encourage success are likely to be more involved in their child's education—to attend school programs, help in course selection, and the like—all of which contribute to student success (Baker and Stevenson, 1986; Steinberg et al., in press; Stevenson and Baker, 1987).

Finally, studies have also shown that the quality of an adolescent's home environment—

as measured simply in terms of the presence of such items as a television set, dictionary, encyclopedia, newspaper, vacuum cleaner, and other indicators of family income—is more strongly correlated with youngsters' level of academic achievement than is the quality of the physical facility of the school they attend, the background and training of their teachers, or the level of teacher salaries paid by the school district (Armor, 1972). A number of researchers have also shown that the extent to which the adolescent's parents provide the youngster with **cultural capital**—by exposing the adolescent to art, music, literature, and so forth—exerts a positve impact on achievement above and beyond the effects of the parents' own level of education (DiMaggio, 1982).

With this in mind, it is important to point out that a disheartening number of young people in this country live in overcrowded, inadequate housing and come from families that are under severe economic and social stress—so much so, that parental encouragement and involvement are often undermined by neighborhood conditions. These obstacles to success disproportionately afflict youngsters from minority backgrounds. Put succinctly, many American youngsters do not grow up in an atmosphere that is conducive to academic achievement.

There is also evidence that friends influence adolescent achievement in addition to parents. But contrary to the notion that the influence of the peer group on adolescent achievement is always negative, recent studies suggest that the impact of friends on adolescents' school performance depends on the academic orientation of the peer group. Having friends who earn high grades and aspire to further education appears to enhance adolescent achievement, whereas having friends who earn low grades or disparage school success may interfere with it (Natriello and McDill, 1986). For example, according to one extensive study of friends in school (Epstein, 1983a), students' grades changed over time in relation to the

Many American young people grow up in environments that present tremendous obstacles to their educational and occupational success. *(Mary Ellen Mark/Archive)*

grades of their friends. Students with best friends who achieved high grades in school were more likely to show improvements in their own grades than students who began at similar levels of achievement but had friends who were not high achievers. Peers also exerted a small but significant influence on each other's college plans. Among low-achieving adolescents, for example, those with high-achieving friends were more likely to plan to continue their education than those with low-achieving friends.

The potential negative impact of friends on achievement is vividly seen in a widely reported study of African-American male peer groups in an inner-city school (Fordham and Ogbu, 1986). These researchers found that bright black students in this school had to live down the "burden of acting white" and face criticism from their peers, who referred to them as "brainiacs." When a small group of these students were placed in an environment in which all their peers were high achievers, the derision and negative labeling did not occur, however.

Situational factors affect occupational as well as educational attainment. In the opinion of some social critics, strong institutional barriers impede the occupational attainment of women and members of ethnic minorities (Ogbu, 1978). These barriers may be especially strong during adolescence, when young people are steered away from some educational and occupational pursuits and toward others—not on the basis of ability or interest but because of gender, socioeconomic background, or race. As we saw in Chapter 6, the ways in which schools determine which students are exposed to which curricula restrict the opportunites of those students who are placed in the slower tracks and perpetuate these students' academic disadvantages. The courses they encounter are likely to be less stimulating and less intellectually enriching than those taken by their peers. And students placed in the slower tracks tend to come disproportionately from minority groups and the economically disadvantaged—partly because their academic test scores warrant remedial placement, but partly as a consequence of their social background (Featherman, 1980).

Thus, although psychological factors play an important role in determining occupational and scholastic success, it is impossible to examine achievement during adolescence thoroughly without taking into account the broader environment in which individuals pursue their educational and occupational careers. Moreover, distinguishing between motivational and environmental factors is hard: They typically go hand in hand. Living in an environment that offers few opportunities for success induces feelings of learned helplessness, which in turn leads individuals to feel that exerting any effort to succeed is futile. Attending school in an environment where achievement is not encouraged engenders attitudes and beliefs inconsistent with striving for achievement. Rather than viewing achievement during adolescence as determined by one single factor, such as ability, it is more accurate to say that patterns of achievement are the result of a cumulative process that includes a long history of experience and socialization in school, in the family, at work, and in the peer group.

## Educational Achievement

Educational achievement is usually defined in one of three ways: the grades students earn in school, their performance on standardized tests of **academic achievement,** or the number of years of schooling completed—a measure of achievement referred to as **educational attainment.** These different measures of educational achievement are, not surprisingly, interrelated, but they are less tied to each other than one would expect.

No one factor adequately accounts for differences in adolescents' levels of educational achievement. Generally speaking, mental ability—as assessed by IQ tests—is highly correlated with performance on achievement tests (not surprisingly, since IQ tests and achievement tests are designed to tap similar abilities), moderately correlated with school grades, and only mildly correlated with educational attainment (Featherman, 1980).

Grades in school—and to an even greater extent, educational attainment—are influenced by a wider range of factors than simply an adolescent's intellectual abilities. Grades, for example, are influenced by teachers' judgments of students' mastery of the material, and these judgments may be influenced by teachers' evaluations of students' effort and behavior in the classroom (Farkas et al., 1990). How many years of school an adolescent completes is likely to be influenced by his or her family background as well as by school performance. Two adolescents may have similar grade-point averages, but if one comes from a poor family and cannot afford to go to college, the two will have different levels of educational attainment. In the words of sociologist David Featherman, "High intelligence begets good grades, and both assist one in acquiring above-average education, but . . . it is obvious that some persons fail to achieve their educational potentials while others ultimately obtain degrees and certification in spite of more modest accomplishments in school or average mental ability" (1980, p. 696).

### THE IMPORTANCE OF SOCIOECONOMIC STATUS

One of the most powerful influences on educational achievement is the socioeconomic status of the adolescent's family. Middle-class adolescents score higher on basic tests of academic skills, earn higher grades in school, and complete more years of schooling than their working-class and lower-class peers (Garbarino and Asp, 1981). Although some of the socioeconomic gaps in school achievement appear to be closing, many disparities between the social classes remain strong, and the importance of socioeconomic status in determining educational achievement remains substantial (Featherman, 1980).

Adolescents who come from lower socioeconomic levels are more likely to score lower than their peers on standardized tests of achievement, and youngsters who come from more advantaged households are more likely to score higher. Similarly, youngsters whose parents have gone to college are more likely to attend college themselves than are those whose parents did not. And those youngsters whose parents completed high school are more likely to attend college than are those whose parents did not (Johnson, 1975). Socioeconomic status, therefore, influences both achievement and attainment and, as a consequence, influences occupational achievement as well. However, you should bear in mind that variations *within* socioeconomic categories are often as substantial as differences *between* categories. Not all youngsters from affluent backgrounds have higher levels of educational achievement than adolescents from poorer families, and many youngsters from economically disadvantaged households go on to receive college and postcollege degrees.

One reason that family background is related to educational achievement is that children from lower socioeconomic levels are more likely to enter elementary school scoring low on tests of basic academic competence. These initial differences are due both to genetic and to environmental factors. Middle-class adults generally have higher IQs than lower-class adults, and this advantage is passed on to middle-class children—both through inheritance and through the benefit that middle-class youngsters receive from growing up under more favorable environmental conditions (Featherman, 1980). Affluent youngsters re-

ceive better health care and better nutrition, for example, both of which contribute to their higher performance on intelligence tests. The disadvantages of poorer youngsters in achievement test scores persist—and may even increase—throughout elementary and secondary school (Coleman et al., 1966; Entwisle and Hayduk, 1988). Because progress in high school depends so heavily on having a solid foundation of basic academic competence, adolescents who enter secondary school without having mastered basic academic skills quickly fall behind. Many then leave high school before graduating.

Studies also suggest that parents from higher social classes are more likely to be involved in their adolescent's education, through formal parent-teacher organizations, like the PTO, and through conferences with their child's teachers (Stevenson and Baker, 1987). They are also more likely to have information about their child's school and to be responsive to their child's school problems and to help select more rigorous courses for their child to take (Baker and Stevenson, 1986). As we noted earlier, adolescents whose parents are involved in their schooling perform better than adolescents whose parents are not, youngsters from higher social classes may achieve more in school than their less advantaged peers (Stevenson and Baker, 1987).

Socioeconomic differences in school achievement—however measured—obviously reflect the cumulative and combined effects of a variety of influences, and it is simplistic to explain group differences in achievement without considering these factors simultaneously. What is perhaps more interesting—and more worthy of scientific study—is to ask what it is about the many youngsters from economically disadvantaged backgrounds who are successful that accounts for their overcoming the tremendous odds against them. Although more research on this subject is sorely needed, several findings suggest that what might be most important is the presence of warm and encouraging parents who raise their children authoritatively, take an interest in their children's academic progress, and hold high aspirations for their children's educational attainment (Bachman, 1970; Simpson, 1962). In other words, positive family relations and parents' encouragement can in some circumstances overcome the negative influence of socioeconomic disadvantage.

## ETHNIC DIFFERENCES IN EDUCATIONAL ACHIEVEMENT

Among the most controversial—and intriguing—findings in research on adolescent achievement are those concerning ethnic differences in school success. On average, the achievement of African-American and Hispanic-American students, virtually however indexed, lags behind that of white students, and all three groups achieve less in school than do Asian-American students. Although some of these differences can be attributed to socioeconomic differences between these ethnic groups, the group disparities persist even after socioeconomic factors are taken into account (Humphries, 1988; Mickelson, 1990; Steinberg, Dornbusch, and Brown, in press; Sue and Okazaki, 1990).

Several theories have been advanced to explain these differences. One set of theories involves the perceptions that adolescents have about the likely pay-off of hard work in school. For example, urban anthropologist John Ogbu (1974) has argued that many minority youth do not believe that educational success will have substantial occupational pay-off for them, because of a prejudicially-imposed "job ceiling" on the career development of African-American and Hispanic-American individuals. Conversely, Asian-American youngsters not only believe in the value of school success, but are very anxious about the possible negative repercussions of *not* doing well in school, both in

Studies of ethnic differences in school performance indicate that Asian-American students, in particular, believe that working hard in school pays off and that not working hard will have severe negative repercussions. Although this precalculus summer school class was open to any student in the school, only Asian-Americans enrolled. *(Rhoda Sidney/ Image Works)*

terms of occupational success and in terms of their parents' disappointment (Chung and Walkey, 1989; Steinberg, Dornbusch and Brown, in press). Moreover, Asian youth believe that the *only* way that they can succeed in mainstream American society is through educational achievement (Sue and Okazaki, 1990).

An alternative, and complementary, view stresses differences in ethnic groups' beliefs about ability. We noted earlier that adolescents who believe that intelligence is malleable are more likely to be intrinsically motivated, mastery oriented, and, as a consequence, academically successful. It is therefore interesting to note that Asian cultures tend to place more emphasis on effort than on ability in explaining school success and are more likely to believe that all students have the capacity to succeed (Hess et al., 1987; Holloway, 1988), and that Asian-American youth spend more than twice the amount of time each week on homework and other school-related activities than do other youth (Steinberg, Dornbusch, and Brown, 1992). One explanation for ethnic differences in performance, then, is that parents and teachers in Asian communities are more likely to socialize adolescents into believing that their success is in their own hands, whereas parents and teachers in black and Hispanic communities are more likely to communicate the message that, although education is important, there is little that minority individuals can do to succeed within a discriminatory society (Mickelson, 1990). Unfortunately, this latter message simply is not true: Not only does educational achievement matter for minority youth, it may make more of a difference for minority youngsters than for their majority counterparts (Wetzel, 1987).

## CHANGES IN EDUCATIONAL ACHIEVEMENT OVER TIME

As noted in Chapter 6, more students are going on to postsecondary education today than ever before. In other words, levels of educational attainment in America have risen substantially over the past half century. For example, whereas in 1937 only 15 percent of the students enrolled in the fifth grade eventually entered college, by 1982, this figure had risen to well over 50 percent. Today, between 50 and 60 percent of recent high school graduates enroll in postsecondary programs (Wetzel, 1987).

These overall trends are encouraging, but several variations from this pattern have drawn the concern of educators in recent years. Notably, although high school graduation rates have increased in recent years among African-American youth, college enrollment rates among minorities have actually declined (De Parle, 1991) (see Figure 12.1). Thus, for example, whereas one-third of black high school graduates enrolled in college in 1976, only one-fourth did so in 1988. Similarly, the proportion of Hispanic high school graduates enrolling in college dropped from 36 percent in 1976 to 27 percent in 1985 (Fiske, 1987). Most experts attribute the decline to cutbacks in financial aid. The decline in minority student college enrollment is all the more troubling in light of other data, discussed later in this chapter, indicating that levels of academic achievement among minority youth, as indexed by standardized tests, have risen more steeply in recent years than scores among nonminority students. For example, the percentage of African-American 17-year-olds reading at an "adept" level tripled between 1975 and 1988 (De Parle, 1991).

Trends in academic achievement, however, have not paralleled trends in educational attainment. Thus, while more students are staying in school, they are not necessarily learning more. For example, as Figures 12.2 and 12.3 indicate, between 1970 and 1980, average scores on the Scholastic Aptitude Test (SAT) declined by about fifty points but rose by about fifteen points between 1980 and 1984 (Con-

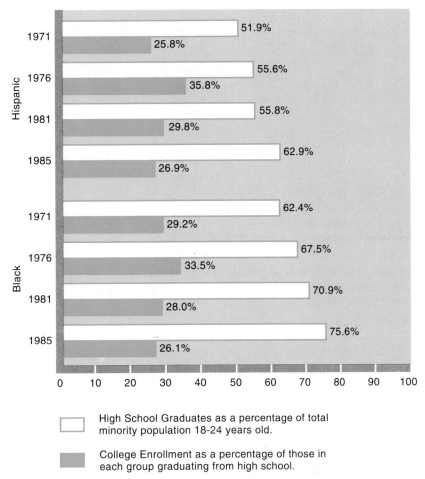

High School Graduates as a percentage of total minority population 18-24 years old.

College Enrollment as a percentage of those in each group graduating from high school.

**FIGURE 12.1**  Although rates of high school graduation among minority youth have increased in recent years, rates of college enrollment have declined. (Census Bureau)

gressional Budget Office, 1986). Scores on other tests of achievement, such as the Iowa Tests of Basic Skills, a widely used standardized test, showed a similar pattern of decline during the late 1960s and 1970s and an increase during the early 1980s (see Figure 12.2 [Congressional Budget office, 1986]). Although scores have been improving, overall achievement levels are not substantially higher now than they were in the early 1970s (Mullis et al., 1990).

The relatively poor showing of American adolescents on standardized tests of achievement was carefully documented in a recent report based on the National Assessment of Educational Progress (NAEP) (Mullis et al., 1990). This national assessment of student achievement is conducted by the federal government, in order to track trends in educational achievement over time. Because the NAEP tests have been administered regularly

Average SAT scores, 1970-1985

**FIGURE 12.2** SAT scores declined between 1970 and 1980, but increased between 1980 and 1984. They have not changed substantially since then. (College Exam Board, 1990)

over the past twenty years, it is possible to compare the achievement levels of today's adolescents with their counterparts two decades ago.

Most analyses of the NAEP data indicate that the main gains in achievement that have occurred during the past decade or so have been in relatively simple skills. In reading and writing, for example, although more than half of all American 13-year-olds today can read well enough to be able to search for specific information and make generalizations from reading material, only 10 percent can understand and summarize relatively complicated information. Fewer than half of all students are able to write a simple report (e.g., on a book or television show) at their grade level, and fewer than one-third are able to write a persuasive essay.

Levels of achievement in math and science show a similar pattern. Thus, while virtually all 17-year-olds can add, subtract, multiply, and divide using whole numbers, only half can perform computations with decimals, fractions, and percents and solve simple equations,

and only 6 percent can use basic algebra. Nearly all 17-year-olds have some simple knowledge about plants and animals, but only 40 percent have any detailed knowledge of science and only 7 percent can use scientific knowledge to draw conclusions.

As is the case in rates of high school graduation, the gap in achievement between white and minority youngsters has narrowed during the past two decades, but a wide disparity still exists. According to NAEP data, across virtually all subject areas, the average African-American or Hispanic-American high school senior is performing at a level comparable to the average white eighth-grader. There is no reason to be sanguine about the performance of white students, however—since the 1970s, their test scores have remained stagnant and U.S. scores on standardized tests are among the lowest in the industrialized world. Three-fourths of all college faculty believe that entering students lack basic skills, and colleges have reported a significant increase in demand for remedial course work for incoming freshmen (Mullis et al., 1990).

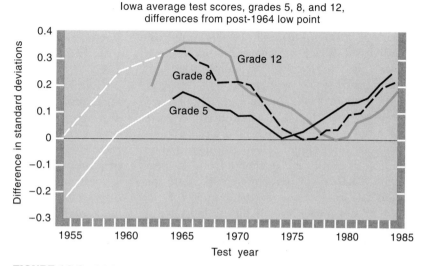

Iowa average test scores, grades 5, 8, and 12, differences from post-1964 low point

**FIGURE 12.3** Adolescents' scores on most standardized tests of achievement, such as the Iowa Tests of Basic Skills, were lower during the 1970s than before or after. (Congressional Budget Office, 1986)

If more American students are remaining in high school, and so many are going on to college, why are their achievement test scores so low? The NAEP report suggests several reasons—among them, that teachers are not

Recent surveys show that fewer than one-third of all American students are able to write a persuasive essay. (Elizabeth Crews/Stock, Boston)

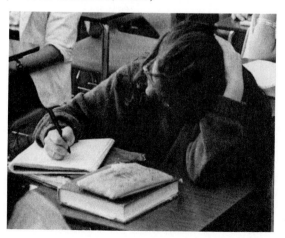

spending enough time on basic instruction in the classroom; that students are not taking advanced courses when they are offered, especially courses in math and science; that parents are not encouraging academic pursuits at home; and that students are not spending sufficient time on their studies outside of school. The average high school senior, for example, spends only about one hour per day on homework (Mullis et al., 1990). Perhaps not surprisingly, students report feeling more unhappy, lethargic, and uninterested while doing homework than during other activities (Leone and Richards, 1989).

## DROPPING OUT OF HIGH SCHOOL

There was a time when leaving high school before graduating did not have the dire consequences that it does today. With changes in the labor force, however, have come changes in the educational requirements for entry into the world of work. Today educational attainment is a powerful predictor of adult occupational success and earnings. Not surprisingly, high school dropouts are far more likely than graduates to live at or near the poverty level, experience unemployment, depend on government-subsidized income maintenance programs, and be involved in delinquent and criminal activity.

Although dropping out of high school is less prevalent now than it was twenty-five years ago, a substantial number of today's adolescents leave high school before graduating. The national dropout rate declined from 40 percent in 1960 to 25 percent in 1965, but the rate began to increase in the late 1970s. In some urban areas, half of all students leave school prematurely (Bryk and Thu, 1989). However, more than half of all youngsters who do not graduate on time eventually complete their high school education by returning to school or through a General Education Development (GED) program. The proportion of individuals who have not completed a high school degree by age 29 is only 14 percent ("Youth and America's Future," 1988).

When dropout rates are examined for different racial groups, we find that African-American youngsters drop out of high school at about the rate of white youngsters (both are near the national average) but that Hispanic youngsters drop out at more than twice the rate of other youth (De Parle, 1991). One reason for this is the large proportion of Hispanic youth who are not English-speaking; a lack of proficiency in English is a major determinant of dropping out (Steinberg et al., 1984).

Given the findings on school achievement discussed earlier, the research evidence on the other correlates of dropping out comes as no surprise. In addition to the prevalence of dropping out among Hispanic youngsters and among youngsters who are not fluent in English, adolescents who leave high school before graduating are more likely to come from lower socioeconomic levels, poor communities, large families, single-parent families, and households where little reading material is available.

In short, adolescents who drop out of school are more likely to come from socially and economically disadvantaged backgrounds (Entwisle, 1990; Rumberger, 1983; Zimiles and Lee, 1991).

Coupled with this socioeconomic disadvantage, adolescents who drop out of high school also are more likely to have had a history of poor school performance, low school involvement, poor performance on standardized tests of achievement and intelligence, and negative school experiences. Many high school dropouts have had to repeat one or more grades in elementary school. By the time youngsters have reached the ninth grade, for example, it is possible to predict—with over 90 percent accuracy—which adolescents will complete high school simply by knowing each individual's age (which indicates whether he or she has been held back in school), IQ, socioeconomic background, and achievement test scores (Walters and Kranzler, 1970). More remarkably, one researcher was able to identify youngsters who would become high school dropouts with 75 percent accuracy at the time the individuals were in the *third* grade, solely on the basis of family background variables, achievement test scores, elementary school grades, and IQ scores (Lloyd, 1978).

The picture that emerges, then, is that dropping out of high school is not so much a decision that is made during the adolescent years but, like other aspects of adolescent achievement, the culmination of a long process. For the dropout, this process is characterized by a history of repeated academic failure and increasing alienation from school.

Although most research on the causes of dropping out has focused on characteristics of adolescents who leave school prematurely, a number of studies have focused on the schools that drop-outs leave. In general, dropping out is less likely in schools in which the environment is orderly, academic pursuits are emphasized, and the faculty is committed. Dropping out is also more frequent in larger schools that group students according to ability (Bryk and Thum, 1989).

## Occupational Achievement

During early and middle adolescence, school is the setting in which achievement is most often expressed. During late adolescence, the focus shifts to the world of careers and work. Although we often think of school and work as separate domains, achievement is one aspect of psychosocial development during adolescence that links them together. Rather than thinking of educational achievement and occupational achievement as separate, it is more useful to think of them as different manifestations of the same basic psychosocial phenomena.

The number of years of schooling an individual completes is the single best indicator of his or her eventual occupational success. It is not simply that adolescents benefit in the labor force by having a high school diploma or a college degree. Although these credentials matter, research shows that each year of education—even without graduating—adds significantly to occupational success. In other words, individuals who have completed three years of college earn more money, on average, than individuals who have completed only one year, even though neither group has a college degree in hand. You may be surprised to learn, however, that *grades* in high school and college are virtually unrelated to occupational success. A few years after graduation, "A" students and "C" students hold similarly prestigious jobs and earn comparable amounts of money (Garbarino and Asp, 1981).

Researchers interested in occupational achievement during adolescence have examined several issues, including the ways in which young people make decisions about their careers and the influences on their occupational

aspirations and expectations. We begin with a look at the development of adolescents' occupational plans.

### THE DEVELOPMENT OF OCCUPATIONAL PLANS

The development of occupational plans during adolescence can be viewed in many respects as paralleling, or even as a part of, the identity development process. As with developing a coherent sense of identity, the development of occupational plans follows a sequence that involves an examination of one's traits, abilities, and interests; a period of experimentation with different work roles; and an integration of influences from one's past (primarily, identification with familial role models) with one's hopes for the future. And as is also the case with identity development, occupational role development is profoundly influenced by the social environment in which it takes place.

For some time, the dominant theoretical viewpoint in the study of the development of occupational plans has been that of Donald Super (1967). Super suggests that occupational plans develop in stages, with adolescence as an important time for the crystallization of plans that are more realistic, less based on fantasy, and more grounded in the adolescent's assessment of his or her talents. Prior to adolescence, individuals express occupational interests, but these are much like fantasies and have little to do with the plans they will eventually make. When children are asked what they want to be when they grow up, they are likely to respond with occupations that are exciting, glamorous, or familiar—a teacher, a policeman, a baseball player, a movie star.

With the advent of more sophisticated thinking capabilities during early adolescence, however, and as the economic and practical realities of adulthood become imminent, young people begin to consider career alternatives in a more systematic fashion. They plan

Educational attainment is an extremely strong determinant of occupational achievement, especially among African-American and Hispanic adolescents. Young people who graduate from college are more successful in the world of work than individuals who do not continue their schooling after high school. *(Janice Fullman/Picture Cube)*

educational and work activities to suit their career interests, and they evaluate career decisions in terms of long- as well as short-term consequences. Instead of merely being attracted to glamorous or exciting jobs, adolescents think about such mundane realities as the need to earn a living.

According to Super, between ages 14 and 18 individuals first begin to crystallize a vocational preference. During this period of **crystallization,** individuals begin to formulate ideas about appropriate work and begin to develop occupational self-conceptions that will guide subsequent educational decisions. Although adolescents may not settle on a particular career at this point, they do begin to narrow their choices according to their interests, values, and abilities. One adolescent may decide that she wants a career in which she works with people. Another may decide that she wants a career in which she can earn a great deal of money. A third may think about a career in science. During this period, the adolescent begins to seek out information on his or her tentative choice and make plans for the future (Osipow, 1973). The process is reminiscent of the sort of role experimentation described by Erik Erikson (1968) in his theory of adolescent identity development. In both cases, during middle adolescence, alternative identities are considered and evaluated on the basis of exploration, experimentation, and self-examination (Grites, 1989).

Following the period of crystallization is a

period of **specification,** occurring roughly between the ages of 18 and 21. During this period, the young person recognizes the need to specify his or her vocational interests and begins to seek appropriate information to accomplish this. In many regards, a similar process is followed during the stage of specification as during the stage of crystallization: alternatives are considered, information is sought, decisions are made, and preferences are consolidated. The chief difference, however, is that during the period of specification, more narrowly defined career pursuits within a general career category are considered (rather than general career categories themselves). For example, during the period of crystallization, a young person may decide that he wants to pursue a career in the field of mental health, without being able to specify a vocational preference within this general category. During the specification stage, he might begin to consider and compare a variety of careers within the mental health profession—social work, educational counseling, clinical psychology, psychiatry, and so on—and make choices among them.

Although the chronological ages given in Super's theory must be taken as only rough guidelines, his perspective is an influential one, and it has shaped the way in which career counselors advise young people. Perhaps most important, Super's perspective reminds us that vocational development comes relatively late during adolescence and that a good deal of growth in this arena takes place during the young adult years. This has become increasingly true in contemporary society, as more and more young people have chosen to continue their education in college and postpone their entrance into a career until their mid-twenties. Changes in the broader environment in which adolescents develop—in this case, changes in the accessibility of higher education—can exert a powerful influence on the developmental course of vocational planning.

## INFLUENCES ON OCCUPATIONAL CHOICES

What makes one individual choose to become an attorney and another, a teacher? Why do some students pursue careers in business while others major in engineering? Researchers have long been interested in the reasons that individuals end up in certain careers. While Super's developmental theory has helped us understand the general stages of career planning, it does not shed light on why certain careers appeal to some individuals but not to others. In other words, Super's theory focuses on *how* and *when* individuals make career choices, rather than on *why* they make the career choices they do.

**The influence of personality traits and interests on occupational plans** Many theorists interested in why people enter different occupational fields have examined the role of personality factors—traits, interests, and values—in the process of career selection. They believe that individuals select careers that match, in one way or another, certain elements of their personality. Perhaps the most widely cited perspective of this sort is that of John Holland (1985).

After years of extensive analysis of jobs and the people who select them, Holland determined that career choices can be viewed as a reflection of basic personality styles. Certain occupational environments are well suited to individuals with certain personalities, and others are not. Successful career choice, in Holland's model, entails the matching of a particular personality type—a given set of interests and personality characteristics—with a vocation that allows the expression of these traits. By answering questions on a standardized personality inventory, an individual can determine which basic personality dimensions are characteristic of himself or herself and can then

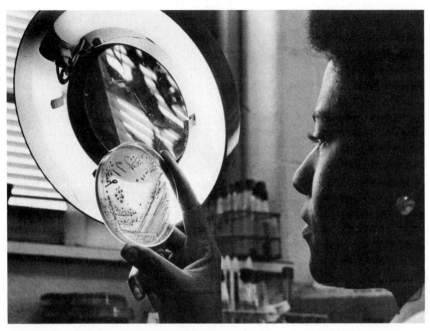

According to John Holland's model of career choice, individuals who are "investigative" are well-suited for jobs that permit the use of conceptual and theoretical skills. Scientists, for example, often have investigative personalities. *(Guy Gillette/Photo Researchers)*

examine directories in which occupations have been classified according to the same typology.

After completing Holland's personality inventory—called the **Self-Directed Search**—an individual better understands his or her vocational profile: which of the personality dimensions are dominant and which are less important. Because different occupations typically offer different degrees of opportunity to express different traits a good career choice, in Holland's view, is one that provides the best fit between a person's personality and a vocation's characteristics. Someone who is artistic, social, and enterprising, for example, would be better suited to a career in acting than in accounting. Other theoretical frameworks focusing on the fit between individual personality characteristics and work environments are popular as well.

There are important limitations to theories of career choice that are based solely on personality traits, however. First, as Jeylan Mortimer and her colleagues have demonstrated (Mortimer and Lorence, 1979), it is clear that interests and abilities are not fixed during adolescence and young adulthood. They continue to develop and change during the adult years. Indeed, one of the most important influences on personality development during adulthood is work itself! Thus through working in a job that emphasizes certain personality characteristics, requires certain abilities, or reinforces certain values, individuals begin to change in these directions. Consequently, a job that may seem like a bad match during early adulthood may, over time, become a good match, as the adult employee grows and changes in response to the work environment.

For example, an individual may not have especially social interests but may, because of a tight job market, end up in a teaching position after graduating from college. Over time, the more he interacts with his students, the more he may come to like the interpersonal aspects of his job. Eventually, he may come to feel that having opportunities for social interaction on the job is very important.

A second problem with theories of career choice that emphasize personality dimensions is that they may underestimate the importance of other factors that influence and shape vocational decisions. Many career decisions are influenced more by individuals' beliefs about what sorts of jobs are "appropriate" for them rather than by interests and preferences. It is all well and good, for example, for an adolescent to discover that he or she is well suited for a career in medicine; but the realization is of little value if the young person's family cannot afford the cost of college or medical school. An adolescent girl may discover, through taking a vocational preference inventory, that she is well suited for work in the area of construction or building, but she may find that her parents, peers, teachers, and potential employers all discourage her from following this avenue of employment. Put most simply, career choices are not made solely on the basis of individual preference; they are the result of an interaction among individual preference, social influence, and important forces in the broader social environment. It is to these influences and forces that we now turn.

## Social and environmental influences on occupational plans

*The influence of parents and peers.* Adolescents' occupational ambitions and achievements are highly correlated with the ambitions and achievements of those around them (Duncan, Featherman, and Duncan, 1972). Youngsters from middle-class families are more likely than their less advantaged peers to aspire to and enter middle-class occupations. In addition, apart from their own socioeconomic status, youngsters who have many friends from middle-class backgrounds are more likely than those who have many friends from lower socioeconomic levels to aspire to high-status occupations (Simpson, 1962).

A variety of explanations have been offered for the fit between adolescents' ambitions and the socioeconomic status of those around them. First and perhaps most important, occupational attainment—the prestige or status an individual achieves in the world of work—depends strongly on educational attainment (Alexander and Eckland, 1975). As we saw earlier, educational attainment is greatly influenced by socioeconomic status. Thus because middle-class adolescents are likely to complete more years of schooling than their lower-class peers, economically advantaged adolescents are more likely to seek and enter higher-status occupations.

Second, middle-class parents, as we noted earlier, are more likely to raise their children in ways that foster the development of strong needs for achievement (Rosen, 1956) and interest in career exploration (Grotevant and Cooper, 1988). The development of achievement motivation, which has an impact on school performance, also has an impact on youngsters' occupational ambitions—both directly (in that individuals with strong needs for achievement will express these needs by aspiring to occupations that provide opportunities to achieve status or wealth) and indirectly, through the effects of achievement motivation on academic achievement (in that youngsters who are successful in school are likely to be encouraged to seek higher-status occupations and engage in identity exploration).

Third, the same opportunities that favor economically advantaged youngsters in school situations—better facilities, more opportunities for enrichment, greater accessibility of higher

Although some young people establish career choices by rejecting their parents' occupations, the majority of adolescents select careers that are similar to, rather than different from, those of their parents. Parent-child similarity in occupational choices is greatest in families with warm, close relationships. *(Eric Roth/Picture Cube)*

education—also favor middle-class youngsters in the world of occupations. Because their parents, for example, are more likely to work in positions of power and leadership, middle-class youngsters often have important family connections and sources of information about the world of work that are less available to youngsters from poorer families. In addition, coming from a family that is economically well-off may provide an adolescent with more time to explore career options and wait for an especially desirable position rather than having to take the first job that becomes available, out of economic necessity.

Fourth, parents, siblings, and other important sources of influence serve as models for adolescents' occupational choices (Grotevant and Cooper, 1988). Although it is true that some young people establish career choices through the explicit rejection of their parents' careers, the weight of the evidence suggests that adolescents' and parents' vocations are more similar than different, particularly when the adolescent's family relationships have been warm and close and when strong identifications have formed. As we saw in our discussion of mothers' employment in Chapter 4, adolescents are especially influenced by the work roles of the parent of the same sex. This finding has become increasingly important as growing numbers of women enter the labor force and hold high-status occupations. Daughters of women who are happily employed outside the home are far more likely themselves to seek careers in addition to marriage and family responsibilities than are adolescent girls whose mothers are not employed (Leslie, 1986). Moreover, young women whose mothers occupy high-status occupations are more likely to do so themselves when they enter the labor force (Hoffman, 1974).

Finally, parents—and to a lesser extent peers—influence adolescents' occupational plans by establishing a value context in which certain occupational choices are encouraged and others are discouraged. According to sociologist Melvin Kohn (1977), middle-class families and middle-class schools encourage children to value autonomy, self-direction, and independence—three features that are more likely to be found in middle-class than in working-class jobs. They are told, implicitly and explicitly, how important it is to have freedom, power, and status. Adolescents who have been raised to value attributes that are characteristic of middle-class jobs will, not surprisingly, seek those attributes when they plan their careers. They will look for jobs that offer independence and power. In working-class families, in contrast, children are more likely to be raised to value obedience and conformity—two characteristics that are highly valued in most working-class jobs. For youngsters from this socioeconomic background, jobs that appeal to these values will be relatively more attractive. They will have been raised to value such things as job security and not having to worry too much about making high-pressured decisions. Indeed, to many working-class youngsters, the high-stress world of the business executive is not at all an attractive career possibility.

### The broader context of occupational choice

Adolescents' occupational choices are made, of course, in a broader context that profoundly influences the nature of their plans. At differ-

ent times, different employment opportunities arise, and young people—particularly by the time they reach the end of their formal schooling—are often very aware of the prospects for employment in different fields. Understandably, they often tailor their plans in response to what they perceive as the needs and future demands of the labor market.

Unfortunately, adolescents also tailor their plans based on their beliefs about what jobs are "acceptable" for individuals of particular social class, ethnicity, or gender. A case in point concerns the occupational choices of young women. Despite the liberalization in sex-role stereotypes that occurred during the past twenty-five years, it is still the case that adolescent girls' vocational choices tend to be concentrated among jobs that have historically been occupied by women, such as secretarial work, teaching, and nursing. In contrast, relatively few adolescent girls plan to enter jobs in science or engineering—occupational sectors that typically have been dominated by men. Moreover, many more adolescent girls than boys express concern about having to balance family and work demands in adulthood, and this further affects their occupational decision making, since they may be reluctant to pursue careers that they believe will interfere with family life (Astin, 1984).

One problem faced by all young people in making career plans is obtaining accurate information about the labor market needs of the future and the appropriate means of pursuing positions in various fields. Psychologist Harold Grotevant, who has studied adolescents' occupational plans extensively (Grotevant and Durrett, 1980), notes that the majority of young people do not have educational plans that are consistent with the educational requirements of the jobs they hope to enter. Even among high school seniors who perceived themselves as having "considerable" knowledge of the fields they planned to enter, approximately one-fifth were planning on too little education and nearly one-third, too much education, given the requirements of the careers to which they aspired. One goal of career educators is to help adolescents make more informed choices about their careers and to free them from stereotypes that constrain their choices.

## Summary

1. Achievement is an important issue during adolescence because society typically designates adolescence as a time for preparation for adult work roles, because individuals now can understand the long-term implications of their educational and career decisions, and because during adolescence, schools begin making distinctions among individuals that potentially have profound effects on their long-term occupational development.

2. Early theories of the development of achievement stressed individual differences in achievement motivation—some individuals were believed to have a stronger "need for achievement" than others. Contemporary theories, however, stress the interaction of motives, beliefs, attributions, and goals as influencing adolescents' achievement orientation. Adolescents who believe that ability is malleable (rather than fixed); who are motivated by intrinsic, rather than extrinsic, rewards; who are confident about their abilities; and who attribute their successes and failures to effort (rather than to ability or luck) achieve more in school than their peers.

3. In addition to the influence of beliefs, motives, attributions, and goals, individuals' level of achievement is also affected by the social context in which they develop. Adolescents whose parents and friends support academic achievement perform better in school than their peers. By far, however, socioeconomic status is the most important contextual influence on achievement: Adolescents from higher social classes perform better in school and complete more years of schooling than their less advantaged counterparts.

4. Recent studies indicate that there are ethnic differences in school achievement above and beyond those attributable to socioeconomic status. In general, Asian-American adolescents outperform Anglo-American students, who in turn do better in school than African-American or Hispanic-American students. One reason for the superior performance of Asian students is that they are more likely to hold beliefs about achievement that are predictive of success in school.

5. The low level of achievement among American youth has been a national concern for some time now. Although some gains in scores on standardized tests of achievement were reported during the mid-1980s, test scores have not improved since that time and the ground that was lost in the late 1960s and early 1970s has not been recovered.

6. About one-quarter of all American adolescents drop out of high school; in some urban school districts, half of all students leave school prematurely. Drop-outs are more likely than their peers to come from economically disadvantaged backgrounds, to come from single-parent homes, and to have had a poor record of school achievement throughout their educational careers. Studies also suggest that the schools these students drop out from are larger, more disorderly, and less academically-focused than other schools.

7. Adolescence is a time for the development of realistic occupational plans. In general, research indicates that adolescents' career choices are influenced by a number of factors, including their personality, their social background, and their perceptions of the labor market and their potential place within it.

## Key Terms

academic
   achievement
achievement
   attributions

consolidation
crystallization
cultural capital

educational
attainment
extrinsic motivation
intrinsic motivation
learned helplessness

motivation
process model
need for achievement
Self-Directed Search
specification

## *For Further Reading*

ELMEN, J. (1991). Achievement orientation in early adolescence: Developmental patterns and social correlates. *Journal of Early Adolescence, 11,* 125–151. A review of the literature on the development of achievement motives in adolescence.

*Explaining the school performance of minority students.* (1987). Special issue of the *Anthropology and Education Quarterly, 18.* An interesting collection of theoretical articles and case studies exploring school performance among minority students.

FEATHERMAN, D. (1980). Schooling and occupational careers: Constancy and change in worldly success. In O. Brim, Jr., and J. Kagan (Eds.), *Constancy and change in human development.* Cambridge: Harvard University Press. An extensive review of the cumulative process of educational and occupational attainment during childhood, adolescence, and adulthood.

HENDERSON, V., AND DWECK, C. (1990). Motivation and achievement. In S. Feldman and G. Elliott (Eds.), *At the threshold: The developing adolescent.* Pp. 308–329. Cambridge: Harvard University Press. A discussion of the role of achievement beliefs and attributions in adolescent school performance.

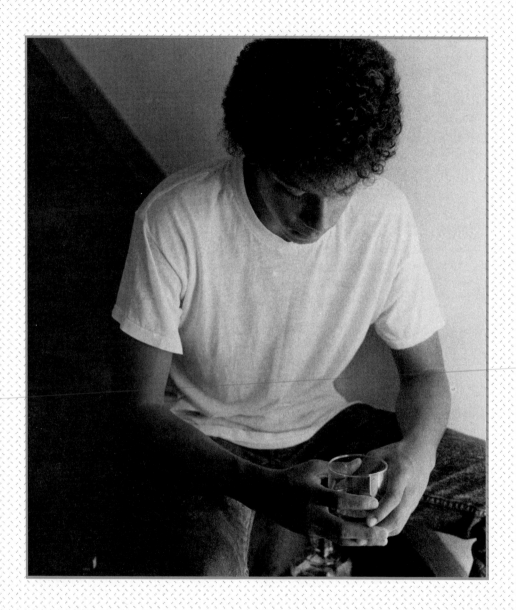

# PSYCHO-SOCIAL PROBLEMS IN ADOLES-CENCE

Although the vast majority of young people move through the adolescent years without experiencing major difficulty, some encounter serious psychological and behavioral problems that disrupt not only their lives but the lives of those around them. Problems such as substance abuse, depression and suicide, eating disorders, and disorders of conduct (including crime and delinquency), while certainly not the norm during adolescence, do affect a worrisome number of teenagers. Moreover, these problems indirectly touch the lives of all of us, either through the personal contact we may have with a troubled young person or indirectly, through increased taxes for community services or heightened anxiety about the safety of our neighborhoods. The young person who drops out of school before graduation, for example, not only jeopardizes his or her own occupational career—reason enough to discourage dropping out of school—but also runs the risk of falling into the welfare system and becoming dependent on public assistance.

In the previous chapters, which examined normative aspects of adolescent psychosocial development, the more problematic aspects of adolescent behavior and development were deliberately de-emphasized, in order to dispel the erroneous stereotype of adolescence as an inherently troubled time. As you now know from reading these chapters, research shows that most individuals emerge from adolescence with positive feelings about themselves and their parents; the ability to form, maintain, and enjoy close relationships with same- and opposite-sex peers; and the basic capabilities needed to take advantage of a range of educational and occupational opportunities. Most settle into adulthood relatively smoothly and begin establishing their work and family careers with little serious difficulty. Although the transition into adulthood may appear forbidding to the young adolescent approaching

many weighty decisions about the future, statistics tell us that for a remarkably high proportion of youth, the transition is relatively peaceful. One in five adolescent girls gets pregnant before she is eighteen, but four in five do not. Twenty percent of students do not complete high school by the societally expected age, but 80 percent do, and more than half of young people who leave school prematurely later receive a high school diploma.

This is not to gloss over the fact that many healthy adolescents at one time or another experience bouts of self-doubt, periods of family squabbling, academic or vocational setbacks, or broken hearts. But it is important to keep in mind as we look at psychosocial probems in adolescence that there is an important distinction between the *normative,* and usually transitory, difficulties that are encountered by many, many young people—and many adults, for that matter—and the serious psychosocial problems that are experienced by a relatively small minority of youth.

## Some General Principles

The mass media like nothing more than to paint extreme pictures of the world in which we live. One way in which this exaggerated view of the world is most obvious is in the presentation of teenage problem behavior. Rarely are portrayals of sex, psychological difficulty, drug use, or delinquency accurate: On television, one experiment with marijuana inevitably leads to drug addiction and school failure. A breakup with a boyfriend is followed by a suicide attempt. An after-school prank develops into a life of crime. A couple's passionate necking session on the beach fades into a commercial, and when the program returns, the adolescent girl is on her way to a life of single parenthood and welfare dependency. Those of you for whom adolescence was not that long ago know that these "facts" about adolescent problem behavior are rarely true, but we are so often bombarded with images of young people in trouble that it is easy for all of us to get fooled into believing that adolescence equals problems.

One of the purposes of this chapter is to put these problems in perspective. It is therefore helpful, before we look at several problems in detail, to lay out some general principles about adolescent psychosocial problems that apply to a range of issues. First, we need to distinguish between *occasional experimentation* and *enduring patterns of dangerous or troublesome behavior*. Research shows that rates of occasional, usually harmless, experimentation far exceed rates of enduring problems. For example, the majority of adolescents experiment with alcohol sometime before high school graduation, and the majority will have been drunk at least once, but, as we shall see, relatively few teenagers will develop drinking problems or permit alcohol to adversely affect their school or personal relationships.

Second, we need to distinguish between problems that have their origins and onset in adolescence and those that have their roots in earlier periods of development. It is true, for example, that some teenagers fall into patterns of criminal or delinquent behavior during adolescence, and for this reason we tend to associate delinquency with the adolescent years. But studies suggest that most teenagers who have recurrent problems with the law had problems at home and at school from an early age; in some samples of delinquents, the problems were evident as early as preschool (Loeber and Stouthamer-Loeber, 1986). In other words, simply because a problem may be displayed *during* adolescence does not mean that it is a problem *of* adolescence.

Third, it is important to remember that some, although not all, of the problems experienced by adolescents are relatively transitory in nature and are resolved by the beginning of adulthood, with few long-term repercussions in most cases. Substance abuse, delinquency, and unemployment are three good examples of problems that tend to follow this pattern: rates of drug and alcohol use, unemployment, and delinquency are all higher within the adolescent and youth population than in the adult population, but most individuals who have abused drugs and alcohol, been unemployed, or committed delinquent acts as teenagers grow up to be sober, employed, law-abiding adults. Individuals for whom problem behavior persists into adulthood are likely to have had a problematic childhood as well as a problematic adolescence. The fact that some of the problems of adolescence seem to disappear on their own with time does not make their prevalence during adolescence any less significant, but it should be kept in mind when rhetoric is hurled back and forth about the "inevitable" decline of civilization at the hands of contemporary youth.

Finally, as should be evident, problem behavior during adolescence is virtually never a direct consequence of going through the normative changes of adolescence itself. Popular theories about "raging hormones" causing oppositional or deviant behavior have no scientific support whatsoever, for example, nor do the widely held beliefs that problem behaviors are manifestations of an inherent need to rebel against authority, or that bizarre behavior results from having an "identity crisis." As you learned in previous chapters, the hormonal changes of puberty have only a modest direct effect on adolescent behavior; rebellion during adolescence is atypical, not normal; and few adolescents experience a tumultuous identity crisis. When a young person exhibits a serious psychosocial problem, such as depression, the worst possible interpretation is that it is a normal part of growing up. It is more likely to be a sign that something is wrong.

In discussions of adolescent problem behavior, it is important to distinguish between occasional experimentation and enduring patterns of dangerous or troublesome behavior. Although the majority of adolescents experiment with alcohol sometime before high school graduation, and the majority will have been drunk at least once, relatively few teenagers will develop drinking problems or permit alcohol to adversely affect their school or interpersonal relationships. *(Harriet Gans/Image Works)*

## Psychosocial Problems: Their Nature and Co-variation

Clinical psychologists and other experts on the development and treatment of psychosocial problems in adolescence typically distinguish between two broad categories of problems: internalizing disorders and externalizing disorders (Achenbach and Edelbrock, 1987). **Internalizing disorders** are those in which the young person's problems are turned inward and manifested in emotional and cognitive symptoms such as depression, anxiety, or in psychosomatic disturbances. (Psychosomatic disorders are physical problems that are at least partially psychological in origin, such as bulimia or anorexia). **Externalizing disorders,** in contrast, are those in which the young person's problems are turned outward and manifested in behavioral problems (some writers use the expression "acting out" to refer to this set of problems). Common externalizing problems in adolescence are delinquency, drug and alcohol abuse, and truancy.

One of the reasons it is helpful to differentiate between internalizing and externalizing disorders is that the specific problems within each broad category are often highly intercorrelated. That is, drug and alcohol abuse is often asssociated with problems such as delinquency, truancy, defiance, sexual promiscuity, and violence (Donovan and Jessor, 1985; Elliott et al., 1989; Newcomb and Bentler, 1989; Osgood et al., 1988). All of these problems are different sorts of manifestations of a lack of impulse control, and adolescents who engage in these behaviors are often described as *under-controlled.*

There is also a good deal of co-variation in internalizing disorders, although this has been less well studied than co-variation among externalizing problems. Nevertheless, it is the case that depressed adolescents are more likely to experience anxiety, panic, suicidal ideation, eating disorders, and other psychosomatic disturbances (Attie and Brooks-Gunn, 1989; Cantwell and Baker, 1991; Colten et al., 1991; Kandel et al., 1991). All of these disorders are manifestations of distress.

Although the distinction between internalizing disorders and externalizing disorders is useful for organizing information about psychosocial problems in adolescence, it is important to bear in mind that some adolescents experience problems in both domains simultaneously. That is, some adolescents who engage in delinquency also suffer from depression (Cantwell and Baker, 1991), and many depressed adolescents also abuse drugs and alcohol (Kandel et al., 1991). Many researchers believe that it is important to distinguish among adolescents who exhibit one specific problem without any others (e.g., depressed adolescents who do not have other internalizing or externalizing problems), adolescents who exhibit more than one problem within the same general category (e.g., drug-abusing delinquent youth), and adolescents who exhibit both internalizing and externalizing problems (e.g., depressed delinquents), since these adolescents may have followed very different pathways to deviance and may require very different types of treatment (Colten et al., 1991; Ensminger, 1990; McCord, 1990).

## PROBLEM BEHAVIOR SYNDROME

During the last decade, researchers have devoted a great deal of attention to studying the co-variation among externalizing problems in adolescence, and a number of theories about the origins of what some experts call "problem behavior syndrome" have been proposed. The most widely cited perspective comes from the work of social psychologist Richard Jessor and his colleagues (Donovan and Jessor, 1985; Jessor and Jessor, 1977). According to **problem behavior theory,** the underlying cause of externalizing problems in adolescence is *unconventionality* in both the adolescent's personality and social environment (Donovan and Jessor, 1985). Unconventional individuals are tolerant of deviance in general, not highly connected to school or to religious institutions, and very liberal in their social views. Unconventional environments are those in which a large number of individuals share these same attitudes. According to Jessor's research, unconventional individuals are more likely to engage in a wide variety of **risk-taking behavior,** including experimentation with illegal drugs, having sex without contraception, delinquent activity, and even risky driving (Jessor, 1987). Thus the reason that so many behavior problems appear to go hand in hand is that unconventional individuals in unconventional environments are likely to engage in all sorts of risky activities.

Although Jessor's theory does not specifically hypothesize what the origins of unconventionality are, a number of possibilities have been proposed. One set of theories, for example, emphasizes the biological underpinnings of risk-taking or unconventionality, and argues that a predisposition toward deviance may actually be inherited (e.g., Mednick et al., 1987; Rowe et al., 1989). A second view stresses biologically-based differences between individuals in arousal and in sensation-seeking (e.g., Zuckerman, 1983). Yet a third viewpoint emphasizes the early family context in which deviance-prone children are reared and presents problem behavior as a sort of "adaptive" response to a hostile environment (Belsky et al., 1991).

An alternative to the view that there is an underlying trait has been proposed by sociologist Denise Kandel. Kandel and her associates argue that different types of deviance have distinctly different origins, but that involvement in a given problem behavior may itself lead to involvement in a second one. For example, the use of illicit drugs other than marijuana (e.g., cocaine, heroin) increases the chances that an adolescent will become premaritally pregnant (Elliott and Morse, 1989; Yamaguchi and Kandel, 1987) or suicidal (Kandel et al., 1991). Thus, problem behaviors may cluster together not only because of an underlying trait such as unconventionality, but because some activities—drug use in particular—lead to involvement in others.

According to a third view, **social control theory** (Gottfredson and Hirschi, 1990; Hirschi, 1969), individuals who do not have strong bonds to society's institutions—such as the family, the school, or the workplace—will be likely to deviate and behave unconventionally in a variety of ways. This view suggests that the apparent clustering of different problem behaviors may stem from an underlying weakness in the attachment of these youngsters to society. This underlying problem leads to the development of an unconventional attitude, to membership in an unconventional peer group, or to involvement in one or several problem behaviors that may set a chain of problem activities in motion. Social control theory helps to explain why behavior problems are not just clustered together, but far more prevalent among poor, inner-city, minority youngsters.

Finally, a number of researchers stress that we should be careful about overstating the case for a problem behavior "syndrome" (McCord, 1990; Osgood et al., 1988). They note that while engaging in one type of behavior problem increases the likelihood of engaging in another, the overlap among behavior problems is far from perfect. Indeed, in one study, it was found that the vast majority of delinquents are *not* serious drug users (Elliott et al., 1989). Such evidence makes it difficult to embrace a theory

that identifies a *single* cause of problem behavior. Like other types of behavior, problem behavior has multiple and complex causes that vary from one individual to the next. It may be just as erroneous to generalize about the "troubled" adolescent as it is to generalize about young people overall.

## STRESS AND COPING

According to recent studies, nearly half of all adolescents report difficulty in coping with stressful situations at home or school (Gans, 1990). These stressors include major life changes (e.g., parental divorce, changing schools, having someone in the family suddenly become seriously ill), chronically stressful conditions (e.g., poverty, a disabling illness, constant family conflict), and day-to-day hassles (e.g., school exams, being teased by friends, and arguments with siblings and parents) (Compas et al., 1987).

For some teenagers, these stressors can lead to internalized disorders, such as anxiety, depression, headaches, and indigestion. For others, the consequences of these stressors are externalized, in behavior and conduct problems or in drug and alcohol abuse. Yet for many adolescents, the very same sources and levels of stress do not seem to be associated with psychological or physical upset at all. Thus, although we tend to think of stress as having negative effects on our well-being, the connection between stress and dysfunction is not clear-cut.

What makes some adolescents more vulnerable to the effects of stress than others? Psychologists point to three sets of factors. First, the effect of any one stressor is exacerbated if it is accompanied by other stressors. Studies show that stress tends to have a multiplicative effect—an adolescent who faces two stressors at the same time (her parents' divorce and having to change schools, for example) is more than twice as likely to experience psychological problems than is someone who has experienced only one of the two same stressors (Rutter, 1978).

Second, adolescents who have sources of social support—who can turn to friends, parents, siblings, or other adults during times of difficulty—seem to be buffered somewhat from the adverse effects of stressful events (Hauser and Bowlds, 1990). For example, an adolescent who has warm and close family relationships is less likely to be distressed by a stressful experience in school or with close friends than is a teenager who has the same stressful experience but less support at home. Similarly, adolescents with close friends seem to be better able to handle stressors such as parental divorce or starting junior high school than are teenagers without close friendships.

Finally, some adolescents use more effective coping strategies than do others. Specialists who study coping strategies distinguish between **problem-focused coping** and **emotion-focused coping** (Compas et al., 1988; Lazarus and Folkman, 1984). Problem-focused coping involves taking steps to change the source of the stress, whereas emotion-focused coping involves efforts to change one's emotional response to the stress. For instance, if you were feeling very worried about an upcoming exam in this course, a problem-focused strategy might be to form a study group with other students in order to review the material, whereas an emotion-focused strategy might be to go out to a movie or to a party in order to take your mind off the test. More often than not, problem-focused coping involves active mastery of the stressor—treatment of the problem—whereas emotion-focused coping involves passive avoidance or distraction—treatment of the symptom.

There are some situations in which emotion-focused coping is quite effective. These tend to be stressful situations that are clearly uncontrollable, such as getting an injection or having to have painful dental work done. In these instances, trying to distract and calm oneself may help alleviate some of the stress. But, in general, research shows that adolescents who employ problem-focused coping strategies are less vulnerable to the detrimental health consequences of stress, especially if the source of the stress is controllable. Adolescents who use problem-focused strategies are better adjusted, less depressed, and less likely to have behavioral problems (Compas et al., 1988; Ebata and Moos, in press).

In this chapter, we examine the nature, prevalence, consequences, and amelioration of four sets of problems typically associated with adolescence: two externalizing disorders—*drug and alcohol use* and *conduct disorders and delinquency*—and two internalizing disorders—*depression and suicide* and *eating disorders*. In each case, we ask three central questions: How many, and which, young people have problems in this domain? What do we know about factors that contribute to problems in this area? And, finally, what approaches to prevention and intervention appear to have the most promise?

## Adolescent Drug and Alcohol Use

Our society sends young people mixed messages about drugs and alcohol. Television programs aimed at preadolescents urge viewers to "Just Say NO!" but the televised football games and adult situation comedies that many of these same viewers watch tell them, no less subtly, that having a good time with friends is virtually impossible without something alcoholic to drink. Many celebrities idolized by teenagers speak out against cocaine and marijuana, but many equally famous stars admit to using these same drugs.

The mixed signals sent to young people about drugs and alcohol reflect, no doubt, the inconsistent way that we view these substances as a society: Some drugs (like alcohol or Val-

# IS "COHORT-CROWDING" A COMMON CAUSE
# OF ADOLESCENT DISTURBANCE?

If you were to graph the rates of many adolescent problems discussed over the period from 1955 to 1990, you would be startled by the degree of similarity in the curves. Between 1960 and 1980, rates of out-of-wedlock births, adolescent drug and alcohol use, juvenile crime, and teenage suicide skyrocketed. Sometime around 1980, each of the four curves began to level off, and following that time, most showed either a pattern of stability or a very slight decline. Although rates of these four problems are still too high today, the remarkable increase in their prevalence that characterized the 1960s and 1970s has clearly abated. Even if we look at something less dramatic—high school seniors' scores on the Scholastic Achievement Test (SAT), for instance—we find a parallel trend: As you have read in Chapter 12, SAT scores worsened between 1960 and 1980, when the decline leveled off. Since that time, scores have remained more or less constant.

Some social scientists believe that the similarities in these indicators of adolescent troubles are more than coincidental. Specifically, they have argued that rates of adolescent problems—from the fatal to the mundane—are related to the size of the adolescent population. The more "crowded" a cohort of adolescents is (a cohort,

as you have read in Chapter 3, is a group of individuals born during the same era), the more prevalent problems will be in that generation. The smaller the size of the cohort, the lower the rate of problems. Predictions made from this **birth-cohort theory** (Easterlin, 1980) about changes in rates of problem behavior over time have been astonishingly accurate.

If you turn back for a moment to page 157, you will see a graph that depicts the percentage of the American population comprised of 15- to 19-year-olds. If you were to add younger adolescents into the figure, the curve would shift slightly to the right, and the peak in the graph would occur around 1980. This increase reflects the movement into adolescence of the "baby boom" cohort, a large group of individuals born during the twenty years following the end of World War II. The picture parallels exactly the pattern found when adolescent problems are graphed: A moderate increase from 1955 until 1960, a dramatic increase between 1960 and 1980, and a decline thereafter. In other words, as the adolescent cohort became more populous, problems increased, but when the growth of this cohort leveled off, so did its rate of problem behavior.

Because rates of adolescent problem behavior are always adjusted for the size of the adolescent

*continued on next page*

ium) are fine, as long as they are not abused, but others (like cocaine or LSD) are not; some drinking (enough to relax at a party) is socially appropriate, but too much (enough to impair an automobile driver) is not; some people (those over 21) are old enough to handle drugs, but others (those under 21) are not. It is easy to see why teenagers do not follow the

dictates of their elders when it comes to alcohol and drugs. How then, should we view drug and alcohol use among teenagers, when our backdrop is a society that much of the time tolerates, if not actively encourages, adults to use these same substances?

As with most of the problem behaviors that are common during adolescence, discussions population (for example, the juvenile crime rate is reported in terms of crimes per 1,000 adolescents), fluctuations over time in *rates* of out-of-wedlock births, drug and alcohol use, crime, or suicide are not due simply to there being more adolescents around to get into trouble. Rather, there appears to be something about being a member of a crowded generation that increases the risk of an individual becoming involved in trouble.

Why should crowdedness increase problem behavior? One explanation is that when a cohort is crowded, its members must compete more fiercely for economic and social resources—for college admissions, for jobs, for marriage partners, for housing—and that this competition intensifies pressure on individuals. While most individuals are able to manage this pressure, some react by turning to drugs, crime, or other self- or socially-destructive behavior. The competition for resources may be enough to push a slightly vulnerable youngster over the edge from health to deviance.

The birth-cohort theory, of course, permits us to make predictions about the future—something social scientists are generally reluctant to do. Although we obviously do not know with any certainty how the next generations of adolescents will fare, an examination of actual and projected population trends gives us some idea of what we may have in store. As you can see from the graph on page 157, the decline in the size of the adolescent population will soon halt. This is because the "baby boom" cohort began having children of their own during the 1970s, and these children—who, by virtue of the sheer size of their parents' cohort, will themselves be members of a crowded cohort—will begin to enter adolescence during the late 1980s and early 1990s. By the year 2000, the size of the adolescent population will be even greater than it was in 1980. These trends suggest that the rate of adolescent problem behavior will begin to rise again during the 1990s and continue to increase as we move toward the end of this century.

Obviously, the size of the adolescent cohort is not the only factor affecting the rate of problem behavior among young people. You can probably think of other explanations for large-scale fluctuations in adolescent problems, including changes in teenagers' access to drugs, changes in the rate of divorce, or widespread changes in attitudes and values that affect adolescents as well as adults. But the birth-cohort theory helps us understand, once again, that it is difficult to make sense out of adolescent behavior without considering the context in which young people grow up. Part of that context includes the number of other individuals who share adolescence with them.

---

of teenage drug and alcohol use are often filled more with rhetoric than with reality. The popular stereotype of contemporary young people is that they use and abuse a wide range of drugs more than their counterparts did previously, that the main reason adolescents use drugs and alcohol is peer pressure, and that the "epidemic" level of drug and alcohol use among American teenagers is behind many of the other problems associated with this age group—including academic underachievement, early pregnancy, suicide, and crime. The simplicity of these assertions is certainly tempting—after all, what could be more reassuring than to identify the "real" culprit (drugs) and the "real" causes (peers) of all of the maladies

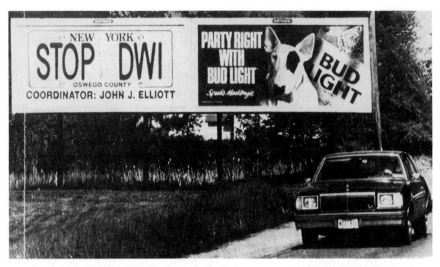

Is there any doubt that our society sends young people mixed messages about drugs and alcohol? On this billboard, an advertisement against driving while intoxicated (DWI) was placed next to one promoting beer consumption. *(Wide World Photos)*

of young people? And what could be even more comforting than the belief that if we simply teach young people to "say no" to their peers, these problems will all disappear?

Unfortunately, what we would like to believe about adolescent drug and alcohol use is not necessarily identical to what the facts are. As we shall see in this section, although there are grains of truth to many of the popular claims about the causes, nature, and consequences of teenage alcohol and drug use, there are many widely held misconceptions about this subject, too.

## PREVALENCE OF DRUG AND ALCOHOL USE

Each year since 1975, a group of researchers from the University of Michigan has surveyed a nationally representative sample of over 16,000 American high school seniors on several aspects of their lifestyle and values, including their use and abuse of a variety of drugs. Because of the size and representative-

ness of the sample of respondents, this survey, called *Monitoring the Future* (Johnston, O'Malley, and Bachman, 1986), is an excellent source of information about patterns of adolescent drug and alcohol use, at least among young people who have not dropped out of school. The most recent statistics available from these researchers are from the graduating class of 1988, and these are summarized in Figure 13.1, which indicates the prevalence and recency of use of eleven types of drugs.

As you can see in Figure 13.1, the two major "legal" drugs—alcohol and cigarettes—are by far the most commonly used substances, both in terms of prevalence (the percentage of teenagers who have *ever* used the drug) and in terms of recency of use (the percentage of teenagers who have used the drug *within the last month*). Nearly all teenagers have tried alcohol, and two-thirds have tried cigarettes. Nearly half of all seniors have tried marijuana, and about one-fifth have smoked marijuana at least once within the last month. After marijuana, however, the percentage of young peo-

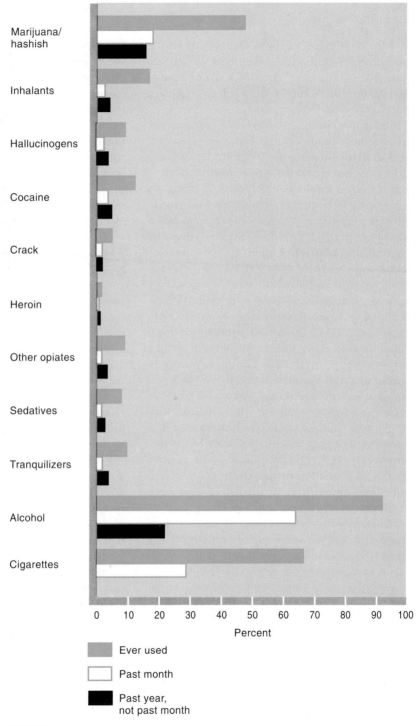

**FIGURE 13.1** Prevalence of recency of use of eleven types of drugs among seniors in the class of 1988. (Johnston et al., 1989)

ple who have tried various other drugs drops precipitously, and the percentage of seniors who have used any of the other drugs within the last month is very small (Johnston et al., 1989).

Prevalence statistics, especially those that tap whether an individual has *ever* tried the substance in question, tell us little about the nature and extent of drug use from the standpoint of adolescents' health and well-being. It is one thing to have tried alcohol or marijuana, but it is something else to use either of these substances so often that one's life and behavior are markedly affected. One of the best ways of examining this issue is to look at the percentage of young people who report using any of these substances daily or nearly daily. When we do so, we find that cigarettes are the only drugs used by a substantial number of high school seniors daily (about 19 percent smoke daily) and that of the remaining drugs, only alcohol and marijuana are used daily by even a modest percentage (5 percent and 3 percent, respectively) of teenagers. Many adults welcome these statistics and find them reassuring—and in some senses they are. More disquieting, however, is that nearly 40 percent of all seniors report having abused alcohol (had more than five drinks in a row) at least once in the past two weeks (Gans, 1990).

Taken together, the findings from these surveys cast doubt on some of the most fervently held stereotypes about adolescent drug use. It is true that many adolescents smoke cigarettes, which is certainly cause for concern, and that many adolescents who drink do so in excess. But the data also indicate that only a very small proportion of young people have serious drug dependency problems (which would lead to daily use) or use hard drugs at all. Moreover, it is very unlikely that drug and alcohol use lurk behind the wide assortment of adolescent problems for which they are so frequently blamed. Rather, the pattern suggests that most adolescents have experimented with alcohol and marijuana, that many have used one or both of these drugs regularly, that alcohol is clearly the drug of choice among teenagers (some of whom drink to excess), and that most teenagers have not experimented with other drugs. From a health and safety standpoint, therefore, education about alcohol and cigarette use and abuse is more urgently needed and may potentially affect a larger percentage of young people than education about any other drug type.

Changes over time in the percentages of seniors reporting daily or near-daily use of marijuana or alcohol are graphed in Figure 13.2. You can see from these figures that the proportion of seniors reporting daily use of marijuana peaked in the late 1970s, declined steadily during the early 1980s, and leveled out during the mid-1980s. The pattern for alcohol is similar, if less striking: Daily alcohol use increased during the mid-1970s, peaked during the late 1970s, declined somewhat during the early 1980s, and has remained essentially unchanged since that time. For the most part, other drugs have followed a similar pattern of either decline or no change in prevalence of use since the early 1980s. One notable exception is cocaine, however, which was used more frequently and more widely by high school seniors during the mid-1980s than previously (Johnston et al., 1986). Cocaine use dropped dramatically between 1986 and 1990, however (see Figure 13.3) (Treaster, 1991).

Several researchers have studied the sequence through which adolescents experiment with different drugs. In general, young people experiment with beer and wine before cigarettes or hard liquor, which precede marijuana use, which in turn precedes the use of other illicit drugs (cocaine, stimulants, LSD) (Kandel, 1980). But although experimentation may follow this sequence, this does not mean that alcohol use invariably *leads to* marijuana use or that marijuana use necessarily *leads to* experimentation with harder drugs. In fact, there is

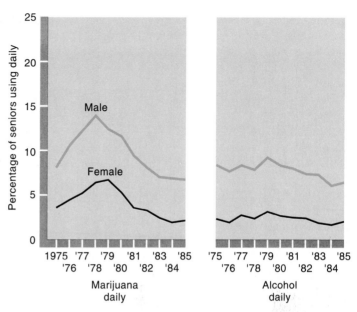

**FIGURE 13.2** Trends in thirty-day prevalance of daily use of marijuana and alcohol. Daily use is defined as use on 20 or more occasions in the past thirty days. (Johnston et al., 1989)

little evidence to support the idea that marijuana is an inevitable "stepping stone" to hard drug use. The fact that such a sequence does exist, however, suggests that virtually all users of hard drugs have also tried alcohol, cigarettes, and marijuana and, moreover, that one way to prevent adolescents from experimenting with more serious drugs is to stop them from experimenting with alcohol and marijuana. In fact, studies show that adolescents who have not experimented with alcohol or marijuana by the time they are 21 are unlikely *ever* to use these or other drugs (Kandel and Logan, 1984). For this reason, alcohol and marijuana are considered "gateway" drugs, in the sense that they form a "gate" through which individuals pass before using harder drugs. Whether an individual passes through the gate, however, is influenced by many other factors beyond his or her previous patterns of drug use.

What to make of this mass of numbers, figures, and trends is not entirely clear. Perhaps the most reasonable reading is that the overall pattern of adolescent drug and alcohol use is not as bad as politicians and the popular media would have us believe but that there nevertheless is little reason to feel complacent. True, drug and alcohol use is lower now than it has been in previous years, but the decline in use that began in the early 1980s has stopped, and cigarette, alcohol, and marijuana use are all still too high, in an absolute sense. Moreover, there is some evidence that experimentation with drugs begins at an earlier age now than previously, so that the problem may not be the prevalence of drug use among high school seniors but, instead, early experimentation with drugs among their younger counterparts. For example, more adolescents begin smoking cigarettes, drinking alcohol, and using marijuana *before* high school than during high school itself

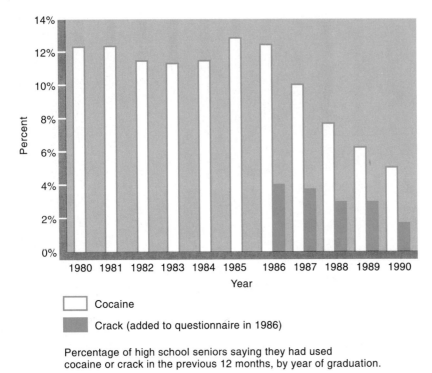

Cocaine

Crack (added to questionnaire in 1986)

Percentage of high school seniors saying they had used
cocaine or crack in the previous 12 months, by year of graduation.

**FIGURE 13.3** Among high school seniors, cocaine use declined dramatically during the late 1980s.

(Johnston et al, 1986). For example, in one recent national survey, more than one-fourth of all eighth-graders reported drinking alcohol regularly, and nearly 10 percent of sixth-graders—11- and 12-year-olds—had consumed five or more drinks consecutively at least once in the previous two weeks (Matza, 1990). Fifteen percent of eighth-grade students report having tried marijuana (Gans, 1990). And the typical adolescent who smokes cigarettes begins in grades 7 or 8 (see Figure 13.4).

The early initiation of drug use among young teenagers and preadolescents is especially disturbing and, unfortunately, has been on the rise (see Figure 13.5) (Matza, 1990). Many psychologists believe that early experimentation with drugs is more harmful than

experimentation at a later age. Younger adolescents may lack the psychological maturity of judgment necessary to use drugs in moderation or under safe circumstances, and younger adolescents may face unique developmental challenges that drug use interferes with (Baumrind and Moselle, 1985). In addition, there is some evidence that heavy drug use may "hurry" adolescents through the psychosocial tasks of adolescence at too fast a pace, thereby interfering with the normal developmental timetable (Newcomb and Bentler, 1988).

Several national surveys have examined ethnic differences in rates of adolescent drug use and abuse. In general, white adolescents are more likely to use drugs and alcohol than mi-

The majority of adolescents who smoke began doing so well before high school. Although adults tend to worry more about teenagers' experimentation with other drugs, cigarette use during adolescence has more harmful long-term health consequences than does experimentation with alcohol or marijuana. *(Mary Ellen Mark Library)*

**FIGURE 13.4**   Most teenagers who begin smoking do so well before high school. (National Adolescent Student Health Survey, Department of Health and Human Services, cited in *The New York Times*, 1990)

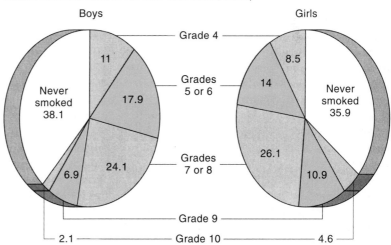

Grades in which students first smoked a cigarette, based on recollections of 10th graders in a 1987 national survey, in percentages.

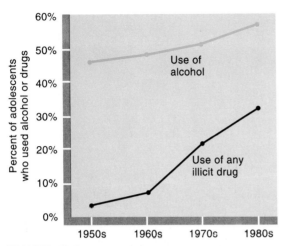

**FIGURE 13.5** Drug use among younger adolescents has increased markedly during the past three decades. (Gans, 1990)

nority youngsters (see Figure 13.6) (Gans, 1990). There is some evidence, however, that Hispanic-American adolescents are at heightened risk for alcohol abuse (Bettes et al., 1990).

## CAUSES AND CONSEQUENCES OF ADOLESCENT DRUG AND ALCOHOL USE

In looking at the causes of drug and alcohol use, it is especially important to keep in mind the distinction between occasional experimentation and regular, problematic use. Because the majority of adolescents have experimented with alcohol and marijuana, one can speculate that occasional alcohol and marijuana use has become normative among American high school students and, consequently, that there are plenty of normal, healthy young people who have used these drugs at least once.

Several studies, in fact, indicate that adolescents who experiment with alcohol and marijuana are as well-adjusted as—if not somewhat better adjusted than—their peers who abstain completely from alcohol and marijuana (e.g., Baumrind, 1991; Shedler and Block, 1990).

This body of research shows quite clearly that it is important to differentiate among adolescents who are frequent drug users (e.g., at least once a week) or hard drug users (i.e., drugs other than alcohol, tobacco, or marijuana); those who experiment with marijuana and alcohol, but who do not use them frequently (i.e., no more than once a month); those who abstain out of irrational fear; and those who abstain out of rational choice (Baumrind, 1991). Experimenters and rational abstainers score higher on measures of psychological adjustment than either frequent users or irrational abstainers. Longer-term follow-up studies also show that moderate alcohol use during adolescence does not have negative long-term effects (Newcomb and Bentler, 1988). Indeed, cigarette use during adolescence has more harmful long-term health consequences than does experimentation with alcohol or marijuana.

These results do not mean that occasional experimentation with drugs during adolescence *leads to* better adjustment, of course. In fact, research shows that the psychological advantages observed among adolescents who experiment with alcohol and marijuana were evident when these individuals were younger children (Shedler and Block, 1990). Taken together, the studies suggest that moderate alcohol and marijuana use has become normative in contemporary society (however troublesome some adults may find this), that these substances are typically used in social situations, and that better adjusted and more interpersonally competent young people are likely to participate in social activities in which alcohol and drugs are present (Burda and Vaux, 1988; Shedler and Block, 1990). Relative to experimenters, abstainers—and "irrational" abstainers in particular—tend to be overcontrolled, narrow in their interests, anxious, and inhibited (Shedler and Block, 1990).

Excessive alcohol or drug use, or, more precisely, alcohol or drug *abuse,* is a different matter. Adolescents who are frequent users of

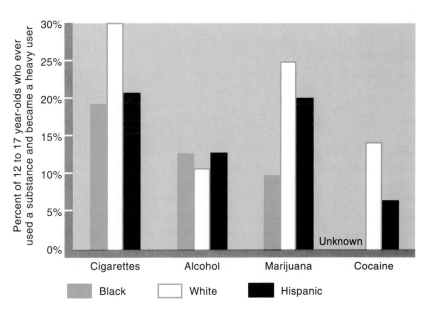

Heavy use is defined as once a week or more except for cigarette use, where it is used in the past month.

**FIGURE 13.6**  White adolescents are more likely to use drugs than are minority youth. (Gans, 1990) drugs score lower on measures of psychological adjustment as teenagers and were more likely to be maladjusted as children (Shedler and Block, 1990). Indeed, a team of researchers who had followed a sample of individuals from preschool into young adulthood reports that at age 7, individuals who would later become frequent drug users as adolescents were described as "not getting along well with other children, not showing concern for moral issues . . . not planful or likely to think ahead, not trustworthy or dependable . . . [and] not self-reliant or confident" (Shedler and Block, 1990, p. 618). As 11-year-olds, these individuals were described as deviant, emotionally labile, stubborn, and inattentive. This study suggests that drug and alcohol abuse during adolescence is probably a symptom of prior psychological disturbance.

During adolescence itself, of course, drug and alcohol abuse is associated with a host of other problems. Young people who abuse drugs and alcohol are more likely to experience problems at school, to experience psychological distress and depression, to engage in "unprotected" sexual activity, and to become involved in dangerous or deviant activities, including crime, delinquency, and truancy (Irwin, 1986; Jessor and Jessor, 1977; Mensch and Kandel, 1988; Newcomb and Bentler, 1989). Alcohol and drugs are typically implicated in adolescent automobile crashes, the leading cause of death and disability among American teenagers (Gans, 1990), and in other fatal and nonfatal accidents, such as drownings, falls, and burns (Irwin, 1986; Wintemute et al., 1987). Adolescent substance abusers also expose themselves to the long-term health risks of excessive drug use that stem from addiction or dependency; in the case of cigarettes, alcohol, and marijuana, these risks are substantial and well-documented—among them, cancer, heart disease, and kidney and liver damage.

Generally, four main sets of "risk factors" for substance abuse have been identified, and

the more risk factors that are present for an individual, the more likely he or she is to use and abuse drugs (Newcomb, Maddahian, and Bentler, 1986). First, individuals with certain personality characteristics—present before adolescence—are more likely to develop drug and alcohol problems than their peers. These characteristics include *anger, impulsivity, depression,* and *achievement problems* (Brook et al., 1986; Shedler and Block, 1990).

Second, individuals with *distant, hostile,* or *conflicted family relationships* are more likely to develop substance abuse problems than are their peers who grow up in close, nurturing families (Barnes, 1984; Flewelling and Bauman, 1990; Needle et al., 1990). Drug-abusing youngsters are also more likely than their peers to have parents who are excessively permissive (perhaps to the point of neglect), uninvolved, or rejecting (Baumrind, 1991; Block et al., 1988; Shedler and Block, 1990). In addition, they are more likely to come from homes in which one or both parents uses drugs or is tolerant of drug use (Brook, Whiteman, and Gordon, 1983; Brook, Whiteman, Gordon, and Brook, 1984; Newcombe, Huba, and Bentler, 1983).

Third, individuals with drug and alcohol probems are more likely to have *friends who also use and tolerate the use of drugs,* both because they are influenced by these friends and because they are drawn to them (Coombs et al., 1991). As you read in Chapter 5, whether and how often adolescents use drugs is an important defining characteristic of peer groups—abstainers tend to have other abstainers as friends, users tend to have other users. Recent studies suggest that drug-using adolescents seek drug-using peers and that drug-using peers encourage even more drug use among their friends (Kandel, 1978).

Finally, adolescents who begin to use drugs a good deal are generally at a point in their own psychological development when they are especially susceptible to the influences around them that may lead them to make the transition into drug use and other deviant behavior (Jessor and Jessor, 1977). Periods of so-called **transition-proneness** are characterized by a high level of tolerance of the probem behavior in question, alienation from school and from family relationships, minimal involvement in religious activity, and general apathy. During transition-prone periods, adolescents are likely to experiment with many different problem behaviors, including drugs, alcohol, and delinquency.

## PREVENTION AND TREATMENT OF DRUG AND ALCOHOL PROBLEMS

Efforts to prevent drug and alcohol use among teenagers focus on one of three factors: the supply of drugs, the environment in which teenagers may be exposed to drugs, and characteristics of the potential drug user (Newcomb and Bentler, 1989). Although a good deal of government spending and media publicity has been devoted to the first of these approaches—that is, to attempts to control or limit the availability of drugs—the consensus among experts is that it is more realistic to try to change adolescents' motivation to use drugs and the environment in which they live, since it has proven virtually impossible to remove drugs totally from society. In addition, the two most commonly used and abused drugs are both legal—cigarettes and alcohol.

Five different types of drug abuse prevention interventions have been tried, either alone or in combination. In two types of programs, drug use is targeted indirectly, by affecting adolescents' psychological development in general or by helping adolescents to develop alternative activities and interests. The idea behind these sorts of efforts is that adolescents who have high self-esteem, for example, or who are gainfully employed, will be less likely to use drugs. Neither of these approaches has been successful, however.

In other programs, the intervention is more directly aimed at preventing drug use. These programs include information-based efforts (in which adolescents are educated about the dangers of drugs), social skills training (in which adolescents are taught how to turn down drugs), and some combination of informational and general psychological intervention (in which adolescents are educated about drug abuse and exposed to a program designed to enhance their self-esteem, for instance) (Newcomb and Bentler, 1989).

Generally speaking, the results of research designed to evaluate these different approaches have not been especially encouraging. Experts are now fairly confident that drug education alone, whether based on rational information or "scare tactics," does not prevent drug use. This is reminiscent of research on sex education, which, as we saw in Chapter 11, shows that informational programs are not effective on their own. Educational programs change individuals' knowledge, but rarely affect their behavior.

The most encouraging results have been found in programs that combine some sort of social competence training with a community-wide intervention aimed not only at adolescents, but at their parents and teachers as well, although these programs have tended to be more successful in reducing cigarette and marijuana use than alcohol use (e.g., Johnson et al., 1990). Overall, most experts agree that efforts designed simply to change the potential adolescent drug user without transforming the environment in which the adolescent lives are not likely to succeed. Despite their intuitive appeal, efforts to help adolescents "Just Say No" have been remarkably unsuccessful.

One of the problems with all prevention programs is that they often do not distinguish between drug *use* and drug *abuse*. As noted earlier, it is abuse, and not occasional use, that is the serious problem. In the words of two leading researchers:

Although it is important to delay the onset of regular drug use as long as possible to allow time for the development of adaptive and effective personal and interpersonal skills, it may be less important to prevent the use of drugs than the abuse, misuse, and problem use of drugs (which place a tremendous burden on the individual and society). It is in this area that prevention programs have been less successful and are in need of continued development. (Newcomb and Bentler, 1989, p. 246)

A similar problem—that is, failing to distinguish between drug use and drug abuse—has plagued treatment efforts aimed at adolescents who are believed to be drug abusers. Indeed, some experts worry that adolescents who are mistakenly enrolled in treatment programs (because their parents have overreacted to the adolescent's normative and probably harmless experimentation with drugs) may end up more alienated and distressed—and more likely to become drug abusers—as a result of the "treatment." Evaluations of treatment programs for adolescents who are genuine drug abusers suggest that efforts that involve the adolescent's family, not just the teenager, are most likely to be successful (Newcomb and Bentler, 1989).

## Juvenile Delinquency and Disorders of Conduct

Although social scientists disagree about the causes and treatment of delinquent behavior during adolescence, there is one point on which there is tremendous agreement—violations of the law are far more common among adolescents and young adults than among any other age segment of the population. Part of this pattern stems from the fact that certain violations, called **status offenses,** are by definition limited to minors. Status offenses, such as truancy, running away from home, or using alcohol, are behaviors that are not against the law for adults but that nevertheless violate established codes of conduct for juveniles. Even if we discount status offenses, however, research shows that both *violent crimes,* such as assault, rape, and murder, and *property crimes,* such as robbery, theft, and arson, increase in frequency between the preadolescent and adolescent years, peak during the high school years, and decline somewhat during young adulthood (Federal Bureau of Investigation, 1986). Individuals under the age of 18, who comprise about one-quarter of the population, account for about *half* of all property crimes, and individuals between the ages of 18 and 24, who comprise a little more than one-tenth of the population, account for nearly half of all violent crimes (U.S. Bureau of the Census, 1985).

Rates of crime among American youth have followed a pattern over time that is similar to that seen when rates of drug use are examined over time. Between 1950 and 1980, roughly speaking, there were steady increases in juvenile arrests for virtually all classes of misbehavior. In the early 1980s, the rate of youthful criminal activity leveled off, and it has remained more or less unchanged since then (FBI, 1990). Because such a large proportion of arrests of juveniles are for property crimes, looking at changes in overall arrest rates over time can be misleading. In fact, when we look specifically at violent crimes, a different, and far more troublesome picture emerges (see Figure 13.7). Between 1965 and 1988, and especially since 1984, the arrest rates for *aggravated assault* (an attack on another person for the purpose of inflicting severe injury, typically with a weapon) and for *murder and nonnegligent manslaughter* increased substantially among young people (FBI, 1990). Increases in violent crime among young people are significant sources of worry to adults, of course. But they also are significant sources of worry to adolescents themselves, who are the age group most likely to be *victims* of crimes such as theft, rob-

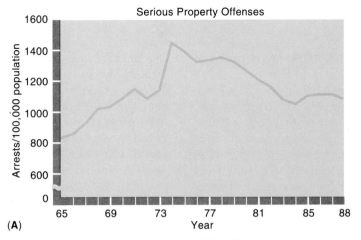

**Serious Property Offenses**

*Serious property offenses* are specified offenses against property (i.e.,burglary, larceny-theft, motor vehicle theft, and arson).

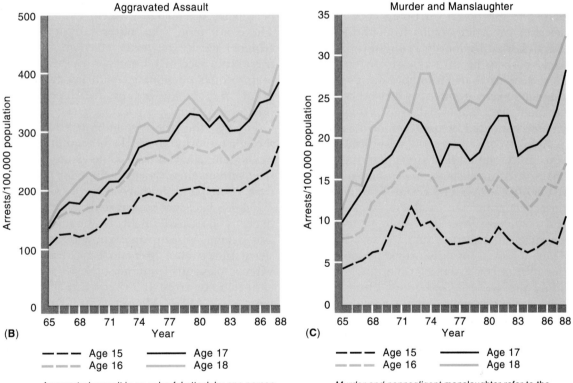

**Aggravated Assault**

- - - Age 15    —— Age 17
- - - Age 16    —— Age 18

*Aggravated assault* is an unlawful attack by one person upon another for the purpose of inflicting severe or aggravated bodily injury. This type of assault usually is accompanied by the use of a weapon or by means likely to produce death or great bodily harm.

**Murder and Manslaughter**

- - - Age 15    —— Age 17
- - - Age 16    —— Age 18

*Murder and nonnegligent* manslaughter refer to the willful (nonnegligent) killing of one human being by another. Note that the scale is different from that for aggravated assault, in order to show the recent increases.

**FIGURE 13.7** Trends in arrest rates. (A) Trends in arrest rates for serious property offenses by persons under age 18 (Office of Technology Assessment, 1991); (B) Trends in arrest rates for aggravated assault by persons age 18 and under (Office of Technology Assessment, 1991); (C) Trends in arrest rates for murder and nonnegligent manslaughter by persons age 18 and under. (Office of Technology Assessment, 1991) bery, rape, and assault (U.S. Department of Justice, 1991).

Most of the data we have on adolescent misbehavior comes from official arrest records. Consequently, it is important to keep in mind that the "official" figures on adolescent crime may both *underreport* and *selectively report* rates of misbehavior. Underreporting results from the fact that many adolescents commit offenses that are undetected by authorities or that are handled outside official reporting procedures—for example, when an adolescent caught shoplifting is reprimanded by the storekeeper instead of being referred to the police. (Only about one-third of crimes are ever reported to the police. [Krisberg et al., 1986].) Selective reporting results from the fact that lower-class and minority youngsters are more likely both to be arrested and to be treated more harshly than are other youngsters who commit similar offenses, so that official statistics may artificially inflate the proportion of crimes committed by poor, minority youth.

An alternative to relying on official records is to go to adolescents directly and ask them about their involvement in various criminal or status offenses. Several researchers have done this, promising the respondents anonymity and confidentiality. The results of these surveys have been surprising, to say the least. They do not necessarily provide a more accurate picture of juvenile crime, but they certainly provide a *different* one. Three conclusions are especially interesting. First, the surveys indicate that a very large proportion of adolescents—between 60 and 80 percent, depending on the survey sample—have engaged in delinquent behavior at one time or another (Gold and Petronio, 1980; Huizinga and Elliot, 1985). Most of these behaviors were not serious crimes, but they nevertheless were genuine status or criminal offenses.

Second, in contrast to official records, which indicate a disproportionate involvement of minority youth in delinquent activities, the sur-

veys indicate that once social class is taken into account, there are relatively few ethnic or racial differences in the prevalence of delinquent activity—in either minor or serious misbehavior. According to data from the 1980 National Youth Survey, for example, nearly equal proportions of white, African-American, and Hispanic-American youth admitted to having committed some type of delinquent activity (65 percent among whites, 72 percent among African-Americans, and 59 percent among Hispanics), and equal proportions admitted having committed a serious crime—about 13 percent in each group. Moreover, there are no racial differences in the prevalence of chronic, or repeat, offenders (Krisberg et al., 1986). There are *social class* differences in serious criminal activity, however, which are often attributed to race or ethnicity. An extensive literature links delinquency with low family income and other indices of disadvantage (McCord, 1990).

Finally, the surveys indicate that even though minority youth do not commit more delinquent behavior than white youth—and do not commit more *serious* delinquent behavior than white youth, either—minority youth are far more likely to be arrested and far more likely to be treated harshly by the juvenile justice system. African-American adolescents are seven times more likely to be arrested than white adolescents for minor offenses and twice as likely to be arrested for serious crimes (Krisberg et al., 1986). Minority youth in general are more likely to be sent to correctional facilities than are white youth who commit similar offenses (Krisberg et al., 1986). Thus the reason for the stereotype of the nonwhite juvenile offender is the higher proportion of arrests in this group, not the higher proportion of delinquent and criminal activity. In addition, the disproportionate number of nonwhite youth living in poverty contributes to racial differences in criminal activity.

Although studies indicate that most adoles-

Surveys indicate that a very large proportion of adolescents—between 60 and 80 percent, depending on the survey sample—have engaged in delinquent behavior at one time or another. Most of these behaviors were not serious crimes, but nevertheless they were chargeable offenses. *(Dorothy Littell/Stock, Boston)*

cents—regardless of their social back-grounds—do *something* that violates the law at one time or another, the vast majority of teen-agers who violate the law do so only once. Thus, while most adolescents have violated the law, a relatively small number of adolescents account for a relatively high proportion of se-rious criminal activity (Gold and Petronio, 1980). It is important, therefore, in thinking about the causes of delinquent behavior, to distinguish between delinquent behavior that is serious and chronic and delinquent behavior that is less worrisome. As you will see momen-tarily, these two sets of delinquent behavior have very different antecedents.

## CAUSES OF DELINQUENT BEHAVIOR

In general, the earlier an adolescent's "criminal career" begins, the more likely he or she is to become a chronic offender, commit serious and violent crimes, and continue committing crimes as an adult. The older an adolescent is when the delinquent activity first appears, the less worrisome his or her behavior is likely to become. For purposes of discussion, therefore, it is helpful to distinguish between youngsters who begin misbehaving before adolescence and those whose delinquent activity first appears during adolescence. The causes and the consequences of delinquency that begins during preadolescence are quite different from those of delinquency that begins during adolescence.

**Undersocialized delinquents** In general, youngsters whose problems with the law begin before adolescence are very psychologically troubled. Most of these delinquents are male, many are poor, and a disproportionate number come from homes in which divorce has occurred. More important, however, chronic delinquents typically come from disorganized families with hostile, neglectful parents who have mistreated their children and failed to instill in them proper standards of behavior or the psychological foundations of self-control (Farrington and West, 1991). The idea that family factors may underlie this type of delinquency—because of either genetic or environmental influences—is supported by observations that preadolescent delinquency tends to run in families. Many adolescents who have been in trouble with the law from an early age have siblings who have had similar problems (Loeber and Stouthamer-Loeber, 1986).

There is also considerable evidence that, apart from family factors, there are individual characteristics that distinguish potential delinquent youngsters from their peers, at a relatively early age. First, and most important, children who become delinquent have histories of aggressive and violent behavior—histories that were identifiable as early as age 8 (Farrington and West, 1991; Kupersmidt and Coie, 1990;

Stattin and Magnusson, 1989). Second, studies show that children who become delinquents are more likely than their peers to suffer from hyperactivity, or as it is officially known, **attention deficit disorder with hyperactivity (ADDH)** (Farrington, 1989; Lambert, 1988; Moffitt, 1990). (ADDH is a syndrome characterized by impulsivity, inattentiveness, restlessness, and inappropriately high levels of activity, especially in learning situations. It is believed to be primarily biological in origin.) Third, children who become delinquent are more likely than their peers to score low in standardized tests of intelligence and to perform poorly in school (Farrington, 1989; Moffitt and Silva, 1988; White et al., 1989).

Because aggressiveness, hyperactivity, and intelligence are relatively stable traits over childhood, there is a great deal of continuity in behavior problems over time. Studies that have followed individuals from childhood through adolescence and into adulthood find very high correlations between behavior problems at one point in time and antisocial behavior later in life (Farrington, 1991; Robins, 1986). It is possible, therefore, to identify at a relatively early age individuals who have what might be termed an **antisocial tendency.** Some social scientists have referred to these youngsters as **undersocialized delinquents** (Gleuck and Gleuck, 1950), because they have not adequately acquired the norms and standards of society. Contrary to popular belief, there is no evidence that these individuals uniformly have low self-esteem, or that raising their self-esteem does anything to diminish their propensity toward misbehavior (McCord, 1990). As you will read, the prognosis for change in this group of adolescents is very grim. Many undersocialized delinquents grow up to be adults diagnosed as suffering from antisocial personality disorder.

**Socialized delinquents** In contrast to youngsters who begin their delinquent careers before adolescence, those who begin after adolescence do not always show signs of psychological abnormality or severe family pathology. Typically, the offenses committed by these youngsters do not develop into serious criminality, and typically these individuals do not violate the law after adolescence. Much of their delinquent activity occurs with peers. Because these individuals have apparently learned the norms and standards of society and are reasonably healthy psychologically, social scientists refer to them as **socialized delinquents** (Miller, 1958).

Current research indicates that some family factors may be associated with socialized delinquency. In particular, there is some evidence that these youngsters are less carefully monitored by their parents (Dornbusch et al., 1985; Patterson and Stouthamer-Loeber, 1984). But there also is evidence that the role of the peer group may be very important (Brown, Clasen, and Eicher, 1986). Specifically, studies show that much of this kind of delinquent activity occurs in group situations in which adolescents are pressured by their friends to go along with the group. In Chapter 9, you read about studies of age differences in susceptibility to peer pressure, which show that susceptibility increases between preadolescence and middle adolescence and then declines. It comes as no surprise, therefore, to discover that much socialized delinquency follows the same pattern: Rates are low during preadolescence, peak during middle adolescence, and drop off as adolescence ends (Berndt, 1979).

An interesting series of studies by Gerald Patterson and his colleagues (Patterson, 1986; Patterson, DeBaryshe, and Ramsey, 1989; Dishion et al., 1991) indicates how family and peer influences may work together in the development of delinquency. Specifically, these researchers have found that poor parental discipline—discipline that is harsh, inconsistent, and lax—during the early elementary school years leads to the association with deviant or antisocial peers, which in turn leads to delinquent behavior. Dysfunctional child-rearing may contribute to the process in two ways. First, adolescents who have distant relationships with their parents are generally more susceptible to peer pressure than other youngsters (Steinberg and Silverberg, 1986). Second, individuals who are raised in dysfunctional ways may develop personality traits that lead children to dislike them—such as aggression—and they may find themselves with few options for friends other than equally disliked and aggressive agemates (Dishion et al., 1991).

**Runaways**   Despite a good deal of attention in the popular media, little empirical research has focused on adolescent runaways. The little research that has been done paints a picture of adolescent runaways different from that portrayed on television melodramas in many significant respects, however. First, the "epidemic" of teenage runaways is grossly overstated. Nationally representative samples of adolescents suggest that between 4 and 10 percent of adolescents have ever run away from home (running away is more common among poor adolescents), and that fewer than half of all runaways have done so more than once. Second, in contrast to images of teenage runaways traveling across the country, surveys indicate that half of all runaways stay within their community, with relatives or friends. Finally, despite frequent portrayals of "long-lost" runaways, half of all runaways return home within a few days, and between 75 and 80 percent return home within a week. Public concern about runaways is high not because the numbers are large, but because of the dangers faced on the streets by the 20 percent who do not return home promptly. These young people are exposed to numerous psychological and physical risks, including prostitution and other criminal behaviors, AIDS and other sexually-transmitted diseases, and drug and alcohol abuse (Windle, 1989).

This young woman lives on the streets of Seattle. Adolescent runaways are exposed to many dangers on the street, among them, prostitution and other criminal behaviors, AIDS and other sexually-transmitted diseases, and drug and alcohol abuse. *(Mary Ellen Mark Library)*

Running away from home is typically considered as another manifestation of problem behavior in general, along with delinquency, aggression, truancy, precocious sexuality, and drug and alcohol use. Consistent with this view, runaways, and repeat runaways in particular, are more likely than other adolescents to be delinquent, to drop out of school, to be aggressive, and to use drugs. The antecedents of running away are similar to those for deviance in general: poverty, low scores on intelligence tests, and family conflict (Garbarino et al., 1986; Windle, 1989).

## TREATMENT AND PREVENTION OF JUVENILE DELINQUENCY

Given the important differences between the causes of undersocialized and socialized delinquency, one would expect that these two groups would be best served by different sorts of preventive and after-the-fact interventions. In order to lower the rate of undersocialized delinquency, we would need to either prevent disruption in family relationships from occurring in the first place or try to repair the psychological damage that these youngsters have suffered because of their upbringing. These strategies are easier proposed than done, however. Our society is hesitant to intervene to prevent family disruption, because we typically wait until we see a sign of trouble in a family before acting. Unfortunately, waiting until after family disruption has occurred before intervening may have little benefit, for research shows that the outlook for delinquents who have begun their criminal careers early is not very good. Various attempts at therapy and other sorts of treatment have not, by and large, proven successful. This is the case for treatment approaches that employ individual psychotherapy, group therapy, and diversion programs designed to remove delinquents from the juvenile justice system (due to the harmful effects of being labeled "delinquent") and provide them with alternative opportunities for productive behavior (McCord, 1990). Programs that attempt to change delinquents' beliefs about the value of aggression as a means for solving problems and teach socially acceptable alternatives to aggression have shown some promise (e.g., Guerra and Slaby, 1990), but even these programs have been only modestly successful in changing offenders' actual behavior (McCord, 1990). Most chronic delinquents go on to commit serious and violent crimes and continue their criminal behavior into adulthood.

The prognosis for the socialized delinquent is somewhat better. Because they have internalized a basic foundation of norms and moral standards, it is easier to help them control their own behavior and stop misbehaving. Three types of strategies have been proposed. First, by helping youngsters learn to resist peer pressure, we can give them the necessary psychological tools to avoid being drawn into misbehavior simply to go along with the crowd (Kaplan, 1983). Second, by training parents to monitor their children more effectively, we can minimize the number of opportunities adolescents have to engage in peer-oriented misbehavior (Loeber and Stouthamer-Loeber, 1986). Finally, by treating delinquency seriously when it occurs—making sure an adolescent knows that his or her misbehavior has definite consequences—we can deter an adolescent from doing the same thing again in the future.

## Depression and Suicide

Most individuals emerge from adolescence confident, with a healthy sense of who they are and where they are headed. But in some in-

stances, the changes and demands of adolescence may leave a teenager feeling helpless, confused, and pessimistic about the future. Although minor fluctuations in self-esteem during early adolescence are commonplace—as you read in Chapter 8—it is not normal for adolescents (or adults, for that matter) to feel a prolonged or intense sense of hopelessness or frustration. Such young people are likely to be psychologically depressed and in need of professional help.

In its mild form, **depression** is probably the most common psychological disturbance among adolescents (Weiner, 1980), but problems in measuring and defining depression make it difficult to say exactly how prevalent the disorder is. It is helpful to distinguish between depressive symptoms and depression as a disorder. Many more individuals have occasional depressive symptoms than suffer from the clinical disorder that is recognized as depression by professionals. According to one large-scale survey, more than half of all adolescents occasionally feel sad and hopeless, more than one-third say they "have nothing to look forward to," and one-third have seriously thought of committing suicide (Gans, 1990) (see Figure 13.8). According to other surveys, about 25 percent of adolescents regularly have depressive feelings, but less than 3 percent of adolescents woud be characterized as severely depressed according to standard diagnostic criteria (Chartier and Ranieri, 1984). There is a dramatic increase in the prevalence of depressive feelings around the time of puberty; depression is half as common during childhood as it is during adolescence. Interestingly, whereas depressive feelings are more common among boys than girls prior to adolescence, depression is much more common among females than males after puberty. This sex difference in the prevalence of depression (see the box on page 449 persists throughout most of adulthood (Gjerde et al., 1988; Petersen et al., 1991).

While minor fluctuations in self-esteem during early adolescence are commonplace, it is not normal for adolescents to feel a prolonged or intense sense of hopelessness or frustration. Such young people are likely to be psychologically depressed and in need of professional help. In its mild form, depression is probably the most common psychological disturbance among adolescents. *(Patt Blue/Archive)*

## THE NATURE OF ADOLESCENT DEPRESSION

Although we typically associate depression with feelings of sadness, there are other symptoms that are important signs of the disturbance, and sadness alone, without any other symptoms, may not indicate depression in the clinical sense of the term. One way of thinking about depression is to consider its four sets of symptoms (Chartier and Ranieri, 1984). Depression has *emotional* manifestations, including dejection, decreased enjoyment of pleasurable activities, and low self-esteem. It has *cognitive* manifestations, such as pessimism and hopelessness. Depressed individuals also have *motivational* symptoms, including apathy and boredom. Finally depression usually has *vegetative,* or physical features, such as a loss of appetite, difficulties sleeping, and loss of energy.

Depression during adolescence is often accompanied by other psychosocial or behavioral problems, which occasionally lead to difficulties in diagnosis or treatment (Kendall et al., 1989). As we noted earlier in the chapter, various types of internalizing disorders—including depression, anxiety, psychosomatic complaints, and eating disorders—tend to co-vary during adolescence. Just as different externalizing problems are hypothesized to reflect an underlying antisocial syndrome, various indicators of internalized distress may be thought of as different manifestations of an underlying factor. This factor, previously labeled "neuroticism," is now referred to as **negative affectivity** (Watson and Kendall, 1989).

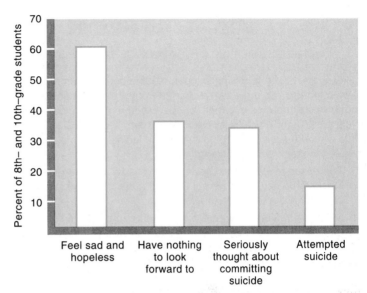

**FIGURE 13.8** Although only 3 percent of adolescents are severely depressed according to standard diagnostic criteria, well over half of all teenagers have felt sad and hopeless at one time or another. (The National Adolescent Student Health Survey, cited in Gans, 1990)

Diagnosing and studying depression among adolescents has been a tricky business for two very different reasons. On the one hand, professionals have been tempted to attribute nearly *all* observable difficulties to unseen depression. In instances of "masked depression," behaviors such as school phobia, running away from home, or anorexia nervosa were thought to hide, or mask, the "real" problem—depression. Now, however, it is widely recognized that not all adolescents with behavior problems are necessarily depressed but, as we saw earlier, that depression and other problems can coexist in some cases (Cantwell and Baker, 1991; Chartier and Ranieri, 1984). In cases in which the main problem seems not to be depression, a careful clinician would certainly want to probe to see if depressive symptoms were present but would not necessarily jump to the conclusion that depression and behavior problems always go hand in hand.

On the other hand, the popular stereotype of adolescents as "normally disturbed" leads many parents and teachers to fail to recognize genuine psychological problems when they appear. You can probably imagine a parent's description of an adolescent daughter who is critical of herself (which can be an emotional manifestation of depression), unduly negative (a possible cognitive manifestation), bored with everything (a possible motivational manifestation), and not very interested in eating (a possible vegetative manifestation). It would be easy for this parent to overlook a potentially very real problem and dismiss her daughter's mood and behavior as normal. Obviously, not all instances of self-criticism or apathy reflect psychological disturbance. But a good rule of thumb is that an individual who displays three or more of the signs of depression for two weeks should probably consult a professional (see Table 13.1).

## TABLE 13.1

### DIAGNOSTIC CRITERIA FOR MAJOR DEPRESSIVE SYNDROME

At least five of the following symptoms have been present during the same 2-week period and represent a change from previous functioning; at least one of the symptoms is either (1) depressed mood, (2) loss of interest or pleasure. (Do not include symptoms that are clearly due to a physical condition, mood-incongruent delusions or hallucinations, incoherence, or marked loosening of associations.)

1. Depressed mood (or can be irritable mood in children and adolescents) most of the day, nearly every day, as indicated either by subjective account or observation by others

2. Markedly diminished interest or pleasure in all, or almost all, activities most of the day, nearly every day (as indicated either by subjective account or observation by others of apathy most of the time)

3. Significant weight loss or weight gain when not dieting (e.g., more than 5% of body weight in a month), or decrease or increase in appetite nearly every day (in children, consider failure to make expected weight gains)

4. Insomnia or hypersomnia nearly every day

5. Psychomotor agitation or retardation nearly every day (observable by others, not merely subjective feelings of restlessness or being slowed down)

6. Fatigue or loss of energy nearly every day

7. Feelings of worthlessness or excessive or inappropriate guilt (which may be delusional) nearly every day (not merely self-reproach or guilt about being sick)

8. Diminished ability to think or concentrate, or indecisiveness, nearly every day (either by subjective account or as observed by others)

9. Recurrent thoughts of death (not just fear of dying), recurrent suicidal ideation without a specific plan, or a suicide attempt or a specific plan for committing suicide

*Source: Diagnostic and Statistical Manual of Mental Disorders* of the American Psychiatric Association (DSMIII-R), from Kendall et al., 1989.

## ADOLESCENT SUICIDE

According to a recent survey, 15 percent of American 10th graders attempted suicide in 1987. Fortunately, the vast majority of these attempts—over 98 percent—are not successful. Nevertheless, the fact that one of three adolescents has contemplated suicide, and one in six has attempted suicide, is frightening and distressing (Gans, 1990).

Contrary to myth, adolescents' suicide attempts are rarely impulsive reactions to immediate distress, such as breaking up with someone. Rather, adolescents who attempt to kill themselves usually have made appeals for help and have tried but have not found emotional support from family or friends. Common warning signs of a suicide attempt are shown in Table 13.2, and advice on how to respond is shown in Table 13.3.

# THE SEXES: WHY ARE THERE SEX DIFFERENCES
# IN RATES OF TEENAGE DEPRESSION?

Before adolescence, boys are somewhat more likely to exhibit depressive symptoms than girls, but after puberty the sex difference in prevalence of depression reverses significantly. From early adolescence until very late in adulthood, women report far more depression than men. Why might adolescence mark a turning point in this pattern?

Psychologists do not have a clear answer at this time. Although the fact that the emergence of a strong sex differential coincides with puberty suggests a biological explanation, there actually is little evidence that the sex difference in depression is directly attributable to sex differences in hormonal changes (Rutter and Garmezy, 1983). More likely, changes in social relationships around the time of puberty may leave girls more vulnerable than boys to some forms of psychological distress, and depression may be a stereotypically feminine way of manifesting it.

Social scientists speculate that the emergence of sex differences in depression has something to do with the social role that the adolescent girl may find herself in as she enters the world of boy-girl relationships. As you read in previous chapters, this role may bring conflict over achievement, due to fears that success will be perceived as unattractive; heightened self-consciousness over physical appearance; and increased concern over popularity with peers. Since many of these feelings may provoke helplessness, hopelessness, and anxiety, adolescent girls may be more susceptible to depressive feelings. To make matters worse, pressures on young women to behave in sex-stereotyped ways, which intensify during adolescence (Hill and Lynch, 1983), may lead girls to adopt some behaviors and dispositions—passivity, dependency, and fragility, for example—that they have been socialized to believe are part of the feminine role.

The *gender intensification hypothesis* is only one explanation for sex differences in the prevalence of depression at adolescence. Two other accounts focus on sex differences in the degree to which adolescence is stressful and on sex differences in the ways that boys and girls cope with stress (Petersen et al., 1991). With respect to the first of these explanations, it is important to note that the link between stress and depression is well-documented (Kessler et al., 1985). Of interest, then is evidence that early adolescence simply may be a more stressful time for girls than boys (Allgood-Merten et al., 1990; Petersen et al., 1991). This is because girls are more likely than boys to experience multiple stressors at the same time (e.g., going through puberty while making the transition into junior high school), because girls are likely to experience more stressful life events than boys, and because the bodily changes of puberty, especially when they occur early in adolescence, are likely to be stressful for girls than boys—as we saw in Chapter 1.

Second, there is evidence that girls are more likely than boys to react to stress by turning their feelings inward—for instance, by ruminating about the problem and feeling helpless—whereas boys are more likely to respond either by distracting themselves or by turning their feelings outward, in aggressive behavior or in drug and alcohol abuse (Gjerde et al., 1988; Nolen-Hoeksema, 1987). This may explain why the prevalence of externalizing disorders is higher in boys while the prevalence of internalizing disorders is higher in girls.

Interestingly, one study that followed children from preschool into adolescence found that the childhood precursors of adolescent depression were different for boys and girls. Girls who would subsequently become depressed were vulnerable, anxious, and low in self-esteem. Boys who would subsequently become depressed, however, were hostile and antisocial (Gjerde and Block, 1991). These writers have suggested that the idea that depression should be viewed as an internalizing disorder may apply to females, but not necessarily to males. Even when males and females suffer from the same underlying problem—such as depression—they may show it in very different ways.

Contrary to myth, adolescents' suicide attempts are rarely impulsive reactions to immediate distress, such as breaking up with someone. Rather, adolescents who attempt to kill themselves usually have made appeals for help and have tried to seek—but have not found—emotional support from family or friends. *(Nancy Hays/Monkmeyer)*

You may have read that suicide is a leading cause of death among young people, but this is primarily because very few young people die from other causes, such as disease. Although the rate of suicide rises rapidly during the middle adolescent years, it continues to rise throughout adulthood, and suicide is a much more common cause of death among adults than it is among young people (Rutter and Garmezy, 1983; Weiner, 1980). Completed suicide is more common among older adults than adolescents and more common among men than women. Attempted suicide, however, is more common during adolescence than during adulthood and far more common among adolescent girls than boys (Rutter and Garmezy, 1983).

Efforts to prevent suicide among adolescents have focused on identifying sets of **risk factors.** Risk factors are characteristics of individuals or their environments that increase the likelihood of their suffering from a particular problem or engaging in a particular behavior—in this case, attempting suicide. The four established sets of risk factors for attempted suicide during adolescence are *having a psychiatric problem,* especially depression or substance abuse, *having a history of suicide in the family,* being under *stress* (especially in the areas of achievement and sexuality), and experiencing *parental rejection, family disruption,* or *extensive family conflict* (Blumenthal and Kupfer, 1988; Rubenstein et al., 1989). Adolescents who have one of these risk factors are significantly more likely to attempt suicide than their peers, and adolescents who have more than one risk factor are dramatically more likely to try to kill themselves.

The adolescent suicide rate increased alarmingly between 1950 and 1980—the suicide rate among 15- to 19-year-olds, for example, quadrupled between 1955 and the end of the 1970s (National Center for Health Statistics, 1982). A variety of explanations have been given for the increase in suicide among American youth, including pressures to grow up earlier, increasing rates of divorce, less contact with adults, high rates of residential mobility, and having to face an unpredictable job market (Bronfenbrenner, 1974; Rutter, 1979). These theories, while intuitively reasonable, however, have not been systematically tested. Moreover, around 1980, the adolescent suicide rate began to level off and has not increased since 1985 (Office of Technology Assessment, 1991). Any theory of the causes of adolescent suicide would have to account for the leveling off of the rate after 1980 as well as for the pre-1980 increase.

Recently, several researchers have noted

## TABLE 13.2

### SUICIDE AMONG ADOLESCENTS: EARLY WARNING SIGNS

1. Direct suicide threats or comments such as "I wish I were dead." "My family would be better off without me." "I have nothing to live for."
2. A previous suicide attempt, no matter how minor. Four out of five people who commit suicide have made at least one previous attempt.
3. Preoccupation with death in music, art, and personal writing.
4. Loss of a family member, pet, or boy/girl friend through death, abandonment, break-up.
5. Family disruptions such as unemployment, serious illness, relocation, divorce.
6. Disturbances in sleeping and eating habits and in personal hygiene.
7. Declining grades and lack of interest in school or hobbies that had previously been important.
8. Drastic changes in behavior patterns, such as a quiet, shy person becoming extremely gregarious.
9. Pervasive sense of gloom, helplessness, and hopelessness.
10. Withdrawal from family members and friends and feelings of alienation from significant others.
11. Giving away prized possessions and otherwise "getting their affairs in order."
12. Series of "accidents" or impulsive, risk-taking behaviors. Drug or alcohol abuse, disregard for personal safety, taking dangerous dares.

*Source:* From "Living with 10- to 15-Year-Olds," A Parent Education Curriculum. © 1984 Center for Early Adolescence, Suite 223, Carr Mill Mall, Carrboro, NC 27510. Reprinted by permission.

that adolescent suicides sometimes occur in clusters—as if there is some sort of contagion effect. A youngster may attempt suicide, and shortly thereafter, a rash of attempts will be reported in the same school district or in nearby communities. This pattern of **cluster suicides** has raised concerns about the advisability of publicizing adolescent suicides and suicide attempts. It was initially thought that publicity surrounding suicide would help increase community awareness of the problem and that such news coverage ultimately would lower the suicide rate. Because a number of studies now demonstrate that publicity increases the likelihood of further suicide attempts, however, this strategy is being reconsidered (Gould and Shaffer, 1986; Phillips and Carstensen, 1986). Instead, efforts are more likely to be aimed at diminishing the pressures, drug problems, and family difficulties believed to lead adolescents to consider taking their life.

### CAUSES AND TREATMENT OF ADOLESCENT DEPRESSION

A variety of theories have been proposed to account for the onset of depression during adolescence, and the current consensus is that depression is likely to be the result of interacting environmental conditions and individual

## TABLE 13.3

### WHAT TO DO, WHAT NOT TO DO WHEN YOU SUSPECT THE DANGER OF SUICIDE

| What to do | What not to do |
| --- | --- |
| 1. Ask direct, straightforward questions in a calm manner. "Are you thinking about hurting yourself?" | 1. Do not ignore warning signs. |
| 2. Assess the seriousness of the suicidal intent by asking questions about feelings, important relationships, who else the person has talked with, and the amount of thought given to the means to be employed. If a gun, pills, rope, or other means has been procured and a specific plan has been developed, the situation is very dangerous. Stay with the person until help arrives. | 2. Do not refuse to talk about suicide if a young person approaches you. |
| | 3. Do not react with horror, disapproval, or repulsion. |
| | 4. Do not offer false reassurances ("Everything will be all right.") or platitudes and simple answers ("You should be thankful for . . ."). |
| 3. Listen and be supportive, without giving false reassurance. | 5. Do not abandon the young person after the crisis has passed or after professional counseling has begun. |
| 4. Encourage the young person to get professional help and assist the person in doing so. | |

*Source:* From "Living with 10- to 15-Year-Olds," A Parent Education Curriculum. © 1984 Center for Early Adolescence, Suite 223, Carr Mill Mall, Carrboro, NC 27510. Reprinted by permission.

predispositions rather than either set of factors alone. Depression may result when individuals who are predisposed toward it are exposed to chronic or acute circumstances that precipitate a depressive reaction. Individuals who are not predisposed toward depression are able to withstand a great deal of stress, for instance, without developing any psychological problems. Other individuals, who have strong predispositions toward the disorder, may become depressed in the face of circumstances that most of us would consider to be quite normal.

Research has focused both on individual predispositions toward depression and on the environmental circumstances likely to precipitate the disorder. Because depression has been found to have a strong genetic component, it is believed that at least some of the predisposition toward depression is biological and may be related to problematic patterns of *neuro-*

*endocrine functioning* (*neuroendocrine* refers to hormonal activity in the brain and nervous system). Other researchers have focused more on the *cognitive set* of depressed individuals, suggesting that people with tendencies toward hopelessness, pessimism, and self-blame are more likely to interpret events in their lives in ways that lead to the development of depression. Some theorists (Noelen-Hoeksema, 1990) believe that these sorts of cognitive sets develop during childhood and play a role in the onset of depression during adolescence.

Researchers who have been more concerned with the environmental determinants of depression have focused on three different sets of conditions. According to one viewpoint, depression is due to some sort of loss—the loss of an important relationship (for example, as a result of parents' divorce or death), the loss of something safe and familiar (moving to a new neighborhood), or the loss of self-esteem (failing at something important) (Weiner, 1980). Other scientists have contrasted the immediate environments of depressed and nondepressed individuals and have found that depressed individuals receive less reinforcement from their activities and relationships (e.g., Lewinsohn, 1975). Finally, chronic or acute stress can trigger psychological distress, of which depression is a likely manifestation (Newcomb et al., 1981). Although these various environmental perspectives on depression are derived from different theories about the causes of psychological distress, they are certainly consistent with each other. An important loss (failing to gain admission to a sought-after college) can be described as a "stressor," for example, or as something that leads to a "reduction in reinforcement." In other words, negative conditions in the environment, broadly defined, may trigger depressive reactions in individuals predisposed in that direction.

You read earlier that the prevalence of depression increases during adolescence. Can these various theories about the causes of depression account for this? For the most part, they can. Biological theorists can point to the hormonal changes of puberty, which are likely to have implications for neuroendocrine activity. Two recent studies, for example, show that depression and **negative affect** in both boys and girls are correlated with various hormones known to change at puberty (Paikoff et al., 1991; Susman et al., 1991). Cognitive theorists can point to the onset of hypothetical thinking at adolescence, which may result in new (and perhaps potentially more depressing) ways of viewing the world. Theorists who emphasize environmental factors draw attention to the new environmental demands of adolescence, such as changing schools or beginning to date, all of which may lead to feelings of loss, heightened stress, or diminished reinforcement (Algood-Marten et al., 1990). Thus there are

many good reasons to expect that the prevalence of depression would increase as individuals pass from childhood into adolescence.

The treatment of depression during adolescence is very similar to its treatment at other points in the life span. Clinicians use a wide range of approaches, including biological therapies employing antidepressant medication (these address the neuroendocrine problem, if one exists); psychotherapies designed to help depressed adolescents understand the roots of their depression, increase the degree to which they experience reinforcement in their daily activities, or chnge the nature of their cognitive set; and family therapies, which focus on changing patterns of family relations that may be contributing to the adolescent's symptoms (Chartier and Ranieri, 1984).

## Eating Disorders

Depression is the most common internalizing disorder observed during adolescence, but it is not the only one. A small, but significant, number of adolescents also suffer from eating disorders. The most common eating disorders among young people are **anorexia nervosa, bulimia,** and **obesity.** In this final section of this chapter, we examine each of these problems.

### ANOREXIA NERVOSA AND BULIMIA

In contemporary America, as the expression goes, one can never be too rich or too thin. Unfortunately, not everyone is genetically or metabolically meant to be as thin as fashion magazines tell people they should be. Some adolescents, especially young women, become so concerned about gaining weight that they take drastic—and dangerous—measures to remain thin. Some go on eating binges and then force themselves to vomit to avoid gaining weight, a pattern associated with an eating disorder called bulimia. In the more severe cases, young women suffering from an eating disorder called anorexia nervosa actually starve themselves in an effort to keep their weight down. Adolescents with these sorts of eating disorders have an extremely disturbed body image. They see themselves as overweight when they are actually underweight. Some anorectic youngsters may lose between 25 percent and 50 percent of their body weight. As you would expect, bulimia and anorexia, if untreated, lead to a variety of serious physical problems; in fact, nearly 20 percent of anorectic teenagers inadvertently starve themselves to death.

Anorexia and bulimia each began to receive a great deal of popular attention during the 1980s, because of their dramatic nature, their concentration in the higher social classes, and their association with celebrity—the singer Karen Carpenter died from anorexia, for instance, and several Hollywood stars, including actress Jane Fonda, revealed histories of bulimia as adolescents or young adults. Perhaps because of this attention, intial reports characterized these eating disorders as being of "epidemic" proportion. In fact, careful unbiased studies indicate that the incidence of genuine anorexia and genuine bulimia is small (Kolata, 1988). Fewer than one-half of 1 percent of adolescents are anorexic, and fewer than 5 percent are bulimic (Howat and Saxton, 1988; Lachenmeyer and Muni, 1988). Anorexia and bulimia are far more common in females than males (indeed, anorexia is almost unheard of among males; when it is diagnosed in males, it typically is seen as a consequence of some other disorder), more common in North America and Western Europe than in other parts of the world, and more common among the affluent and better educated (Condit, 1990). Anorexia and bulimia are rarely seen before puberty.

Although the incidence of anorexia and bulimia is small, the proportion of adolescents who are unhappy with their body shape or weight is not. This is especially the case among female adolescents, which no doubt accounts for the greater incidence of anorexia and bulimia among young women than men. In one recent study, for example, more than one-third of girls whose weight was considered normal by medical and health standards believed that they were overweight—including 5 percent who actually were underweight by medical criteria. (Less than 7 percent of normal weight boys, and *no* underweight boys, described themselves as overweight.) In this study, more than 70 percent of the girls reported that they would like to be thinner than they are (as opposed to one-third of the boys), and more than 80 percent said that being thinner would make them happier, more successful, and more popular (Paxton et al., 1991). Not surprisingly, dissatisfaction with one's body is likely to lead to the development of eating problems (Attie and Brooks-Gunn, 1989).

Several theories have been proposed to account for the onset of anorexia and bulimia during adolescence (see Condit, 1990). One perspective emphasizes the biological basis for anorexia, in particular, since there is strong evidence that anorexia is both genetically and hormonally influenced (Holland et al., 1988; Leibowitz, 1983). Unfortunately, it is difficult in hormonal studies to separate cause and effect: Changes in hormone levels can affect weight loss, but starvation and dieting also affect hormone levels.

A second view emphasizes psychological factors. Some theorists have proposed that anorexia is related to the adolescent's attempts to assert her autonomy within an overly controlling family system (Bruch, 1973; Minuchin et al., 1978). Others have suggested that anorexia is a sort of "avoidance" mechanism that reflects the young woman's fears of entering adulthood (Crisp, 1983). (One of the consequences of starvation during early adolescence is that pubertal development is severely delayed [Surbey, 1987].) Still others have pointed to links between anorexia and other internalized disorders, such as depression, since many anorexic women display depressive symptoms (Munoz and Amado, 1986). The suggestion here is that anorexia may simply be a specific manifestation of internalized distress. In addition, there is some evidence that the same medications that are successful in treating depression is useful in treating anorexia (Corbit, 1990).

Finally, because anorexia and bulimia are ten times more common in females than males and far more common in some societies and social classes than others, it is likely that broader social forces are a main factor in the development of these eating disorders (Brumberg, 1988). One interesting study showed, for example, how bulimia became socially "contagious" in a college sorority (Crandall, 1988). This researcher found that over the course of the academic year, women's eating behavior became more and more like that of her sorority friends—even in a sorority in which binge eating was the norm.

Just because cultural conditions contribute to the development of anorexia nervosa doesn't mean that individual characteristics do not play a role as well. It may be the case that cultural conditions predispose women more than men toward these eating disorders and that, within the population of adolescent women, those who have certain psychological traits (proneness to depression, for example) or familial characteristics (overcontrolling parents, for example) may be more likely to develop problems. The onset of eating disorders, like so many aspects of adolescent development, cannot be understood apart from the context in which young people live.

A variety of therapeutic approaches have been employed successfully in the treatment of anorexia and bulimia, including individual psychotherapy and congitive-behavior modification, group therapy, family therapy, and, more recently, the use of antidepressant med-

ication (Agras, et al., 1989; Condit, 1990; Vigersky, 1977). The treatment of anorexia often requires hospitalization intitially in order to ensure that starvation does not progress to fatal or near-fatal levels (Mitchell, 1985).

## OBESITY

Although it is far less glamorous and less well-publicized than anorexia or bulimia, **obesity** is a more common eating disorder. According to recent national surveys, about 5 percent of adolescents in the United States are obese—that is, they are more than 20 percent over the maximum recommended weight for their height—and an additional 15 percent are seriously overweight (Gans, 1990). Because adolescence is a time of dramatic change in physical appearance, the young person's self-image is very much tied to his or her body image. Deviation from the "ideal" physique can lead to loss of self-esteem and other problems in the adolescent's self-image. In particular, being overweight can be a painful source of embarrassment to teenagers, who are unusually self-conscious about their appearance. In addition, obesity during adolescence places the individual at much higher risk for other health problems, including hypertension (high blood pressure), high cholesterol levels, and diabetes. Nearly 80 percent of obese adolescents will be obese adults and suffer the disadvantages associated with obesity.

Although a variety of nutritional and behavioral factors can lead to weight gain during adolescence, gaining weight can sometimes result directly from the physical changes of puberty. Not only does the ratio of body fat to muscle increase markedly during puberty, but the body's **basal metabolism rate** also drops about 15 percent. The basal metabolism rate is the minimum amount of energy one uses when one is resting. One's weight is partly dependent on this ratio. Do you know people who seem to be able to eat as much as they want without gaining weight? Adolescents whose basal metabolism rate is high can eat more during the course of a day without gaining weight than their peers whose rate is low, because individuals with high metabolic rates naturally burn off more calories. Because basal metabolism normally decreases during adolescence, many individuals who are not overweight as children develop weight problems as teenagers. In fact, obesity is about three times more common during adolescence than during childhood (Paulsen, 1972). Often, a program of intense physical exercise combined with proper nutrition can help youngsters lose weight (Brody, 1987).

## Summary

1. Although the vast majority of individuals do not develop serious psychological or social problems during the adolescent years, a significant minority do. Psychologists find it useful to distinguish between internalizing disorders (in which problems are turned inward) and externalizing disorders (in which problems are expressed outward).

2. There is a great deal of co-variation among different psychosocial problems during adolescence within the broad internalizing and externalizing disorder categories. Adolescents who engage in delinquency, for example, are more likely than their peers to be truant, to use and abuse drugs, engage in precocious sexual behavior, and commit acts of aggression— a pattern called problem behavior syndrome. Conversely, adolescents who suffer from depression are more likely than their peers to feel anxiety and other symptoms of negative affectivity.

3. Among contemporary adolescents, alcohol and cigarettes are still the drugs of choice, although a substantial number of young people have experimented with marijuana as well. Research indicates a clear need to distinguish between experimentation with alcohol and marijuana (which has not been shown to be harmful) and regular or heavy use (which has). Adolescents who abuse alcohol and other drugs are more likely to come from hostile family environments, to have friends who use drugs, and to have other problems, in school as well as in interpersonal relationships.

4. Adolescents account for a disproportionately high number of crimes, including violent crimes. Research shows that chronic offenders are more likely than other adolescents to come from poor families, to have had childhood histories of aggressive behavior, to have been diagnosed as hyperactive, and to score low on standardized tests of intelligence and achievement. Because few approaches to the treatment of chronic offenders have proven successful, many efforts today are being directed at prevention.

5. Depression is the most common internalizing disorder of adolescence, afflicting about 3 percent of the adolescent population in its most severe form, but more than 25 percent of adolescents in more minor forms. More remarkably, surveys show that one of every six adolescents has attempted suicide. Although males are more likely to suffer from depression during childhood, depression is much more common among females after puberty—a sex difference that persists into adulthood. The current consensus is that depression is the result of an interacting set of environmental conditions (especially stress and loss) and individual predispositions.

6. Eating disorders comprise a second set of internalizing disorders seen at adolescence. The most life-threatening, anorexia nervosa, fortunately, is quite rate. Bulimia, a disorder characterized by binge eating and self-induced vomiting, is more common. Both anorexia and bulimia are far more common among females, in Western societies, and among women from affluent and well-educated families. Obesity is a more common eating disorder that also has important psychological and physical health

implications. The causes of eating disorders are, like depression, both biological and environmental.

## Key Terms

antisocial tendency

anorexia nervosa

attention deficit disorder with hyperactivity (ADDH)

birth-cohort theory

bulimia

depression

emotion-focused coping

externalizing disorders

internalizing disorders

negative affectivity

obesity

problem behavior theory

problem-focused coping

risk factors

risk-taking behavior

social control theory

socialized delinquency

status offenses

transition-proneness

unsocialized delinquency

## For Further Reading

BROOKS-GUNN, J., AND PETERSEN, A. (EDS.) (1991). The emergence of depressive symptoms during adolescence. *Journal of Youth and Adolescence, 20* (whole issue). A recent collection of research articles on the nature of adolescent depression.

BRUMBERG, J. (1988). *Fasting girls: The emergence of anorexia as a modern disease.* Cambridge: Harvard University Press. A historical look at the social origins and "invention" of anorexia.

JESSOR, R. (1984). Adolescent development and behavioral health. In J. Matarazzo, S. Weiss, J. Herd, N. Miller, and S. Weiss (Eds.), *Behavioral health: A handbook of health enhancement and disease prevention.* New York: Wiley. An excellent summary of problem behavior theory, by the theory's author.

MCCORD, J. (1990). Problem behaviors. In S. Feldman and G. Elliot (Eds.), *At the threshold: The developing adolescent.* Cambridge: Harvard University Press. An overview of the literature on problem behavior during adolescence.

SHEDLER, J., AND BLOCK, J. (1990). Adolescent drug use and psychological health: A longitudinal inquiry. *American Psychologist, 45,* 612–630. A controversial study showing that experimenting with drugs and alcohol during adolescence is not psychologically harmful.

# THEORETICAL PERSPECTIVES ON ADOLESCENCE

I t is useful to organize theoretical perspectives on adolescence around an issue that has long dominated discussions about the nature of this period of the life span: To what extent is adolescence shaped by the fundamental biological changes of the period, and to what extent is it defined by the environment in which the individual develops? Whereas some theories construe adolescence as a biologically defined period, others view it as contextually determined. Still others fall somewhere between the two extremes of this continuum. The purpose of this brief overview is not to argue for one approach over another, but rather, to demonstrate how each of these views has helped us gain a better understanding of the nature of adolescence.

## BIOLOGICAL THEORIES

The fact that biological change during adolescence is noteworthy is not a matter of dispute. How important this biological change is in defining the psychosocial issues of the period is, however, in dispute. Theorists who have taken a biological, or more accurately, *biosocial* view of adolescence stress the hormonal and physical changes of puberty as driving forces. The most important biosocial theorist was G. Stanley Hall (1904), considered the "father" of the scientific study of adolescence.

Hall, who was very much influenced by the work of Charles Darwin, the author of the theory of evolution, believed that the development of the individual paralleled the development of the human species, a notion referred to as his theory of **recapitulation.** Infancy, in his view, was equivalent to the time during our evolution when we were primitive, like animals. Adolescence, in contrast, was seen as a time that paralleled the evolution of our species into civilization. For Hall, the development of the individual through these stages was determined primarily by instinct—by bio-

logical and genetic forces within the person, and hardly influenced by the environment.

The most important legacy of Hall's view of adolescence is the notion that adolescence is inevitably a period of **storm and stress.** He believed that the hormonal changes of puberty cause upheaval, both for the individual and for those around the young person. Because this turbulence was biologically determined, it was unavoidable. The best that society could do was to find ways of managing the young person whose "raging hormones" would invariably lead to difficulties.

Although scientists no longer believe that adolescence is an inherently stressful period, much contemporary work continues to emphasize the role that biological factors play in shaping the adolescent experience. Indeed, the study of the impact of puberty on adolescent psychosocial development has been, and continues to be, a central question for the field. In addition, current work from the biosocial tradition explores the genetic bases of individual differences in adolescence as well as the sociobiological bases of adolescent behavior.

## ORGANISMIC THEORIES

Our next stop on the continuum is in the domain of **organismic theorists.** Like biosocial theorists, organismic theorists also stress the importance of the biological changes of adolescence. But unlike their biosocial counterparts, organismic theories also take into account the ways in which contextual forces interact with and modify the impact of these biological imperatives.

If you have had previous coursework in developmental psychology, you have encountered the major organismic theorists, since they have long dominated the study of development. Three of these theorists, in particular, have had a great influence over the study of adolescence: Sigmund Freud (1938), Erik Erikson (1968), and Jean Piaget (Inhelder and Piaget, 1958). Although each of these theorists is classified as organismic, the theories they developed emphasized different aspects of individual growth and development.

For Freud, development was best understood in terms of the **psychosexual conflicts** that arise at different points in development. In **psychoanalytic theory,** adolescence is also seen as a time of upheaval—as was the case in Hall's view. According to Freud, the hormonal changes of puberty upset the psychic balance that had been achieved during the prior psychosexual stage, called "latency." Because the hormonal changes of puberty were responsible for marked increases in sexual drive, the adolescent was temporarily thrown into a period of intrapsychic crisis, and old psychosexual conflicts, long buried in the unconscious, were revived. Freud and his followers believed that the main challenge of adolescence was to restore a psychic balance and resolve these conflicts. Although the process was driven by the hormonal changes of puberty, the specific conflicts faced by the young person were seen as dependent on his or her early experiences in the family.

Freud himself actually had very little to say specifically about adolescence. But his daughter, Anna Freud (1958), extended much of her father's thinking to the study of development during the second decade of life. Today, this work is carried on by **neo-Freudians,** such as Peter Blos (1979), whose theories of adolescent development we explore in detail in Chapter 9.

In Erikson's theory, the emphasis was on the **psychosocial crises** characteristic of each period of growth. Like Freud, Erikson also believed that internal, biological developments moved the individual from one developmental stage to the next. But unlike Freud, Erikson stressed the psychosocial, rather than the psychosexual, conflicts faced by the individual at

each point in time. Whereas Freud emphasized the development of the **id**—that part of the psyche believed to be dominated by instinctual urges, Erikson emphasized the development of the **ego**—that part of the psyche believed to regulate thought, emotion, and behavior.

Erikson proposed eight stages in psychosocial development, each characterized by a specific "crisis" that arose at that point in development because of the interplay between the internal forces of biology and the unique demands of society. In Erikson's theory, which we look at in detail in Chapter 8, adolescence is seen as a period that revolves around the crisis of "identity versus identity diffusion," a crisis that is shaped both by the changes of puberty and the specific demands that society places on young people. According to Erikson, the challenge of adolescence is to resolve the identity crisis successfully, and emerge from the period with a coherent sense of who one is and where one is headed.

Freud and Erikson both emphasized emotional and social development. For Piaget, development could best be understood by examining changes in the nature of thinking, or cognition. Piaget believed that as children mature, they pass through stages of cognitive development, and in each stage, from birth to adolescence, their ways of thinking are qualitatively distinct. According to his view, understanding the distinctive features of thought and reasoning at each stage can give us insight into the overall development of the individual at that point in time.

In Piaget's theory, which is discussed in detail in Chapter 2, adolescence marks the transition from concrete to abstract thought. According to this model, adolescence is the period in which individuals become capable of thinking in hypothetical terms, a development which permits a wide expansion of logical abilities. As you will see, many of the familiar changes in behavior we associate with adolescence have been attributed to these changes in cognitive abilities. Piaget's views have been applied to the study of moral development, social development, and education.

As is the case with the other organismic theories, Piaget's theory of cognitive development emphasizes the interplay between biological and contextual forces. The development of higher-order thinking in adolescence, for example, is influenced both by the internal biological changes of the developmental period and by changes in the intellectual environment encountered by the individual.

## LEARNING THEORIES

As we move across the theoretical continuum from extreme biological views to extreme environmental ones, we encounter a group of theories that shift the emphasis from biological forces to contextual ones. Whereas organismic theorists tend to emphasize the interaction between biological change and environmental demand, learning theorists stress the context in which behavior takes place. The capacity of the individual to learn from experience is assumed to be a biological given. What is of interest to **learning theorists** is the content of what is learned.

Learning theorists are not especially developmental in their approach, and, as a consequence, have little to say specifically about adolescence as a developmental period. Indeed, for learning theorists, the basic processes of human behavior are the same in adolescence as they are during other periods of the life span. But learning theorists have been extremely influential in the study of adolescent development because they have helped us understand how the specific environment in which an adolescent lives can shape the individual's behavior.

There are two general categories of learning theorists. One group, called **behaviorists,** emphasizes the processes of reinforcement and punishment as the main influences on adolescent behavior. The main proponent of this view was B. F. Skinner (1953), whose theory of **operant conditioning** has had a tremendous impact on the entire field of psychology. Within an operant conditioning framework, **reinforcement** is defined as the process through which a behavior is made more likely to occur again, whereas **punishment** is defined as the process through which a behavior is made less likely to occur again. From this vantage point, adolescent behavior can be seen as nothing more or less than the product of the various reinforcements and punishments to which the individual has been exposed. An adolescent who strives to do well in school, for example, does so because she has been reinforced for this behavior, or punished for not behaving this way, in the past.

A related approach is taken by **social learning theorists.** Social learning theorists, such as Albert Bandura (Bandura and Walters, 1959), also emphasize the ways in which adolescents learn how to behave. But in contrast to behaviorists, social learning theorists place more weight on the processes of **modeling** and **observational learning.** That is, adolescents learn how to behave not simply by being reinforced and punished by forces in the environment, but by watching and imitating those around them. As you will read throughout the text, social learning approaches to adolescence have been very influential in explaining how adolescents are affected by the child-rearing methods employed by their parents and by the influence, or pressure, of their peers.

## SOCIOLOGICAL THEORIES

The emphasis within the biosocial, organismic, and learning theories is mainly on forces within the individual, or within the individual's specific environment, shaping his or her development and behavior. In contrast, sociological theories of adolescence attempt to understand how adolescents, as a group, come of age in society. Instead of emphasizing differences among individuals in their biological make-ups or their experiences in the world, sociological theories of adolescence emphasize the factors that all adolescents, or groups of adolescents—by virtue of their sharing age, ethnicity, gender, or some other demographic feature—have in common.

Sociological theories of adolescence have often focused on relations between the generations and have tended to emphasize the difficulties young people have in making the transition from adolescence into adulthood, especially in industrialized society. Two themes have dominated these discussions. One, concerning the **marginality** of young people, emphasizes the difference in power that exists between the adult and adolescent generations. Two important thinkers in this vein are Kurt Lewin (1951) and Edgar Friedenberg (1959). Although the view that adolescents are "second-class citizens" was more influential forty years ago than today, contemporary applications of this viewpoint stress the fact that many adolescents are prohibited from occupying meaningful roles in society and therefore experience frustration and restlessness. Some theorists have argued that adults have forced adolescents into occupying one and only one role—that of student—which is an inherently powerless and "infantilizing" position for young people. This was one explanation given for the student movements of the 1960s (e.g., Braungart, 1980).

A modification of this view focuses on differences *within* the adolescent population. According to this viewpoint, the adolescent's **social class,** or socioeconomic status, as it is formally known, structures his or her experience of growing up. Theorists such as August Hollingshead (1949/1975) or Robert Havighurst (1952) have emphasized the fact that the experience of adolescence differs markedly as a function of the young person's family background. They argue that it is impossible to generalize about the "nature" of adolescence because it varies so much depending on the resources of the adolescent's family.

The other theme in sociological theories of adolescence concerns intergenerational conflict, or as it is more commonly known, the **generation gap.** Theorists such as Karl Mannheim (1952) and James Coleman (1962) stressed the fact that adolescents and adults grow up under different social circumstances and therefore develop different sets of attitudes, values, and beliefs. As a consequence, there is inevitable tension between the adolescent and adult generations. Some, like Coleman, have gone so far as to argue that adolescents develop a different cultural viewpoint—a **counterculture**—that may be hostile to the values or beliefs of adult society.

Although sociological theories of adolescence clearly place the emphasis on the broader context in which adolescents come of age, there is still a theme of inevitability that runs through their approach. Mannheim, for example, believed that because modern society changed so rapidly, there would always be problems between generations because each cohort came into adulthood with different experiences and beliefs. Similarly, Lewin believed that marginality was an inherent feature of adolescence because adults always control more resources and have more power than young people.

## HISTORICAL AND ANTHROPOLOGICAL APPROACHES

Our final stop on the continuum takes us to the extreme environmental position. Historians and anthropologists who study adolescence share with sociologists an interest in the broader context in which young people come of age, but they take a much more relativistic stance. Historical perspectives, such as those offered by Glen Elder (1980) or Joseph Kett

(1977), stress the fact that adolescence as a developmental period has varied considerably from one historical era to another. As a consequence, it is impossible to generalize about such issues as the degree to which adolescence is stressful, the developmental tasks of the period, or the nature of intergenerational relations. Historians would say that it all depends on the social, political, and economic forces present at the time. Even something as "basic" to our view of adolescence as the "identity crisis," they say, is a social invention that arose because of industrialization and the prolongation of schooling. Before the industrial revolution, when most adolescents followed in their parents' occupation, "crises" over identity did not exist.

One group of theorists has taken this viewpoint to its logical extreme. These theorists, called **inventionists,** argue that adolescence is *entirely* a social invention (Bakan, 1972). Inventionists believe that the way in which we divide the life cycle into stages—drawing a boundary between childhood and adolescence, for example—is nothing more than a reflection of the political, economic, and social circumstances in which we live. They point out that, although puberty has been a feature of development for as long as humans have lived, it was not until the rise of compulsory education that we began treating adolescents as a special and distinct group. This suggests that social conditions, not biological givens, define the nature of adolescent development.

A similar theme is echoed by anthropologists who study adolescence, the most important of whom were Ruth Benedict (1934) and Margaret Mead (1928). Benedict and Mead, whose work is examined in Chapter 3, pointed out that societies vary considerably in the ways in which they view and structure adolescence. As a consequence, they viewed adolescence as a culturally defined experience—stressful and difficult in societies that saw it this way, calm and peaceful in societies that had an alternative vision. Benedict, in particular, drew a distinction between **continuous** and **discontinuous** societies. In continuous societies (typically, nonindustrialized societies with little social change), the transition from adolescence to adulthood is gradual and peaceful. In discontinuous societies (typically, industrialized societies characterized by rapid social change), the transition into adulthood is abrupt and difficult.

# *Glossary*

**academic achievement** Achievement that is measured by standardized tests of scholastic ability or knowledge

**achievement** The psychosocial domain concerning behaviors and feelings in evaluative situations

**achievement attributions** The beliefs one holds about the causes of one's successes and failures

**activational role of hormones** The process through which changes in hormone levels, especially at puberty, stimulate changes in the adolescent's behavior, appearance, or growth

**adolescent growth spurt** The dramatic increase in height and weight that occurs during puberty

**adolescent health** A new field of study and health-care devoted to understanding the health-care needs of individuals during the second decade of life

**adrenal androgens** A group of hormones, secreted by the adrenal gland, which affect growth and behavior at puberty

**adrenal cortex** A part of the adrenal gland which secretes many of the hormones that stimulate bodily change at puberty

**age of majority** The designated age at which an individual is recognized as an adult member of the community

**AIDS (autoimmune deficiency syndrome)** A disease, transmitted by means of bodily fluids, that devastates the immune system.

**anchoring** The process through which status hierarchies are formed in peer groups

**androgen** One of the sex hormones secreted by the gonads, found in both sexes, but in higher levels among males than among females following puberty

**androgynous** Possessing both highly masculine and highly feminine traits

**anorexia nervosa** An eating disorder found chiefly among young women, characterized by dramatic and severe self-induced weight loss

**antisocial tendency** The presumed psychosocial constellation that underlies various types of externalizing disorders, including delinquency, aggression, and drug use

**anxious-avoidant attachment** An insecure attachment between infant and caregiver, characterized by indifference on the part of the infant toward the caregiver

**anxious-resistant attachment** An insecure attachment between infant and caregiver, characterized by distress at separation and anger at reunion

**aptitude test** A test designed to predict a student's future performance in school, such as the Scholastic Aptitude Test (SAT)

**asynchronicity of growth** The fact that different parts of the body grow at different rates at puberty, which sometimes results in the appearance of gawkiness or awkwardness during early adolescence

**attachment** The strong affectional bond that develops between an infant and caregiver

**attention deficit disorder with hyperactivity (ADDH)** A biologically-based psychological disorder characterized by impulsivity, inattentiveness, and restlessness, often in school situations; ADDH is a risk factor for antisocial behavior in adolescence

**authoritarian parenting** A style of parenting characterized by punitive, absolute, and forceful discipline, in which a premium is placed on obedience and conformity

**authoritative parenting** A style of parenting characterized by warmth, firm control, and rational, issue-oriented discipline, in which emphasis is placed on the development of self-direction

**autoerotic behavior** Sexual behavior that is experienced alone, such as masturbation or sexual fantasizing

**automatization** The mechanism through which

various cognitive processes become automatic, or second nature

**autonomy**  The psychosocial domain concerning the development and expression of independence

**barometric self-esteem**  The aspect of self-esteem that fluctuates across situations

**basal metabolism rate**  The minimum amount of energy used by the body during a resting state

**baseline self-esteem**  The aspect of self-esteem that is relatively stable across situations and over time

**behavioral autonomy**  The capacity to make independent decisions and follow through with them

**behavioral decision theory**  An approach to understanding adolescent risk-taking, in which behaviors are seen as the outcome of systematic decision-making processes

**behaviorists**  Learning theorists who emphasize the role of concrete stimuli in shaping behavior

**biculturalism**  The successful maintenance of an identification with more than one cultural background

**birth-cohort theory**  A theory that links an individual's behavior to his or her membership in a particular cohort

**brother-sister avoidance**  The avoidance of any contact or interaction between brothers and sisters from the onset of puberty until one or both persons are married—part of the process of social redefinition at adolescence in many societies

**bulimia**  An eating disorder found chiefly among young women, characterized primarily by a pattern of binge eating and self-induced vomiting

**care orientation**  In Carol Gilligan's theory of moral development, a moral orientation that emphasizes responding to others' needs

**case study**  A study that amasses detailed information about one or a few people

**child protectionists**  Individuals who argued, early in the twentieth century, that adolescents needed to be kept out of the labor force in order to protect them from the hazards of the workplace

**chlorosis**  An eating disorder of adolescent women prevalent at the turn of the century; also referred to as the "green sickness" because of the greenish tinge it produced in the complexion

**chlamydia**  A sexually transmitted disease caused by a parasite

**cliques**  Small, tightly knit groups of between two and twelve friends, generally of the same sex and age

**cofigurative cultures**  Cultures in which the socialization of young people is accomplished not only through contact with elders but also through contact between people of the same age

**cognitive-developmental (Piagetian)**  A perspective on development, based on the work of Piaget, that takes a qualitative, stage-theory approach

**community service**  The involvement of young people in activities that serve some social or economic need of society

**comprehensive high school**  An educational institution that evolved during the first half of this century, offering a varied curriculum and designed to meet the needs of a diverse population of adolescents

**concrete operations**  The third stage of cognitive development, according to Piaget, spanning the period roughly between age 6 and early adolescence

**constraining interactions**  According to Stuart Hauser's model of family processes, interactions that discourage open expression and the exchange of ideas

**continuous transition**  A passage into adulthood in which adult roles and statuses are entered into gradually

**conventional moral reasoning**  The second level of moral development, according to Kohlberg, which develops during late childhood and early adolescence; characterized by reasoning that is based on the rules and conventions of society

**correlational study**  An assessment of the extent to which two or more factors are related

**counterculture**  A set of values and norms, typically associated with adolescents, that is hostile to the values and norms of adult society

**critical thinking**  Thinking that is in-depth, analytical, and discriminating

**cross-pressure study**  A research strategy employed in the study of behavioral autonomy, in which adolescents are asked to choose between conforming to the wishes of peers and the wishes of adults

**cross-sectional study** A study that compares two or more groups of individuals at one point in time

**crowds** Large, loosely organized groups of young people, composed of several cliques and typically organized around a common shared activity

**crystallization** According to Super, the stage during which individuals, typically between the ages of 14 and 18, first begin to formulate their ideas about appropriate occupations

**cultural capital** The resources provided within a family through the exposure of the adolescent to art, music, literature, and other elements of "high culture"

**date rape** Being forced by a date to have sex against one's will

**depression** A psychological disturbance characterized by low self-esteem, decreased motivation, sadness, and difficulty finding pleasure in formerly enjoyable activities

**detachment** In psychoanalytic theory, the process through which adolescents sever emotional attachments to their parents or other authority figures

**developmental readiness** The idea that adolescents may be more psychologically ready for certain experiences at one point in development than at another

**discontinuous transition** A passage into adulthood in which adult roles and statuses are entered into abruptly

**displacement hypothesis** The hypothesis that leisure activities displace the more "important" tasks of adolescence

**divided attention** The process of paying attention to two or more stimuli at the same time

**early adolescence** The period spanning roughly ages 11 through 14, corresponding approximately to the junior high or middle school years.

**educational attainment** The number of years of schooling completed by an individual

**ego** In psychoanalytic theory, the part of the psyche that regulates thought, behavior, and emotion

**ego development** The maturation of the ability to function autonomously and in relationships with others

**emotional autonomy** The establishment of more adultlike and less childish close relationships with family members and peers

**emotion-focused coping** Reaction to stress in which one attempts to change one's emotional response to the stressor, such as avoidance or distraction; effective in situations in which the source of stress is uncontrollable

**enabling interactions** According to Stuart Hauser's model of family processes, interactions that encourage open expression and the exchange of ideas

**endocrine system** The system of the body that produces, circulates, and regulates hormones

**epiphysis** The closing of the ends of the long bones in the body, which terminates growth in height; one of the markers of the end of puberty

**estrogen** One of the sex hormones secreted by the gonads, found in both sexes, but in higher levels among females than among males following puberty

**ethnic identity** The aspect of one's sense of identity concerning ancestry or racial group membership

**ethnography** A type of research in which individuals are observed in their natural settings

**externalizing disorders** Psychosocial problems that are manifested in a turning of the symptoms outward, as in aggression or delinquency

**extrinsic motivation** Motivation based on the rewards one will receive for successful performance

**extrusion** The practice of separating children from their parents and requiring them to sleep in other households—part of the process of social redefinition at adolescence in many societies

**family life cycle** The sequence of phases through which families develop as their needs and concerns change

**feedback loop** A cycle through which two or more bodily functions respond to and regulate each other, such as that formed by the hypothalamus, the pituitary gland, and the gonads

**Forgotten Half** The approximately one-half of all American adolescents who do not enroll in college; they have been neglected by researchers and policy-makers

**formal operations** The fourth stage of cognitive

development, according to Piaget, spanning the period from early adolescence through adulthood

**functional community** According to James Coleman, a community in which parents, teachers, and adolescents all share similar values and attitudes

**Gender Intensification Hypothesis** The idea that pressures to behave in sex-appropriate ways intensify during adolescence

**generation gap** The popular phrase for the alleged conflict between young people and adults over values and attitudes

**gonadotropins** Substances that stimulate the gonads to release sex hormones

**gonorrhea** A sexually transmitted disease caused by a bacterium

**herpes** A sexually transmitted disease caused by a virus

**higher-order thinking** Thinking that involves analyzing, evaluating, and interpreting information, rather than simply memorizing it

**homophobia** The unwarranted fear of homosexuals or homosexuality

**human immunodeficiency virus (HIV)** The virus responsible for AIDS, transmitted through bodily fluids

**hypothalamus** A part of the lower brain stem that controls the functioning of the pituitary gland.

**id** In psychoanalytic theory, the part of the psyche dominated by instinctual urges

**identity** The psychosocial domain concerning feelings and thoughts about the self

**identity diffusion (identity confusion)** The incoherent, disjointed, incomplete sense of self characteristic of not having resolved the crisis of identity successfully

**identity foreclosure** The premature establishment of a sense of identity, before sufficient role experimentation has occurred

**identity versus identity diffusion** According to Erikson, the normative crisis characteristic of the fifth stage of psychosocial development, predominant during adolescence

**imaginary audience** The belief, often brought on by the heightened self-consciousness of early adolescence, that everyone is watching and evaluating one's behavior

**impression formation** The aspect of thinking that concerns the ways in which individuals' judgments of other people are formed and organized

**indifferent parenting** A style of parenting characterized by low warmth and low demandingness

**indulgent parenting** A style of parenting characterized by high warmth but low demandingness

**individuation** The progressive sharpening of one's sense of being an autonomous, independent person

**information processing** A perspective on cognition that derives from the study of artificial intelligence and attempts to explain cognitive development in terms of the growth of specific components of the thinking process (for example, memory)

**initiation** The ceremonial induction of the young person into adulthood

**intergenerational conflict** Tensions often thought to be inherent in relations between the adolescent and adult generations; thought by most scholars to have been overestimated

**internal working model** The implicit model of interpersonal relationships an individual employs through life, believed to be shaped by early attachment experiences

**internalizing disorders** Psychosocial problems that are manifested in a turning of the symptoms inward, as in depression or anxiety

**intimacy** The psychosocial domain concerning the formation, maintenance, and termination of close relationships

**intimcy versus isolation** According to Erikson, the normative crisis characteristic of the sixth psychosocial stage of development, predominant during young adulthood

**intrinsic motivation** Motivation based on the pleasure one will experience from mastering a task

**inventionists** Theorists who argue that the period of adolescence is mainly a social inventon

**junior high school** An educational institution designed during the early era of public secondary education, in which young adolescents are schooled separately from older adolescents

**justice orientation** In Carol Gilligan's theory of moral development, a moral orientation that emphasizes fairness and objectivity

**late adolescence (youth)** The period spanning roughly ages 18 through 21, corresponding approximately to the college years

**learned helplessness** The acquired belief that one is not able to influence events through one's own efforts or actions

**learning theories** Psychological theories that emphasize the acquisition of behavior through learning

**long-term memory** The ability to recall something from a long time ago

**longitudinal study** A study following the same group of individuals over time

**mainstreaming** The integration of students with educational handicaps into regular classrooms.

**marginal man** Kurt Lewin's term that refers to the transitional nature of adolescence—poised on the margin of adulthood

**marginality** The situation of being on the margin of the mainstream society, an experience more common among minority youth

**menarche** The time of first menstruation, one of the important changes to occur among females during puberty

**metacognition** The process of thinking about thinking itself

**middle adolescence** The period spanning roughly ages 15 through 18, corresponding approximately to the high school years

**middle school** An educational institution housing seventh- and eighth-grade students with adolescents who are one or two years younger

**midlife crisis** A psychological crisis over identity believed to occur between the ages of 35 and 45, the age range of most adolescents' parents

**modeling** Imitation

**motivation process model** A theory of adolescent achievement that stresses the interaction of beliefs, motives, goals, and attributions

**need for achievement** A need that influences the extent to which an individual strives for success in evaluative situations

**need for integration into adult society** According to Sullivan, the chief interpersonal need of late adolescence

**need for intimacy** According to Sullivan, the chief interpersonal need of preadolescence

**needs for sexual contact and for a loving relationship with a peer of the other sex** According to Sullivan, the chief interpersonal needs of early adolescence

**negative affectivity** The presumed underlying cause of internalizing disorders, characterized by high levels of subjective distress

**negative identity** The selection of an identity that is obviously undesirable in the eyes of significant others and the broader community

**neo-Freudians** Theorists who have followed in, and expanded on, the psychoanalytic tradition

**obesity** The condition of being more than twenty percent overweight

**observational learning** The process of learning by watching others

**occupational deviance** The commission of acts at work that are illegal or unethical

**operant conditioning** The process through which behavior is shaped through reinforcement and punishment

**organismic theories** Psychological theories that emphasize the interaction between biological and environmental forces

**organizational role of hormones** The process through which early exposure to hormones, especially prenatally, organizes the brain or other organs in anticipation of later changes in behavior or patterns of growth

**ovaries** The female gonads

**overmanning** The presence of too many individuals relative to the number of opportunities available for participation in the activities of a setting

**parental demandingness** According to Diana Baumrind, one of the two important dimensions of parenting; *demandingness* refers to the degree to which the parent expects and demands mature, responsible behavior from the child

**parental responsiveness** According to Diana Baumrind, one of the two important dimensions of parenting; *responsiveness* refers to the degree to which the parent responds to the child's needs in an accepting, supportive manner

**participant observation** A research technique in which the researcher "infiltrates" a group of individuals in order to study their behavior and relationships

**particularistic norms**   Guidelines for behavior that vary from one individual to another; more commonly found in less industrialized societies

**peak height velocity**   The point at which the adolescent is growing most rapidly

**peer groups**   Groups of individuals of approximately the same age

**peer pressure**   The perceived influences of one's agemates or friends to go along with their behavior

**permissive societies**   Societies in which sexual activity during childhood and adolescence is not greatly restrained

**personal fable**   An adolescent's belief that he or she is unique and therefore not subject to the rules that govern other people's behavior

**personal responsibility**   The ability to take responsibility for oneself and manage one's own affairs

**pituitary gland**   One of the chief glands responsible for regulating levels of hormones in the body

**popularity**   The degree to which an individual is liked by his or her peers

**postfigurative cultures**   Cultures in which the socialization of young people is accomplished almost exclusively through contact between children and their elders

**preconventional moral reasoning**   The first level of moral development, according to Kohlberg, typical of children and characterized by reasoning that is based on the rewards and punishments associated with different courses of action

**prefigurative cultures**   Cultures in which young people socialize their elders, rather than vice versa

**premature affluence**   Having more income than one can manage maturely

**preoperational period**   The second stage of cognitive development, according to Piaget, spanning roughly ages 2 through 5

**principled reasoning**   The third level of moral development, according to Kohlberg, which may develop during late adolescence; characterized by reasoning that is based on abstract moral principles

**problem behavior theory**   A theory that suggests that the covariation among various types of externalizing disorders is due to an underlying trait of unconventionality

**problem-focused coping**   Reaction to stress in which one attempts to change the source of stress, such as attempting to master a difficult challenge; effective in situations in which the source of stress is controllable

**propositional logic**   An abstract system of logic that forms the basis for formal operational thinking

**psychoanalytic theory**   Freud's theory of development

**psychometric**   A perspective on cognitive development concerned primarily with the measurement of quantitative changes in intelligence through the use of standardized tests

**psychosexual conflicts**   In Freud's theory, the intrapsychic tensions that drive human behavior

**psychosocial**   Referring to aspects of development that are both psychological and social in nature, such as developing a sense of identity or sexuality

**psychosocial crises**   In Erikson's theory, the conflicts that structure the various stages of development

**psychosocial moratorium**   A period of time during which individuals are free from excessive obligations and responsibilities and can therefore experiment with different roles and personalities

**puberty**   The biological changes of adolescence

**punishment**   The process that leads to a decrease in the likelihood that a specific behavior will occur

**pursuit of satisfaction**   According to Sullivan, the basic biological tendency that pushes individuals toward pleasurable, satisfying, or life-sustaining experiences

**pursuit of security**   According to Sullivan, the basic psychological tendency that pushes individuals toward the safety of secure interpersonal relationships

**recapitulation**   In Hall's theory, the notion that individual development parallels the evolution of the species

**reference group**   A group against which an individual compares himself or herself

**reinforcement**   The process that leads to an increase in the likelihood that a specific behavior will occur

**relationship maturity**   The level of sophistication and intimacy of one's closest relationships

**restrictive societies**   Societies in which adolescents

are pressured to refrain from sexual activity until they have married or undergone a formal rite of passage into adulthood

**risk-taking behavior**   Behavior that is pursued simply because it is risky. Risk-taking is thought to be linked to adolescent problem behavior

**rite of passage**   A ceremony or ritual marking an individual's transition from one social status to another, and especially, marking the young person's transition into adulthood

**role taking**   The aspect of thinking concerning the assessment of others' thoughts and feelings

**school climate**   The overall atmosphere that pervades a school or classroom

**school-based health centers**   A new approach to the delivery of health care services to adolescents, which places health care providers in offices located in or adjacent to schools

**secondary sex characteristics**   The manifestations of sexual maturation at puberty, including the development of breasts, the growth of facial and body hair, and changes in the voice

**secular trend**   The tendency, over the past two centuries, for individuals to be larger in stature and to reach puberty earlier, due primarily to improvements in health and nutrition

**secure attachment**   A healthy attachment between infant and caregiver, characterized by trust

**selective attention**   The process through which we focus on one stimulus while tuning out another

**self-conceptions**   The collection of traits and attributes individuals use to describe or characterize themselves

**self-consciousness**   The degree to which an individual is preoccupied with his or her self-image

**Self-Directed Search**   A personality inventory developed by Holland used to help individuals better understand their vocational interests

**self-esteem**   The degree to which individuals feel positively or negatively about themselves

**self-fulfilling prophecy**   The idea that individuals' behavior is influenced by what we expect of them

**self-image stability**   The degree to which an individual feels that his or her self-image changes from day to day

**self-reliance**   Subjective feelings of one's ability to function autonomously

**semirestrictive societies**   Societies in which pressures against adolescent sexual activity exist but are not vigilantly enforced

**sense of identity**   The extent to which individuals feel secure about who they are and who they are becoming

**sensorimotor**   The first stage of cognitive development, according to Piaget, spanning the period roughly between birth and age 2

**serial monogamy**   Having a series of sexual relationships over time in which one is monogamous within each relationship

**set point**   A physiological level or setting (of a specific hormone, for example) that the body attempts to maintain through a self-regulating system

**sex cleavage**   The separation of girls and boys into different cliques, common during late childhood and early adolescence

**sex-role transcendence**   The capacity to look beyond sex-roles as defining individuals' experiences

**sexuality**   The psychosocial domain concerning the development and expression of sexual feelings

**sexual socialization**   The process through which adolescents are exposed to and educated about sexuality

**sexually transmitted disease (STD)**   Any of a group of diseases, including gonorrhea, herpes, chlamydia, and AIDS, passed on through sexual contact

**short-term memory**   The ability to remember something for a very brief period of time

**significant others**   The people most important in an individual's life

**social class**   The social position of an individual or family in society as determined by wealth, power, reputation, or achievement

**social cognition**   The aspect of cognition that concerns thinking about other people, interpersonal relationships, and social institutions

**social competence training**   Psychological interventions designed to enhance adolescents' social skills

**social control theory**   A theory of delinquency that links deviance with the absence of bonds to society's main institutions

**social conventions**   The norms that govern everyday behavior in social situations

**social learning theorists** Learning theorists who emphasize the role of modeling and observational learning

**social network** The people an individual interacts with most regularly

**social redefinition** The process through which an individual's position or status is redefined by society

**social responsibility** The ability to cooperate with and take responsibility for others

**social support** The extent to which one receives emotional or instrumental assistance from one's social network

**socialized delinquency** Delinquent activity that is primarily the result of conforming to one's peer group

**sociocenter** The highly popular member of a peer group who is generally the best at keeping interpersonal relationships in the group smooth

**sociosexual behavior** The aspect of sexual behavior that is merged with social relationships

**specification** According to Super, the stage during which individuals, typically between the ages of 18 and 21, first begin to consider narrowly defined occupational pursuits

**standardized test** A carefully developed test that allows individual scores to be compared with established norms

**status** The degree to which an individual is perceived as a leader by his or her peers

**status offenses** Violations of the law that pertain to minors but not to adults

**storm and stress** Hall's phrase that refers to the inevitable turmoil of adolescence

**student engagement** The extent to which students are psychologically committed to learning and mastering material in school

**Tanner stages** A widely used system to describe the five stages of pubertal development

**task leader** The high-status member of a peer group who is generally the best at planning and implementing the group's activities

**teenager** A term coined about fifty years ago to refer to young people; it connoted a more frivolous and lighthearted image than the term *adolescent*

**testes** The male gonads

**testosterone** One of the sex hormones secreted by the gonads, found in both sexes but in higher levels among males than females

**thyroid** One of the many glands secreting the hormones that stimulate bodily growth at puberty

**tracking** The grouping of students, according to ability, into different levels of classes within the same school grade

**transition-proneness** A social and psychological period of heightened readiness to try new behaviors, especially problem behaviors

**triarchic theory of intelligence** Robert Sternberg's theory of intelligence, in which three different types of intelligence are examined: componential intelligence, experiential intelligence, and contextual intelligence

**universalistic norms** Guidelines for behavior that apply to all members of a community; more common in industrialized societies

**unsocialized delinquency** Delinquent activity that is primarily the result of inadequate socialization

**value autonomy** The establishment of an independent set of values and beliefs

**youth** Today, a term used to refer to individuals between the ages of 18 and 22; it once referred to individuals between the ages of 12 and 24

**youth unemployment** The unemployment of young people, especially 16- to 24-year-olds who are not enrolled in school

# References

Achenbach, T., and Edelbrock, C. (1987). *The manual for the Youth Self-Report and Profile*. Burlington, Vt.: University of Vermont.

Adams, G., and Fitch, S. (1982). Ego stage and identity status development: A cross-sequential analysis. *Journal of Personality and Social Psychology, 43*, 574–583.

Adams, G., and Jones, R. (1983). Female adolescents' identity development: Age comparisons and perceived child-rearing experience. *Developmental Psychology, 19*, 249–256.

Adelson, J. (1972). The political imagination of the young adolescent. In J. Kagan and R. Coles (Eds.), *Twelve to sixteen: Early adolescence*. New York: Norton.

Adelson, J. (1979). The generalization gap. *Psychology Today*, 33–37.

Adler, M. (1982). *The Paideia proposal: An educational manifesto*. New York: Macmillan.

Agras, W. S., Schneider, J., Arnow, B., Raeburn, S., and Telch, C. (1989). Cognitive-behavioral and response-prevention treatments for bulimia nervosa. *Journal of Consulting and Clinical Psychology, 57*, 215–221.

Ainsworth, M., Blehar, M., Waters, E., and Wall, S. (1978). *Patterns of attachment*. Hillsdale, N.J.: Erlbaum.

Alexander, K., and Cook, M. (1982). Curricula and coursework: A surprise ending to a familiar story. *American Sociological Review, 47*, 626–640.

Alexander, K., and Eckland, B. (1975). School experience and status attainment. In S. Dragastin and G. Elder, Jr. (Eds.), *Adolescence in the life cycle*. Washington, D.C.: Hemisphere.

Alexander, C., Ensminger, M., Kim, Y., Smith, B. J., Johnson, K., and Dolan, L. (1989). Early sexual activity among adolescents in small towns and rural areas: Race and gender patterns. *Family Planning Perspectives, 21*, 261–266.

Alexander, K., Natriello, G., and Pallas, A. (1985). For whom the cognitive bell tolls: The impact of dropping out on cognitive performance. *American Sociological Review, 50*, 409–420.

Allgood-Merten, B., Lewinsohn, P., and Hops, H. (1990). Sex differences and adolescent depression. *Journal of Abnormal Psychology, 99*, 55–63.

Allison, S., and Furstenberg, F. F. (1989). How marital dissolution affects children: Variations by age and sex. *Developmental Psychology, 25*, 540–549.

Ames, C., and Archer, J. (1988). Achievement goals in the classroom: Students' learning strategies and motivation processes. *Journal of Educational Psychology, 80*, 260–267.

Andersson, T., and Magnusson, D. (1990). Biological maturation in adolescence and the development of drinking habits and alcohol abuse among young males: A prospective longitudinal study. *Journal of Youth and Adolescence, 19*, 33–42.

Apter, T. (1990). *Altered loves: Mothers and daughters during adolescence*. New York: St. Martin's Press.

Archer, S. (1982). The lower age boundaries of identity development. *Child Development, 53*, 1551–1556.

Archer, S. (1989). Gender differences in identity development: Issues of process, domain, and timing. *Journal of Adolescence, 12*, 117–138.

Armor, D. (1972). School and family effects on black and white achievement: A reexamination of the USOE data. In F. Mosteller and D. Moynihan (Eds.), *On equality of educational opportunity*. New York: Random House.

Armsden, G., and Greenberg, M. (1987). The inventory of parent and peer attachment: Individual differences and their relationship to psychological well-being in adolescence. *Journal of Youth and Adolescence, 16*, 427–453.

Aro, H., and Taipale, V. (1987). The impact of timing of puberty on psychosomatic symptoms among fourteen- to sixteen-year-old Finnish girls. *Child Development, 58*, 261–268.

Astin, H. (1984). The meaning of work in women's lives: A sociopsychological model of career choice and work behavior. *Counseling Psychologist, 12,* 117–126.

Attie, I., and Brooks-Gunn, J. (1989). The development of eating problems in adolescent girls: A longitudinal study. *Developmental Psychology, 25,* 70–79.

Bachman, J. (1970). *Youth in transition.* (Vol. 2). *The impact of family background and intelligence on tenth-grade boys.* Ann Arbor: Institute for Social Research, University of Michigan.

Bachman, J. (1983, Summer). Premature affluence: Do high school students earn too much? *Economic Outlook USA,* 64–67.

Bachman, J., Bare, D., and Frankie, E. (1986). Correlates of employment among high school seniors. Paper available from the Institute for Social Research, University of Michigan, Ann Arbor.

Bachman, J., and O'Malley, P. (1986). Self-concepts, self-esteem, and educational experiences: The frog pond revisited (again). *Journal of Personality and Social Psychology, 50,* 35–46.

Bakan, D. (1972). Adolescence in America: From idea to social fact. In J. Kagan and R. Coles (Eds.), *Twelve to sixteen: Early adolescence.* New York: Norton.

Bakan, D. (1966). *The duality of human existence.* Chicago: Rand McNally.

Baker, D., and Stevenson, D. (1986). Mothers' strategies for school achievement: Managing the transition to high school. *Sociology of Education, 59,* 156–167.

Baker, S., and Gore, T. (1989, May 29). Some reasons for 'wilding.' *Newsweek,* pp. 6–7.

Baker, L., and Brown, A. (1984). Metacognitive skills and reading. In P. Pearson (Ed.), *Handbook of reading research* (Part 2). New York: Longman.

Bandura, A., and Walters, R. (1959). *Adolescent aggression.* New York: Ronald Press.

Bradwick, J., and Douvan, E. (1971). Ambivalence: The socialization of women. In V. Gernick and B. Moran (Eds.), *Women in sexist society: Studies in power and powerlessness.* New York: Basic Books.

Barenboim, C. (1981). The development of person perception in childhood and adolescence: From behavioral comparisons to psychological constructs to psychological comparisons. *Child Development, 52,* 129–144.

Barker, R., and Gump, P. (1964). *Big school, small school: High school size and student behavior.* Stanford, Calif.: Stanford University Press.

Barnes, E. (1980). The black community as the source of positive self-concept for black children: A theoretical perspective. In R. Jones (Ed.), *Black psychology.* Pp. 106–130. New York: Harper & Row.

Baron, J., and Sternberg, R. (1987). *Teaching thinking skills: Theory and practice.* New York: Freeman.

Barringer, F. (1991, June 7). Changes in U.S. households: Single parents and solitude. *The New York Times,* p. 1 and ff.

Barringer, F. (1990, August 17). After long decline, teen births are up. *The New York Times,* p. A14.

Barton, P. (1989). *Earning and learning.* Princeton, N.J.: National Assessment of Educational Progress, Educational Testing Service.

Baruch, G., Barnett, R., and Rivers. C. (1983). *Lifeprints.* New York: McGraw-Hill.

Baumeister, R., and Tice, D. (1986). How adolescence became the struggle for self: A historical transformation of psychological development. Pp. 183–201. In J. Suls and A. Greenwald (Eds.), *Psychological perspectives on the self.* (Vol. 3). Hillsdale, N.J.: Erlbaum.

Baumrind, D. (1987). Parental disciplinary patterns and social competence in children. *Youth and Society, 9,* 239–276.

Baumrind, D. (1991). The influence of parenting style on adolescent competence and substance use. *Journal of Early Adolescence, 11,* 56–95.

Baumrind, D. (1991). Parenting styles and adolescent development. In J. Brooks-Gunn, R. Lerner, and A. C. Petersen (Eds.), *The encyclopedia of adolescence.* Pp. 746–758. New York: Garland.

Baumrind, D., and Moselle, K. (1985). A developmental perspective on adolescent drug abuse. *Advances in Alcohol and Substance Abuse, 4,* 41–67.

Beardslee, W., Schultz, L., and Selman, R. (1987). Level of social-cognitive development, adaptive functioning, and *DSM-III* diagnoses in adolescent offspring of parents with affective disorders: Implications of the development of the capacity for mutuality. *Developmental Psychology, 23,* 807–815.

Bell, A., Weinberg, M., and Hammersmith, S.

(1981). *Sexual preference: Its development in men and women.* Bloomington, Ind.: Indiana University Press.

Belsky, J., Steinberg, L., and Draper, P. (1991). Childhood experience, interpersonal development, and reproductive strategy: An evolutionary theory of socialization. *Child Development 62*, 647–670.

Bem, S. (1975). Sex-role adaptability: One consequence of psychological androgyny. *Journal of Personality and Social Psychology, 31*, 634–643.

Benedict, R. (1934). *Patterns of culture.* Boston: Houghton Mifflin.

Bennett, G. (1919). *The junior high school.* Baltimore: Warwick and York.

Bennett, S. (1987). *New dimensions in research on class size and academic achievement.* Madison, Wis.: National Center on Effective Secondary Schools.

Benson, P., Donahue, M., and Erickson, J. (1989). Adolescence and religion: Review of the literature from 1970–1986. *Research in the Social Scientific Study of Religion, 1,* 153–181.

Berkowitz, M. (1985). The role of discussion in moral education. In M. Berkowitz and F. Oser (Eds.), *Moral education: Theory and application.* Pp. 197–218. Hillsdale, N.J.: Erlbaum.

Bernard, J. (1973). *The future of marriage.* New York: Bantam.

Berndt, T. (1979). Developmental changes in conformity to peers and parents. *Developmental Psychology, 15,* 608–616.

Berndt, T. (1981). Relations between social cognition, nonsocial cognition, and social behavior: The case of friendship. In J. Flavell and L. Ross (Eds.), *Social cognitive development: Frontiers and possible futures.* Cambridge: Cambridge University Press.

Berndt, T. (1982). The features and effects of friendship in early adolescence. *Child Development, 53,* 1447–1460.

Berndt, T. (1987). Changes in friendship and school adjustment after the transition to junior high school. Paper presented at the biennial meeting of the Society for Research in Child Development, Baltimore.

Berndt, T., and Perry, T. B. (1990). Distinctive features and effects of early adolescent friendships. In R. Montemayor, G. Adams, and T. Gullota

(Eds.), *Advances in adolescence research* (Vol. 2). Pp. 269–287. Beverly Hills, Calif.: Sage.

Bettes, B., Dusenbury, L., Kerner, J., James-Ortiz, and Botvin, G. (1990). Ethnicity and psychosocial factors in alcohol and tobacco use in adolescence. *Child Development, 61,* 557–565.

Bigelow, B., and LaGaipa, J. (1975). Children's written descriptions of friendship. *Developmental Psychology, 11,* 857–858.

Biller, H. (1981). Father absence, divorce, and personality development. In M. Lamb (Ed.), *The role of the father in child development* (2nd ed.). New York: Wiley.

Billy, J., Landale, N., Grady, W., and Zimmerle, D. (1988). Effects of sexual activity on adolescent social and psychological development. *Social Psychology Quarterly, 51,* 190–212.

Block, J., Block, J., and Keyes, S. (1988). Longitudinally foretelling drug usage in adolescence: Early childhood personality and environmental precursors. *Child Development, 59,* 336–355.

Bloom, A. (1987). *The closing of the American mind.* New York: Simon and Schuster.

Blos, P. (1967). The second individuation process of adolescence. In R. S. Eissler et al. (Eds.), *Psychoanalytic study of the child* (Vol. 15). New York: International Universities Press.

Blum, R., Resnick, M., and Stark, T. (1990). Factors associated with the use of court bypass by minors to obtain abortions. *Family Planning Perspectives, 22,* 158–160.

Blumenthal, S., and Kupfer, D. (1988). Overview of early detection and treatment strategies for suicidal behavior in young people. *Journal of Youth and Adolescence, 17,* 1–24.

Blyth, D., Hill, J., and Smyth, C. (1981). The influence of older adolescents on younger adolescents: Do grade-level arrangements make a difference in behaviors, attitudes, and experiences? *Journal of Early Adolescence, 1,* 85–110.

Blyth, D., Hill, J., and Thiel, K. (1982). Early adolescents' significant others: Grade and gender differences in perceived relationships with familial and non-familial adults and young people. *Journal of Youth and Adolescence, 11,* 425–450.

Blyth, D., Simmons, R., Bulcroft, R., Felt, D., Van Cleave, E., and Bush, D. (1980). The effects of physical development on self-image and satisfaction with body image for early adolescent males. In F. G. Simmons (Ed.), *Handbook of community and mental health* (Vol. 2). Greenwich, Conn.: JAI Press.

Blyth, D., Simmons, R., and Zakin, D. (1985). Satisfaction with body image for early adolescent females: The impact of pubertal timing within different school environments. *Journal of Youth and Adolescence, 14,* 227–236.

Bogenschneider, K., and Steinberg, L. (1989, August). Maternal employment and adolescent achievement: A process model. Paper presented as a part of a symposium entitled "Maternal Employment and Child Outcomes: New Perspectives on 'Process' Issues," at the annual meeting of the American Psychological Association, New Orleans.

Bohrnstedt, G., and Felson, R. (1983). Explaining the relations among children's actual and perceived performances and self-esteem: A comparison of several causal models. *Journal of Personality and Social Psychology, 45,* 43–56.

Boldizar, J., Wilso, K., and Deemer, D. (1989). Gender, life experiences, and moral judgment development: A process-oriented approach. *Journal of Personality and Social Psychology, 57,* 229–238.

Bourne, E. (1978a). The state of research on ego identity: A review and appraisal. Part I. *Journal of Youth and Adolescence, 7,* 223–251.

Bourne, E. (1978b). The state of research on ego identity: A review and appraisal. Part II. *Journal of Youth and Adolescence, 7,* 371–392.

Bowlby, J. (1969). *Attachment and loss* (Vol. 1). *Attachment.* New York: Basic Books.

Boyer, E. (1983). *High school.* New York: Harper & Row.

Boyer, E. (1986). Transition from school to college. *Phi Delta Kappan, December,* 293–287.

Braddock, J. (1985). School desegregation and black assimilation. *Journal of Social Issues, 41,* 9–22.

Bradley, L., and Bradley, G. (1977). The academic achievement of black students in desegregated schools: A critical review. *Review of Educational Research, 47,* 399–449.

Braungart, R. (1980). Youth movements. In J. Adelson (Ed.), *Handbook of adolescent psychology.* Pp. 560–597. New York: Wiley.

Brittain, C. (1963). Adolescent choices and parent/

peer cross-pressures. *American Sociological Review, 28,* 385–391.

Brody, J. (1986, December 16). Effeminacy and homeosexuality. *The New York Times,* p. 17.

Brody, J. (1987, June 3). Personal health column. *The New York Times.*

Bronfenbrenner, U. (1967). Response to pressure from peers versus adults among Soviet and American school children. *International Journal of Psychology, 2,* 199–207.

Bronfenbrenner, U. (1974). The origins of alienation. *Scientific American, 231,* 53–61.

Bronfenbrenner, U. (1975). Reality and research in the ecology of human development. *Proceedings of the American Philosophical Society, 119,* 439–469.

Bronfenbrenner, U. (1979). *The ecology of human development.* Cambridge: Harvard University Press.

Brook, J., Whiteman, M., and Gordon, A. (1983). Stages of drug use in adolescence: Personality, peer, and family correlates. *Developmental Psychology, 19,* 269–277.

Brook, J., Whiteman, M., Gordon, A., and Brook, D. (1984). Paternal determinants of female adolescent's marijuana use. *Developmental Psychology, 20,* 1032–1043.

Brook, J., Whitman, M., Gordon, A., and Cohen, P. (1986). Dynamics of childhood and adolescent personality traits and adolescent drug use. *Developmental Psychology, 22,* 403–414.

Brooks-Gunn, J. (1987). Pubertal processes and girls' psychological adaptation. In R. Lerner and T. Fochs (Eds.), *Biological-psychosocial interactions in early adolescence: A life-span perspective.* Pp. 123–153. Hillsdale, N.J.: Erlbaum.

Brooks-Gunn, J. (1989). Pubertal processes and the early adolescent transition. In W. Damon (Ed.), *Child development today and tommorrow.* Pp. 155–176. San Francisco: Jossey-Bass.

Brooks-Gunn, J., and Furstenberg, F., Jr. (1989). Adolescent sexual behavior. *American Psychologist, 44,* 249–257.

Brooks-Gunn, J., and Reiter, E. (1990). The role of pubertal processes. In S. Feldman and G. Elliott (Eds.), *At the threshold: The developing adolescent.* Pp. 16–23. Cambridge: Harvard University Press.

Brooks-Gunn, J., Boyer, C., and Hein, K. (1988). Preventing HIV infection and AIDS in children and adolescents. *American Psychologist, 43,* 958–964.

Brooks-Gunn, J., and Pedtersen, A. (Eds.) (1991). *The emergence of depressive symptoms during adolescence. Journal of Youth and Adolescence, 20* (whole issue).

Brooks-Gunn, J., and Ruble, D. (1979). The social and psychological meaning of menarche. Paper presented at the biennial meeting of the Society for Research in Child Development, San Francisco.

Brooks-Gunn, J., and Ruble, D. (1982). The development of menstrual-related beliefs and behaviors during early adolescence. *Child Development, 53,* 1567–1577.

Brooks-Gunn, J., and Warren, M. (1985). The effects of delayed menarche in different contexts: Dance and nondance students. *Journal of Youth and Adolescence, 14,* 285–300.

Brooks-Gunn, J., Warren, M., and Rosso, J. (1991). The impact of pubertal and social events upon girls' problem behavior. *Journal of Youth and Adolescence.*

Brophy, J. (1979). Teacher behavior and its effects. *Journal of Educational Psychology, 71,* 733–750.

Broverman, I., Vogel, S., Broverman, D., Clarkson, F., and Rosenkrantz, P. (1972). Sex-role stereotypes: A current appraisal. *Journal of Social Issues, 28,* 59–78.

Brown, A. (1975). The development of memory: Knowing, knowing about knowing, and knowing how to know. In H. Reese (Ed.), *Advances in child development and behavior* (Vol. 10). New York: Academic Press.

Brown, B. (1990). Peer groups. In S. Feldman and G. Elliott (Eds.), *At the threshold: The developing adolescent.* Pp. 171–196. Cambridge: Harvard University Press.

Brown, B., Clasen, D., and Eicher, S. (1986). Perceptions of peer pressure, peer conformity dispositions, and self-reported behavior among adolescents. *Developmental Psychology, 22,* 521–530.

Brown, B., Lamborn, S., and Newmann, F. (in press). "You live and you learn": The place of school engagement in the lives of teenagers. In F. Newmann (Ed.), *Student engagement and achievement in American high schools.* New York: Teachers College Press.

Brown, B., and Mounts, N. (1989, April). Peer group structures in single versus multiethnic high schools. Paper presented at the biennial meeting of the Society for Research in Child Development, Kansas City.

Brubacher, J., and Rudy, W. (1976). *Higher education in transition* (3rd ed.). New York: Harper & Row.

Bruch, H. (1973). *Eating disorders.* New York: Basic Books.

Brumberg, J. (1982). Chlorotic girls, 1870–1920: A historical perspective on female adolescence. *Child Development, 53,* 1468–1477.

Brumberg, J. (1988). *Fasting girls: The emergence of anorexia as a modern disease.* Cambridge: Harvard University Press.

Bryk, A., and Thum, Y. (1989). The effects of high school organization on dropping out: An exploratory investigation. *American Educational Research Journal, 26,* 353–383.

Buchanan, C. M., and Maccoby, E. (1990, March). Characteristics of adolescents and their families in three custodial arrangements. Paper presented at the biennial meeting of the Society for Research on Adolescence, Atlanta.

Buchanan, M., and Robbins, C. (1990). Early adult psychological consequences for males of adolescent pregnancy and its resolution. *Journal of Youth and Adolescence, 19,* 413–424.

Buhrmester, D., and Furman, W. (1987). The development of companionship and intimacy. *Child Development, 58,* 1101–1113.

Bulcroft, R. (1991). The value of physical change in adolescence: Consequences for the parent-adolescent exchange relationship. *Journal of Youth and Adolescence, 20,* 89–106.

Bullough, V. (1981). Age at menarche: A misunderstanding. *Science, 213,* 365–366.

Bumpass, L., and McLanahan, S. (1987, April). Unmarried motherhood: A note on recent trends, composition and black-white differences. Paper presented at the annual meeting of the Population Association of America, Chicago.

Burchinal, L. (1965). Trends and prospects for young marriages in the U.S. *Journal of Marriage and the Family, 27,* 243–254.

Burda, P., and Vaux, A. (1988). Social drinking in supportive contexts among college males. *Journal of Youth and Adolescence, 17,* 165–172.

Burleson, B. (1982). The development of comforting communication skills in childhood and adolescence. *Child Development, 53,* 1578–1588.

Butler, R., and Nissan, M. (1975). Who is afraid of success? And why? *Journal of Youth and Adolescence, 4,* 259–270.

Cairns, R., Cairns, B., Neckerman, H., Ferguson, L., and Gariepy, J. (1989). Growth and aggression: 1. Childhood to early adolescence. *Developmental Psychology, 25,* 320–330.

Campbell, A. (1968). The role of family planning in the reduction of poverty. *Journal of Marriage and the Family, 30,* 236–245.

Campbell, B. (1977). The impact of school desegregation: An investigation of three mediating factors. *Youth and Society, 9,* 79–111.

Campbell, E., Adams, G., and Dobson, W. (1984). Familial correlates of identity formation in late adolescence: A study of the predictive utility of connectedness and individuality in family relations. *Journal of Youth and Adolescence, 13,* 509–526.

Cantwell, D., and Baker, L. (1991). Manifestations of depressive affect in adolescence. *Journal of Youth and Adolescence, 20,* 121–134.

Carnegie Council on Adolescent Development. (1989). *Turning points: Preparing youth for the 21st century.* New York: Carnegie Corporation of New York.

Carns, D. (1973). Talking about sex: Notes on first coitis and the double sexual standard. *Journal of Marriage and the Family, 35,* 677–688.

Case, R. (1985). *Intellectual development: Birth to adulthood.* New York: Academic Press.

Casper, L. (1990). Does family interaction prevent adolescent pregnancy? *Family Planning Perspectives, 22,* 109–114.

Caspi, A., and Moffitt, T. (in press). Individual differences and personal transitions: The sample case of girls at puberty.

Caspi, A., Elder, Jr., G., and Bem, D. (1987). Moving against the world: Life-course patterns of explosive children. *Developmental Psychology, 23,* 308–313.

Cauce, A. (1987). School and peer competence in early adolescence: A test of domain-specific self-perceived competence. *Developmental Psychology, 23,* 287–291.

Chandler, M. (1987). The Othello effect: Essay on the emergence and eclipse of skeptical doubt. *Human Development, 30,* 137–159.

Charner, I., and Fraser, B. (1987). *Youth and work.* Washington, D.C.: William T. Grant Foundation Commission on Work, Family, and Citizenship.

Chartier, G., and Ranieri, D. (1984). Adolescent depression: Concepts, treatments, prevention. In P. Karoly and J. Steffen (Eds.), *Adolescent behavior disorders: Foundations and contemporary concerns.* Lexington, MA: Lexington.

Children's Defense Fund. (1989). *Service opportunities for youths.* Washington: Children's Defense Fund.

Chilman, C. (1980, November). Social and psychological research concerning adolescent childbearing: 1970–1980. *Journal of Marriage and the Family,* pp. 793–805.

Chilman, C. (1986). Some psychosocial aspects of adolescent sexual and contraceptive behaviors in a changing American society. In J. Lancaster and B. Hamburg (Eds.), *School-age pregnancy and parenthood: Biosocial dimensions.* New York: Aldine de Gruyter.

Christopher, F. S., and Roosa, M. (1990). An evaluation of an adolescent pregnancy prevention program: Is "Just say no" enough? *Family Relations, 39,* 68–72.

Chung, R., and Walkey, F. (1989). Educational and achievement aspirations of New Zealand Chinese and European secondary school students. *Youth and Society, 21,* 139–152.

Church, R. (1976). *Education in the United States.* New York: Free Press.

Clark, R., and Delia, J. (1976). The development of functional persuasive skills in childhood and early adolescence. *Child Development, 47,* 1008–1014.

Clasen, D., and Brown, B. (1985). The multidimensionality of peer pressure in adolescence. *Journal of Youth and Adolescence, 14,* 451–468.

Clausen, J. (1975). The social meaning of differential physical and sexual maturation. In S. E. Dragastin and G. H. Elder, Jr. (Eds.), *Adolescence in the life cycle.* New York: Halsted Press.

Clayton, R., and Bokemeier, J. (1980, November). Premarital sex in the seventies. *Journal of Marriage and the Family,* pp. 759–775.

Coe, C., Hayashi, K., and Levine, S. (1988). Hormones and behavior at puberty: Activation or concatenation. In M. Gunnar and W. A. Collins (Eds.), *The Minnesota Symposia on Child Psychology* (Vol. 21, pp. 17–41). Hillsdale, N.J.: Erlbaum.

Cohen, Y. (1964). *The transition from childhood to adolescence.* Chicago: Aldine.

Colby, A., Kohlberg, L., Gibbs, J., and Lieberman, M. (1983). A longitudinal study of moral judgment. *Monographs of the Society for Research in Child Development, 48* (Serial No. 200).

Coleman, J. (1961). *The adolescent society.* Glencoe, Ill.: Free Press.

Coleman, J. (1980). Friendship and the peer group in adolescence. In J. Adelson (Ed.), *Handbook of adolescent psychology.* New York: Wiley.

Coleman, J., Campbell, E., Hobson, C., McPartland, J., Mood, A., Weinfeld, F., and York, R. (1966). *Equality of educational opportunity.* Washington, D.C.: U.S. Government Printing Office.

Coleman, J., and Hoffer, T. (1987). *Public and private high schools: The impact of communities.* New York: Basic Books.

Coleman, J., Hoffer, T., and Kilgore, S. (1982). *High school achievement: Public, Catholic and other private schools compared.* New York: Basic Books.

Coll, C., Hoffman, J., and Oh, W. (1987). The social ecology and early parenting of Caucasian adolescent mothers. *Child Development, 58,* 955–963.

College Exam Board. (1988). *Scholastic aptitude test performance.* Princeton, N.J.: College Exam Board.

Collins, W. A. (1990). Parent-child relationships in the transition to adolescence: Continuity and change in interaction, affect, and cognition. In R. Montemayor, G. Adams, and T. Gullotta (Eds.), *Advances in adolescent development: Vol. 2. The transition from childhood to adolescence.* Pp. 85–106. Beverly Hills, Calif.: Sage.

Collins, W. A. (1988). Research on the transition to adolescence: Continuity in the study of developmental processes. In M. Gunnar (Ed.), *21st Minnesota Symposium on Child Psychology.* Pp. 1–15. Hillsdale, N.J.: Erlbaum.

Colten, M., Gore, S., and Aseltine, Jr., R. (1991). The patterning of distress and disorder in a community sample of high school aged youth. In M. Colten and S. Gore (Eds.). *Adolescent stress: Causes and consequences.* Pp. 157–180. New York: Aldine de Gruyter.

Committee for the Study of National Service.

(1980). *National youth service: What's at stake?* Washington, D.C.: Potomac Institute.

Compas, B., Davis, G., Forsythe, C., and Wagner, B. (1987). Assessment of major and daily stressful life events during adolescence: The Adolescent Perceived Events Scale. *Journal of Consulting and Clinical Psychology, 55,* 534–541.

Compas, B., Malcarne, V., and Fondacaro, K. (1988). Coping with stressful events in children and young adolescents. *Journal of Consulting and Clinical Psychology, 56,* 405–411.

Conant, J. (1959). *The American high school today.* New York: McGraw-Hill.

Condit, V. (1990). Anorexia nervosa: Levels of causation. *Human Nature, 1,* 391–413.

Conger, J. (1975). Current issues in adolescent development. In *Master lectures on developmental psychology.* Washington, D.C.: American Psychological Association.

Conger, J. (1977). *Adolescence and youth* (2nd ed.). New York: Harper & Row.

Conger, J. (1981). Freedom and commitment: Families, youth, and social change. *American Psychologist, 36,* 1475–1484.

Congressional Budget Office (1986). *Trends in educational achievement.* Washington: U.S. Congress.

Coombs, R., Paulson, M., and Richardson, M. (1991). Peer vs. parental influence in substance use among Hispanic and Anglo children and adolescents. *Journal of Youth and Adolescence, 20,* 73–88.

Cooper, C. (1988). Commentary: The role of conflict in adolescent parent relationships. In M. Gunnar (Ed.), *21st Minnesota Symposium on Child Psychology.* Pp. 181–187. Hillsdale, N.J.: Erlbaum.

Cooper, C., Grotevant, H., and Condon, S. (1983). Individuality and connectedness in the family as a context for adolescent identity formation and role taking skill. In H. Grotevant and C. Cooper (Eds.), *Adolescent development in the family.* San Francisco: Jossey-Bass.

Crandall, C. (1988). Social contagion of binge eating. *Journal of Personality and Social Psychology, 55,* 588–598.

Crisp, A. (1983). Some aspects of the psychopathology of anorexia nervosa. In P. Darby, P. Garfinkel, D. Garner, and D. Cosina (Eds.), *Anorexia nervosa: Recent developments in research.* Pp. 15–28. New York: Alan R. Liss.

Crites, H. (1989). Career differentiation in adolescence. In D. Stern and D. Eichorn (Eds.), *Adolescence and work*. Hillsdale, N.J.: Erlbaum.

Crockett, L., and Dorn, L. (1987). Young adolescents' pubertal status and reported heterosocial interaction. Paper presented at the biennial meeting of the Society for Research in Child Development, Baltimore.

Cross, W. (1978). The Thomas and Cook models of psychological nigrescence: A literature review. *Journal of Black Psychology, 4,* 13–31.

Crouter, A., MacDermid, S., McHale, S., and Perry-Jenkins, M. (1990). Parental monitoring and perceptions of children's school performance and conduct in dual- and single-earner families. *Developmental Psychology, 26,* 649–657.

Csikszentmihalyi, M., and Larson, R. (1984). *Being adolescent.* New York: Basic Books.

Cutrona, C. (1982). Transition to college: Loneliness and the process of social adjustment. In L. Peplau and D. Perlman (Eds.), *Loneliness: A sourcebook of current theory, research, and therapy.* New York: Wiley.

Cvetkovich, G., Grote, B., Bjorseth, A., and Sarkissian, J. (1975). On the psychology of adolescents' use of contraceptives. *Journal of Sex Research, 11,* 256–270.

Damico, R. (1984). Does working in high school impair academic progress? *Sociology of Education, 57,* 157–164.

Daniels, D., Dunn, J., Furstenberg, F., Jr., and Plomin, R. (1985). Environmental differences within the family and adjustment differences within pairs of adolescent siblings. *Child Development, 56,* 764–774.

Danner, F., and Day, M. (1977). Eliciting formal operations. *Child Development, 48,* 1600–1606.

Darabi, K., and Ortiz, V. (1987). Childbearing among young Latino women in the United States. *American Journal of Public Health, 77,* 25–28.

Davis, K. (1940). The sociology of parent-youth conflict. *American Sociological Review, 5,* 523–525.

Demorest, A., Meyer, C., Phelps, E., Gardner, H., and Winner, E. (1984). Words speak louder than actions: Understanding deliberately false remarks. *Child Development, 55,* 1527–1534.

DeParle, J. (1991, June 9). Without fanfare, Blacks march to greater high school success. *The New York Times,* p. 1 and ff.

Devereux, E. (1970). The role of peer group experience in moral development. In J. Hill (Ed.), *Minnesota Symposium on Child Psychology* (Vol. 4). Minneapolis: University of Minnesota Press.

Diaz, R., and Berndt, T. (1982). Children's knowledge of a best friend: Fact or fancy? *Developmental Psychology, 18,* 787–794.

DiClemente, R. (1990). The emergence of adolescents as a risk group for Human Immunodeficiency Virus infection. *Journal of Adolescent Research, 5,* 7–17.

DiClemente, R., Boyer, C., and Morales, E. (1988). Minorities and AIDS: Knowledge, attitudes, and misconceptions among Black and Latino adolescents. *American Journal of Public Health, 78,* 55–57.

Dickenson, G. (1975). Dating behavior of black and white adolescents before and after desegregation. *Journal of Marriage and the Family, 37,* 602–608.

DiMaggio, P. (1982). Cultural capital and school success: The impact of status culture participation on the grades of U.S. high school students. *American Sociological Review, 47,* 189–201.

Dishion, T., Patterson, G., Stoolmiller, M., and Skinner, M. (1991). Family, school, and behavioral antecedents to early adolescent involvement with antisocial peers. *Developmental Psychology, 27,* 172–180.

Dodge, K. (1986). A social information-processing model of social competence in children. In M. Perlmutter (Ed.), *Minnesota Symposium on Child Psychology* (Vol. 18, pp. 77–125). Hillsdale, N.J.: Erlbaum.

Donovan, J., and Jessor, R. (1985). Structure of problem behavior in adolescence and young adulthood. *Journal of Consulting and Clinical Psychology, 53,* 890–904.

Dornbusch, S., Carlsmith, J., Gross, R., Martin, J., Jennings, D., Rosenberg, A., and Duke, P. (1981). Sexual development, age, and dating: A comparison of biological and social influences upon one set of behaviors. *Child Development, 52,* 179–185.

Dornbusch, S., Carlsmith, J., Bushwall, S., Ritter, P., Leiderman, P., Hastorf, A., and Gross, R. (1985). Single parents, extended households, and the control of adolescents. *Child Development, 56,* 326–341.

Dornbusch, S., Ritter, P., Liederman, P., Roberts, D., and Fraleigh, M. (1987). The relation of parenting style to adolescent school performance. *Child Development, 58,* 1244–1257.

Douvan, E., and Adelson, J. (1966). *The adolescent experience.* New York: Wiley.

Dreyer, P. (1982). Sexuality during adolescence. In B. Wolman (Ed.), *Handbook of developmental psychology.* Englewood Cliffs, N.J.: Prentice-Hall.

DuBois, D., and Hirsch, B. (1990). School and neighborhood friendship patterns of blacks and whites in early adolescence. *Child Development, 61,* 524–536.

Duncan, O., Featherman D., and Duncan, B. (1972). *Socioeconomic background and achievement.* New York: Semmar Press.

Duncan, P., Ritter, P., Dornbusch, S., Gross, R., and Carlsmith, J. (1985). The effects of pubertal timing on body image, school behavior, and deviance. *Journal of Youth and Adolescence, 14,* 227–236.

Dunn, S., Putallaz, M., Sheppard, B., and Lindstrom, R. (1987). Social support and adjustment in gifted adolescents. *Journal of Educational Psychology, 79,* 467–473.

Dusek, J., and Flaherty, J. (1981). The development of the self-concept during the adolescent years. *Monographs of the Society for Research in Child Development, 46* (Serial No. 191).

Dweck, C., and Light, B. (1980). Learned helplessness and intellectual achievement. In J. Garber and M. Seligman (Eds.), *Human helplessness.* New York: Academic Press.

Dweck, C., and Wortman, C. (1980). Achievement, test anxiety, and learned helplessness: Adaptive and maladaptive cognitions. In H. Krohne and L. Laux (Eds.), *Achievement, stress, and anxiety.* Washington, D.C.: Hemisphere.

Dyk, P., and Adams, G. (1990). Identity and intimacy: An initial investigation of three theoretical models using cross-lag panel correlations. *Journal of Youth and Adolescence, 19,* 91–110.

Easterlin, R. (1980). *Birth and fortune.* New York: Basic Books.

Ebata, A., and Moos, R. (in press). Coping and adjustment in distressed and healthy adolescents. *Journal of Applied Developmental Psychology.*

Eccles, J., Adler, T., and Meece, J. (1984). Sex differences in achievement: A test of alternate theories. *Journal of Personality and Social Psychology, 46,* 26–43.

Eccles, J., and Midgley, C. (1990). Changes in academic motivation and self-perception during early adolescence. In R. Montemayor, G. Adams, and T. Gullotta (Eds.), *Advances in adolescent development.* (Vol. 2). *The transition from childhood to adolescence.* Pp. 134–155. Beverly Hills, Calif.: Sage.

Eccles, J., Midgley, C., and Adler, T. (1984). Grade-related changes in the school environment: Effects on achievement motivation. In J. Nicholls (Eds.), *Advances in motivation and achievement.* Pp. 283–331. Greenwich, Conn.: JAI Press.

Eder, D., and Parker, S. (1987). The cultural production and reproduction of gender: The effect of extracurricular activities on peer-group culture. *Sociology of Education, 60,* 200–213.

Elder, G., Jr. (1974). *Children of the Great Depression.* Chicago: University of Chicago Press.

Elder, G., Jr. (1980). Adolescence in historical perspective. In J. Adelson (Ed.), *Handbook of adolescent psychology.* New York: Wiley.

Elder, G. H., Jr., Caspi, A., and van Nguyen, T. (1986). Resourceful and vulnerable children: Family influences in stressful times. In R. Silbereisen, K. Eyferth, and G. Rudinger (Eds.), *Development as action in context.* Heidelberg: Springer.

Elder, G. H., Jr., van Nguyen, T., and Caspi, A. (1985). Linking family hardship to children's lives. *Child Development, 56,* 361–375.

Elkind, D. (1967). Egocentrism in adolescence. *Child Development, 38,* 1025–1034.

Elkind, D. (1978). Understanding the young adolescent. *Adolescence, 13,* 127–134.

Elkind, D. (1982). *The hurried child.* New York: Addison-Wesley, 1982.

Elkind, D. (1985). Egocentrism redux. *Developmental Review, 5,* 218–226.

Elkind, D., Barocas, R., and Rosenthal, R. (1968). Combinatorial thinking in adolescents from graded and ungraded classrooms. *Perceptual and Motor Skills, 27,* 1015–1018.

Elliott, D., Huizinga, D., and Menard, S. (1989). *Multiple problem youth: Delinquency, substance abuse, and mental health problems.* New York: Springer-Verlag.

Elliott, D., and Morse, B. (1989). Delinquency and drug use as risk factors in teenage sexual activity. *Youth and Society, 21*, 32–57.

Elmen, J. (1991). Achievement orientation in early adolescence: Developmental patterns and social correlates. *Journal of Early Adolescence, 11*, 125–151.

Elster, A., Lamb, M., Peters, L., Kahn, J., and Tavare, J. (1987). Judicial involvement and conduct problems of fathers of infants born to adolescent mothers. *Pediatrics, 79*, 230–234.

Enright, R., Levy, V., Harris, D., and Lapsley, D. (1987). Do economic conditions influence how theorists view adolescents? *Journal of Youth and Adolescence, 16*, 541–560.

Ensminger, M. (1990). Sexual activity and problem behaviors among Black, urban adolescents. *Child Development, 61*, 2032–2046.

Entwisle, D. (1990). Schools and the adolescent. In S. Feldman and G. Elliott (Eds.), *At the threshold: The developing adolescent*. Pp. 197–224. Cambridge: Harvard University Press.

Entwisle, D., and Hayduk, L. (1988). Lasting effects of elementary school. *Sociology of Education, 61*, 147–159.

Epstein, J. (1983a). Selecting friends in contrasting secondary school environments. In J. Epstein and N. Karweit (Eds.), *Friends in school*. New York: Academic Press.

Erikson, E. (1959). Identity and the life cycle. *Psychological Issues, 1*, 1–171.

Erikson, E. (1963). *Childhood and society*. New York: Norton.

Erikson, E. (1968). *Identity: Youth and crisis*. New York: Norton.

Erickson, M. F., Sroufe, L. A., and Egeland, B. (1985). The relationship between quality of attachment and behavior problems in preschool in a high-risk sample. Growing Points of Attachment Theory and Research: *Monographs of the Society for Research in Child Development, 50*, 147–193.

Evans, E., Rutberg, J., Sather, C., and Turner, C. (1990). Content analysis of contemporary teen magazines for adolescent females. Paper presented at the meeting of the American Educational Research Association, Boston, April.

Eveleth, P., and Tanner, J. (1976). *Worldwide variation in human growth*. New York: Cambridge University Press.

Farkas, G., Grobe, R., and Shuan, Y. (1990). Cultural resources and school success: Gender, ethnicity, and poverty groups within an urban school district. *American Sociological Review, 55*, 127–142.

Farel, A. (1982). *Early adolescence and religion: A status study*. Carrboro, N.C.: Center for Early Adolescence.

Farrington, D. (1990). Implications of criminal career research for the prevention of offending. *Journal of Adolescence, 13*, 93–113.

Farrington, D. (1989). Early predictors of adolescent aggression and adult violence. *Violence and Victims, 4*, 79–100.

Farrington, D. (1991). Childhood aggression and adult violence: Early precursors and later-life outcomes. In D. Pepler and K. Rubin (Eds.), *The development and treatment of childhood aggression*. Pp. 5–29. Hillsdale, N.J.: Erlbaum.

Farrington, D., and West, D. (1991). The Cambridge Study in Delinquent Development: A long-term follow-up of 411 London males. In H. Kerner and G. Kaiser (Eds.), *Criminality: Personality, behavior, and life history*. Pp. 115–138. New York: Springer-Verlag.

Fauber, R., Forehand, R., McCombs, A., and Wierson, M. (1990). A mediational model of the impact of marital conflict on adolescent adjustment in intact and divorced families: The role of disrupted parenting. *Child Development, 61*, 1112–1123.

Featherman, D. (1980). Schooling and occupational careers: Constancy and change in worldly success. In O. Brim, Jr., and J. Kagan (Eds.), *Constancy and change in human development*. Cambridge, Mass.: Harvard University Press.

Federal Bureau of Investigation. (1986). *Uniform crime reports for the United States*. Washington, D.C.: U.S. Government Printing Office.

Federal Bureau of Investigation (FBI). (1990). *Age-specific arrest rates and race-specific arrest rates for selected offenses 1965–1988*. Washington, D.C.: U.S. Government Printing Office.

Feingold, A. (1988). Cognitive gender differences are disappearing. *American Psychologist, 43*, 95–103.

Feldman, S., and Gehring, T. (1988). Changing perceptions of family cohesion and power across adolescence. *Child Development, 59*, 1034–1045.

Feldman, S., and Quatman, T. (1988). Factors influencing age expectations for adolescent autonomy: A study of early adolescents and parents. *Journal of Early Adolescence, 8.*

Feldstein, M., and Ellwood, D. (1982). Teenage unemployment: What is the problem? In R. Freeman and D. Wise (Eds.), *The youth labor market problem: Its nature, causes, and consequences.* Chicago: University of Chicago Press.

Felson, R., and Zielinski, M. (1989). Children's self-esteem and parental support. *Journal of Marriage and the Family, 51,* 727–735.

Fennema, E., and Peterson, P. (1985). Autonomous learning behavior: A possible explanation of gender-related differences in mathematics. In P. Peterson, L. Wilkinson, and M. Hallinan, *The social context of instruction.* Orlando: Academic Press.

Fennema, E., and Sherman, J. (1977). Sex-related differences in mathematics achievement, spatial visualization, and affective factors. *American Educational Research Journal, 14,* 51–71.

Ferrell, M., Tolone, W., and Walsh, R. (1977). Maturational and societal changes in the sexual double-standard: A panel analysis (1967–1971; 1970–1974). *Journal of Marriage and the Family, 39,* 255–271.

Fine, G. (1981). Friends, impression management, and preadolescent behavior. In S. Asher and J. Gottman (Eds.), *The development of children's friendships.* Cambridge: Cambridge University Press.

Fine, F. (1987). *With the boys.* Chicago: University of Chicago Press.

Fine, G., Mortimer, J., and Roberts, D. (1990). Leisure, work, and the mass media. In S. Feldman and G. Elliott (Eds.), *At the threshold: The developing adolescent.* Pp. 225–252. Cambridge: Harvard University Press.

Fischoff, B. (1988). Judgment and decision making. In R. Sternberg and E. Smith (Eds.), *The psychology of human thought.* Pp. 153–187. New York: Cambridge University Press.

Fisher, T. (1989). An extension of the findings of Moore, Peterson, and Furstenberg [1986] regarding family sexual communication and adolescent sexual behavior. *Journal of Marriage and the Family, 51,* 637–639.

Fiske, E. (1987, November 12). Colleges open new minority drive. *The New York Times,* p. 12.

Flanagan, C. (1990). Change on family work status: Effects on parent-adolescent decision making. *Child Development, 61,* 163–177.

Flewelling, R., and Bauman, K. (1990). Family structure as a predictor of initial substance use and sexual intercourse in early adolescence. *Journal of Marriage and the Family, 52,* 171–181.

Ford, C., and Beach, F. (1951). *Patterns of sexual behavior.* New York: Harper & Row.

Ford, M. (1982). Social cognition and social competence in adolescence. *Developmental Psychology, 18,* 323–340.

Ford, M. (1987). Processes contributing to adolescent social competence. In M. Ford and D. Ford (Eds.), *Humans as self-constructing living systems.* Hillsdale, N.J.: Erlbaum.

Ford, M., and Lowery, C. (1986). Gender differences in moral reasoning: A comparison of the use of justice and care orientations. *Journal of Personality and Social Psychology, 50,* 777–783.

Fordham, C., and Ogbu, J. (1986). Black students' school success: Coping with the burden of "acting white." *Urban Review, 18,* 176–206.

Forehand, R., Thomas, A. M., Wierson, M., Brody, G., and Fauber, R. (1990). Role of maternal functioning and parenting skills in adolescent functioning following parental divorce. *Journal of Abnormal Psychology, 99,* 278–283.

Foster-Clark, F. and Blyth, D. (1987). Predicting adolescents' drug use: The role of personal and social network characteristics. Paper presented at the biennial meeting of the Society for Research in Child Development, Baltimore.

Fowler, J. (1981). *Stages of faith.* New York: Harper & Row.

Frank, S., Pirsch, L., and Wright, V. (1990). Late adolescents' perceptions of their relationships with their parents: Relationships among deidealization, autonomy, relatedness, and insecurity and implications for adolescent adjustment and ego identity status. *Journal of Youth and Adolescence, 19,* 571–588.

Franklin, K., Janoff-Bulman, R., and Roberts, J. (1990). Long-term impact of parental divorce on optimism and trust: Changes in general assumptions or narrow beliefs? *Journal of Personality and Social Psychology, 59,* 743–755.

Freeman, R., and Wise, D. (Eds.). (1982). *The youth labor market problem: Its nature, causes, and consequences.* Chicago: University of Chicago Press.

Freud, A. (1958). Adolescence. *Psychoanalytic Study of the Child, 13*, 255–278.

Freud A. (1969). Adolescence as a developmental disturbance. In G. Caplan and S. Lebovici (Eds.), *Adolescence: Psychosocial perspectives.* Pp. 5–10. New York: Basic Books.

Freud, S. (1938). *An outline of psychoanalysis.* London: Hogarth Press.

Fried, M., and Fried, M. (1980). *Transitions: Four rituals in eight cultures.* New York: Norton.

Friedenberg, E. (1967). *Coming of age in America.* New York: Vintage Books.

Friedenberg, E. (1959). *The vanishing adolescent.* Boston: Beacon Press.

Friedenberg, E. (1965). *The dignity of youth and other atavisms.* Boston: Beacon Press.

Frisch, R. (1983). Fatness, puberty, and fertility: The effects of nutrition and physical training on menarche and ovulation. In J. Brooks-Gunn and A. Petersen (Eds.), *Girls at puberty.* New York: Plenum.

Furbey, L., and Beyth-Marom, R. (1990). *Risk taking in adolescence: A decision-making perspective.* Washington, D.C.: Carnegie Council on Adolescent Development.

Furstenberg, F. (1990). Coming of age in a changing family system. In S. Feldman and G. Elliott (Eds.), *At the threshold: The developing adolescent.* Pp. 147–170. Cambridge: Harvard University Press.

Furstenberg, F., Jr. (1991). As the pendulum swings: Teenage childbearing and social concern. *Family Relations, 40*, 127–138.

Furstenberg, F., Jr., et al. (1987). Race differences in the timing of adolescent intercourse. *American Sociological Review, 52*, 511–518.

Furstenberg, F., Brooks-Gunn, J., and Chase-Landsdale, L. (1989). Teenaged pregnancy and childbearing. *American Psychologist, 44*, 313–320.

Furstenberg, F., Jr., Brooks-Gunn, J., and Morgan, S. (1987). *Adolescent mothers in later life.* New York: Cambridge University Press.

Furstenberg, F., Jr., Moore, K., and Peterson, J. (1985). Sex education and sexual experience among adolescents. *American Journal of Public Health, 75*, 1331–1332.

Furstenberg, F., Jr. Morgan, S. P., and Allison, P. (1987). Paternal participation and children's well-being after marital dissolution. *American Sociological Review, 52*, 695–701.

Furstenberg, F., Peterson, J., Nord, C., and Zill, N. (1983). The life course of children of divorce: Marital disruption and parental contact. *American Sociological Review, 48*, 125–129.

Gaddis, A., and Brooks-Gunn, J. (1985). The male experience of pubertal change. *Journal of Youth and Adolescence, 14*, 61–70.

Gagne, E. (1985). *The cognitive psychology of school learning.* Boston: Little Brown.

Gagnon, J. (1972). The creation of the sexual in early adolescence. In J. Kagan and R. Coles (Eds.), *Twelve to sixteen: Early adolescence.* New York: Norton.

Galambos, N., Almeida, D., and Petersen, A. (in press). Masculinity, femininity, and sex role attitudes in early adolescence: Exploring gender intensification. *Child Development.*

Galambos, N., and Garbarino, J. (1985). Adjustment of unsupervised children in a rural setting. *Journal of Genetic Psychology, 146*, 227–231.

Galambos, N., and Maggs, J. (in press). Out-of-school care of young adolescents and self-reported behavior. *Developmental Psychology.*

Galambos, N., and Maggs, J. (1990). Putting mothers' work-related stress in perspective: Mothers and adolescents in dual-earner families. *Journal of Early Adolescence, 10*, 313–328.

Galambos, N., and Silbereisen, R. (1987). Income change, parental life outlook, and adolescent expectations for job success. *Journal of Marriage and the Family, 49*, 141–149.

Gallatin, J. (1975). *Adolescence and individuality.* New York: Harper & Row.

Galotti, K. (1989). Gender differences in self-reported moral reasoning: A review and new evidence. *Journal of Youth and Adolescence, 18*, 475–488.

Galotti, K., Kozberg, S., and Farmer, M. (1991). Gender and developmental differences in adolescents' conceptions of moral reasoning. *Journal of Youth and Adolescence, 20*, 13–30.

Gamoran, A. (1987). The stratification of high school learning opportunities. *Sociology of Education, 60*, 135–155.

Gamoran, A., and Mare, R. (1989). Secondary school tracking and educational inequality: Compensation, reinforcement, or neutrality? *American Journal of Sociology, 94,* 1146–1183.

Gans, J. (1990). *America's adolescents: How healthy are they?* Chicago: American Medical Association.

Garbarino, J., and Asp, C. (1981). *Successful schools and competent students.* Lexington, Mass.: Lexington Books.

Garbarino, J., Boston, N., Raber, S., Russell, R., and Crouter, A. (1978). The social maps of children approaching adolescence: Studying the ecology of youth development. *Journal of Youth and Adolescence, 7,* 417–428.

Garbarino, J., Sebes, J., and Schellenbach, C. (1984). Families at risk for destructive parent-child relations in adolescence. *Child Development, 55,* 174–183.

Garbarino, J., Wilson, J., and Garbarino, J. (1986). The adolescent runaway. In J. Garbarino and J. Sebes (Eds.), *Troubled youth, troubled families.* Pp. 315–351. New York; Aldine.

Gardner, H. (1983). *Frames of mind.* New York: Basic Books.

Gargiulo, J., Attie, I., Brooks-Gunn, J., and Warren, M. (1987). Girls' dating behavior as a function of social context and maturation. *Developmental Psychology, 23,* 730–737.

Gavin, L., and Furman, W. (1989). Age differences in adolescents' perceptions of their peer groups. *Developmental Psychology, 25,* 827–834.

Gerrard, M. (1987). Sex, sex guilt, and contraceptive use revisted: The 1980s. *Journal of Personality and Social Psychology, 52,* 975–980.

Gilligan, C. (1982). *In a different voice.* Cambridge: Harvard University Press.

Gilligan, C. (1986). Adolescent development reconsidered. Paper presented at the Invitational Conference on Health Futures of Adolescents, Daytona Beach, Florida.

Ginzberg, E. (1977). The job problem. *Scientific American, 237,* 43–51.

Gjerde, P., Block, J., and Block, J. (1988). Depressive symptoms and personality during late adolescence: Gender differences in the externalization-internalization of symptom expression. *Journal of Abnormal Psychology, 97,* 475–486.

Gjerde, P., and Block, J. (1991). Preadolescent antecedents of depressive symptomatology at age 18: A prospective study. *Journal of Youth and Adolescence, 20,* 217–232.

Glazer, R., and Bassok, M. (1989). Learning theory and the study of instruction. *Annual Review of Psychology, 40.* Palo Alto, Calif.: Annual Reviews.

Glenbard East *Echo.* (1984). *Teenagers themselves.* New York: Adama Books.

Glueck, S., and Glueck, E. (1950). *Unraveling juvenile delinquency.* New York: Commonwealth Fund.

Gold, M., and Petronio, R. (1980). Delinquent behavior in adolescence. In J. Adelson (Ed.), *Handbook of adolescent psychology.* New York: Wiley.

Gold, M., and Yanof, D. (1985). Mothers, daughters, and girlfriends. *Journal of Personality and Social Psychology, 49,* 654–659.

Goleman, D. (1988, September 22). Studies play down dangers to latch key children. *The New York Times,* p. B12.

Good, T., and Brophy, J. (1948). *Looking in classrooms.* New York: Harper & Row.

Goodchilds, J., and Zellman, G. (1984). Sexual signalling and sexual aggression in adolescent relationships. In N. M. Malamuth and E. D. Donnerstein (Eds.), *Pornography and sexual aggression.* New York: Academic Press.

Goodlad, J. (1984). *A place called school.* New York: McGraw-Hill.

Gordon, M., and Miller, R. (1984). Going steady in the 1980s: Exclusive relationships in six Connecticut high schools. *Sociology and Social Research, 68,* 463–479.

Gore, T. (1987). *Raising PG kids in an X-rated society.* Nashville, Tenn.: Abingdon Press.

Gottfredson, D. (1985). Youth employment, crime, and schooling: A longitudinal study of a national sample. *Developmental Psychology, 21,* 419–432.

Gottfredson, M., and Hirschi, T. (1990). *A general theory of crime.* Stanford, Calif.: Stanford University Press.

Gould, M., and Shaffer, D. (1986). The impact of suicide in television movies. *New England Journal of Medicine, 351,* 690–694.

Gove, W. (1972). The relationships between sex roles, marital status, and mental illness. *Social Forces, 51,* 34–44.

Graham, E. (1988, January 19). As kids gain power of purse, marketing takes aim at them. *The Wall Street Journal,* p. 1 and ff.

Gray, W. and Hudson, L. (1984). Formal operations and the imaginary audience. *Developmental Psychology, 20,* 619–627.

Green, R. (1980). Homosexuality. In H. Kaplan, A. Freedman, and B. Sadock (Eds.), *Comprehensive textbook of psychiatry.* (Vol. 2) (3rd ed.). Baltimore: Williams & Wilkins.

Green, R. (1987). *The 'Sissy Boy' syndrome and the development of homosexuality.* New Haven: Yale University Press.

Greenberg, M., Siegel, J., and Leitch, C. (1983). The nature and importance of attachment relationships to parents and peers during adolescence. *Journal of Youth and Adolescence, 12,* 373–386.

Greenberger, E. (1982). Education and the acquisition of psychosocial maturity. In D. McClelland (Ed.), *The development of social maturity.* New York: Irvington Publishers.

Greenberger, E., and Sorenson, A. (1974). Toward a concept of psychosocial maturity. *Journal of Youth and Adolescence, 3,* 329–358.

Greenberger, E., and Steinberg, L. (1981). The workplace as a context for the socialization of youth. *Journal of Youth and Adolescence, 10,* 185–210.

Greenberger, E., and Steinberg, L. (1983). Sex differences in early work experience: Harbinger of things to come? *Social Forces, 62,* 467–486.

Greenberger, E., and Steinberg, L. (1986). *When teenagers work: The psychological and social costs of adolescent employment.* New York: Basic Books.

Greenberger, E., Steinberg, L., and Ruggiero, M. (1982). A job is a job is a job . . . Or is it? Behavioral observations in the adolescent workplace. *Work and Occupations, 9,* 79–96.

Greenberger, E., Steinberg, L., and Vaux, A. (1981). Adolescents who work: Health and behavioral consequences of job stress. *Developmental Psychology, 17,* 691–703.

Greenberger, E., Steinberg, L., Vaux, A., and McAuliffe, S. (1980). Adolescents who work: Effects of part-time employment on family and peer relations. *Journal of Youth and Adolescence, 9,* 189–202.

Greenfield, P., Bruzzone, L., Koyamatsu, K., Satuloff, W., Nixon, K., Brodie, M., and Kingsdale, D. (1987). What is rock music doing to the minds of our youth? A first experimental look at the effects of rock music lyrics and music videos. *Journal of Early Adolescence, 7,* 315–329.

Grief, E., and Ulman, K. (1982). The psychological impact of menarche on early adolescent females: A review of the literature. *Child Development. 53,* 1413–1430.

Grotevant, H., and Cooper, C. (1986). Individuation in family relationships: A perspective on individual differences in the development of identity and role-taking skill in adolescence. *Human Development, 29,* 82–100.

Grotevant, H., and Cooper, C. (1988). The role of family experience in career exploration during adolescence. In P. Baltes, D. Featherman, and R. Lerner (Eds.), *Life-span development and behavior* (Vol. 8). Hillsdale, N.J.: Erlbaum.

Grotevant, H., and Durrett, M. (1980). Occupational knowledge and career development in adolescence. *Journal of Vocational Behavior, 17,* 171–182.

Grotevant, H., and Thorbecke, W. (1982). Sex differences in styles of occupational identity formation in late adolescence. *Developmental Psychology, 18,* 396–405.

Grumbach, M., Roth, J., Kaplan, S., and Kelch, R. (1974). Hypothalamic-pituitary regulation of puberty in man: Evidence and concepts derived from clinical research. In M. Grumbach, G. Grave, and F. Mayer (Eds.), *Control of the onset of puberty.* New York: Wiley.

Guerra, N., and Slaby, R. (1990). Cognitive mediators of aggression in adolescent offenders: 2. Intervention. *Developmental Psychology, 26,* 269–277.

Haan, N., Smith, M., and Block, J. (1986). Moral reasoning of young adults: Political-social behavior, family background, and personality correlates. *Journal of Personality and Social Psychology, 10,* 183–201.

Hafetz, E. (1976). Parameters of sexual maturity in man. In E. Hafetz (Ed.), *Perspectives in human reproduction.* (Vol. 3) *Sexual maturity: Physiological and clinical parameters.* Ann Arbor, Mich.: Ann Arbor Science Publishers.

Hall, G. S. (1904). *Adolescence.* New York: Appleton.

Hallinan, M. (1981). Recent advances in sociometry. In S. Asher and J. Gottman (Eds.), *The development of children's friendship.* New York: Cambridge University Press.

Hallinan, M., and Sorensen, A. (1987). Ability

grouping and sex differences in mathematics achievement. *Sociology of Education, 60,* 63–72.

Hallinan, M., and Teixeira, R. (1987). Opportunities and constraints: Black-white differences in the formation of interracial friendships. *Child Development, 58,* 1358–1371.

Hallinan, M., and Williams, R. (1989). Interracial friendship choices in secondary schools. *American Sociological Review, 54,* 67–78.

Hamburg, D. (1986). *Preparing for life: The critical transition of adolescence.* New York: Carnegie Corporation of New York.

Hamilton, S. (1990). *Apprenticeship for adulthood.* New York: Free Press.

Hanson, S., and Ginsburg, A. (1988). Gaining ground: Values and high school success. *American Educational Research Journal, 25,* 334–365.

Hanson, S., Myers, D., and Ginsburg, A. (1987). The role of responsibility and knowledge in reducing teenage out-of-wedlock childbearing. *Journal of Marriage and the Family, 49,* 241–256.

Hardy, J., Duggan, A., Masnyk, K., and Pearson, C. (1989). Fathers of children born to young urban mothers. *Family Planning Perspectives, 21,* 159–163.

Harter, S. (1990). Identity and self development. In S. Feldman and G. Elliott (Eds.). *At the threshold: The developing adolescent.* Pp. 352–387. Cambridge: Harvard University Press.

Harter, S., Whitesell, N., and Kowalski, P. (1991). The effects of educational transitions on children's perceptions of competence and motivational orientation. Manuscript submitted for publication. Department of Psychology, University of Denver.

Hartnagel, T., and Krahn, H. (1989). High school dropouts, labor market success, and criminal behavior. *Youth and Society, 20,* 416–444.

Hartup, W. (1983). Peer relations. In E. M. Hetherington (Ed.), *Handbook of child psychology; Socialization, personality, and social development* (Vol. 4). New York: Wiley.

Hauser, S., and Bowlds, M. (1990). Stress, coping, and adaptation. In S. Feldman and G. Elliott (Eds.), *At the threshold: The developing adolescent.* Pp. 388–413. Cambridge: Harvard University Press.

Hauser, S., and Kasendorf, E. (1983). *Black and white identity formation.* Malabar, Fla.: Robert E. Kreiger.

Hauser, S., Powers, S., and Noam, G. (1991). *Adolescents and their families.* New York: Free Press.

Havighurst, R. (1952). *Developmental tasks and education.* New York: McKay.

Hayes, C. (Ed.) (1987). *Risking the future: Adolescent sexuality, pregnancy, and childbearing* (Vol. 1). Washington, D.C.: National Academy Press.

Hein, K. (1988). *AIDS in adolescence: A rationale for concern.* Washington, D.C: Carnegie Council on Adolescent Development.

Hein, K. (1988). *Issues in adolescent health: An overview.* Washington, D.C.: Carnegie Council on Adolescent Development.

Henderson, V., and Dweck, C. (1990). Motivation and achievement. In S. Feldman and G. Elliott (Eds.), *At the threshold: The developing adolescent.* Pp. 308–329. Cambridge: Harvard University Press.

Hess, R., Chih-Mei, C., and Mcdevitt, T. (1987). Cultural variations in family beliefs about children's performance in mathematics: Comparisons among People's Republic of China, Chinese-American, and Caucasian-American families. *Journal of Educational Psychology, 79,* 179–188.

Hetherington, E. (1981). Children and divorce. In R. Henderson (Ed.), *Parent-child interaction: Theory, research, and prospects.* New York: Academic Press.

Hetherington, E. M. (1991). The role of individual differences and family relationships in children's coping with divorce and remarriage. In P. Cowan and E. M. Hetherington, (Eds.), *Advances in family research.* (Vol. 2). *Family transitions.* Hillsdale, N.J.: Erlbaum.

Hetherington, E. M. (1990, March). Studying family transitions: Families, lives, and videotapes. Presidential address presented at the biennial meeting of the Society for Research on Adolescence. Atlanta, Georgia.

Hetherington, E. M., Stanley-Hagan, M., and Anderson, E. (1989). Marital transitions: A child's perspective. *American Psychologist, 44,* 303–312.

Heyns, B. (1982). *Summer learning and the effects of schooling.* New York: Academic Press.

Higgins, A., and Turnure, J. (1984). Distractibility and concentration of attention in children's development. *Child Development, 44,* 1799–1810.

Hightower, E. (1990). Adolescent interpersonal and familial predictors of positive mental health at midlife. *Journal of Youth and Adolescence, 19,* 257–276.

Hill, C., Rubin, Z., and Peplau, L. (1979). Breakups before marriage: The end of 103 affairs. In G. Levinger and O. Moles (Eds.), *Divorce and separation.* New York: Basic Books.

Hill, J. (1980). The family. In M. Johnson (Ed.), *Toward adolescence: The middle school years* (Seventy-ninth yearbook of the National Society for the Study of Education). Chicago: University of Chicago Press.

Hill, J. (1983). Early adolescence: A framework. *Journal of Early Adolescence, 3,* 1–21.

Hill, J., and Holmbeck, G. (1986). Attachment and autonomy during adolescence. In G. Whitehurst (Ed.), *Annals of child development.* Greenwich, Conn.: JAI Press.

Hill, J., Holmbeck, G., Marlow, L., Green, T., and Lynch, M. (1985a). Pubertal status and parent-child relations in families of seventh-grade boys. *Journal of Early Adolescence, 5,* 31–44.

Hill, J., Holmbeck, G., Marlow, L., Green, T., and Lynch, M. (1985b). Menarcheal status and parent-child relations in families of seventh-grade boys. *Journal of Youth and Adolescence, 14,* 301–316.

Hill, J., and Lynch, M. (1983). The intensification of gender-related role expectations during early adolescence. In J. Brooks-Gunn and A. Petersen (Eds.), *Female puberty.* New York: Plenum Press.

Hill, J., and Palmquist, W. (1978). Social cognition and social relations in early adolescence. *International Journal of Behavioral Development, 1,* 1–36.

Hirsch, B., and DuBois, D. (1991). Self-esteem in early adolescence: The identification and prediction of contrasting longitudinal trajectories. *Journal of Youth and Adolescence, 20,* 53–72.

Hirschi, T. (1969). *Cause of delinquency.* Berkeley: University of California Press.

Hodgkinson, H. (1985). *All one system: Demographics of education, kindergarten through graduate school.* Washington, D.C.: Institute for Educational Leadership.

Hoffman, L. (1974). Effects of maternal employment on the child: A review of the research. *Developmental Psychology, 10,* 204–228.

Hoffman, L. (1977). Fear of success in 1965 and 1974: A follow-up study. *Journal of Consulting and Clinical Psychology, 45,* 310–321.

Hoffman, M. (1980). Moral development in adolescence. In J. Adelson (Ed.), *Handbook of adolescent psychology.* New York: Wiley.

Hogue, A. (1991). Adolescence and sexual abuse: Theoretical and empirical issues. Unpublished manuscript, Dept. of Psychology, Temple University, Philadelphia.

Holland, J. (1985). *Making vocational choice: A theory of careers.* (2nd ed.). Englewood Cliffs, N.J.: Prentice-Hall.

Holland, A., Sicotte, N., and Treasure, L. (1988). Anorexia nervosa: Evidence for a genetic basis. *Journal of Psychosomatic Research, 32,* 561–571.

Hollingshead, A. (1975). *Elmtown's youth and Elmtown revisited.* New York: Wiley. (Orig. pub. 1949.)

Holloway, S. (1988). Concepts of ability and effort in Japan and the United States. *Review of Educational Research, 58,* 327–345.

Holmbeck, G., and Hill, J. (in press). Conflictive engagement, positive affect, and menarche in families with seventh-grade girls. *Child Development.*

Holmbeck, G., and Hill, J. (1988). Storm and stress beliefs about adolescence: Prevalence, self-reported antecedents, and effects of an undergraduate course. *Journal of Youth and Adolescence, 17,* 285–306.

Holmbeck, G., and O'Donnell, K. (in press). Longitudinal study of discrepancies between maternal and adolescent perceptions of decision-making and desired behavioral autonomy. In R. Paikoff and W. A. Collins (Eds.), *New directions for child development: Shared views of the family during adolescence.* San Francisco: Jossey-Bass.

Holstein, C. (1972). The relation of children's moral judgment level to that of their parents and to communication patterns in the family. In R. Smart and M. Smart (Eds.), *Readings in child development and relationships.* New York: Macmillan.

Howat, P., and Saxton, A. (1988). The incidence of bulimic behavior in a secondary and university school population. *Journal of Youth and Adolescence, 17,* 221–232.

Huizinga, D., and Elliot, D. (1985). *Juvenile offenders prevalence, offender incidence, and arrest rates by race.* Boulder, Colo.: Institute of Behavioral Science.

Humphries, L. (1988). Trends in levels of academic achievement of blacks and other minorities. *Intelligence, 12,* 231–260.

Hunt, M. (1974). *Sexual behavior in the 1970s.* Chicago: Playboy Press.

Hunt, J., and Hunt, L. (1977). Racial inequality and self-image: Identity maintenance as identity diffusion. *Sociology and Social Research, 61,* 539–559.

Hunter, F. (1984). Socializing procedures in parent-child and friendship relations during adolescence. *Developmental Psychology, 18,* 806–811.

Hunter, F., and Youniss, J. (1982). Changes in functions of three relations during adolescence. *Developmental Psychology, 18,* 806–811.

Huston, A., and Alvarez, M. (1990). The socialization context of gender role development in early adolescence. In R. Montemayor, G. Adams, and T. Gullotta (Eds.), *Advances in adolescent development.* (Vol. 2). *The transition from childhood to adolescence.* Pp. 156–179. Beverly Hills, Calif.: Sage.

Hyde, J., and Linn, M. (1988). Are there sex differences in verbal abilities?: A meta-analysis. *Psychological Bulletin, 104,* 53–69.


Inhelder, B., and Piaget, J. (1958). *The growth of logical thinking from childhood to adolescence.* New York: Basic Books.

Inhoff-Germain, G., Arnold, G., Nottelmann, E., Susman, E., Cutler, G., Jr., and Chrousos, G. (1988). Relations between hormone levels and observational measures of aggressive behavior of young adolescents in family interactions. *Developmental Psychology, 24,* 129–139.

Irwin, C. (1986). Biopsychosocial correlates of risk-taking behavior during adolescence: Can the physician intervene? *Journal of Adolescent Health Care, 7,* 82–96.

Ishiyama, I., and Chabassol, D. (1985). Adolescents' fear of social consequences of academic success as a function of age and sex. *Journal of Youth and Adolescence, 14,* 37–46.


Jacklin, C. (1989). Female and male: Issues of gender. *American Psychologist, 44,* 127–133.

Jackson, A., and Hornbeck, D. (1989). Educating young adolescents. *American Psychologist, 44,* 831–836.

Jessor, R. (1987). Risky driving and adolescent problem behavior: An extension of problem-behavior theory. *Alcohol, Drugs, and Driving, 3,* 1–11.

Jessor, R., Costa, F., Jessor, L., and Donovan, J. (1983). Time of first intercourse: A prospective study. *Journal of Personality and Social Psychology, 44,* 608–626.

Jessor, R., and Jessor, S. (1977). *Problem behavior and psychosocial development: A longitudinal study of youth.* New York: Academic Press.

Johnson, E., and Meade, A. (1987). Developmental patterns of spatial ability: An early sex difference. *Child Development, 58,* 725–740.

Johnson, C. A., Pentz, M., Weber, M., Dwyer, J., Baer, N., MacKinnon, D., Hansen, W., and Flay, B. (1990). Relative effectiveness of comprehensive community programming for drug abuse prevention with high-risk and low-risk adolescents. *Journal of Consulting and Clinical Psychology, 58,* 447–456.

Johnson, S. (1975). *Update on education: A digest of the National Assessment of Education Progress.* Denver: The Education Commission of the States.

Johnston, L., Bachman, J., and O'Malley, P. (1982). *Monitoring the future: Questionnaire responses from the nation's high school seniors, 1981.* Ann Arbor, Mich.: Institute for Social Research.

Johnston, L., Bachman, J., and O'Malley, P. (1986). *Monitoring the future: Questionnaire responses from the nation's high school seniors, 1985.* Ann Arbor, Mich.: Institute for Social Research.

Johnston, L., O'Malley, P., and Bachman, J. (1986). *Drug use among American high school students, college students, and other young adults: National trends through 1985.* Washington: National Institute on Drug Abuse.

Johnston, L., O'Malley, P., and Bachman, J. (1989). *Drug use, drinking, and smoking: National survey results from high school, college, and young adult populations 1975–1988.* Rockville, Md.: National Institute on Drug Abuse.

Jones, E., et al. (1987). *Teenage pregnancy in industrialized countries.* New Haven: Yale University Press.

Jones, H. (1949). Adolescence in our society. In *The family in a democratic society* (Anniversary papers of the Community Service Society of New York). New York: Columbia University Press.

Jones, M. C. (1957). The later careers of boys who were early- or late-maturing. *Child Development, 28,* 113–128.

Jones, M. C. (1965). Psychological correlates of somatic development. *Child Development, 36,* 899–911.

Jones, M. C., and Bayley, N. (1950). Physical maturing among boys as related to behavior. *Journal of Educational Psychology, 41,* 129–148.

Jones, M. C., and Mussen, P. (1958). Self-conceptions, motivations, and inter-personal attitudes of early- and late-maturing girls. *Child Development, 29,* 491–501.

Josselson, R. (1980). Ego development in adolescence. In J. Adelson (Ed.), *Handbook of adolescent psychology.* New York: Wiley.

Josselson, R., Greenberger, E., and McConochie, D. (1977a). Phenomenological aspects of psychosocial maturity in adolescence. Part I: Boys. *Journal of Youth and Adolescence, 6,* 25–56.

Josselson, R., Greenberger, E., and McConochie, D. (1977b). Phenomenological aspects of psychosocial maturity in adolescence. Part II: Girls. *Journal of Youth and Adolescence, 6,* 145–167.

Kagan, J., and Coles, R. (Eds.). (1972). *Twelve to sixteen: Early adolescence.* New York: Norton.

Kahn, S., Zimmerman, G., Csikszentmihalyi, M., and Getzels, J. (1985). Relations between identity in young adulthood and intimacy in midlife. *Journal of Personality and Social Psychology, 49,* 1316–1322.

Kahneman, D., Slovic, P., and Tversky, A. (Eds.). (1982). *Judgment under uncertainty: Heuristics and biases.* New York: Cambridge University Press.

Kallen, D., and Stephenson, J. (1982). Talking about sex revisited. *Journal of Youth and Adolescence, 11,* 11–24.

Kandel, D. (1978). Homophily, selection, and socialization in adolescent friendships. *American Journal of Sociology, 84,* 427–436.

Kandel, D. (1980). Drug and drinking behavior among youth. *Annual Review of Sociology, 6,* 235–285.

Kandel, D., and Lesser, G. (1972). *Youth in two worlds.* San Francisco: Jossey-Bass.

Kandel, D., and Logan (1984). Patterns of drug use from adolescence to young adulthood: I. Periods of risk for initiation, continued use, and discontinuation. *American Journal of Public Health, 74,* 660–666.

Kandel, D., Raveis, V., and Davies, M. (1991). Suicidal ideation in adolescence: Depression, substance abuse, and other risk factors. *Journal of Youth and Adolescence, 20,* 289–310.

Kaplan, L. (1983). *Coping with peer pressure.* New York: Rosen.

Katchadourian, H. (1990). Sexuality. In S. Feldman and G. Elliot (Eds.), *At the threshold: The developing adolescent.* Pp. 330–351. Cambridge: Harvard University Press.

Katz, M. (1975). *The people of Hamilton, Canada West: Family and class in a mid-nineteenth-century city.* Cambridge: Harvard University Press.

Katz, P. (1979). The development of female identity. *Sex Roles, 5,* 155–178.

Kavrell, A., and Petersen, A. (1984). Patterns of achievement in early adolescence. *Advances in Motivation and Achievement, 2,* 1–35.

Keating, D. (1980). Thinking processes in adolescence. In J. Adelson (Ed.), *Handbook of adolescent psychology.* New York: Wiley.

Keating, D. (1990). Adolescent thinking. In S. Feldman and G. Elliott (Eds.), *At the threshold: The developing adolescent.* Pp. 54–89. Cambridge: Harvard University Press.

Keating, D., and Clark, L. (1980). Development of physical and social reasoning in adolescence. *Developmental Psychology, 16,* 23–30.

Kegeles, S., Adler, N., and Irwin, C., Jr. (1988). Sexually active adolescents and condoms: Changes over one year in knowledge, attitudes and use. *American Journal of Public Health, 78,* 460–461.

Kelley, J., and de Armaa, A. (1989). Social relationships in adolescence: Skill development and training. In J. Worell and F. Danner (Eds.). *The adolescent as decision-maker.* San Diego: Academic Press.

Kendall, P., Cantwell, D., and Kazdin, A. (1989). Depression in children and adolescents: Assessment issues and recommendations. *Cognitive Therapy and Research, 13,* 109–146.

Keniston, K. (1970). Youth: A "new" stage of life. *American Scholar, 39,* 631–641.

Kenny, M. (1987). The extent and function of parental attachment among first-year college students. *Journal of Youth and Adolescence, 16,* 17–27.

Kessen, W. (Ed.). (1975). *Childhood in China.* New Haven: Yale University Press.

Kessler, R., Price, R., and Wortmann, C. (1985). Social factors in psychopathology: Stress, social support, and coping processes. *Annual Review of Psychology, 36,* 351–372.

Kett, J. (1977). *Rise of passage: Adolescence in America, 1790 to the present.* New York: Basic Books.

King, K., Balswick, J., and Robinson, I. (1977). The continuing premarital sexual revolution among college females. *Journal of Marriage and the Family, 39,* 455–459.

Kinsey, A., Pomeroy, W., and Martin, C. (1948). *Sexual behavior in the human male.* Philadelphia: Saunders.

Kirby, D., Harvey, P., Claussenius, D., and Novar, M. (1989). A direct mailing to teenage males about condom use: Its impact on knowledge, attitudes and sexual behavior. *Family Planning Perspectives, 21,* 12–18.

Kirkendall, L. (1981). Sex education in the United States: A historical perspective. In L. Brown (Ed.), *Sex education in the eighties.* New York: Plenum.

Kite, M. (1984). Sex differences in attitudes towards homosexuals: A meta-analytic review. *Journal of Homosexuality, 10,* 69–81.

Kneisel, P. (1987). Social support preferences of female adolescents in the context of interpersonal stress. Paper presented at the biennial meeting of the Society for Research in Child Development, Baltimore.

Kobak, R., and Sceery, A. (1988). Attachment in late adolescence: Working models, affect regulation, and representations of self and others. *Child Development, 59,* 135–146.

Kohlberg, L. (1976). Moral stages and moralization: The cognitive-development approach. In T. Lickona (Ed.), *Moral development and behavior.* New York: Holt, Rinehart & Winston.

Kohlberg, L., and Gilligan, C. (1972). The adolescent as philosopher: The discovery of the self in a post-conventional world. In J. Kagan and R. Coles (Eds.), *Twelve to sixteen: Early adolescence.* New York: Norton.

Kohn, M. (1977). *Class and conformity* (2nd ed.). Chicago: University of Chicago Press.

Kolata, G. (1988, August 25). Epidemic of dangerous eating disorders may be false alarm. *The New York Times,* p. B16.

Krisberg, B., Schwartz, I., Fishman, G., Eisikovits, Z., and Guttman, E. (1986). *The incarceration of minority youth.* Minneapolis: Hubert H. Humphrey Institute of Public Affairs, National Council on Crime and Delinquency.

Krosnick, J., and Judd, C. (1982). Transitions in social influence at adolescence: Who induces cigarette smoking? *Developmental Psychology, 18,* 359–368.

Kuhn, D., Langer, J., Kohlberg, L., and Haan, N. (1977). The development of formal operations in logical and moral judgment. *Genetic Psychology Monographs, 95,* 97–188.

Kupersmidt, J., and Coie, J. (1990). Preadolescent peer status, aggression, and school adjustment as predictors of externalizing problems in adolescence. *Child Development, 61,* 1350–1362.

Kurdek, L., and Sinclair, R. (1988). Relation of eighth graders' family structure, gender, and family environment with academic performance and school behavior. *Journal of Educational Psychology, 80,* 90–94.

Kutner, L. (1988, July 14). When young adults head back home. *The New York Times,* p. C8.

Lachenmeyer, J., and Muni, P. (1988). Eating disorders in a nonclinical adolescent population. *Adolescence, 23,* 313–322.

Lambert, N. (1988). Adolescent outcomes for hyperactive children. *American Psychologist, 43,* 786–799.

Lamborn, S., Mounts, N., Steinberg, L., and Dornbusch, S. (1991). Patterns of competence and adjustment among adolescents from authoritative, authoritarian, indulgent, and neglectful families. *Child Development, 62,* 1049–1065.

Lapsley, D. (1989). Continuity and discontinuity in adolescent social cognitive development. In R. Montemayor, G. Adams, and T. Gullota (Eds.), *Advances in adolescence research.* (Vol. 2). Beverly Hills, Calif.: Sage.

Lapsley, D., Enright, R., and Serlin, R. (1985). Toward a theoretical perspective on the legislation of adolescence. *Journal of Early Adolescence, 5,* 441–466.

Lapsley, D., and Murphy, M. (1985). Another look at the theoretical assumption of adolescent egocentrism. *Developmental Review, 5,* 201–217.

Larkin, R. W. (1979). *Suburban youth in cultural crisis.* New York: Oxford.

Larson, R., and Richards, M. (Eds.). The changing life space of early adolescence. *Journal of Youth and Adolescence, 18 (6).* [A special issue of the journal devoted to a series of studies of how adolescents spend their time.]

Larson, R., Kubey, R., and Colletti, J. (1989). Changing channels: Early adolescent media choices and shifting investments in family and friends. *Journal of Youth and Adolescence, 18,* 583–600.

Larson, R., and Lampman-Petraitis, C. (1989). Daily emotional states as reported by children and adolescents. *Child Development, 60,* 1250–1260.

Lau, S. (1990). Crisis and vulnerability in adolescent development. *Journal of Youth and Adolescence, 19,* 111–132.

Lazarus, R., and Folkman, S. (Eds.) (1984). *Stress, appraisal, and coping.* New York: Springer.

Lee, V., and Bryk, A. (1989). A multilevel model of the social distribution of high school achievement. *Sociology of Education, 62,* 172–192.

Lee, V., and Bryk, A. (1988). Curriculum tracking as mediating the social distribution of high school achievement. *Sociology of Education, 61,* 78–94.

Leibowitz, S. (1983). Hypothalamic catecholamine systems controlling eating behavior: A potential model for anorexia nervosa. In P. Darby, P. Garfinkel, D. Garner, and D. Cosina (Eds.), *Anorexia nervosa: Recent developments in research.* Pp. 221–229. New York: Alan R. Liss.

Leming, J. (1987). Rock music and the socialization of moral values in early adolescence. *Youth and Society, 18,* 363–383.

Lempers, J., Clark-Lempers, D., and Simons, R. (1989). Economic hardship, parenting, and distress in adolescence. *Child Development, 60,* 25–49.

Leone, C., and Richards, M. (1989). Classwork and homework in early adolescence: The ecology of achievement. *Journal of Youth and Adolescence, 18,* 531–548.

Lerner, J., Hertzog, C., Hooker, K., Hassibi, M., and Thomas, A. (1988). A longitudinal study of negative emotional states and adjustment from early childhood through adolescence. *Child Development, 59,* 356–366.

Leslie, L. (1986). The impact of adolescent females' assessments of parenthood and employment on plans for the future. *Journal of Youth and Adolescence, 15,* 29–49.

Levinson, D. (1978). *The seasons of a man's life.* New York: Knopf.

Levitz-Jones, E., and Orlofsky, J. (1985). Separation-individuation and intimacy capacity in college women. *Journal of Personality and Social Psychology, 49,* 156–169.

Lewin, K. (1948). *Resolving social conflict.* New York: Harper.

Lewin, K. (1951). *Field theory and social science.* New York: Harper & Row.

Lewin-Epstein, N. (1981). *Youth employment during high school.* Washington, D.C.: National Center for Education Statistics.

Lewinsohn, P. (1975). The behavioral study and treatment of depression. In M. Herson, R. Eisler, and P. Miller (Eds.), *Progress in behavior modifications.* New York: Academic Press.

Lewis, C. (1981). How adolescents approach decisions: Changes over grades seven to twelve and policy implications. *Child Development, 52,* 538–544.

Lewis, C. Minors' competence to consent to abortion. *American Psychologist, 41,* 84–88.

Lewis, M., Feiring, C., McGuffog, C., and Jaskir, J. (1984). Predicting psychopathology in six-year-olds from early social relations. *Child Development, 55,* 123–136.

Lewis, R., and Spanier, G. (1979). Theorizing about the quality and stability of marriage. In W. Burr, R. Hill, I. Nye, and I. Reiss (Eds.), *Contemporary theories about the family.* Glencoe, Ill.: Free Press.

Lightfoot, S. (1983). *The good high school.* New York: Basic Books.

Linn, M. (1987). Establishing a research base for scientific education: Challenges, trends, and recommendations. *Journal of Research in Science Teaching, 24,* 191–216.

Linney, J., and Seidman, E. (1989). The future of schooling. *American Psychologist, 44,* 336–340.

Lipsitz, J. (1977). *Growing up forgotten.* Lexington, Mass.: Lexington Books.

Livesley, W., and Bromley, D. (1973). *Person perception in childhood and adolescence.* New York: Wiley.

Livson, N., and Peskin, H. (1980). Perspectives on adolescence from longitudinal research. In J. Adelson (Ed.), *Handbook of adolescent psychology.* New York: Wiley.

Lloyd, D. (1978). Prediction of school failure from third-grade data. *Educational Psychological Measurement, 38,* 1193–1200.

Loeber, R., and Stouthamer-Loeber, M. (1986). Family factors as correlates and predictors of juvenile conduct problems and delinquency. In M. Tonry and N. Morris (Eds.), *Crime and justice.* Vol. 7. Chicago: University of Chicago Press.

Long, B. (1989). Heterosexual involvement of unmarried undergraduate females in relation to self-evaluations. *Journal of Youth and Adolescence, 18,* 489–500.

Long, L., and Long, T. (1983). *The handbook for latchkey children and their parents.* New York: Berkeley Books.

Louis, K., and Smith, B. (in press). Breaking the iron law of social class: The renewal of teachers' professional status and engagement. In F. Newmann (Ed.), *Student engagement and achievement in American high schools.* New York: Teachers College Press.

Lynn, D. (1966, November). The process of learning parental and sex-role identification. *Journal of Marriage and the Family,* 446–470.

McCabe, M. (1984). Toward a theory of adolescent dating. *Adolescence, 19,* 159–169.

McCall, R., Applebaum, M., and Hogarty, P. (1973). Developmental changes in mental performance. *Monographs of the Society for Research in Child Development, 38* (Serial No. 150).

McClelland, D. (1961). *The achieving society.* Princeton, N.J.: Van Nostrand.

McClelland, D., Atkinson, J., Clark, R., and Lowell, E. (1953). *The achievement motive.* New York: Appleton-Century-Crofts.

McClintock, M. (1980). Major gaps in menstrual cycle research: Behavioral and physiological controls in a biological context. In P. Komenich, M. McSweeney, J. Noack, and N. Elder (Eds.), *The menstrual cycle.* (Vol. 2). Pp. 7–23. New York: Springer.

McCord, J. (1990). *Problem behaviors.* In S. Feldman and G. Elliot (Eds.), *At the threshold: The developing adolescent.* Pp. 414–430. Cambridge: Harvard University Press.

McGovern, K., Arkowitz, H., and Gilmore, S. (1975). Evaluation of social skill training programs for college dating inhibitions. *Journal of Counseling Psychology, 22,* 505–512.

McLanahan, S., and Bumpass, L. (1988). Intergenerational consequences of family disruption. *American Journal of Sociology, 94,* 130–152.

McNeil, L. (1984). *Lowering expectations: The impact of student employment on classroom knowledge.* Madison, WI: Wisconsin Center for Education Research.

Maccoby, E. (1990). Gender and relationships: A developmental account. *American Psychologist, 45,* 513–520.

Maccoby, E. (1988). Gender as a social category. *Developmental Psychology, 24,* 755–775.

Maccoby, E., and Martin, J. (1983). Socialization in the context of the family: Parent-child interaction. In E. M. Hetherington (Ed.), *Handbook of child psychology; Socialization, personality, and social development.* (Vol. 4). New York: Wiley.

Magnusson, D., Stattin, H., and Allen, V. (1986). Differential maturation among girls and its relation to social adjustment in a longitudinal perspective. In P. Baltes, D. Featherman, and R. Lerner (Eds.) *Life span development and behavior.* (Vol. 7). Hillsdale, N.J.: Erlbaum.

Mahoney, E. (1983). *Human sexuality.* New York: McGraw-Hill.

Mannheim, K. (1952). The problem of generations. In K. Mannheim (Ed.), *Essays on the sociology of knowledge.* London: Routledge and Kegan Paul.

Marcia, J. (1966). Development and validation of ego identity status. *Journal of Personality and Social Psychology, 3,* 551–558.

Marcia, J. (1976). Identity six years after: A follow-up study. *Journal of Youth and Adolescence, 5,* 145–150.

Marcia, J. (1980). Identity in adolescence. In J. Adelson (Ed.), *Handbook of adolescent psychology.* New York: Wiley.

Mare, R. Winship, C., and Kubitschek, W. (1984). The transition from youth to adult: Understanding the age pattern of employment. *American Journal of Sociology, 90,* 326–358.

Marini, M. (1984). The order of events in the transition to adulthood. *Sociology of Education, 57,* 63–84.

Markus, H., and Nurius, P. (1986). Possible selves. *American Psychologist, 41,* 954–969.

Marsh, H. (1989). Sex differences in the development of verbal and mathematical constructs: The High School and Beyond Study. *American Educational Research Journal, 26,* 191–225.

Marsh, H. (1989). Age and sex effects in multiple dimensions of self-concept: Preadolescence to early adulthood. *Journal of Educational Psychology, 81,* 417–430.

Marsiglio, W. (1987). Adolescent fathers in the United States: Their initial living arrangements, marital experience and educational outcomes. *Family Planning Perspectives, 19,* 240–251.

Marshall, W. (1978). Puberty. In F. Falkner and J. Tanner (Eds.), *Human growth* (Vol. 2). New York: Plenum Press.

Martin, B. (1990). The transmission of relationship difficulties from one generation to the next. *Journal of Youth and Adolescence, 19*, 181–200.

Masnick, G., and Bane, M. (1980). *The nation's families: 1960–1990.* Boston: Auburn House.

Massad, C. (1981). Sex role identity and adjustment during adolescence. *Child Development, 52*, 1290–1298.

Matas, L., Arend, R., and Sroufe, L. (1978). Continuity in adaptation in the second year: The relationship between quality of attachment and later competence. *Child Development, 49*, 547–556.

Matza, M. (1990, November 24). More pre-teens drinking, more teens are alcoholics. *The Philadelphia Inquirer*, p. 1-A.

Mazor, A., and Enright, R. (1988). The development of the individuation process from a social cognitive perspective. *Journal of Adolescence, 11*, 29–47.

Mazor, A., Shamir, R., and Ben-Moshe, J. (1990). The individuation process from a social-cognitive perspective in kibbutz adolescents. *Journal of Youth and Adolescence, 19*, 73–90.

Mead, M. (1928). *Coming of age in Samoa.* New York: Morrow.

Mechanic, D. (1983). Adolescent health and illness behavior: Review of the literature and a new hypothesis for the study of stress. *Journal of Human Stress, 9*, 4–13.

Mednick, S., Gabrielli, W., and Hitchings, B. (1987). Genetic factors in the etiology of criminal behavior. In S. Mednick, T. Moffitt, and S. Stack (Eds.), *The causes of crime: New biological approaches.* Pp. 74–91. Cambridge: Cambridge University Press.

Medrich, E., Roizen, J., Rubin, V., and Buckley, S. (1982). *The serious business of growing up.* Berkeley: University of California Press.

Mensch, B., and Kandel, D. (1988). Dropping out of high school and drug involvement. *Sociology of Education, 61*, 95–113.

Mickelson, R. (1990). The attitude-achievement paradox among black adolescents. *Sociology of Education, 63*, 44–61.

Midgley, C., Feldlaufer, H., and Eccles, J. (1988). The transition to junior high school: Beliefs of pre- and posttransition teachers. *Journal of Youth and Adolescence, 17*, 543–562.

Miller, B., and Bingham, R. (1989). Family configuration in relation to the sexual behavior of female adolescents. *Journal of Marriage and the Family, 51*, 499–506.

Miller, J., and Yung, S. (1990). The role of allowances in adolescent socialization. *Youth and Society, 17*, 57–63.

Miller, N. (1928). *The child in primitive society.* New York: Brentano.

Miller, P., and Simon, W. (1980). The development of sexuality in adolescence. In J. Adelson (Ed.), *Handbook of adolescent psychology.* New York: Wiley.

Miller, R., and Gordon, M. (1986). The decline in formal dating: A study in six Connecticut high schools. *Marriage and Family Review, 10*, 139–156.

Miller, W. (1958). Lower-class culture as a generating milieu of gang delinquency. *Journal of Social Issues, 14*, 5–19.

Millstein, S. (1988). *The potential of school-linked centers to promote adolescent health and development.* Washington, D.C.: Carnegie Council on Adolescent Development.

Minuchin, S., Rosman, B., and Baker, L. (1978). *Psychosomatic families: Anorexia nervosa in context.* Cambridge: Harvard University Press.

Mitchell, B., Wister, A., and Burch, T. (1989). The family environment and leaving the parental home. *Journal of Marriage and the Family, 51*, 605–613.

Mitchell, E. (Ed.). (1985). *Anorexia nervosa and bulimia: Diagnosis and treatment.* Minneapolis: University of Minnesota Press.

Modell, J., Furstenberg, F., Jr., and Hershberg, T. (1976). Social change and transitions to adulthood in historical perspective. *Journal of Family History, 1*, 7–32.

Modell, J., and Goodman, M. (1990). Historical perspectives. In S. Feldman and G. Elliott (Eds.), *At the threshold: The developing adolescent.* Pp. 93–122. Cambridge: Harvard University Press.

Moffitt, T. (1990). Juvenile delinquency and attention deficit disorder: Boys' developmental trajectories from age 3 to age 15. *Child Development, 61*, 893–910.

Moffitt, T., and Silva, P. (1988). IQ and delinquency: A direct test of the differential detection hypothesis. *Journal of Abnormal Psychology, 97*, 330–333.

Moll, R. (1986). *Playing the private college admissions game.* New York: Penguin.

Monahan, L., Kuhn, D., and Shaver, P. (1974). Intrapsychic versus cultural explanations of the "fear of success" motive. *Journal of Personality and Social Psychology, 29,* 60–64.

Montemayor, R. (1984). Maternal employment and adolescents' relations with parents, siblings, and peers. *Journal of Youth and Adolescence, 13,* 543–557.

Montemayor, R. (1986). Family variation in parent-adolescent storm and stress. *Journal of Adolescent Research, 1,* 15–31.

Montemayor, R., Brown, B., and Adams, G. (1985). Changes in identity status and psychological adjustment after leaving home and entering college. Paper presented at the biennial meeting of the Society for Research in Child Development, Toronto.

Montemayor, R., and Eisen, M. (1977). The development of self-conceptions from childhood to adolescence. *Developmental Psychology, 13,* 314–319.

Moore, K., Nord, C., and Peterson, J. (1989). Nonvoluntary sexual activity among adolescents. *Family Planning Perspectives, 21,* 110–114.

Moore, K., Peterson, J., and Furstenberg, F., Jr. (1986). Parental attitudes and the occurrence of early sexual activity. *Journal of Marriage and the Family, 48,* 777–782.

Moos, R. (1978). A typology of junior high and high school classrooms. *American Educational Research Journal, 15,* 53–66.

Mortimer, J., and Finch, M. (1986). The effects of part-time work on adolescent self-concept and achievement. In P. Borman and J. Reisman (Eds.), *Becoming a worker.* Norwood: Ablex.

Mortimer, J., Finch, M., Shanahan, M., and Ryu, S. (1990). Work experience, mental health, and behavioral adjustment in adolescence. Paper presented at the biennial meeting of the Society for Research on Adolescence, Atlanta, March.

Mortimer, J., and Lorence, J. (1979). Work experience and occupational value socialization: A longitudinal study. *American Journal of Sociology, 84,* 1361–1385.

Mullis, I., Owen, E., and Phillips, G. (1990). *America's challenge: Accelerating academic achievement. A summary of findings from 20 years of NAEP.* Washington, D.C.: U.S. Department of Education.

Mullis, I., Owen, E., and Phillips, G. (1990). *America's challenge: Accelerating academic achievement.*

Princeton, N.J.: National Assessment of Educational Progress, Educational Testing Service.

Muñoz, R., and Amado, H. (1986). Anorexia nervosa: An affective disorder. In F. Larocca (Ed.), *Eating disorders.* Pp. 13–19. San Francisco: Jossey-Bass.

Munro, G., and Adams, G. (1977). Ego-identity formation in college students and working youth. *Developmental Psychology, 13,* 523–524.

Mussen, P., and Jones, M. C. (1957). Self-conceptions, motivations, and interpersonal attitudes of late- and early-maturing boys. *Child Development, 28,* 243–256.

Mussen, P. and Jones, M. C. (1958). The behavior-inferred motivations of late- and early-maturing boys. *Child Development, 29,* 61–67.

Myers, J., Lindentthal, J., and Pepper, M. (1975). Life events, social integration, and psychiatric symptomatology. *Journal of Health and Social Behavior, 16,* 421–429.


National Center on Education and the Economy. (1990). *America's choice: High skills or low wages!* Washington, D.C.: National Center on Education and the Economy.

National Center for Health Statistics. (1982). *Vital Statistics of the United States.* Washington, D.C.: U.S. Government Printing Office.

National Commission on Excellence in Education. (1983). *A nation at risk: The imperative for educational reform.* Washington, D.C.: U.S. Department of Education.

National Commission on Youth. (1980). *The transition of youth to adulthood: A bridge too long.* Boulder, Colo.: Westview Press.

Natriello, G., and McDill, E. (1986). Performance standards, student effort on homework, and academic achievement. *Sociology of Education, 59,* 18–31.

Natriello, G., Pallas, A., and Alexander, K. (1989). On the right track? Curriculum and academic achievement. *Sociology of Education, 62,* 109–118.

Needle, R., Su., S., and Doherty, W. (1990). Divorce, remarriage, and adolescent substance use: A prospective study. *Journal of Marriage and the Family, 52,* 157–169.

Neimark, E. (1975). Intellectual development during adolescence. In F. Horowitz (Ed.), *Review of child development research* (Vol. 4). Chicago: University of Chicago Press.

Neugarten, B., and Datan, N. (1974). The middle years. In S. Arieti (Ed.), *American handbook of psychiatry* (2nd ed.). (Vol. 1, Part 3). New York: Basic Books.

*New York Times.* (1991, January 30). Only one U.S. family in four is 'traditional,' p. A19.

Newcomb, M., and Bentler, P. (1989). Substance use and abuse among children and teenagers. *American Psychologist, 44,* 242–248.

Newcomb, M., and Bentler, P. (1988). Impact of adolescent drug use and social support on problems of young adults: A longitudinal study. *Journal of Abnormal Psychology, 97,* 64–75.

Newcomb, M., Huba, G., and Bentler, P. (1981). A multidimensional assessment of stressful life events among adolescents: Derivation and correlates. *Journal of Health and Social Behavior, 22,* 400–415.

Newcomb, M., Huba, G., and Bentler, P. (1983). Mothers' influence on the drug use of their children: Confirmatory tests of direct modeling and mediational theories. *Developmental Psychology, 19,* 714–726.

Newcomb, M., Maddahain, E., and Bentler, P. (1986). Risk factors for drug use among adolescents: Concurrent and longitudinal analyses. *American Journal of Public Health, 76,* 525–531.

Newcombe, N., and Dubas, J. (1987). Individual differences in cognitive ability: Are they related to timing of puberty? In R. Lerner and T. Foch (Eds.), *Biological-psychosocial interactions in early adolescence.* Pp. 249–302. Hillsdale, N.J.: Erlbaum.

Newcomer, S., and Udry, J. R. (1985). Oral sex in an adolescent population. *Archives of Sexual Behavior, 14,* 41–56.

Newcomber, S., and Udry, J. (1987). Parental marital status effects on adolescent sexual behavior. *Journal of Marriage and the Family, 49,* 235–240.

Newmann, F. (in press). Higher order thinking and prospects for classroom thoughtfulness. In F. Newmann (Ed.), *Student engagement and achievement in American high schools.* New York: Teachers College Press.

Newmann, B., and Newmann, P. (1976). Early adolescence and its conflict: Group identity versus alienation. *Adolescence, 11,* 261–274.

Nielsen, L. (1991). *Adolescence: A contemporary view* (2nd ed.). New York: Holt, Rinehart, Winston.

Nightingale, E., and Wolverton, L. (1988). *Adolescent rolelessness in modern society.* Washington, D.C.: Carnegie Council on Adolescent Development.

Nolen-Hoeksema, S. (1987). Sex differences in unipolar depression: Evidence and theory. *Psychological Bulletin, 101,* 259–282.

Nolen-Hoeksema, S. (1990). *Sex differences in depression.* Stanford, Calif.: Stanford University Press.

Noller, P., and Callan, V. (1990). Adolescents' perceptions of the nature of their communication with parents. *Journal of Youth and Adolescence, 19,* 349–362.

Nordheimer, J. (1990, October 18). Stepfathers: The shoes rarely fit. *The New York Times,* pp. C1 and ff.

Nottlemann, E., Inhoff-Germain, G., Susman, E., and Chrousos, G. (in press). Hormones and behavior at puberty. In J. Bancroft (Ed.), *Adolescence and puberty.* New York: Oxford University Press.

Nottlemann, E., Susman, E., Inhoff-Germain, G., and Chrousos, G. (1987). Concurrent and predictive relations between hormone levels and social-emotional functioning in early adolescence. Paper presented at the biennial meeting of the Society for Research in Child Development, Baltimore.

O'Brien, S., and Bierman, K. (1988). Conceptions and perceived influence of peer groups: Interviews with preadolescents and adolescents. *Child Development, 59,* 1360–1365.

Office of Technology Assessment, U.S. Congress. (1991). *Adolescent health.* (Vol. 1). *Summary and policy options.* Washington, D.C.: U.S. Government Printing Office.

Ogbu, J. (1974). *The next generation: An ethnography of education in an urban neighborhood.* New York: Academic Press.

Ogbu, J. (1978). *Minority education and caste.* New York: Academic Press.

O'Malley, P., and Bachman, J. (1983). Self-esteem: Change and stability between ages 13 and 23. *Developmental Psychology, 19,* 257–268.

Orlofsky, J., Marcia, J., and Lesser, I. (1973). Ego identity status and the intimacy versus isolation crisis of young adulthood. *Journal of Personality and Social Psychology, 27,* 211–219.

Osgood, D. W., Johnston, L., O'Malley, P., and Bachman, J. (1988). The generality of deviance in late adolescence and early adulthood. *American Sociological Review, 53,* 81–93.

Osipow, S. (1973). *Theories of career development* (2nd ed.). New York: Appleton-Century-Crofts.

Overton, W. (1985). Scientific methodologies and the competence-moderator-performance issue. In E. Neimark, R. DeLisi, and J. Newman (Eds.), *Moderators of competence.* Pp. 15–41.

Paige, K. (1983). A bargaining theory of menarcheal responses in preindustrialized cultures. In J. Brooks-Gunn and A. Petersen (Eds.), *Girls at puberty.* New York: Plenum.

Paikoff, R., Brooks-Gunn, J., and Warren, M. (1991). Effects of girls' hormonal status on depressive and aggressive symptoms over the course of one year. *Journal of Youth and Adolescence, 20,* 191–216.

Pallas, A., Natriello, G., and McDill, E. (1989). The changing nature of the disadvantaged population: Current dimensions and future trends. *Educational Researcher, 18,* 16–22.

Pantages, T., and Creedon, C. (1978). Studies of college attrition: 1950–1975. *Review of Educational Research, 48,* 49–101.

Parke, R. (1988). Families in life-span perspective: A multilevel developmental approach. In E. M. Hetherington and M. Perlmutter (Eds.), *Child development in life-span perspective.* Pp. 159–190. Hillsdale, N.J.: Erlbaum.

Parsons, J., Eccles, Adler, T., and Kaczala, C. (1982). Socialization of achievement attitudes and beliefs: Parental influences. *Child Development, 53,* 310–321.

Patterson, G. (1986). Performance models for antisocial boys. *American Psychologist, 41,* 432–444.

Patterson, G., DeBaryshe, B., and Ramsey, E. (1989). A developmental perspective on antisocial behavior. *American Psychologist, 44,* 329–335.

Patterson, G., and Stouthamer-Loeber, M. (1984). The correlation of family management practices and delinquency. *Child Development, 55,* 1299–1307.

Paulsen, E. (1972). Obesity in children and adolescents. In H. Barnett and A. Einhorn (Eds.), *Pediatrics.* New York: Appleton-Century-Crofts.

Paulsen, K., and Johnson, M. (1983). Sex role attitudes and mathematical ability in 4th-, 8th-, and 11th-grade students from a high socioeconomic area. *Developmental Psychology, 19,* 210–214.

Paxton, S., Wertheim, E., Gibbons, K., Szmukler, G., Hillier, L., and Petrovich, J. (1991). Body image satisfaction, dieting beliefs, and weight loss behaviors in adolescent girls and boys. *Journal of Youth and Adolescence, 20,* 361–380.

Peel, E. (1971). *The nature of adolescent judgment.* London: Staples Press.

Peplau, L., Rubin, Z., and Hill, C. (1977). Sexual intimacy in dating relationships. *Journal of Social Issues, 33,* 86–109.

Perry, W. (1970). *Forms of intellectual and ethical development in the college years.* New York: Holt.

Peskin, H. (1967). Pubertal onset and ego functioning: A psychoanalytic approach. *Journal of Abnormal Psychology, 72,* 1–15.

Peskin, H. (1973). Influence of the developmental schedule of puberty on learning and ego functioning. *Journal of Youth and Adolescence, 2,* 273–290.

Petersen, A. (in press). A longitudinal investigation of adolescents' changing perceptions of pubertal timing. *Developmental Psychology.*

Petersen, A. (1985). Pubertal development as a cause of disturbance: Myths, realities, and unanswered questions. *Genetic, Social, and General Psychology Monographs, 111,* 205–232.

Petersen, A. (1988). Adolescent development. *Annual Review of Psychology, 39,* 583–607.

Petersen, A., Graber, J., and Sullivan, P. (1990, March). Pubertal timing and problem behavior: Variations in effects. Paper presented at the biennial meeting of the Society for Research on Adolescence, Atlanta.

Petersen, A., Sarigiani, P., and Kennedy, R. (1991). Adolescent depression: Why more girls? *Journal of Youth and Adolescence, 20,* 247–272.

Petersen, A., and Taylor, B. (1980). The biological approach to adolescence: Biological change and psychological adaptation. In J. Adelson (Ed.), *Handbook of adolescent psychology.* New York: Wiley.

Peterson, J., and Zill, N. (1986). Marital disruption, parent-child relationships, and behavior problems in children. *Journal of Marriage and the Family, 48,* 295–307.

Phillips, D., and Carstensen, L. (1986). Clustering of teenage suicides after television news stories about suicide. *New England Journal of Medicine, 315,* 685–689.

Phinney, J., and Alipuria, L. (1987). Ethnic identity in older adolescents from four ethnic groups. Paper presented at the biennial meeting of the Society for Research in Child Development, Baltimore.

Phinney, J., Lochner, B., and Murphy, R. (in press). Ethnic identity development and psychological adjustment in adolescence. In A. Stiffman and L. Davis (Eds.), *Advances in adolescent mental health.* Vol. 5. *Ethnic issues.* Greenwich, Conn.: JAI Press.

Plomin, R., and Fulker, D. (1987). Behavioral genetics and development in early adolescence. In R. Lerner and T. Fochs (Eds.), *Biological-psychosocial interactions in early adolescence.* Pp. 63–94. Hillsdale, N.J.: Erlbaum.

Powell, A., Farrar, E., and Cohen, D. (1985). *The shopping mall high school.* Boston: Houghton Mifflin.

Powers, S., and Wagner, M. (1984). Attributions for school achievement of middle school students. *Journal of Early Adolescence, 4,* 215–222.

President's Science Advisory Committee. (1974). *Youth: Transition to adulthood.* Chicago: University of Chicago Press.

Prinsky, L., and Rosenbaum, J. (1987). Leer-ics or lyrics? *Youth and Society, 18,* 384–394.

Rebecca, M., Hefner, R., and Oleshansky, B. (1976). A model of sex-role transcendence. *Journal of Social Issues, 32,* 197–206.

Reiss, I. (1960). *Premarital sexual standards in America.* New York: Free Press.

Renken, B., Egeland, B., Marvinney, D., Mangelsdorf, S., and Sroufe, L. A. (1989). Early childhood antecedents of aggression and passive withdrawal in early elementary school. *Journal of Personality, 57,* 257–282.

Resnick, L. (1987). *Education and learning to think:* Washington, D.C.: National Academy Press.

Rest, J. (1983). Morality. In J. Flavell and E. Markman (Eds.), *Handbook of child psychology.* (Vol. III). *Cognitive development.* New York: Wiley.

Rest, J., Davison, M., and Robbins, S. (1978). Age trends in judging moral issues: A review of cross-sectional, longitudinal, and sequential studies of the Defining Issues Test. *Child Development, 49,* 263–279.

Reubens, B., Harrison, J., and Rupp, K. (1981). *The youth labor force, 1945–1995: A cross-national analysis.* Totowa, N.J.: Allanheld, Osmun, and Co.

Rice, K. (1990). Attachment in adolescence: A nar-

rative and meta-analytic review. *Journal of Youth and Adolescence, 19,* 511–538.

Richards, M., Boxer, A., Petersen, A., and Albrecht, R. (1990). Relation of weight to body image in pubertal girls and boys from two communities. *Developmental Psychology, 26,* 313–321.

Richardson, J., Dwyer, K., McGuigan, K., Hansen, W., Dent, C., Johnson, C., Sussman, S., Brannon, B., and Flay, B. (1989). Substance use among eighth-grade students who take care of themselves after school. *Pediatrics, 84,* 556–566.

Rierdan, J., Koff, E., and Stubbs, M. (1989). Timing of menarche, preparation, and initial menstrual experience: Replication and further analyses in prospective study. *Journal of Youth and Adolescence, 18,* 413–426.

Rigsby, L. C., and McDill, E. L. (1975). Value orientations of high school students. In H. R. Stub (Ed.), *The sociology of education: A sourcebook* (3rd ed.) Pp. 53–74. Homewood, Ill.: Dorsey Press.

Riley, T., Adams, G., and Neilsen, E. (1984). Adolescent egocentrism: The association among imaginary audience behavior, cognitive development, and parental support and rejection. *Journal of Youth and Adolescence, 13,* 401–438.

Rivara, F., Sweeney, P., and Henderson, B. (1987). Risk of fatherhood among Black teenage males. *American Journal of Public Health, 77,* 203–205.

Robbins, C., Kaplan, H., and Martin, S. (1985, August). Antecedents of pregnancy among unmarried adolescents. *Journal of Marriage and the Family,* pp. 567–583.

Robins, L. (1986). Changes in conduct disorder over time. In D. Farran and J. McKinney (Eds.), *Risk in intellectual and psychosocial development.* Pp. 227–259. New York: Academic Press.

Rodgers, J., and Rowe, D. (1988). Influence of siblings on adolescent sexual behavior. *Developmental Psychology, 24,* 722–728.

Rodman, H., Pratto, D., and Nelson, R. (1988). Toward a definition of self-care children: A commentary on Steinberg (1986). *Developmental Psychology, 24,* 292–294.

Roosa, M., and Christopher, F. S. (in press). Evaluation of an abstinence-only adolescent pregnancy prevention program: A replication. *Family Relations.*

Rosen, B. (1956). The achievement syndrome: A

psychocultural dimension of social stratification. *American Sociological Review, 21,* 203–211.

Rosen, B., and Aneshensel, C. (1975). The chameleon syndrome. *Journal of Marriage and the Family, 38,* 605–617.

Rosen, B., and D'Andrade, R. (1959). The psychosocial origins of achievement motivation. *Sociometry, 22,* 185–218.

Rosenbaum, J. (1976). *Making inequality: The hidden curriculum of high school tracking.* New York: Wiley.

Rosenberg, M. (1975). The dissonant context and the adolescent self-concept. In S. Dragastin and G. Elder, Jr. (Eds.), *Adolescence in the life cycle.* Washington, D.C.: Hemisphere.

Rosenberg, M. (1986). Self concept from middle childhood through adolescence. In J. Suls and A. Greenwald (Eds.), *Psychological perspectives on the self* (Vol. 3). Hillsdale, N.J.: Erlbaum.

Rosenberg, M., and Simmons, R. (1972). *Black and white self-esteem: The urban school child.* Washington, D.C.: American Sociological Association.

Rosenthal, D., and Feldman, S. (1991). The acculturation of Chinese immigrants: Effects on family functioning of length of residence in two cultural contexts. Unpublished manuscript, Department of Psychology, University of Melbourne, Victoria, Australia.

Rosenthal, R., and Jacobson, E. (1968). *Pygmalion in the classroom.* New York: Holt, Rinehart & Winston.

Rotbart, D. (1981, March 2). Allowances stay flat, candy rises—And kids lose their innocence. *Wall Street Journal,* p. 1 and ff.

Rousseau, J. (1911). *Emile* (B. Foxley, trans.). London: Dent. (Originally published 1762).

Rowe, D., Rodgers, J., Meseck-Bushey, S., and St. John, C. (1989). Sexual behavior and nonsexual deviance: A sibling study of their relationship. *Developmental Psychology, 25,* 61–69.

Rubenstein, J., Heeren, T., Housman, D., Rubin, C., and Stechler, G. (1989). Suicidal behavior in "normal" adolescents: Risk and protective factors. *American Journal of Orthopsychiatry, 59,* 59–71.

Rubin, Z. (1980). *Children's friendships.* Cambridge: Harvard University Press.

Ruble, D., and Brooks-Gunn, J. (1982). The experience of menarche. *Child Development, 53,* 1557–1566.

Ruggiero, M., Greenberger, E., and Steinberg, L.

(1982). Occupational deviance among first-time workers. *Youth and Society, 13,* 423–448.

Rumberger, R. (1983). Dropping out of high school: The influence of race, sex, and family background. *American Educational Research Journal, 20,* 199–220.

Rutter, M. (1978). Protective factors in children's responses to stress and disadvantage. In M. Kent and J. Rolf (Eds.), *Primary prevention of psychopathology.* (Vol. 3). *Promoting social competence and coping in children.* Hanover, N.J.: University Press of New England.

Rutter, M. (1983). School effects on pupil progress: Research findings and policy implications. *Child Development, 54,* 1–29.

Rutter, M., and Garmezy, N. (1983). Developmental psychopathology. In E. M. Hetherington (Ed.), *Handbook of child psychology.* (Vol. IV). *Socialization, personality, and social development.* New York: Wiley.

Rutter, M., Maugham, B., Mortimore, P., and Ouston, J. (1979). *Fifteen thousand hours: Secondary schools and their effects on children.* London: Open Books.

Ryan, R. M., and Lynch, J. H. (1989). Emotional autonomy versus detachment: Revisiting the vicissitudes of adolescence and young adulthood. *Child Development, 60,* 340–356.

Safer, D. (1986). The stress of secondary school for vulnerable students. *Journal of Youth and Adolescence, 15,* 405–417.

St. John, N. (1975). *School desegregation outcomes for children.* New York: Wiley.

Salinger, J. D. (1964). *The catcher in the rye.* New York: Bantam.

Savin-Williams, R. (1976). An ethological study of dominance formation and maintenance in a group of human adolescents. *Child Development, 47,* 972–979.

Savin-Williams, R. (1979). Dominance hierarchies in groups of adolescents. *Child Development, 50,* 923–935.

Savin-Williams, R. (1988). Theoretical perspectives accounting for adolescent homosexuality. *Journal of Adolescent Health Care, 9,* 95–104.

Savin-Williams, R. (1989). Coming out to parents and self-esteem among gay and lesbian youths. *Journal of Homosexuality, 17,* 1–35.

Savin-Williams, R., and Berndt, T. (1990). Friendship and peer relations. In S. Feldman and G. Elliott (Eds.), *At the threshold: The developing adolescent*. Pp. 277–307. Cambridge: Harvard University Press.

Savin-Williams, R., and Demo, D. (1983). Situational and transituational determinants of adolescent self-feelings. *Journal of Personality and Social Psychology, 44,* 824–833.

Savin-Williams, R., and Demo, D. (1984). Developmental change and stability in adolescent self-concept. *Developmental Psychology, 20,* 1100–1110.

Schiff, A., and Knopf, I. (1985). The effects of task demands on attention allocation in children of different ages. *Child Development, 56,* 621–630.

Schofield, J. (1981). Complementary and conflicting identities: Images and interaction in an interracial school. In S. Asher and J. Gottman (Eds.), *The development of children's friendships.* Cambridge: Cambridge University Press.

Scott, C., and Owen, R. (1990, March). Similarities and differences in sexuality socialization of males in three cultural/ethnic groups. Paper presented at the biennial meeting of the Society for Research on Adolescence, Atlanta.

Seginer, R. (1983). Parents' educational expectations and children's academic achievements: A literature review. *Merrill-Palmer Quarterly, 29,* 1–23.

Selman, R. (1980). *The growth of interpersonal understanding: Developmental and clinical analyses.* New York: Academic Press.

Sessa, F., and Steinberg, L. (1991). Family structure and the development of autonomy in adolescence. *Journal of Early Adolescence, 11,* 38–55.

Sharabany, R., Gershoni, R., and Hofman, J. (1981). Girlfriend, boyfriend: Age and sex differences in intimate friendship. *Developmental Psychology, 17,* 800–808.

Shaver, P., Furnam, W., and Buhrmester, D. (1985). Transition to college: Network changes, social skills, and loneliness. In S. Duck and D. Perlman (Eds.), *Understanding personal relationships: An interdisciplinary approach.* Pp. 193–219. London: Sage.

Shavit, Y., and Featherman, D. (1988). School, tracking, and teenage intelligence. *Sociology of Education, 61,* 42–51.

Shaw, M., and White, D. (1965). The relationship between child-parent identification and academic underachievement. *Journal of Clinical Psychology, 21,* 10–13.

Shayne, V., and Kaplan, B. (1988). AIDS education for adolescents. *Youth and Society, 20,* 180–208.

Shedler, J., and Block, J. (1990). Adolescent drug use and psychological health: A longitudinal inquiry. *American Psychologist, 45,* 612–630.

Shipman, G. (1971). The psychodynamics of sex education. In R. E. Muuss (Ed.), *Adolescent behavior and society.* New York: Random House.

Shrum, W., Cheek, N., Jr., and Hunter, S. MacD. (1988). Friendship in school: Gender and racial homophily. *Sociology of Education, 61,* 227–239.

Siegler, R. (1988). Individual differences in strategy choices: Good students, not-so-good students, and perfectionists. *Child Development, 59,* 833–851.

Siegler, R., Liebert, D., and Liebert, R. (1973). Inhelder and Piaget's pendulum problem: Teaching adolescents to act as scientists. *Developmental Psychology, 9,* 97–101.

Silbereisen, R., Kracke, B., and Crockett, L. (1990, March). Timing of maturation and adolescent substance use. Paper presented at the biennial meeting of the Society for Research on Adolescence, Atlanta.

Silbereisen, R., Petersen, A., Albrecht, H., and Kracke, B. (1989). Maturational timing and the development of problem behavior: Longitudinal studies in adolescence. *Journal of Early Adolescence.*

Silverberg, S. (1986). Psychological well-being of parents with early adolescent children. Unpublished doctoral dissertation. Department of Child and Family Studies, University of Wisconsin–Madison.

Silverberg, S., and Steinberg, L. (1990). Psychological well-being of parents at midlife: The impact of early adolescent children. *Developmental Psychology, 26,* 658–666.

Simmons, R., and Blyth, D. (1987). *Moving into adolescence.* New York: Aldine de Gruyter.

Simmons, R., Blyth, D., and McKinney, K. (1983). The social and psychological effects of puberty on white females. In J. Brooks-Gunn and A. Petersen (Eds.), *Girls at puberty.* New York: Plenum Press.

Simmons, R., Blyth, D., Van Cleave, E., and Bush, D. (1979). Entry into early adolescence: The impact of school structure, puberty, and early dating on self-esteem. *American Sociological Review, 44,* 948–967.

Simmons, R., Brown, L., Bush, D., and Blyth, D. (1978). Self-esteem and achievement of black and white adolescents. *Social Problems, 26,* 86–96.

Simmons, R., Burgeson, R., Carlton-Ford, S., and Blyth, D. (1987). The impact of cumulative change in early adolescence. *Child Development, 58,* 1220–1234.

Simmons, R., and Rosenberg, F. (1975). Sex, sex roles, and self-image. *Journal of Youth and Adolescence, 4,* 229–258.

Simmons, R., Rosenberg, F., and Rosenberg, M. (1973). Disturbance in the self-image at adolescence. *American Sociological Review, 38,* 553–568.

Simon, W., Berger, A., and Gagnon, J. (1972). Beyond anxiety and fantasy: The coital experience of college youth. *Journal of Youth and Adolescence, 1,* 203–222.

Simon, W., and Gagnon, J. (1969). On psychosexual development. In D. Goslin (Ed.), *Handbook of socialization theory and research.* Chicago: Rand McNally.

Simpson, R. (1962). Parental influence, anticipatory socialization, and social mobility. *American Sociological Review, 27,* 517–522.

Sizer, T. (1984). *Horace's compromise.* Boston: Houghton Mifflin.

Skinner, B. F. (1953). *Science and human behavior.* New York: Free Press.

Small, S. (1988). Parental self-esteem and its relationship to childrearing practices, parent-adolescent interaction, and adolescent behavior. *Journal of Marriage and the Family, 50,* 1063–1072.

Small, S., Eastman, G., and Cornelius, S. (1988). Adolescent autonomy and parental stress. *Journal of Youth and Adolescence, 17,* 377–391.

Smetana, J. (1988). Adolescents' and parents' conceptions of parental authority. *Child Development, 59,* 321–335.

Smetana, J. (1988). Concepts of self and social convention: Adolescents' and parents' reasoning about hypothetical and actual family conflicts. In M. Gunnar (Ed.), *21st Minnesota Symposium on Child Psychology.* Pp. 79–122. Hillsdale, N.J.: Erlbaum.

Smetana, J. (1989). Adolescents' and parents' reasoning about actual family conflict. *Child Development, 60,* 1052–1067.

Smetana, J., Yau, J., and Hanson, S. (in press). Conflict resolution in families with adolescents. *Journal of Research on Adolescence.*

Smith, E., and Udry, J. (1985). Coital and non-coital sexual behaviors of white and black adolescents. *American Journal of Public Health, 75,* 1200–1203.

Smith, E., Udry, J., and Morris, N. (1985). Pubertal development and friends: A biosocial explanation of adolescent sexual behavior. *Journal of Health and Social Behavior, 26,* 183–192.

Smollar, J., and Youniss, J. (1985). Transformation in adolescents' perceptions of parents. Paper presented at the biennial meeting of the Society for Research in Child Development, Baltimore.

Sobesky, W. (1983). The effects of situational factors on moral judgments. *Child Development, 54,* 575–584.

Sorensen, R. (1973). *Adolescent sexuality in contemporary society.* New York: World Book.

Spanier, G. (1976). Formal and informal sex education as determinants of premarital sexual behavior. *Archives of Sexual Behavior, 5,* 39–67.

Spence, J., and Helmreich, R. (1978). *Masculinity and femininity: Their psychological dimensions, correlates, and antecedents.* Austin: University of Texas Press.

Spencer, M., and Dornbusch, S. (1990). Challenges in studying minority youth. In S. Feldman and G. Elliot (Eds.), *At the threshold: The developing adolescent.* Pp. 123–146. Cambridge: Harvard University Press.

Sroufe, L. A. (1979). The coherence of individual development. *American Psychologist, 34,* 834–841.

Stattin, H., and Magnusson, D. (1989). The role of early aggressive behavior in the frequency, seriousness, and types of later crime. *Journal of Consulting and Clinical Psychology, 57,* 710–718.

Steinberg, L. (1981). Transformations in family relations at puberty. *Developmental Psychology, 17,* 833–840.

Steinberg, L. (1986). Latchkey children and susceptibility to peer pressure: An ecological analysis. *Developmental Psychology, 22,* 433–439.

Steinberg, L. (1987a). The impact of puberty on family relations: Effects of pubertal status and pubertal timing. *Developmental Psychology, 23,* 451–460.

Steinberg, L. (1987b, September). Bound to bicker: Pubescent primates leave home for good reasons. Our teens stay with us and squabble. *Psychology Today,* 36–39.

Steinberg, L. (1987). Recent research on the family

at adolescence: The extent and nature of sex differences. *Journal of Youth and Adolescence, 16,* 191–198.

Steinberg, L. (1988). Simple solutions to a complex problem: A reply to Rodman, Pratto, and Nelson (1988). *Developmental Psychology, 24,* 295–296.

Steinberg, L. (1988). Reciprocal relation between parent-child distance and pubertal maturation. *Developmental Psychology, 24,* 122–128.

Steinberg, L. (1990). Autonomy, conflict, and harmony in the family relationship. In S. Feldman and G. Elliot (Eds.), *At the threshold: The developing adolescent.* Pp. 255–276. Cambridge: Harvard University Press.

Steinberg, L., Blinn, P., and Chan, K. (1984). Dropping out among language minority youth. *Review of Educational Research, 54,* 113–132.

Steinberg, L., and Dornbusch, S. (1991). Negative correlates of part-time work in adolescence: Replication and elaboration. *Developmental Psychology, 27,* 304–313.

Steinberg, L., Dornbusch, S., and Brown, B. (in press). Ethnic differences in adolescent achievement in ecological perspective. *American Psychologist.*

Steinberg, L., Elmen, J, and Mounts, N. (1989). Authoritative parenting, psychosocial maturity, and academic success among adolescence. *Child Development, 60,* 1424–1436.

Steinberg, L., Greenberger, E., Garduque, L., and McAuliffe, S. (1982). Adolescents in the labor force: Some costs and benefits to schooling and learning. *Educational Evaluation and Policy Analysis, 4,* 363–372.

Steinberg, L., Greenberger, E., Garduque, L., Ruggiero, M., and Vaux, A. (1982). Effects of working on adolescent development. *Developmental Psychology, 18,* 385–395.

Steinberg, L., Lamborn, S., Dornbusch, S. and Darling, N. (in press). Impact of parenting practices on adolescent achievement: Authoritative parenting, school involvement, and encouragement to succeed. *Child Development.*

Steinberg, L., and Levine, A. (1990). *You and your adolescent: A parent's guide for ages 10 to 20.* New York: Harper & Row.

Steinberg, L., Mounts, N., Lamborn, S., and Dornbusch, S. (1991). Authoritative parenting and adolescent adjustment across various ecological niches. *Journal of Research on Adolescence, 1,* 19–36.

Steinberg, L., and Silverberg, S. (1986). The vicissitudes of autonomy in early adolescence. *Child Development, 57,* 841–851.

Steinberg, L., and Silverberg, S. (1987). Influences on marital satisfaction during the middle stages of the family life cycle. *Journal of Marriage and the Family, 49,* 751–760.

Sternberg, R. (1977). *Intelligence, information processing, and analogical reasoning: The componential analysis of human abilities.* Hillsdale, N.J.: Erlbaum.

Sternberg, R. (1988). *The triarchic mind.* New York: Viking Penguin.

Sternberg, R., and Nigro, G. (1980). Developmental patterns in the solution of verbal analogies. *Child Development, 51,* 27–38.

Sternberg, R., and Rifkin, B. (1979). The development of analogical reasoning processes. *Journal of Experimental Child Psychology, 27,* 195–232.

Stevens, J. (1988). Social support, locus of control, and parenting in three low-income groups of mothers: Black teenagers, Black adults, and White adults. *Child Development, 59,* 635–642.

Stevenson, D., and Baker, D. (1987). The family-school relation and the child's school performance. *Child Development, 58,* 1348–1357.

Studer, M., and Thornton, A. (1987). Adolescent religiosity and contraceptive usage. *Journal of Marriage and the Family, 49,* 117–128.

Sue, S., and Okazaki, S. (1990). Asian-American educational achievements: A phenomenon in search of an explanation. *American Psychologist, 45,* 913–920.

Sullivan, H. S. (1953a). *The interpersonal theory of psychiatry.* New York: Norton.

Sullivan, H. S. (1953b). *Conceptions of modern psychiatry.* New York: Norton.

Sullivan, K., and Sullivan, A. (1980). Adolescent-parent separation. *Developmental Psychology, 16,* 93–99.

Super, D. (1967). *The psychology of careers.* New York: Harper & Row.

Surbey, M. (1987). Anorexia nervosa, amenorrhea, and adaptation. *Ethology and Sociobiology, 8,* 475–615.

Surbey, M. (1990). Family composition, stress, and human menarche. In F. Bercovitch and T. Zeigler (Eds.), *The socioendocrinology of primate reproduction.* New York: Alan R. Liss.

Susman, E., Dorn, L., and Chrousos, G. (1991). Negative affect and hormone levels in young adolescents: Concurrent and predictive perspectives. *Journal of Youth and Adolescence, 20,* 167–190.

Susman, E., Inhoff-Germain, G., Nottlemann, E., Loriaux, D., Cutler, G., Jr., and Chrousos, G. (1987). Hormones, emotional dispositions, and aggressive attributes in young adolescents. *Child Development, 58,* 1114–1134.

Tanner, D. (1972). *Secondary education.* New York: Macmillan.

Tanner, J. (1972). Sequence, tempo, and individual variation in growth and development of boys and girls aged twelve to sixteen. In J. Kagan and R. Coles (Eds.), *Twelve to sixteen: Early adolescence.* New York: Norton.

Teti, D., and Lamb, M. (1989). Socioeconomic and marital outcomes of adolescent marriage, adolescent childbirth, and their co-occurrence. *Journal of Marriage and the Family, 51,* 203–212.

Teti, D., Lamb, M., and Elster, A. (1987). Long-range socioeconomic and marital consequences of adolescent marriage in three cohorts of adult males. *Journal of Marriage and the Family, 49,* 499–506.

Tobin-Richards, M. (1985). Sex differences and similarities in heterosexual activity in early adolescence. Paper presented at the biennial meeting of the Society for Research in Child Development, Toronto.

Torney-Purta, J. (1990). Youth in relation to social institutions. In S. Feldman and G. Elliot (Eds.), *At the threshold: The developing adolescent.* Pp. 457–478. Cambridge: Harvard University Press.

Treaster, J. (1991, February 25). Drop in youths' cocaine use may reflect a societal shift. *The New York Times,* p. A14.

Treboux, D., and Busch-Rossnagel, N. (1990a). Social network influences on adolescent sexual attitudes and behaviors. *Journal of Adolescent Research, 5,* 175–189.

Treboux, D., and Busch-Rossnagel, N. (1990b, March). Age differences in social network influences on the sexual attitudes and behavior of female adolescents. Paper presented at the biennial meeting of the Society for Research on Adolescence, Atlanta.

Trussell, J. (1989). Teenage pregnancy in the United States. *Family Planning Perspectives, 21,* 262–269.

Turiel, E. (1978). The development of concepts of social structure: Social convention. In J. Glick and K. A. Clarke-Stewart (Eds.), *The development of social understanding.* New York: Gardner.

Udry, J. (1987). Hormonal and social determinants of adolescent sexual initiation. In J. Bancroft (Ed.), *Adolescence and puberty.* New York: Oxford University Press.

Udry, J. R., and Billy, J. (1987). Initiation of coitus in early adolescence. *American Sociological Review, 52,* 841–855.

Udry, J., Billy, J., Morris, N., Gruff, T., and Raj, M. (1985). Serum androgenic hormones motivate sexual behavior in boys. *Fertility and Sterility, 43,* 90–94.

Udry, J., Talbert, L., and Morris, N. (1986). Biosocial foundations for adolescent female sexuality. *Demography, 23,* 217–230.

Uhlenberg, P., and Eggebeen, D. (1986). The declining well-being of American adolescents. *Public Interest, 82,* 25–38.

U.S. Bureau of the Census. (1982, June). *Marital status and living arrangements: March 1981.* Washington, D.C.: U.S. Department of Commerce.

U.S. Bureau of the Census. (1985). *Statistical abstract of the United States.* Washington, D.C.: U.S. Government Printing Office.

U.S. Department of Commerce, Bureau of the Census. (1940). *Characteristics of the population.* Washington, D.C.: U.S. Government Printing Office.

U.S. Department of Justice. (1991). *Criminal victimization in the United States, 1988.* Washington, D.C.: U.S. Government Printing Office.

Vandell, D., and Corasaniti, M. (1988). The relation between third graders' after-school care and social, academic, and emotional functioning. *Child Development, 59,* 868–875.

Vanfossen, B., Jones, J., and Spade, J. (1987). Curriculum tracking and status maintenance. *Sociology of Education, 60,* 104–122.

Varenne, H. (1982). Jocks and freaks: The symbolic structure of the expression of social interaction among American senior high school students. In G. Spindler (Ed.), *Doing the ethnography of schooling.* Pp. 213–235. New York: Holt, Rinehart, and Winston.

Vener, A., and Stewart, C. (1974). Adolescent sexual behavior in Middle America revisited: 1970–1973. *Journal of Marriage and the Family, 36,* 728–735.

Ventura, S. (1984). Trends in teenage child bearing, United States, 1970–81. *Vital and Health Statistics Series.* (Vol. 21). Washington, D.C.: U.S. Government Printing Office.

Vigersky, R. (Ed.). (1977). *Anorexia nervosa.* New York: Raven Press.

Vrazzo, F. (1990, November 8). More teen girls sexually active, study finds. *The Philadelphia Inquirer,* p. 1 and ff.


Waber, D. (1977). Sex differences in mental abilities, hemispheric lateralization, and rate of physical growth at adolescence. *Developmental Psychology, 13,* 29–38.

Waite, L., Goldscheider, F., and Witsberger, C. (1986). Nonfamily living and the erosion of traditional family orientations among young adults. *American Sociological Review, 51,* 541–554.

Walker, L., de Vries, B., and Trevethan, S. (1987). Moral stages and moral orientations in real-life and hypothetical dilemmas. *Child Development, 58,* 842–858.

Wallerstein, J. S., and Blakeslee, S. (1989). *Second chances.* New York: Ticknor & Fields.

Wallerstein, J., and Kelley, J. (1974). The effects of parental divorce: The adolescent experience. In E. Anthony and A. Koupernik (Eds.), *The child in his family: Children as a psychiatric risk.* (Vol. 3). New York: Wiley.

Walters, H., and Kranzler, G. (1970). Early identification of the school dropout. *School Counselor, 18,* 97–104.

Waterman, A. (1982). Identity development from adolescence to adulthood: An extension of theory and a review of research. *Developmental Psychology, 18,* 341–358.

Waterman, A., Geary, P., and Waterman, A. (1974). A longitudinal study of changes in ego identity status from the freshman to the senior year at college. *Developmental Psychology, 10,* 387–392.

Waterman, A., and Goldman, J. (1976). A longitudinal study of ego identity development at a liberal arts college. *Journal of Youth and Adolescence, 5,* 361–369.

Waterman, A., and Waterman, M. (1971). A longitudinal study of changes in ego identity status during the freshman year at college. *Developmental Psychology, 5,* 167–173.

Watson, D., and Kendall, P. (1989). Understanding anxiety and depression: Their relation to negative and positive affective states. In P. Kendall (Ed.), *Anxiety and depression.* Pp. 3–26. New York: Academic Press.

Weideger, P. (1976). *Menstruation and menopause.* New York: Knopf.

Weiner, I. (1980). Psychopathology in adolescence. In J. Adelson (Ed.), *Handbook of adolescent psychology.* New York: Wiley.

Weinmann, L., Steinberg, L., and Dornbusch, S. Impact of divorce and remarriage on adolescent adjustment. Unpublished manuscript, Department of Psychology, Temple University.

Weiss, R. (1974). The provisions of social relationships. In Z. Rubin (Ed.), *Doing unto others.* Englewood Cliffs, N.J.: Prentice-Hall.

Weiss, R. (1979). Growing up a little faster: The experience of growing up in a single parent household. *Journal of Social Issues, 35,* 97–111.

Weissberg, R., Caplan, M., and Sivo, P. (1989). A new conceptual framework for establishing school-based social competence promotion programs. In L. Bond, B. Compas, and C. Swift (Eds.), *Prevention in the schools.* Menlo Park, Calif.: Sage.

Westoff, C. (1988). Unintended pregnancy in America and abroad. *Family Planning Perspectives, 20,* 254–261.

Wetzel, J. (1987). *American youth: A statistical snapshot.* New York: William T. Grant Foundation Commission on Work, Family, and Citizenship.

White, K., Speisman, J., and Costos, D. (1983). Young adults and their parents. In H. Grotevant and C. Cooper (Eds.), *Adolescent development in the family.* San Francisco: Jossey-Bass.

White, J., Moffitt, T., and Silva, P. (1989). A prospective replication of the protective effects of IQ in subjects at high risk for juvenile delinquency. *Journal of Consulting and Clinical Psychology, 57,* 719–724.

White, L., and Brinkerhoff, D. (1981). The sexual division of labor: Evidence from childhood. *Social Forces, 60,* 170–181.

Whiting, B., and Whiting, J. (1975). *Children of six cultures.* Cambridge, Mass.: Harvard University Press.

William T. Grant Foundation Commission on Work, Family, and Citizenship. (1988). *The forgotten half:*

*Non-college youth in America*. Washington: William T. Grant Foundation Commission on Work, Family, and Citizenship.

Willits, F. (1988). Adolescent behavior and adult success and well-being. *Youth and Society, 20,* 68–69.

Wilson, F. (1985). The impact of school desegregation programs on white public-school enrollment, 1968–1976. *Sociology of Education, 58,* 137–153.

Wilson, T., and Linville, P. (1985). Improving the performance of college freshmen with attributional techniques. *Journal of Personality and Social Psychology, 49,* 287–293.

Wilson, W. (1987). *The truly disadvantaged: The inner city, the underclass, and public policy.* Chicago: University of Chicago Press.

Wiltfang, G., and Scarbecz, M. (1990). Social class and adolescents' self-esteem: Another look. *Social Psychology Quarterly, 53,* 174–183.

Windle, M. (1989). Substance use and abuse among adolescent runaways: A four-year follow-up study. *Journal of Youth and Adolescence, 18,* 331–344.

Wintemute, G., Kraus, J., Teret, S., and Wright, M. (1987). Drowning in childhood and adolescence: A population-based study. *American Journal of Public Health, 77,* 830–832.

Winterbottom, M. (1958). The relation of need for achievement to learning experiences in independence and mastery. In J. Atkinson (Ed.), *Motives in fantasy, action, and society.* Princeton, N.J.: Van Nostrand.

Wintre, M., Hicks, R., McVey, G., and Fox, J. (1988). Age and sex differences in choice of consultant for various types of problems. *Child Development, 59,* 1046–1055.

Wirtz, P., Rohrbeck, C., Charner, I., and Fraser, B. (1987). Intense employment while in high school: Are teachers, guidance counselors, and parents misguiding academically-oriented adolescents? Paper available from the Graduate Institute for Policy Education and Research, The George Washington University, Washington, D.C.

Wolfe, T. (1976, August 23) The "me" decade and the third great awakening. *New York,* pp. 26–40.

Wright, M. R. (1989). Body image satisfaction in adolescent girls and boys: A longitudinal study. *Journal of Youth and Adolescence, 18,* 71–84.

Wuthnow, R., and Glock, C. (1973). Religious loyalty, defection, and experimentation among college youth. *Journal for the Scientific Study of Religion, 12,* 157–180.

Yamaguichi, K., and Kandel, D. (1987). Drug use and other determinants of premarital pregnancy and its outcome: A dynamic analysis of competing life events. *Journal of Marriage and the Family, 49,* 257–270.

Yankelovich, D. (1974). *The new morality: A profile of American youth in the 1970s.* New York: McGraw-Hill.

Young, H., and Ferguson, L. (1979). Developmental changes through adolescence in the spontaneous nomination of reference groups as a function of decision context. *Journal of Youth and Adolescence, 8,* 239–252.

Youniss, J., and Smollar, J. (1985). *Adolescent relations with mothers, fathers, and friends.* Chicago: University of Chicago Press.

Youth and America's Future. (1988). *The forgotten half: Non-college youth in America.* Washington: William T. Grant Foundation Commission on Works, Family, and Citizenship.

Yussen, S. (1976). Moral reasoning from the perspective of others. *Child Development, 47,* 551–555.

Zabin, L., Hirsch, M., Smith, E., Streett, R., and Hardy, J. (1986). Evaluation of a pregnancy prevention program for urban teenagers. *Family Planning Perspectives, 16,* 119–126.

Zabin, L., Hirsch, M., and Emerson, M. (1989). When urban adolescents choose abortion: Effects on education, psychological status and subsequent pregnancy. *Family Planning Perspectives, 21,* 248–255.

Zabin, L., et al. (1986). Ages of physical maturation and first intercourse. *Demography, 23,* 595–605.

Zajonc, R. (1976). Family configuration and intelligence. *Science, 192,* 227–236.

Zeldin, R., Small, S., and Savin-Williams, R. (1982). Prosocial interactions in two mixed-sex adolescent groups. *Child Development, 53,* 1492–1498.

Zelnick, M., and Kantner, L. (1973). Sex and contraception among unmarried teenagers. In C.

Westoff et al. (Eds.), *Toward the end of growth: Population in America*. Englewood Cliffs, N.J.: Prentice-Hall.

Zelnick, M., Kantner, J., and Ford, K. (1981). *Sex and pregnancy in adolescence*. Beverly Hills, Calif.: Sage.

Zill, N. (1984). *Happy, healthy and insecure*. New York: Doubleday.

Zimiles, H., and Lee, V. (1991). Adolescent family structure and educational progress. *Developmental Psychology, 27,* 314–320.

Zimring, F. (1982). *The changing legal world of adolescence*. New York: Free Press.

Zuckerman, M. (Ed.). (1983). *Biological basis of sensation seeking, impulsivity, and anxiety*. Hillsdale, N.J.: Erlbaum.

# Acknowledgments

| | |
|---|---|
| Figures 1.1 and 1.4 | From M. Grumbach, J. Roth, S. Kaplan, and R. Kelch, "Hypothalamic-pituitary Regulations of Puberty in Man: Evidence and Concepts Derived from Clinical Research," in M. Grumbach, G. Grave, and F. Mayer, (Eds). *Control of the Onset of Puberty*, John Wiley & Sons, 1974. |
| Figure 1.3 | Adapted from W. Marshall, "Puberty," in F. Falkner and J. Tanner, (Eds.), *Human Growth*, Vol. 2, 1978. Reprinted by permission of Plenum Publishing Corporation, 1978. |
| Figures 1.5 and 1.7 | Adapted from J. Tanner, "Sequence, Tempo, and Individual Variation in Growth and Development of Boys and Girls Aged Twelve to Sixteen," in J. Kagan and R. Coles, (Eds.), *Twelve to Sixteen: Early Adolescence*, W. W. Norton & Co., Inc., 1972. |
| Figure 1.6 | From N. M. Morris and J. R. Udry, "Validation of a Self-Administered Instrument to Assess State of Adolescent Development," *Journal of Youth and Adolescence*, Vol. 9, 1980, pp. 275–276. Reprinted by permission of Plenum Publishing Corporation. |
| Box, p. 34 | Copyright © 1972 by Nora Ephron. Reprinted from *Crazy Salad: Some Things About Women*, by Nora Ephron, by permission of Alfred A. Knopf, Inc. |
| Figures 1.9, 1.10, and 1.11 | Adapted from P. Eveleth and J. Tanner, *World-wide Variation in Human Growth*, Cambridge University Press, 1976. |
| Figure 1.8 | From W. A. Marshall and J. M. Tanner, "Variations in the Pattern of Pubertal Changes in Girls," *Archives of Disease in Childhood*, Vol. 44, 1969, pp. 291. Reprinted by permission of the British Medical Association. |
| Figure 1.12 | Figure adapted from *Being Adolescent: Conflict and Growth in the Teenage Years* by Mihaly Csikszentmihalyi and Reed Larson. Copyright © 1984 by Basic Books, Inc. Reprinted by permission of Basic Books, a division of HarperCollins Publishers Inc. |
| Box, p. 59; Quote, p. 286; Box, p. 341 | From *Teenage Romance: Or How to Die of Embarrassment* by Delia Ephron. Illustrated by Edward Koren. Copyright © 1981 by Delia Ephron (text). Illustrations copyright © 1981 by Edward Koren. Used by permission of Viking Penguin, a division of Penguin Books USA Inc. |
| Figure 2.3 | From R. McCall, M. Applebaum, and P. Hogarty, "Developmental Changes in Mental Performance," *Monographs of the Society for Research in Child Development*, 38 (Serial No. 150), 1973. Copyright © by The Society for Research in Child Development, Inc. |
| Figure 4.6 | From W. Furman and D. Buhrmester, "Children's Perceptions of the Personal Relationships in their Social Networks," *Developmental Psychology*, 21, 1985, pp. 1016–1024. Reprinted by permission of the author. |
| Figure 6.2 | Adapted from R. Barker and P. Gump, *Big School, Small School: High School Size and Student Behavior*, 1964. Reprinted by permission of Stanford University Press. |

| | |
|---|---|
| Figure 7.1 | Figure from *Being Adolescent* by Mihalyi Csikszentmihalyi and Reed Larson. Copyright © 1984 by Basic Books, Inc. Reprinted by permission of Basic Books, a division of HarperCollins Publishers. |
| Table 7.2 | From J. Bachman, "Premature Affluence: Do High School Students Earn Too Much?" Reprinted from *Economic Outlook USA*, Summer 1983, by special permission. Copyright 1983 by The University of Michigan. |
| Figure 8.1 | From B. Hirsch and D. DuBois, "Self-esteem in Early Adolescence: The Identification and Prediction of Contrasting Longitudinal Trajectories," *Journal of Youth and Adolescence*, Vol. 20, 1991, pp. 53–72. Reprinted by permission of Plenum Publishing Corporation. |
| Figure 10.2 | From F. Hunter and J. Youniss, "Changes in Functions of Three Relations During Adolescence," *Developmental Psychology, 18*, 1982, pp. 806–811. Copyright © 1982 by the American Psychological Association. Reprinted by permission of the American Psychological Association and the author. |
| Figure 11.3 | From J. E. Gans, D. A. Blyth, A. E. Elster, and L. L. Gaveras, *America's Adolescents: How Healthy Are They?* Chicago: IL: American Medical Association, 1990. |
| Tables 13.2 and 13.3 | From *Living with 10- to 15-Year-Olds: A Parent Education Curriculum*, Revised Edition. Carrboro, N.C.: Center for Early Adolescence, The University of North Carolina at Chapel Hill, 1991. Used with permission. |
| Figure 13.2 | "Fading Cocaine Use in High Schools," *The New York Times*, January 25, 1991. Copyright © 1991 by The New York Times Company. Reprinted by permission. |
| Figure 13.4 | "When Youngsters Light Up," *The New York Times*, December 11, 1990. Copyright © 1990 by the New York Times Company. Reprinted by permission. |
| Figures 13.5, 13.6, and 13.8 | From J. E. Gans, D. A. Blyth, A. E. Elster, and L. L. Gaveras, *America's Adolescents: How Healthy Are They?* Chicago, IL: American Medical Association, 1990. |
| Box, p. 233 | From J. Montgomery, "Low, Pay, Bossy Bosses Kill Kids' Enthusiasm for Food-Service Jobs," *The Wall Street Journal*, March 15, 1979, pp. 1 ff. Reprinted by permission of *The Wall Street Journal*, © 1979 Dow Jones & Company, Inc. All Rights Reserved Worldwide. |
| Quote p. 254 | Reprinted by permission of the publishers from *At the Threshold: The Developing Adolescent*, edited by Shirley S. Feldman and Glen R. Elliot, Cambridge, Mass.: Harvard University Press, Copyright © 1990 by the President and Fellows of Harvard College. |
| Box p. 271 | From *The Member of the Wedding* by Carson McCullers. Copyright 1946 by Carson McCullers. Copyright © renewed 1974 by Floria V. Lasky. Reprinted by permission of Houghton Mifflin Company. All rights reserved. |
| Figure in box p. 337 | Adapted from R. Sharabany, R. Gershoni, and J. Hofman, "Girlfriend, Boyfriend: Age and Sex Differences in Intimate Friendship," *Developmental Psychology, 17*, 1981, pp. 800–808. Copyright © 1981 by the American Psychological Association. Reprinted by permission of the American Psychological Association and the author. |

# NAME INDEX